# INFORMATION
# PLEASE
## BOOK OF
## SPORTS FACTS
## AND RECORDS
# 1983

## INFORMATION PLEASE PUBLISHERS
## A DIVISION OF
# A&W PUBLISHERS, INC.
## NEW YORK

# FOREWORD

This comprehensive factbook has been created by the editors of *Information Please Almanac* as one of a series of general reference books, and it is intended to give readers easy access to all the important information they need to know on virtually every popular sport today in a single, concise, easy-to-use text. The major sports are arranged in their seasonal sequence under special section headings such as "Football," "Basketball," "Hockey," and "Figure Skating." All sports entries are listed alphabetically in the table of contents.

In addition to presenting a wealth of data on players and team records, the *Information Please Book of Sports Facts and Records* answers the questions sports fans frequently ask, such as: How much do top tennis stars earn? When was the first ice hockey game played? What was major league baseball attendance in 1982?

Everyone who watches or reads about sports will enjoy this fascinating book. It is designed to increase the reader's understanding of the sports world and will provide fans with many hours of reading pleasure.

In preparing the material used throughout these pages, every effort has been made to ensure accuracy. The editors have drawn upon the vast resources of the *Information Please Almanac*, long recognized as the most reliable, up-to-date source of information for almost four decades.

An Information Please Book

Published by
A&W Publishers, Inc.
95 Madison Avenue
New York, NY 10016

Manufactured in the United States of America

Library of Congress Catalog Card Number:
82-074429

ISBN: 0-89479-123-0

# CONTENTS

## Sports Personalities

A name in parentheses is the original name or form of name. Localities are places of birth. Dates of birth appear as month/day/year. **Boldface** years in parentheses are dates of **(birth-death)**.
Information has been gathered from many sources, including the individuals themselves. However, the *Information Please Almanac* cannot guarantee the accuracy of every individual item.

Aaron, Hank (Henry) (baseball); Mobile, Ala., 2/5/1934
Abdul-Jabbar, Kareem (Lewis Ferdinand Alcindor, Jr.) (basketball); New York City, 4/16/1947
Adderly, Herbert A. (football); Philadelphia, 6/8/1939
Alcindor, Lew. See Abdul-Jabbar
Ali, Muhammad (Cassius Clay) (boxing); Louisville, Ky., 1/18/1942
Allen, Dick (Richard Anthony) (baseball); Wampum, Pa., 3/8/1942
Allison, Bobby (Robert Arthur) (auto racing); Hueytown, Ala., 12/3/1937
Alworth, Lance (football); Houston, 8/3/1940
Anderson, Donny (Gary Donny) (football); Brooklyn, N.Y., 4/3/1949
Anderson, Ken (football); Batavia, Ill., 2/15/1949
Anderson, Sparky (George) (baseball); Bridgewater, S.D., 2/22/1934
Andretti, Mario (auto racing); Montona, Trieste, Italy, 2/28/1940
Anthony, Earl (bowling); Kent, Wash., 4/27/1938
Appling, Luke (baseball); High Point, N.C., 4/2/1907
Arcaro, Eddie (George Edward) (jockey); Cincinnati, 2/19/1916
Ashe, Arthur (tennis); Richmond, Va., 7/10/1943
Austin, Tracy (tennis); Rolling Hills, Calif., 12/2/1962
Babashoff, Shirley (swimming); Whittier, Calif., 1/31/1957
Baer, Max (boxer); Omaha, Neb. **(1909–1959)**
Bakken, Jim (James Leroy) (football); Madison, Wis., 11/2/1940
Banks, Ernie (baseball); Dallas, 1/31/1931
Bannister, Roger (runner); Harrow, England, 3/24/1929
Barry, Rick (Richard) (basketball); Elizabeth, N.J., 3/28/1944
Bauer, Hank (Henry) (baseball); East St. Louis, Ill., 7/31/1922
Baugh, Sammy (football); Temple, Tex., 3/17/1914
Bayi, Filbert (runner); Karratu, Tanganyika, 6/23/1953
Baylor, Elgin (basketball); Washington, D.C., 9/16/1934
Beamon, Bob (long jumper); New York City, 8/2/1946
Beliveau, Jean (hockey); Three Rivers, Quebec, Canada, 8/31/1931
Beman, Deane (golf); Washington, D.C., 4/22/1938
Bench, Johnny (Johnny Lee) (baseball); Oklahoma City, 12/7/1947
Berg, Patty (Patricia Jane) (golf); Minneapolis, 2/13/1918
Berning, Susie Maxwell (golf); Pasadena, Calif., 7/22/1941
Berra, Yogi (Lawrence) (baseball); St. Louis, 5/12/1925
Biletnikoff, Frederick (football); Erie, Pa., 2/23/1943
Bird, Larry (basketball); French Lick, Ind., 12/7/1956
Blaik, Earl H. (football); Detroit, 2/15/1897
Blanda, George Frederick (football); Youngwood, Pa., 9/17/1927
Blue, Vida (baseball); Mansfield, La., 7/28/1949
Borg, Björn (tennis); Stockholm, 6/6/1956
Boros, Julius (golf); Fairfield, Conn., 3/3/1920
Bossy, Mike (hockey); Montreal, 1/22/1957
Boston, Ralph (long jumper); Laurel, Miss., 5/9/1939
Bradley, Bill (William Warren) (basketball); Crystal City, Mo., 7/28/1943
Bradshaw, Terry (football); Shreveport, La., 9/2/1948
Breedlove, Craig (Norman) (speed driving); Los Angeles, 3/23/1938
Brett, George (baseball); Glendale, W. Va., 5/15/1953
Brock, Louis Clark (baseball); El Dorado, Ark., 6/18/1939
Brown, Jimmy (football); St. Simon Island, Ga., 2/17/1936
Brown, Larry (football); Clairton, Pa., 9/19/1947
Brumel, Valeri (high jumper); Tolbuzino, Siberia, 4/14/1942
Bryant, Rosalyn Evette (track); Chicago, 1/7/1956
Burton, Michael (swimming); Des Moines, Iowa, 7/3/1947
Butkus, Dick (Richard Marvin) (football); Chicago, 12/9/1942
Campanella, Roy (baseball); Homestead, Pa., 11/19/1921
Campbell, Earl (football); Tyler, Tex., 3/29/1955
Caponi, Donna Maria (golf); Detroit, 1/29/1945
Cappelletti, Gino (football); Keewatin, Minn., 3/26/1934
Carew, Rod (Rodney Cline) (baseball); Gatun, Panama, 10/1/1945
Carlos, John (sprinter); New York City, 6/5/1945
Carlton, Steven Norman (baseball); Miami, Fla., 12/22/1944
Carner, Joanne Gunderson (Mrs. Don) (golf); Kirkland, Wash., 3/4/1939
Casals, Rosemary (tennis); San Francisco, 9/16/1948
Casper, Billy (golf); San Diego, Calif., 6/24/1931
Caulkins, Tracy (swimming); Wimona, Minn., 1/11/63
Cauthen, Steve (jockey); Covington, Ky., 5/1/1960
Chamberlain, Wilt (Wilton) (basketball); Philadelphia, 8/21/1936
Chapot, Frank (equestrian); Camden, N.J., 2/24/1934
Chinaglia, Giorgio (soccer); Carrara, Italy 1/24/1947
Clarke, Bobby (Robert Earle) (hockey); Flin Flon, Manitoba, Canada, 8/13/1949

Clay, Cassius. See Ali, Muhammad
Clemente, Roberto Walker (baseball); Carolina, Puerto Rico **(1934–1972)**
Cobb, Tyrus Raymond (Ty) (baseball); Narrows, Ga. **(1886–1961)**
Cochran, Barbara Ann (skiing); Claremont, N.H., 1/4/1951
Cochran, Marilyn (skiing); Burlington, Vt., 2/7/1950
Cochran, Robert (skiing); Claremont, N.H., 12/11/1951
Coe, Sebastian Newbold (track); London, England, 9/29/1956
Colavito, Rocky (Rocco Domenico) (baseball); New York City, 8/10/1933
Comaneci, Nadia (gymnast); Onesti, Romania, 11/12/1961
Connors, Jimmy (James Scott) (tennis); East St. Louis, Ill., 9/2/1952
Cordero, Angel (jockey); Santurce, Puerto Rico, 5/8/1942
Cournoyer, Yvan Serge (hockey); Drummondville, Quebec, Canada, 11/22/1943
Court, Margaret Smith (tennis); Albury, New South Wales, Australia, 7/16/1942
Cousy, Bob (basketball); New York City, 8/9/1928
Crenshaw, Ben (golf); Austin, Tex., 1/11/1952
Cronin, Joe (baseball executive); San Francisco, 10/12/1906
Cruyff, Johan (soccer); Amsterdam, Netherlands, 4/25/47
Csonka, Larry (Lawrence Richard) (football); Stow, Ohio, 12/25/1946
Dancer, Stanley (harness racing); New Egypt, N.J., 7/25/1927
Dark, Alvin (baseball); Comanche, Okla., 1/7/1922
Davenport, Willie (track); Troy, Ala., 6/6/1943
Dawson, Leonard Ray (football); Alliance, Ohio, 6/20/1935
Dean, Dizzy (Jay Hanna) (baseball); Lucas, Ark. **(1911–1974)**
DeBusschere, Dave (basketball); Detroit, 10/16/1940
Delvecchio, Alex Peter (hockey); Fort William, Ontario, Canada, 12/4/1931
Demaret, Jim (golf); Houston, 5/10/1910
Dempsey, Jack (William H.) (boxing); Manassa, Colo., 6/24/1895
DeVicenzo, Roberto (golf); Buenos Aires, 4/14/1923
Dibbs, Edward George (tennis); Brooklyn, N.Y., 2/23/1951
Dietz, James W. (rowing); New York, N.Y., 1/12/1949
DiMaggio, Joe (baseball); Martinez, Calif., 11/25/1914
Dionne, Marcel (hockey); Drummondville, Quebec, Canada, 8/3/1951
Dominguin, Luis Miguel (matador); Madrid, 12/9/1926
Dorsett, Tony (football); Rochester, Pa., 4/7/1954
Dryden, Kenneth (hockey); Hamilton, Ontario, Canada, 8/4/1947
Drysdale, Don (baseball); Van Nuys, Calif., 7/23/1936
Duran, Roberto (boxing); Panama City 6/16/1951
Durocher, Leo (baseball); West Springfield, Mass., 7/27/1906
Durr, François (tennis); Algiers, Algeria, 12/25/1942
El Cordobés, (Manuel Benítez Pérez) (matador); Palma del Río, Córdoba, Spain, 5/4/1936(?)
Elder, Lee (golf); Dallas, 7/14/1934
Emerson, Roy (tennis); Kingsway, Australia, 11/3/1936
Ender, Kornelia (swimming); Plauen, East Germany, 10/25/1958
Erving, Julius (Dr. J) (basketball); Roosevelt, N.Y., 2/22/1950
Esposito, Phil (Philip Anthony) (hockey); Sault Ste. Marie, Ontario, Canada, 2/20/1942
Evans, Lee (runner); Mandena, Calif., 2/25/1947
Ewbank, Weeb (football); Richmond, Ind., 5/6/1907
Feller, Robert (Bobby) (baseball); Van Meter, Iowa, 11/3/1918
Feuerbach, Allan Dean (track); Preston, Iowa, 1/12/1948
Finley, Charles O. (sportsman); Ensley, Ala., 2/22/1918
Fischer, Bobby (chess); Chicago, 3/9/1943
Fitzsimmons, Bob (Robert Prometheus) (boxer); Cornwall, England **(1862–1917)**
Fleming, Peggy Gale (ice skating); San Jose, Calif., 7/27/1948
Ford, Whitey (Edward) (baseball); New York City, 10/21/1928
Foreman, George (boxing); Marshall, Tex., 1/10/1949
Fosbury, Richard (high jumper); Portland, Ore., 3/6/1947
Fox, Nellie (Jacob Nelson) (baseball); St. Thomas, Pa. **(1927–1975)**
Foxx, James Emory (baseball); Sudlersville, Md., **(1907–1967)**
Foyt, A. J. (auto racing); Houston, 1/16/1935
Francis, Emile (hockey); North Battleford, Sask., 9/13/1926
Fratianne, Linda (figure skating); Los Angeles, 8/2/1960
Frazier, Joe (boxing); Beauford, S.C., 1/17/1944
Frazier, Walt (basketball); Atlanta, 3/29/1945
Frick, Ford C. (baseball); Wawaka, Ind., **(1894–1978)**
Furniss, Bruce (swimming); Fresno, Calif., 5/27/1957
Gable, Dan (wrestling); Waterloo, Iowa; 10/25/1945

Gabriel, Roman (football); Wilmington, N.C., 8/5/1940
Gallagher, Michael Donald (skiing); Yonkers, N.Y., 10/3/1941
Gehrig, Lou (Henry Louis Gehrig) (baseball); New York City **(1903–1941)**
Gehringer, Charlie (baseball); Fowlerville, Mich., 5/11/1903
Geoffrion, Bernie (Boom Boom) (hockey); Montreal, 2/14/1931
Gerulaitis, Vitas (tennis); Brooklyn, N.Y., 7/26/1954
Giacomin, Ed (hockey); Sudbury, Ontario, Canada, 6/6/1939
Gibson, Bob (baseball); Omaha, Neb., 11/9/1935
Gifford, Frank (football); Santa Monica, Calif., 8/16/1930
Gilbert, Rod (Rodrique) (hockey); Montreal, 7/1/1941
Giles, Warren (baseball executive); Tiskilwa, Ill., **(1896–1979)**
Gilmore, Artis (basketball); Chipley, Fla., 9/21/1949
Glance, Harvey (track); Phenix City, Ala., 3/28/1957
Gonzalez, Pancho (tennis); Los Angeles, 5/9/1928
Goodell, Brian Stuart (swimming); Stockton, Calif., 4/2/1959
Goodrich, Gail (basketball); Los Angeles, 4/23/1943
Goolagong Cawley, Evonne (tennis); Griffith, Australia, 7/31/1951
Gottfried, Brian (tennis); Baltimore, Md., 1/27/1952
Graham, David (golf); Windsor, Australia; 5/23/1946
Graham, Otto Everett (football); Waukegan, Ill., 12/6/1921
Grange, Red (Harold) (football); Forksville, Pa., 6/13/1904
Green, Hubert (golf); Birmingham, Ala., 12/28/1946
Greene, Charles E. (sprinter); Pine Bluff, Ark., 3/21/1945
Gretzky, Wayne (hockey); Brantford, Ont., 1/26/1961
Griese, Bob (Robert Allen) (football); Evansville, Ind., 2/3/1945
Grove, Lefty (Robert Moses) (baseball); Lonaconing, Md., **(1900–1975)**
Groza, Lou (football); Martins Ferry, Ohio, 1/25/1924
Guidry, Ronald Ames (baseball); Lafayette, La., 8/28/1950
Gunter, Nancy Richey (tennis); San Angelo, Tex., 8/23/1942
Halas, George (football); Chicago, 2/2/1895
Hall, Gary (swimming); Fayetteville, N.C., 8/7/1951
Hamill, Dorothy (figure skater); Chicago, 1956(?)
Hammond, Kathy (runner); Sacramento, Calif., 11/2/1951
Harris, Franco (football); Ft. Dix, N.J., 3/7/1950
Hartack, William, Jr. (jockey); Colver, Pa., 12/9/1932
Haughton, William (harness racing); Gloversville, N.Y., 11/2/1923
Havlicek, John (basketball); Martins Ferry, Ohio, 4/8/1940
Hayes, Elvin (basketball); Rayville, La., 11/17/1945
Haynie, Sandra (golf); Fort Worth, 6/4/1943
Heiden, Eric (speed skater); Madison, Wis., 6/14/1958
Hencken, John (swimming); Culver City, Calif., 5/29/1954
Henderson, Rickey (baseball); Chicago, 12/25/1958
Henie, Sonja (ice skater); Oslo **(1912–1969)**
Hernandez, Keith (baseball); San Francisco, 10/20/1953
Hickcox, Charles (swimming); Phoenix, Ariz., 2/6/1947
Hines, James (sprinter); Dumas, Ark., 9/10/1946
Hodges, Gil (baseball); Princeton, Ind. **(1924–1972)**
Hogan, Ben (golf); Dublin, Tex., 8/13/1912
Holmes, Larry (boxing); Cuthert, Ga., 11/3/1949
Hornsby, Rogers (baseball); Winters, Tex. **(1896–1963)**
Hornung, Paul (football); Louisville, Ky., 12/23/1935
Houk, Ralph (baseball); Lawrence, Kan., 8/9/1919
Howard, Elston (baseball); St. Louis **(1929–1980)**
Howe, Gordon (hockey); Floral, Sask., Canada, 3/31/1928
Howell, Jim Lee (football); Lonoke, Ark., 9/27/1914
Hubbell, Carl (baseball); Carthage, Mo., 6/22/1903
Huff, Sam (Robert Lee) (football); Morgantown, W. Va., 10/4/1934
Hull, Bobby (hockey); Point Anne, Ontario, Canada, 1/3/1939
Hunter, Jim (Catfish) (baseball); Hertford, N.C., 4/8/1946
Huntley, Joni (track); McMinnville, Ore., 8/4/1956
Hutson, Donald (football); Pine Bluff, Ark., 1/31/1913
Insko, Del (harness racing); Amboy, Minn., 7/10/1931
Irwin, Hale (golf); Joplin, Mo., 6/3/1945
Jackson, Reggie (baseball); Wyncote, Pa., 5/18/1946
Jeffries, James J. (boxer); Carroll, Ohio **(1875–1953)**
Jenkins, Ferguson Arthur (baseball); Chatham, Ontario, Canada, 12/13/1943
Jenner, (W.) Bruce (track); Mt. Kisco, N.Y., 10/28/1949
Jezek, Linda (swimming); Palo Alto, Calif., 3/10/1960
Johnson, Earvin (Magic) (basketball); E. Lansing, Mich., 8/14/1959
Johnson, Anthony (rowing); Washington, D.C., 11/16/1940
Johnson, Jack (John Arthur Johnson) (boxer); Galveston, Tex. **(1876–1946)**
Johnson, Rafer (decathlon); Hillsboro, Tex., 8/18/1935
Jones, Deacon (David) (football); Eatonville, Fla., 12/9/1938
Juantoreno, Alberto (track); Santiago, Cuba, 12/3/1951
Jurgensen, Sonny (football); Wilmington, N.C., 8/23/1934
Kaat, Jim (baseball); Zeeland, Mich., 11/7/1938
Kaline, Al (Albert) (baseball); Baltimore, 12/19/1934
Keino, Kipchoge (runner); Kapchemoiymo, Kenya, 1/?/1940
Kelly, Leroy (football); Philadelphia, 5/20/1942
Kelly, Red (Leonard Patrick) (hockey); Simcoe, Ontario, Canada, 7/9/1927
Killebrew, Harmon (baseball); Payette, Idaho, 6/29/1936
Killy, Jean-Claude (skiing); Saint-Cloud, France, 8/30/1943
Kilmer, Bill (William Orland) (football); Topeka, Kan., 9/5/1939

King, Billie Jean (Billie Jean Moffitt) (tennis); Long Beach, Calif., 11/22/1943
Kinsella, John (swimming); Oak Park, Ill., 8/26/1952
Kodes, Jan (tennis); Prague, 3/1/1946
Kolb, Claudia (swimming); Hayward, Calif., 12/19/1949
Koosman, Jerry Martin (baseball); Appleton, Minn., 12/23/1942
Korbut, Olga (gymnast); Grodno, Byelorussia, U.S.S.R., 5/16/1955
Koufax, Sandy (Sanford) (baseball); Brooklyn, N.Y., 12/30/1935
Kramer, Jack (tennis); Las Vegas, Nev., 8/1/1921
Kramer, Jerry (football); Jordan, Mont., 1/23/1936
Kuhn, Bowie Kent (baseball); Takoma Park, Md., 10/28/1926
Kwalik, Ted (Thaddeus John) (football); McKees Rocks, Pa., 4/15/1947
Lafleur, Guy Damien (hockey); Thurson, Quebec, Canada, 8/20/1951
Laird, Ronald (walker); Louisville, Ky., 5/31/1935
Lamonica, Daryle (football); Fresno, Calif., 7/17/1941
Landis, Kenesaw Mountain (1st baseball commissioner); Millville, Ohio **(1866–1944)**
Landry, Tom (football); Mission, Tex., 9/11/1924
Landy, John (runner); Australia, 4/4/1930
Larrieu, Francie (track); Palo Alto, Calif., 11/28/1952
Lasorda, Tom (baseball); Norristown, Pa., 9/22/1927
Laver, Rod (tennis); Rockhampton, Australia, 8/9/1938
Lendl, Ivan (tennis); Prague, 3/7/1960
Leonard, Benny (Benjamin Leiner) (boxer); New York City **(1896–1947)**
Leonard, Sugar Ray (boxing); Wilmington, N.C., 5/17/1956
Lewis, Carl (track); Willingboro, N.J., 7/1/1961
Linehan, Kim (swimming); Bronxville, N.Y., 12/11/1962
Liquori, Marty (runner); Montclair, N.J., 9/11/1949
Little, Floyd Douglas (football); New Haven, Conn., 7/4/1942
Little, Lou (football); Leominster, Mass., **(1893–1979)**
Littler, Gene (golf); San Diego, Calif., 11/16/1920
Lloyd, Chris Evert (Christine Marie) (tennis); Fort Lauderdale, Fla., 12/21/1954
Lombardi, Vince (football); Brooklyn, N.Y. **(1913–1970)**
Longden, Johnny (horse racing); Wakefield, England, 2/14/1907
Lopez, Al (baseball); Tampa, Fla., 8/20/1908
Lopez, Nancy (golf); Torrance, Calif., 1/6/1957
Louis, Joe (Joe Louis Barrow) (boxing); Lafayette, Ala. **(1914–1981)**
Lynn, Frederic Michael (baseball); Chicago, Ill., 2/3/1952
Lynn, Janet (figure skating); Rockford, Ill., 4/6/1953
Mack, Connie (Cornelius Alexander McGillicuddy) (baseball executive); East Brookfield, Mass. **(1862–1956)**
Mackey, John (football); New York City, 9/24/1941
Mahovlich, Frank (Francis William) (hockey); Timmins, Ontario, Canada, 1/10/1938
Mahre, Phil (skiing); White Pass, Wash., 5/10/1957
Mann, Carol (golf); Buffalo, N.Y., 2/3/1941
Manning, Madeline (runner); Cleveland, 1/11/1948
Mantle, Mickey Charles (baseball); Spavinaw, Okla., 10/20/1931
Marciano, Rocky (boxing); Brockton, Mass. **(1923–1969)**
Marichal, Juan (baseball); Laguna Verde, Montecristi, Dominican Republic, 10/20/1937
Maris, Roger (baseball); Hibbing, Minn., 9/10/1934
Martin, Billy (Alfred Manuel) (baseball); Berkeley, Calif., 5/16/1928
Martin, Rick (Richard Lionel) (hockey); Verdun, Quebec, Canada, 7/26/1951
Mathews, Ed (Edwin) (baseball); Texarkana, Tex., 10/13/1931
Matson, Randy (shot putter); Kilgore, Tex., 3/5/1945
Mays, Willie (baseball); Westfield, Ala., 5/6/1931
McAdoo, Bob (basketball); Greensboro, N.C., 9/25/1951
McCarthy, Joe (Joseph Vincent) (baseball); Philadelphia **(1887–1978)**
McCovey, Willie Lee (baseball); Mobile, Ala., 1/10/1938
McEnroe, John Patrick, Jr. (tennis); Wiesbaden, Germany, 2/16/1959
McGraw, John Joseph (baseball); Truxton, N.Y. **(1873–1934)**
McLain, Dennis (baseball); Chicago, 3/24/1944
McMillan, Kathy Laverne (track); Raeford, N.C., 11/7/1957
Merrill, Janice (track); New London, Conn., 6/18/1962
Meyer, Deborah (swimming); Haddonfield, N.J., 8/14/1952
Middlecoff, Cary (golf); Halls, Tenn., 1/6/1921
Mikita, Stan (hockey); Sokolce, Czechoslovakia, 5/20/1940
Milburn, Rodney, Jr. (hurdler); Opelousas, La., 5/18/1950
Miller, Johnny (golf); San Francisco, 4/29/1947
Montgomery, Jim (swimming); Madison, Wis., 1/24/1955
Moore, Archie (boxing); Benoit, Miss., 12/13/1916
Morgan, Joe Leonard (baseball); Bonham, Tex., 9/19/1943
Morrall, Earl (football); Muskegon, Mich., 5/17/1934
Morton, Craig L. (football); Flint, Mich., 2/5/1943
Mosconi, Willie (pocket billiards); Philadelphia, 6/27/1913
Moser, Annemarie. See Proell, Annemarie
Moses, Edward Corley (track); Dayton, Ohio, 8/31/1958
Munson, Thurman (baseball); Akron, Ohio, **(1947–1979)**
Murphy, Calvin (basketball); Norwalk, Conn., 5/9/1948
Musial, Stan (baseball); Donora, Pa., 11/21/1920
Myers, Linda (archery); York, Pa., 6/19/1947
Naber, John (swimming); Evanston, Ill., 1/20/1956
Namath, Joe (Joseph William) (football); Beaver Falls, Pa., 5/31/1943
Nastase, Ilie (tennis); Bucharest, 7/19/1946

Navratilova, Martina (tennis); Prague, 10/18/1956
Nehemiah, Renaldo (track); Newark, N.J., 3/24/1959
Nelson, Cindy (skiing); Lutsen, Minn. 8/19/1955
Newcombe, John (tennis); Sydney, Australia, 5/23/1943
Niekro, Phil (baseball); Lansing, Ohio, 4/1/1939
Nicklaus, Jack (golf); Columbus, Ohio, 1/21/1940
North, Lowell (yachting); Springfield, Mo., 12/2/1929
Oerter, Al (discus thrower); New York City, 9/19/1936
Okker, Tom (tennis); Amsterdam, 2/22/1944
Oldfield, Barney (racing driver); Fulton County, Ohio **(1878–1946)**
Oliva, Tony (Pedro) (baseball); Pinar Del Rio, Cuba, 7/20/1940
Olsen, Merlin Jay (football); Logan, Utah, 9/15/1940
O'Malley, Walter (baseball executive); New York City **(1903–1979)**
Orantes, Manuel (tennis); Granada, Spain, 2/6/1949
Orr, Bobby (hockey); Parry Sound, Ontario, Canada, 3/20/1948
Ovett, Steve (track); Brighton, England, 10/9/1955
Owens, Jesse (track); Decatur, Ala. **(1914–1980)**
Pace, Darrell (archery); Cincinnati, 10/23/1956
Paige, Satchel (Leroy) (baseball); Mobile, Ala., **(1906–1982)**
Palmer, Arnold (golf); Latrobe, Pa., 9/10/1929
Palmer, James Alvin (baseball); New York City, 10/15/1945
Parent, Bernard Marcel (hockey); Montreal, 4/3/1945
Park, Brad (Douglas Bradford) (hockey); Toronto, Ontario, Canada, 7/6/1948
Parseghian, Ara (football); Akron, Ohio, 5/21/1923
Pasarell, Charles (tennis); San Juan, Puerto Rico, 2/12/1944
Patterson, Floyd (boxing); Waco, N.C., 1/4/1935
Peete, Calvin (golf); Detroit, Mich., 7/18/1943
Pelé (Edson Arantes do Nascimento) (soccer); Tres Coracoes, Brazil, 10/23/1940
Perry, Gaylord (baseball); Williamston, N.C., 9/13/1938
Perry, Jim (baseball); Williamston, N.C., 9/15/1938
Pettit, Bob (basketball); Baton Rouge, La., 12/12/1932
Petty, Richard Lee (auto racing); Randleman, N.C., 7/2/1937
Pincay, Laffit, Jr. (jockey); Panama City, Panama, 12/29/1946
Plante, Jacques (hockey); Shawinigan Falls, Quebec, Canada, 1/17/1929
Player, Gary (golf); Johannesburg, South Africa, 11/1/1935
Plunkett, Jim (football); San Jose, Calif., 12/5/1947
Potvin, Denis Charles (hockey); Hull, Quebec, Canada, 10/29/1953
Powell, Boog (baseball); Lakeland, Fla., 8/17/1941
Prefontaine, Steve Roland (runner); Coos Bay, Ore. **(1951–1975)**
Proell, Annemarie Moser (Alpine skier); Kleinarl, Austria, 3/27/1953
Ralston, Dennis (tennis); Bakersfield, Calif., 7/27/1942
Rankin, Judy Torluemke (golf); St. Louis, Mo., 2/18/1945
Ratelle, Jean (Joseph Gilbert Yvon Jean) (hockey); St. Jean, Quebec, Canada, 10/29/1953
Rawls, Betsy (Elizabeth Earle) (golf); Spartanburg, S.C., 5/4/1928
Reed, Willis (basketball); Hico, La., 6/25/1942
Reese, Pee Wee (Harold) (baseball); Ekron, Ky., 7/23/1919
Richard, Maurice (hockey); Montreal, 8/14/1924
Riessen, Martin (tennis); Hinsdale, Ill., 12/4/1941
Rigney, William (baseball); Alameda, Calif., 1/29/1918
Rizzuto, Phil (baseball); New York City, 9/25/1918
Roark, Helen Wills Moody (tennis); Centerville, Calif., 10/6/1906
Robertson, Oscar (basketball); Charlotte, Tenn., 11/24/1938
Robinson, Arnie (track); San Diego, Calif., 4/7/1948
Robinson, Brooks (baseball); Little Rock, Ark., 5/18/1937
Robinson, Frank (baseball); Beaumont, Tex., 8/31/1935
Robinson, Jackie (baseball); Cairo, Ga. **(1919–1972)**
Robinson, Larry Clark (hockey); Marvelville, Ontario, Canada, 6/2/1951
Robinson, (Sugar) Ray (boxing); Detroit, 5/3/1920
Rockne, Knute Kenneth (football); Voss, Norway **(1888–1931)**
Rockwell, Martha (skiing); Providence, R.I., 4/26/1944
Rono, Harry (track); Kiptaragon, Kenya, 2/12/1952
Rose, Pete (Peter Edward) (baseball); Cincinnati, 4/14/1942
Rosenbloom, Maxie (boxing); New York City **(1904–1976)**
Rosewall, Ken (tennis); Sydney, Australia, 11/2/1934
Rote, Kyle (football); San Antonio, 10/27/1928
Rozelle, Pete (Alvin Ray) (commissioner of National Football League); South Gate, Calif., 3/1/1926
Rudolph, Wilma Glodean (sprinter); St. Bethlehem, Tenn., 6/23/1940
Russell, Bill (basketball); Monroe, La., 2/12/1934
Ruth, Babe (George Herman Ruth) (baseball); Baltimore **(1895–1948)**
Rutherford, Johnny (auto racing); Fort Worth, 3/12/1938
Ryan, Nolan (Lynn Nolan, Jr.) (baseball); Refugio, Tex., 1/31/1947
Ryon, Luann (archery); Long Beach, Calif., 1/13/1953
Ryun, Jim (runner); Wichita, Kan., 4/29/1947
Salazar, Alberto (track); Havana, 8/7/1958
Santana, Manuel (Manuel Santana Martinez) (tennis); Chamartín, Spain, 5/10/1938
Sayers, Gale (football); Wichita, Kan., 5/30/1943
Schmidt, Mike (baseball); Dayton, Ohio, 9/27/1949
Schoendienst, Al (Albert) (baseball); Germantown, Ill., 2/2/1923
Scholander, Donald (swimming); Charlotte, N.C., 4/30/1946
Seagren, Bob (Robert Lloyd) (pole vaulter); Pomona, Calif., 10/17/1946
Seaver, Tom (baseball); Fresno, Calif., 11/17/1944

Seidler, Maren (track); Brooklyn, N.Y., 6/11/1962
Shoemaker, Willie (jockey); Fabens, Tex., 8/19/1931
Shorter, Frank (runner); Munich, Germany, 10/31/1947
Shula, Don (Donald Francis) (football); Grand River, Ohio, 1/4/1930
Silvester, Jay (discus thrower); Tremonton, Utah, 2/27/1937
Simpson, O. J. (Orenthal James) (football); San Francisco, 7/9/1947
Sims, Billy (football); St. Louis, 9/18/1955
Smith, Bubba (Charles Aaron) (football); Orange, Tex., 2/28/1945
Smith, Ronnie Ray (sprinter); Los Angeles, 3/28/1949
Smith, Stanley Roger (tennis); Pasadena, Calif., 12/14/1946
Smith, Tommie (sprinter); Clarksville, Tex., 6/5/1944
Smoke, Marcia Jones (canoeing); Oklahoma City, 7/18/1941
Snead, Sam (golf); Hot Springs, Va., 5/27/1912
Sneva, Tom (auto racing); Spokane, Wash., 6/1/1948
Snider, Duke (Edwin) (baseball); Los Angeles, 9/19/1926
Solomon, Harold (tennis); Washington, D.C., 9/17/1952
Spahn, Warren (baseball); Buffalo, N.Y., 4/23/1921
Speaker, Tristram (baseball); Hubbard City, Tex. **(1888–1958)**
Spinks, Leon (boxing); St. Louis, 7/11/1953
Spitz, Mark (swimming); Modesto, Calif., 2/10/1950
Stabler, Kenneth (football); Foley, Ala., 12/25/1945
Stagg, Amos Alonzo (football); West Orange, N.J. **(1862–1965)**
Stargell, Willie (Wilver Dornell) (baseball); Earlsboro, Okla., 3/6/1941
Starr, Bart (football); Montgomery, Ala., 1/9/1934
Staubach, Roger (football); Cincinnati, 2/5/1942
Steinkraus, William C. (equestrian); Cleveland, 10/12/1925
Stenerud, Jan (football); Fetsund, Norway, 11/26/1942
Stengel, Casey (Charles Dillon) (baseball); Kansas City, Mo. **(1891–1975)**
Stenmark, Ingemar (Alpine skier); Tarnaby, Sweden, 3/18/1956
Stockton, Richard LaClede (tennis); New York City, 2/18/1951
Stones, Dwight Edwin (track); Los Angeles, 12/6/1953
Sullivan, John Lawrence (boxer); Boston **(1858–1918)**
Sutton, Don (Donald Howard) (baseball); Clio, Ala., 4/2/1945
Swann, Lynn (football); Alcoa, Tenn., 3/7/1952
Tanner, Leonard Roscoe III (tennis); Chattanooga, Tenn., 10/15/1951
Tarkenton, Fran (Francis) (football); Richmond, Va., 2/3/1940
Tebbetts, Birdie (George R.) (baseball); Nashua, N.H., 11/10/1914
Thoeni, Gustavo (Alpine skier); Trafoi, Italy, 2/28/1951
Thompson, David (basketball); Shelby, N.C., 7/13/1954
Thorpe, Jim (James Francis Thorpe) (all-around athlete); nr. Prague, Okla. **(1888–1953)**
Tilden, William Tatem II (tennis); Philadelphia **(1893–1953)**
Tittle, Y. A. (Yelberton Abraham) (football); Marshall, Tex., 10/24/1926
Toomey, William (decathlon); Philadelphia, 1/10/1939
Trevino, Lee (golf); Dallas, 12/1/1939
Tunney, Gene (James J.) (boxing); New York City **(1898–1978)**
Tyus, Wyomia (runner); Griffin, Ga., 8/29/1945
Unitas, John (football); Pittsburgh, 5/7/1933
Unser, Al (auto racing); Albuquerque, N. Mex., 5/29/1939
Unser, Bobby (auto racing); Albuquerque N. Mex., 2/20/1934
Valenzuela, Fernando (baseball); Sonora, Mexico, 11/1/1960
Van Brocklin, Norm (football); Eagle Butte, S. Dak., 3/15/1926
Vilas, Guillermo (tennis); Mar del Plata, Argentina, 8/17/1952
Viren, Lasse (track); Myrskyla, Finland, 7/12/1949
Wade, Virginia (tennis); Bournemouth, England, 7/10/1945
Wagner, Honus (John Peter Honus) (baseball); Carnegie, Pa. **(1867–1955)**
Walcott, Jersey Joe (Arnold Cream) (boxing); Merchantville, N.J., 1/31/1914
Walton, Bill (basketball); La Mesa, Calif., 11/5/1952
Watson, Martha Rae (track); Long Beach, Calif., 8/19/1946
Watson, Tom (golf); Kansas City, Mo., 9/4/1949
Weaver, Earl (baseball); St. Louis, 8/14/1930
Webster, Alex (football); Kearny, N.J., 4/19/1931
Weiskopf, Tom (golf); Massillon, Ohio, 11/9/1942
Weiss, George (baseball executive); New Haven, Conn. **(1895–1972)**
Weissmuller, Johnny (swimmer and actor); Windber, Pa., 6/2/1904
West, Jerry (basketball); Cheylan, W. Va., 5/28/1938
White, Willye B. (long jumper); Money, Miss., 1/1/1936
Whitworth, Kathy (golf); Monahans, Tex., 9/27/1939
Wilkens, Mac Maurice (track); Eugene, Ore., 11/15/1950
Wilkins, Lennie (basketball); 11/25/1937
Wilkinson, Bud (football); Minneapolis, 4/23/1916
Williams, Dick (baseball); St. Louis, 5/7/1929
Williams, Ted (baseball); San Diego, Calif., 8/30/1918
Wills, Maury (baseball); Washington, D.C., 10/2/1932
Winfield, Dave (baseball); St. Paul, Minn., 10/3/1951
Wohlhuter, Richard C. (runner); Geneva, Ill. 12/23/1945
Woodhead, Cynthia (swimming); Riverside, Calif., 2/7/1964
Wottle, David James (runner); Canton, Ohio, 8/7/1950
Wright, Mickey (Mary Kathryn) (golf); San Diego, Calif., 2/14/1935
Yarborough, Cale (William Caleb) (auto racing); Timmonsville, S.C., 3/27/1939
Yastrzemski, Carl (baseball); Southampton, N.Y., 8/22/1939
Young, Cy (Denton True Young) (baseball); Gilmore, Ohio **(1867–1955)**
Young, Sheila (speed skater, bicycle racer); Detroit, 10/14/1950

# THE OLYMPIC GAMES

(W)—Site of Winter Games. (S)—Site of Summer Games

| | | | | | | |
|---|---|---|---|---|---|---|
| 1896 | Athens | 1936 | Garmisch-Partenkirchen (W) | 1968 | Mexico City (S) | |
| 1900 | Paris | 1936 | Berlin (S) | 1972 | Sapporo, Japan (W) | |
| 1904 | St. Louis | 1948 | St. Moritz (W) | 1972 | Munich (S) | |
| 1906 | Athens | 1948 | London (S) | 1976 | Innsbruck, Austria (W) | |
| 1908 | London | 1952 | Oslo (W) | 1976 | Montreal (S) | |
| 1912 | Stockholm | 1952 | Helsinki (S) | 1980 | Lake Placid (W) | |
| 1920 | Antwerp | 1956 | Cortina d'Ampezzo, Italy (W) | 1980 | Moscow (S) | |
| 1924 | Chamonix (W) | 1956 | Melbourne (S) | 1984 | Sarajevo, Yugoslavia (W) | |
| 1924 | Paris (S) | 1960 | Squaw Valley, Calif. (W) | 1984 | Los Angeles (S) | |
| 1928 | St. Moritz (W) | 1960 | Rome (S) | 1988 | Calgary, Alberta (W) | |
| 1928 | Amsterdam (S) | 1964 | Innsbruck, Austria (W) | 1988 | Seoul, South Korea (S) | |
| 1932 | Lake Placid (W) | 1964 | Tokyo (S) | | | |
| 1932 | Los Angeles (S) | 1968 | Grenoble, France (W) | | | |

The first Olympic Games of which there is record occurred in 776 B.C. and consisted of one event, a great foot race of about 200 yards held on a plain by the River Alpheus (now the Ruphia) just outside the little town of Olympia in Greece. It was from that date that the Greeks began to keep their calendar by "Olympiads," the four-year spans between the celebrations of the famous games.

The modern Olympic Games, which started in Athens in 1896, are the result of the devotion of a French educator, Baron Pierre de Coubertin, to the idea that, since young people and athletics have gone together down the ages, education and athletics might well go hand-in-hand toward a better international understanding.

At the top of the organization responsible for the Olympic movement and the staging of the Games every four years is the International Olympic Committee (IOC). Other important roles are played by National Olympic Committees in each participating country, international sports federations, and the Organizing Committee of the host city.

In 1979, the IOC consisted of 89 members, elected by the IOC itself. Its headquarters are in Lausanne, Switzerland. The president of the IOC is Juan Antonio Samaranch of Spain.

The Olympic motto is "Citius, Altius, Fortius"— "Faster, Higher, Stronger." The Olympic symbol is five interlocking circles colored blue, yellow, black, green, and red, on a white background, representing the five continents. At least one of these colors appears in the national flag of every country.

## Summer Games

### TRACK AND FIELD—MEN

#### 100-Meter Dash

| | | |
|---|---|---|
| 1896 | Thomas Burke, United States | 12s |
| 1900 | Francis W. Jarvis, United States | 10.8s |
| 1904 | Archie Hahn, United States | 11s |
| 1906 | Archie Hahn, United States | 11.2s |
| 1908 | Reginald Walker, South Africa | 10.8s |
| 1912 | Ralph Craig, United States | 10.8s |
| 1920 | Charles Paddock, United States | 10.8s |
| 1924 | Harold Abrahams, Great Britain | 10.6s |
| 1928 | Percy Williams, Canada | 10.8s |
| 1932 | Eddie Tolan, United States | 10.3s |
| 1936 | Jesse Owens, United States | 10.3s[1] |
| 1948 | Harrison Dillard, United States | 10.3s |
| 1952 | Lindy Remigino, United States | 10.4s |
| 1956 | Bobby Morrow, United States | 10.5s |
| 1960 | Armin Hary, Germany | 10.2s |
| 1964 | Robert Hayes, United States | 10s |
| 1968 | James Hines, United States | 9.9s |
| 1972 | Valery Borzov, U.S.S.R. | 10.14s |
| 1976 | Hasely Crawford, Trinidad and Tebago | 10.06s |
| 1980 | Allan Wells, Britain | 10.25s |

1. Wind assisted.

#### 200-Meter Dash

| | | |
|---|---|---|
| 1900 | John Tewksbury, United States | 22.2s |
| 1904 | Archie Hahn, United States | 21.6s |
| 1908 | Robert Kerr, Canada | 22.6s |
| 1912 | Ralph Craig, United States | 21.7s |
| 1920 | Allan Woodring, United States | 22s |
| 1924 | Jackson Scholz, United States | 21.6s |
| 1928 | Percy Williams, Canada | 21.8s |
| 1932 | Eddie Tolan, United States | 21.2s |
| 1936 | Jesse Owens, United States | 20.7s |
| 1948 | Melvin E. Patton, United States | 21.1s |
| 1952 | Andrew Stanfield, United States | 20.7s |
| 1956 | Bobby Morrow, United States | 20.6s |
| 1960 | Livio Berruti, Italy | 20.5s |
| 1964 | Henry Carr, United States | 20.3s |
| 1968 | Tommie Smith, United States | 19.8s |
| 1972 | Valery Borzov, U.S.S.R. | 20s |
| 1976 | Don Quarrie, Jamaica | 20.23s |
| 1980 | Pietro Mennea, Italy | 20.19s |

#### 400-Meter Dash

| | | |
|---|---|---|
| 1896 | Thomas Burke, United States | 54.2s |
| 1900 | Maxwell Long, United States | 49.4s |
| 1904 | Harry Hillman, United States | 49.2s |
| 1906 | Paul Pilgrim, United States | 53.2s |
| 1908 | Wyndham Halswelle, Great Britain (walkover) | 50s |
| 1912 | Charles Reidpath, United States | 48.2s |
| 1920 | Bevil Rudd, South Africa | 49.6s |
| 1924 | Eric Liddell, Great Britain | 47.6s |
| 1928 | Ray Barbuti, United States | 47.8s |
| 1932 | William Carr, United States | 46.2s |
| 1936 | Archie Williams, United States | 46.5s |
| 1948 | Arthur Wint, Jamaica, B.W.I. | 46.2s |
| 1952 | George Rhoden, Jamaica, B.W.I. | 45.9s |
| 1956 | Charles Jenkins, United States | 46.7s |
| 1960 | Otis Davis, United States | 44.9s |
| 1964 | Mike Larrabee, United States | 45.1s |
| 1968 | Lee Evans, United States | 43.8s |
| 1972 | Vincent Matthews, United States | 44.66s |
| 1976 | Alberto Juantorena, Cuba | 44.26s |
| 1980 | Viktor Markin, U.S.S.R. | 44.60s |

#### 800-Meter Run

| | | |
|---|---|---|
| 1896 | Edwin Flack, Australia | 2m11s |
| 1900 | Alfred Tysoe, Great Britain | 2m1.4s |
| 1904 | James Lightbody, United States | 1m56s |
| 1906 | Paul Pilgrim, United States | 2m1.2s |
| 1908 | Mel Sheppard, United States | 1m52.8s |
| 1912 | Ted Meredith, United States | 1m51.9s |

| | | |
|---|---|---|
| 1920 | Albert Hill, Great Britain | 1m53.4s |
| 1924 | Douglas Lowe, Great Britain | 1m52.4s |
| 1928 | Douglas Lowe, Great Britain | 1m51.8s |
| 1932 | Thomas Hampson, Great Britain | 1m49.8s |
| 1936 | John Woodruff, United States | 1m52.9s |
| 1948 | Malvin Whitfield, United States | 1m49.2s |
| 1952 | Malvin Whitfield, United States | 1m49.2s |
| 1956 | Tom Courtney, United States | 1m47.7s |
| 1960 | Peter Snell, New Zealand | 1m46.3s |
| 1964 | Peter Snell, New Zealand | 1m45.1s |
| 1968 | Ralph Doubell, Australia | 1m44.3s |
| 1972 | David Wottle, United States | 1m45.9s |
| 1976 | Alberto Juantorena, Cuba | 1m43.5s |
| 1980 | Steve Ovett, Britain | 1m45.4s |

## 1,500-Meter Run

| | | |
|---|---|---|
| 1896 | Edwin Flack, Australia | 4m33.2s |
| 1900 | Charles Bennett, Great Britain | 4m6s |
| 1904 | James Lightbody, United States | 4m5.4s |
| 1906 | James Lightbody, United States | 4m12s |
| 1908 | Mel Sheppard, United States | 4m3.4s |
| 1912 | Arnold Jackson, Great Britain | 3m56.8s |
| 1920 | Albert Hill, Great Britain | 4m1.8s |
| 1924 | Paavo Nurmi, Finland | 3m53.6s |
| 1928 | Harry Larva, Finland | 3m53.2s |
| 1932 | Luigi Beccali, Italy | 3m51.2s |
| 1936 | Jack Lovelock, New Zealand | 3m47.8s |
| 1948 | Henri Eriksson, Sweden | 3m49.8s |
| 1952 | Joseph Barthel, Luxembourg | 3m45.2s |
| 1956 | Ron Delany, Ireland | 3m41.2s |
| 1960 | Herb Elliott, Australia | 3m35.6s |
| 1964 | Peter Snell, New Zealand | 3m38.1s |
| 1968 | Kipchoge Keino, Kenya | 3m34.9s |
| 1972 | Pekka Vasala, Finland | 3m36.3s |
| 1976 | John Walker, New Zealand | 3m39.17s |
| 1980 | Sebastian Coe, Britain | 3m38.4s |

## 5,000-Meter Run

| | | |
|---|---|---|
| 1912 | Hannes Kolehmainen, Finland | 14m36.6s |
| 1920 | Joseph Guillemot, France | 14m55.6s |
| 1924 | Paavo Nurmi, Finland | 14m31.2s |
| 1928 | Willie Ritola, Finland | 14m38s |
| 1932 | Lauri Lehtinen, Finland | 14m30s |
| 1936 | Gunnar Hockert, Finland | 14m22.2s |
| 1948 | Gaston Reiff, Belgium | 14m17.6s |
| 1952 | Emil Zatopek, Czechoslovakia | 14m6.6s |
| 1956 | Vladimir Kuts, U.S.S.R. | 13m39.6s |
| 1960 | Murray Halberg, New Zealand | 13m43.4s |
| 1964 | Bob Schul, United States | 13m48.8s |
| 1968 | Mohamed Gammoudi, Tunisia | 14m.05s |
| 1972 | Lasse Viren, Finland | 13m26.4s |
| 1976 | Lasse Viren, Finland | 13m24.76s |
| 1980 | Miruts Yifter, Ethiopia | 13m21s |

## 5-Mile Run

| | | |
|---|---|---|
| 1906 | H. Hawtrey, Great Britain | 26m26.2s |
| 1908 | Emil Voigt, Great Britain | 25m11.2s |

## 10,000-Meter Run

| | | |
|---|---|---|
| 1912 | Hannes Kolehmainen, Finland | 31m20.8s |
| 1920 | Paavo Nurmi, Finland | 31m45.8s |
| 1924 | Willie Ritola, Finland | 30m23.2s |
| 1928 | Paavo Nurmi, Finland | 30m18.8s |
| 1932 | Janusz Kusocinski, Poland | 30m11.4s |
| 1936 | Ilmari Salminen, Finland | 30m15.4s |
| 1948 | Emil Zatopek, Czechoslovakia | 29m59.6s |
| 1952 | Emil Zatopek, Czechoslovakia | 29m17s |
| 1956 | Vladimir Kuts, U.S.S.R. | 28m45.6s |
| 1960 | Peter Bolotnikov, U.S.S.R. | 28m32.2s |
| 1964 | Billy Mills, United States | 28m24.4s |
| 1968 | Naftali Temu, Kenya | 29m27.4s |
| 1972 | Lasse Viren, Finland | 27m38.4s |
| 1976 | Lasse Viren, Finland | 27m40.38s |

| | | |
|---|---|---|
| 1980 | Miruts Yifter, Ethiopia | 27m42.7s |

## Marathon

| | | |
|---|---|---|
| 1896 | Spiridon Loues, Greece | 2h58m50s |
| 1900 | Michel Teato, France | 2h59m45s |
| 1904 | Thomas Hicks, United States | 3h28m53s |
| 1906 | William J. Sherring, Canada | 2h51m23.65s |
| 1908 | John J. Hayes, United States | 2h55m18.4s |
| 1912 | Kenneth McArthur, South Africa | 2h36m54.8s |
| 1920 | Hannes Kolehmainen, Finland | 2h32m35.8s |
| 1924 | Albin Stenroos, Finland | 2h41m22.6s |
| 1928 | A. B. El Ouafi, France | 2h32m57s |
| 1932 | Juan Zabala, Argentina | 2h31m36s |
| 1936 | Kitei Son, Japan | 2h29m19.2s |
| 1948 | Delfo Cabrera, Argentina | 2h34m51.6s |
| 1952 | Emil Zatopek, Czechoslovakia | 2h23m3.2s |
| 1956 | Alain Mimoun, France | 2h25m |
| 1960 | Abebe Bikila, Ethiopia | 2h15m16.2s |
| 1964 | Abebe Bikila, Ethiopia | 2h12m11.2s |
| 1968 | Mamo Wold, Ethiopia | 2h20m26.4s |
| 1972 | Frank Shorter, United States | 2h12m19.8s |
| 1976 | Walter Cierpinski, East Germany | 2h09m55s |
| 1980 | Walter Cierpinski, East Germany | 2h11m3s |

## 110-Meter Hurdles

| | | |
|---|---|---|
| 1896 | Thomas Curtis, United States | 17.6s |
| 1900 | Alvin Kraenzlein, United States | 15.4s |
| 1904 | Frederick Schule, United States | 16s |
| 1906 | R. G. Leavitt, United States | 16.2s |
| 1908 | Forrest Smithson, United States | 15s |
| 1912 | Frederick Kelly, United States | 15.1s |
| 1920 | Earl Thomson, Canada | 14.8s |
| 1924 | Daniel Kinsey, United States | 15s |
| 1928 | Sydney Atkinson, South Africa | 14.8s |
| 1932 | George Saling, United States | 14.6s |
| 1936 | Forrest Towns, United States | 14.2s |
| 1948 | William Porter, United States | 13.9s |
| 1952 | Harrison Dillard, United States | 13.7s |
| 1956 | Lee Calhoun, United States | 13.5s |
| 1960 | Lee Calhoun, United States | 13.8s |
| 1964 | Hayes Jones, United States | 13.6s |
| 1968 | Willie Davenport, United States | 13.3s |
| 1972 | Rodney Milburn, United States | 13.24s |
| 1976 | Guy Drut, France | 13.30s |
| 1980 | Thomas Munkett, East Germany | 13.39s |

## 200-Meter Hurdles

| | | |
|---|---|---|
| 1900 | Alvin Kraenzlein, United States | 25.4s |
| 1904 | Harry Hillman, United States | 24.6s |

## 400-Meter Hurdles

| | | |
|---|---|---|
| 1900 | John Tewksbury, United States | 57.6s |
| 1904 | Harry Hillman, United States | 53s |
| 1908 | Charles Bacon, United States | 55s |
| 1920 | Frank Loomis, United States | 54s |
| 1924 | F. Morgan Taylor, United States | 52.6s |
| 1928 | Lord David Burghley, Great Britain | 53.4s |
| 1932 | Robert Tisdall, Ireland | 51.8s[1] |
| 1936 | Glenn Hardin, United States | 52.4s |
| 1948 | Roy Cochran, United States | 51.1s |
| 1952 | Charles Moore, United States | 50.8s |
| 1956 | Glenn Davis, United States | 50.1s |
| 1960 | Glenn Davis, United States | 49.3s |
| 1964 | Rex Cawley, United States | 49.6s |
| 1968 | David Hemery, Great Britain | 48.1s |
| 1972 | John Akii-Bua, Uganda | 47.8s |
| 1976 | Edwin Moses, United States | 47.64 |
| 1980 | Volker Beck, East Germany | 48.70s |

1. Record not allowed.

## 2,500-Meter Steeplechase

| | | |
|---|---|---|
| 1900 | George Orton, United States | 7m34s |
| 1904 | James Lightbody, United States | 7m39.6s |

### 3,000-Meter Steeplechase

| | | |
|---|---|---|
| 1920 | Percy Hodge, Great Britain | 10m0.4s |
| 1924 | Willie Ritola, Finland | 9m33.6s |
| 1928 | Toivo Loukola, Finland | 9m21.8s |
| 1932 | Volmari Iso-Hollo, Finland | 10m33.4s[1] |
| 1936 | Volmari Iso-Hollo, Finland | 9m3.8s |
| 1948 | Thure Sjoestrand, Sweden | 9m4.6s |
| 1952 | Horace Ashenfelter, United States | 8m45.4s |
| 1956 | Chris Brasher, Great Britain | 8m41.2s |
| 1960 | Zdzislaw Krzyskowiak, Poland | 8m34.2s |
| 1964 | Gaston Roelants, Belgium | 8m30.8s |
| 1968 | Amos Biwott, Kenya | 8m51s |
| 1972 | Kipchoge Keino, Kenya | 8m23.6s |
| 1976 | Anders Gardervd, Sweden | 8m08.02s |
| 1980 | Bronislaw Malinowski, Poland | 8m9.7s |

1. About 3,450 meters—extra lap by error.

### Cross-Country

| | | |
|---|---|---|
| 1912 | Hannes Kolehmainen, Finland (8,000 meters) | 45m11.6s |
| 1920 | Paavo Nurmi, Finland (10,000 meters) | 27m15s |
| 1924 | Paavo Nurmi, Finland (10,000 meters) | 32m54.8s |

### Cross-Country Team Races

| | | Pts. |
|---|---|---|
| 1912 | Sweden (8,000 meters) | 10 |
| 1920 | Finland (10,000 meters) | 10 |
| 1924 | Finland (10,000 meters) | 11 |

### 1,500-Meter Walk

| | | |
|---|---|---|
| 1906 | George V. Bonhag, United States | 7m12.6s |

### 3,000-Meter Walk

| | | |
|---|---|---|
| 1920 | Ugo Frigerio, Italy | 13m14.2s |

### 10,000-Meter Walk

| | | |
|---|---|---|
| 1912 | George Goulding, Canada | 46m28.4s |
| 1920 | Ugo Frigerio, Italy | 48m6.2s |
| 1924 | Ugo Frigerio, Italy | 47m49s |
| 1948 | John Mikaelsson, Sweden | 45m13.2s |
| 1952 | John Mikaelsson, Sweden | 45m2.8s |

### 20,000-Meter Walk

| | | |
|---|---|---|
| 1956 | Leonid Spirin, U.S.S.R. | 1h31m27.4s |
| 1960 | Vladimir Golubnichy, U.S.S.R. | 1h34m7.2s |
| 1964 | Ken Mathews, Great Britain | 1h29m34s |
| 1968 | Vladimir Golubnichy, U.S.S.R. | 1h33m58.4s |
| 1972 | Peter Frenkel, East Germany | 1h26m42.4s |
| 1976 | Daniel Bautista, Mexico | 1h24m40.6s |
| 1980 | Maurizio Damiliano, Italy | 1h23m35.5s |

### 50,000-Meter Walk

| | | |
|---|---|---|
| 1932 | Thomas W. Green, Great Britain | 4h50m10s |
| 1936 | Harold Whitlock, Great Britain | 4h30m41.1s |
| 1948 | John Ljunggren, Sweden | 4h41m52s |
| 1952 | Giuseppe Dordoni, Italy | 4h28m7.8s |
| 1956 | Norman Read, New Zealand | 4h30m42.8s |
| 1960 | Donald Thompson, Great Britain | 4h25m30s |
| 1964 | Abdon Pamich, Italy | 4h11m12.4s |
| 1968 | Christoph Hohne, East Germany | 4h20m13.6s |
| 1972 | Bern Kannernberg, West Germany | 3h56m11.6s |
| 1980 | Hartwig Gauder, East Germany | 3h49m24s |

### 400-Meter Relay (4 x 100)

| | | |
|---|---|---|
| 1912 | Great Britain | 42.4s |
| 1920 | United States | 42.2s |
| 1924 | United States | 41s |
| 1928 | United States | 41s |
| 1932 | United States | 40s |
| 1936 | United States | 39.8s |
| 1948 | United States | 40.6s |
| 1952 | United States | 40.1s |
| 1956 | United States | 39.5s |
| 1960 | Germany | 39.5s |
| 1964 | United States | 39s |
| 1968 | United States | 38.2s |
| 1972 | United States | 38.19s |
| 1976 | United States | 38.33s |
| 1980 | U.S.S.R. | 38.26s |

### 1,600-Meter Relay (200–200–400–800)

| | | |
|---|---|---|
| 1908 | United States | 3m29.4s |

### 1,600-Meter Relay (4 x 400)

| | | |
|---|---|---|
| 1912 | United States | 3m16.6s |
| 1920 | Great Britain | 3m22.2s |
| 1924 | United States | 3m16s |
| 1928 | United States | 3m14.2s |
| 1932 | United States | 3m8.2s |
| 1936 | Great Britain | 3m9s |
| 1948 | United States | 3m10.4s |
| 1952 | Jamaica, B.W.I. | 3m3.9s |
| 1956 | United States | 3m4.8s |
| 1960 | United States | 3m2.2s |
| 1964 | United States | 3m0.7s |
| 1968 | United States | 2m56.1s |
| 1972 | Kenya | 2m59.8s |
| 1976 | United States | 2m58.65s |
| 1980 | U.S.S.R. | 3m01.1s |

### Team Race

| | | Pts. |
|---|---|---|
| 1900 | Great Britain (5,000 meters) | 26 |
| 1904 | United States (4 miles) | 27 |
| 1908 | Great Britain (3 miles) | 6 |
| 1912 | United States (3,000 meters) | 9 |
| 1920 | United States (3,000 meters) | 10 |
| 1924 | Finland (3,000 meters) | 9 |

### Standing High Jump

| | | |
|---|---|---|
| 1900 | Ray Ewry, United States | 5 ft 5 in. |
| 1904 | Ray Ewry, United States | 4 ft 11 in. |
| 1906 | Ray Ewry, United States | 5 ft 1⅝ in. |
| 1908 | Ray Ewry, United States | 5 ft 2 in. |
| 1912 | Platt Adams, United States | 5 ft 4⅛ in. |

### Running High Jump

| | | |
|---|---|---|
| 1896 | Ellery Clark, United States | 5 ft 11¼ in. |
| 1900 | Irving Baxter, United States | 6 ft 2¾ in. |
| 1904 | Samuel Jones, United States | 5 ft 11 in. |
| 1906 | Con Leahy, Ireland | 5 ft 9⅞ in. |
| 1908 | Harry Porter, United States | 6 ft 3 in. |
| 1912 | Alma Richards, United States | 6 ft 4 in. |
| 1920 | Richmond Landon, United States | 6 ft 4¼ in. |
| 1924 | Harold Osborn, United States | 6 ft 5 15/16 in. |
| 1928 | Robert W. King, United States | 6 ft 4⅜ in. |
| 1932 | Duncan McNaughton, Canada | 6 ft 5⅝ in. |
| 1936 | Cornelius Johnson, United States | 6 ft 7 15/16 in. |
| 1948 | John Winter, Australia | 6 ft 6 in. |
| 1952 | Walter Davis, United States | 6 ft 8 5/16 in. |
| 1956 | Charles Dumas, United States | 6 ft 11¼ in. |
| 1960 | Robert Shavlakadze, U.S.S.R. | 7 ft 1 in. |
| 1964 | Valeri Brumel, U.S.S.R. | 7 ft 1¾ in. |
| 1968 | Dick Fosbury, United States | 7 ft 4¼ in. |
| 1972 | Yuri Tarmak, U.S.S.R. | 7 ft 3¾ in. |
| 1976 | Jacek Wszola, Poland | (2.25m) 7 ft 4½ in. |
| 1980 | Gerd Wessig, East Germany | 7ft 8¾ in. |

### Standing Long Jump

| | | |
|---|---|---|
| 1900 | Ray Ewry, United States | 10 ft 6⅖ in. |
| 1904 | Ray Ewry, United States | 11 ft 4⅞ in. |
| 1906 | Ray Ewry, United States | 10 ft 10 in. |
| 1908 | Ray Ewry, United States | 10 ft 11¼ in. |
| 1912 | Constantin Tsicilitiras, Greece | 11 ft ¼ in. |

**Long Jump**

| | | |
|---|---|---|
| 1896 | Ellery Clark, United States | 20 ft 9¾ in. |
| 1900 | Alvin Kraenzlein, United States | 23 ft 6⅞ in. |
| 1904 | Myer Prinstein, United States | 24 ft 1 in. |
| 1906 | Myer Prinstein, United States | 23 ft 7½ in. |
| 1908 | Frank Irons, United States | 24 ft 6½ in. |
| 1912 | Albert Gutterson, United States | 24 ft 11¼ in. |
| 1920 | William Petterssen, Sweden | 23 ft 5½ in. |
| 1924 | DeHart Hubbard, United States | 24 ft 5⅛ in. |
| 1928 | Edward B. Hamm, United States | 25 ft 4¾ in. |
| 1932 | Edward Gordon, United States | 25 ft ¾ in. |
| 1936 | Jesse Owens, United States | 26 ft $5\frac{5}{16}$ in. |
| 1948 | Willie Steele, United States | 25 ft 8 in. |
| 1952 | Jerome Biffle, United States | 24 ft 10 in. |
| 1956 | Gregory Bell, United States | 25 ft 8¼ in. |
| 1960 | Ralph Boston, United States | 26 ft 7¾ in. |
| 1964 | Lynn Davies, Great Britain | 26 ft 5¾ in. |
| 1968 | Bob Beamon, United States | 29 ft 2½ in. |
| 1972 | Randy Williams, United States | 27 ft ½ in. |
| 1976 | Arnie Robinson, United States | (8.35m) 24 ft 7¾ in. |
| 1980 | Lutz Dombrowski, Poland | 28 ft ¼ in. |

**Standing Triple Jump**

| | | |
|---|---|---|
| 1900 | Ray Ewry, United States | 34 ft 8½ in. |
| 1904 | Ray Ewry, United States | 34 ft 7¼ in. |

**Triple Jump**

| | | |
|---|---|---|
| 1896 | James B. Connolly, United States | 45 ft |
| 1900 | Myer Prinstein, United States | 47 ft 4¼ in. |
| 1904 | Myer Prinstein, United States | 47 ft |
| 1906 | P. G. O'Connor, Ireland | 46 ft 2 in. |
| 1908 | Timothy Ahearne, Great Britain | 48 ft 11¼ in. |
| 1912 | Gustaf Lindblom, Sweden | 48 ft 5⅛ in. |
| 1920 | Vilho Tuulos, Finland | 47 ft 6⅞ in. |
| 1924 | Archie Winter, Australia | 50 ft 11⅛ in. |
| 1928 | Mikio Oda, Japan | 49 ft $10\frac{13}{16}$ in. |
| 1932 | Chuhei Nambu, Japan | 51 ft 7 in. |
| 1936 | Naoto Tajima, Japan | 52 ft 5⅞ in. |
| 1948 | Arne Ahman, Sweden | 50 ft 6¼ in. |
| 1952 | Adhemar da Silva, Brazil | 53 ft 2½ in. |
| 1956 | Adhemar da Silva, Brazil | 53 ft 7½ in. |
| 1960 | Jozef Schmidt, Poland | 55 ft 1¾ in. |
| 1964 | Jozef Schmidt, Poland | 55 ft 3¼ in. |
| 1968 | Viktor Saneyev, U.S.S.R. | 57 ft ¾ in. |
| 1972 | Viktor Saneyev, U.S.S.R. | 56 ft 11 in. |
| 1976 | Viktor Saneyev, U.S.S.R. | (17.29m) 56 ft 8¾ in. |
| 1980 | Jaak Uudmae, U.S.S.R. | 56 ft 11⅛ in. |

**Pole Vault**

| | | |
|---|---|---|
| 1896 | William Hoyt, United States | 10 ft 9¾ in. |
| 1900 | Irving Baxter, United States | 10 ft 9⅞ in. |
| 1904 | Charles Dvorak, United States | 11 ft 6 in. |
| 1906 | Fernand Gouder, France | 11 ft 6 in. |
| 1908 | Alfred Gilbert, United States, and Edward Cook, United States (tie) | 12 ft 2 in. |
| 1912 | Harry Babcock, United States | 12 ft 11½ in. |
| 1920 | Frank Foss, United States | 13 ft $5\frac{9}{16}$ in. |
| 1924 | Lee Barnes, United States | 12 ft 11½ in. |
| 1928 | Sabin W. Carr, United States | 13 ft 9⅜ in. |
| 1932 | William Miller, United States | 14 ft 1⅞ in. |
| 1936 | Earle Meadows, United States | 14 ft 3¼ in. |
| 1948 | Guinn Smith, United States | 14 ft 1¼ in. |
| 1952 | Robert Richards, United States | 14 ft 11⅛ in. |
| 1956 | Robert Richards, United States | 14 ft 11½ in. |
| 1960 | Don Bragg, United States | 15 ft 5⅛ in. |
| 1964 | Fred Hansen, United States | 16 ft 8¾ in. |
| 1968 | Bob Seagren, United States | 17 ft 8½ in. |
| 1972 | Wolfgang Nordwig, East Germany | 18 ft ½ in. |
| 1976 | Tadeusz Slusarski, Poland | (5.50m) 18 ft ½ in. |
| 1980 | Wladyslaw Kozakiewicz, Poland | 18 ft 11½ in. |

**16-lb Shot-Put**

| | | |
|---|---|---|
| 1896 | Robert Garrett, United States | 36 ft 9¾ in. |
| 1900 | Richard Sheldon, United States | 46 ft 3⅛ in. |
| 1904 | Ralph Rose, United States | 48 ft 7 in. |
| 1906 | Martin Sheridan, United States | 40 ft 4⅘ in. |
| 1908 | Ralph Rose, United States | 46 ft 7½ in. |
| 1912 | Pat McDonald, United States | 50 ft 4 in. |
| 1920 | Ville Porhola, Finland | 48 ft 7⅛ in. |
| 1924 | Clarence Houser, United States | 49 ft 2½ in. |
| 1928 | John Kuck, United States | 52 ft $11\frac{11}{16}$ in. |
| 1932 | Leo Sexton, United States | 52 ft $6\frac{3}{16}$ in. |
| 1936 | Hans Woellke, Germany | 53 ft 1¾ in. |
| 1948 | Wilbur Thompson, United States | 56 ft 2 in. |
| 1952 | Parry O'Brien, United States | 57 ft 1½ in. |
| 1956 | Parry O'Brien, United States | 60 ft 11 in. |
| 1960 | Bill Nieder, United States | 64 ft 6¾ in. |
| 1964 | Dallas Long, United States | 66 ft 8¼ in. |
| 1968 | Randy Matson, United States | 67 ft 4¾ in. |
| 1972 | Wladyslaw Komar, Poland | 69 ft 6 in. |
| 1976 | Udo Beyer, East Germany | (21.05m) 69 ft ¾ in. |
| 1980 | Vladimir Kiselyov, U.S.S.R. | 70 ft ½ in. |

**16-lb Shot-Put (Both Hands)**

| | | |
|---|---|---|
| 1912 | Ralph Rose, United States | 90 ft 5⅜ in. |

**Discus Throw**

| | | |
|---|---|---|
| 1896 | Robert Garrett, United States | 95 ft 7½ in. |
| 1900 | Rudolf Bauer, Hungary | 118 ft 2⅞ in. |
| 1904 | Martin Sheridan, United States | 128 ft 10½ in. |
| 1906 | Martin Sheridan, United States | 136 ft ⅓ in. |
| 1908 | Martin Sheridan, United States | 134 ft 2 in. |
| 1912 | Armas Taipale, Finland | 145 ft $\frac{9}{16}$ in. |
| 1920 | Elmer Niklander, Finland | 146 ft 7 in. |
| 1924 | Clarence Houser, United States | 151 ft 5¼ in. |
| 1928 | Clarence Houser, United States | 155 ft 2⅘ in. |
| 1932 | John Anderson, United States | 162 ft 4⅞ in. |
| 1936 | Ken Carpenter, United States | 165 ft 7⅜ in. |
| 1948 | Adolfo Consolini, Italy | 173 ft 2 in. |
| 1952 | Simeon Iness, United States | 180 ft 6½ in. |
| 1956 | Al Oerter, United States | 184 ft 10½ in. |
| 1960 | Al Oerter, United States | 194 ft 2 in. |
| 1964 | Al Oerter, United States | 200 ft 1½ in. |
| 1968 | Al Oerter, United States | 212 ft 6 in. |
| 1972 | Ludvik Danek, Czechoslovakia | 211 ft 3 in. |
| 1976 | Mac Wilkins, United States | (67.5m) 221 ft 5 in. |
| 1980 | Viktor Rashchupkin, U.S.S.R. | 218 ft 8 in. |

**Discus Throw—Greek Style**

| | | |
|---|---|---|
| 1906 | Werner Jaervinen, Finland | 115 ft 4 in. |
| 1908 | Martin Sheridan, United States | 124 ft 8 in. |

**Discus Throw (Both Hands)**

| | | |
|---|---|---|
| 1912 | Armas Taipale, Finland | 271 ft 10⅛ in. |

**Javelin Throw**

| | | |
|---|---|---|
| 1906 | Eric Lemming, Sweden | 175 ft 6 in. |
| 1908 | Eric Lemming, Sweden | 179 ft 10½ in. |
| 1912 | Eric Lemming, Sweden | 198 ft 11¼ in. |
| 1920 | Jonni Myyra, Finland | 215 ft 9¾ in. |
| 1924 | Jonni Myyra, Finland | 206 ft 6¾ in. |
| 1928 | Eric Lundquist, Sweden | 218 ft 6⅛ in. |
| 1932 | Matti Jarvinen, Finland | 238 ft 7 in. |
| 1936 | Gerhard Stoeck, Germany | 235 ft $8\frac{5}{16}$ in. |
| 1948 | Kaj Rautavaara, Finland | 228 ft 10½ in. |
| 1952 | Cy Young, United States | 242 ft ¾ in. |
| 1956 | Egil Danielsen, Norway | 281 ft 2¼ in. |
| 1960 | Viktor Tsibulenko, U.S.S.R. | 277 ft 8⅜ in. |
| 1964 | Pauli Nevala, Finland | 271 ft 2¼ in. |
| 1968 | Janis Lusis, U.S.S.R. | 295 ft 7 in. |
| 1972 | Klaus Wolfermann, West Germany | 296 ft 10 in. |
| 1976 | Miklos Nemeth, Hungary | (94.58m) 310 ft 4 in. |
| 1980 | Dainis Kula, U.S.S.R. | 299 ft 2⅜ in. |

**Javelin Throw—Free Style**

| | | |
|---|---|---|
| 1908 | Eric Lemming, Sweden | 178 ft 7½ in. |

### Javelin Throw (Both Hands)

| | | |
|---|---|---|
| 1912 | Julius Saaristo, Finland | 358 ft 11½ in. |

### 16-lb Hammer Throw

| | | |
|---|---|---|
| 1900 | John Flanagan, United States | 167 ft 4 in. |
| 1904 | John Flanagan, United States | 168 ft 1 in. |
| 1908 | John Flanagan, United States | 170 ft 4¼ in. |
| 1912 | Matt McGrath, United States | 179 ft 7⅛ in. |
| 1920 | Pat Ryan, United States | 173 ft 5⅝ in. |
| 1924 | Fred Tootell, United States | 174 ft 10¼ in. |
| 1928 | Patrick O'Callaghan, Ireland | 168 ft 7½ in. |
| 1932 | Patrick O'Callaghan, Ireland | 176 ft 11⅛ in. |
| 1936 | Karl Hein, Germany | 185 ft 4 in. |
| 1948 | Imre Nemeth, Hungary | 183 ft 11½ in. |
| 1952 | Jozsef Csermak, Hungary | 197 ft 11⁹⁄₁₆ in. |
| 1956 | Harold Connolly, United States | 207 ft 2¾ in. |
| 1960 | Vasily Rudenkov, U.S.S.R. | 220 ft 1⅝ in. |
| 1964 | Romuald Klim, U.S.S.R. | 228 ft 9½ in. |
| 1968 | Gyula Zsivotzky, Hungary | 240 ft 8 in. |
| 1972 | Anatoly Bondarchuk, U.S.S.R. | 247 ft 8½ in. |
| 1976 | Yuri Sedykh, U.S.S.R. | (77.52m) 254 ft 4 in. |
| 1980 | Yuri Sedykh, U.S.S.R. | (81.80m) 268 ft 4½ in. |

### Throwing the Stone (14 lbs.)

| | | |
|---|---|---|
| 1906 | Nicolas Georgantas, Greece | 65 ft 4⅕ in. |

### 56-lb Weight Throw

| | | |
|---|---|---|
| 1904 | Etienne Desmarteau, Canada | 34 ft 4 in. |
| 1920 | Pat McDonald, United States | 36 ft 11⅝ in. |

### All-Around

| | | |
|---|---|---|
| 1904 | Thomas Kiely, Great Britain | 6,036 pts. |

### Pentathlon

| | | |
|---|---|---|
| 1906 | H. Mellander, Sweden | 24 pts. |
| 1912 | Ferdinand Bie, Norway | 21 pts. |
| 1920 | Eero Lehtonen, Finland | 14 pts. |
| 1924 | Eero Lehtonen, Finland | 16 pts. |

### Decathlon

| | | |
|---|---|---|
| 1912 | Hugo Wieslander, Sweden | 7,724.495 pts. |
| 1920 | Helge Lovland, Norway | 6,804.35 pts. |
| 1924 | Harold Osborn, United States | 7,710.775 pts. |
| 1928 | Paavo Yrjola, Finland | 8,053.29 pts. |
| 1932 | James Bausch, United States | 8,462.23 pts. |
| 1936 | Glenn Morris, United States | 7,900 pts.[1] |
| 1948 | Robert B. Mathias, United States | 7,139 pts. |
| 1952 | Robert B. Mathias, United States | 7,887 pts. |
| 1956 | Milton Campbell, United States | 7,937 pts. |
| 1960 | Rafer Johnson, United States | 8,392 pts. |
| 1964 | Willi Holdorf, Germany | 7,887 pts.[1] |
| 1968 | Bill Toomey, United States | 8,193 pts. |
| 1972 | Nikolai Avilov, U.S.S.R. | 8,454 pts. |
| 1976 | Bruce Jenner, United States | 8,618 pts. |
| 1980 | Daley Thompson, Britain | 8,495 pts. |

1. Point system revised.

### Tug of War

| | | | |
|---|---|---|---|
| 1904 | United States | 1912 | Sweden |
| 1906 | Germany | 1920 | Great Britain |
| 1908 | Great Britain | | |

## TRACK AND FIELD—WOMEN

### 100-Meter Dash

| | | |
|---|---|---|
| 1928 | Elizabeth Robinson, United States | 12.2s |
| 1932 | Stella Walsh, Poland | 11.9s |
| 1936 | Helen Stephens, United States | 11.5s |
| 1948 | Fanny Blankers-Koen, Netherlands | 11.9s |
| 1952 | Marjorie Jackson, Australia | 11.5s |
| 1956 | Betty Cuthbert, Australia | 11.5s |
| 1960 | Wilma Rudolph, United States | 11s |
| 1964 | Wyomia Tyus, United States | 11.4s |
| 1968 | Wyomia Tyus, United States | 11s |
| 1972 | Renate Stecher, East Germany | 11.07s |
| 1976 | Annegret Richter, West Germany | 11.08s |
| 1980 | Lyudmila Kondratyeva, U.S.S.R. | 11.06s |

### 200-Meter Dash

| | | |
|---|---|---|
| 1948 | Fanny Blankers-Koen, Netherlands | 24.4s |
| 1952 | Marjorie Jackson, Australia | 23.7s |
| 1956 | Betty Cuthbert, Australia | 23.4s |
| 1960 | Wilma Rudolph, United States | 24s |
| 1964 | Edith McGuire, United States | 23s |
| 1968 | Irena Szewinska, Poland | 22.5s |
| 1972 | Renate Stecher, East Germany | 22.4s |
| 1976 | Baerbel Eckert, East Germany | 22.37s |
| 1980 | Barbara Wockel, East Germany | 22.03s |

### 400-Meter Dash

| | | |
|---|---|---|
| 1964 | Betty Cuthbert, Australia | 52s |
| 1968 | Colette Besson, France | 52s |
| 1972 | Monika Zehrt, East Germany | 51.08s |
| 1976 | Irena Szewinska, Poland | 49.29s |
| 1980 | Marita Koch, East Germany | 48.88s |

### 800-Meter Run

| | | |
|---|---|---|
| 1928 | Lina Radke, Germany | 2m16.8s |
| 1960 | Ljudmila Shevcova, U.S.S.R. | 2m4.3s |
| 1964 | Ann Packer, Great Britain | 2m1.1s |
| 1968 | Madeline Manning, United States | 2m0.9s |
| 1972 | Hildegard Falck, West Germany | 1m58.6s |
| 1976 | Tatiana Kazankina, U.S.S.R. | 1m54.94s |
| 1980 | Nadezhda Olizarenko, U.S.S.R. | 1m53.5s |

### 1,500-Meter Run

| | | |
|---|---|---|
| 1972 | Ludmila Bragina, U.S.S.R. | 4m01.4s |
| 1976 | Tatiana Kazankina, U.S.S.R. | 4m05.48s |

### 80-Meter Hurdles

| | | |
|---|---|---|
| 1932 | Mildred Didrikson, United States | 11.7s |
| 1936 | Trebisonda Valla, Italy | 11.7s |
| 1948 | Fanny Blankers-Koen, Netherlands | 11.2s |
| 1952 | Shirley S. de la Hunty, Australia | 10.9s |
| 1956 | Shirley S. de la Hunty, Australia | 10.7s |
| 1960 | Irina Press, U.S.S.R. | 10.8s |
| 1964 | Karin Balzer, Germany | 10.5s[1] |
| 1968 | Maureen Caird, Australia | 10.3s |

1. Wind assisted.

### 100-Meter Hurdles

| | | |
|---|---|---|
| 1972 | Annelie Ehrhardt, East Garmany | 12.59s |
| 1976 | Johanna Schaller, East Germany | 12.77s |
| 1980 | Vera Komisova, U.S.S.R. | 12.56s |

### 400-Meter Relay

| | | |
|---|---|---|
| 1928 | Canada | 48.4s |
| 1932 | United States | 47s |
| 1936 | United States | 46.9s |
| 1948 | Netherlands | 47.5s |
| 1952 | United States | 45.9s |
| 1956 | Australia | 44.5s |
| 1960 | United States | 44.5s |
| 1964 | Poland | 43.6s |
| 1968 | United States | 42.8s |
| 1972 | West Germany | 42.81s |
| 1976 | East Germany | 42.55s |
| 1980 | East Germany | 41.60s |

### 1,600-Meter Relay

| | | |
|---|---|---|
| 1972 | East Germany | 3m23s |
| 1976 | East Germany | 3m19.23s |
| 1980 | U.S.S.R. | 3m20.2s |

### Running High Jump

| | | |
|---|---|---|
| 1928 | Ethel Catherwood, Canada | 5 ft 3 in. |
| 1932 | Jean Shiley, United States | 5 ft 5¼ in. |
| 1936 | Ibolya Csak, Hungary | 5 ft 3 in. |
| 1948 | Alice Coachman, United States | 5 ft 6⅛ in. |
| 1952 | Ester Brand, South Africa | 5 ft 5¾ in. |
| 1956 | Mildred McDaniel, United States | 5 ft 9¼ in. |
| 1960 | Iolanda Balas, Romania | 6 ft ¾ in. |
| 1964 | Iolanda Balas, U.S.S.R. | 6 ft 2¾ in. |
| 1968 | Miloslava Rezkova, Czechoslovakia | 5 ft 11¾ in. |
| 1972 | Ulrike Meyfarth, West Germany | 6 ft 3⅝ in. |
| 1976 | Rosemarie Ackerman, E. Germany | (1.93m) 6 ft 4 in. |
| 1980 | Sara Simeoni, Italy | 6 ft 5½ in. |

### Long Jump

| | | |
|---|---|---|
| 1948 | Olga Gyarmati, Hungary | 18 ft 8¼ in. |
| 1952 | Yvette Williams, New Zealand | 20 ft 5¾ in. |
| 1956 | Elzbieta Krzesinska, Poland | 20 ft 9¾ in. |
| 1960 | Vera Krepkina, U.S.S.R. | 20 ft 10¾ in. |
| 1964 | Mary Rand, Great Britain | 22 ft 2 in. |
| 1968 | Viorica Ciscopoleanu, Romania | 22 ft 4½ in. |
| 1972 | Heidemarie Rosendahl, West Germany | 22 ft 3 in. |
| 1976 | Angela Voigt, East Germany | (6.72m) 22 ft ½ in. |
| 1980 | Tatiana Kolpakova, U.S.S.R. | 23 ft 2 in. |

### Shot-Put

| | | |
|---|---|---|
| 1948 | Micheline Ostermeyer, France | 45 ft 1½ in. |
| 1952 | Galina Zybina, U.S.S.R. | 50 ft 1½ in. |
| 1956 | Tamara Tishkyevich, U.S.S.R. | 54 ft 5 in. |
| 1960 | Tamara Press, U.S.S.R. | 56 ft 9⅞ in. |
| 1964 | Tamara Press, U.S.S.R. | 59 ft 6 in. |
| 1968 | Margitta Gummel, East Germany | 64 ft 4 in. |
| 1972 | Nadezhda Chizhova, U.S.S.R. | 69 ft |
| 1976 | Ivanka Christova, Bulgaria | (21.16m) 69 ft 5 in. |
| 1980 | Ilona Sluplanek, East Germany | 73 ft 6 in. |

### Discus Throw

| | | |
|---|---|---|
| 1928 | Helena Konopacka, Poland | 129 ft 11⅞ in. |
| 1932 | Lillian Copeland, United States | 133 ft 2 in. |
| 1936 | Gisela Mauermayer, Germany | 156 ft $3\frac{3}{16}$ in. |
| 1948 | Micheline Ostermeyer, France | 137 ft 6½ in. |
| 1952 | Nina Romaschkova, U.S.S.R. | 168 ft $8\frac{7}{16}$ in. |
| 1956 | Olga Fikotova, Czechoslovakia | 176 ft 1½ in. |
| 1960 | Nina Ponomareva, U.S.S.R. | 180 ft 8¼ in. |
| 1964 | Tamara Press, U.S.S.R. | 187 ft 10¾ in. |
| 1968 | Lia Manoliu, Romania | 191 ft 2½ in. |
| 1972 | Faina Melnik, U.S.S.R. | 218 ft 7 in. |
| 1976 | Evelin Schlaak, East Germany | (69.0m) 226 ft 4 in. |
| 1980 | Evelin Jahl, East Germany | 229 ft 6½ in. |

### Javelin Throw

| | | |
|---|---|---|
| 1932 | Mildred Didrikson, United States | 143 ft 4 in. |
| 1936 | Tilly Fleischer, Germany | 148 ft 2¾ in. |
| 1948 | Herma Bauma, Austria | 149 ft 6 in. |
| 1952 | Dana Zatopek, Czechoslovakia | 165 ft 7 in. |
| 1956 | Inessa Janzeme, U.S.S.R. | 176 ft 8 in. |
| 1960 | Elvira Ozolina, U.S.S.R. | 183 ft 8 in. |
| 1964 | Mihaela Penes, Romania | 198 ft 7½ in. |
| 1968 | Angela Nemeth, Hungary | 198 ft 0 in. |
| 1972 | Ruth Fuchs, East Germany | 209 ft 7 in. |
| 1976 | Ruth Fuchs, East Germany | (65.94m) 216 ft 4 in. |
| 1980 | Maria Colon, Cuba | 224 ft 5 in. |

### Pentathlon

| | | |
|---|---|---|
| 1964 | Irina Press, U.S.S.R. | 5,246 pts. |
| 1968 | Ingrid Becker, West Germany | 5,098 pts. |
| 1972 | Mary Peters, Britain | 4,801 pts. |
| 1976 | Siegrun Siegl, East Germany | 4,745 pts. |
| 1980 | Nadyezhda Tkachenko, U.S.S.R. | 5,083 pts. |

## SWIMMING—MEN

### 50-Yard Freestyle

| | | |
|---|---|---|
| 1904 | Zoltan de Halmay, Hungary | 28s |

### 100 Meters Freestyle

| | | |
|---|---|---|
| 1896 | Alfred Hajos, Hungary | 1m22.2s |
| 1904 | Zoltan de Halmay, Hungary | 1m2.8s[1] |
| 1906 | Charles Daniels, United States | 1m13s |
| 1908 | Charles Daniels, United States | 1m5.6s |
| 1912 | Duke P. Kahanamoku, United States | 1m3.4s |
| 1920 | Duke P. Kahanamoku, United States | 1m1.4s |
| 1924 | John Weissmuller, United States | 59s |
| 1928 | John Weissmuller, United States | 58.6s |
| 1932 | Yasuji Miyazaki, Japan | 58.2s |
| 1936 | Ferenc Csik, Hungary | 57.6s |
| 1948 | Walter Ris, United States | 57.3s |
| 1952 | Clarke Scholes, United States | 57.4s |
| 1956 | Jon Henricks, Australia | 55.4s |
| 1960 | John Devitt, Australia | 55.2s |
| 1964 | Don Schollander, United States | 53.4s |
| 1968 | Michael Wenden, Australia | 52.2s |
| 1972 | Mark Spitz, United States | 51.22s |
| 1976 | Jim Montgomery, United States | 49.99s |
| 1980 | Jorg Woithe, East Germany | 50.40s |

1. 100 yards.

### 200-Meter Freestyle

| | | |
|---|---|---|
| 1900 | Frederick Lane, Australia | 2m25.2s |
| 1904 | Charles Daniels, United States | 2m44.2s[1] |
| 1968 | Michael Wenden, Australia | 1m55.2s |
| 1972 | Mark Spitz, United States | 1m52.78s |
| 1976 | Bruce Furniss, United States | 1m50.29s |
| 1980 | Sergei Kopliakov, U.S.S.R. | 1m49.81s |

1. 220 yards.

### 400-Meter Freestyle

| | | |
|---|---|---|
| 1896 | Paul Neumann, Austria | 8m12.6s[1] |
| 1904 | Charles Daniels, United States | 6m16.2s[2] |
| 1906 | Otto Sheff, Austria | 6m23.8s |
| 1908 | Henry Taylor, Great Britain | 5m36.8s |
| 1912 | George Hodgson, Canada | 5m24.4s |
| 1920 | Norman Ross, United States | 5m26.8s |
| 1926 | Jonn Weissmuller, United States | 5m4.2s |
| 1928 | Albert Zorilla, Argentina | 5m1.6s |
| 1932 | Clarence Crabbe, United States | 4m48.4s |
| 1936 | Jack Medica, United States | 4m44.5s |
| 1948 | William Smith, United States | 4m41s |
| 1952 | Jean Boiteux, France | 4m30.7s |
| 1956 | Murray Rose, Australia | 4m27.3s |
| 1960 | Murray Rose, Australia | 4m18.3s |
| 1964 | Don Schollander, United States | 4m12.2s |
| 1968 | Mike Burton, United States | 4m9s |
| 1972 | Bradford Cooper, Australia[3] | 4m00.27s |
| 1976 | Brian Goodell, United States | 3m51.93s |
| 1980 | Vladimir Salnikov, U.S.S.R. | 3m51.31s |

1. 500 meters. 2. 440 yards. 3. Rick DeMont, United States, won but was disqualified following day for medical reasons.

### 1,200-Meter Freestyle

| | | |
|---|---|---|
| 1896 | Alfred Hajos, Hungary | 18m22.2s |

### 1,500 Meters Freestyle

| | | |
|---|---|---|
| 1904 | Emil Rausch, Germany | 27m18.2s[1] |
| 1906 | Henry Taylor, Great Britain | 28m28s[2] |
| 1908 | Henry Taylor, Great Britain | 22m48.4s |
| 1912 | George Hodgson, Canada | 22m |
| 1920 | Norman Ross, United States | 22m23.2s |
| 1924 | Andrew Charlton, Australia | 20m6.6s |
| 1928 | Arne Borg, Sweden | 19m51.8s |
| 1932 | Kusuo Kitamura, Japan | 19m12.4s |
| 1936 | Noboru Terada, Japan | 19m13.7s |

| 1948 | James McLane, United States | 19m18.5s |
|---|---|---|
| 1952 | Ford Konno, United States | 18m30s |
| 1956 | Murray Rose, Australia | 17m58.9s |
| 1960 | Jon Konrads, Australia | 17m19.6s |
| 1964 | Robert Windle, Australia | 17m1.7s |
| 1968 | Michael Burton, United States | 16m38.9s |
| 1972 | Mike Burton, United States | 15m52.58s |
| 1976 | Brian Goodell, United States | 15m02.4s |
| 1980 | Vladimir Salnikov, U.S.S.R. | 14m58.27s |

1. One mile. 2. 1,600 meters.

## 4,000-Meter Freestyle

| 1900 | John Jarvis, Great Britain | 58m24s |
|---|---|---|

## 100-Meter Backstroke

| 1904 | Walter Brack, Germany | 1m16.8s[1] |
|---|---|---|
| 1908 | Arno Bieberstein, Germany | 1m24.6s |
| 1912 | Harry Hebner, United States | 1m21.2s |
| 1920 | Warren Kealoha, United States | 1m15.2s |
| 1924 | Warren Kealoha, United States | 1m13.2s |
| 1928 | George Kojac, United States | 1m8.2s |
| 1932 | Masaji Kiyokawa, Japan | 1m8.6s |
| 1936 | Adolph Kiefer, United States | 1m5.9s |
| 1948 | Allen Stack, United States | 1m6.4s |
| 1952 | Yoshinobu Oyakawa, United States | 1m5.4s |
| 1956 | David Thiele, Australia | 1m2.2s |
| 1960 | David Thiele, Australia | 1m1.9s |
| 1968 | Roland Matthes, East Germany | 58.7s |
| 1972 | Roland Matthes, East Germany | 56.58s |
| 1976 | John Naber, United States | 55.49s |
| 1980 | Bengt Baron, Sweden | 56.53s |

1. 100 yards

## 200-Meter Backstroke

| 1900 | Ernst Hoppenberg, Germany | 2m47s |
|---|---|---|
| 1964 | Jed Graef, United States | 2m10.3s |
| 1968 | Roland Matthes, East Germany | 2m9.6s |
| 1972 | Roland Matthes, East Germany | 2m2.82s |
| 1976 | John Naber, United States | 1m59.19s |
| 1980 | Sandor Wladar, Hungary | 2:01.93s |

## 100-Meter Breaststroke

| 1968 | Donald McKenzie, United States | 1m7.7s |
|---|---|---|
| 1972 | Nobutaka Taguchi, Japan | 1m4.94s |
| 1976 | John Hencken, United States | 1m03.11s |
| 1980 | Duncan Goodhew, Britain | 1m03.34s |

## 200-Meter Breaststroke

| 1908 | Frederick Holman, Great Britain | 3m9.2s |
|---|---|---|
| 1912 | Walter Bathe, Germany | 3m1.8s |
| 1920 | Haken Malmroth, Sweden | 3m4.4s |
| 1924 | Robert Skelton, United States | 2m56.6s |
| 1928 | Yoshiyuki Tsuruta, Japan | 2m48.8s |
| 1932 | Yoshiyuki Tsuruta, Japan | 2m45.4s |
| 1936 | Tetsuo Hamuro, Japan | 2m41.5s |
| 1948 | Joseph Verdeur, United States | 2m39.3s |
| 1952 | John Davies, Australia | 2m34.4s |
| 1956 | Masaru Furukawa, Japan | 2m34.7s |
| 1960 | Bill Mulliken, United States | 2m37.4s |
| 1964 | Ian O'Brien, Australia | 2m27.8s |
| 1968 | Felipe Munoz, Mexico | 2m28.7s |
| 1972 | John Hencken, United States | 2m21.55s |
| 1976 | David Willkie, Britain | 2m15.11s |
| 1980 | Robertas Zulpa, U.S.S.R. | 2m15.85s |

## 400-Meter Breaststroke

| 1904 | Georg Zacharias, Germany | 7m23.6s[1] |
|---|---|---|
| 1912 | Walter Bathe, Germany | 6m29.6s |
| 1920 | Haken Malmroth, Sweden | 6m31.8s |

1. 440 yards

## 100-Meter Butterfly

| 1968 | Douglas Russell, United States | 55.9s |
|---|---|---|
| 1972 | Mark Spitz, United States | 54.27s |
| 1976 | Matt Vogel, United States | 54.35s |
| 1980 | Par Arvidsson, Sweden | 54.92s |

## 200-Meter Butterfly

| 1956 | Bill Yorzyk, United States | 2m19.3s |
|---|---|---|
| 1960 | Mike Troy, United States | 2m12.8s |
| 1964 | Kevin Berry, Australia | 2m6.6s |
| 1968 | Carl Robie, United States | 2m8.7s |
| 1972 | Mark Spitz, United States | 2m00.7s |
| 1976 | Mike Bruner, United States | 1m59.23s |
| 1980 | Sergei Fesenko, U.S.S.R. | 1m59.76s |

## 200-Meter Individual Medley

| 1968 | Charles Hickcox, United States | 2m12s |
|---|---|---|
| 1972 | Gunnar Larsson, Sweden | 2m7.17s |

## 400-Meter Individual Medley

| 1964 | Dick Roth, United States | 4m45.4s |
|---|---|---|
| 1968 | Charles Hickcox, United States | 4m48.4s |
| 1972 | Gunnar Larsson, Sweden | 4m31.98s |
| 1976 | Rod Strachan, United States | 4m23.68s |
| 1980 | Aleksandr Sidorenko, U.S.S.R. | 4m22.8s |

## 60-Meter Underwater

| 1900 | de Vaudeville, France | 1m53.4s |
|---|---|---|

## 200-Meter Obstacle

| 1900 | Frederick Lane, Australia | 2m38.4s |
|---|---|---|

## Relays

| 1900 | Germany (200 meters, 5 men) | 32 pts. |
|---|---|---|
| 1904 | United States (200 yards) | 2m4.6s |
| 1906 | Hungary (1,000 meters) | 16m52.4s |

## 400-Meter Freestyle Relay

| 1964 | United States | 3m32.2s |
|---|---|---|
| 1968 | United States | 3m31.7s |
| 1972 | United States | 3m26.42s |

## 800-Meter Freestyle Relay

| 1908 | Great Britain | 10m55.6s |
|---|---|---|
| 1912 | Australia | 10m11.2s |
| 1920 | United States | 10m4.4s |
| 1924 | United States | 9m53.4s |
| 1928 | United States | 9m36.2s |
| 1932 | Japan | 8m58.4s |
| 1936 | Japan | 8m51.5s |
| 1948 | United States | 8m46s |
| 1952 | United States | 8m31.1s |
| 1956 | Australia | 8m23.6s |
| 1960 | United States | 8m10.2s |
| 1964 | United States | 7m52.1s |
| 1968 | United States | 7m52.3s |
| 1972 | United States | 7m35.78s |
| 1976 | United States | 7m23.22s |
| 1980 | U.S.S.R. | 7m23.50s |

## 400-Meter Medley Relay

| 1960 | United States | 4m5.4s |
|---|---|---|
| 1964 | United States | 3m58.4s |
| 1968 | United States | 3m54.9s |
| 1972 | United States | 3m48.16s |
| 1976 | United States | 3m42.22s |
| 1980 | Australia | 3m45.70s |

## Springboard Dive

|  |  | Points |
|---|---|---|
| 1908 | Albert Zuerner, Germany | 85.5 |

| 1912 | Paul Guenther, Germany | 79.23 |
| 1920 | Louis Kuehn, United States | 675 |
| 1924 | Albert White, United States | 696.4 |
| 1928 | Pete Desjardins, United States | 185.04 |
| 1932 | Michael Galitzen, United States | 161.38 |
| 1936 | Richard Degener, United States | 163.57 |
| 1948 | Bruce Harlan, United States | 163.64 |
| 1952 | David Browning, United States | 205.59 |
| 1956 | Robert Clotworthy, United States | 159.56 |
| 1960 | Gary Tobian, United States | 170.00 |
| 1964 | Ken Sitzberger, United States | 159.90 |
| 1968 | Bernard Wrightson, United States | 170.15 |
| 1972 | Vladimir Vasin, U.S.S.R. | 594.09 |
| 1976 | Phil Boggs, United States | 619.05 |
| 1980 | Alexsandr Portnov, U.S.S.R. | 905.02 |

### Platform Dive

| | | Points |
|---|---|---|
| 1904 | G. E. Sheldon, United States | 12.75 |
| 1906 | Gottlob Walz, Germany | 156 |
| 1908 | Hjalmar Johansson, Sweden | 83.75 |
| 1912 | Erik Adlerz, Sweden | 73.94 |
| 1920 | Clarence Pinkston, United States | 100.67 |
| 1924 | Albert White, United States | 487.3 |
| 1928 | Pete Desjardins, United States | 98.74 |
| 1932 | Harold Smith, United States | 124.80 |
| 1936 | Marshall Wayne, United States | 113.58 |
| 1948 | Samuel Lee, United States | 130.05 |
| 1952 | Samuel Lee, United States | 156.28 |
| 1956 | Joaquin Capilla, Mexico | 152.44 |
| 1960 | Bob Webster, United States | 165.56 |
| 1964 | Bob Webster, United States | 148.58 |
| 1968 | Klaus Dibiasi, Italy | 164.18 |
| 1972 | Klaus Dibiasi, Italy | 504.12 |
| 1976 | Klaus Dibiasi, Italy | 600.51 |
| 1980 | Falk Hoffman, E. Germany | 835.65 |

### Plain High Dive

| | | Points |
|---|---|---|
| 1912 | Erik Adlerz, Sweden | 40 |
| 1920 | Arvid Wallman, Sweden | 7 |
| 1924 | Richard Eve, Australia | 160 |

### Plunge for Distance

| 1904 | W. E. Dickey, United States | 62 ft 6 in. |

## SWIMMING—WOMEN

### 100 Meters Freestyle

| 1912 | Fanny Durack, Australia | 1m22.2s |
| 1920 | Ethelda Bleibtrey, United States | 1m13.6s |
| 1924 | Ethel Lackie, United States | 1m12.4s |
| 1928 | Albina Osipowich, United States | 1m11s |
| 1932 | Helene Madison, United States | 1m6.8s |
| 1936 | Hendrika Mastenbroek, Netherlands | 1m5.9s |
| 1948 | Greta Andersen, Denmark | 1m6.3s |
| 1952 | Katalin Szoke, Hungary | 1m6.8s |
| 1956 | Dawn Fraser, Australia | 1m2s |
| 1960 | Dawn Fraser, Australia | 1m1.2s |
| 1964 | Dawn Fraser, Australia | 59.5s |
| 1968 | Marge Jan Henne, United States | 1m |
| 1972 | Sandra Neilson, United States | 58.59s |
| 1976 | Kornelia Ender, East Germany | 55.65s |
| 1980 | Barbara Krause, East Germany | 54.79s |

### 200-Meter Freestyle

| 1968 | Debbie Meyer, United States | 2m10.5s |
| 1972 | Shane Gould, Australia | 2m3.56s |
| 1976 | Kornelia Ender, East Germany | 1m59.26s |
| 1980 | Barbara Krause, East Germany | 1m58.33s |

### 400-Meter Freestyle

| 1920 | Ethelda Bleibtrey, United States | 4m34s[1] |
| 1924 | Martha Norelius, United States | 6m2.2s |
| 1928 | Martha Norelius, United States | 5m42.8s |
| 1932 | Helene Madison, United States | 5m28.5s |
| 1936 | Hendrika Mastenbroek, Netherlands | 5m26.4s |
| 1948 | Ann Curtis, United States | 5m17.8s |
| 1952 | Valerie Gyenge, Hungary | 5m12.1s |
| 1956 | Lorraine Crapp, Australia | 4m54.6s |
| 1960 | Chris von Saltza, United States | 4m50.6s |
| 1964 | Ginny Duenkel, United States | 4m43.3s |
| 1968 | Debbie Meyer, United States | 4m31.8s |
| 1972 | Shane Gould, Australia | 4m19.04s |
| 1976 | Petra Thumer, East Germany | 4m09.89s |
| 1980 | Ines Diers, East Germany | 4m08.76s |

1. 300 meters.

### 800-Meter Freestyle

| 1968 | Debbie Meyer, United States | 9m24s |
| 1972 | Keena Rothhammer, United States | 8m53.68s |
| 1976 | Petra Thumer, East Germany | 8m37.14s |
| 1980 | Michelle Ford, Australia | 8m28.90s |

### 100-Meter Backstroke

| 1924 | Sybil Bauer, United States | 1m23.2s |
| 1928 | Marie Braun, Netherlands | 1m22s |
| 1932 | Eleanor Holm, United States | 1m19.4s |
| 1936 | Dina Senff, Netherlands | 1m18.9s |
| 1948 | Karen Harup, Denmark | 1m14.4s |
| 1952 | Joan Harrison, South Africa | 1m14.3s |
| 1956 | Judy Grinham, Great Britain | 1m12.9s |
| 1960 | Lynn Burke, United States | 1m9.3s |
| 1964 | Cathy Ferguson, United States | 1m7.7s |
| 1968 | Kaye Hall, United States | 1m6.2s |
| 1972 | Melissa Belote, United States | 1m5.78s |
| 1976 | Ulrike Richter, East Germany | 1m01.83s |
| 1980 | Rica Reinisch, East Germany | 1m00.86s |

### 200-Meter Backstroke

| 1968 | Pokey Watson, United States | 2m24.8s |
| 1972 | Melissa Belote, United States | 2m19.19s |
| 1976 | Ulrike Richter, East Germany | 2m13.43s |
| 1980 | Rica Reinisch, East Germany | 2m11.77s |

### 100-Meter Breaststroke

| 1968 | Djurdjica Bjedov, Yugoslavia | 1m15.8s |
| 1972 | Catherine Carr, United States | 1m13.58s |
| 1976 | Hannelore Anke, East Germany | 1m11.16s |
| 1980 | Ute Geweniger, East Germany | 1m10.22s |

### 200-Meter Breaststroke

| 1924 | Lucy Morton, Great Britain | 3m33.2s |
| 1928 | Hilde Schrader, Germany | 3m12.6s |
| 1932 | Clare Dennis, Australia | 3m6.3s |
| 1936 | Hideko Maehata, Japan | 3m3.6s |
| 1948 | Nel van Vliet, Netherlands | 2m57.2s |
| 1952 | Eva Szekely, Hungary | 2m51.7s |
| 1956 | Ursala Happe, Germany | 2m53.1s |
| 1960 | Anita Lonsbrough, Great Britain | 2m49.5s |
| 1964 | Galina Prozumenschikova, U.S.S.R. | 2m46.4s |
| 1968 | Sharon Wichman, United States | 2m44.4s |
| 1972 | Beverly Whitfield, Australia | 2m41.71s |
| 1976 | Marina Koshevaia, U.S.S.R. | 2m33.35s |
| 1980 | Lina Kachushite, U.S.S.R. | 2m29.54s |

### 100-Meter Butterfly

| 1956 | Shelley Mann, United States | 1m11s |
| 1960 | Carolyn Schuler, United States | 1m9.5s |
| 1964 | Sharon Stouder, United States | 1m4.7s |
| 1968 | Lynn McClements, Australia | 1m5.5s |
| 1972 | Mayumi Aoki, Japan | 1m3.34s |
| 1976 | Kornelia Ender, East Germany | 1m00.13s |
| 1980 | Caren Metschuck, East Germany | 1m00.42s |

## 200-Meter Butterfly

| | | |
|---|---|---|
| 1968 | Ada Kok, Netherlands | 2m24.7s |
| 1972 | Karen Moe, United States | 2m15.57s |
| 1976 | Andrea Pollack, East Germany | 2m11.41s |
| 1980 | Ines Geissler, East Germany | 2m10.44s |

## 200-Meter Individual Medley

| | | |
|---|---|---|
| 1968 | Claudia Kolb, United States | 2m24.7s |
| 1972 | Shane Gould, Australia | 2m23.07s |

## 400-Meter Individual Medley

| | | |
|---|---|---|
| 1964 | Donna de Varona, United States | 5m18.7s |
| 1968 | Claudia Kolb, United States | 5m8.5s |
| 1972 | Gail Neall, Australia | 5m2.97s |
| 1976 | Ulrike Tauber, East Germany | 4m42.77s |
| 1980 | Petra Schneider, East Germany | 4m36.29s |

## 400-Meter Freestyle Relay

| | | |
|---|---|---|
| 1912 | Great Britain | 5m52.8s |
| 1920 | United States | 5m11.6s |
| 1924 | United States | 4m58.8s |
| 1928 | United States | 4m47.6s |
| 1932 | United States | 4m38s |
| 1936 | Netherlands | 4m36s |
| 1948 | United States | 4m29.2s |
| 1952 | Hungary | 4m24.4s |
| 1956 | Australia | 4m17.1s |
| 1960 | United States | 4m8.9s |
| 1964 | United States | 4m3.8s |
| 1968 | United States | 4m2.5s |
| 1972 | United States | 3m55.19s |
| 1976 | United States | 3m44.82s |
| 1980 | East Germany | 3m42.71s |

## 400-Meter Medley Relay

| | | |
|---|---|---|
| 1960 | United States | 4m41.1s |
| 1964 | United States | 4m33.9s |
| 1968 | United States | 4m28.3s |
| 1972 | United States | 4m20.75s |
| 1976 | East Germany | 4m07.95s |
| 1980 | East Germany | 4m06.67s |

## Springboard Dive

| | | Points |
|---|---|---|
| 1920 | Aileen Riggin, United States | 539.90 |
| 1924 | Elizabeth Becker, United States | 474.5 |
| 1928 | Helen Meany, United States | 78.62 |
| 1932 | Georgia Coleman, United States | 87.52 |
| 1936 | Marjorie Gestring, United States | 89.27 |
| 1948 | Victoria M. Draves, United States | 108.74 |
| 1952 | Patricia McCormick, United States | 147.30 |
| 1956 | Patricia McCormick, United States | 142.36 |
| 1960 | Ingrid Kramer, Germany | 155.81 |
| 1964 | Ingrid Kramer Engel, Germany | 145.00 |
| 1968 | Sue Gossick, United States | 150.77 |
| 1972 | Micki King, United States | 450.03 |
| 1976 | Jennifer Chandler, United States | 506.19 |
| 1980 | Irina Kalinina, U.S.S.R. | 725.91 |

## Platform Dive

| | | Points |
|---|---|---|
| 1912 | Greta Johansson, Sweden | 39.9 |
| 1920 | Stefani Fryland, Denmark | 34.60 |
| 1924 | Caroline Smith, United States | 166 |
| 1928 | Elizabeth B. Pinkston, United States | 31.60 |
| 1932 | Dorothy Poynton, United States | 40.26 |
| 1936 | Dorothy Poynton Hill, United States | 33.92 |
| 1948 | Victoria M. Draves, United States | 68.87 |
| 1952 | Patricia McCormick, United States | 79.37 |
| 1956 | Patricia McCormick, United States | 84.85 |
| 1960 | Ingrid Kramer, Germany | 91.28 |

## DISTRIBUTION OF MEDALS
## 1980 SUMMER GAMES

| | Gold | Silver | Bronze | Total |
|---|---|---|---|---|
| Soviet Union | 80 | 70 | 47 | 197 |
| East Germany | 47 | 36 | 43 | 126 |
| Bulgaria | 8 | 16 | 16 | 40 |
| Hungary | 7 | 10 | 15 | 32 |
| Poland | 3 | 14 | 14 | 31 |
| Romania | 6 | 6 | 13 | 25 |
| Britain | 5 | 7 | 9 | 21 |
| Cuba | 8 | 7 | 5 | 20 |
| Italy | 8 | 3 | 4 | 15 |
| France | 6 | 5 | 3 | 14 |
| Czechoslovakia | 2 | 2 | 9 | 13 |
| Sweden | 3 | 3 | 6 | 12 |
| Australia | 2 | 2 | 5 | 9 |
| Yugoslavia | 2 | 3 | 4 | 9 |
| Finland | 3 | 1 | 4 | 8 |
| Spain | 1 | 3 | 2 | 6 |
| Denmark | 2 | 1 | 2 | 5 |
| Austria | 1 | 3 | 1 | 5 |
| North Korea | 0 | 3 | 2 | 5 |
| Brazil | 2 | 0 | 2 | 4 |
| Ethiopia | 2 | 0 | 2 | 4 |
| Mongolia | 0 | 2 | 2 | 4 |
| Netherlands | 0 | 1 | 3 | 4 |
| Mexico | 0 | 1 | 3 | 4 |
| Greece | 1 | 0 | 2 | 3 |
| Jamaica | 0 | 0 | 3 | 3 |
| Switzerland | 2 | 0 | 0 | 2 |
| Tanzania | 0 | 2 | 0 | 2 |
| Ireland | 0 | 1 | 1 | 2 |
| Belgium | 1 | 0 | 1 | 1 |
| India | 1 | 0 | 0 | 1 |
| Zimbabwe | 1 | 0 | 0 | 1 |
| Venezuela | 1 | 0 | 0 | 1 |
| Uganda | 0 | 1 | 0 | 1 |
| Guyana | 0 | 0 | 1 | 1 |
| Lebanon | 0 | 0 | 1 | 1 |

| | | |
|---|---|---|
| 1964 | Lesley Bush, United States | 99.80 |
| 1968 | Milena Duchkova, Czechoslovakia | 109.59 |
| 1972 | Ulrika Knape, Sweden | 390.00 |
| 1976 | Elena Vaytsekhovskaia, U.S.S.R. | 406.59 |
| 1980 | Martina Jaschke, East Germany | 596.25 |

## BOXING

(U.S. winners only)

(U.S. boycotted Olympics in 1980)

### Flyweight—112 Pounds (51 kilograms)

| | | | |
|---|---|---|---|
| 1904 | George V. Finnegan | 1952 | Nate Brooks |
| 1920 | Frank De Genaro | 1976 | Leo Randolph |
| 1924 | Fidel La Barba | | |

### Bantamweight—119 pounds (54 kg)

1904   O.L. Kirk

### Featherweight—126 pounds (57 kg)

| | | | |
|---|---|---|---|
| 1904 | O.L. Kirk | 1924 | Jackie Fields |

### Lightweight—132 Pounds (60 kg)

| | | | |
|---|---|---|---|
| 1904 | H.J. Spanger | 1968 | Ronnie Harris |
| 1920 | Samuel Mosberg | 1976 | Howard Davis |

### Light Welterweight—140 Pounds (63.5 kg)

| | | | |
|---|---|---|---|
| 1952 | Charles Adkins | 1976 | Ray Leonard |
| 1972 | Ray Seales | | |

**Welterweight—148 Pounds (67 kg)**

| | | | |
|---|---|---|---|
| 1904 | Al Young | 1932 | Edward Flynn |

**Light Middleweight—157 Pounds (71 kg)**

| | |
|---|---|
| 1960 | Wilbert McClure |

**Middleweight—165 Pounds (75 kg)**

| | | | |
|---|---|---|---|
| 1904 | Charles Mayer | 1960 | Eddie Crook |
| 1932 | Carmen Barth | 1976 | Mike Spinks |
| 1952 | Floyd Patterson | | |

**Light Heavyweight—179 Pounds (81 kg)**

| | | | |
|---|---|---|---|
| 1920 | Edward Eagan | 1960 | Cassius Clay |
| 1952 | Norvel Lee | 1976 | Leon Spinks |
| 1956 | James Boyd | | |

**Heavyweight (unlimited)**

| | | | |
|---|---|---|---|
| 1904 | Sam Berger | 1964 | Joe Frazier |
| 1952 | Edward Sanders | 1968 | George Foreman |
| 1956 | Pete Rademacher | | |

## BASKETBALL—MEN

| | | | |
|---|---|---|---|
| 1904 | United States | 1960 | United States |
| 1936 | United States | 1964 | United States |
| 1948 | United States | 1968 | United States |
| 1952 | United States | 1972 | U.S.S.R. |
| 1956 | United States | 1976 | United States |
| | | 1980 | Yugoslavia |

## BASKETBALL—WOMEN

| | |
|---|---|
| 1976 | U.S.S.R. |
| 1980 | U.S.S.R. |

# Winter Games

## FIGURE SKATING—MEN

| | |
|---|---|
| 1908 | Ulrich Salchow, Sweden |
| 1920 | Gillis Grafstrom, Sweden |
| 1924 | Gillis Grafstrom, Sweden |
| 1928 | Gillis Grafstrom, Sweden |
| 1932 | Karl Schaefer, Austria |
| 1936 | Karl Schaefer, Austria |
| 1948 | Richard Button, United States |
| 1952 | Richard Button, United States |
| 1956 | Hayes Alan Jenkins, United States |
| 1960 | David Jenkins, United States |
| 1964 | Manfred Schnelldorfer, Germany |
| 1968 | Wolfgang Schwarz, Austria |
| 1972 | Ondrej Nepela, Czechoslovakia |
| 1976 | John Curry, Great Britain |
| 1980 | Robin Cousins, Great Britain |

## FIGURE SKATING—WOMEN

| | |
|---|---|
| 1908 | Madge Syers, Britain |
| 1920 | Magda Julin–Maurey, Sweden |
| 1924 | Herma Szabo-Planck, Austria |
| 1928 | Sonja Henie, Norway |
| 1932 | Sonja Henie, Norway |
| 1936 | Sonja Henie, Norway |
| 1948 | Barbara Ann Scott, Canada |
| 1952 | Jeannette Altwegg, Great Britain |
| 1956 | Tenley Albright, United States |
| 1960 | Carol Heiss, United States |
| 1964 | Sjoukje Dijkstra, Netherlands |
| 1968 | Peggy Fleming, United States |
| 1972 | Beatrix Schuba, Austria |
| 1976 | Dorothy Hamill, United States |
| 1980 | Anett Poetzsch, East Germany |

## SPEED SKATING—MEN
(U.S. winners only)

**500 Meters**

| | | |
|---|---|---|
| 1924 | Charles Jewtraw | 44.0 |
| 1932 | John A. Shea | 43.4 |
| 1952 | Kenneth Henry | 43.2 |
| 1964 | Terrence McDermott | 40.1 |
| 1980 | Eric Heiden | 38.03 |

**1,000 Meters**

| | | |
|---|---|---|
| 1976 | Peter Mueller | 1:19.32 |
| 1980 | Eric Heiden | 1:15.18 |

**1,500 Meters**

| | | |
|---|---|---|
| 1932 | John A. Shea | 2:57.5 |
| 1980 | Eric Heiden | 1:55.44 |

**5,000 Meters**

| | | |
|---|---|---|
| 1932 | Irving Jaffee | 9:40.8 |
| 1980 | Eric Heiden | 7:02.29 |

**10,000 Meters**

| | | |
|---|---|---|
| 1932 | Irving Jaffee | 19:13.6 |
| 1980 | Eric Heiden | 14:28.13 |

## SPEED SKATING—WOMEN

**500 Meters**

| | | |
|---|---|---|
| 1972 | Anne Henning | 43.33 |
| 1976 | Sheila Young | 42.76 |

**1,500 Meters**

| | | |
|---|---|---|
| 1972 | Dianne Holum | 2:20.85 |

## HEIDEN FIRST ATHLETE TO WIN 5 GOLD MEDALS IN WINTER GAMES

Eric Heiden of Madison, Wis., became the first athlete to win five gold medals in the Winter Olympics when he swept the 1980 speed skating events at Lake Placid, N.Y. The 21-year-old Heiden captured the 500-, 1,000-, 1,500-, 5,000-, and 10,000-meter events. He set an Olympic record in each event and capped his performance on Feb. 23 with a world record of 14 minutes 28.13 seconds in the 10,000-meter race, breaking the mark set in 1977 by Viktor Leskin of the Soviet Union by 16.20 seconds.

Lydia Skoblikova of the Soviet Union was the only other athlete to sweep an Olympic speed skating program. She captured all four female events in the 1964 Winter Games at Innsbruck, Austria.

The weekend after his gold-medal sweep, Heiden failed in his attempt to win a fourth straight world title, at Heerenveen, the Netherlands. He was dethroned by 22-year-old Hilbert van der Duim of the host country.

## SKIING, ALPINE—MEN

### Downhill

| | | |
|---|---|---|
| 1948 | Henri Oreiller, France | 2m55.0s |
| 1952 | Zeno Colo, Italy | 2m30.8s |
| 1956 | Anton Sailer, Austria | 2m52.2s |
| 1960 | Jean Vuarnet, France | 2m06.2s |
| 1964 | Egon Zimmermann, Austria | 2m18.16s |
| 1968 | Jean-Claude Killy, France | 1m59.85s |
| 1972 | Bernhard Russi, Switzerland | 1m51.43s |
| 1976 | Franz Klammer, Austria | 1m45.72s |
| 1980 | Leonhard Stock, Austria | 1m45.50s |

### Slalom

| | | |
|---|---|---|
| 1948 | Edi Reinalter, Switzerland | 2m10.3s |
| 1952 | Othmar Schneider, Austria | 2m00.0s |
| 1956 | Anton Sailer, Austria | 194.7 pts. |
| 1960 | Ernst Hinterseer, Austria | 2m08.9s |
| 1964 | Josef Stiegler, Austria | 2m10.13 |
| 1968 | Jean-Claude Killy, France | 1m39.73s |
| 1972 | Francisco Fernandez Ochoa, Spain | 1m49.27s |
| 1976 | Piero Gros, Italy | 2m03.29s |
| 1980 | Ingemar Stenmark, Sweden | 1m44.26s |

### Giant Slalom

| | | |
|---|---|---|
| 1952 | Stein Eriksen, Norway | 2m25.0s |
| 1956 | Anton Sailer, Austria | 3m00.1s |
| 1960 | Roger Staub, Switzerland | 1m48.3s |
| 1964 | Francois Bonlieu, France | 1m46.71s |
| 1968 | Jean-Claude Killy, France | 3m29.28s |
| 1972 | Gustavo Thoeni, Italy | 3m09.52s |
| 1976 | Heini Hemmi, Switzerland | 3m26.97s |
| 1980 | Ingemar Stenmark, Sweden | 2m40.74s |

## SKIING, ALPINE—WOMEN

### Downhill

| | | |
|---|---|---|
| 1948 | Hedi Schlunegger, Switzerland | 2m28.3s |
| 1952 | Trude Jochum-Beiser, Austria | 1m47.1s |
| 1956 | Madeleine Berthod, Switzerland | 1m40.1s |
| 1960 | Heidi Biebl, Germany | 1m37.6s |
| 1964 | Christl Haas, Austria | 1m55.39s |
| 1968 | Olga Pall, Austria | 1m40.87s |
| 1972 | Marie-Therese Nadig, Switzerland | 1m36.68s |
| 1976 | Rosi Mittermeier, West Germany | 1m46.16s |
| 1980 | Annemarie Proell Moser, Austria | 1m37.52s |

### Slalom

| | | |
|---|---|---|
| 1948 | Gretchen Fraser, United States | 1m57.2s |
| 1952 | Andrea Mead Lawrence, United States | 2m10.6s |
| 1956 | Renee Colliard, Switzerland | 112.3 pts. |

| | | |
|---|---|---|
| 1960 | Anne Heggtveigt, Canada | 1m49.6s |
| 1964 | Christine Goitschel, France | 1m29.86s |
| 1968 | Marielle Goitschel, France | 1m25.86s |
| 1972 | Barbara Cochran, United States | 1m31.24s |
| 1976 | Rosi Mittermeier, West Germany | 1m30.54s |
| 1980 | Hanni Wenzel, Liechtenstein | 1m25.09s |

### Giant Slalom

| | | |
|---|---|---|
| 1952 | Andrea M. Lawrence, United States | 2m06.8s |
| 1956 | Ossi Reichert, Germany | 1m56.5s |
| 1960 | Yvonne Ruegg, Switzerland | 1m39.9s |
| 1964 | Marielle Goitschel, France | 1m52.24s |
| 1968 | Nancy Greene, Canada | 1m51.97s |
| 1972 | Marie-Therese Nadig, Switzerland | 1m29.90s |
| 1976 | Kathy Kreiner, Canada | 1m29.13s |
| 1980 | Hanni Wenzel, Liechtenstein | 2m41.66s |

## ICE HOCKEY

| | | | | |
|---|---|---|---|---|
| 1920 | Canada | | 1956 | U.S.S.R. |
| 1924 | Canada | | 1960 | United States |
| 1928 | Canada | | 1964 | U.S.S.R. |
| 1932 | Canada | | 1968 | U.S.S.R. |
| 1936 | Great Britain | | 1972 | U.S.S.R. |
| 1948 | Canada | | 1976 | U.S.S.R. |
| 1952 | Canada | | 1980 | United States |

## SKIING, NORDIC, JUMPING

### 90-Meter Hill

| | | Points |
|---|---|---|
| 1924 | Jacob T. Thams, Norway | 227.5 |
| 1928 | Alfred Andersen, Norway | 230.5 |
| 1932 | Birger Ruud, Norway | 228.0 |
| 1936 | Birger Ruud, Norway | 232.0 |
| 1948 | Peter Hugsted, Norway | 228.1 |
| 1952 | A. Bergmann, Norway | 226.0 |
| 1956 | Antti Hyvarinen, Finland | 227.0 |
| 1960 | Helmut Recknagel, Germany | 227.2 |
| 1964 | Toralf Engan, Norway | 230.7 |
| 1968 | Vladimir Beloussov, U.S.S.R. | 231.3 |
| 1972 | Wojciech Fortuna, Poland | 219.9 |
| 1976 | Karl Schnabl, Austria | 234.8 |
| 1980 | Jouko Tormanen, Finland | 271.0 |

### Small Hill (70 meters)

| | | |
|---|---|---|
| 1964 | Veikko Kankkonen, Finland | 229.9 |
| 1968 | Jiri Raska, Czechoslovakia | 216.5 |
| 1972 | Yukio Kasaya, Japan | 244.2 |
| 1976 | Hans-Georg Aschenbach, East Germany | 252.0 |
| 1980 | Anton Innauer, Austria | 266.3 |

## AMERICAN HOCKEY TEAM SCORES BIGGEST UPSET IN GAMES

The United States hockey team, made up of college and minor-league players, stunned the hockey world and stirred patriotic fervor among Americans everywhere with a 4–3 upset triumph in the Winter Olympics over the Soviet Union, considered by experts as the finest hockey team in the world—amateur or professional.

The Soviet team was heavily favored to win the Olympic gold medal at Lake Placid, N.Y., for a fifth straight time. The Americans were rated seventh among the 12 national teams and were given virtually no chance of gaining the final round. The 20-man American squad was coached by Herb Brooks, the coach of the University of Minnesota team. He instituted a new style for the Americans, stressing speed and puck control, tactics generally employed by European teams. The Americans opened their unbeaten streak with a 2–2 tie against Sweden in the first round, then stormed to victories over Romania, Czechoslovakia, West Germany, and Norway. Their upset of the Russians came in the first game of the final round on a goal by Mike Eruzione, the team captain from Winthrop, Mass.

They captured the gold medal with a 4–2 victory over Finland and touched off a national celebration and a surge of patriotism seldom seen in American sports. The triumph came at a time when the Olympic movement was under fire and the United States threatened to boycott the Summer Games in Moscow because of the Soviet invasion of Afghanistan. Only once before, in 1960 at Squaw Valley, Calif., had an American team won an Olympic hockey gold medal.

## HOW U.S. HOCKEY ADVANCED TO OLYMPIC TITLE
### FINAL STANDING

|  | W | L | T | Pts | GF | GA |
|---|---|---|---|---|---|---|
| United States | 2 | 0 | 1 | 5 | 10 | 7 |
| Soviet Union | 2 | 1 | 0 | 4 | 16 | 8 |
| Sweden | 0 | 2 | 2 | 2 | 7 | 14 |
| Finland | 0 | 2 | 1 | 1 | 7 | 11 |

(The top two teams in the Red Division and the two top teams in the Blue Division of the preliminary round-robin advanced to the final, where the Red Division teams played the Blue Division teams. The records of the teams who played each other in their own divisions were counted in the final standing.)

### Results of Final Round Games

United States 4, Soviet Union 3
Sweden 3, Finland 3
United States 4, Finland 2
Soviet Union 9, Sweden 2

### Consolation for Fifth Place

Czechoslovakia 6, Canada 1

## PRELIMINARY ROUND STANDING
### Red Division

|  | W | L | T | Pts | GF | GA |
|---|---|---|---|---|---|---|
| Soviet Union | 5 | 0 | 0 | 10 | 51 | 11 |
| Finland | 3 | 2 | 0 | 6 | 26 | 18 |
| Canada | 3 | 2 | 0 | 6 | 28 | 12 |
| Poland | 2 | 3 | 0 | 4 | 15 | 23 |
| Holland | 1 | 3 | 1 | 3 | 16 | 43 |
| Japan | 0 | 4 | 1 | 1 | 7 | 36 |

### Blue Division

|  | W | L | T | Pts | GF | GA |
|---|---|---|---|---|---|---|
| Sweden | 4 | 0 | 1 | 9 | 26 | 7 |
| United States | 4 | 0 | 1 | 9 | 25 | 10 |
| Czechoslovakia | 3 | 2 | 0 | 6 | 34 | 16 |
| Romania | 1 | 3 | 1 | 3 | 13 | 29 |
| West Germany | 1 | 4 | 0 | 2 | 21 | 30 |
| Norway | 0 | 4 | 1 | 1 | 9 | 36 |

(Top two teams in each division advanced to final round. Third place teams played for fifth.)

### Results of Preliminary Round Games Involving U.S.

United States 2, Sweden 2
United States 7, Czechoslovakia 3
United States 5, Norway 1
United States 7, Romania 2
United States 4, West Germany 2

## DISTRIBUTION OF MEDALS
## 1980 WINTER GAMES

|  | Gold | Silver | Bronze | Total |
|---|---|---|---|---|
| Soviet Union | 10 | 6 | 6 | 22 |
| East Germany | 9 | 7 | 7 | 23 |
| United States | 6 | 4 | 2 | 12 |
| Norway | 1 | 3 | 6 | 10 |
| Finland | 1 | 5 | 3 | 9 |
| Austria | 3 | 2 | 2 | 7 |
| West Germany | 0 | 2 | 3 | 5 |
| Switzerland | 1 | 1 | 3 | 5 |
| Liechtenstein | 2 | 2 | 0 | 4 |
| Netherlands | 1 | 2 | 1 | 4 |
| Sweden | 3 | 0 | 1 | 4 |
| Italy | 0 | 2 | 0 | 2 |
| Canada | 0 | 1 | 1 | 2 |
| Britain | 1 | 0 | 0 | 1 |
| Hungary | 0 | 1 | 0 | 1 |
| Japan | 0 | 1 | 0 | 1 |
| Bulgaria | 0 | 0 | 1 | 1 |
| Czechoslovakia | 0 | 0 | 1 | 1 |
| France | 0 | 0 | 1 | 1 |

Total countries competing: 37.

### Scoring of U.S. Victory Over Soviet Union

| United States | 2 | 0 | 2 | — | 4 |
|---|---|---|---|---|---|
| Soviet Union | 2 | 1 | 0 | — | 3 |

**FIRST PERIOD**—1, Soviet Union, Krutov (Kasatonov), 9:12; 2, United States, Schneider (Pavelich), 14:03; 3, Soviet Union, Makarov (A. Golikov), 17:34; 4, United States, Johnson (Christian, Silk), 19:59.
**SECOND PERIOD**—5, Soviet Union, Maltsev (Krutiv), power-play goal, 2:18
**THIRD PERIOD**—6, United States, Johnson (Silk), power-play goal, 8:39; 7, United States, Eruzione (Pavelich, Harrington), 10:00
**SHOTS ON GOAL**—United States on Tretiak, Myshkin, 8, 2, 6—16. Soviet Union on Craig, 18, 12, 9—39

### Scoring of U.S. Gold Medal Victory Over Finland

| United States | 0 | 1 | 3 | — | 4 |
|---|---|---|---|---|---|
| Finland | 1 | 1 | 0 | — | 2 |

**FIRST PERIOD**—1, Finland, Porvari (Leinonen, Litma) 9:20
**SECOND PERIOD**—2, United States, Christoff (unassisted), 4:39; 3, Finland, Leinonen (Haapalainen, Kimalainen), power-play goal, 6:30
**THIRD PERIOD**—4, United States, Verchota (Christian), 2:25; 5, McClanahan (Johnson, Christian), 6:05; 6, United States, Johnson, (Christoff), shorthanded goal, 16:25
**SHOTS ON GOAL**—United States on Valtonen, 14, 8, 7—29. Finland on Craig, 7, 6, 10—23.

## AMERICAN SWIMMERS RACE AGAINST OLYMPIC CLOCK

Forty-eight hours after the Olympic swimming competition in Moscow ended, United States swimmers, who had boycotted the Games, protesting the Soviet intervention in Afghanistan, took to the water at Irvine, Calif., hoping to shatter records in the United States Championships and Olympic Trials. Organizers erected a huge scoreboard showing the Olympic times in each event so swimmers and spectators could make comparisons as to how the Americans would have fared had they chosen to go to Moscow.

In a sport they usually dominated, the Americans registered three world records, and on a basis of comparative times, showed they would have won six of 11 gold medals in men's events and four of 11 in women's events had they competed in the Olympics. The world records shattered at Irvine were by Craig Beardsley of Gainesville, Fla., in the 200-meter butterfly (1:58.46); Bill Barrett of Alpharetta, Ga., in the 200 individual medley (2:03.24); and Mary T. Meagher, a 15-year-old from Cincinnati, in the 200 butterfly (2:06.37).

# Other 1980 Olympic Games Champions

## SUMMER

### Archery
Men—Tomi Polkolainen, Finland
Women—Keto Losaberodze, U.S.S.R.

### Boxing
106 lb—Shamil Sabyrov, U.S.S.R.
112 lb—Petar Lessov, U.S.S.R.
119 lb—Juan Hernandez, Cuba
126 lb—Rudi Fink, E. Ger.
132 lb—Angel Herrera, Cuba
140 lb—Patrizio Oliva, Italy
148 lb—Andres Aldama, Cuba
157 lb—Armando Martinez, Cuba
165 lb—Jose Gomez, Cuba
179 lb—Slobodan Kacar, Yugoslavia
Heavyweight—Teofilo Stevenson, Cuba

### Canadian Canoeing
500 m—Sergei Postrekhin, U.S.S.R.
1,000 m—Lubomir Lubenov, Bulgaria
500-m pairs—Laszlo Foltan and Istvan Vaskutl, Hungary
1,000-m pairs—Ivan Potzalchin and Toma Simionov, Romania

### Kayak—Men
500 m—Vladimir Parfenovich, U.S.S.R.
1,000 m—Rudiger Helm, E. Ger.
500-m pairs—Vladimir Parfenovich and Sergei Chukhrai, U.S.S.R.
1,000-m pairs—Vladimir Parfenovich and Sergei Chukhrai, U.S.S.R.
1,000-m fours—E. Ger.

### Kayak—Women
500 m—Birgit Fischer, E. Ger.
500-m pairs—Carsta Genauss and Martina Dischof, E. Ger.

### Cycling
1,000 m—Lothar Thoms, E. Ger.
Sprint—Lutz Hesslich, E. Ger.
Pursuit—Robert Dill-Bondi, Switzerland
Team pursuit—U.S.S.R.
Road Race—Sergei Soukhoroutchenkov, U.S.S.R.
Team road race—U.S.S.R.

### Equestrian
Dressage—Elisabeth Theurer, Austria
Dressage team—U.S.S.R.
Jumping—Jan Kowalczky, Poland
Team jumping—U.S.S.R.
3-Day event—Federico Euro Roman, Italy
Team 3-day event—U.S.S.R. (Aleksandr Blinov, Yuri Salnikov, Valeri Volkov)

### Fencing
Foil—Vladimir Smirnov, U.S.S.R.
Team foil—France
Epee—Johan Harmenberg, Sweden
Team epee—France
Saber—Viktor Krovopuskov, U.S.S.R.
Team saber—France
Women's foil—Pascale Trinquet, France
Women's team foil—France

### Gymnastics—Men
All-around—Aleksandr Dityatin, U.S.S.R.
Floor exercises—Roland Bruckner, E. Ger.
Horizontal bar—Stoyan Deltchev, Bulgaria
Parallel bars—Aleksandr Tkachyov, U.S.S.R.
Pommel horse—Zoltan Magyar, Hungary
Rings—Aleksandr Dityatin, U.S.S.R.
Vault—Nikolai Andrianov, U.S.S.R.
Team all-around—U.S.S.R.

### Gymnastics—Women
All-around—Yelena Davydova, U.S.S.R.
Balance beam—Nadia Comaneci, Romania
Floor exercises—Nelli Kim, U.S.S.R., and Nadia Comaneci, Romania, tie
Uneven bars—Maxi Gnauck, E. Ger.
Vault—Natalya Shaposhnikova, U.S.S.R.
Team all-round—U.S.S.R.

### Judo
132 lb—Thierry Rey, France
143 lb—Nikolai Solodukhin, U.S.S.R.
157 lb—Ezio Gamba, Italy
172 lb—Shota Khabarell, U.S.S.R.
190 lb—Juerg Roethilsberger, Switzerland
209 lb—Robert Van De Walle, Belgium
Over 209 lb—Angelo Parisi, France
Open—Dietmar Lorenz, East Germany

### Modern Pentathlon
Individual—Anatoly Starostin, U.S.S.R.
Team—U.S.S.R.

### Rowing—Men
Singles—Pertti Karppinen, Finland
Doubles—Joachim Dreifke and Klaus Kroppelien, E. Ger.
Pairs—Bernd and Jorg Landvoigt, E. Ger.
Pairs with coxswain—Harald Jahrling-Friedrich-Wilhelm Ulrich-Georg Spohr, E. Ger.
Fours—Jurgen Thiele-Andreas Decker-Stefan Semmier-Siegfried Brietzke, E. Ger.
Fours with coxswains—Dieter Wemdisch-Ullrich Diessner-Walter Diessner-Gottfried Dohn-Andreas Gregor, E. Ger.
Quadruple sculls—Frank Dunba-Karstn Bunk-Uwe Heppner-Martin Winter, E. Ger.
Eights—Bernd Krauss-Hans-Peter Koppe-Ulrich Kons-Jorg Friedrich-Jens Doberschutz-Ulrich Karnatz-Uwe Duhring-Bernd Hoing-Klaus-Dieter Ludwig, E. Ger.

### Rowing—Women
Singles—Sanda Toma, Romania
Doubles—Yelena Khloptseva and Larisa Popova, U.S.S.R.
Pairs—Ute Steindorf and Cornelia Klier, E. Ger.
Fours with coxswains—Romona Kapheim

-Silvia Frohlich-Angelika Noack-Romy Saalfeld-Kirsten Wenzel, E. Ger.
Quadruple sculls—Sybille Reinhardt-Jutta Ploch-Jutta Lau-Roswietha Zobelt-Liane Buhr, E. Ger.
Eights—Martina Boesler-Kersten Neisser-Christiane Kopke-Brigit Schutz-Gabriele Kuhn-Ilona Richter-Marita Sandig-Karin Metze-Marina Wilke, E. Ger.

### Shooting
Free pistol—Aleksandr Melentev, U.S.S.R.
Rapid-fire pistol—Corneliu Ion, Romania
Small-bore rifle, prone—Karoly Varga, Hungary
Small-bore rifle, 3 positions—Viktor Vlasov, U.S.S.R.
Rifle, running game target—Igor Sokolov, U.S.S.R.
Trap—Luciano Giovannetti, Italy
Skeet—Hans Kjeld Rasmussen, Denmark

### Weight Lifting
114 lb—Kanybek Osmonaliev, U.S.S.R.
123 lb—Daniel Nunez, Cuba
132 lb—Viktor Mazin, U.S.S.R.
149 lb—Yanko Roussev, Bulgaria
165 lb—Assen Zlatev, Bulgaria
182 lb—Yurik Vardanyan, U.S.S.R.
198 lb—Peter Baczako, Hungary
220 lb—Ata Zaremba, Czechoslovakia
242 lb—Leonid Taranenko, U.S.S.R.

### Wrestling—Freestyle
106 lb—Claudio Pollio, Italy
115 lb—Anatoly Belogiazov, U.S.S.R.
126 lb—Sergei Belogiazov, U.S.S.R.
137 lb—Magomrdgasan Abushev, U.S.S.R.
149 lb—Salpulla Absaidov, U.S.S.R.
163 lb—Valentin Raitchev, Bulgaria
181 lb—Ismail Abilov, Bulgaria
198 lb—Sanasar Oganesyan, U.S.S.R.
220 lb—Ilya Mate, U.S.S.R.
Over 220 lb—Sosian Andlev, U.S.S.R.

### Wrestling—Greco-Roman
106 lb—Saksylik Ushkempirov, U.S.S.R.
114 lb—Vakhtang Blagidze, U.S.S.R.
125 lb—Shamil Sherikov, U.S.S.R.
136 lb—Stillanos Migiakis, Greece
150 lb—Stefan Rusu, Romania
163 lb—Ferenc Kocsis, Hungary
180 lb—Gennady Korban, U.S.S.R.
198 lb—Norbert Nottny, Hungary
220 lb—Gheorghi Raikov, Bulgaria
Over 220 lb—Aleksandr Kolchinsky, U.S.S.R.

### Yachting
Finn—Esko Rechardt, Finland
Flying Dutchman—Alesandro Abascal and Miguel Noguer, Spain
470 Class—Marcos Soares and Eduardo Penido, Brazil
Soling—Poul Richard, Erik Hansen and

Valdemar Bandolowski, Denmark
Star—Valentin Mankin and Aleksandr Muzyschenko, U.S.S.R.
Tornado—Alexandre Welter and Lars Bjorkstrom, Brazil

**Team Champions**
Field hockey, men—India
Field hockey, women—Zimbabwe
Handball, men—E. Ger.
Handball, women—U.S.S.R.

Soccer—Czechoslovakia
Volleyball, men—U.S.S.R.
Volleyball, women—U.S.S.R.
Water polo—U.S.S.R.

## WINTER

**Biathlon**
Individual—(10 km): Frank Ullrich, East Germany (20 km): Anatoly Alabyev, Soviet Union
Relay—Soviet Union (Vladimir Aliken, Aleksandr Tikhonov, Vladimir Barnaschov, and Anatoly Alabyev)

**Bobsledding**
2–Man—Erich Schaerer and Josef Benz, Switzerland
4–Man—East Germany (Meinhard Nehmer, Bogdan Musiol, Bernhard Germeshausen, and Hans Jurgen Gerhardt)

**Figure Skating**
Men—Robin Cousins, Great Britain
Women—Anett Poetzsch, East Germany
Pairs—Irina Rodnina and Aleksandr Zaitsev, Soviet Union
Dance—Natalya Linichuk and Gennadi Karponosov, Soviet Union

**Speed Skating—Men**
500 m—Eric Heiden, Madison, Wis.
1,000 m—Eric Heiden, Madison, Wis.
1,500 m—Eric Heiden, Madison, Wis.
5,000 m—Eric Heiden, Madison, Wis.
10,000 m—Eric Heiden, Madison, Wis.

**Speed Skating—Women**
500 m—Karin Enke, East Germany
1,000 m—Natalya Petruseva, Soviet Union

1,500 m—Annie Borckink, Netherlands
3,000 m—Bjoerg Eva Jensen, Norway

**Hockey**
Team—United States

**Luge**
Men—Bernhard Glass, East Germany
Doubles—Hans Rinn and Norbert Hahn, East Germany
Women—Vera Zozulya, Soviet Union

**Skiing, Nordic—Men**
Combined—Ulrich Wehling, East Germany
70–m jump—Anton Innauer, Austria
90–m jump—Jouko Tormanen, Finland

**Cross–Country Skiing—Men**
15 km—Thomas Wassberg, Sweden
30 km—Nikolai Zimyatov, Soviet Union
50 km—Nikolai Zimyatov, Soviet Union
40–km relay—Soviet Union (Vasily Rochev, Nikolai Bazhukov, Yevgeny Beliaev, and Nikolai Zimyatov)

**Cross–Country Skiing—Women**
5 km—Raisa Smetanina, Soviet Union
10 km—Barbara Petzold, East Germany
20–km relay—East Germany (Marlies Rostock, Carola Anding, Veronika Hesse, and Barbara Petzold)

## JAMES E. SULLIVAN MEMORIAL AWARD WINNERS
(Amateur Athlete of Year Chosen in Amateur Athletic Union Poll)

| | | | | | | |
|---|---|---|---|---|---|---|
| 1930 | Robert Tyre Jones, Jr. | Golf | 1956 | Patricia McCormick | Diving |
| 1931 | Bernard E. Berlinger | Track and field | 1957 | Bobby Jo Morrow | Track and field |
| 1932 | James A. Bausch | Track and field | 1958 | Glenn Davis | Track and field |
| 1933 | Glenn Cunningham | Track and field | 1959 | Parry O'Brien | Track and field |
| 1934 | William R. Bonthron | Track and field | 1960 | Rafer Johnson | Track and field |
| 1935 | W. Lawson Little, Jr. | Golf | 1961 | Wilma Rudolph Ward | Track and field |
| 1936 | Glenn Morris | Track and field | 1962 | Jim Beatty | Track and field |
| 1937 | J. Donald Budge | Tennis | 1963 | John Pennel | Track and field |
| 1938 | Donald R. Lash | Track and field | 1964 | Don Schollander | Swimming |
| 1939 | Joseph W. Burk | Rowing | 1965 | Bill Bradley | Basketball |
| 1940 | J. Gregory Rice | Track and field | 1966 | Jim Ryun | Track and field |
| 1941 | Leslie MacMitchell | Track and field | 1967 | Randy Matson | Track and field |
| 1942 | Cornelius Warmerdam | Track and field | 1968 | Debbie Meyer | Swimming |
| 1943 | Gilbert L. Dodds | Track and field | 1969 | Bill Toomey | Decathlon |
| 1944 | Ann Curtis | Swimming | 1970 | John Kinsella | Swimming |
| 1945 | Felix (Doc) Blanchard | Football | 1971 | Mark Spitz | Swimming |
| 1946 | Y. Arnold Tucker | Football | 1972 | Frank Shorter | Marathon |
| 1947 | John B. Kelly, Jr. | Rowing | 1973 | Bill Walton | Basketball |
| 1948 | Robert B. Mathias | Track and field | 1974 | Rick Wohlhuter | Track |
| 1949 | Richard T. Button | Figure skating | 1975 | Tim Shaw | Swimming |
| 1950 | Fred Wilt | Track and field | 1976 | Bruce Jenner | Track and field |
| 1951 | Robert E. Richards | Track and field | 1977 | John Naber | Swimming |
| 1952 | Horace Ashenfelter | Track and field | 1978 | Tracy Caulkins | Swimming |
| 1953 | Major Sammy Lee | Diving | 1979 | Kurt Thomas | Gymnastics |
| 1954 | Malvin Whitfield | Track and field | 1980 | Eric Heiden | Speed skating |
| 1955 | Harrison Dillard | Track and field | 1981 | Carl Lewis | Track and field |

# FOOTBALL

The pastime of kicking around a ball goes back beyond the limits of recorded history. Ancient savage tribes played football of a primitive kind. There was a ball-kicking game played by Athenians, Spartans, and Corinthians 2500 years ago, which the Greeks called *Episkuros*. The Romans had a somewhat similar game called *Harpastum* and are supposed to have carried the game with them when they invaded the British Isles in the First Century, B.C.

Undoubtedly the game known in the United Stated as Football traces directly to the English game of Rugby, though the modifications have been many. Informal football was played on college lawns well over a century ago, and an annual Freshman-Sophomore series of "scrimmages" began at Yale in 1840. The first formal intercollegiate football game was the Princeton-Rutgers contest at New Brunswick, N.J., on Nov. 6, 1869, with Rutgers winning by 6 goals to 4.

In those days, games were played with 25, 20, 15, or 11 men on a side. In 1880, there was a convention at which Walter Camp of Yale persuaded the delegates to agree to a rule calling for 11 players on a side. The game grew so rough that it was attacked as brutal, and some colleges abandoned the sport. Conditions were so bad in 1906 that President Theodore Roosevelt called a meeting of Yale, Harvard, and Princeton representatives at the White House in the hope of reforming and improving the game. The outcome was that the game, with the forward pass introduced and some other modifications of the rules inserted, became faster and cleaner.

The first professional game was played in 1895 at Latrobe, Pa. The National Football League was founded in 1921. The All-American Conference went into action in 1946. At the end of the 1949 season the two circuits merged, retaining the name of the older league. In 1960, the American Football League, began operations. In 1970, the leagues merged.

## College Football

### NATIONAL COLLEGE FOOTBALL CHAMPIONS

The "National Collegiate A. A. Football Guide" recognizes as unofficial national champion the team selected each year by press association polls. Where The Associated Press poll (of writers) does not agree with the United Press International poll (of coaches), the guide lists both teams selected.

| | | | | | | | | | |
|---|---|---|---|---|---|---|---|---|---|
| 1937 | Pittsburgh | 1948 | Michigan | | Ohio State | 1967 | So. California | 1976 | Pittsburgh |
| 1938 | Texas Christian | 1949 | Notre Dame | 1958 | Louisiana State | 1968 | Ohio State | 1977 | Notre Dame |
| 1939 | Texas A & M | 1950 | Oklahoma | 1959 | Syracuse | 1969 | Texas | 1978 | Alabama and |
| 1940 | Minnesota | 1951 | Tennessee | 1960 | Minnesota | 1970 | Texas and Ne- | | So. California |
| 1941 | Minnesota | 1952 | Michigan State | 1961 | Alabama | | braska | 1979 | Alabama |
| 1942 | Ohio State | 1953 | Maryland | 1962 | So. California | 1971 | Nebraska | 1980 | Georgia |
| 1943 | Notre Dame | 1954 | Ohio State and | 1963 | Texas | 1972 | So. California | 1981 | Clemson |
| 1944 | Army | | U.C.L.A. | 1964 | Alabama | 1973 | Notre Dame | | |
| 1945 | Army | 1955 | Oklahoma | 1965 | Alabama and | 1974 | Oklahoma and | | |
| 1946 | Notre Dame | 1956 | Oklahoma | | Michigan State | | So. California | | |
| 1947 | Notre Dame | 1957 | Auburn and | 1966 | Notre Dame | 1975 | Oklahoma | | |

### ARMY-NAVY SERIES RECORD SINCE 1962

| | | | | | |
|---|---|---|---|---|---|
| 1962 | Navy 34, Army 14 | 1969 | Army 27, Navy 0 | 1976 | Navy 38, Army 10 |
| 1963 | Navy 21, Army 15 | 1970 | Navy 11, Army 7 | 1977 | Army 17, Navy 14 |
| 1964 | Army 11, Navy 8 | 1971 | Army 24, Navy 23 | 1978 | Navy 28, Army 0 |
| 1965 | Army 7, Navy 7 | 1972 | Army 23, Navy 15 | 1979 | Navy 31, Army 7 |
| 1966 | Army 20, Navy 7 | 1973 | Navy 51, Army 0 | 1980 | Navy 33, Army 6 |
| 1967 | Navy 19, Army 14 | 1974 | Navy 19, Army 0 | 1981 | Army 3, Navy 3 |
| 1968 | Army 21, Navy 14 | 1975 | Navy 30, Army 6 | | |

### RECORD OF ANNUAL MAJOR BOWL COLLEGE FOOTBALL GAMES

**Rose Bowl**
(At Pasadena, Calif.)

| | | | | | |
|---|---|---|---|---|---|
| | | 1924 | Navy 14, Washington 14 | 1939 | So. California 7, Duke 3 |
| | | 1925 | Notre Dame 27, Stanford 10 | 1940 | So. California 14, Tennessee 0 |
| | | 1926 | Alabama 20, Washington 19 | 1941 | Stanford 21, Nebraska 13 |
| 1902 | Michigan 49, Stanford 0 | 1927 | Alabama 7, Stanford 7 | 1942 | Oregon State 20, Duke 16[1] |
| 1916 | Washington State 14, Brown 0 | 1928 | Stanford 7, Pittsburgh 6 | 1943 | Georgia 9, U.C.L.A. 0 |
| 1917 | Oregon 14, Pennsylvania 0 | 1929 | Georgia Tech 8, California 7 | 1944 | So. California 29, Washington 0 |
| 1918 | Mare Island Marines 19, Camp Lewis 7 | 1930 | So. California 47, Pittsburgh 14 | 1945 | So. California 25, Tennessee 0 |
| | | 1931 | Alabama 24, Washington State 0 | 1946 | Alabama 34, So. California 14 |
| 1919 | Great Lakes 17, Mare Island Marines 0 | 1932 | So. California 21, Tulane 12 | 1947 | Illinois 45, U.C.L.A. 14 |
| | | 1933 | So. California 35, Pittsburgh 0 | 1948 | Michigan 49, So. California 0 |
| 1920 | Harvard 7, Oregon 6 | 1934 | Columbia 7, Stanford 0 | 1949 | Northwestern 20, California 14 |
| 1921 | California 28, Ohio State 0 | 1935 | Alabama 29, Stanford 13 | 1950 | Ohio State 17, California 14 |
| 1922 | Washington and Jefferson 0, California 0 | 1936 | Stanford 7, So. Methodist 0 | 1951 | Michigan 14, California 6 |
| | | 1937 | Pittsburgh 21, Washington 0 | 1952 | Illinois 40, Stanford 7 |
| 1923 | So. California 14, Penn State 3 | 1938 | California 13, Alabama 0 | 1953 | So. California 7, Wisconsin 0 |

1954  Michigan State 28, U.C.L.A. 20
1955  Ohio State 20, So. California 7
1956  Michigan State 17, U.C.L.A. 14
1957  Iowa 35, Oregon State 19
1958  Ohio State 10, Oregon 7
1959  Iowa 38, California 12
1960  Washington 44, Wisconsin 8
1961  Washington 17, Minnesota 7
1962  Minnesota 21, U.C.L.A. 3
1963  So. California 42, Wisconsin 37
1964  Illinois 17, Washington 7
1965  Michigan 34, Oregon State 7
1966  U.C.L.A. 14, Michigan State 12
1967  Purdue 14, So. California 13
1968  So. California 14, Indiana 3
1969  Ohio State 27, So. California 16
1970  So. California 10, Michigan 3
1971  Stanford 27, Ohio State 17
1972  Stanford 13, Michigan 12
1973  So. California 42, Ohio State 17
1974  Ohio State 42, So. California 21
1975  So. California 18, Ohio State 17
1976  U.C.L.A. 23, Ohio State 10
1977  So. California 14, Michigan 6
1978  Washington 27, Michigan 20
1979  So. California 17, Michigan 10
1980  So. California 17, Ohio State 16
1981  Michigan 23, Washington 6
1982  Washington 28, Iowa 0
1. Played at Durham, N.C.

## Orange Bowl

(At Miami)

1933  Miami (Fla.) 7, Manhattan 0
1934  Duquesne 33, Miami (Fla.) 7
1935  Bucknell 26, Miami (Fla.) 0
1936  Catholic 20, Mississippi 19
1937  Duquesne 13, Mississippi State 12
1938  Auburn 6, Michigan State 0
1939  Tennessee 17, Oklahoma 0
1940  Georgia Tech 21, Missouri 7
1941  Mississippi State 14, Georgetown 7
1942  Georgia 40, Texas Christian 26
1943  Alabama 37, Boston College 21
1944  Louisiana State 19, Texas A&M 14
1945  Tulsa 26, Georgia Tech 12
1946  Miami (Fla.) 13, Holy Cross 6
1947  Rice 8, Tennessee 0
1948  Georgia Tech 20, Kansas 14
1949  Texas 41, Georgia 28
1950  Santa Clara 21, Kentucky 13
1951  Clemson 15, Miami (Fla.) 14
1952  Georgia Tech 17, Baylor 14
1953  Alabama 61, Syracuse 6
1954  Oklahoma 7, Maryland 0
1955  Duke 34, Nebraska 7
1956  Oklahoma 20, Maryland 6
1957  Colorado 27, Clemson 21
1958  Oklahoma 48, Duke 21
1959  Oklahoma 21, Syracuse 6
1960  Georgia 14, Missouri 0
1961  Missouri 21, Navy 14
1962  Louisiana State 25, Colorado 7
1963  Alabama 17, Oklahoma 0
1964  Nebraska 13, Auburn 7
1965  Texas 21, Alabama 17
1966  Alabama 39, Nebraska 28
1967  Florida 27, Georgia Tech 12
1968  Oklahoma 26, Tennessee 24
1969  Penn State 15, Kansas 14
1970  Penn State 10, Missouri 3

1971  Nebraska 17, Louisiana State 12
1972  Nebraska 38, Alabama 6
1973  Nebraska 40, Notre Dame 6
1974  Penn State 16, Louisiana State 9
1975  Notre Dame 13, Alabama 11
1976  Oklahoma 14, Michigan 6
1977  Ohio State 27, Colorado 10
1978  Arkansas 31, Oklahoma 6
1979  Oklahoma 31, Nebraska 24
1980  Oklahoma 24, Florida State 7
1981  Oklahoma 18, Florida State 17
1982  Clemson 22, Nebraska 15

## Sugar Bowl

(At New Orleans)

1935  Tulane 20, Temple 14
1936  Texas Christian 3, Louisiana State 2
1937  Santa Clara 21, Louisiana State 14
1938  Santa Clara 6, Louisiana State 0
1939  Texas Christian 15, Carnegie Tech 7
1940  Texas A & M 14, Tulane 13
1941  Boston College 19, Tennessee 13
1942  Fordham 2, Missouri 0
1943  Tennessee 14, Tulsa 7
1944  Georgia Tech 20, Tulsa 18
1945  Duke 29, Alabama 26
1946  Oklahoma A & M 33, St. Mary's (Calif.) 13
1947  Georgia 20, North Carolina 10
1948  Texas 27, Alabama 7
1949  Oklahoma 14, North Carolina 6
1950  Oklahoma 35, Louisiana State 0
1951  Kentucky 13, Oklahoma 7
1952  Maryland 28, Tennessee 13
1953  Georgia Tech 24, Mississippi 7
1954  Georgia Tech 42, West Virginia 19
1955  Navy 21, Mississippi 0
1956  Georgia Tech 7, Pittsburgh 0
1957  Baylor 13, Tennessee 7
1958  Mississippi 39, Texas 7
1959  Louisiana State 7, Clemson 0
1960  Mississippi 21, Louisiana State 0
1961  Mississippi 14, Rice 6
1962  Alabama 10, Arkansas 3
1963  Mississippi 17, Arkansas 13
1964  Alabama 12, Mississippi 7
1965  Louisiana State 13, Syracuse 10
1966  Missouri 20, Florida 18
1967  Alabama 34, Nebraska 7
1968  Louisiana State 20, Wyoming 13
1969  Arkansas 16, Georgia 2
1970  Mississippi 27, Arkansas 22
1971  Tennessee 34, Air Force Academy 13
1972  Oklahoma 40, Auburn 22
1973  Oklahoma 14, Penn State 0
1974  Notre Dame 24, Alabama 23
1975  Nebraska 13, Florida 10
1976  Alabama 13, Penn State 6
1977  Pittsburgh 27, Georgia 3
1978  Alabama 35, Ohio State 6
1979  Alabama 14, Penn State 7
1980  Alabama 24, Arkansas 9
1981  Georgia 17, Notre Dame 10
1982  Pittsburgh 24, Georgia 20

## Cotton Bowl

(At Dallas)

1937  Texas Christian 16, Marquette 6
1938  Rice 28, Colorado 14

1939  St. Mary's (Calif.) 20, Texas Tech. 13
1940  Clemson 6, Boston College 3
1941  Texas A & M 13, Fordham 12
1942  Alabama 29, Texas A & M 21
1943  Texas 14, Georgia Tech 7
1944  Randolph Field 7, Texas 7
1945  Oklahoma A & M 34, Texas Christian 0
1946  Texas 40, Missouri 27
1947  Louisiana State 0, Arkansas 0
1948  So. Methodist 13, Penn State 13
1949  So. Methodist 21, Oregon 13
1950  Rice 27, North Carolina 13
1951  Tennessee 20, Texas 14
1952  Kentucky 20, Texas Christian 7
1953  Texas 16, Tennessee 0
1954  Rice 28, Alabama 6
1955  Georgia Tech 14, Arkansas 6
1956  Mississippi 14, Texas Christian 13
1957  Texas Christian 28, Syracuse 27
1958  Navy 20, Rice 7
1959  Air Force 0, Texas Christian 0
1960  Syracuse 23, Texas 14
1961  Duke 7, Arkansas 6
1962  Texas 12, Mississippi 7
1963  Louisiana State 13, Texas 0
1964  Texas 28, Navy 6
1965  Arkansas 10, Nebraska 7
1966  Louisiana State 14, Arkansas 7
1967  Georgia 24, So. Methodist 9
1968  Texas A & M 20, Alabama 16
1969  Texas 36, Tennessee 13
1970  Texas 21, Notre Dame 17
1971  Notre Dame 24, Texas 11
1972  Penn State 30, Texas 6
1973  Texas 17, Alabama 13
1974  Nebraska 19, Texas 3
1975  Penn State 41, Baylor 20
1976  Arkansas 31, Georgia 10
1977  Houston 30, Maryland 21
1978  Notre Dame 38, Texas 10
1979  Notre Dame 35, Houston 34
1980  Houston 17, Nebraska 14
1981  Alabama 30, Baylor 2
1982  Texas 14, Alabama 12

## Gator Bowl

(At Jacksonville, Fla. Played on Saturday nearest New Year's Day of year indicated)

1953  Florida 14, Tulsa 13
1954  Texas Tech 35, Auburn 13
1955  Auburn 33, Baylor 13
1956  Vanderbilt 25, Auburn 13
1957  Georgia Tech 21, Pittsburgh 14
1958  Tennessee 3, Texas A & M 0
1959  Mississippi 7, Florida 3
1960  Arkansas 14, Georgia Tech 7
1961  Florida 13, Baylor 12
1962  Penn State 30, Georgia Tech 15
1963  Florida 17, Penn State 7
1964  No. Carolina 35, Air Force 0
1965  Florida State 36, Oklahoma 19
1966  Georgia Tech 31, Texas Tech 21
1967  Tennessee 18, Syracuse 12
1968  Penn State 17, Florida State 17
1969  Missouri 35, Alabama 10
1970  Florida 14, Tennessee 13
1971  Auburn 35, Mississippi 28
1972  Georgia 7, North Carolina 3
1973  Auburn 24, Colorado 3
1974  Texas Tech 28, Tennessee 19

| 1975 | Auburn 27, Texas 3 | 1979 | Clemson 17, Ohio State 15 |
| 1976 | Maryland 13, Florida 0 | 1980 | North Carolina 17, Michigan 15 |
| 1977 | Notre Dame 20, Penn State 9 | 1981 | Pittsburgh 37, South Carolina 9 |
| 1978 | Pittsburgh 34, Clemson 3 | 1982 | North Carolina 31, Arkansas 27 |

## RESULTS OF OTHER 1981 SEASON BOWL GAMES

Bluebonnet (Houston)—Michigan 33, U.C.L.A. 14
California Bowl (Fresno, Calif.)—Toledo 27, San Jose State 25
Fiesta (Tempe, Ariz.)—Penn State 26, Southern California 10
Hall of Fame (Birmingham, Ala.)—Mississippi State 10, Kansas 0
Holiday (San Diego)—Brigham Young 38, Washington State 36
Independence (Shreveport, La.)—Texas A. and M. 33, Oklahoma State 16

Liberty (Memphis)—Ohio State 31, Navy 28
Garden State (East Rutherford, N.J.)—Tennessee 28, Wisconsin 21
Peach (Atlanta)—West Virginia 26, Florida 6
Sun (El Paso)—Oklahoma 40, Houston 14
Tangerine (Orlando, Fla.)—Missouri 19, Southern Mississippi 17

## HEISMAN MEMORIAL TROPHY WINNERS

The Heisman Memorial Trophy is presented annually by the Downtown Athletic Club of New York City to the nation's outstanding college football player, as determined by a poll of sportswriters and sportscasters.

| 1935 | Jay Berwanger, Chicago | 1952 | Billy Vessels, Oklahoma | 1968 | O. J. Simpson, Southern California |
| 1936 | Larry Kelley, Yale | 1953 | Johnny Lattner, Notre Dame | | |
| 1937 | Clinton Frank, Yale | 1954 | Alan Ameche, Wisconsin | 1969 | Steve Owens, Oklahoma |
| 1938 | Davey O'Brien, Texas Christian | 1955 | Howard Cassady, Ohio State | 1970 | Jim Plunkett, Stanford |
| 1939 | Nile Kinnick, Iowa | 1956 | Paul Hornung, Notre Dame | 1971 | Pat Sullivan, Auburn |
| 1940 | Tom Harmon, Michigan | 1957 | John Crow, Texas A & M | 1972 | Johnny Rodgers, Nebraska |
| 1941 | Bruce Smith, Minnesota | 1958 | Pete Dawkins, Army | 1973 | John Cappelletti, Penn State |
| 1942 | Frank Sinkwich, Georgia | 1959 | Billy Cannon, Louisiana State | 1974–75 | Archie Griffin, Ohio State |
| 1943 | Angelo Bertelli, Notre Dame | 1960 | Joe Bellino, Navy | 1976 | Tony Dorsett, Pittsburgh |
| 1944 | Leslie Horvath, Ohio State | 1961 | Ernie Davis, Syracuse | 1977 | Earl Campbell, Texas |
| 1945 | Felix Blanchard, Army | 1962 | Terry Baker, Oregon State | 1978 | Billy Sims, Oklahoma |
| 1946 | Glenn Davis, Army | 1963 | Roger Staubach, Navy | 1979 | Charles White, Southern California |
| 1947 | Johnny Lujack, Notre Dame | 1964 | John Huarte, Notre Dame | | |
| 1948 | Doak Walker, So. Methodist | 1965 | Mike Garrett, Southern California | 1980 | George Rogers, South Carolina |
| 1949 | Leon Hart, Notre Dame | | | 1981 | Marcus Allen, Southern California |
| 1950 | Vic Janowicz, Ohio State | 1966 | Steve Spurrier, Florida | | |
| 1951 | Dick Kazmaier, Princeton | 1967 | Gary Beban, U.C.L.A. | | |

## COLLEGE FOOTBALL HALL OF FAME

(Kings Island, Interstate 71, Kings Mills, Ohio)

(Date given is player's last year of competition)

### Players

Abell, Earl—Colgate, 1915
Agase, Alex—Purdue/Illinois, 1946
Agganis, Harry—Boston Univ., 1952
Albert, Frank—Stanford, 1941
Aldrich, Chas. (Ki)—T.C.U., 1938
Aldrich, Malcolm—Yale, 1921
Alexander, John—Syracuse, 1920
Ameche, Alan (Horse)—Wisconsin, 1954
Anderson, H. (Hunk)—Notre Dame, 1921
Bacon, C. Everett—Wesleyan, 1912
Bagnell, Francis (Reds)—Penn, 1950
Baker, Hobart (Hobey)—Princeton, 1913
Baker, Terry—Oregon State, 1962
Ballin, Harold—Princeton, 1914
Banker, Bill—Tulane, 1929
Barnes, Stanley—S. California, 1921
Barrett, Charles—Cornell, 1915
Baston, Bert—Minnesota, 1916
Battles, Cliff—W. Va. Wesleyan, 1931
Baugh, Sammy—Texas Christian U., 1936
Bausch, James—Kansas, 1930
Beckett, John—Oregon, 1913
Bednarik, Chuck—Pennsylvania, 1948
Bellini, Joe—Navy, 1960
Benbrook, A.—Michigan, 1911
Bertelli, A.—Notre Dame, 1943
Berry, Charlie—Lafayette, 1924
Berwanger, John (Jay)—Chicago, 1935
Bettencourt, Larry—St. Mary's, 1927

Blanchard, Felix (Doc)—Army, 1946
Bock, Ed—Iowa State, 1938
Bomar, Lynn—Vanderbilt, 1924
Bomeisler, Doug (Bo)—Yale, 1913
Booth, Albie—Yale, 1931
Borries, Fred—Navy, 1934
Bosely, Bruce—West Virginia, 1955
Bottari, Vic—California, 1939
Boynton, Ben—Williams, 1920
Brewer, Charles—Harvard, 1895
Brooke, George—Pennsylvania, 1895
Brown, Gordon—Yale, 1900
Brown, John, Jr.—Navy, 1913
Brown, Johnny Mack—Alabama, 1925
Brown, Raymond (Tay)—So. California, 1932
Bunker, Paul—Army, 1902
Butler, Robert—Wisconsin, 1912
Cafego, George—Tennessee, 1939
Cagle, Chris—SW La./Army, 1929
Cain, John—Alabama, 1932
Cameron, Eddie—Wash. & Lee, 1924
Campbell, David C.—Harvard, 1901
Cannon, Jack—Notre Dame, 1929
Carideo, Frank—Notre Dame, 1930
Caroline, J.C.—Illinois, 1954
Carney, Charles—Illinois, 1921
Carpenter, Bill—Army, 1959
Carpenter, C. Hunter—VPI, 1905
Carroll, Charles—Washington, 1928

Casey, Edward L.—Harvard, 1919
Cassady, Howard—Ohio State, 1955
Chamberlain, Guy—Nebraska, 1915
Christman, Paul—Missouri, 1940
Clark, Earl (Dutch)—Colo. College, 1929
Clevenger, Zora—Indiana, 1903
Cochran, Gary—Princeton, 1895
Cody, Josh—Vanderbilt, 1920
Coleman, Don—Mich. State, 1951
Conerly, Chuck—Mississippi, 1947
Connor, George—Notre Dame, 1947
Corbin, W.—Yale, 1888
Corbus, William—Stanford, 1933
Cowan, Hector—Princeton, 1889
Coy, Edward H. (Tad)—Yale, 1909
Crawford, Fred—Duke, 1933
Crow, John D.—Texas A&M, 1957
Crowley, James—Notre Dame, 1924
Cutter, Slade—Navy, 1934
Czarobski, Ziggie—Notre Dame, 1947
Dalrymple, Gerald—Tulane, 1931
Daniell, James—Ohio State, 1941
Dawkins, Pete—Army, 1958
Dalton, John—Navy, 1912
Daly, Charles—Harvard/Army, 1902
Daniell, Averell—Pittsburgh, 1936
Davies, Tom—Pittsburgh, 1921
Davis, Ernest—Syracuse, 1961
Davis, Glenn—Army, 1946
Davis, Robert T.—Georgia Tech, 1947

DesJardien, Paul—Chicago, 1914
Devine, Aubrey—Iowa, 1921
DeWitt, John—Princeton, 1903
Dobbs, Glenn—Tulsa, 1942
Dodd, Bobby—Tennessee, 1930
Donchess, Joseph—Pittsburgh, 1929
Dougherty, Nathan—Tennessee, 1909
Drahos, Nick—Cornell, 1940
Driscoll, Paddy—Northwestern, 1917
Drury, Morley—So. California, 1927
Dudley, William (Bill)—Virginia, 1941
Eckersall, Walter—Chicago, 1906
Edwards, Turk—Washington State, 1931
Edwards, William—Princeton, 1900
Eichenlaub, R.—Notre Dame, 1913
Evans, Ray—Kansas, 1947
Exendine, Albert—Carlisle, 1908
Falaschi, Nello—Santa Clara, 1937
Fears, Tom—Santa Clara/UCLA, 1947
Feathers, Beattie—Tennessee, 1933
Fenimore, Robert—Oklahoma State, 1947
Fenton, G.E. (Doc)—La. State U., 1910
Ferraro, John—So. California, 1944
Fesler, Wesley—Ohio State, 1930
Fincher, Bill—Georgia Tech, 1920
Fish, Hamilton—Harvard, 1909
Fisher, Robert—Harvard, 1911
Flowers, Abe—Georgia Tech, 1920
Fortmann, Daniel—Colgate, 1935
Francis, Sam—Nebraska, 1936
Franco, Edmund (Ed)—Fordham, 1937
Frank, Clint—Yale, 1937
Franz, Rodney—California, 1949
Friedman, Benny—Michigan, 1926
Gain, Bob—Kentucky, 1950
Gallarneau, Hugh—Stanford, 1941
Garbisch, Edgar—Army, 1924
Gelbert, Charles—Pennsylvania, 1896
Geyer, Forest—Oklahoma, 1915
Giel, Paul—Minnesota, 1953
Gifford, Frank—So. California, 1951
Gilbert, Walter—Auburn, 1936
Gipp, George—Notre Dame, 1920
Gladchuk, Chet—Boston College, 1940
Goldberg, Marshall—Pittsburgh, 1938
Goodreault, Gene—Boston College, 1940
Gordon, Walter—California, 1918
Graham, Otto—Northwestern, 1943
Grange, Harold (Red)—Illinois, 1925
Grayson, Robert—Stanford, 1935
Gulick, Merel—Hobart, 1929
Guyon, Joe—Georgia Tech, 1919
Hale, Edwin—Mississippi Col, 1921
Hamilton, Robert (Bones)—Stanford, 1935
Hamilton, Tom—Navy, 1925
Hanson, Vic—Syracuse, 1926
Hardwick, H. (Tack)—Harvard, 1914
Hare, T. Truxton—Pennsylvania, 1900
Harley, Chick—Ohio State, 1919
Harmon, Tom—Michigan, 1940
Harpster, Howard—Carnegie Tech, 1928
Hart, Edward J.—Princeton, 1911
Hart, Leon—Notre Dame, 1949
Hazel, Homer—Rutgers, 1924
Healey, Ed—Dartmouth, 1916
Heffelfinger, W. (Pudge)—Yale, 1891
Hein, Mel—Washington State, 1930
Henry, Wilber—Wash. & Jefferson, 1919
Herschberger, Clarence—Chicago, 1899
Herwig, Robert—California, 1937
Heston, Willie—Michigan, 1904
Hickman, Herman—Tennessee, 1931
Hickok, William—Yale, 1895

Hill, Dan—Duke, 1938
Hillebrand, A.R. (Doc)—Princeton, 1900
Hinkey, Frank—Yale, 1894
Hinkle, Carl—Vanderbilt, 1937
Hinkle, Clark—Bucknell, 1932
Hirsch, Elroy—Wis./Mich., 1943
Hitchcock, James—Auburn, 1932
Hoffman, Frank—Notre Dame, 1931
Hogan, James J.—Yale, 1904
Holland, Jerome (Brud)—Cornell, 1938
Hollenbeck, William—Penn., 1908
Holovak, Michael—Boston College, 1942
Horrell, Edwin—California, 1924
Horvath, Les—Ohio State, 1944
Howe, Arthur—Yale, 1911
Howell, Millard (Dixie)—Alabama, 1934
Hubbard, Cal—Centenary, 1926
Hubbard, John—Amherst, 1906
Hubert, Allison—Alabama, 1925
Huff, Robert Lee (Sam)—W. Va., 1955
Humble, Weldon G.—Rice, 1946
Hunt, Joel—Texas A&M, 1927
Huntington, Ellery—Colgate, 1914
Hutson, Don—Alabama, 1934
Ingram, James—Navy, 1906
Isbell, Cecil—Purdue, 1937
Jablonsky, Harvey—Wash. U./Army, 1933
Janowicz, Vic—Ohio State, 1951
Jenkins, Darold—Missouri, 1941
Joesting, Herbert—Minnesota, 1927
Johnson, James—Carlisle, 1903
Jones, Calvin—Iowa, 1955
Jones, Gomer—Ohio State, 1935
Juhan, Frank—Univ. of South, 1910
Justice, Charlie—North Carolina, 1949
Kaer, Mort—So. California, 1926
Kavanaugh, Kenneth—La. State U., 1939
Kaw, Edgar—Cornell, 1922
Kazmaier, Richard—Princeton, 1951
Keck, James—Princeton, 1921
Kelley, Larry—Yale, 1936
Kelly, William—Montana, 1926
Ketcham, Henry—Yale, 1913
Killinger, William—Penn State, 1922
Kimbrough, John—Texas A&M, 1940
Kinard, Frank—Mississippi, 1937
King, Phillip—Princeton, 1893
Kinnick, Nile—Iowa, 1939
Kipke, Harry—Michigan, 1923
Kirkpatrick, John Reed—Yale, 1910
Kitzmiller, John—Oregon, 1929
Koch, Barton—Baylor, 1931
Kitner, Malcolm—Texas, 1942
Kramer, Ron—Michigan, 1956
Lach, Steve—Duke, 1941
Lane, Myles—Dartmouth, 1927
Lattner, Joseph J.—Notre Dame, 1953
Lauricella, Hank—Tennessee, 1952
Lautenschlaeger—Tulane, 1925
Layden, Elmer—Notre Dame, 1924
Layne, Bobby—Texas, 1947
Lea, Langdon—Princeton, 1895
LeBaron, Eddie—Univ. of Pacific, 1949
Leech, James—Va. Mil. Inst., 1920
Lilly, Bob—Texas Christian, 1960
Lio, Augie—Georgetown, 1940
Locke, Gordon—Iowa, 1922
Lourie, Don—Princeton, 1921
Luckman, Sid—Columbia, 1938
Lujack, John—Notre Dame, 1947
Lund, J.L. (Pug)—Minnesota, 1934
Macomber, Bart—Illinois, 1915
MacLeod, Robert—Dartmouth, 1938
Maegle, Dick—Rice, 1954

Mahan, Edward W.—Harvard, 1915
Mallory, William—Yale, 1893
Mann, Gerald—So. Methodist, 1927
Markov, Vic—Washington, 1937
Marshall, Robert—Minnesota, 1907
Matson, Ollie—San Fran. U., 1952
Matthews, Ray—Texas Christ. U., 1928
Maulbetsch, John—Michigan, 1914
Mauthe, J.L. (Pete)—Penn State 1912
Maxwell, Robert—Chi./Swarthmore, 1906
McAfee, George—Duke, 1939
McColl, William F.—Stanford, 1951
McCormick, James B.—Princeton, 1907
McDowall, Jack—No. Car. State, 1927
McElhenny, Hugh—Washington, 1951
McEver, Gene—Tennessee, 1931
McEwan, John—Minn./Army, 1916
McFadden, J.B.—Clemson, 1939
McClung, Thomas L.—Yale, 1891
McGinley, Edward—Pennsylvania, 1924
McGovern, J.—Minnesota, 1910
McGraw, Thurman—Colorado State, 1949
McLaren, George—Pittsburgh, 1918
McMillan, Dan—U.S.C./Calif., 1922
McMillin, A.N. (Bo)—Centre, 1921
McWhorter, Robert—Georgia, 1913
Mercer, Leroy—Pennsylvania, 1912
Meredith, Don—Southern Methodist, 1959
Metzger, Bert—Notre Dame, 1930
Mickal, Abe—La. State U., 1935
Miller, Creighton—Notre Dame, 1943
Miller, Don—Notre Dame, 1925
Miller, Edgar (Rip)—Notre Dame, 1924
Miller, Eugene—Penn State, 1913
Milstead, Century—Wabash, Yale 1923
Minds, John—Pennsylvania, 1897
Moffatt, Alex—Princeton, 1884
Montgomery, Cliff—Columbia, 1933
Moomaw, Donn—U.C.L.A., 1952
Morley, William—Columbia, 1903
Morris, George—Georgia Tech, 1952
Morton, William—Dartmouth, 1931
Muller, Harold (Brick)—Calif., 1922
Nagurski, Bronko—Minnesota, 1929
Nevers, Ernie—Stanford, 1925
Newell, Marshall—Harvard, 1893
Newman, Harry—Michigan, 1932
Nobis, Tommy—Texas, 1965
Nomellini, Leo—Minnesota, 1949
Oberlander, Andrew—Dartmouth, 1925
O'Brien, Davey—Texas Christ. U., 1938
O'Dea, Pat—Wisconsin, 1899
O'Hearn, J.—Cornell, 1915
Oliphant, Elmer—Purdue/Army, 1917
Olsen, Merlin—Utah State, 1961
Oosterbaan, Ben—Michigan, 1927
O'Rourke, Charles—Boston College, 1940
Orsi, John—Colgate, 1931
Osgood, W.D.—Cornell/Penn, 1895
Osmanski, William—Holy Cross, 1938
Owens, Jim—Oklahoma, 1949
Parilli, Vito (Babe)—Kentucky, 1951
Parker, Clarence (Ace)—Duke, 1936
Parker, Jackie—Miss. State, 1953
Parker, James—Ohio State, 1956
Pazzetti, V.J.—Wes./Lehigh, 1912
Peabody, Endicott—Harvard, 1941
Peck, Robert—Pittsburgh, 1916
Pennock, Stanley B.—Harvard, 1914
Pfann, George—Cornell, 1923
Phillips, H.D.—U. of South, 1904

Pingel, John—Michigan State, 1938
Pihos, Pete—Indiana, 1945
Pinckert, Ernie—So. California, 1931
Poe, Arthur—Princeton, 1899
Pollard, Fritz—Brown, 1916
Poole, Barney—Miss./Army, 1947
Pregulman, Merv—Michigan, 1943
Price, Eddie—Tulane, 1949
Pund, Henry—Georgia Tech, 1928
Ramsey, Gerrard—Wm. & Mary, 1942
Reeds, Claude—Oklahoma, 1913
Reid, William—Harvard, 1900
Rentner, Ernest—Northwestern, 1932
Reynolds, Robert—Stanford, 1935
Richter, Les—California, 1951
Rinehart, Charles—Lafayette, 1897
Rodgers, Ira—West Virginia, 1919
Rogers, Edward L.—Minnesota, 1903
Rosenberg, Aaron—So. California, 1934
Rote, Kyle—So. Methodist, 1950
Routt, Joe—Texas A&M., 1937
Salmon, Louis—Notre Dame, 1904
Sauer, George—Nebraska, 1933
Sayers, Gale—Kansas, 1964
Scarlett, Hunter—Pennsylvania, 1909
Schoonover, Wear—Arkansas, 1929
Schreiner, Dave—Wisconsin, 1942
Schultz, Adolf (Germany)—Mich., 1908
Schwab, Frank—Lafayette, 1922
Schwartz, Marchmont—Notre Dame, 1931
Schwegler, Paul—Washington, 1931
Scott, Clyde—Arkansas, 1949
Scott, Tom—Virgina, 1953
Seibels, Henry—Sewanee, 1899
Shelton, Murray—Cornell, 1915
Shevlin, Tom—Yale, 1905
Shively, Bernie—Illinois, 1926
Simons, Claude—Tulane, 1934
Sington, Fred—Alabama, 1930
Sinkwich, Frank—Georgia, 1942
Skladany, Joe—Pittsburgh, 1933
Slater, F.F. (Duke)—Iowa, 1921
Smith, Bruce—Minnesota, 1941

Smith, Ernie—So. California, 1932
Smith, Harry—So. California, 1939
Smith, John (Clipper)—Notre Dame, 1927
Smith, Vernon—Georgia, 1931
Snow, Neil—Michigan, 1901
Spears, Clarence W.—Dartmouth, 1915
Spears, W.D.—Vanderbilt, 1927
Sprackling, William—Brown, 1911
Sprague, M. (Bud)—Texas/Army, 1928
Stafford, Harrison—Texas, 1932
Stagg, Amos Alonzo—Yale, 1889
Staubach, Roger—Navy, 1963
Steffen, Walter—Chicago, 1908
Stein, Herbert—Pittsburgh, 1921
Steuber, Robert—Missouri, 1943
Stevens, Mal—Yale, 1923
Stinchcomb, Gaylord—Ohio State, 1920
Stevenson, Vincent—Pennsylvania, 1905
Strong, Ken—New York Univ., 1928
Strupper, George—Georgia Tech, 1917
Stuhldreher, Harry—Notre Dame, 1924
Stydahar, Joe—West Virginia, 1935
Suffridge, Robert—Tennessee, 1940
Sundstrom, Frank—Cornell, 1923
Swanson, Clarence—Nebraska, 1921
Swiacki, Bill—Holy Cross/Colombia, 1947
Swink, Jim—Texas Christian, 1956
Taliaferro, George—Indiana, 1948
Thompson, Joe—Pittsburgh, 1907
Thorne, Samuel B.—Yale, 1906
Thorpe, Jim—Carlisle, 1912
Ticknor, Ben—Harvard, 1930
Tigert, John—Vanderbilt, 1904
Tinsley, Gaynell—La. State U., 1936
Tipton, Eric—Duke, 1938
Tonnemaker, Clayton—Minnesota, 1949
Torrey, Robert—Pennsylvania, 1906
Travis, Ed Tarkio—Missouri, 1920
Trippi, Charles—Georgia, 1946
Tryon, J. Edward—Colgate, 1925
Utay, Joe—Texas A&M, 1907
Van Brocklin, Norm—Oregon, 1948
Van Sickel, Dale—Florida, 1929
Van Surdam, Henderson—Wesleyan, 1905

Very, Dexter—Penn State, 1912
Vessels, Billy—Oklahoma, 1931
Wagner, Huber—Pittsburgh, 1913
Walker, Doak—So. Methodist, 1949
Wallace, Bill—Rice, 1935
Walsh, Adam—Notre Dame, 1924
Warburton, I. (Cotton)—So. Calif., 1934
Ward, Robert (Bob)—Maryland, 1951
Warner, William—Cornell, 1903
Washington, Ken—U.C.L.A., 1939
Wedemeyer, Herman J.—St. Mary's, 1947
Weekes, Harold—Columbia, 1902
Weir, Ed—Nebraska, 1925
Welch, Gus—Carlisle, 1914
Weller, John—Princeton, 1935
Wendell, Percy—Harvard, 1913
West, D. Belford—Colgate, 1919
Weyand, Alex—Army, 1915
Wharton, Charles—Pennsylvania, 1896
Wheeler, Arthur—Princeton, 1894
White, Byron (Whizzer)—Colorado, 1937
Whitmire, Don—Alabama/Navy, 1944
Wickhorst, Frank—Navy, 1926
Widseth, Ed—Minnesota, 1936
Wildung, Richard—Minnesota, 1942
Williams, James—Rice, 1949
Willis, William—Ohio State, 1945
Wilson, George—Washington, 1925
Wilson, Harry—Penn State/Army, 1923
Wistert, Albert A.—Michigan, 1942
Wistert, Al—Michigan, 1949
Wistert, Frank (Whitey)—Mich., 1933
Wood, Barry—Harvard, 1931
Wojciechowicz, Alex—Fordham, 1936
Wyant, Andrew—Bucknell/Chicago, 1894
Wyatt, Bowden—Tennessee, 1938
Wyckoff, Clint—Cornell, 1896
Yoder, Lloyd—Carnegie Tech, 1926
Young, Claude (Buddy)—Illinois, 1946
Young, Harry—Wash. & Lee, 1916
Zarnas, Gus—Ohio State, 1937

## Coaches

Bill Alexander
Dr. Ed Anderson
Ike Armstrong
Matty Bell
Hugo Bezdek
Dana X. Bible
Bernie Bierman
Earl (Red) Blaik
Charles W. Caldwell
Walter Camp
Len Casanova
Frank Cavanaugh
Fritz Crisler
Bob Devaney
Gil Dobie
Michael Donohue
Gus Dorais

Charles (Rip) Engle
Don Faurot
Jake Gaither
Ernest Godfrey
Jack Harding
Edward K. Hall
Richard Harlow
Jesse Harper
Percy Haughton
John W. Heisman
R. A. (Bob) Higgins
Orin E. Hollingberry
William Ingram
Morley Jennings
Howard Jones
L. (Biff) Jones
Thomas (Tad) Jones

Ralph (Shug) Jordan
Andy Kerr
Frank Leahy
George E. Little
Lou Little
El (Slip) Madigan
Herbert McCracken
Daniel McGugin
DeOrmond (Tuss) McLaughry
L. R. (Dutch) Meyer
Bernie Moore
Scrappy Moor
Ray Morrison
George A. Munger
Clarence Munn
William Murray
Ed (Hooks) Mylin

Earle (Greasy) Neale
Jess Neely
Robert Neyland
Homer Norton
Frank (Buck) O'Neill
Bennie Owen
Ara Parseghian
James Phalea
E. N. Robinson
Knute Rockne
E. L. (Dick) Romney
William W. Roper
George F. Sanford
Francis A. Schmidt
Floyd (Ben) Schwartzwalder
Clark Shaughnessy
Buck Shaw

Andrew L. Smith
Carl Snavely
Amos A. Stagg
Jock Sutherland
Frank W. Thomas
John H. Vaught
Wallace Wade
Lynn Waldorf
Glenn (Pop) Warner
E. E. (Tad) Wieman
John W. Wilce
Bud Wilkinson
Henry L. Williams
George W. Woodruff
Fielding H. Yost
Robert Zuppke

## MAJOR COLLEGE FOOTBALL RECORDS (1940–1981)

(Opposing teams are listed in parentheses. *Source:* National Collegiate Sports Services)

**LONGEST PLAYS**
**Rushing**

| | Yards |
|---|---|
| Kelsey Finch, Tennessee (Florida) 1977 | 99 |
| Ralph Thompson, W. Tex. State (Wichita State) 1970 | 99 |
| Max Anderson, Arizona State (Wyoming) 1967 | 99 |
| Gale Sayers, Kansas (Nebraska) 1963 | 99 |
| Granville Amos, Virginia M. I. (Wm. & Mary) 1964 | 98 |
| Jim Thacker, Davidson (George Washington) 1952 | 98 |
| Bill Powell, California (Oregon State) 1951 | 98 |
| Al Yannelli, Bucknell (Delaware) 1946 | 98 |
| Meredith Warner, Iowa State (Iowa Pre-Flight) 1943 | 98 |

Methodist (Ohio State) 1968 and Dave Wilson, Illinois (Ohio State) 1980
Most passes completed—43, Dave Wilson, Illinois (Ohio State) 1980 and Rich Campbell, California (Florida) 1980
Most passes caught—22, Jay Miller, Brigham Young (New Mexico) 1973

### Scoring

|  | Years | Td | Pat | Fg | Pts |
|---|---|---|---|---|---|
| Tony Dorsett, Pittsburgh | 1973–76 | 59[1] | 2 | 0 | 356[1] |
| Glenn Davis, Army | 1943–46 | 59[1] | 0 | 0 | 354 |

| Art Luppino, Arizona | 1953–56 | 48 | 49 | 0 | 337 |
|---|---|---|---|---|---|
| Steve Owens, Oklahoma | 1967–69 | 56 | 0 | 0 | 336 |
| Wilford White, Arizona State | 1947–50 | 48 | 27 | 4 | 327 |
| Ed Marinaro, Cornell | 1969–71 | 52 | 6 | 0 | 318 |
| Pete Johnson, Ohio State | 1973–76 | 53 | 0 | 0 | 318 |
| Ted Brown, North Carolina State | 1975–78 | 51 | 6 | 0 | 312 |
| Eddie Talboom, Wyoming | 1948–50 | 34 | 99 | 0 | 303 |

1. Record.

## N.C.A.A. DIVISION II AND III FOOTBALL RECORDS (1942–1981)

### LONGEST PLAYS
#### Rushing

|  | Yards |
|---|---|
| Kevin Doherty, Mass. Maritime (New Haven) 1980 | 99 |
| Fred Deutsch, Springfield (Wagner) 1977 | 99 |
| Sam Hallston, Albany State, N.Y. (Norwich) 1977 | 99 |
| Sammy Croom, San Diego (Azusa Pacific) 1972 | 99 |
| John Stenger, Swarthmore (Widener) 1970 | 99 |
| Jed Knuttila, Hamline (St. Thomas) 1968 | 99 |
| Dave Lanoha, Colorado College (Texas Lutheran) 1967 | 99 |
| Tom Pabst, Cal–Riverside (Cal. Tech) 1965 | 99 |
| George Phillips, Concord (Davis and Elkins) 1961 | 99 |
| Gerry White, Connecticut (Rhode Island) 1960 | 99 |
| Leo Williams, St. Augustine's (Morris) 1960 | 99 |
| George Phelps, Cornell College (Monmouth) 1959 | 99 |
| Mark Lydon, Tufts (Bowdoin) 1958 | 99 |
| David Wells, Tufts (Williams) 1956 | 99 |
| Jack Moskal, Western Reserve (Case Tech) 1954 | 99 |
| Lou Mariano, Kent State (Western Reserve) 1954 | 99 |
| Ron Temple, Chico State (Southern Oregon) 1953 | 99 |
| Ellis Horton, Eureka (Rose–Hulman) 1952 | 99 |
| Pat Abbruzzi, Rhode Island (New Hampshire) 1951 | 99 |

#### Field Goals

| Joe Duren, Arkansas State (McNeese State) 1974 | 63 |
|---|---|
| Dom Antonini, Glassboro State (Salisbury State) 1976 | 62 |
| Mike Flater, Colorado Mines (Western State) 1973 | 62 |
| Duane Christian, Cameron (Southwestern Oklahoma) 1976 | 61 |
| Mike Wood, Southeast Missouri (Lincoln) 1975 | 61 |
| Bill Shear, Cortland State (Hobart) 1966 | 61 |

#### Passing

|  | Yards |
|---|---|
| John Guercio–Tom Bennett, C.W. Post (Juniata) 1980 | -99 |
| Mike Moroski–Calvin Ellison, California-Davis (Puget Sound) 1978 | 99 |
| Rich Boling–Lewis Borsellino, DePauw (Valparaiso) 1976 | 99 |
| John Wicinski–Donnell Lipford, John Carroll (Allegheny) 1975 | 99 |
| Jack Berry–Mercer West, Washington and Lee (Hampden–Sydney) 1974 | 99 |
| Gary Shope–Rick Rudolph, Juniata (Moravian) 1973 | 99 |
| Gary Dusenberg–Harvey King, North Park (Illinois Wesleyan) 1970 | 99 |
| Bob Janesko–Frank Stankiewicz, Emporia (Pittsburg State) 1969 | 99 |
| John Williams–Bill Carter, N.M. Highlands (North Colorado) 1964 | 99 |
| Carl Meyers–Roger Sayers, Nebraska-Omaha (Drake) 1963 | 99 |

#### Punts

| Earl Hurst, Emporia State (Central Missouri) 1964 | 97 |
|---|---|
| Gary Frens, Hope (Olivet) 1966 | 96 |
| Jim Jarrett, North Dakota (South Dakota) 1957 | 96 |
| Elliot Mills, Carleton (Monmouth) 1970 | 93 |

| Kaspar Fitins, Taylor (Georgetown, Ky.) 1966 | 93 |
|---|---|
| Leeroy Sweeney, Pomona (Cal–Riverside) 1960 | 93 |

### CAREER LEADERS
#### Rushing

|  | Years | Plays | Yds | Avg |
|---|---|---|---|---|
| Chris Cobb, Eastern Illinois | 1976–79 | 930 | 5,042[1] | 5.42 |
| Jerry Linton, Panhandle State | 1959–62 | 648 | 4,839 | 7.47 |
| John VanWagner, Mich. Tech. | 1973–76 | 958 | 4,788 | 5.00 |
| Rich Kowalski, Hobart | 1972–75 | 907 | 4,631 | 5.11 |
| Don Aleksiewicz, Hobart | 1969–72 | 819 | 4,525 | 5.53 |
| Dale Mills, NE Missouri | 1957–60 | 751 | 4,502 | 5.99 |
| Leo Lewis, Lincoln (Mo.) | 1951–54 | 623 | 4,458 | 7.16 |
| Bernie Peeters, Luther | 1968–71 | 1,072[1] | 4,435 | 4.14 |
| Larry Schreiber, Tenn. Tech. | 1966–69 | 878 | 4,421 | 5.04 |
| Brad Rowland, McMurry | 1947–50 | 683 | 4,347 | 6.36 |
| Vincent Allen, Indiana State | 1973–77 | 832 | 4,335 | 5.21 |
| Bill Rhodes, Colorado Western | 1953–56 | 506 | 4,294 | 8.49[1] |
| Lem Harkey, Col. of Emporia | 1951–54 | 502 | 4,232 | 8.43 |

1. Record.

#### Scoring

|  | Years | Td | Pat | Fg | Pts |
|---|---|---|---|---|---|
| Walter Payton, Jackson State | 1971–74 | 66[1] | 53 | 5 | 464[1] |
| Dale Mills, NE Missouri | 1957–60 | 64 | 23 | 0 | 407 |
| Garney Henley, Huron | 1956–59 | 63 | 16 | 0 | 394 |
| Leo Lewis, Lincoln (Mo.) | 1951–54 | 64 | 0 | 0 | 384 |
| Billy Johnson, Widener | 1971–73 | 62 | 0 | 0 | 372 |
| Tank Younger, Grambling | 1945–48 | 60 | 9 | 0 | 369 |

1. Record

#### Passing

|  | Years | Cmp | Pct | Yds | Td |
|---|---|---|---|---|---|
| Jim Lindsey, Abilene Chr. | 1967–70 | 642[1] | .519 | 8,521[1] | 61 |
| Bob Caress, Bradley | 1962–65 | 610 | .528 | 7,115 | 64 |
| Dan Miles, So. Oregon | 1964–67 | 577 | .662[1] | 6,531 | 52 |
| George Bork, N. Illinois | 1960–63 | 577 | .640 | 6,782 | 60 |
| Mike Hoston, St. Joseph's | 1978–81 | 576 | .559 | 6,815 | 57 |
| Curt Strasheim, Southwest St. | 1978–81 | 568 | .526 | 5,837 | 29 |
| Craig Soloman, Southwestern Tennessee | 1975–78 | 542 | .530 | 7,314 | 71 |
| Ron Meehan, Towson State | 1977–80 | 529 | .527 | 6,164 | 31 |
| Kim McQuilken, Lehigh | 1971–73 | 516 | .558 | 6,996 | 37 |
| Tim Von Dulm, Portland St. | 1969–70 | 500 | .541 | 5,967 | 51 |
| Greg Cavanaugh, St. Norbert | 1977–80 | 489 | .499 | 5,442 | 37 |
| Doug Williams, Grambling | 1974–77 | 484 | .480 | 8,411 | 93[1] |

1. Record.

| | |
|---|---|
| Stanley Howell, Miss. State (Southern Miss.) 1979 | 98 |
| Mark Malone, Arizona State (Utah State) 1979 | 98 |
| Steve Atkins, Maryland (Clemson) 1978 | 98 |

## Punt Returns

| | Yards |
|---|---|
| Jimmy Campagna, Georgia (Vanderbilt) 1952 | 100 |
| Hugh McElhenny, Washington (So. Cal.) 1951 | 100 |
| Frank Brady, Navy (Maryland) 1951 | 100 |
| Bert Rechichar, Tennessee (Wash. & Lee) 1950 | 100 |
| Eddie Macon, Pacific (Boston U.) 1950 | 100 |
| Richie Luzzi, Clemson (Georgia) 1968 | 100[1] |
| Don Guest, California (Washington State) 1966 | 100[1] |

1. Return of a field goal attempt.

## Passing

| | Yards |
|---|---|
| Chris Collingsworth—Derrick Gaffney, Florida (Rice) 1977 | 99 |
| Terry Peel—Robert Ford, Houston (San Diego St.) 1972 | 99 |
| Terry Peel—Robert Ford, Houston (Syracuse) 1970 | 99 |
| Colin Clapton—Eddie Jenkins, Holy Cross (Boston U.) 1970 | 99 |
| Bo Burris—Warren McVea, Houston (Wash. St.) 1966 | 99 |
| Fred Owens—Jack Ford, Portland (St. Mary's) 1947 | 99 |
| Jeff Martin—Mark Flaker, Drake (N.M. State) 1976 | 98 |
| Pete Woods—Joe Stewart, Missouri (Nebraska) 1976 | 98 |
| Dan Hagemann—Jack Steptoe, Utah (New Mexico) 1976 | 98 |
| Bruce Shaw—Pat Kenny, N.C. State (Penn State) 1972 | 98 |
| Jerry Rhome—Jeff Jordan, Tulsa (Wichita State) 1963 | 98 |
| Bob Dean—Norman Dawson, Cornell (Navy) 1947 | 98 |

## Punts

| | Yards |
|---|---|
| Pat Brady, Nevada-Reno (Loyola, L. A.) 1950 | 99 |
| George O'Brien, Wisconsin (Iowa) 1952 | 96 |
| John Hadl, Kansas (Oklahoma) 1959 | 94 |
| Carl Knox, Texas Christian (Oklahoma State) 1947 | 94 |
| Preston Johnson, SMU (Pittsburgh) 1940 | 94 |

## Field Goals

| | Yards |
|---|---|
| Joe Williams, Wichita State (So. Illinois) 1978 | 67 |
| Steve Little, Arkansas (Texas) 1977 | 67 |
| Russell Erxleben, Texas (Rice) 1977 | 67 |
| Tony Franklin, Texas A&M (Baylor) 1976 | 65 |
| Russell Erxleben, Texas (Oklahoma) 1977 | 64 |
| Tony Franklin, Texas A&M (Baylor) 1976 | 64 |
| Morten Andersen, Mich. State (Ohio State) 1981 | 63 |
| Clark Kemble, Colorado State (Arizona) 1975 | 63 |
| Dan Christopulos, Wyoming (Colorado State) 1977 | 62 |
| Iseed Khoury, North Texas State (Richmond) 1977 | 62 |
| Dave Lawson, Air Force Academy (Iowa State) 1975 | 62 |
| Steve Little, Arkansas (Tulsa) 1976 | 61 |
| Wayne Latimer, Virginia Tech (Florida State) 1975 | 61 |
| Ray Guy, Southern Mississippi (Utah State) 1972 | 61 |

## CAREER LEADERS
## Rushing

| | Years | Plays | Yds | Avg |
|---|---|---|---|---|
| Tony Dorsett, Pittsburgh | 1973–76 | 1,074[1] | 6,082[1] | 5.66 |
| Charles White, So. Calif. | 1976–79 | 1,023 | 5,598 | 5.47 |
| Archie Griffin, Ohio State | 1972–75 | 845 | 5,177 | 6.13 |
| George Rogers, So. Calif. | 1977–80 | 902 | 4,958 | 5.50 |
| Ed Marinaro, Cornell | 1969–71 | 918 | 4,715 | 5.14 |
| Marcus Allen, So. Calif. | 1978–81 | 893 | 4,682 | 5.24 |
| Ted Brown, No. Carolina State | 1975–78 | 860 | 4,602 | 5.35 |
| Terry Miller, Oklahoma State | 1974–77 | 847 | 4,582 | 5.41 |
| Earl Campbell, Texas | 1974–77 | 765 | 4,443 | 5.81 |
| Amos Lawrence, North Carolina | 1977–80 | 881 | 4,391 | 4.98 |
| Joe Morris, Syracuse | 1978–81 | 813 | 4,299 | 5.29 |
| Jerome Persell, Western | | | | |

| | | | | |
|---|---|---|---|---|
| Mich. | 1976–78 | 842 | 4,190 | 4.98 |
| Stump Mitchell, Citadel | 1977–80 | 756 | 4,062 | 5.37 |
| Charles Alexander, L.S.U. | 1975–78 | 855 | 4,035 | 4.72 |
| Darrin Nelson, Stanford | 1977–78 1980–81 | 703 | 4,033 | 5.74 |

1. Record.

## Passing

| | Years | Cmp | Pct | Yds | Td |
|---|---|---|---|---|---|
| Mark Herrmann, Purdue | 1977–80 | 717[1] | .589 | 9,188 | 62 |
| Jim McMahon, Brigham Young | 1977–78 1980–81 | 653 | .616 | 9,536[1] | 84[1] |
| Chuck Hixson, Southern Methodist | 1968–70 | 642 | .576 | 7,179 | 40 |
| Joe Adams, Tennessee State | 1977–80 | 604 | .549 | 8,649 | 81 |
| John Reaves, Florida | 1969–71 | 603 | .535 | 7,549 | 54 |
| Jack Thompson, Washington State | 1975–78 | 601 | .553 | 7,818 | 53 |
| Ed Luther, San Jose State | 1976–79 | 600 | .537 | 7,190 | 47 |
| Rich Campbell, California | 1977–80 | 574 | .644[1] | 6,933 | 33 |
| Randy Hertel, Rice | 1977–80 | 561 | .500 | 6,161 | 38 |
| Gene Swick, Toledo | 1972–75 | 556 | .593 | 7,267 | 44 |
| Marc Wilson, Brigham Young | 1977–79 | 535 | .571 | 7,637 | 61 |
| Jim Plunkett, Stanford | 1968–70 | 530 | .551 | 7,544 | 52 |
| John Elway, Stanford | 1979–81 | 512 | .609 | 6,107 | 54 |
| Tommy Kramer, Rice | 1973–76 | 507 | .489 | 6,197 | 37 |

1. Record.

## Total Offense

| | Years | Plays | Yds | Tdr[1] |
|---|---|---|---|---|
| Jim McMahon, Brigham Young | 1977–78 1980–81 | 1,325 | 9,723[2] | 94[2] |
| Mark Herrmann, Purdue | 1977–80 | 1,354 | 8,444 | 63 |
| Gene Swick, Toledo | 1972–75 | 1,579[2] | 8,074 | 63 |
| Joe Adams, Tennessee State | 1977–80 | 1,256 | 7,972 | 86 |
| Jim Plunkett, Stanford | 1968–70 | 1,174 | 7,887 | 62 |
| Art Schlichter, Ohio State | 1978–81 | 1,316 | 7,869 | n.a. |
| Jack Thompson, Washington State | 1975–78 | 1,345 | 7,698 | 63 |
| Marc Wilson, Brigham Young | 1977–79 | 1,183 | 7,602 | 68 |
| John Reaves, Florida | 1969–71 | 1,258 | 7,283 | 58 |
| Steve Brown, Appalachian State | 1977–80 | 1,160 | 7,129 | 49 |
| Ed Luther, San Jose State | 1976–79 | 1,230 | 6,981 | 55 |
| Chuck Hixson, Southern Methodist | 1968–70 | 1,358 | 6,884 | 50 |
| Pat Sullivan, Auburn | 1969–71 | 970 | 6,884 | 71 |

1. Touchdowns responsible for—scored or passed for. 2. Record. n.a.—not available.

## Pass Receiving

| | Years | Rec | Yds | Td |
|---|---|---|---|---|
| Howard Twilley, Tulsa | 1963–65 | 261[1] | 3,343 | 32 |
| Darren Nelson, Stanford | 1977–78 1980–81 | 214 | 2,368 | 16 |
| Ron Sellers, Florida State | 1966–68 | 212 | 3,598[1] | 23 |
| Gerald Harp, Western Carolina | 1977–80 | 197 | 3,305 | 26 |
| Phil Odle, Brigham Young | 1965–67 | 181 | 2,548 | 25 |
| Tim Delaney, San Diego State | 1968–70 | 180 | 2,535 | 22 |

1. Record.

## BEST SINGLE-GAME PERFORMANCES

Most yards, rushing—356, Eddie Lee Ivery, Georgia Tech (Air Force) 1978

Most yards, total offense—599, Virgil Carter, Brigham Young (Texas–El Paso) 1966

Most yards, passing—621, Dave Wilson, Illinois (Ohio State) 1980

Most yards, pass receiving—349, Chuck Hughes, Texas–El Paso (North Texas State) 1965

Most points scored—44, Jim McMahon, Brigham Young, 1981

Most passes attempted—69, Chuck Hixson, Southern

## Pass Receiving

| | Years | Rec | Yards | Td |
|---|---|---|---|---|
| Bill Stromberg, Johns Hopkins | 1978–81 | 258[1] | 3,776 | 39 |
| Chris Myers, Kenyon | 1967–70 | 253 | 3,897 | 33 |
| Bruce Cerone, Yankton–Emporia St. | 1966–67 1968–1969 | 241[1] | 4,354[1] | 49[1] |
| Harold Roberts, Austin Peay | 1967–70 | 232 | 3,005 | 31 |
| Jerry Hendren, Idaho | 1967–69 | 230 | 3,435 | 27 |
| Terry Fredenberg, Wis.–Milwaukee | 1965–68 | 206 | 2,789 | 24 |
| Rick Fry, Occidental | 1974–77 | 200 | 3,073 | 18 |
| Jay True, DePauw | 1977–80 | 195 | 2,567 | 12 |
| Bill Wick, Carroll (Wis.) | 1966–69 | 190 | 2,967 | 20 |
| Don Hutt, Boise State | 1971–73 | 187 | 2,716 | 30 |

1. Record.

## MOST POINTS IN SEASON

| | Yards | Tds | PAT | Fg | Pts |
|---|---|---|---|---|---|
| Terry Metcalf, Long Beach St. | 1971 | 29[1] | 4 | 0 | 178 |
| Jim Switzer, Coll. Emporia | 1963 | 28 | 0 | 0 | 168 |

| Carl Herakovich, Rose Polytech | 1958 | 25 | 18 | 0 | 168 |
|---|---|---|---|---|---|
| Ted Scown, Sul Ross State | 1948 | 28 | 0 | 0 | 168 |
| Eddie McGovern, Rose Polytech | 1942 | 23 | 27 | 0 | 165 |
| Leon Burns, Long Beach State | 1969 | 27 | 2 | 0 | 164 |

1. Record.

## Total Offense

| | Years | Plays | Yds |
|---|---|---|---|
| Jim Lindsey, Abilene Christian | 1967–70 | 1,510[1] | 8,385[1] |
| Doug Williams, Grambling | 1974–77 | 1,072 | 8,195 |
| Donald Smith, Langston | 1958–61 | 998 | 7,376 |
| Bruce Upstill, Coll. Emporia | 1960–63 | 922 | 7,122 |
| Mike Houston, St. Joseph's (Ind.) | 1978–81 | 1,298 | 7,104 |
| Craig Solomon, SW Tennessee | 1975–78 | 1,261 | 7,055 |
| Clay Sampson, Denison | 1977–80 | 1,225 | 6,920 |
| Kim McQuilken, Lehigh | 1971–73 | 991 | 6,878 |
| Bob Caress, Bradley | 1962–65 | 1,361 | 6,757 |

1. Record.

## N.C.A.A. 1981 CHAMPIONSHIP PLAYOFFS

### DIVISION I–AA
**Semifinals**
Eastern Kentucky 23, Boise State 17
Idaho State 41, South Carolina State 12

**Championship**
Idaho State 34, Eastern Kentucky 23

### DIVISION II
**First Round**
Shippensburg (Pa.) State 40, Virginia Union 27
Northern Michigan 55, Elizabeth City (N.C.) State 6
Southwest Texas State 38, Jacksonville State 22
North Dakota State–Fargo 24, Puget Sound 10

**Semifinals**
Southwest Texas State 62, Northern Michigan 0
North Dakota State 18, Shippensburg State 6

**Championship**
Southwest Texas State 42, North Dakota State 13

### DIVISION III
**Semifinals**
Widener 23, Montclair State 12
Dayton 38, Lawrence Univ. 0

**Championship**
Widener 17, Dayton 10

## NATIONAL ASSOCIATION OF INTERCOLLEGIATE ATHLETICS 1981 CHAMPIONSHIPS

### DIVISION I
**Semifinals**
Elon (N.C.) 41, Hillsdale (Mich.) 13
Pittsburg (Kan.) State won by forfeit from Cameron, Okla.

**Championship**
Elon 3, Pittsburg State 0

### DIVISION II
**Championship**
Austin College 24, Concordia (Minn.) 24

# *Professional Football*

## NATIONAL FOOTBALL LEAGUE FINAL STANDING 1981

### AMERICAN CONFERENCE
**Eastern Division**

| | W | L | T | Pct | Pts | OP |
|---|---|---|---|---|---|---|
| Miami | 11 | 4 | 1 | .719 | 345 | 275 |
| New York Jets[1] | 10 | 5 | 1 | .657 | 355 | 287 |
| Buffalo[1] | 10 | 6 | 0 | .625 | 311 | 276 |
| Baltimore | 2 | 14 | 0 | .125 | 259 | 533 |
| New England | 2 | 14 | 0 | .125 | 322 | 370 |

**Central Division**

| Cincinnati | 12 | 4 | 0 | .750 | 421 | 304 |
|---|---|---|---|---|---|---|
| Pittsburgh | 8 | 8 | 0 | .500 | 356 | 297 |
| Houston | 7 | 9 | 0 | .438 | 281 | 355 |
| Cleveland | 5 | 11 | 0 | .313 | 276 | 375 |

**Western Division**

| San Diego | 10 | 6 | 0 | .625 | 478 | 390 |
|---|---|---|---|---|---|---|
| Denver | 10 | 6 | 0 | .625 | 321 | 289 |
| Kansas City | 9 | 7 | 0 | .563 | 343 | 290 |
| Seattle | 6 | 10 | 0 | .375 | 322 | 388 |

1. Wild card qualifier for playoffs.

**Playoffs:** Buffalo 31, New York Jets 27; Cincinnati 28, Buffalo 21; San Diego 41, Miami 38 (overtime).
**Conference championship:** Cincinnati 27, San Diego 7.

### NATIONAL CONFERENCE
**Eastern Division**

| | W | L | T | Pct | Pts | OP |
|---|---|---|---|---|---|---|
| Dallas | 12 | 4 | 0 | .750 | 367 | 277 |
| Philadelphia[1] | 10 | 6 | 0 | .625 | 368 | 221 |
| New York Giants[1] | 9 | 7 | 0 | .563 | 295 | 257 |
| Washington | 8 | 8 | 0 | .500 | 347 | 349 |
| St. Louis | 7 | 9 | 0 | .438 | 315 | 408 |

**Central Division**

| | | | | | | |
|---|---|---|---|---|---|---|
| Tampa Bay | 9 | 7 | 0 | .563 | 315 | 268 |
| Detroit | 8 | 8 | 0 | .500 | 397 | 322 |
| Green Bay | 8 | 8 | 0 | .500 | 324 | 361 |
| Minnesota | 7 | 9 | 0 | .438 | 325 | 369 |
| Chicago | 6 | 10 | 0 | .375 | 253 | 324 |

**Western Division**

| | | | | | | |
|---|---|---|---|---|---|---|
| San Francisco | 13 | 3 | 0 | .813 | 357 | 250 |
| Atlanta | 7 | 9 | 0 | .438 | 426 | 355 |

| | | | | | | |
|---|---|---|---|---|---|---|
| Los Angeles | 6 | 10 | 0 | .375 | 303 | 351 |
| New Orleans | 4 | 12 | 0 | .250 | 207 | 378 |

1. Wild card qualifier for playoffs.

**Playoffs:** New York Giants 27, Philadelphia 21; San Francisco 38, New York Giants 24; Dallas 38, Tampa Bay 0.

**Conference championship:** San Francisco 28, Dallas 27.

## LEAGUE CHAMPIONSHIP—SUPER BOWL XVI
### (Jan. 24, 1982; at Silverdome, Pontiac, Mich.; Attendance 81,270)

**Scoring**

| | 1st Q | 2nd Q | 3rd Q | 4th Q | Final |
|---|---|---|---|---|---|
| San Francisco (NFC) | 7 | 13 | 0 | 6 | 26 |
| Cincinnati (ACF) | 0 | 0 | 7 | 14 | 21 |

**Scoring**—San Francisco: Touchdowns: Montana, 1–yard run; Cooper, 11–yard pass from Montana. Conversions: Wersching 2 (kicks). Field goals: Wersching 4, 22 yards, 26 yards, 40 yards, and 23 yards. Cincinnati: Touchdowns: Anderson, 4–yard run; Ross, 4–yard pass from Anderson; Ross, 3–yard pass from Anderson. Conversions: Breech 3 (kicks).

**Statistics of the Game**

| | San Francisco | Cincinnati |
|---|---|---|
| First downs | 20 | 24 |
| Yards gained rushing | 127 | 72 |
| Yards gained passing | 148 | 284 |
| Passes completed | 14 | 25 |
| Passes intercepted by | 2 | 0 |
| Punts | 4–46 | 3–44 |
| Ball lost, fumbles | 1 | 2 |
| Yards penalized | 65 | 57 |

## SUPER BOWLS I–XVI[1]

| Game | Date | Winner | Loser | Site | Attendance |
|---|---|---|---|---|---|
| XVI | Jan. 24, 1982 | San Francisco (NFC) 26 | Cincinnati (AFC) 21 | Silverdome, Pontiac, Mich. | 81,270 |
| XV | Jan. 25, 1981 | Oakland (AFC) 27 | Philadelphia (NFC) 10 | Superdome, New Orleans | 75,500 |
| XIV | Jan. 20, 1980 | Pittsburgh (AFC) 31 | Los Angeles (NFC) 19 | Rose Bowl, Pasadena | 103,985 |
| XIII | Jan. 21, 1979 | Pittsburgh (AFC) 35 | Dallas (NFC) 31 | Orange Bowl, Miami | 79,484 |
| XII | Jan. 15, 1978 | Dallas (NFC) 27 | Denver (AFC) 10 | Superdome, New Orleans | 75,583 |
| XI | Jan. 9, 1977 | Oakland (AFC) 32 | Minnesota (NFC) 14 | Rose Bowl, Pasadena | 103,424 |
| X | Jan. 18, 1976 | Pittsburgh (AFC) 21 | Dallas (NFC) 17 | Orange Bowl, Miami | 80,187 |
| IX | Jan. 12, 1975 | Pittsburgh (AFC) 16 | Minnesota (NFC) 6 | Tulane Stadium, New Orleans | 80,997 |
| VIII | Jan. 13, 1974 | Miami (AFC) 24 | Minnesota (NFC) 7 | Rice Stadium, Houston | 71,882 |
| VII | Jan. 14, 1973 | Miami (AFC) 14 | Washington (NFC) 7 | Memorial Coliseum, Los Angeles | 90,182 |
| VI | Jan. 16, 1972 | Dallas (NFC) 24 | Miami (AFC) 3 | Tulane Stadium, New Orleans | 81,591 |
| V | Jan. 17, 1971 | Baltimore (AFC) 16 | Dallas (NFC) 13 | Orange Bowl, Miami | 79,204 |
| IV | Jan. 11, 1970 | Kansas City (AFL) 23 | Minnesota (NFL) 7 | Tulane Stadium, New Orleans | 80,562 |
| III | Jan. 12, 1969 | New York (AFL) 16 | Baltimore (NFL) 7 | Orange Bowl, Miami | 75,389 |
| II | Jan. 14, 1968 | Green Bay (NFL) 33 | Oakland (AFL) 14 | Orange Bowl, Miami | 75,546 |
| I | Jan. 15, 1967 | Green Bay (NFL) 35 | Kansas City (AFL) 10 | Memorial Coliseum, Los Angeles | 61,946 |

1. Super Bowls I to IV were played before the American Football League and National Football League merged into the NFL, which was divided into two conferences, the NFC and AFC.

## NATIONAL LEAGUE CHAMPIONS

| Year | Champion (W-L-T) | Year | Champion (W-L-T) | Year | Champion (W-L-T) |
|---|---|---|---|---|---|
| 1921 | Chicago Bears (Staley's) (10–1–1) | 1925 | Chicago Cardinals (11–2–1) | 1929 | Green Bay Packers (12–0–1) |
| 1922 | Canton Bulldogs (10–0–2) | 1926 | Frankford Yellow Jackets (14–1–1) | 1930 | Green Bay Packers (10–3–1) |
| 1923 | Canton Bulldogs (11–0–1) | 1927 | New York Giants (11–1–1) | 1931 | Green Bay Packers (12–2–0) |
| 1924 | Cleveland Indians (7–1–1) | 1928 | Providence Steamrollers (8–1–2) | 1932 | Chicago Bears (7–1–6) |

| Year | Eastern Conference winners (W-L-T) | Western Conference winners (W-L-T) | League champion playoff results |
|---|---|---|---|
| 1933 | New York Giants (11–3–0) | Chicago Bears (10–2–1) | Chicago Bears 23, New York 21 |
| 1934 | New York Giants (8–5–0) | Chicago Bears (13–0–0) | New York 30, Chicago Bears 13 |
| 1935 | New York Giants (9–3–0) | Detroit Lions (7–3–2) | Detroit 26, New York 7 |
| 1936 | Boston Redskins (7–5–0) | Green Bay Packers (10–1–1) | Green Bay 21, Boston 6 |
| 1937 | Washington Redskins (8–3–0) | Chicago Bears (9–1–1) | Washington 28, Chicago Bears 21 |
| 1938 | New York Giants (8–2–1) | Green Bay Packers (8–3–0) | New York 23, Green Bay 17 |
| 1939 | New York Giants (9–1–1) | Green Bay Packers (9–2–0) | Green Bay 27, New York 0 |
| 1940 | Washington Redskins (9–2–0) | Chicago Bears (8–3–0) | Chicago Bears 73, Washington 0 |
| 1941 | New York Giants (8–3–0) | Chicago Bears (10–1–1)[2] | Chicago Bears 37, New York 9 |

| 1942 | Washington Redskins (10–1–1) | Chicago Bears (11–0–0) | Washington 14, Chicago Bears 6 |
|------|------|------|------|
| 1943 | Washington Redskins (6–3–1)[2] | Chicago Bears (8–1–1) | Chicago Bears 41, Washington 21 |
| 1944 | New York Giants (8–1–1) | Green Bay Packers (8–2–0) | Green Bay 14, New York 7 |
| 1945 | Washington Redskins (8–2–0) | Cleveland Rams (9–1–0) | Cleveland 15, Washington 14 |
| 1946 | New York Giants (7–3–1) | Chicago Bears (8–2–1) | Chicago Bears 24, New York 14 |
| 1947 | Philadelphia Eagles (8–4–0)[2] | Chicago Cardinals (9–3–0) | Chicago Cardinals 28, Philadelphia 21 |
| 1948 | Philadelphia Eagles (9–2–1) | Chicago Cardinals (11–1–0) | Philadelphia 7, Chicago Cardinals 0 |
| 1949 | Philadelphia Eagles (11–1–0) | Los Angeles Rams (8–2–2) | Philadelphia 14, Los Angeles 0 |
| 1950[1] | Cleveland Browns (10–2–0)[2] | Los Angeles Rams (9–3–0)[2] | Cleveland 30, Los Angeles 28 |
| 1951[1] | Cleveland Browns (11–1–0) | Los Angeles Rams (8–4–0) | Los Angeles 24, Cleveland 17 |
| 1952[1] | Cleveland Browns (8–4–0) | Detroit Lions (9–3–0)[2] | Detroit 17, Cleveland 7 |
| 1953 | Cleveland Browns (11–1–0) | Detroit Lions (10–2–0) | Detroit 17, Cleveland 16 |
| 1954 | Cleveland Browns (9–3–0) | Detroit Lions (9–2–1) | Cleveland 56, Detroit 10 |
| 1955 | Cleveland Browns (9–2–1) | Los Angeles Rams (8–3–1) | Cleveland 38, Los Angeles 14 |
| 1956 | New York Giants (8–3–1) | Chicago Bears (9–2–1) | New York 47, Chicago Bears 7 |
| 1957 | Cleveland Browns (9–2–1) | Detroit Lions (8–4–0)[3] | Detroit 59, Cleveland 14 |
| 1958 | New York Giants (9–3–0)[2] | Baltimore Colts (9–3–0) | Baltimore 23, New York 17[3] |
| 1959 | New York Giants (10–2–0) | Baltimore Colts (9–3–0) | Baltimore 31, New York 16 |
| 1960 | Philadelphia Eagles (10–2–0) | Green Bay Packers (8–4–0) | Philadelphia 17, Green Bay 13 |
| 1961 | New York Giants (10–3–1) | Green Bay Packers (11–3–0) | Green Bay 37, New York 0 |
| 1962 | New York Giants (12–2–0) | Green Bay Packers (13–1–0) | Green Bay 16, New York 7 |
| 1963 | New York Giants (11–3–0) | Chicago Bears (11–1–2) | Chicago 14, New York 10 |
| 1964 | Cleveland Browns (10–3–1) | Baltimore Colts (12–2–0) | Cleveland 27, Baltimore 0 |
| 1965 | Cleveland Browns (11–3–0) | Green Bay Packers (11–3–1)[2] | Green Bay 23, Cleveland 12 |
| 1966 | Dallas Cowboys (10–3–1) | Green Bay Packers (12–2–0) | Green Bay 34, Dallas 27 |
| 1967 | Dallas Cowboys (9–5–0)[2] | Green Bay Packers (9–4–1)[2] | Green Bay 21, Dallas 17 |
| 1968 | Cleveland Browns (10–4–0)[2] | Baltimore Colts (13–1–0)[2] | Baltimore 34, Cleveland 0 |
| 1969 | Cleveland Browns (10–3–1)[2] | Minnesota Vikings (12–2–0)[2] | Minnesota 27, Cleveland 7 |

1. League was divided into American and National Conferences, 1950–52 and again in 1970, when leagues merged. 2. Won divisional playoff. 3. Won at 8:15 of sudden death overtime period.

## NATIONAL CONFERENCE CHAMPIONS

| Year | Eastern Division | Central Division | Western Division | Champion |
|------|------|------|------|------|
| 1970 | Dallas Cowboys (10–4–0) | Minnesota Vikings (12–2–0) | San Francisco 49ers (10–3–1) | Dallas |
| 1971 | Dallas Cowboys (11–3–0) | Minnesota Vikings (11–3–0) | San Francisco 49ers (9–5–0) | Dallas |
| 1972 | Washington Redskins (11–3–0) | Green Bay Packers (10–4–0) | San Francisco 49ers (8–5–1) | Washington |
| 1973 | Dallas Cowboys (10–4–0) | Minnesota Vikings (12–2–0) | Los Angeles Rams (12–2–0) | Minnesota |
| 1974 | St. Louis Cardinals (10–4–0) | Minnesota Vikings (10–4–0) | Los Angeles Rams (10–4–0) | Minnesota |
| 1975 | St. Louis Cardinals (11–3–0) | Minnesota Vikings (12–2–0) | Los Angeles Rams (12–2–0) | Dallas |
| 1976 | Dallas Cowboys (12–2–0) | Minnesota Vikings (11–2–1) | Los Angeles Rams (10–3–1) | Minnesota |
| 1977 | Dallas Cowboys (12–2–0) | Minnesota Vikings (9–5–0) | Los Angeles Rams (10–4–0) | Dallas |
| 1978 | Dallas Cowboys (12–4–0) | Minnesota Vikings (8–7–1) | Los Angeles Rams (12–4–0) | Dallas |
| 1979 | Dallas Cowboys (11–5–0) | Tampa Bay Buccaneers (10–6–0) | Los Angeles Rams (9–7–0) | Los Angeles |
| 1980 | Philadelphia Eagles (12–4–0) | Minnesota Vikings (9–7–0) | Atlanta Falcons (12–4–0) | Philadelphia |
| 1981 | Dallas Cowboys (12–4–0) | Tampa Bay Buccaneers (9–7–0) | San Francisco 49ers (13–3–0) | San Francisco |

## AMERICAN CONFERENCE CHAMPIONS

| Year | Eastern Division | Central Division | Western Division | Champion |
|------|------|------|------|------|
| 1970 | Baltimore Colts (11–2–1) | Cincinnati Bengals (8–6–0) | Oakland Raiders (8–4–2) | Baltimore |
| 1971 | Miami Dolphins (10–3–1) | Cleveland Browns (9–5–0) | Kansas City Chiefs (10–3–1) | Miami |
| 1972 | Miami Dolphins (14–0–0) | Pittsburgh Steelers (11–3–0) | Oakland Raiders (10–3–1) | Miami |
| 1973 | Miami Dolphins (12–2–0) | Cincinnati Bengals (10–4–0) | Oakland Raiders (9–4–1) | Miami |
| 1974 | Miami Dolphins (11–3–0) | Pittsburgh Steelers (10–3–1) | Oakland Raiders (12–2–0) | Pittsburgh |
| 1975 | Baltimore Colts (10–4–0) | Pittsburgh Steelers (12–2–0) | Oakland Raiders (12–2–0) | Pittsburgh |
| 1976 | Baltimore Colts (11–3–0) | Pittsburgh Steelers (10–4–0) | Oakland Raiders (13–1–0) | Oakland |
| 1977 | Baltimore Colts (10–4–0) | Pittsburgh Steelers (9–5–0) | Denver Broncos (12–2–0) | Denver |
| 1978 | New England Patriots (11–5–0) | Pittsburgh Steelers (14–2–0) | Denver Broncos (10–6–0) | Pittsburgh |
| 1979 | Miami Dolphins (10–6–0) | Pittsburgh Steelers (12–4–0) | San Diego Chargers (12–4–0) | Pittsburgh |
| 1980 | Buffalo Bills (11–5–0) | Cleveland Browns (11–5–0) | San Diego Chargers (11–5–0) | Oakland |
| 1981 | Miami Dolphins (11–4–1) | Cincinnati Bengals (12–4–0) | San Diego Chargers (10–6–0) | Cincinnati |

## AMERICAN LEAGUE CHAMPIONS

| Year | Eastern Division (W-L-T) | Western Division (W-L-T) | League champion, playoffs results |
|------|------|------|------|
| 1960 | Houston Oilers (10–4–0) | Los Angeles Chargers (10–4–0) | Houston 24, Los Angeles 16 |
| 1961 | Houston Oilers (10–3–1) | San Diego Chargers (12–2–0) | Houston 10, San Diego 3 |
| 1962 | Houston Oilers (11–3–0) | Dallas Texans (11–3–0) | Dallas 20, Houston 17[1] |
| 1963 | Boston Patriots (8–6–1)[2] | San Diego Chargers (11–3–0) | San Diego 51, Boston 10 |
| 1964 | Buffalo Bills (12–2–0) | San Diego Chargers (8–5–1) | Buffalo 20, San Diego 7 |

| | | |
|---|---|---|
| 1965 | Buffalo Bills (10–3–1) | San Diego Chargers (9–2–3) | Buffalo 23, San Diego 0 |
| 1966 | Buffalo Bills (9–4–1) | Kansas City Chiefs (11–2–1) | Kansas City 31, Buffalo 7 |
| 1967 | Houston Oilers (9–4–1) | Oakland Raiders (13–1–0) | Oakland 40, Houston 7 |
| 1968 | New York Jets (11–3–0) | Oakland Raiders (12–2–0)[2] | New York 27, Oakland 23 |
| 1969 | New York Jets (10–4–0) | Oakland Raiders (12–1–1) | Kansas City 17, Oakland 7[3] |

1. Won at 2:45 of second sudden death overtime period. 2. Won divisional playoff. 3. Kansas City defeated New York, 13–6, and Oakland defeated Houston, 56–7, in interdivisional playoffs.

## NATIONAL FOOTBALL LEAGUE GOVERNMENT

**Commissioner's Office:** Pete Rozelle, commissioner; Don Weiss, executive director; Bill Ray, treasurer; Jay Moyer, counsel to commissioner; Jan Van Duser, director of operations; Jim Heffernan, director of public relations; Joe Browne, director of information; Warren Welsh, director of security; Charles R. Jackson, assistant director of security; Joel Bussert, director of personnel; Art McNally, supervisor of officials; Peter Hadhazy, administrative coordinator; Val Pinchbeck, Jr., director of broadcasting; Jim Steeg, director of special events.

**American Conference:** Lamar Hunt, president; Al Ward, assistant to the president; Fran Connors, director of information.

**National Conference:** George Halas, president; Joe Rhein, assistant to the president; Dick Maxwell, director of information.

## PRO FOOTBALL HALL OF FAME

### (National Football Museum, Canton, Ohio)

Teams named are those with which player is best identified; figures in parentheses indicate number of playing seasons.

| | | | | |
|---|---|---|---|---|
| Adderley, Herb, defensive back, Packers, Cowboys (12) | 1961–72 | Guyon, Joe, back, 6 teams (8) | 1919–27 |
| Alworth, Lance, wide receiver, Chargers, Cowboys (11) | 1962–72 | Halas, George, N.F.L. founder, owner and coach, Staleys and Bears, end (11) | 1919–67 |
| Atkins, Doug, defensive end, Browns, Bears, Saints (17) | 1953–69 | Healey, Ed, tackle, Bears (8) | 1920–27 |
| Badgro, Morris, end, N.Y. Yankees, Giants, Bklyn. Dodgers (8) | 1927, 1930–36 | Hein, Mel, center, Giants (15) | 1931–45 |
| Battles, Cliff, back, Redskins (6) | 1932–37 | Henry, Wilbur (Pete), tackle, Bulldogs, Giants (8) | 1920–28 |
| Baugh, Sammy, quarterback, Redskins (16) | 1937–52 | Herber, Arnie, Qback, Packers, Giants (13) | 1930–45 |
| Bednarik, Chuck, center-linebacker, Eagles (14) | 1949–62 | Hewitt, Bill, end, Bears, Eagles (9) | 1932–43 |
| Bell, Bert, N.F.L. founder, owner Eagles and Steelers, N.F.L. Commissioner | 1946–59 | Hinkle, Clarke, fullback, Packers (10) | 1932–41 |
| Berry, Raymond, end, Colts (13) | 1955–67 | Hirsch, Elroy (Crazy Legs), back, end, Rams (12) | 1946–57 |
| Bidwell, Charles W., owner Chicago Cardinals | 1933–47 | Hubbard, R. (Cal), tackle, Giants, Packers (9) | 1927–36 |
| Blanda, George, quarterback–kicker, Bears, Oilers, Raiders (27) | 1949–75 | Huff, Sam, linebacker, Giants, Redskins (13) | 1956–67, 1969 |
| Brown, Jim, fullback, Browns (9) | 1957–65 | Hunt, Lamar, Founder A.F.L., owner Texans, Chiefs | 1959 — |
| Brown, Paul E., coach, Browns (1946–62), Bengals (1968–75) | 1946–75 | Hutson, Don, end, Packers (11) | 1935–45 |
| Brown, Roosevelt, tackle, Giants (13) | 1953–65 | Jones, David (Deacon), defensive end, Rams, Chargers, Redskins (14) | 1961–74 |
| Butkus, Dick, linebacker, Bears (19) | 1965–73 | Kiesling, Walt, guard 6 teams (13) | 1926–38 |
| Canadeo, Tony, back, Packers (11) | 1941–52 | Kinard, Frank (Bruiser), tackle, Dodgers (9) | 1938–47 |
| Carr, Joe, president N.F.L. (18) | 1921–39 | Lambeau, Earl (Curly), N.F.L. founder, coach, end, back, Packers (11) | 1919–53 |
| Chamberlin, Guy, end 4 teams (9) | 1919–27 | Lane, Richard (Night Train), defensive back, Rams, Cardinals, Lions (14) | 1952–65 |
| Christiansen, Jack, defensive back, Lions (8) | 1951–58 | Lary, Yale, defensive back, punter, Lions (11) | 1952–64 |
| Clark, Earl (Dutch), Qback, Spartans, Lions (7) | 1931–38 | Lavelli, Dante, end, Browns (11) | 1946–56 |
| Connor, George, tackle, linebacker, Bears (8) | 1948–55 | Layne, Bobby, Qback, Bears, Lions, Steelers (15) | 1948–62 |
| Conzelman, Jimmy, Qback 5 teams (10), owner | 1921–48 | Leemans, Alphonse (Tuffy), back, Giants (8) | 1936–43 |
| Davis, Willie, defensive end, Packers (10) | 1960–69 | Lilly, Bob, defensive tackle, Cowboys (14) | 1961–74 |
| Donovan, Art, defensive tackle, Colts (12) | 1950–61 | Lombardi, Vince, coach, Packers, Redskins (11) | 1959–70 |
| Driscoll, John (Paddy), Qback, Cards, Bears (11) | 1919–29 | Luckman, Sid, quarterback, Bears (12) | 1939–50 |
| Dudley, Bill, back, Steelers, Lions, Redskins (9) | 1942–53 | Lyman, Roy (Link), tackle, Bulldogs, Bears (11) | 1922–34 |
| Edwards, Albert Glen (Turk), tackle, Redskins (9) | 1932–40 | Mara, Tim, N.F.L. founder, owner Giants | 1925–59 |
| Ewbank, Weeb, coach Colts, Jets (20) | 1954–73 | Marchetti, Gino, defensive end, Colts (14) | 1952–66 |
| Fears, Tom, end, Rams (9); coach, Saints | 1948–56 | Marshall, George P., N.F.L. founder, owner Redskins | 1932–65 |
| Flaherty, Ray, end, Yankees, Giants (9); coach, Redskins, Yankees (14) | 1928–49 | Matson, Ollie, back, Cardinals, Rams, Lions, Eagles (14) | 1952–66 |
| Ford, Len, end, def. end, Browns, Packers (11) | 1948–58 | McAfee, George, back, Bears (8) | 1940–50 |
| Fortmann, Daniel J., guard, Bears (8) | 1936–43 | McElhenny, Hugh, back, 49ers, Vikings, Giants (13) | 1952–64 |
| George, Bill, linebacker, Bears, Rams (15) | 1952–66 | McNally, John (Blood), back, 7 teams (15) | 1925–39 |
| Gifford, Frank, back, Giants (12) | 1952–64 | Michalske, August, guard, Yankees, Packers (13) | 1926–37 |
| Graham, Otto, quarterback, Browns (10) | 1946–55 | Millner, Wayne, end, Redskins (7) | 1936–45 |
| Grange, Harold (Red), back, Bears, Yankees (9) | 1925–34 | Mix, Ron, tackle, Chargers (11) | 1960–71 |
| Gregg, Forrest, tackle, Packers (15) | 1956–71 | Moore, Lenny, back, Colts (12) | 1956–67 |
| Groza, Lou, place-kicker, tackle, Browns (21) | 1946–67 | Motley, Marion, fullback, Browns, Steelers (9) | 1946–55 |
| | | Musso, George, guard-tackle, Bears (12) | 1933–44 |
| | | Nagurski, Bronko, fullback, Bears (9) | 1930–43 |

Neale, Earle (Greasy), coach, Eagles — 1941–50
Nevers, Ernie, fullback, Chicago Cardinals (5) — 1926–31
Nitschke, Ray, linebacker, Packers (15) — 1958–72
Nomellini, Leo, defensive tackle, 49ers (14) — 1950–63
Olsen, Merlin, defensive tackle, Rams (15) — 1962–76
Otto, Jim, center, Raiders (15) — 1960–74
Owen, Steve, tackle, Giants (9), coach, Giants (13) — 1924–53
Parker, Clarence (Ace), quarterback, Dodgers (7) — 1937–46
Parker, Jim, guard, tackle, Colts (11) — 1957–67
Perry, Joe, fullback, 49ers, Colts (16) — 1948–63
Pihos, Pete, end, Eagles (9) — 1947–55
Ray, Hugh, Shorty, N.F.L. advisor — 1938–52
Reeves, Dan, owner Rams — 1941–71
Ringo, Jim, center, Packers (15) — 1953–67
Robustelli, Andy, def. end, Rams, Giants (14) — 1951–64
Rooney, Art, N.F.L. founder, owner Steelers — 1933— 
Sayers, Gale, back, Bears (7) — 1965–71
Schmidt, Joe, linebacker, Lions (13) — 1953–65
Starr, Bart, quarterback, coach, Packers (16) — 1956–71

Stautner, Ernie, defensive tackle, Steelers (14) — 1950–63
Strong, Ken, back, Giants, Yankees (14) — 1929–47
Stydahar, Joe, tackle, Bears (9); coach, Rams, Cardinals (5) — 1936–54
Taylor, Jim, fullback, Packers, Saints (10) — 1958–67
Thorpe, Jim, back, 7 teams (12) — 1915–28
Tittle, Y. A., Qback, Colts, 49ers, Giants (17) — 1948–64
Trafton, George, center, Bears (13) — 1920–32
Trippi, Charley, back, Chicago Cardinals (9) — 1947–55
Tunnell, Emlen, def. back, Giants, Packers (14) — 1948–61
Turner, Clyde (Bulldog), center, Bears (13) — 1940–52
Unitas, John, quarterback, Colts (18) — 1956–73
Van Brocklin, Norm, Qback, Rams, Eagles (12) — 1949–60
Van Buren, Steve, back, Eagles (8) — 1944–51
Waterfield, Bob, quarterback, Rams (8) — 1945–52
Willis, Bill, Guard, Browns (8) — 1946–53
Wilson, Larry, defensive back, Cardinals (13) — 1960–72
Wojciechowicz, Alex, center, Lions, Eagles (13) — 1938–50

## N.F.L. INDIVIDUAL LIFETIME, SEASON, AND GAME RECORDS

(American Football League records were incorporated into N.F.L. records after merger of the leagues)

### All-Time Leading Touchdown Scorers

|  | Yrs | Rush | Pass rec | Returns | TD |
|---|---|---|---|---|---|
| Jim Brown | 9 | 106 | 20 | 0 | 126 |
| Lenny Moore | 12 | 63 | 48 | 2 | 113 |
| Don Hutson | 11 | 3 | 99 | 3 | 105 |
| Jim Taylor | 10 | 83 | 10 | 0 | 93 |
| Franco Harris | 10 | 84 | 7 | 0 | 91 |
| Bobby Mitchell | 11 | 18 | 65 | 8 | 91 |
| Leroy Kelly | 10 | 74 | 13 | 3 | 90 |
| Charley Taylor | 13 | 11 | 79 | 0 | 90 |
| Don Maynard | 15 | 0 | 88 | 0 | 88 |
| Lance Alworth | 11 | 2 | 85 | 0 | 85 |

### All-Time Leading Passers

|  | Comp | Pct comp | Yds | TD | Int | Rating |
|---|---|---|---|---|---|---|
| Roger Staubach | 1,685 | 57.0 | 22,700 | 153 | 109 | 83.5 |
| Sonny Jurgensen | 2,433 | 57.1 | 32,224 | 255 | 189 | 82.8 |
| Len Dawson | 2,136 | 57.1 | 28,711 | 239 | 183 | 82.6 |
| Ken Anderson | 2,036 | 57.5 | 25,562 | 160 | 124 | 80.5 |
| Fran Tarkenton | 3,686 | 57.0 | 47,003 | 342 | 266 | 80.5 |
| Bart Starr | 1,808 | 57.4 | 24,718 | 152 | 138 | 80.3 |
| Bert Jones | 1,382 | 56.1 | 17,663 | 122 | 97 | 79.1 |
| Dan Fouts | 1,849 | 57.7 | 24,256 | 145 | 142 | 78.4 |
| Johnny Unitas | 2,830 | 54.6 | 40,239 | 290 | 253 | 78.2 |
| Otto Graham | 872 | 55.7 | 13,499 | 88 | 94 | 78.1 |

The passing ratings are based on performance standards established for completion percentage, interception percentage, touchdown percentage, and average pass gain. Passers are allocated points according to how their marks compare with those standards. This listing is based on 1,500 or more pass attempts.

### All-Time Leading Receivers

|  | Yrs | Pass rec | Yds | Avg |
|---|---|---|---|---|
| Charley Taylor | 13 | 649 | 9,110 | 14.0 |
| Don Maynard | 15 | 633 | 11,834 | 18.7 |
| Raymond Berry | 13 | 631 | 9,275 | 14.7 |
| Fred Biletnikoff | 14 | 589 | 8,974 | 12.7 |
| Harold Jackson | 14 | 571 | 10,246 | 17.9 |
| Lionel Taylor | 10 | 567 | 7,195 | 12.7 |
| Lance Alworth | 11 | 542 | 10,266 | 18.9 |
| Bobby Mitchell | 11 | 521 | 7,954 | 15.3 |
| Harold Carmichael | 11 | 516 | 7,923 | 15.4 |
| Billy Howton | 12 | 503 | 8,459 | 16.8 |
| Tommy McDonald | 12 | 495 | 8,410 | 17.0 |
| Charlie Joiner | 13 | 485 | 8,476 | 17.0 |

### All-Time Leading Scorers

|  | Yrs | TD | FG | PAT | Pts |
|---|---|---|---|---|---|
| George Blanda | 26 | 9 | 335 | 943 | 2,002 |
| Jim Turner | 16 | 1 | 304 | 521 | 1,439 |
| Jim Bakken | 17 | 0 | 282 | 534 | 1,380 |
| Fred Cox | 15 | 0 | 282 | 519 | 1,365 |
| Lou Groza | 17 | 1 | 234 | 641 | 1,349 |
| Jan Stenerud | 15 | 0 | 304 | 432 | 1,344 |
| Gino Cappelletti | 11 | 42 | 176 | 350 | 1,130[1] |
| Don Cockroft | 13 | 0 | 216 | 432 | 1,080 |
| Garo Yepremian | 14 | 0 | 210 | 444 | 1,074 |
| Bruce Gossett | 11 | 0 | 219 | 374 | 1,031 |

1. Includes four 2-point conversions.

### All-Time Leading Rushers

|  | Yrs | Att | Yds | Avg |
|---|---|---|---|---|
| Jim Brown | 9 | 2,359 | 12,312 | 5.2 |
| O.J. Simpson | 11 | 2,404 | 11,236 | 4.7 |
| Franco Harris | 10 | 2,462 | 10,339 | 4.2 |
| Walter Payton | 7 | 2,204 | 9,608 | 4.4 |
| Jim Taylor | 10 | 1,941 | 8,597 | 4.4 |
| Joe Perry | 14 | 1,737 | 8,378 | 4.8 |
| Larry Csonka | 11 | 1,891 | 8,081 | 4.3 |
| John Riggins | 10 | 1,861 | 7,536 | 4.0 |
| Leroy Kelly | 10 | 1,727 | 7,274 | 4.2 |
| John Henry Johnson | 13 | 1,571 | 6,803 | 4.3 |

## Scoring

Most points scored, lifetime—2,002, George Blanda, Chicago Bears, 1949–58; Baltimore, 1950; Houston, 1960–66; Oakland, 1967–75 (9tds, 943 pat, 335 fgs).

Most points, season—176, Paul Hornung, Green Bay, 1960 (15 td, 41 pat, 15 fg).

Most points, game—40, Ernie Nevers, Chicago Cardinals, 1929 (6 td, 4 pat).

Most points, per quarter—29, Don Hutson, Green Bay, 1945 (4 td, 5 pat).

Most touchdowns, lifetime—126, Jim Brown, Cleveland, 1957–65.

Most touchdowns, season—23, O.J. Simpson, Buffalo, 1975.

Most touchdowns, game—6, Ernie Nevers, Chicago Cardinals, 1929; William Jones, Cleveland, 1951; Gale Sayers, Chicago Bears, 1965.

Most points after touchdown, lifetime—943, George Blanda, Chicago Bears, 1949–58; Baltimore, 1950; Houston, 1960–66; Oakland, 1967–75.

Most points after touchdown, game—9, Pat Harder, Chicago Cardinals, 1948; Bob Waterfield, Los Angeles, 1950; Charlie Gogolak, Washington, 1966.

Most consecutive points after touchdown—234, Tommy Davis, San Francisco, 1959–65.

Most points after touchdown, no misses, season—56, Danny Villanueva, Dallas, 1966.

Most field goals, lifetime—335, George Blanda, Chicago Bears 1949–58; Baltimore, 1950; Houston, 1960–66; Oakland 1967–75.

Most field goals, season—34, Jim Turner, New York Jets, 1968.

Most field goals, game—7, Jim Bakken, St. Louis, 1967.

Longest field goal—63 yards, Tom Dempsey, New Orleans, 1970.

## Rushing

Most yards gained, lifetime—12,312, Jim Brown, Cleveland, 1957–65.

Most yards gained, season—2,003, O. J. Simpson, Buffalo, 1973.

Most yards gained, game—275, Walter Payton, Chicago, 1977.

Most touchdowns, lifetime—106, Jim Brown, Cleveland, 1957–65.

Most touchdowns, season—19, Earl Campbell, Houston, 1979; Jim Taylor, Green Bay, 1962; Chuck Muncie, San Diego, 1981.

Most touchdowns, game—6, Ernie Nevers, Chicago Cardinals, 1929.

Longest run from scrimmage—97 yards, Andy Uram, Green Bay, 1939; Bob Gage, Pittsburgh, 1949 (both for touchdowns).

## Passing

Most passes completed, lifetime—3,686, Fran Tarkenton, Minnesota, 1961–66, 72–78; New York Giants, 1967–71.

Most passes completed, season—360, Dan Fouts, San Diego, 1981.

Most passes completed, game—42, Richard Todd, New York Jets, 1980.

Most consecutive passes completed—17, Bert Jones, Baltimore, 1974.

Most yards gained, lifetime—47,003, Fran Tarkenton, Minnesota, 1961–66, 72–78; New York Giants, 1967–71.

Most yards gained, season—4,802, Dan Fouts, San Diego, 1981.

Most yards gained, game—554, Norm Van Brocklin, Los Angeles, 1951

Most touchdown passes, lifetime—342, Fran Tarkenton, Minnesota, 1961–66, 72–78; New York Giants, 1967–71.

Most touchdown passes, season—36, George Blanda, Houston, 1961; Y. A. Tittle, New York Giants, 1963.

Most touchdown passes, game—7, Sid Luckman, Chicago Bears, 1943; Adrian Burk, Philadelphia, 1954; George Blanda, Houston 1961; Y.A. Tittle, New York Giants, 1963; Joe Kapp, Minnesota, 1969.

Most consecutive games, touchdown passes—47, John Unitas, Baltimore.

Most consecutive passes attempted, none intercepted—294, Bart Starr, Green Bay, 1964–65.

Longest pass completion—99 yards, Frank Filchock (to Andy Farkas), Washington, 1939; George Izo (to Bob Mitchell), Washington, 1963; Karl Sweetan (to Pat Studstill), Detroit, 1966; Sonny Jurgensen (to Gerry Allen), Washington, 1968, (all for touchdowns).

Most pass receptions, lifetime—649, Charley Taylor, Washington, 1964–75, 1977.

Most pass receptions, season—101, Charley Hennigan, Houston, 1964.

Most pass receptions, game—18, Tom Fears, Los Angeles, 1950.

Most consecutive games, pass receptions—127, Harold Carmichael, Philadelphia, 1972–80.

Most yards gained, pass receptions, lifetime—11,834, Don Maynard, New York Giants, 1958; New York Jets, 1960–72; St. Louis, 1973.

Most yards gained receptions, season—1,746, Charley Hennigan, Houston, 1961.

Most yards gained receptions, game—303, Jim Benton, Cleveland Rams, 1945.

Most touchdown pass receptions, lifetime—99, Don Hutson, Green Bay, 1935–45.

Most touchdown pass receptions, season—17, Don Hutson, Green Bay, 1942; Elroy Hirsch, Los Angeles, 1951; Bill Groman, Houston, 1961.

Most touchdown pass receptions, game—5, Bob Shaw, Chicago Cards, 1950.

Most consecutive games, touchdown pass receptions—11, Elroy Hirsch, Los Angeles, 1950–51; Buddy Dial, Pittsburgh, 1959–60.

Most pass interceptions, lifetime—81, Paul Krause, Washington, 1964–67; Minnesota, 1968–79.

Most pass interceptions, season—14, Richard (Night Train) Lane, Los Angeles, 1952.

Most pass interceptions, game—4, by 15 players.

Longest pass interception return—102 yards, Bob Smith, Chicago Bears, 1949; Erich Barnes, New York Giants, 1961; Gary Barbaro, Kansas City, 1977; Louis Breeden, Cincinnati, 1981.

## Kicking

Longest punt—98 yards, Steve O'Neal, New York Jets, 1969.

Highest average punting, lifetime—45.10 yards, Sammy Baugh, Washington, 1937–52.

Longest punt return—98 yards, Gil LeFebvre, Cincinnati Reds, 1933; Charlie West, Minnesota, 1968; Dennis Morgan, Dallas, 1974.

Longest kick-off return—106 yards, Roy Green, St. Louis, 1979; Al Carmichael, Green Bay, 1956; Noland Smith, Kansas City, 1967.

# TABLE TENNIS

## U.S. OPEN CHAMPIONSHIPS—1982

Men's singles—Zoran Kosanovic, Canada
Women's singles—Kayoko Kawahigashi, Japan
Men's doubles—Danny and Ricky Seemiller, Pittsburgh

Women's doubles—Shin Deuk Hwa and Jung Kyung, South Korea
Mixed doubles—Koichi Kawamura and Tomoko Tamura, Japan
Men's team—Japan
Women's team—South Korea

## TEAM NICKNAMES AND HOME FIELD STADIUM CAPACITIES

### AMERICAN CONFERENCE

#### Eastern Division

| | | |
|---|---|---|
| Baltimore Colts | Memorial Stadium (G) | 60,020 |
| Buffalo Bills | Rich Stadium (AT) | 80,020 |
| Miami Dolphins | Orange Bowl (G) | 75,449 |
| New England Patriots | Schaefer Stadium (ST) | 61,297 |
| New York Jets | Shea Stadium (G) | 60,000 |

#### Central Division

| | | |
|---|---|---|
| Cincinnati Bengals | Riverfront Stadium (AT) | 56,200 |
| Cleveland Browns | Cleveland Stadium (G) | 80,385 |
| Houston Oilers | Astrodome (AT) | 50,000 |
| Pittsburgh Steelers | Three Rivers Stadium (TT) | 50,350 |

#### Western Division

| | | |
|---|---|---|
| Denver Broncos | Mile High Stadium (G) | 75,087 |
| Kansas City Chiefs | Arrowhead Stadium (TT) | 78,094 |
| Los Angeles Raiders[1] | Memorial Coliseum (G) | 73,999 |
| San Diego Chargers | San Diego Stadium (G) | 52,552 |
| Seattle Seahawks | Kingdome (AT) | 64,752 |

1. Moved franchise to Los Angeles for 1982 season.
NOTE: Stadium playing surfaces in parentheses: AT = Astro-Turf; G = grass; ST = Super Turf; TT = TartanTurf.

### NATIONAL CONFERENCE

#### Eastern Division

| | | |
|---|---|---|
| Dallas Cowboys | Texas Stadium (TT) | 65,101 |
| New York Giants | Giants Stadium (AT)[1] | 76,500 |
| Philadelphia Eagles | Veterans Stadium (AT) | 66,052 |
| St. Louis Cardinals | Busch Mem. Stadium (AT) | 51,392 |
| Washington Redskins | R. F. Kennedy Stadium (G) | 55,031 |

1. At East Rutherford, N.J.

#### Central Division

| | | |
|---|---|---|
| Chicago Bears | Soldier Field (AT) | 58,064 |
| Detroit Lions | Pontiac Silverdome (AT) | 80,638 |
| | Lambeau Field (G) | 56,267 |
| Green Bay Packers | Milwaukee Stadium (G) | 55,958 |
| Minnesota Vikings | Metropolitan Stadium (G) | 48,446 |
| Tampa Bay Buccaneers | Tampa Stadium (G) | 72,112 |

#### Western Division

| | | |
|---|---|---|
| Atlanta Falcons | Atlanta-Fulton Stadium (G) | 60,489 |
| Los Angeles Rams[1] | Anaheim Stadium (G) | 70,000 |
| New Orleans Saints | Louisiana Superdome (AT) | 71,330 |
| San Francisco 49ers | Candlestick Park (G) | 61,246 |

1. Moved to Anaheim Stadium at start of 1980 season.

# FISHING

## WORLD ALL-TACKLE FISHING RECORDS

### Caught With Rod and Reel in Fresh Water

*Source:* International Game Fish Association

| Species | lb-oz | Length | Girth | Where caught | Year | Angler |
|---|---|---|---|---|---|---|
| Bass, Largemouth | 22–4 | 32½" | 28½" | Montgomery Lake, Ga. | 1932 | George W. Perry |
| Bass, Peacock | 21 | — | — | Orinoco River, Colombia | 1981 | David Orndorf |
| Bass, Redeye | 8–3 | 23" | 16½" | Flint River, Ga. | 1977 | David A. Hubbard |
| Bass, Rock | 3 | 13½" | 10¾" | York River, Ontario | 1974 | Peter Gulgin |
| Bass, Smallmouth | 11–15 | .27" | 21⅔" | Dale Hollow Lake, Ky. | 1955 | David L. Hayes |
| Bass, Spotted | 8–15 | — | — | Smith Lake, Ala. | 1978 | Philip C. Terry Jr. |
| Bass, Striped (landlocked) | 59–12 | — | — | Colorado River, Ariz. | 1977 | Frank W. Smith |
| Bass, White | 5–9 | — | — | Colorado River, Texas | 1977 | David S. Cordill |
| Bass, Whiterock | 20–6 | — | — | Savannah River, Ga. | 1978 | Danny Wood |
| Bass, Yellow | 2–4 | 16¼" | 12¾" | Lake Monroe, Ind. | 1977 | Donald L. Stalker |
| Bluegill | 4–12 | 15" | 18¼" | Ketona Lake, Ala. | 1950 | T. S. Hudson |
| Bowfin | 21–8 | — | — | Florence, N.C. | 1980 | Robert L. Harmon |
| Buffalo, Bigmouth | 70–5 | — | — | Bussey Brake, Bastrop, La. | 1980 | Delbert Sisk |
| Buffalo, Smallmouth | 51 | — | — | Lawrence, Kan. | 1979 | Scott Butler |
| Bullhead, Black | 8 | 24" | 17¾" | Lake Waccabuc, N.Y. | 1951 | Kani Evans |
| Bullhead, Brown | 5–8 | — | — | Veal Pond, Ga. | 1975 | Jimmy Andrews |
| Bullhead, Yellow | 3 | — | — | Nelson Lake, Wis. | 1977 | Mark Nessman |
| Burbot | 18–4 | — | — | Pickford, Mich. | 1980 | Thomas Courtemanche |
| Carp | 55–5 | 42" | 31" | Clearwater Lake, Minn. | 1952 | Frank J. Ledwein |
| Catfish, Blue | 97 | 57" | 37" | Missouri River, S.D. | 1959 | Edward B. Elliott |
| Catfish, Channel | 58 | 47¼" | 29⅛" | Santee-Cooper Res., S.C. | 1964 | W. B. Whaley |
| Catfish, Flathead | 79–8 | 44" | 27" | White River, Ind. | 1966 | Glenn T. Simpson |
| Catfish, White | 10–5 | 25" | 17½" | Raritan River, N.J. | 1976 | L. W. Lomerson |
| Char, Arctic | 29–11 | 39¾" | 26" | Arctic River, N.W.T. | 1968 | Jeanne P. Branson |
| Crappie, Black | 6 | — | — | Seaplane Canal, Westwego, La. | 1969 | Lettie Theresa Robertson |
| Crappie, White | 5–3 | 21" | 19" | Enid Dam, Miss. | 1957 | Fred L. Bright |
| Dolly Varden | 3–13 | — | — | Unalaklett River, Alaska | 1980 | Roy Lawson |
| Drum, Freshwater | 54–8 | 31½" | 29" | Nickajack Lake, Tenn. | 1972 | Benny E. Hull |
| Gar, Alligator | 279 | 93" | — | Rio Grande River, Tex. | 1951 | Bill Valverde |
| Gar, Florida | 21–3 | — | — | Boca Raton, Fla. | 1981 | Jeff Sabol |
| Gar, Longnose | 50–5 | 72¼" | 22½" | Trinity River, Texas | 1954 | Townsend Miller |
| Gar, Shortnose | 3–5 | — | — | Lake Francis Case, S.D. | 1977 | J. Pawlowski |
| Grayling, Arctic | 5–15 | 29⅞" | 15⅛" | Katseyedie River, N.W.T. | 1967 | Jeanne P. Branson |
| Huchen | 70–12 | — | — | Carinthia, Austria | 1980 | Martin F. Esterl |
| Inconnu | 33–9 | — | — | Kobuk River, Alaska | 1981 | John A. Berg |
| Kokanee | 6–9 | 24½" | 14½" | Priest Lake, Idaho | 1975 | Jerry Verge |

| Species | lb–oz | Length | Girth | Where caught | Year | Angler |
|---|---|---|---|---|---|---|
| Muskellunge | 69–15 | 64½" | 31¾" | St. Lawrence River, N.Y. | 1957 | Arthur Lawton |
| Muskellunge, Tiger | 51–3 | — | — | Lac Vieux–Desert, Wis./Mich. | 1919 | John A. Knobla |
| Perch, White | 4–12 | 19½" | 13" | Messalonskee Lake, Me. | 1949 | Mrs. Earl Small |
| Perch, Yellow | 4–3 | — | — | Bordentown, N.J. | 1865 | Dr. C. C. Abbot |
| Pickerel, Eastern chain | 9–6 | 31" | 14" | Homerville, Ga. | 1961 | Baxley McQuaig, Jr. |
| Pike, Northern | 62–8 | — | — | Reuss-Weiher, Richenbach, Switz. | 1979 | Jurg Notzli |
| Redhorse, Northern | 3–11 | — | — | Missouri River, S.D. | 1977 | Philip Laumeyer |
| Redhorse, Silver | 5–13 | — | — | Betsie River, Frankfort, Mich. | 1980 | Darrell T. Hasler |
|  | 5–14 | — | — | Shelbyville, Ind. | 1980 | Ernest Harley Jr. |
| Salmon, Atlantic | 79–2 | — | — | Tana River, Norway | 1928 | Henrik Henriksen |
| Salmon, Chinook | 93 | 50" | 39" | Kelp Bay, Alaska | 1977 | Howard C. Rider |
| Salmon, Chum | 27–3 | 39³⁄₈" | 24½" | Raymond Cove, Alaska | 1977 | Robert A. Jahnke |
| Salmon Landlocked | 22–8 | 36" | — | Sebago Lake, Me. | 1907 | Edward Blakely |
| Salmon, Pink | 12–9 | — | — | Moose and Kenai Rivers, Alaska | 1974 | Steven Alan Lee |
| Salmon, Sockeye | 7–14 | — | — | American River, Alaska | 1981 | Brooke P. Halsey Jr. |
| Sauger | 8–12 | 28" | 15" | Lake Sakakawea, N.D. | 1971 | Mike Fischer |
| Shad, American | 9–4 | — | — | Delaware River, Pa. | 1979 | J. Edward Whitman |
|  | 9–4 | — | — | Connecticut River, Wilson, Conn. | 1981 | Edward William Cypus |
| Splake | 16–12 | — | — | Island Lake, Colo. | 1973 | Del Canty |
| Sturgeon | 407 | — | — | Sacramento River, Colusa, Calif. | 1979 | Raymond Pittenger |
| Sturgeon, White | 360 | 111" | 86" | Snake River, Idaho | 1956 | Willard Cravens |
| Sunfish, Green | 2–2 | 14¾" | 14" | Stockton Lake, Mo. | 1971 | Paul M. Dilley |
| Sunfish, Redbreast | 1–8 | 11" | 12⁵⁄₈" | Suwannee River, Fla. | 1977 | Tommy D. Cason, Jr. |
| Sunfish, Redear | 4–8 | 16¼" | 17¾" | Chase City, Va. | 1970 | Maurice E. Ball |
| Trout, Brook | 14–8 | 31½" | 11½" | Nipigon River, Ontario | 1916 | Dr. W. J. Cook |
| Trout, Brown | 35–15 | — | — | Nahuel Haupi, Argentina | 1952 | Eugenio Cavaglia |
| Trout, Bull | 32 | — | — | Lake Pend Oreille, Idaho | 1949 | N.L. Higgins |
| Trout, Cutthroat | 41 | 39" | — | Pyramid Lake, Nev. | 1925 | John Skimmerhorn |
| Trout, Golden | 11 | 28" | 16" | Cook's Lake, Wyo. | 1948 | Charles S. Reed |
| Trout, Lake | 65 | 52" | 38" | Great Bear Lake, N.W.T. | 1970 | Larry Daunis |
| Trout, Rainbow or Steelhead | 42–2 | 43" | 23½" | Bell Island, Alaska | 1970 | David R. White |
| Trout, Sunapee | 11–8 | 33" | 21" | Lake Sunapee, N.H. | 1954 | Ernest Theoharis |
| Trout, Tiger | 20–13 | — | — | Lake Michigan, Wis. | 1978 | Pete M. Friedlan |
| Walleye | 25 | 41" | 29" | Old Hickory Lake, Tenn. | 1960 | Mabry Harper |
| Warmouth | 2–2 | — | — | Douglas Swamp, S.C. | 1973 | Willie Singletary |
| Whitefish, Lake | 13–15 | — | — | Meaford, Ontario | 1981 | Wayne Caswell |
| Whitefish, Mountain | 5 | 19" | 14" | Athabasca River, Alberta, Can. | 1963 | Orville Welch |
| Whitefish, Round | 3–4 | — | — | Leland Harbor, Mich. | 1977 | Vernon A. Bauer |

## Caught With Rod and Reel in Salt Water

*Source:* International Game Fish Association

| Species | lb–oz | Length | Girth | Where caught | Year | Angler |
|---|---|---|---|---|---|---|
| Albacore | 88–2 | — | — | Canary Islands | 1977 | Siegfried Dickemann |
| Amberjack | 155–10 | — | — | Challenger Bank, Bermuda | 1981 | Joseph Dawson |
| Barracuda | 83 | 72¼" | 29" | Lagos, Nigeria | 1952 | K. J. W. Hackett |
| Bass, Black Sea | 8–12 | — | — | Oregon Inlet, N.C. | 1979 | Joe W. Mizelle Sr. |
| Bass, Giant Sea | 563–8 | 89" | 72" | Anacapa Island, Calif. | 1968 | J. D. McAdam, Jr. |
| Bass, Striped | 76 | — | — | Montauk, Long Island, N.Y. | 1981 | Robert A. Rocchetta |
| Blackfish (Tautog) | 21–6 | 31½" | 23½" | Cape May, N.J. | 1954 | R. N. Sheafer |
| Bluefish | 31–12 | 47" | 23" | North Carolina | 1972 | James M. Hussey |
| Bonefish | 19 | — | — | Zululand, S. Africa | 1962 | Brian W. Batchelor |
| Bonito, Atlantic | 16–12 | — | — | Canary Islands | 1980 | Rolf Fredderies |
| Bonito, Pacific | 23–8 | 35¼" | 23¼" | Victoria, Mahe | 1975 | Mrs. Anne Cochain |
| Cobia | 110–5 | — | — | Mombasa, Kenya | 1964 | Eric Tinworth |
| Cod | 98–12 | 63" | 41" | Isle of Shoals, N.H. | 1969 | Alphonse Bielevich |
| Conger | 39–7 | — | — | Pornichet–La Baule, France | 1980 | Jean–Claude Guilmineau |
| Dolphin | 87 | 81²⁄₃" | 28" | Papagallo Gulf, Costa Rica | 1976 | Manual Salazar |
| Drum, Black | 113–1 | 53⅛" | 43½" | Lewes, Del. | 1975 | G. M. Townsend |
| Drum, Red | 90 | 55½" | 38¼" | Rodanthe, N.C. | 1973 | Elvin Hooper |
| Flounder, Summer | 22–7 | — | — | Montauk, N.Y. | 1975 | Charles Nappi |
| Halibut, Atlantic | 250 | — | — | Gloucester, Mass. | 1981 | Louis P. Sirard |
| Halibut, California | 42 | — | — | Santa Rosa Island, Calif. | 1981 | Jerry Yahiro |
| Halibut, Pacific | 235 | — | — | Juneau, Alaska | 1980 | Norbert U. Koch |
| Jack, Crevalle | 51 | — | — | Lake Worth, Fla. | 1978 | Stephen Schwenk |
| Jack, Horse–eye | 23–2 | — | — | Cancun, Mexico | 1981 | Norman A. Carpenter |
| Jewfish | 680 | 85½" | 66" | Fernandina Beach, Fla. | 1961 | Lynn Joyner |
| Kawakawa | 26 | — | — | Merimbula, N.S.W., Australia | 1980 | Wally Elfring |
| Mackerel, King | 90 | — | — | Key West, Florida | 1976 | Norton I. Thomton |
| Marlin, Black | 1560 | 174" | 81" | Cabo Blanco, Peru | 1953 | A. C. Glassel, Jr. |
| Marlin, Atlantic Blue | 1282 | 176" | 76½" | St. Thomas, Virgin Islands | 1977 | Larry Martin |
| Marlin, Pacific Blue | 1153 | 176" | 73" | Ritidian Point, Guam | 1969 | Greg G. Perez |
| Marlin, Striped | 417–8 | 139½" | 52½" | Cavalli Island, New Zealand | 1977 | Phillip Bryers |
| Marlin, White | 181–14 | — | — | Victoria, Brazil | 1979 | Evandro Luiz Coser |

| Species | Weight | Length | Length | Location | Year | Angler |
|---|---|---|---|---|---|---|
| Permit | 51–8 | — | — | Lake Worth, Fla. | 1978 | William M. Kenney |
| Pollack | 16–1 | — | — | Plymouth, England | 1978 | Peter J. Peck |
| Pollack (virens) | 46–7 | 50½" | 30" | Brielle, N.J. | 1975 | John T. Holton |
| Pompano, African | 41–8 | — | — | Fort Lauderdale, Fla. | 1979 | Wayne Sommers |
| Roosterfish | 114 | 64" | 33" | La Paz, Mexico | 1960 | Abe Sackheim |
| Runner, Rainbow | 33–10 | 55¼" | 22½" | Clarion Island, Mexico | 1976 | R. A. Mikkelsen |
| Sailfish, Atlantic | 128–1 | 106¼" | 34¼" | Luanda, Angola, Africa | 1974 | Harm Steyn |
| Sailfish, Pacific | 221 | 129" | — | Santa Cruz Is., Galapagos Is. | 1947 | C. W. Stewart |
| Seabass, White | 83–12 | 65½" | 34" | San Felipe, Mexico | 1953 | L. C. Baumgardner |
| Seatrout, Spotted | 16 | 32½" | 21¾" | Mason's Beach, Va. | 1977 | William G. Katko |
| Shark, Blue | 437 | — | — | Catherine Bay, Australia | 1976 | Peter Hyde |
| Shark, Hammerhead | 717 | — | — | Jacksonville Beach, Fla. | 1980 | Richard Edward Morse |
| Shark, Mako | 1080 | — | — | Montauk, N.Y. | 1979 | James L. Melanson |
| Shark, Porbeagle | 465 | 111" | 56" | Padstow, Cornwall, England | 1976 | Jorge Potier |
| Shark, Thresher | 802 | — | — | Tutukaka, New Zealand | 1981 | Dianne North |
| Shark, Tiger | 1780 | 166½" | 103" | Cherry Grove, S.C. | 1964 | Walter Maxwell |
| Shark, White | 2664 | 202" | 114" | South Australia | 1959 | Alfred Dean |
| Skipjack, Black | 14–8 | — | — | Baja, Mexico | 1977 | Lorraine Carlton |
| Snapper, Cubera | 60–12 | — | — | Miami Beach, Fla. | 1980 | Dr. Richard A. Klein |
| Snook | 53–10 | — | — | Costa Rica | 1978 | Gilbert Ponzi |
| Spearfish | 90–13 | — | — | Madeira Island, Portugal | 1980 | Joseph Larkin |
| Swordfish | 1182 | 179¼" | 78" | Iquique, Chile | 1953 | L. E. Marron |
| Tanguigue | 85–6 | — | — | Western Australia | 1978 | Barry Wrightson |
| Tarpon | 283 | 85⅗" | — | Lake Maracaibo, Venezuela | 1956 | M. Salazar |
| Tautog (See Blackfish) | | | | | | |
| Trevally, Giant | 116 | — | — | American Samoa | 1978 | William G. Foster |
| Tuna, Yellowfin | 388–12 | — | — | Mexico | 1977 | Curt Wiesenhutter |
| Tuna, Atlantic Bigeye | 375–8 | — | — | Ocean City, Md. | 1977 | Cecil Browne |
| Tuna, Blackfin | 42 | — | — | Bermuda | 1978 | Alan J. Card |
| Tuna, Bluefin | 1496 | — | — | Nova Scotia, Canada | 1979 | Ken Fraser |
| Tuna, Dog–tooth | 194 | — | — | Kwan-Tall Island, Korea | 1980 | Kim Chul |
| Tuna, Longtail | 60 | — | — | Bermagui, Australia | 1975 | N. Noel Webster |
| Tuna, Pacific Big-Eyed | 435 | 93" | 63½" | Cabo Blanco, Peru | 1957 | R.V. A. Lee |
| Tuna, Skipjack | 39–15 | 39" | 28" | Walker City, Bahamas | 1952 | R. Drowley |
| | 40 | 38¾" | 27½" | Baie du Tambeau, Mauritius | 1971 | Joseph R. Cabache |
| Tuna, Southern Bluefin | 348–5 | — | — | Whakatane, New Zealand | 1981 | Rex Wood |
| Tunny, Little | 27 | 39" | 22" | Key Largo, Fla. | 1976 | William E. Allison |
| Wahoo | 149 | — | — | Cat Cay, Bahamas | 1962 | John Pirovano |
| Weakfish | 17–14 | — | — | Rye, N.Y. | 1980 | William N. Herold |
| Yellowtail, California | 71–15 | — | — | Alijos Rocks, Mexico | 1979 | Michael Carpenter |
| Yellowtail, Southern | 111 | — | — | Bay of Islands, New Zealand | 1961 | A. F. Plim |

# CHESS

## WORLD CHAMPIONS

| | |
|---|---|
| 1894–1921 | Emanuel Lasker, Germany |
| 1921–27 | Jose R. Capablanca, Cuba |
| 1927–35 | Alexander A. Alekhine, U.S.S.R. |
| 1935–37 | Dr. Max Euwe, Netherlands |
| 1937–46 | Alexander A. Alekhine, U.S.S.R.[1] |
| 1948–57 | Mikhail Botvinnik, U.S.S.R. |
| 1957–58 | Vassily Smyslov, U.S.S.R. |
| 1958–60 | Mikhail Botvinnik, U.S.S.R. |
| 1960–61 | Mikhail Tal, U.S.S.R. |
| 1961–63 | Mikhail Botvinnik, U.S.S.R. |
| 1963–68 | Tigran Petrosian, U.S.S.R. |
| 1969–71 | Boris Spassky, U.S.S.R. |
| 1972–74 | Bobby Fischer, Los Angeles |
| 1975 | Bobby Fischer[2]; Anatoly Karpov, U.S.S.R. |
| 1976–82 | Anatoly Karpov, U.S.S.R.[3] |

1. Alekhine, a French citizen, died while champion. 2. Relinquished title. 3. In 1978, Karpov defeated Viktor Korchnoi 6 games to 5.

## UNITED STATES CHAMPIONS

| | |
|---|---|
| 1909–36 | Frank J. Marshall, New York |
| 1936–44 | Samuel Reshevsky, New York[1] |
| 1944–46 | Arnold S. Denker, New York |
| 1946 | Samuel Reshevsky, Boston |
| 1948 | Herman Steiner, Los Angeles |
| 1951–52 | Larry Evans, New York |
| 1954–57 | Arthur Bisguier, New York |
| 1958–61 | Bobby Fischer, Brooklyn, N.Y. |
| 1962 | Larry Evans, New York |
| 1963–67 | Bobby Fischer, New York |
| 1968 | Larry Evans, New York |
| 1969–71 | Samuel Reshevsky, Spring Valley, N.Y. |
| 1972 | Robert Byrne, Ossining, N.Y. |
| 1973 | Lubomir Kavelek, Washington; John Grefe, San Francisco |
| 1974–77 | Walter Browne, Berkeley, Calif. |
| 1978–79 | Lubomir Kavelek, New York |
| 1980 | Tie, Walter Browne, Berkeley, Calif. Larry Christiansen, Modesto, Calif. Larry Evans, Reno, Nev. |
| 1981–82[2] | Tie, Walter Browne Yasser Seirawan, Seattle, Wash. |

1. In 1942, Isaac I. Kashdan of New York was co-champion for a while because of a tie with Reshevsky in that year's tournament. Reshevsky won the play-off. 2. Championship not contested in 1982.

# BASKETBALL

Basketball may be the one sport whose exact origin is definitely known. In the winter of 1891–92, Dr. James Naismith, an instructor in the Y.M.C.A. Training College (now Springfield College) at Springfield, Mass., deliberately invented the game of basketball in order to provide indoor exercise and competition for the students between the closing of the football season and the opening of the baseball season. He affixed peach baskets overhead on the walls at opposite ends of the gymnasium and organized teams to play his new game in which the purpose was to toss an association (soccer) ball into one basket and prevent the opponents from tossing the ball into the other basket. The game is fundamentally the same today, though there have been improvements in equipment and some changes in rules.

Because Dr. Naismith had eighteen available players when he invented the game, the first rule was: "There shall be nine players on each side." Later the number of players became optional, depending upon the size of the available court, but the five-player standard was adopted when the game spread over the country. United States soldiers brought basketball to Europe in World War I, and it soon became a world-wide sport.

## College Basketball

### NATIONAL COLLEGIATE A.A. CHAMPIONS

| | | | | | | | |
|---|---|---|---|---|---|---|---|
| 1939 | Oregon | 1949 | Kentucky | 1959 | California | 1975 | U.C.L.A. |
| 1940 | Indiana | 1950 | C.C.N.Y. | 1960 | Ohio State | 1976 | Indiana |
| 1941 | Wisconsin | 1951 | Kentucky | 1961 | Cincinnati | 1977 | Marquette |
| 1942 | Stanford | 1952 | Kansas | 1962 | Cincinnati | 1978 | Kentucky |
| 1943 | Wyoming | 1953 | Indiana | 1963 | Loyola (Chicago) | 1979 | Michigan State |
| 1944 | Utah | 1954 | La Salle | 1964 | U.C.L.A. | 1980 | Louisville |
| 1945 | Oklahoma A & M | 1955 | San Francisco | 1965 | U.C.L.A. | 1981 | Indiana |
| 1946 | Oklahoma A & M | 1956 | San Francisco | 1966 | Texas Western | 1982 | North Carolina |
| 1947 | Holy Cross | 1957 | North Carolina | 1967–73 | U.C.L.A. | | |
| 1948 | Kentucky | 1958 | Kentucky | 1974 | No. Carolina State | | |

### NATIONAL INVITATION TOURNAMENT (NIT) CHAMPIONS

| | | | | | | | |
|---|---|---|---|---|---|---|---|
| 1939 | Long Island U. | 1951 | Brigham Young | 1962 | Dayton | 1973 | Virginia Tech |
| 1940 | Colorado | 1952 | La Salle | 1963 | Providence | 1974 | Purdue |
| 1941 | Long Island U. | 1953 | Seton Hall | 1964 | Bradley | 1975 | Princeton |
| 1942 | West Virginia | 1954 | Holy Cross | 1965 | St. John's (Bklyn.) | 1976 | Kentucky |
| 1943–44 | St. John's (Bklyn.) | 1955 | Duquesne | 1966 | Brigham Young | 1977 | St. Bonaventure |
| 1945 | DePaul | 1956 | Louisville | 1967 | So. Illinois | 1978 | Texas |
| 1946 | Kentucky | 1957 | Bradley | 1968 | Dayton | 1979 | Indiana |
| 1947 | Utah | 1958 | Xavier (Cincinnati) | 1969 | Temple | 1980 | Virginia |
| 1948 | St. Louis | 1959 | St. John's (Bklyn.) | 1970 | Marquette | 1981 | Tulsa |
| 1949 | San Francisco | 1960 | Bradley | 1971 | North Carolina | 1982 | Bradley |
| 1950 | C.C.N.Y. | 1961 | Providence | 1972 | Maryland | | |

### N.C.A.A. MAJOR COLLEGE INDIVIDUAL SCORING RECORDS

**Single Season Averages**

| Player, Team | Year | G | FG | FT | Pts | Avg |
|---|---|---|---|---|---|---|
| Pete Maravich, Louisiana State | 1969–70 | 31 | 522[1] | 337 | 1381[1] | 44.5[1] |
| Pete Maravich | 1968–69 | 26 | 433 | 282 | 1148 | 44.2 |
| Pete Maravich | 1967–68 | 26 | 432 | 274 | 1138 | 43.8 |
| Frank Selvy, Furman | 1953–54 | 29 | 427 | 355[1] | 1209 | 41.7 |
| Johnny Neumann, Mississippi | 1970–71 | 23 | 366 | 191 | 923 | 40.1 |
| Freeman Williams, Portland State | 1976–77 | 26 | 417 | 176 | 1010 | 38.8 |
| Billy McGill, Utah | 1961–62 | 26 | 394 | 221 | 1009 | 38.8 |
| Calvin Murphy, Niagara | 1967–68 | 24 | 337 | 242 | 916 | 38.2 |
| Austin Carr, Notre Dame | 1969–70 | 29 | 444 | 218 | 1106 | 38.1 |

1. Record.

### LONGEST FIELD GOAL IN COLLEGE BASKETBALL

What was the longest field goal ever scored in a college basketball game? Would you believe 89 ft 3 in.? That's only 4 ft 9 in. short of the regulation length of a court. It happened on January 21, 1980, at Tallahassee, Fla., and the shooter was Les Henson, a 6-ft-6-in. senior forward for Virginia Tech. He took the shot with only two seconds left in the game against Florida State and gave the Gobblers a 79–77 victory. Henson had just grabbed a rebound off the Florida State boards about a foot from the baseline. The normally left-handed-shooting Henson unleashed a right-handed shot in desperation and it went in. At first the shot was reported as 93 ft, but a later measurement established it at 89–3. "It was eerie while the ball was in the air," Henson later recalled. "Everything was quiet, you couldn't hear a thing in the arena. At first, I thought it was going to hit one of the light fixtures, but it didn't, and then it just swished through the hoop." It bettered the previous longest scoring shot of 88 ft by Rudy Williams of Providence College against Rhode Island on February 17, 1979.

# N.C.A.A. CAREER SCORING TOTALS

## Division I

| Player, Team | Last year | G | FG | FT | Pts | Avg |
|---|---|---|---|---|---|---|
| Pete Maravich, Louisiana State | 1970 | 83 | 1387[1] | 893[1] | 3667[1] | 44.2[1] |
| Austin Carr, Notre Dame | 1971 | 74 | 1017 | 526 | 2560 | 34.6 |
| Oscar Robertson, Cincinnati | 1960 | 88 | 1052 | 869 | 2973 | 33.8 |
| Calvin Murphy, Niagara | 1970 | 77 | 947 | 654 | 2548 | 33.1 |
| Dwight Lamar[2] | 1973 | 57 | 768 | 326 | 1862 | 32.7 |
| Frank Selvy, Furman | 1954 | 78 | 922 | 694 | 2538 | 32.5 |
| Rick Mount, Purdue | 1970 | 72 | 910 | 503 | 2323 | 32.3 |
| Darrel Floyd, Furman | 1956 | 71 | 868 | 545 | 2281 | 32.1 |
| Nick Werkman, Seton Hall | 1964 | 71 | 812 | 649 | 2273 | 32.0 |

1. Record. 2. Also played two seasons in college division.

## Division II

| Player, Team | Last year | G | FG | FT | Pts | Avg |
|---|---|---|---|---|---|---|
| Travis Grant, Kentucky State | 1972 | 121 | 1760[1] | 525 | 4045[1] | 33.4[1] |
| John Rinka, Kenyon | 1970 | 99 | 1261 | 729 | 3251 | 32.8 |
| Florindo Vieira, Quinnipiac | 1957 | 69 | 761 | 741 | 2263 | 32.8 |
| Willie Shaw, Lane | 1964 | 76 | 960 | 459 | 2379 | 31.3 |
| Mike Davis, Virginia Union | 1969 | 89 | 1014 | 730 | 2758 | 31.0 |
| Henry Logan, Western Carolina | 1968 | 107 | 1263 | 764 | 3290 | 30.7 |
| Willie Scott, Alabama State | 1969 | 103 | 1277 | 601 | 3155 | 30.6 |
| Gregg Northington, Alabama State | 1972 | 75 | 894 | 403 | 2191 | 29.2 |
| Bob Hopkins, Grambling | 1956 | 126 | 1403 | 953 | 3759 | 29.8 |

1. Record.

# TOP SINGLE-GAME SCORING MARKS

| Player, Team (Opponent) | Yr | Pts | Player, Team (Opponent) | Yr | Pts |
|---|---|---|---|---|---|
| Selvy, Furman (Newberry) | 1954 | 100[1] | Floyd, Furman (Morehead) | 1955 | 67 |
| Williams, Portland State (Rocky Mtn.) | 1978 | 81 | Maravich, LSU (Tulane) | 1969 | 66 |
| Mlkvy, Temple (Wilkes) | 1951 | 73 | Handlan, W & L (Furman) | 1951 | 66 |
| Williams, Portland State (So. Oregon) | 1977 | 71 | Roberts, Oral Roberts (N.C. A&T) | 1977 | 66 |
| Maravich, LSU (Alabama) | 1970 | 69 | Williams, Portland State (Geo. Fox Coll.) | 1978 | 66 |
| Murphy, Niagara (Syracuse) | 1969 | 68 | Roberts, Oral Roberts (Oregon) | 1977 | 65 |

1. Record.

# NATIONAL COLLEGIATE ATHLETIC ASSOCIATION (N.C.A.A.)—1982

## DIVISION I

### First Round—East

James Madison 55, Ohio State 48
Northeastern 63, St. Joseph's 62
St. John's 66, Pennsylvania 56
Wake Forest 74, Old Dominion 57

### First Round—Mideast

Indiana 94, Robert Morris 62
Middle Tennessee 50, Kentucky 44
Tennessee 61, Southwestern Louisiana 57
Tennessee–Chattanooga 58, North Carolina State 51

### First Round—Midwest

Boston College 70, San Francisco 66
Houston 94, Alcorn State 84
Kansas State 77, Northern Illinois 68
Marquette 67, Evansville 62

### First Round—West

Iowa 70, Northeastern Louisiana 63
Pepperdine 99, Pittsburgh 88
West Virginia 102, North Carolina A and T 72
Wyoming 61, Southern California 58

### Second Round—East

Alabama 69, St. John's 68
Memphis State 56, Wake Forest 55

North Carolina 52, James Madison 50
Villanova 76, Northeastern 72 (3 overtimes)

### Second Round—Mideast

Alabama–Birmingham 80, Indiana 70
Louisville 81, Middle Tennessee 56
Minnesota 62, Tennessee–Chattanooga 61
Virginia 54, Tennessee 51

### Second Round—Midwest

Boston College 82, De Paul 75
Houston 78, Tulsa 74
Kansas State 65, Arkansas 64
Missouri 73, Marquette 69

### Second Round—West

Fresno State 50, West Virginia 46
Georgetown 51, Wyoming 43
Idaho 69, Iowa 67 (overtime)
Oregon State 70, Pepperdine 51

### Third Round—East

Villanova 70, Memphis State 66 (overtime)
North Carolina 74, Alabama 69

### Third Round—Mideast

Alabama–Birmingham 68, Virginia 66
Louisville 67, Minnesota 61

**Third Round—Midwest**
Boston College 69, Kansas State 65
Houston 79, Missouri 78

**Third Round—West**
Georgetown 58, Fresno State 40
Oregon State 60, Idaho 42

**Regional Finals**
East—North Carolina 70, Villanova 60
Mideast—Louisville 75, Alabama–Birmingham 68
Midwest—Houston 99, Boston College 92
West—Georgetown 69, Oregon State 45

**National Semifinals**
(New Orleans, March 27, 1982)
North Carolina 68, Houston 63
Georgetown 50, Louisville 46
Third Place—Not contested.

**National Final**
(New Orleans, March 29, 1982)
North Carolina 63, Georgetown 62

**DIVISION II**
Semifinals
District of Columbia 76, Bakersfield State 71
Florida Southern 90, Kentucky Wesleyan 89 (2 overtimes)

**Third Place**
Kentucky Wesleyan 77, Bakersfield State 66

**Championship**
(Springfield, Mass., March 20, 1982)
District of Columbia 73, Florida Southern 63

**DIVISION III**
Semifinals
Potsdam State 50, Brooklyn College 49
Wabash 68, Stanislaus State 64

**Third Place**
Brooklyn College 68, Stanislaus State 62 (overtime)

**Championship**
(Grand Rapids, Mich., March 20, 1982)
Wabash 83, Potsdam State 62

**JUNIOR COLLEGES**
Championship
(Hutchinson, Kan., March 20, 1982)
Midland (Tex.) College 93, Miami-Dade (Fla.) 88

## ASSOCIATION FOR INTERCOLLEGIATE ATHLETICS FOR WOMEN
### (A.I.A.W.—1982)

**QUARTERFINALS**
Texas 73, Wisconsin 61
Villanova 87, Delta State 72
Rutgers 83, Minnesota 75
Wayland Baptist 85, California 70

**NATIONAL SEMIFINALS**
(Philadelphia, March 26, 1982)
Texas 82, Wayland Baptist 63
Rutgers 83, Villanova 75

**THIRD PLACE**
Villanova 90, Wayland Baptist 81

**CHAMPIONSHIP**
(Philadelphia, March 28, 1982)
Rutgers 83, Texas 77

**DIVISION II**
Final
(Charleston, S.C., March 27, 1982)
Francis Marion College (S.C.) 92, College of Charleston (S.C.) 83

**DIVISION III**
Final
(Cedar Rapids, Iowa, March 27, 1982)
Concordia (Minn.) 73, Mount Mercy (Iowa) 72

## WOMEN'S COLLEGE BASKETBALL—1982

### N.C.A.A. CHAMPIONSHIPS*

**First Round—East**
Cheyney State 75, Auburn 64
Kansas State 78, Stephen F. Austin 75
North Carolina State 75, Northwestern 71
Old Dominion 75, St. Peter's 42

**First Round—Mideast**
Memphis State 72, Mississippi 70
Penn State 96, Clemson 75
Southern California 99, Kent State 55
Tennessee 72, Jackson State 56

**First Round—Midwest**
Arizona State 97, Georgia 77
Kentucky 88, Illinois 80
Louisiana Tech 114, Tennessee Tech 53
South Carolina 79, East Carolina 54

**First Round—West**
Drake 90, Ohio State 79
Long Beach State 95, Howard 57

Maryland 82, Stanford 48
Missouri 59, Oregon 53

**Second Round—East**
Cheyney State 74, North Carolina State 61
Kansas State 76, Old Dominion 67

**Second Round—Mideast**
Southern California 73, Penn State 70
Tennessee 78, Memphis State 63

**Second Round—Midwest**
Kentucky 73, South Carolina 69
Louisiana Tech 92, Arizona State 54

**Second Round—West**
Drake 91, Long Beach State 78
Maryland 80, Missouri 68

**Regional Finals**
East—Cheyney State 93, Kansas State 71
Mideast—Tennessee 91, Southern California 90 (overtime)

Midwest—Louisiana Tech 82, Kentucky 60
West—Maryland 89, Drake 78

**NATIONAL SEMIFINALS**
(Norfolk, Va., March 26, 1982)
Cheyney State 76, Maryland 66
Louisiana Tech 69, Tennessee 46

**CHAMPIONSHIP**
(Norfolk, Va., March 28, 1982)
Louisiana Tech 76, Cheyney State 62

**DIVISION II**
Final
(Springfield, Mass., March 20, 1982)
California State Poly-Pomona 93, Tuskegee 74

*First year of tournament.

## NATIONAL INVITATION TOURNAMENT (N.I.T.)—1982

**Semifinals**
(March 22, 1982, Madison Square Garden, New York)
Bradley 84, Oklahoma 68
Purdue 61, Georgia 60
Third Place—Not contested

**Championship**
(March 24, 1982, Madison Square Garden, New York)
Bradley 67, Purdue 58

## A.A.U. CHAMPIONSHIP—MEN

(Portland, Ore., March 28, 1982)

**Semifinals**
Brewster Packing (Seattle) 124, Houston Flyers 116
Marathon Oil (Lexington, Ky.) 116, Sports in Action (Wash.) 96

**Championship**
Brewster Packing 93, Marathon Oil 91

## N.B.A. ALL-ROOKIE TEAM—1982

Buck Williams, New Jersey Nets; Isiah Thomas, Detroit Pistons; Kelly Tripucka, Detroit Pistons; Jay Vincent, Dallas Mavericks; Jeff Ruland, Washington Bullets

## LEADING N.C.A.A. SCORERS—1981-1982
### Division I

| | FG | FT | Pts | Avg |
|---|---|---|---|---|
| Harry Kelly, Texas Southern | 336 | 190 | 862 | 29.7 |
| Ricky Pierce, Rice | 314 | 177 | 805 | 26.8 |
| Dan Callandrillo, Seton Hall | 250 | 198 | 698 | 25.9 |
| Kevin Magee, California-Irvine | 272 | 188 | 732 | 25.2 |
| Quintin Dailey, San Francisco | 286 | 183 | 755 | 25.2 |
| Willie Jackson, Centenary | 273 | 147 | 693 | 23.9 |
| Mitchell Wiggins, Florida State | 223 | 77 | 523 | 23.8 |
| Perry Moss, Northeastern | 279 | 152 | 710 | 23.7 |
| Melvin McLaughlin, Central Mich. | 255 | 71 | 581 | 23.2 |
| Joe Jakubick, Akron | 235 | 124 | 594 | 22.8 |
| Steve Barker, Samford | 222 | 140 | 584 | 22.5 |
| Terry Cummings, De Paul | 244 | 136 | 624 | 22.3 |
| Terry Teagle, Baylor | 259 | 104 | 622 | 22.2 |
| Steve Burtt, Iona | 251 | 182 | 684 | 22.1 |
| Wayne Sappleton, Loyola (Ill.) | 238 | 162 | 638 | 22.0 |
| Mark McNamara, California | 231 | 131 | 593 | 22.0 |

## NATIONAL ASSOCIATION OF INTERCOLLEGIATE ATHLETICS—1982

**Round of 16**
Kearney (Neb.) State 77, Hanover (Ind.) 76
Saginaw Valley (Mich.) 67, Southern Tech (Ga.) 61 (overtime)
South Carolina-Spartanburg 63, St. Mary's (Tex.) 53
Henderson State (Ark.) 70, Moorhead State (Minn.) 61
Biola (Calif.) 62, Quincy (Ill.) 56
Hampton Institute (Va.) 63, Central Washington 49
Wisconsin-Eau Claire 91, St. Thomas Aquinas (N.Y.) 77
Western Oregon 63, Briar Cliff (Iowa) 55

**Quarterfinals**
Biola 42, Saginaw Valley 40
Hampton Institute 70, Henderson State 66
South Carolina-Spartanburg 76, Wisconsin-Eau Claire 64
Kearney State 97, Western Oregon 95

**Semifinals**
South Carolina-Spartanburg 68, Hampton Institute 54
Biola 84, Kearney State 75

**Third Place**
Hampton Institute 98, Kearney State 94

**Championship**
South Carolina-Spartanburg 51, Biola 38

# Professional Basketball

## NATIONAL BASKETBALL ASSOCIATION CHAMPIONS

*Source:* Matt Winick, Director of Media Information, National Basketball Association
The National Basketball Association was originally the Basketball Association of America. It took its current name in 1949 when it merged with the National Basketball League.

| Season | Eastern Conference (W-L) | Western Conference (W-L) | Playoff Champions[1] |
|---|---|---|---|
| 1946–47 | Washington Capitols (49–11) | Chicago Stags (39–22) | Philadelphia Warriors |
| 1947–48 | Philadelphia Warriors (27–21) | St. Louis Bombers (29–19) | Baltimore Bullets |
| 1948–49 | Washington Capitols (38–22) | Rochester Royals (45–15) | Minneapolis Lakers |
| 1949–50 | Syracuse Nationals (51–13) | Indianapolis Olympians (39–25) | Minneapolis Lakers |
| 1950–51 | Philadelphia Warriors (40–26) | Minneapolis Lakers (44–24) | Rochester Royals |
| 1951–52 | Syracuse Nationals (40–26) | Rochester Royals (41–25) | Minneapolis Lakers |
| 1952–53 | New York Knickerbockers (47–23) | Minneapolis Lakers (48–22) | Minneapolis Lakers |
| 1953–54 | New York Knickerbockers (44–28) | Minneapolis Lakers (46–26) | Minneapolis Lakers |
| 1954–55 | Syracuse Nationals (43–29) | Ft. Wayne Pistons (43–29) | Syracuse Nationals |
| 1955–56 | Philadelphia Warriors (45–27) | Ft. Wayne Pistons (37–35) | Philadelphia Warriors |
| 1956–57 | Boston Celtics (44–28) | St. Louis Hawks (34–38) | Boston Celtics |

| Season | Eastern Conference (W-L) | Western Conference (W-L) | Playoff Champions[1] |
|--------|--------------------------|--------------------------|----------------------|
| 1957–58 | Boston Celtics (48–23) | St. Louis Hawks (41–31) | St. Louis Hawks |
| 1958–59 | Boston Celtics (52–20) | St. Louis Hawks (49–23) | Boston Celtics |
| 1959–60 | Boston Celtics (59–16) | St. Louis Hawks (46–29) | Boston Celtics |
| 1960–61 | Boston Celtics (57–22) | St. Louis Hawks (51–28) | Boston Celtics |
| 1961–62 | Boston Celtics (60–20) | Los Angeles Lakers (54–26) | Boston Celtics |
| 1962–63 | Boston Celtics (58–22) | Los Angeles Lakers (53–27) | Boston Celtics |
| 1963–64 | Boston Celtics (59–21) | San Francisco Warriors (48–32) | Boston Celtics |
| 1964–65 | Boston Celtics (62–18) | Los Angeles Lakers (49–31) | Boston Celtics |
| 1965–66 | Philadelphia 76ers (55–25) | Los Angeles Lakers (45–35) | Boston Celtics |
| 1966–67 | Philadelphia 76ers (68–13) | San Francisco Warriors (44–37) | Philadelphia 76ers |
| 1967–68 | Philadelphia 76ers (62–20) | St. Louis Hawks (56–26) | Boston Celtics |
| 1968–69 | Baltimore Bullets (57–25) | Los Angeles Lakers (55–27) | Boston Celtics |
| 1969–70 | New York Knickerbockers (60–22) | Atlanta Hawks (48–34) | New York Knicks |
| 1970–71 | Baltimore Bullets (42–40) | Milwaukee Bucks (66–16) | Milwaukee Bucks |
| 1971–72 | New York Knickerbockers (48–34) | Los Angeles Lakers (69–13) | Los Angeles Lakers |
| 1972–73 | New York Knickerbockers (57–25) | Los Angeles Lakers (69–22) | New York Knicks |
| 1973–74 | Boston Celtics (56–26) | Milwaukee Bucks (59–23) | Boston Celtics |
| 1974–75 | Washington Bullets (60–22) | Golden State Warriors (48–34) | Golden State Warriors |
| 1975–76 | Boston Celtics (54–28) | Phoenix Suns (42–40) | Boston Celtics |
| 1976–77 | Philadelphia 76ers (50–32) | Portland Trail Blazers (49–33) | Portland Trail Blazers |
| 1977–78 | Washington Bullets (44–38) | Seattle Super Sonics (47–35) | Washington Bullets |
| 1978–79 | Washington Bullets (54–28) | Seattle Super Sonics (52–30) | Seattle Super Sonics |
| 1979–80 | Philadelphia 76ers (59–23) | Los Angeles Lakers (60–22) | Los Angeles Lakers |
| 1980–81 | Boston Celtics (62–20) | Phoenix Suns (57–25) | Boston Celtics |
| 1981–82 | Boston Celtics (63–19) | Los Angeles Lakers (57–25) | Los Angeles Lakers |

1. Playoffs may involve teams other than conference winners.

## INDIVIDUAL N.B.A. SCORING CHAMPIONS

| Season | Player, Team | G | FG | FT | Pts | Avg |
|--------|--------------|---|----|----|----|-----|
| 1953–54 | Neil Johnston, Philadelphia Warriors | 72 | 591 | 577 | 1759 | 24.4 |
| 1954–55 | Neil Johnston, Philadelphia Warriors | 72 | 521 | 589 | 1631 | 22.7 |
| 1955–56 | Bob Pettit, St. Louis Hawks | 72 | 646 | 557 | 1849 | 25.7 |
| 1956–57 | Paul Arizin, Philadelphia Warriors | 71 | 613 | 591 | 1817 | 25.6 |
| 1957–58 | George Yardley, Detroit Pistons | 72 | 673 | 655 | 2001 | 27.8 |
| 1958–59 | Bob Pettit, St. Louis Hawks | 72 | 719 | 667 | 2105 | 29.2 |
| 1959–60 | Wilt Chamberlain, Philadelphia Warriors | 72 | 1065 | 577 | 2707 | 37.6 |
| 1960–61 | Wilt Chamberlain, Phildelphia Warriors | 79 | 1251 | 531 | 3033 | 38.4 |
| 1961–62 | Wilt Chamberlain, Philadelphia Warriors | 80 | 1597 | 835 | 4029 | 50.4 |
| 1962–63 | Wilt Chamberlain, San Francisco Warriors | 80 | 1463 | 660 | 3586 | 44.8 |
| 1963–64 | Wilt Chamberlain, San Francisco Warriors | 80 | 1204 | 540 | 2948 | 36.9 |
| 1964–65 | Wilt Chamberlain, San Francisco Warriors-Phila. 76ers | 73 | 1063 | 408 | 2534 | 34.7 |
| 1965–66 | Wilt Chamberlain, Philadelphia 76ers | 79 | 1074 | 501 | 2649 | 33.5 |
| 1966–67 | Rick Barry, San Francisco Warriors | 78 | 1011 | 753 | 2775 | 35.6 |
| 1967–68 | Dave Bing, Detroit Pistons | 79 | 835 | 472 | 2142 | 27.1 |
| 1968–69 | Elvin Hayes, San Diego Rockets | 82 | 930 | 467 | 2327 | 28.4 |
| 1969–70 | Jerry West, Los Angeles Lakers | 74 | 831 | 647 | 2309 | 31.2 |
| 1970–71 | Lew Alcindor,[1] Milwaukee Bucks | 82 | 1063 | 470 | 2596 | 31.7 |
| 1971–72 | Kareem Abdul-Jabbar, Milwaukee Bucks | 81 | 1159 | 504 | 2822 | 34.8 |
| 1972–73 | Nate Archibald, Kansas City-Omaha Kings | 80 | 1028 | 663 | 2719 | 34.0 |
| 1973–74 | Bob McAdoo, Buffalo Braves | 74 | 901 | 459 | 2261 | 30.8 |
| 1974–75 | Bob McAdoo, Buffalo Braves | 82 | 1095 | 641 | 2831 | 34.5 |
| 1975–76 | Bob McAdoo, Buffalo Braves | 78 | 934 | 559 | 2427 | 31.1 |
| 1976–77 | Pete Maravich, New Orleans Jazz | 73 | 886 | 501 | 2273 | 31.1 |
| 1977–78 | George Gervin, San Antonio Spurs | 82 | 864 | 504 | 2232 | 27.2 |
| 1978–79 | George Gervin, San Antonio | 80 | 947 | 471 | 2365 | 29.6 |
| 1979–80 | George Gervin, San Antonio | 78 | 1024 | 505 | 2585 | 33.1 |
| 1980–81 | Adrian Dantley, Utah Jazz | 80 | 909 | 632 | 2452 | 30.7 |
| 1981–82 | George Gervin, San Antonio | 79 | 993 | 555 | 2551 | 32.3 |

1. (Kareem Abdul-Jabbar).

## N.B.A. LIFETIME LEADERS
(Through 1981–1982 season)

### Scoring

| | Yrs | FG | FT | Pts | | | | | |
|---|-----|----|----|----|---|---|---|---|---|
| | | | | | Elvin Hayes | 14 | 10,394 | 5,074 | 25,8 |
| | | | | | Rick Barry* | 14 | 9,695 | 5,713 | 25, |
| | | | | | Jerry West | 14 | 9,016 | 7,160 | 25, |
| Wilt Chamberlain | 14 | 12,681 | 6,057 | 31,419 | Dan Issel* | 12 | 8,828 | 5,570 | 23, |
| Kareem Adbul-Jabbar | 13 | 11,568 | 4,952 | 28,088 | Elgin Baylor | 14 | 8,693 | 5,763 | 23, |
| Oscar Robertson | 14 | 9,508 | 7,694 | 26,710 | Julius Erving* | 11 | 9,004 | 4,744 | 22,8 |
| John Havlicek | 16 | 10,513 | 5,369 | 26,395 | | | | | |

| Hal Greer | 15 | 8,504 | 4,578 | 21,586 |
| Walt Bellamy | 14 | 7,914 | 5,113 | 20,941 |
| Bob Pettit | 11 | 7,349 | 6,182 | 20,880 |

*Includes statistics compiled in the American Basketball Association.

## Scoring Average

(400 games or 10,000 points minimum)

| | Games | Pts | Avg |
|---|---|---|---|
| Wilt Chamberlain | 1,045 | 31,419 | 30.1 |
| Kareem Abdul–Jabbar | 1,011 | 28,088 | 27.8 |
| Elgin Baylor | 846 | 23,149 | 27.4 |
| Jerry West | 932 | 25,192 | 27.0 |
| Bob Pettit | 792 | 20,880 | 26.4 |
| George Gervin* | 752 | 19,736 | 26.2 |
| Julius Erving* | 882 | 22,851 | 25.9 |
| Oscar Robertson | 1,040 | 26,710 | 25.7 |
| Bob McAdoo | 640 | 16,184 | 25.3 |
| David Thompson* | 516 | 12,728 | 24.7 |
| Pete Maravich | 658 | 15,948 | 24.2 |
| Rick Barry | 794 | 18,395 | 23.2 |
| Elvin Hayes | 1,141 | 25,865 | 22.7 |

*Includes statistics compiled in the American Basketball Association.

## Rebounds

| Wilt Chamberlain | 23,924 |
|---|---|
| Bill Russell | 21,620 |
| Elvin Hayes | 15,403 |
| Nate Thurmond | 14,464 |
| Walt Bellamy | 14,241 |
| Kareem Abdul–Jabbar | 13,826 |
| Wes Unseld | 13,769 |
| Jerry Lucas | 12,942 |
| Bob Pettit | 12,849 |
| Paul Silas | 12,357 |

## N.B.A. ALL-DEFENSIVE TEAM—1982

Forwards—Bobby Jones, Philadelphia, and Dan Roundfield, Atlanta

Center—Caldwell Jones, Philadelphia

Guards—Michael Cooper, Los Angeles, and Dennis Johnson, Phoenix

## Free-Throw Percentage

(1,400 free throws made minimum)

| | Att | FT | Pct |
|---|---|---|---|
| Rick Barry | 4,243 | 3,818 | .900 |
| Calvin Murphy | 3,714 | 3,307 | .890 |
| Bill Sharman | 3,557 | 3,143 | .884 |
| Mike Newlin | 3,456 | 3,005 | .870 |
| Fred Brown | 2,053 | 1,761 | .858 |
| Larry Siegfried | 1,945 | 1,662 | .854 |
| Ricky Sobers | 1,959 | 1,655 | .845 |
| Dolph Schayes | 8,273 | 6,979 | .844 |
| Jack Marin | 2,852 | 2,405 | .843 |
| Flynn Robinson | 2,061 | 1,722 | .836 |

## Field-Goal Percentage

(2,000 field goals minimum)

| | Att | FG | Pct |
|---|---|---|---|
| Artis Gilmore | 5,827 | 3,425 | .588 |
| Kareem Abdul–Jabbar | 20,741 | 11,568 | .558 |
| Bobby Jones | 4,584 | 2,540 | .554 |
| Adrian Dantley | 7,387 | 4,039 | .547 |
| Walter Davis | 5,792 | 3,150 | .544 |
| Marques Johnson | 5,875 | 3,177 | .541 |
| Swen Nater | 4,255 | 2,302 | .541 |
| Wilt Chamberlain | 23,497 | 12,681 | .540 |
| Bernard King | 5,712 | 3,050 | .534 |
| Cliff Ray | 4,450 | 2,333 | .524 |
| George Gervin | 10,351 | 5,404 | .522 |
| Walt Bellamy | 15,340 | 7,914 | .516 |

## Assists

| Oscar Robertson | 9,887 |
|---|---|
| Lenny Wilkens | 7,211 |
| Bob Cousy | 6,955 |
| Guy Rodgers | 6,917 |
| Jerry West | 6,238 |
| John Havlicek | 6,114 |
| Nate Archibald | 5,907 |
| Dave Bing | 5,397 |
| Kevin Porter | 5,268 |
| Norm Van Lier | 5,217 |
| Walt Frazier | 5,040 |

## N.B.A. MOST VALUABLE PLAYERS

| 1956 | Bob Pettit |
| 1957 | Bob Cousy |
| 1958 | Bill Russell |
| 1959 | Bob Pettit |
| 1960 | Wilt Chamberlain |
| 1961–63 | Bill Russell |
| 1964 | Oscar Robertson |
| 1965 | Bill Russell |
| 1966–68 | Wilt Chamberlain |
| 1969 | Wes Unseld |
| 1970 | Willis Reed |
| 1971–72 | Lew Alcindor (Kareem Abdul-Jabbar) |
| 1973 | Dave Cowens |
| 1974 | Kareem Abdul-Jabbar, Milwaukee |
| 1975 | Bob McAdoo, Buffalo |
| 1976–77 | Kareem Abdul-Jabbar, Los Angeles |
| 1978 | Bill Walton, Portland |
| 1979 | Moses Malone, Houston |
| 1980 | Kareem Abdul-Jabbar, Los Angeles |
| 1981 | Julius Erving, Philadelphia |
| 1982 | Moses Malone, Houston |

## N.B.A. TEAM RECORDS

Most points, game—173, Boston vs. Minneapolis, 1959
Most points, quarter—58, Buffalo vs. Boston, 1968
Most points, half—97, Atlanta vs. San Diego, 1970
Most points, overtime period—22, Detroit vs. Cleveland, 1973
Most field goals, game—72, Boston, 1959
Most field goals, quarter—23, Boston, 1959; Buffalo, 1972
Most field goals, half—40, Boston, 1959; Syracuse, 1963; Atlanta, 1979
Most assists, game—53, Milwaukee, 1978
Most rebounds, game—112, Philadelphia, 1959
Most points, both teams, game—337 (San Antonio 171, Milwaukee 166), 3 overtimes, San Antonio, March 6, 1982
Most points, both teams, quarter—96 (Boston 52, Minneapolis 44), 1959; (Detroit 53, Cincinnati 43), 1972
Most points, both teams, half—170 (Philadelphia 90, Cincinnati 80), Philadelphia, 1971
Longest winning streak—33, Los Angeles, 1971–72
Longest losing streak—20, Philadelphia, 1973
Longest winning streak at home—36, Philadelphia, 1966–67
Most games won, season—69, Los Angeles, 1971–72
Most games lost, season—73, Philadelphia, 1972–73
Highest average points per game—126.5, Denver, 1981–82

## N.B.A. INDIVIDUAL RECORDS

Most points, game—100, Wilt Chamberlain, Philadelphia vs. New York at Hershey, Pa., 1962

Most points, quarter—33, George Gervin, San Antonio, 1978

Most points, half—59, Wilt Chamberlain, Philadelphia, 1962

Most free throws, game—28, Wilt Chamberlain, Philadelphia, vs. New York at Hershey, Pa. 1962

Most free throws, quarter—14, Rick Barry, San Francisco, 1966

Most free throws, half—19, Oscar Robertson, Cincinnati, 1964

Most field goals, game—28, Wilt Chamberlain, Philadelphia, 1962

Most consecutive field goals, game—18, Wilt Chamberlain, San Francisco, 1963; Wilt Chamberlain, Philadelphia, 1967

Most assists, game—29, Kevin Porter, New Jersey Nets, 1978

Most rebounds, game—55, Wilt Chamberlain, Philadelphia, 1963

## NATIONAL BASKETBALL ASSOCIATION
## FINAL STANDING OF THE CLUBS—1981–1982

### EASTERN CONFERENCE
**Atlantic Division**

|  | W | L | Pct | Scoring For | Agst |
|---|---|---|---|---|---|
| Boston Celtics | 63 | 19 | .768 | 112.0 | 105.6 |
| Philadelphia 76ers | 58 | 24 | .707 | 111.2 | 105.5 |
| New Jersey Nets | 44 | 38 | .537 | 106.7 | 106.0 |
| Washington Bullets | 43 | 39 | .524 | 103.5 | 102.6 |
| New York Knicks | 33 | 49 | .402 | 106.2 | 108.9 |

**Central Division**

|  | W | L | Pct | Scoring For | Agst |
|---|---|---|---|---|---|
| Milwaukee Bucks | 55 | 27 | .671 | 108.4 | 102.9 |
| Atlanta Hawks | 42 | 40 | .512 | 101.0 | 100.5 |
| Detroit Pistons | 39 | 43 | .476 | 111.1 | 112.0 |
| Indiana Pacers | 35 | 47 | .427 | 102.2 | 104.0 |
| Chicago Bulls | 34 | 48 | .415 | 106.6 | 108.6 |
| Cleveland Cavaliers | 15 | 67 | .183 | 103.2 | 111.7 |

### WESTERN CONFERENCE
**Midwest Division**

|  | W | L | Pct | Scoring For | Agst |
|---|---|---|---|---|---|
| San Antonio Spurs | 48 | 34 | .585 | 113.1 | 110.8 |
| Denver Nuggets | 46 | 36 | .561 | 126.5 | 126.0 |
| Houston Rockets | 46 | 36 | .561 | 105.9 | 105.9 |
| Kansas City Kings | 30 | 52 | .366 | 107.1 | 110.2 |
| Dallas Mavericks | 28 | 54 | .341 | 104.6 | 109.0 |
| Utah Jazz | 25 | 57 | .305 | 110.9 | 116.6 |

**Pacific Division**

|  | W | L | Pct | Scoring For | Agst |
|---|---|---|---|---|---|
| Los Angeles Lakers | 57 | 25 | .695 | 114.6 | 109.8 |
| Seattle SuperSonics | 52 | 30 | .634 | 107.3 | 103.1 |
| Phoenix Suns | 46 | 36 | .561 | 106.2 | 102.7 |
| Golden State Warriors | 45 | 37 | .549 | 110.9 | 109.8 |
| Portland Trail Blazers | 42 | 40 | .512 | 109.8 | 109.2 |
| San Diego Clippers | 17 | 65 | .207 | 108.5 | 115.9 |

## N.B.A. PLAYOFFS—1982

### EASTERN CONFERENCE
**First Round**

Washington defeated New Jersey, 2 games to 0
Philadelphia defeated Atlanta, 2 games to 0

**Semifinal Round**

Boston defeated Washington, 4 games to 1
Philadelphia defeated Milwaukee,.4 games to 2

**Conference Finals**

Philadelphia defeated Boston, 4 games to 3
  May 9—Boston 121, Philadelphia 81
  May 12—Philadelphia 121, Boston 113
  May 15—Philadelphia 99, Boston 97
  May 16—Philadelphia 119, Boston 94
  May 19—Boston 114, Philadelphia 85
  May 21—Boston 88, Philadelphia 75
  May 23—Philadelphia 120, Boston 106

### WESTERN CONFERENCE
**First Round**

Seattle defeated Houston, 2 games to 1
Phoenix defeated Denver, 2 games to 1

**Semifinal Round**

Los Angeles defeated Phoenix, 4 games to 0
San Antonio defeated Seattle, 4 games to 1

**Conference Finals**

Los Angeles defeated San Antonio, 4 games to 0
  May 9—Los Angeles 128, San Antonio 117
  May 11—Los Angeles 110, San Antonio 101
  May 14—Los Angeles 118, San Antonio 108
  May 15—Los Angeles 128, San Antonio 123

### Championship

Los Angeles defeated Philadelphia, 4 games to 2
  May 27—Los Angeles 124, Philadelphia 117[1]
  May 30—Philadelphia 110, Los Angeles 94[1]
  June 1—Los Angeles 129, Philadelphia 108
  June 3—Los Angeles 111, Philadelphia 101
  June 6—Philadelphia 135, Los Angeles 102[1]
  June 8—Los Angeles 114, Philadelphia 104
  1. At Philadelphia.

### FIELD-GOAL LEADERS—1981–1982
(Minimum 300 FG made)

|  | FG | Att | Pct |
|---|---|---|---|
| Artis Gilmore, Chicago | 546 | 837 | .652 |
| Steve Johnson, Kansas City | 395 | 644 | .613 |
| Buck Williams, New Jersey | 513 | 881 | .582 |
| Kareem Abdul–Jabbar, Los Angeles | 753 | 1,301 | .579 |
| Calvin Natt, Portland | 515 | 894 | .576 |
| Adrian Dantley, Utah | 904 | 1,586 | .570 |
| Bernard King, Golden State | 740 | 1,307 | .566 |
| Bobby Jones, Philadelphia | 416 | 737 | .564 |
| Bill Cartwright, New York | 390 | 694 | .562 |
| Jeff Ruland, Washington | 420 | 749 | .561 |

### FREE-THROW LEADERS—1981–1982
(Minimum 125 FT made)

|  | FT | Att | Pct |
|---|---|---|---|
| Kyle Macy, Phoenix | 152 | 169 | .899 |
| Charlie Criss, San Diego | 141 | 159 | .887 |
| John Long, Detroit | 238 | 275 | .865 |
| George Gervin, San Antonio | 555 | 642 | .864 |
| Larry Bird, Boston | 328 | 380 | .863 |
| James Silas, Cleveland | 246 | 286 | .860 |
| Mike Newlin, New York | 126 | 147 | .857 |
| Kiki Vandeweghe, Detroit | 347 | 405 | .857 |
| Kevin Grevey, Washington | 165 | 193 | .855 |
| Jack Sikma, Seattle | 447 | 523 | .855 |

## LEADING SCORERS—1981–1982

| | G | FG | FT | Pts | Avg |
|---|---|---|---|---|---|
| George Gervin, San Antonio | 79 | 993 | 555 | 2,551 | 32.3 |
| Moses Malone, Houston | 81 | 945 | 630 | 2,520 | 31.1 |
| Adrian Dantley, Utah | 81 | 904 | 648 | 2,457 | 30.3 |
| Alex English, Denver | 82 | 855 | 372 | 2,082 | 25.4 |
| Julius Erving, Philadelphia | 81 | 780 | 411 | 1,974 | 24.4 |
| Kareem Abdul–Jabbar, Los Angeles | 76 | 753 | 312 | 1,818 | 23.9 |
| Gus Williams, Seattle | 80 | 773 | 320 | 1,875 | 23.4 |
| Bernard King, Golden State | 79 | 740 | 352 | 1,833 | 23.2 |
| World B. Free, Golden State | 78 | 650 | .479 | 1,789 | 22.9 |
| Larry Bird, Boston | 77 | 711 | 328 | 1,761 | 22.9 |
| Dan Issel, Denver | 81 | 651 | 546 | 1,852 | 22.9 |
| John Long, Detroit | 69 | 637 | 238 | 1,514 | 21.9 |
| Kelly Tripucka, Detroit | 82 | 636 | 495 | 1,772 | 21.6 |
| Kiki Vandeweghe, Denver | 82 | 706 | 347 | 1,760 | 21.5 |
| Jay Vincent, Dallas | 81 | 719 | 293 | 1,732 | 21.4 |
| Jamaal Wilkes, Los Angeles | 82 | 744 | 246 | 1,734 | 21.1 |
| David Thompson, Portland | 79 | 681 | 280 | 1,642 | 20.8 |

## BLOCKED-SHOTS LEADERS—1981–1982
(Minimum 70 games or 100 blocked shots)

| | G | No. | Avg |
|---|---|---|---|
| George Johnson, San Antonio | 75 | 234 | 3.12 |
| Wayne Rollins, Atlanta | 79 | 224 | 2.84 |
| Kareem Abdul–Jabbar, Los Angeles | 76 | 207 | 2.72 |
| Artis Gilmore, Chicago | 82 | 221 | 2.70 |
| Robert Parish, Boston | 80 | 192 | 2.40 |
| Kevin McHale, Boston | 82 | 185 | 2.26 |
| Herb Williams, Indiana | 82 | 178 | 2.17 |
| Terry Tyler, Detroit | 82 | 160 | 1.95 |
| Caldwell Jones, Philadelphia | 81 | 146 | 1.80 |
| Julius Erving, Philadelphia | 81 | 141 | 1.74 |

## ASSISTS LEADERS—1981–1982
(Minimum 70 games or 400 assists)

| | G | No. | Avg. |
|---|---|---|---|
| Johnny Moore, San Antonio | 79 | 762 | 9.6 |
| Earvin Johnson, Los Angeles | 78 | 743 | 9.5 |
| Maurice Cheeks, Philadelphia | 79 | 667 | 8.4 |
| Nate Archibald, Boston | 68 | 541 | 8.0 |
| Norm Nixon, Los Angeles | 82 | 652 | 8.0 |
| Isiah Thomas, Detroit | 72 | 565 | 7.8 |
| Rickey Green, Utah | 81 | 630 | 7.8 |
| Geoff Huston, Cleveland | 78 | 590 | 7.6 |
| Kelvin Ransey, Portland | 78 | 555 | 7.1 |
| Michael Ray Richardson, New York | 82 | 572 | 7.0 |

## STEALS LEADERS—1981–1982
(Minimum 70 games or 125 steals)

| | G | No. | Avg |
|---|---|---|---|
| Earvin Johnson, Los Angeles | 78 | 208 | 2.67 |
| Maurice Cheeks, Philadelphia | 79 | 209 | 2.65 |
| Michael Ray Richardson, New York | 82 | 213 | 2.60 |
| Quinn Buckner, Milwaukee | 70 | 174 | 2.49 |
| Ray Williams, New Jersey | 82 | 199 | 2.43 |
| Rickey Green, Utah | 81 | 185 | 2.28 |
| Gus Williams, Seattle | 80 | 172 | 2.15 |
| Isiah Thomas, Detroit | 72 | 150 | 2.08 |
| Johnny Moore, San Antonio | 79 | 163 | 2.06 |
| Don Buse, Indiana | 82 | 164 | 2.00 |

## 3-POINT FIELD-GOAL LEADERS—1981–1982
(Minimum 25 made)

| | FG | Att | Pct |
|---|---|---|---|
| Campy Russell, New York | 25 | 57 | .439 |
| Andrew Toney, Philadelphia | 25 | 59 | .424 |
| Kyle Macy, Phoenix | 39 | 100 | .390 |
| Brian Winters, Milwaukee | 36 | 93 | .387 |
| Don Buse, Indiana | 73 | 189 | .386 |
| Mike Dunleavy, Houston | 33 | 86 | .384 |
| Mark Aguirre, Dallas | 25 | 71 | .352 |
| Kevin Grevey, Washington | 28 | 82 | .341 |
| Mike Bratz, San Antonio | 46 | 138 | .333 |
| Joey Hassett, Golden State | 71 | 214 | .332 |

## REBOUND LEADERS—1981–1982
(Minimum 70 games or 800 rebounds)

| | G | Off | Def | Total | Avg |
|---|---|---|---|---|---|
| Moses Malone, Houston | 81 | 558 | 630 | 1,188 | 14.7 |
| Jack Sikma, Seattle | 82 | 223 | 815 | 1,038 | 12.7 |
| Buck Williams, New Jersey | 82 | 347 | 658 | 1,005 | 12.3 |
| David Thompson, Portland | 79 | 258 | 663 | 921 | 11.7 |
| Maurice Lucas, New York | 80 | 274 | 629 | 903 | 11.3 |
| Phil Smith, Golden State | 74 | 279 | 534 | 813 | 11.0 |
| Larry Bird, Boston | 77 | 200 | 637 | 837 | 10.9 |
| Robert Parish, Boston | 80 | 288 | 578 | 866 | 10.8 |
| Artis Gilmore, Chicago | 82 | 224 | 611 | 835 | 10.2 |
| Leonard Robinson, Phoenix | 74 | 202 | 519 | 721 | 9.7 |

## N.B.A. ALL-STAR TEAM—1982

| First Team | Pos. | Second Team |
|---|---|---|
| Larry Bird, Boston | F | Alex English, Denver |
| Julius Erving, Philadelphia | F | Bernard King, Golden State |
| Moses Malone, Houston | C | Robert Parish, Boston |
| George Gervin, San Antonio | G | Earvin (Magic) Johnson, Los Angeles |
| Gus Williams, Seattle | G | Sidney Moncrief, Milwaukee |

# ARCHERY

## NATIONAL ARCHERY ASSOCIATION CHAMPIONSHIPS
(Oxford, Ohio, Aug. 2–6, 1982)

| Men's Division | Pts |
|---|---|
| Richard McKinney, Glendale, Ariz. | 2,616 |
| Edwin Eliason, Seattle | 2,571 |
| Philip Hoelle, Smithtown, N.Y. | 2,523 |
| Larry Smith, Shrewsbury, Pa. | 2,523 |
| Gerry Pylypchuk, Brooklyn, N.Y. | 2,514 |

| Women's Division | Pts |
|---|---|
| Luann Ryon, Riverside, Calif. | 2,541 |
| Ruth Rowe, Gaithersburg, Md. | 2,511 |
| Nanby Myrick, Huntington Beach, Calif. | 2,487 |
| Trena King, Cutlerville, Mich. | 2,487 |
| Eileen Pylypchuck, Brooklyn, N.Y. | 2,483 |

| Other Champions | Pts |
|---|---|
| Intermediate boys—Johnny Kazak, Aurora, Ill. | 2,449 |
| Intermediate girls—Becky Liggett, Muncie, Ind. | 2,466 |
| Junior boys—James Swanson, Brighton, Mich. | 2,428 |
| Junior girls—Angela Nusz, Wrightsville, Pa. | 2,314 |
| Cadet boys—Scott Raunigk, Wilmington, Del. | 2,543 |
| Cadet girls—Lara Corya, Anderson, Ind. | 2,213 |

| Crossbow | Pts |
|---|---|
| Men's division—Ervin Myers, Dallastown, Pa. | 3,361 |
| Women's division—Carol Pelosi, Greenbelt, Md. | 3,260 |
| King's round—Ervin Myers | 56 |
| Queen's round—Carol Pelosi | 36 |

# HOCKEY

Ice hockey, by birth and upbringing a Canadian game, is an offshoot of field hockey. Some historians say that the first ice hockey game was played in Montreal in December 1879 between two teams composed almost exclusively of McGill University students, but others assert that earlier hockey games took place in Kingston, Ontario, or Halifax, Nova Scotia. In the Montreal game of 1879, there were fifteen players on a side, who used an assortment of crude sticks to keep the puck in motion. Early rules allowed nine men on a side, but the number was reduced to seven in 1886 and later to six.

The first governing body of the sport was the Amateur Hockey Association of Canada, organized in 1887. In the winter of 1894–95, a group of college students from the United States visited Canada and saw hockey played. They became enthused over the game and introduced it as a winter sport when they returned home. The first professional league was the International Hockey League, which operated in northern Michigan in 1904–06.

Until 1910, professionals and amateurs were allowed to play together on "mixed teams," but this arrangement ended with the formation of the first "big league," the National Hockey Association, in eastern Canada in 1910. The Pacific Coast League was organized in 1911 for western Canadian hockey. The league included Seattle and later other American cities. The National Hockey League replaced the National Hockey Association in 1917. Boston, in 1924, was the first American city to join that circuit. The league expanded to include western cities in 1967. The Stanley Cup was competed for by "mixed teams" from 1894 to 1910, thereafter by professionals. It was awarded to the winner of the N.H.L. playoffs from 1926–67 and now to the league champion. The World Hockey Association was organized in October 1972 and was dissolved after the 1978–79 season when the N.H.L. absorbed four of the teams.

## STANLEY CUP WINNERS

Emblematic of World Professional Championship; N.H.L. Championship after 1967

| | | | | | |
|---|---|---|---|---|---|
| 1894 | Montreal A.A.A. | 1922 | Toronto St. Patricks | 1947–49 | Toronto Maple Leafs |
| 1895 | Montreal Victorias | 1923 | Ottawa Senators | 1950 | Detroit Red Wings |
| 1896 | Winnipeg Victorias | 1924 | Montreal Canadiens | 1951 | Toronto Maple Leafs |
| 1897–99 | Montreal Victorias | 1925 | Victoria Cougars | 1952 | Detroit Red Wings |
| 1900 | Montreal Shamrocks | 1926 | Montreal Maroons | 1953 | Montreal Canadiens |
| 1901 | Winnipeg Victorias | 1927 | Ottawa Senators | 1954–55 | Detroit Red Wings |
| 1902 | Montreal A.A.A. | 1928 | N.Y. Rangers | 1956–60 | Montreal Canadiens |
| 1903–05 | Ottawa Silver Seven | 1929 | Boston Bruins | 1961 | Chicago Black Hawks |
| 1906 | Montreal Wanderers | 1930–31 | Montreal Canadiens | 1962–64 | Toronto Maple Leafs |
| 1907 | Kenora Thistles[1] | 1932 | Toronto Maple Leafs | 1965–66 | Montreal Canadiens |
| 1907 | Mont. Wanderers[2] | 1933 | N.Y. Rangers | 1967 | Toronto Maple Leafs |
| 1908 | Montreal Wanderers | 1934 | Chicago Black Hawks | 1968–69 | Montreal Canadiens |
| 1909 | Ottawa Senators | 1935 | Montreal Maroons | 1970 | Boston Bruins |
| 1910 | Montreal Wanderers | 1936–37 | Detroit Red Wings | 1971 | Montreal Canadiens |
| 1911 | Ottawa Senators | 1938 | Chicago Black Hawks | 1972 | Boston Bruins |
| 1912–13 | Quebec Bulldogs | 1939 | Boston Bruins | 1973 | Montreal Canadiens |
| 1914 | Toronto | 1940 | N.Y. Rangers | 1974–75 | Philadelphia Flyers |
| 1915 | Vancouver Millionaires | 1941 | Boston Bruins | 1976–79 | Montreal Canadiens |
| 1916 | Montreal Canadiens | 1942 | Toronto Maple Leafs | 1980–82 | New York Islanders |
| 1917 | Seattle Metropolitans | 1943 | Detroit Red Wings | 1. January. 2. March. | |
| 1918 | Toronto Arenas | 1944 | Montreal Canadiens | | |
| 1919 | No champion | 1945 | Toronto Maple Leafs | | |
| 1920–21 | Ottawa Senators | 1946 | Montreal Canadiens | | |

## NATIONAL HOCKEY LEAGUE YEARLY TROPHY WINNERS

### The Hart Trophy—Most Valuable Player

| | | | |
|---|---|---|---|
| 1924 | Frank Nighbor, Ottawa | 1946 | Max Bentley, Chicago |
| 1925 | Billy Burch, Hamilton | 1947 | Maurice Richard, Montreal Canadiens |
| 1926 | Nels Stewart, Montreal Maroons | 1948 | Buddy O'Connor, New York Rangers |
| 1927 | Herb Gardiner, Montreal Canadiens | 1949 | Sid Abel, Detroit |
| 1928 | Howie Morenz, Montreal Canadiens | 1950 | Chuck Rayner, New York Rangers |
| 1929 | Roy Worters, New York Americans | 1951 | Milt Schmidt, Boston |
| 1930 | Nels Stewart, Montreal Maroons | 1952–53 | Gordon Howe, Detroit |
| 1931–32 | Howie Morenz, Montreal Canadiens | 1954 | Al Rollins, Chicago |
| 1933 | Eddie Shore, Boston | 1955 | Ted Kennedy, Toronto |
| 1934 | Aurel Joliat, Montreal Canadiens | 1956 | Jean Beliveau, Montreal Canadiens |
| 1935–36 | Eddie Shore, Boston | 1957–58 | Gordon Howe, Detroit |
| 1937 | Babe Siebert, Montreal Canadiens | 1959 | Andy Bathgate, New York Rangers |
| 1938 | Eddie Shore, Boston | 1960 | Gordon Howe, Detroit |
| 1939 | Toe Blake, Montreal Canadiens | 1961 | Bernie Geoffrion, Montreal Canadiens |
| 1940 | Ebbie Goodfellow, Detroit | 1962 | Jacques Plante, Montreal Canadiens |
| 1941 | Bill Cowley, Boston | 1963 | Gordon Howe, Detroit |
| 1942 | Tom Anderson, New York Americans | 1964 | Jean Beliveau, Montreal Canadiens |
| 1943 | Bill Cowley, Boston | 1965–66 | Bobby Hull, Chicago |
| 1944 | Babe Pratt, Toronto | 1967–68 | Stan Mikita, Chicago |
| 1945 | Elmer Lach, Montreal Canadiens | 1969 | Phil Esposito, Boston |

1970–72    Bobby Orr, Boston
1973    Bobby Clarke, Philadelphia
1974    Phil Esposito, Boston
1975–76    Bobby Clarke, Philadelphia
1977–78    Guy Lafleur, Montreal
1979    Bryan Trottier, N.Y. Islanders
1980    Wayne Gretzky, Edmonton
1981    Wayne Gretzky, Edmonton
1982    Wayne Gretzky, Edmonton

## Vezina Trophy—Leading Goalkeeper

1956–60    Jacques Plante, Montreal
1961    Johnny Bower, Toronto
1962    Jacques Plante, Montreal
1963    Glenn Hall, Chicago
1964    Charlie Hodge, Montreal
1965    Terry Sawchuk–Johnny Bower, Toronto
1966    Lorne Worsley–Charlie Hodge, Montreal
1967    Glenn Hall–Denis DeJordy, Chicago
1968    Lorne Worsley–Rogatien Vachon, Montreal
1969    Glenn Hall–Jacques Plante, St. Louis
1970    Tony Esposito, Chicago
1971    Ed Giacomin–Gilles Villemure, New York
1972    Tony Esposito–Gary Smith, Chicago
1973    Ken Dryden, Montreal
1974    Bernie Parent, Philadelphia, and Tony Esposito, Chicago
1975    Bernie Parent, Philadelphia
1976    Ken Dryden, Montreal
1977–79    Ken Dryden–Michel Larocque, Montreal
1980    Bob Sauve–Don Edwards, Buffalo
1981    Richard Sevigny, Denis Herron and Michel Larocque, Montreal
1982    Billy Smith, New York Islanders

## James Norris Trophy—Defenseman

1954    Red Kelly, Detroit
1955–58    Doug Harvey, Montreal
1959    Tom Johnson, Montreal
1960–62    Doug Harvey, Montreal, New York (62)
1963–65    Pierre Pilote, Chicago
1966    Jacques Laperriere, Montreal
1967    Harry Howell, New York
1968–75    Bobby Orr, Boston
1976    Denis Potvin, N.Y. Islanders
1977    Larry Robinson, Montreal
1978    Denis Potvin, N.Y. Islanders
1980    Larry Robinson, Montreal
1981    Randy Carlyle, Pittsburgh
1982    Doug Wilson, Chicago

## Lady Byng Trophy—Sportsmanship

1960    Don McKenney, Boston
1961    Red Kelly, Detroit
1962–63    Dave Keon, Toronto
1964    Ken Wharram, Chicago
1965    Bobby Hull, Chicago
1966    Alex Delvecchio, Detroit
1967–68    Stan Mikita, Chicago
1969    Alex Delvecchio, Detroit
1970    Phil Goyette, St. Louis
1971    John Bucyk, Boston
1972    Jean Ratelle, New York
1973    Gil Perreault, Buffalo
1974    John Buyck, Boston
1975    Marcel Dionne, Detroit
1976    Jean Ratelle, N.Y. Rangers–Boston
1977    Marcel Dionne, Los Angeles
1978    Butch Goring, Los Angeles
1979    Bob MacMillan, Atlanta
1980    Wayne Gretzky, Edmonton
1981    Rick Kehoe, Pittsburgh
1982    Rick Middleton, Boston

## Calder Trophy—Rookie

1962    Bobby Rousseau, Montreal
1963    Kent Douglas, Toronto
1964    Jacques Laperriere, Montreal
1965    Roger Crozier, Detroit
1966    Brit Selby, Toronto
1967    Bobby Orr, Boston
1968    Derek Sanderson, Boston
1969    Danny Grant, Minnesota
1970    Tony Esposito, Chicago
1971    Gilbert Perreault, Buffalo
1972    Ken Dryden, Montreal
1973    Steve Vickers, New York Rangers
1974    Denis Potvin, N.Y. Islanders
1975    Eric Vail, Atlanta
1976    Bryan Trottier, N.Y. Islanders
1977    Willi Plett, Atlanta
1978    Mike Bossy, N.Y. Islanders
1979    Bobby Smith, Minnesota
1980    Ray Bourque, Boston
1981    Peter Stastny, Quebec
1982    Dale Hawerchuk, Winnipeg

## Art Ross Trophy—Leading scorer

1955    Bernie Geoffrion, Montreal
1956    Jean Beliveau, Montreal
1957    Gordie Howe, Detroit
1958–59    Dickie Moore, Montreal
1960    Bobby Hull, Chicago
1961    Bernie Geoffrion, Montreal
1962    Bobby Hull, Chicago
1963    Gordie Howe, Detroit
1964–65    Stan Mikita, Chicago
1966    Bobby Hull, Chicago
1967–68    Stan Mikita, Chicago
1969    Phil Esposito, Boston
1970    Bobby Orr, Boston
1971–74    Phil Esposito, Boston
1975    Bobby Orr, Boston
1976–78    Guy Lafleur, Montreal
1979    Bryan Trottier, N.Y. Islanders
1980    Marcel Dionne, Los Angeles
1981    Wayne Gretzky, Edmonton
1982    Wayne Gretzky, Edmonton

## N.H.L. CHAMPIONS
### Prince of Wales Trophy

1939    Boston
1940    Boston
1941    Boston
1942    New York
1943    Detroit
1944–47    Montreal
1948    Toronto
1948–55    Detroit
1956    Montreal
1957    Detroit
1958–62    Montreal
1963    Toronto
1964    Montreal
1965    Detroit
1966    Montreal
1967    Chicago

### Eastern Division

1968–69    Montreal
1970    Chicago
1971    Boston
1972    Boston
1973    Montreal
1974    Boston

| Prince of Wales Conference | |
|---|---|
| 1975 | Buffalo |
| 1976–79 | Montreal |
| 1980 | Buffalo |
| 1981 | Montreal |
| 1982 | New York Islanders |

**CAMPBELL BOWL**
**Western Division**

| 1968 | Philadelphia |
|---|---|
| 1969 | St. Louis |
| 1970 | St. Louis |
| 1971–73 | Chicago |
| 1974 | Philadelphia |

**Clarence Campbell Conference**

| 1975 | Philadelphia |
|---|---|
| 1976–77 | Philadelphia |
| 1978–79 | N.Y. Islanders |
| 1980 | Philadelphia |
| 1981 | New York Islanders |
| 1982 | Edmonton |

# NATIONAL HOCKEY LEAGUE
## Final Standing of the Clubs—1981–1982

### PRINCE OF WALES CONFERENCE
**Patrick Division**

| | W | L | T | GF | GA | Pts |
|---|---|---|---|---|---|---|
| New York Islanders | 54 | 16 | 10 | 385 | 250 | 118 |
| New York Rangers | 39 | 27 | 14 | 316 | 306 | 92 |
| Philadelphia Flyers | 38 | 31 | 11 | 325 | 313 | 87 |
| Pittsburgh Penguins | 31 | 36 | 13 | 310 | 337 | 75 |
| Washington Capitals | 26 | 41 | 13 | 319 | 338 | 65 |

**Adams Division**

| | W | L | T | GF | GA | Pts |
|---|---|---|---|---|---|---|
| Montreal Canadiens | 46 | 17 | 17 | 360 | 223 | 109 |
| Boston Bruins | 43 | 27 | 10 | 323 | 285 | 96 |
| Buffalo Sabres | 39 | 26 | 15 | 307 | 273 | 93 |
| Quebec Nordiques | 33 | 31 | 16 | 356 | 345 | 82 |
| Hartford Whalers | 21 | 41 | 18 | 264 | 351 | 60 |

### CLARENCE CAMPBELL CONFERENCE
**Norris Division**

| | W | L | T | GF | GA | Pts |
|---|---|---|---|---|---|---|
| Minnesota North Stars | 37 | 23 | 20 | 346 | 288 | 94 |
| Winnipeg Jets | 33 | 33 | 14 | 319 | 332 | 80 |
| St. Louis Blues | 32 | 40 | 8 | 315 | 349 | 72 |
| Chicago Black Hawks | 30 | 38 | 12 | 332 | 363 | 72 |
| Toronto Maple Leafs | 20 | 44 | 16 | 298 | 380 | 56 |
| Detroit Red Wings | 21 | 47 | 12 | 271 | 350 | 54 |

**Smythe Division**

| | W | L | T | GF | GA | Pts |
|---|---|---|---|---|---|---|
| Edmonton Oilers | 48 | 17 | 15 | 417 | 295 | 111 |
| Vancouver Canucks | 30 | 33 | 17 | 290 | 286 | 77 |
| Calgary Flames | 29 | 34 | 17 | 334 | 345 | 75 |
| Los Angeles Kings | 24 | 41 | 15 | 314 | 369 | 63 |
| Colorado Rockies | 18 | 49 | 13 | 241 | 362 | 49 |

## Stanley Cup Playoffs—1982

**Preliminary Round**

New York Islanders defeated Pittsburgh Penguins, 3 games to 2
New York Rangers defeated Philadelphia Flyers, 3 games to 1
Quebec Nordiques defeated Montreal Canadiens, 3 games to 2
Boston Bruins defeated Buffalo Sabres, 3 games to 1
Vancouver Canucks defeated Calgary Flames, 3 games to 0
Chicago Black Hawks defeated Minnesota North Stars, 3 games to 1
St. Louis Blues defeated Winnipeg Jets, 3 games to 1
Los Angeles Kings defeated Edmonton Oilers, 3 games to 2

**Quarterfinal Round**

New York Islanders defeated New York Rangers, 4 games to 2
Chicago defeated St. Louis, 4 games to 2
Vancouver defeated Los Angeles, 4 games to 1
Quebec defeated Boston, 4 games to 3

**Semifinal Round**

New York Islanders defeated Quebec, 4 games to 0
April 27—New York 4, Quebec 1[1]
April 29—New York 5, Quebec 2[1]
May 1—New York 5, Quebec 4 (overtime)
May 4—New York 4, Quebec 2
1. At Nassau Coliseum, Uniondale, New York.
Vancouver defeated Chicago, 4 games to 1
April 27—Vancouver 2, Chicago 1 (2 overtimes)[1]
April 29—Chicago 4, Vancouver 1[1]
May 1—Vancouver 4, Chicago 3
May 4—Vancouver 5, Chicago 3
May 6—Vancouver 6, Chicago 2[1]
1. At Chicago.

**Championship**

New York Islanders defeated Vancouver, 4 games to 0
May 8—New York 6, Vancouver 5 (overtime)[1]
May 11—New York 6, Vancouver 4[1]
May 13—New York 3, Vancouver 0

May 16—New York 3, Vancouver 1
1. At Nassau Coliseum, Uniondale, New York.

## N.H.L. LEADING SCORERS—1981–1982

| | GP | G | A | Pts |
|---|---|---|---|---|
| Wayne Gretzky, Edmonton | 80 | 92 | 120 | 212 |
| Mike Bossy, New York Islanders | 80 | 64 | 83 | 147 |
| Peter Stastny, Quebec | 80 | 46 | 93 | 139 |
| Dennis Maruk, Washington | 80 | 60 | 76 | 136 |
| Bryan Trottier, N.Y. Islanders | 80 | 50 | 79 | 129 |
| Denis Savard, Chicago | 80 | 32 | 87 | 119 |
| Marcel Dionne, Los Angeles | 78 | 50 | 67 | 117 |
| Bobby Smith, Minnesota | 80 | 43 | 71 | 114 |
| Dino Ciccarelli, Minnesota | 76 | 55 | 52 | 107 |
| Dave Taylor, Los Angeles | 78 | 39 | 67 | 106 |
| Glenn Anderson, Edmonton | 80 | 38 | 67 | 105 |
| Dale Hawerchuk, Winnipeg | 80 | 45 | 58 | 103 |
| Mike Rogers, New York Rangers | 80 | 38 | 65 | 103 |
| Neal Broten, Minnesota | 73 | 38 | 59 | 97 |
| Real Cloutier, Quebec | 67 | 37 | 60 | 97 |
| Rick Middleton, Boston | 75 | 51 | 43 | 94 |
| John Tonelli, N.Y. Islanders | 80 | 35 | 58 | 93 |
| Barry Pederson, Boston | 80 | 44 | 48 | 92 |
| Ken Linseman, Philadelphia | 79 | 24 | 68 | 92 |
| Bernie Federko, St. Louis | 74 | 30 | 62 | 92 |
| Morris Lukowich, Winnipeg | 77 | 43 | 49 | 92 |
| Blaine Stoughton, Hartford | 80 | 52 | 39 | 91 |
| Brian Propp, Philadelphia | 80 | 44 | 47 | 91 |

## N.H.L. ALL-STAR TEAMS—1982

| First Team | Pos. | Second Team |
|---|---|---|
| Billy Smith, New York Islanders | G | Grant Fuhr, Edmonton |
| Doug Wilson, Chicago | D | Paul Coffey, Edmonton |
| Ray Bourque, Boston | D | Brian Engblom, Montreal |
| Wayne Gretzky, | C | Bryan Trottier, |

| Edmonton Mark Messier, | LW | New York Islanders John Tonelli, |
|---|---|---|
| Edmonton Mike Bossy, New York Islanders | RW | New York Islanders Rick Middleton, Boston |

## OTHER N.H.L. AWARDS—1982

Selke (Best defensive forward)—Steve Kasper, Boston
Smythe (Most valuable in playoffs)—Mike Bossy, New York Islanders

## N.H.L. LEADING GOALTENDERS—1981–1982

| | G | Min | GA | Avg |
|---|---|---|---|---|
| Denis Herron, Montreal | 27 | 1,547 | 68 | 2.64 |
| Rick Wamsley, Montreal | 38 | 2,206 | 101 | 2.75 |
| Bill Smith, New York Islanders | 46 | 2,685 | 133 | 2.97 |
| Roland Melanson, N.Y. Islanders | 36 | 2,115 | 114 | 3.23 |
| Grant Fuhr, Edmonton | 48 | 2,847 | 157 | 3.31 |
| Richard Brodeur, Vancouver | 52 | 3,010 | 168 | 3.35 |
| Mario Baron, Boston | 44 | 2,515 | 144 | 3.44 |
| Gilles Meloche, Minnesota | 51 | 3,026 | 175 | 3.47 |
| Don Edwards, Buffalo | 62 | 3,500 | 205 | 3.51 |
| Ed Mio, New York Rangers | 25 | 1,500 | 89 | 3.56 |
| Rogie Vachon, Boston | 38 | 2,165 | 132 | 3.66 |
| Don Beaupre, Minnesota | 29 | 1,634 | 101 | 3.71 |
| Pete Peeters, Philadelphia | 44 | 2,591 | 160 | 3.71 |
| Steve Weeks, N.Y. Rangers | 49 | 2,852 | 179 | 3.77 |

**Top Team Averages**

| | | | | |
|---|---|---|---|---|
| Montreal (Holden, Herron, Wamsley Sevigny) | 80 | 4,800 | 223 | 2.79 |
| New York Islanders (Smith, Melanson) | 80 | 4,800 | 250 | 3.13 |

## N.H.L. CAREER SCORING LEADERS

(Listed in order of total points scored; figures in parentheses indicate the top 10 in goals scored)

| | Yrs | Games | G | A | Pts |
|---|---|---|---|---|---|
| Gordie Howe (1) | 26 | 1,767 | 801 | 1,049 | 1,850 |
| Phil Esposito (2) | 18 | 1,282 | 717 | 873 | 1,590 |
| Stan Mikita (6) | 22 | 1,394 | 541 | 926 | 1,467 |
| John Bucyk (4) | 23 | 1,540 | 556 | 813 | 1,369 |
| Alex Delvecchio | 24 | 1,549 | 456 | 825 | 1,281 |
| Jean Ratelle (9) | 21 | 1,281 | 491 | 776 | 1,267 |
| Norm Ullman (10) | 20 | 1,410 | 490 | 739 | 1,229 |
| Jean Beliveau (8) | 20 | 1,125 | 507 | 712 | 1,219 |
| Marcel Dionne[1] | 11 | 857 | 488 | 692 | 1,180 |
| Bobby Hull (3) | 16 | 1,063 | 610 | 560 | 1,170 |
| Frank Mahovlich (7) | 18 | 1,181 | 533 | 570 | 1,103 |
| Guy Lafleur[1] | 11 | 794 | 459 | 636 | 1,095 |
| Bobby Clarke[1] | 13 | 991 | 318 | 747 | 1,065 |
| Henri Richard | 20 | 1,256 | 358 | 688 | 1,046 |
| Rod Gilbert | 18 | 1,065 | 406 | 615 | 1,021 |
| Gil Perreault[1] | 12 | 871 | 391 | 610 | 1,001 |
| Dave Keon[1] | 18 | 1,296 | 396 | 590 | 986 |
| Andy Bathgate | 17 | 1,069 | 349 | 624 | 973 |
| Maurice Richard (5) | 18 | 978 | 544 | 421 | 965 |
| Darryl Sittler[1] | 12 | 879 | 403 | 545 | 948 |
| Bobby Orr | 12 | 657 | 207 | 645 | 915 |

1. Still active in N.H.L.

## AMATEUR LEAGUES—1982

International League—Regular season: Toledo. Playoffs: Toledo defeated Saginaw, 4 games to 1, in final.
Western League—Regular season: Eastern Division: Lethbridge; Western Division: Portland. Playoffs: Portland defeated Regina, 4 games to 1, in final.
Ontario Major League—Regular season: Leyden Division: Ottawa; Emms Division: Kitchener. Playoffs: Kitchener defeated Ottawa 9-1 in points (Kitchener won 4 games and 1 was tied in final 5–game series).
Quebec Major League—Regular season: Sherbrooke. Playoffs: Sherbrooke defeated T-Rivieres, 4 games to 0, in final.
Memorial Cup—Kitchener.

## MINOR LEAGUE HOCKEY CHAMPIONS
### American League—1982

| | W | L | T | GF | GA | Pts |
|---|---|---|---|---|---|---|
| **Northern Division** | | | | | | |
| New Brunswick Hawks | 48 | 21 | 11 | 338 | 227 | 107 |
| Maine Mariners | 47 | 26 | 7 | 325 | 272 | 101 |
| Nova Scotia Voyageurs | 35 | 35 | 10 | 330 | 313 | 80 |
| Springfield Indians | 32 | 43 | 5 | 278 | 319 | 69 |
| Fredericton Express | 20 | 55 | 5 | 275 | 408 | 45 |
| **Southern Division** | | | | | | |
| Binghamton Dusters | 46 | 28 | 6 | 329 | 266 | 98 |
| Rochester Americans | 40 | 31 | 9 | 325 | 286 | 89 |
| New Haven Nighthawks | 39 | 33 | 8 | 292 | 276 | 86 |
| Hershey Bears | 36 | 38 | 6 | 316 | 347 | 78 |
| Adirondack Red Wings | 34 | 37 | 9 | 299 | 285 | 77 |
| Erie Blades | 22 | 52 | 6 | 317 | 425 | 50 |

**CALDER CUP PLAYOFFS**
**Quarterfinals**

New Brunswick defeated Adirondack, 3 games to 2
Nova Scotia defeated Maine, 3 games to 1
Binghamton defeated Hershey, 3 games to 2
Rochester defeated New Haven, 3 games to 1

**Semifinals**

Binghamton defeated Rochester, 4 games to 1
New Brunswick defeated Nova Scotia, 4 games to 1

**Final**

New Brunswick defeated Binghamton, 4 games to 1

### Central League—1981–1982

| | W | L | T | GF | GA | Pts |
|---|---|---|---|---|---|---|
| **Northern Division** | | | | | | |
| Salt Lake City Golden Eagles | 47 | 30 | 3 | 368 | 329 | 97 |
| Cincinnati Tigers | 46 | 30 | 4 | 375 | 340 | 96 |
| Indianapolis Checkers | 42 | 33 | 5 | 319 | 259 | 89 |
| Nashville South Stars | 41 | 35 | 4 | 313 | 319 | 86 |
| **South Division** | | | | | | |
| Wichita Wind | 44 | 33 | 3 | 343 | 289 | 91 |
| Tulsa Oilers | 43 | 36 | 1 | 355 | 324 | 87 |
| Dallas Black Hawks | 37 | 37 | 6 | 394 | 382 | 80 |
| Oklahoma City Stars | 25 | 54 | 1 | 300 | 397 | 51 |
| Fort Worth Texans | 20 | 57 | 3 | 273 | 401 | 43 |

**ADAMS CUP PLAYOFFS**
**Semifinals**

Dallas defeated Salt Lake City, 4 games to 2
Indianapolis defeated Wichita, 4 games to 0

**Final**

Indianapolis defeated Dallas, 4 games to 2

## COLLEGE CHAMPIONS—1982

N.C.A.A. Division I (Providence, R.I.)—Final: North Dakota defeated Wisconsin, 5–2. Third place: Northeastern defeated New Hampshire, 10–4. Semifinals: North Dakota defeated Northeastern, 6–2; Wisconsin defeated New Hampshire, 5–0.

E.CA.C. Division I—Final: Northeastern defeated Harvard, 5–2. Semifinals: Northeastern defeated New Hampshire, 4–2; Harvard defeated Clarkson, 7–1. Quarterfinals: Clarkson defeated Colgate, 7–4; Northeastern defeated St. Lawrence, 5–3; New Hampshire defeated Providence, 4–2; Harvard defeated Boston College, 2–0.

C.C.H.A.—Final: Michigan State defeated Notre Dame, 4–1. Third place: Bowling Green defeated Michigan Tech, 2–1. Semifinals: Notre Dame defeated Bowling Green, 8–5; Michigan State defeated Michigan Tech, 3–2.

W.C.H.A.—Final: Wisconsin defeated North Dakota in two–game total–goals series, 12–1.

# BOWLING

## AMERICAN BOWLING CONGRESS CHAMPIONS

| Year | Singles | All-events | Year | Singles | All-events |
|------|---------|------------|------|---------|------------|
| 1959 | Ed Lubanski | Ed Lubanski | 1971 | Al Cohn | Al Cohn |
| 1960 | Paul Kulbaga | Vince Lucci | 1972 | Bill Pointer | Mac Lowry |
| 1961 | Lyle Spooner | Luke Karen | 1973 | Ed Thompson | Ron Woolet |
| 1962 | Andy Renaldo | Billy Young | 1974 | Gene Krause | Bob Hart |
| 1963 | Fred Delello | Bus Owalt | 1975 | Jim Setser | Bobby Meadows |
| 1964 | Jim Stefanich | Les Zikes, Jr. | 1976 | Mike Putzer | Jim Lindquist |
| 1965 | Ken Roeth | Tom Hathaway | 1977 | Frank Gadaleto | Bud Debenham |
| 1966 | Don Chapman | John Wilcox | 1978 | Rich Mersek | Chris Cobus |
| 1967 | Frank Perry | Gary Lewis | 1979 | Rick Peters | Bob Basacchi |
| 1968 | Wayne Kowalski | Vince Mazzanti | 1980 | Mike Eaton | Steve Fehr |
| 1969 | Greg Campbell | Eddie Jackson | 1981 | Rob Vital | Rod Toft |
| 1970 | Jake Yoder | Mike Berlin | 1982 | Bruce Bohm | Rich Wonders |

## PROFESSIONAL BOWLERS ASSOCIATION

### National Championship Tournament

| | | | | | | | |
|------|------|------|------|------|------|------|------|
| 1960 | Don Carter | 1966 | Wayne Zahn | 1972 | Johnny Guenther | 1978 | Warren Nelson |
| 1961 | Dave Soutar | 1967 | Dave Davis | 1973 | Earl Anthony | 1979 | Mike Aulby |
| 1962 | Carmen Salvino | 1968 | Wayne Zahn | 1974 | Earl Anthony | 1980 | Johnny Petraglia |
| 1963 | Billy Hardwick | 1969 | Mike McGrath | 1975 | Earl Anthony | 1981 | Earl Anthony |
| 1964 | Bob Strampe | 1970 | Mike McGrath | 1976 | Paul Colwell | 1982 | Earl Anthony |
| 1965 | Dave Davis | 1971 | Mike Lemongello | 1977 | Tommy Hudson | | |

## BOWLING PROPRIETORS' ASSOCIATION OF AMERICA—MEN

### United States Open[1]

| | | | | | | | |
|------|------|------|------|------|------|------|------|
| 1971 | Mike Lemongello | 1974 | Larry Laub | 1977 | Johnny Petraglia | 1980 | Steve Martin |
| 1972 | Don Johnson | 1975 | Steve Neff | 1978 | Nelson Burton, Jr. | 1981 | Marshall Holman |
| 1973 | Mike McGrath | 1976 | Paul Moser | 1979 | Joe Berardi | 1982 | Dave Husted |

1. Replaced All-Star tournament and is rolled as part of B.P.A. tour.

## WOMEN'S INTERNATIONAL BOWLING CONGRESS CHAMPIONS

| Year | Singles | All-events | Year | Singles | All-events |
|------|---------|------------|------|---------|------------|
| 1959 | Mae Bolt | Pat McBride | 1971 | Mary Scruggs | Lorrie Nichols |
| 1960 | Marge McDaniels | Judy Roberts | 1972 | D. D. Jacobson | Mildred Martorella |
| 1961 | Elaine Newton | Evelyn Teal | 1973 | Bobby Buffaloe | Toni Calvery |
| 1962 | Martha Hoffman | Flossie Argent | 1974 | Shirley Garms | Judy C. Soutar |
| 1963 | Dot Wilkinson | Helen Shablis | 1975 | Barbara Leicht | Virginia Norton |
| 1964 | Jean Havlish | Jean Havlish | 1976 | Bev Shonk | Betty Morris |
| 1965 | Doris Rudell | Donna Zimmerman | 1977 | Akiko Yamaga | Akiko Yamaga |
| 1966 | Gloria Bouvia | Kate Helbig | 1978 | Mae Bolt | Annese Kelly |
| 1967 | Gloria Paeth | Carol Miller | 1979 | Betty Morris | Betty Morris |
| 1968 | Norma Parks | Susie Reichley | 1980 | Betty Morris | Cheryl Robinson |
| 1969 | Joan Bender | Helen Duval | 1981 | Virginia Norton | Virginia Norton |
| 1970 | Dorothy Fothergill | Dorothy Fothergill | 1982 | Gracie Freeman | Aleta Rzepecki |

## WIBC QUEENS TOURNAMENT CHAMPIONS

| | | | | | | | |
|------|------|------|------|------|------|------|------|
| 1961 | Janet Harman | 1967 | Mildred Martorella | 1973 | Dorothy Fothergill | 1979 | Donna Adamek |
| 1962 | Dorothy Wilkinson | 1968 | Phyllis Massey | 1974 | Judy Soutar | 1980 | Donna Adamek |
| 1963 | Irene Monterosso | 1969 | Ann Feigel | 1975 | Cindy Powell | 1981 | Katsuko Sugimoto |
| 1964 | D.D. Jacobson | 1970 | Mildred Martorella | 1976 | Pamela Buckner | 1982 | Katsuko Sugimoto |
| 1965 | Betty Kuczynski | 1971 | Mildred Martorella | 1977 | Dana Stewart | | |
| 1966 | Judy Lee | 1972 | Dorothy Fothergill | 1978 | Loa Boxberger | | |

## BOWLING PROPRIETORS' ASSOCIATION OF AMERICA—WOMEN

### United States Open[1]

| | | | | | |
|---|---|---|---|---|---|
| 1971 | Paula Carter | 1974 | Pat Costello (Calif.) | 1977 | Betty Morris | 1980 | Pat Costello (Calif.) |
| 1972 | Lorrie Nichols | 1975 | Paula Carter | 1978 | Donna Adamek | 1981 | Donna Adamek |
| 1973 | Mildred Martorella | 1976 | Patty Costello (Pa.) | 1979 | Diana Silva | 1982 | Shinobu Saitoh |

1. Replaced All-Star tournament.

### AMERICAN BOWLING CONGRESS TOURNAMENT—1982
(Baltimore, Md., Feb. 6-May 16, 1982)

**Regular Division**

| | |
|---|---|
| Singles—Bruce Bohm, Chicago | 748 |
| Doubles—Rich Wonders, Racine, Wis., and Darold Meisel, Milwaukee | 1,364 |
| All events—Rich Wonders, Racine, Wis. | 2,076 |
| Team—Carl's Bowlers Paddock, Cincinnati | 3,268 |
| Team All events—Kender No. 1, Milwaukee | 9,498 |
| Booster Team—Charlotte B.A. No. 1, Charlotte, N.C. | 2,734 |

### MASTERS TOURNAMENT—1982
(Baltimore, Md., May 11-15, 1982)

Singles—Joe Berardi, Brooklyn, N.Y. (defeated Ted Hannahs, Zanesville, Ohio, 236–216, in final)
Third place—Sam Maccarone, Glassboro, N.J.
Fourth place—Tom Baker, Buffalo, N.Y.
Fifth place—Steve Fehr, Cincinnati

### WOMEN'S INTERNATIONAL BOWLING CONGRESS—1982
(St. Louis, Mo., April 3-June 18, 1982)

**Open Division**

| | |
|---|---|
| Singles—Gracie Freeman, Alexandria, Va. | 652 |
| Doubles—Tie between Pat Costello, Fremont, Calif., and Donna Adamek, Duarte, Calif., and Shirley Hintz, Merritt Island, Fla., and | |
| Lisa Wrathgeber, Palmetto, Fla. | 1,264 |
| All events—Aleta Rzepecki, Detroit, Mich. | 1,905 |
| Team—Zavakos Realtors, Dayton, Ohio | 2,961 |

**Division I**

| | |
|---|---|
| Singles—Jan Sammon, Davenport, Iowa | 650 |
| Doubles—Bridgett Basiak, Chesterton, Ind., and Donna Oldaker, Lake Station, Ind. | 1,211 |
| All events—Elmere Harrison, Chalmette, La. | 1,770 |
| Team—Century Lanes, Hampton, Va. | 2,856 |

**Division II**

| | |
|---|---|
| Singles—Sammie Gray, Martin, Tenn. | 582 |
| Doubles—Gloria Tayek, Crystal Lake, Ill., and Gayle Comerer, Elgin, Ill. | 1,067 |
| All events—Brenda Draper, Auburn, Neb. | 1,672 |
| Team—Baldwin State Bank, Baldwin City, Kan. | 2,526 |

### WIBC QUEENS TOURNAMENT—1982

Winner—Katsuko Sugimoto, Tokyo, Japan
(defeated Nikki Giamulias, Vallajo, Calif., in final)

### COLLEGIATE
**Association of College Unions–International**
(St. Louis, April 15, 1982)

| | |
|---|---|
| Singles—Melisa Day, Ball State | 575 |
| Doubles—Melisa Day, Ball State, and Donna Kolb, Western Illinois | 1,118 |
| All events—Melisa Day, Ball State | 1,698 |

# WEIGHT LIFTING

## U.S. WEIGHTLIFTING FEDERATION MEN'S NATIONAL CHAMPIONSHIPS
(Glenbrook, Ill., May 29-30, 1982)

| | Snatch | C&J[1] | Total[2] |
|---|---|---|---|
| 114 lb—Brian Okada, Wailuku, Hawaii | 72.5 | 97.5 | 170 |
| 123 lb—Albert Hood, Los Angeles | 97.5 | 117.5 | 215 |
| 132 lb—Philip Sanderson, Billings, Mont. | 105 | 135 | 240 |
| 148 lb—Don Abrahamson, San Jose, Calif. | 127.5 | 157.5 | 285 |
| 165 lb—Cal Schake, Butler, Pa. | 147.5 | 167.5 | 315 |
| 181 lb—Curt White, Colorado Springs, Colo | 150 | 172.5 | 322.5 |
| 198 lb—Kevin Winter, San Jose, Calif. | 155 | 185 | 340 |
| 220 lb—Ken Clark, Pacifica, Calif. | 157.5 | 210 | 367.5 |
| 242 lb—Jeff Nichels, Chicago | 182.5[3] | 217.5 | 400 |
| Over 242 lb—Mario Martinez, San Francisco | 170 | 210 | 380 |

1. Clean and Jerk. 2. All results in kilograms. 3. American record.

## WOMEN'S NATIONAL CHAMPIONSHIPS
(St. Charles Park District, St. Charles, Ill., April 4, 1982)

| | Snatch | C&J[1] | Total[2] |
|---|---|---|---|
| 97 lb—Pam Bickler, Milwaukee, Wis. | 32.5 | 42.5 | 75 |
| 105.8 lb—Michelle Evris, Garfield, Ohio | 47.5 | 60 | 107.5 |
| 114.5 lb—Rachel Silverman, Berkeley, Calif. | 52.5 | 65 | 117.5 |
| 123 lb—Mary Beth Cervenak, U.S. Air Force Base, Colo. | 52.5 | 72.5 | 125 |
| 132 lb—Diane Redgate, Delaware | 47.5 | 62.5 | 110 |
| 148¾ lb—Judy Glenney, Farmington, N.M. | 77.5 | 90 | 167.5 |
| 165¼ lb—Karen Tarter, Harrison, N.Y. | 62.5 | 85 | 147.5 |
| 181¾ lb—Mary Hyden, Jefferson City, Mo. | 60 | 80 | 140 |
| Over 181¾ lb—Lorna Griffin, Huntington Beach, Calif. | 75 | 100 | 175 |

1. Clean and Jerk. 2. All results in kilograms.

# SKIING

## ALPINE WORLD CUP OVERALL WINNERS

| | Men | Women | Team |
|---|---|---|---|
| 1967 | Jean-Claude Killy, France | Nancy Greene, Canada | France |
| 1968 | Jean-Claude Killy, France | Nancy Greene, Canada | France |
| 1969 | Karl Schranz, Austria | Gertrude Gabl, Austria | Austria |
| 1970 | Karl Schranz, Austria | Michel Jacot, France | France |
| 1971 | Gustavo Thoeni, Italy | Annemarie Proell, Austria | France |
| 1972 | Gustavo Thoeni, Italy | Annemarie Proell, Austria | France |
| 1973 | Gustavo Thoeni, Italy | Annemarie Proell Moser, Austria | Austria |
| 1974 | Piero Gros, Italy | Annemarie Proell Moser, Austria | Austria |
| 1975 | Gustavo Thoeni, Italy | Annemarie Proell Moser, Austria | Austria |
| 1976 | Ingemar Stenmark, Sweden | Rosi Mittermaier, West Germany | Austria |
| 1977 | Ingemar Stenmark, Sweden | Lise-Marie Morerod, Switzerland | Austria |
| 1978 | Ingemar Stenmark, Sweden | Hanni Wenzel, Liechtenstein | Austria |
| 1979 | Peter Luescher, Switzerland | Annemarie Proell Moser, Austria | Austria |
| 1980 | Andreas Wenzel, Liechtenstein | Hanni Wenzel, Liechtenstein | Liechtenstein |
| 1981 | Phil Mahre, United States | Marie-Theres Nadig, Switzerland | Switzerland |
| 1982 | Phil Mahre, United States | Erika Hess, Switzerland | Austria |

## UNITED STATES CHAMPIONSHIPS—1982

### ALPINE

**Men's Events**

| | |
|---|---|
| Downhill—Steve Hegg, Olympic Valley, Calif. | 1:54.05 |
| Slalom—Francois Jodoin, Ste. Adele, Quebec, Canada | 1:33.90 |
| Leading American—Felix McGrath, Norwich, Vt. | 1:34.21 |
| Giant slalom—Canceled because of bad weather | |

**Women's Events**

| | |
|---|---|
| Downhill—Cindy Oak, Orchard Park, N.Y. | 1:15.58 |
| Slalom—Tara McKinney, Olympic Valley, Calif. | 1:29.91 |
| Giant slalom—Canceled because of bad weather | |

### NORDIC

**Men's Cross-Country**

| | |
|---|---|
| 15 kilometers—Bill Koch, Putney, Vt. | 47:11.18 |
| 30 kilometers—Stan Dunklee, Brattleboro, Vt. | 1:32:38.9 |
| 50 kilometers—Tim Caldwell, Putney, Vt. | 2:11:47.1 |
| Relay—East (Bruce Likely, Dan Simoneau, Howie Bean) | 1:33:23.3 |
| Veterans 10 km—Paul Daly | 30:31 |
| Veterans 30 km—Paul Daly | 1:43:28 |

**Women's Cross-Country**

| | |
|---|---|
| 5 kilometers—Lynn Spencer Galanes, Vermont | 18:56.5 |
| 10 kilometers—Lynn Spencer Galanes | 34:15.1 |
| 20 kilometers—Lynn Spencer Galanes | 58:25.1 |
| Relay—East (Leslie Bancroft, Beth Paxson, Lindsay Putnam) | 49:18.3 |
| Veterans 5 km—Linda Stetson, Pittsfield, Mass. | 21:09 |
| Veterans 15 km—Draha Strnad, Portchester, N.Y. | 1:06.38 |

### FREESTYLE

**Men's Event**

Ballet—Ian Edmondson, Grand Rapids, Mich.
Moguls—Frank Beddor III, Chanhassen, Minn.
Aerials—Wayne Hilterbrand, Salem, Ore.
Combined—Frank Beddor III

**Women's Events**

Ballet—Jan Bucher, Salt Lake City, Utah
Moguls—Hilary Engisch, Williston, Vt.
Aerials—Hayley Wolff, New York City
Combined—Hayley Wolff

## COLLEGIATE

### Men—N.C.A.A.

(Lake Placid, N.Y. March 6, 1982)

Slalom—Gale Shaw, Dartmouth
Giant Slalom—Seth Bayer, Colorado
Cross-country—Egil Nilsen, Colorado
Cross-country relay—Colorado
Team—Colorado

## WORLD CHAMPIONSHIPS—1982

### ALPINE

(Schladming, Austria, Jan. 31–Feb. 7, 1982)

**Men's Events**

| | |
|---|---|
| Downhill—Harti Weirather, Austria | 1:55.10 |
| Slalom—Ingemar Stenmark, Sweden | 1:48.48 |
| Giant slalom—Steve Mahre, Yakima, Wash. | 2:38.80 |
| Combined—Michel Vion, France | 12.64 pts |

**Women's Events**

| | |
|---|---|
| Downhill—Gerry Sorensen, Canada | 1:37.47 |
| Slalom—Erika Hess, Switzerland | 1:41.60 |
| Giant slalom—Erika Hess | 2:37.17 |
| Combined—Erika Hess | 8.99 pts |

### NORDIC

(Oslo, Norway, Feb. 17–27, 1982)

**Jumping**

| | |
|---|---|
| 70-meter—Armin Kogler, Austria (237 ft 11 in. and 241–2) | 249.3 pts |
| 90-meter—Matti Nykanen, Finland (355–9, 336–3) | 257.9 pts |

**Combined**

| | |
|---|---|
| 70-meter jump—Hubert Schwartz, West Germany | 221.7 pts |
| 15-km cross-country—Tom Sandberg, Norway | 40:06 |
| Combined—Tom Sandberg, Norway (13th in jump, 1st in run) | 426.600 pts |

**Men's Cross-Country**

| | |
|---|---|
| 15 kilometers—Oddvar Bra, Norway | 38:52.5 |
| 30 kilometers—Thomas Eriksson, Sweden | 1:21:52.3 |
| 50 kilometers—Thomas Wassberg, Sweden | 2:32:00.9 |
| 40-km relay—Norway and Soviet Union (tie) | 1:56:27.6 |

### Women's Cross-Country

| | |
|---|---|
| 5 kilometers—Berit Aunli, Norway | 14:30.2 |
| 10 kilometers—Berit Aunli, Norway | 29:25.9 |
| 20 kilometers—Raisa Smetanina, Soviet Union | 1:06:16.9 |
| 20–km relay—Norway | 1:02.15.9 |

## ALPINE WORLD CUP—1982

### Overall—Men

| | Pts |
|---|---|
| Phil Mahre, Yakima, Wash. | 309 |
| Ingemar Stenmark, Sweden | 211 |
| Steve Mahre, Yakima, Wash. | 183 |
| Peter Mueller, Switzerland | 132 |
| 8—Steve Podborski, Canada | 115 |

### Overall—Women

| | Pts |
|---|---|
| Erika Hess, Switzerland | 297 |
| Irene Epple, West Germany | 282 |
| Christin Cooper, Sun Valley, Idaho | 198 |
| Maria Epple, West Germany | 166 |
| 5—Cindy Nelson, Reno, Nev. | 158 |
| 9—Tamara McKinney, Olympic Valley, Calif. | 116 |

### Event Leaders—Men

| | Pts |
|---|---|
| Downhill—Steve Podborski,* Canada | 115 |
| 2—Peter Mueller, Switzerland | 115 |
| 3—Harti Weirather, Austria | 97 |
| *Won title with more finishes in top three in races. | |
| Slalom—Phil Mahre, Yakima, Wash. | 120 |
| 2—Ingemar Stenmark, Sweden | 110 |
| 3—Steve Mahre, Yakima, Wash. | 92 |
| Giant Slalom—Phil Mahre, Yakima, Wash. | 105 |
| 2—Ingemar Stenmark, Sweden | 101 |
| 3—Marc Girardelli, Luxembourg | 77 |
| 7—Steve Mahre, Yakima, Wash. | 66 |
| Combined—Phil Mahre, Yakima, Wash. | 75 |
| 2—Andreas Wenzel, Liechtenstein | 60 |
| 3—Evan Hole, Norway | 37 |

### Event Leaders—Women

| | Pts |
|---|---|
| Downhill—Marie Cecile Gros–Gaudenier, France | 87 |
| 2—Doris de Agostini, Switzerland | 84 |
| 3—Holly Flanders, Deerfield, N.H. | 84 |
| Slalom—Erika Hess, Switzerland | 125 |
| 2—Ursula Konzett, Liechtenstein | 100 |
| 3—Christin Cooper, Sun Valley, Idaho | 88 |
| Giant Slalom—Irene Epple, West Germany | 120 |
| 2—Maria Epple, West Germany | 110 |
| 3—Erika Hess, Switzerland | 105 |
| 4—Tamara McKinney, Olympic Valley, Calif. | 74 |
| 5—Christin Cooper, Sun Valley, Idaho | 68 |
| 7—Cindy Nelson, Reno, Nev. | 47 |
| Combined—Irene Epple, West Germany | 70 |
| 2—Erika Hess, Switzerland | 45 |
| 3—Lea Soelkner, Austria | 41 |

## NORDIC WORLD CUP—1982

### Overall-Men

| | Pts |
|---|---|
| Cross-country | |
| 1—Bill Koch, Guilford, Vt. | 121 |
| 2—Thomas Wassberg, Sweden | 114 |
| 3—Harri Kirvesniemi, Finland | 106 |
| Jumping | |
| 1—Armin Kogler, Austria | 189 |
| 2—Hubert Neuper, Austria | 174 |
| 3—Horst Bulau, Canada | 150 |

## ALPINE NATIONS CUP—1982

| | Pts |
|---|---|
| Overall—Austria | 1,492 |
| Switzerland | 1,423 |
| United States | 1,196 |
| West Germany | 677 |
| Italy | 547 |
| France | 526 |
| Liechtenstein | 447 |
| Canada | 433 |
| Sweden | 362 |
| Yugoslavia | 284 |

# WRESTLING

## A.A.U. NATIONAL CHAMPIONSHIPS—1982

### Freestyle

(Lincoln, Neb., April 29–May 1, 1982)

105.5 lb—Bill Rosado, Sunkist Kids
114.5 lb—Bob Weaver, New York Athletic Club
125.5 lb—Gene Mills, New York A.C.
136.5 lb—Lee Roy Smith, Cowboy Wrestling Club
149.5 lb—Andy Rein, Wisconsin Wrestling Club
163 lb—Lee Kemp, Wisconsin Wrestling Club
180.5 lb—Bruce Kinseth, Hawkeye Wrestling Club
198 lb—Bill Scherr, Nebraska Olympic Club
220 lb—Greg Gibson, United States Marines
Heavyweight—Bruce Baumgartner, New York A.C.
Team—New York A.C. (85 points)
Outstanding wrestler—Lee Roy Smith

### Greco-Roman

(Cincinnati, Ohio, May 7–8, 1982)

105.5 lb—T.J. Jones, United States Navy
114.5 lb—Mark Fuller, Little C Athletic Club
125.5 lb—Dan Mello, United States Marines
136.5 lb—Frank Famiano, Adirondack 3-Style Club
149.5 lb—Doug Yeats, Canada
163 lb—John Matthews, Michigan Wrestling Club
180.5 lb—Tom Press, Minnesota Wrestling Club
198 lb—Steve Fraser, Michigan Wrestling Club
220 lb—Greg Gibson, United States Marines
Heavyweight—Pete Lee, Grand Rapids, Mich.
Team—United States Marines (58 points)
Outstanding wrestler—Dan Mello

## WORLD CUP CHAMPIONSHIPS—1982

### Freestyle

(Toledo, Ohio, March 27–28, 1982)

105.5 lb—Adam Cuestas, United States
114.5 lb—Joe Gonzales, United States
125.5 lb—Sergei Beloglazov, Soviet Union
136.5 lb—Viktor Alexeev, Soviet Union
149.5 lb—Makhail Kharachura, Soviet Union
163 lb—Lee Kemp, United States
180.5 lb—Mark Schultz, United States
198 lb—Clark Davis, Canada
220 lb—Magomed Magomedov, Soviet Union
Heavyweight—Salman Chasimikov, Soviet Union
Team—United States; 2. Soviet Union. 3. Canada. 4. South Korea. 5. Africa.

# SPEED SKATING

## U.S. OUTDOOR CHAMPIONS

### Men

| | |
|---|---|
| 1959–60 | Ken Bartholomew |
| 1961 | Ed Rudolph |
| 1962 | Floyd Bedbury |
| 1963 | Tom Gray |
| 1964 | Neil Blatchford |
| 1965–66 | Rich Wurster |
| 1967 | Mike Passarella |
| 1968–70 | Peter Cefalu |
| 1971 | Jack Walters |
| 1972 | Barth Levy |
| 1973 | Mike Woods |
| 1974 | Leigh Barczewski, Mike Passarella |
| 1975 | Rich Wurster |
| 1976 | John Wurster |
| 1977 | Jim Chapin |
| 1978 | Bill Heinkel |
| 1979 | Erik Henriksen |
| 1980 | Greg Oly |
| 1981 | Tom Grannes |
| 1982 | Greg Oly |

### Women

| | |
|---|---|
| 1960 | Mary Novak |
| 1961 | Jean Ashworth |
| 1962 | Jean Omelenchuk |
| 1963 | Jean Ashworth |
| 1964 | Diane White |
| 1965 | Jean Omelenchuk |
| 1966 | Diane White |
| 1967 | Jean Ashworth |
| 1968 | Helen Lutsch |
| 1969 | Sally Blatchford |
| 1970–71 | Sheila Young |
| 1972 | Ruth Moore, Nancy Thorne |
| 1973 | Nancy Class |
| 1974 | Kris Garbe |
| 1975 | Nancy Swider |
| 1976 | Connie Carpenter |
| 1977 | Liz Crowe |
| 1978 | Paula Class, Betsy Davis |
| 1979 | Gretchen Byrnes |
| 1980 | Shari Miller |
| 1981 | Lisa Merrifield |
| 1982 | Lisa Merrifield |

## WORLD SPEED SKATING RECORDS

### Men

| Distance | Time | Skater | Place | Year |
|---|---|---|---|---|
| 500 m | 0:36.91 | Yevgeny Kulikov, U.S.S.R. | Alma–Ata, U.S.S.R. | 1981 |
| 1,000 m | 1:13.39 | Gaetan Boucher, Canada | Davos, Switzerland | 1981 |
| 1,500 m | 1:55.18 | Jan Egil Storholt, Norway | Medeo, U.S.S.R. | 1977 |
| 3,000 m | 4:04.01 | Eric Heiden, U.S. | Inzell, Austria | 1978 |
| 5,000 m | 6:54.66 | Aleksandr Baranov, U.S.S.R. | Alma-Ata, U.S.S.R. | 1982 |
| 10,000 m | 14:23.59 | Thomas Gustafsson, Sweden | Oslo, Norway | 1982 |

### Women

| Distance | Time | Skater | Place | Year |
|---|---|---|---|---|
| 500 m | 0:40.18 | Christa Rothenburger, E. Germany | Alma-Ata, U.S.S.R. | 1981 |
| 1,000 m | 1:20.81 | Natalya Petruseva, U.S.S.R. | Alma-Ata, U.S.S.R. | 1981 |
| 1,500 m | 2:05.39 | Natalya Petruseva, U.S.S.R. | Alma-Ata, U.S.S.R. | 1981 |
| 3,000 m | 4:21.70 | Gabi Schoenbrunn, E. Germany | Alma-Ata, U.S.S.R. | 1981 |

## WORLD CHAMPIONSHIPS—1982

### Men

(Assen, the Netherlands, Feb. 20–21, 1982)

| | |
|---|---|
| Champion—Hilbert van der Duim, Netherlands | 168.410 pts |
| 500 m—Gaetan Boucher, Canada | 0:38.53 |
| 1,500 m—Hilbert van der Duim | 2:00.59 |
| 5,000 m—Dmitri Bochkarev, Soviet Union | 7:13.64 |
| 10,000 m—Dmitri Bochkarev | 14:55.2 |

### Women

(Inzell, Germany, Feb. 13–14, 1982)

| | |
|---|---|
| Champion—Karin Busch, East Germany | 168.271 pts |
| 500 m—Karin Busch | 0:40.81 |
| 1,000 m—Karin Busch | 1:20.98 |
| 1,500 m—Karin Busch | 2:05.79 |
| 3,000 m—Andrea Schone, East Germany | 4:24.26 |

## WORLD SPRINT CHAMPIONSHIPS—1982

(Alkmaar, the Netherlands, Feb. 6–7, 1982)

| | |
|---|---|
| Men's champion—Sergei Khlebnikov, Soviet Union | 154.250 pts |
| Women's champion—Natalya Petruseva, Soviet Union | 167.985 pts |

## U.S. OUTDOOR CHAMPIONS

(St. Paul, Minn., Feb. 6–7, 1982)

Men—Greg Oly, Minneapolis, Minn.
Women—Lisa Merrifield, Butte, Mont.
Intermediate men—Michael Ralston, Streamwood, Ill.
Intermediate women—Bonnie Blair, Champaign, Ill.
Junior boys—David Silk, Butte, Mont.
Junior girls—Ann Hills, Shoreview, Minn.

## U.S. INDOOR CHAMPIONS

(St. Louis, Mo., March 13–14, 1982)

Men—Tie, Jack Mortell, Evanston, Ill., and Paul Jacobs, Park Ridge, Ill.
Women—Lydia Stephans, Northbrook, Ill.
Intermediate men—Andy Gabel, Northbrook, Ill.
Intermediate women—Lisa Parfitt, Alpena, Mich.
Junior boys—Marty Pierce, St. Francis, Wis.
Junior girls—Michelle Fang, Arlington Heights, Ill.

## NORTH AMERICAN OUTDOOR CHAMPIONS

(Lake Placid, N.Y., Feb. 13–14, 1982)

Men—Kevin O'Brien, Prince Edward Island
Women—Katie Class, St. Paul, Minn.
Intermediate men—Michael Ralston, Streamwood, Ill.
Intermediate women—Rhonda Reinke, Milwaukee, Wis.
Junior boys—Tony Meibock, Fairview Park, Ohio
Junior girls—Susan Auch, Manitoba, Canada

## NORTH AMERICAN INDOOR CHAMPIONS

(Sherbrooke, Quebec, March 27–28, 1982)

Men—Louis Baril, Quebec, Canada
Women—Susan Hellingwerf, Quebec, Canada
Intermediate men—Robert Tremblay, Quebec, Canada
Intermediate women—Tie, Lisa Parfitt, Alpena, Mich., and M-Josee Martin, Quebec, Canada
Junior boys—Benoit Lamarche, Quebec, Canada
Junior girls—Susan Auch, Manitoba, Canada

# SPORTS ORGANIZATIONS AND INFORMATION BUREAUS

**Amateur Athletic Union of the U.S.** 3400 West 86th St., Indianapolis, Indiana 46862

**Amateur Fencers League of America.** 601 Curtis St., Albany, Calif. 94706

**Amateur Hockey Association of the U.S.** 10 Lake Circle, Colorado Springs, Colo. 80906

**Amateur Skating Union of the U.S.** 4423 West Deming Place, Chicago, Ill. 60639

**Amateur Softball Association.** 2801 N.E. 50th St., P.O. Box 11437, Oklahoma City, Okla. 73111

**Amateur Trapshooting Association of America.** Vandalia, Ohio 45377

**American Amateur Baseball Congress.** 212 Plaza Building, 2855 W. Market St., Akron, Ohio 44313

**American Association (baseball).** P.O. Box 382, Wichita, Kan. 67201

**American Bowling Congress.** 5301 South 76th St., Greendale, Wis. 53129

**American Canoe Association.** P.O. Box 248, Lorton, Va. 22079

**American Hockey League.** 31 Elm St., Suite 533, Springfield, Mass. 01103

**American Horse Shows Association.** 527 Madison Ave., New York, N.Y. 10022

**American Kennel Club.** 51 Madison Ave., New York, N.Y. 10010

**American League (baseball).** 280 Park Ave., New York, N.Y. 10017

**American Motorcycle Association.** 33 Collingwood Rd., Westerville, Ohio, 43081

**American Power Boat Association.** 17640 East 9-Mile Rd., P.O. Box 377, East Detroit, Mich. 48021

**American Water Ski Association.** State Route 550 at Carl Floyd Road, P.O. Box 191, Winter Haven, Fla. 33880

**Association of Intercollegiate Athletics for Women.** 1201 16th St. N.W., Washington, D.C.

**Athletics Congress, The.** 3400 West 86th St., Indianapolis, Ind. 46268

**Baseball Commissioner.** 75 Rockefeller Plaza, New York, N.Y. 10019

**Baseball Hall of Fame.** Cooperstown, N.Y.

**Bowling Proprietors' Association of America.** P.O. Box 5802, Arlington, Texas 76011

**Central Hockey League.** 5740 Oakland Ave., St. Louis, Mo. 63110

**Championship Auto Racing Teams (CART).** 2655 Woodward Ave., Suite 275, Bloomfield Hills, Mich. 48013

**Eastern College Athletic Conference.** P.O. Box 3, Centerville, Mass. 02632

**Elias Sports Bureau.** 500 Fifth Ave., New York, N.Y. 10036

**Fish and Wildlife Service.** Department of the Interior, Washington, D.C. 20240

**Football Hall of Fame (college).** Kings Mills, Ohio 45034

**Football Hall of Fame (pro).** Canton, Ohio 44708

**Intercollegiate (Big Ten) Conference (1896).** 1111 Plaza Dr., Schaumburg, Ill. 60195

**International Amateur Athletic Federation.** 62 Upper Richmond Rd., Putney, London, SW15 2 SL, England

**International Game Fish Association.** 3000 East Las Olas Blvd., Fort Lauderdale, Fla. 33316

**International League (baseball).** Box 608, Grove City, Ohio 43123

**International Motor Sports Association.** P.O. Box 805, Fairfield, Conn. 06430

**International Olympic Committee.** Chateau de Vidy, Lausanne, Switzerland

**The Jockey Club.** 380 Madison Ave., New York, N.Y. 10017

**Ladies Professional Golf Association.** 919 Third Ave., New York, N.Y. 10022

**Little League Baseball.** Williamsport, Pa. 17701

**National Archery Association.** 1951 Geraldson Drive, Lancaster, Pa. 17601

**National Association for Girls and Women in Sports.** 1201 16th St. N.W., Washington, D.C.

**National Association of Amateur Oarsmen.** 4 Boathouse Row, Philadelphia, Pa. 19130

**National Association of Intercollegiate Athletics.** 1221 Baltimore St., Kansas City, Mo. 64105

**National Association of Professional Baseball Leagues (minors).** P.O. Box A, St. Petersburg, Fla. 33731

**National Association for Stock Car Auto Racing.** P.O. Box K, Daytona Beach, Fla. 32015

**National Baseball Congress.** Wichita, Kan. 67201

**National Basketball Association.** Olympic Tower, 645 Fifth Ave., New York, N.Y. 10022

**National Collegiate Athletic Association.** P.O. Box 1906, Shawnee Mission, Kan. 66222

**National Duck Pin Bowling Congress.** 711–14th St. N.W., Washington, D.C. 20005

**National Field Archery Association.** Rt. 2, Box 514, Redlands, Calif. 92373

**National Football Foundation.** 201 East 42nd St., New York, N.Y. 10017. *See also:* Football Hall of Fame (college)

**National Football League.** 410 Park Ave., New York, N.Y. 10022

**National Hockey League.** 922 Sun Life Bldg., Montreal, Que., Canada

**National Horseshoe Pitchers Association.** Route 5, Lucasville, Ohio 45648

**National Hot Rod Association.** P.O. Box 150, North Hollywood, Calif. 91603

**National Junior College Athletic Association.** P.O. Box 1586, Hutchinson, Kan. 67501

**National Lawn Tennis Hall of Fame.** Newport Casino, Newport, R.I., 02840

**National League (baseball).** 1 Rockefeller Plaza, New York, N.Y. 10019

**National Rifle Association of America.** 1600 Rhode Island Ave., N.W., Washington, D.C. 20036

**National Skeet Shooting Association.** P.O. Box 28188, San Antonio, Tex. 78228

**New York Racing Association.** P.O. Box 90, Jamaica, N.Y. 11417

**New York State Athletic Commission** (boxing). 270 Broadway, New York, N.Y.

**National Shuffleboard Association.** 5612 Plattsburg Road, Springfield, Ohio, 45505

**North American Yacht Racing Union.** *See* United States Yacht Racing Union

**North American Soccer League.** 1133 Avenue of the Americas, New York, N.Y. 10036

**Pacific Coast League (baseball).** 2509 South Shannon Drive, Tempe, Ariz., 85282

**Professional Bowlers Association.** 1720 Merriman Road, Akron, Ohio 44313

**Professional Golfers' Association of America.** Box 12458, Lake Park, Fla. 33403

**Rodeo Cowboys Association.** 2929 W. 19th Ave.,

Denver, Colo. 80204

**Roller Skating Rink Operators Association.** P.O. Box 81846, Lincoln, Neb. 68501

**Sports Car Club of America.** 6750 S. Emporia St., Englewood, Colo. 80112

**Thoroughbred Racing Associations of the U.S.** 3000 Marcus Ave., Lake Success, N.Y. 11040

**Track and Field Hall of Fame.** Charleston, W. Va.

**United States of America Roller Skating Confederation.** 7700 "A" St., Lincoln, Neb. 68501

**United States Auto Club.** 4910 West 16th St., Speedway, Ind. 46224

**United States Badminton Association.** P.O. Box 237, Swartz Creek, Mich. 48473

**U.S. Chess Federation.** 186 Route 9W, New Windsor, N.Y. 12550

**U.S. Cycling Federation.** Box 669, Wall Street Station, New York, N.Y. 10005

**U.S. Figure Skating Association.** Sears Crescent Building, Suite 500, City Hall, Boston, Mass. 02108

**U.S. Golf Association.** Far Hills, N.J. 07931

**U.S. Handball Association.** 4101 Dempster St., Skokie, Ill. 60077

**U.S. Men's Curling Association.** 12822 Water Street, Duluth, Minn., 55008

**U.S. Olympic Committee.** 1750 East Boulder Street, Colorado Springs, Colo. 80909

**U.S. Olympic Training Center.** P.O. Box 4000, Colorado Springs, Colo. 80930

**U.S. Parachute Association.** 806–15th St. N.W., Washington, D.C. 20005

**U.S. Polo Association.** 1301 W. 22nd St., Oak Brook, Ill. 60521

**U.S. Ski Association.** P.O. Box 100, Park City, Utah 84060

**U.S. Ski Team.** P.O. Box 100, Park City, Utah 84060

**U.S. Soccer Federation.** 350 Fifth Ave., New York, N.Y. 10001

**U.S. Squash Racquets Association.** 211 Ford Road, Bala-Cynwyd, Pa., 19004

**U.S. Table Tennis Association.** 3466 Bridgeland Drive, Bridgeland Square Building, St. Louis, Mo. 63044

**U.S. Tennis Association.** 51 E. 42nd St., New York, N.Y. 10017

**U.S. Touch and Flag Football Association.** 2705 Normandy Drive, Youngstown, Ohio, 49511

**U.S. Trotting Association.** 750 Michigan Ave., Columbus, Ohio 43215

**U.S. Volleyball Association.** 1750 East Boulder St., Colorado Springs, Colo. 80909

**U.S. Women's Curling Association.** 635 Chatham Road, Glenview, Ill. 60025

**U.S. Yacht Racing Union.** P.O. Box 209, Goat Island, Newport, R.I. 02840

**Women's International Bowling Congress.** 5301 S. 76th St., Greendale, Wis. 53129

---

# STANDARD MEASUREMENTS IN SPORTS

## BASEBALL

**Home plate to pitcher's box:** 60 feet 6 inches.

**Plate to second base:** 127 feet $3\frac{3}{8}$ inches.

**Distance from base to base (home plate included):** 90 feet.

**Size of bases:** 15 inches by 15 inches.

**Pitcher's plate:** 24 inches by 6 inches.

**Batter's box:** 4 feet by 6 feet.

**Home plate:** 17 inches by 12 inches by 12 inches, cut to a point at rear.

**Home plate to backstop:** Not less than 60 feet (recommended).

**Weight of ball:** Not less than 5 ounces nor more than $5\frac{1}{4}$ ounces.

**Circumference of ball:** Not less than 9 inches nor more than $9\frac{1}{4}$ inches.

**Bat:** Must be round, not over $2\frac{3}{4}$ inches in diameter at thickest part, nor more than 42 inches in length, and of solid wood in one piece or laminated wood.

## FOOTBALL

(N.C.A.A.)

**Length of field:** 120 yards. (including 10 yards of end zone at each end).

**Width of field:** $53\frac{1}{3}$ yards (160 feet).

**Height of goal posts:** At least 20 feet.

**Height of crossbar:** 10 feet.

**Width of goal posts (above crossbar):** 23 feet 4 inches, inside to inside, and not more than 24 feet, outside to outside.

**Length of ball:** $10\frac{7}{8}$ to $11\frac{7}{16}$ inches (long axis).

**Circumference of ball:** $20\frac{3}{4}$ to $21\frac{1}{4}$ inches (middle); $27\frac{3}{4}$ to $28\frac{1}{2}$ inches (long axis).

## LAWN TENNIS

**Size of court:** Rectangle 78 feet long and 27 feet wide (singles); 78 feet long and 36 feet wide (doubles).

**Height of net:** 3 feet in center, gradually rising to reach 3-foot 6-inch posts at a point 3 feet outside each side of court.

**Ball:** Shall be more than $2\frac{1}{2}$ inches and less than $2\frac{5}{8}$ inches in diameter and weight more than 2 ounces and less than $2\frac{1}{16}$ ounces.

**Service line:** 21 feet from net.

## HOCKEY

**Size of rink:** 200 feet long by 85 feet wide surrounded by a wooden wall not less than 40 inches and not more than 48 inches above level of ice.

**Size of goal:** 6 feet wide by 4 feet in height.

**Puck:** 1 inch thick and 3 inches in diameter; made of vulcanized rubber; weight $5\frac{1}{2}$ to 6 ounces.

**Length of stick:** Not more than 58 inches from heel to end of shaft nor 12$\frac{1}{2}$ inches from heel to end of blade. Blade should not be more than 3 inches in width but not less than 2 inches, except goal keeper's stick, which shall not exceed $3\frac{1}{2}$ inches in width except at the heel, where it must not exceed $4\frac{1}{2}$ inches.

## BOWLING

**Lane dimensions:** Overall length 62 feet $10\frac{3}{16}$ inches, measuring from foul line to pit (not including tail plank), with $\frac{1}{2}$ inch tolerance permitted. Foul line to center of No. 1 pinspot 60 feet, with $\frac{1}{2}$ inch tolerance permitted. Lane width, $41\frac{1}{2}$ inches with a tolerance of a $\frac{1}{2}$ inch permitted. Approach, not less than 15 feet. Gutters, $9\frac{5}{16}$ inches wide with $\frac{3}{16}$ plus or $\frac{5}{16}$ minus tolerances permitted.

**Ball:** Circumference, not more than 27 inches. Weight, 16 pounds maximum.

## GOLF

**The ball, specifications:** Broadened to require that the ball be designed to perform as if it were spherically symmetrical. The weight of the ball shall not be greater than 1.620 ounces avoirdupois, and the size shall not be less than 1.680 inches in diameter.

**Velocity of ball:** Not greater than 250 feet per second when tested on U.S.G.A. apparatus, with 2 percent tolerance.

**Hole:** 4¼ inches in diameter and at least 4 inches deep.

**Clubs:** 14 is the maximum number permitted.

## BASKETBALL
(National Collegiate A.A. Rules)

**Playing court:** College: 94 feet long by 50 feet wide (ideal dimensions). High School: 84 feet long by 50 feet wide (ideal inside dimensions).

**Baskets:** Rings 18 inches in inside diameter, with white cord 12-mesh nets, 15 to 18 inches in length. Each ring is made of metal, is not more than ⅝ of an inch in diameter, and is bright orange in color.

**Height of basket:** 10 feet (upper edge).

**Weight of ball:** Not less than 20 ounces nor more than 22.

**Circumference of ball:** No greater than 30 inches and not less than 29½.

**Free-throw line:** 15 feet from the face of the backboard, 2 inches wide.

## BOXING

**Ring:** Professional matches take place in an area not less than 18 nor more than 24 feet square including apron. It is enclosed by four covered ropes, each not less than one inch in diameter. The floor has a 2-inch padding of Ensolite (or equivalent) underneath ring cover that extends at least 6 inches beyond the roped area in the case of elevated rings. For U.S.A./A.B.F. boxing, not less than 16 nor more than 20 feet square within the ropes. The floor must extend beyond the ring ropes not less than 2 feet. The ring posts shall be connected to the three ring ropes with the extension not shorter than 18 inches and must be properly padded.

**Gloves:** In professional fights, not less than 8-ounce gloves generally are used. U.S.A./A.B.F., not less than 10 ounces for all divisions; for international competition not less than 8 ounces.

# FIGURE SKATING

## WORLD CHAMPIONS

**Men**

| | | | | | |
|---|---|---|---|---|---|
| 1960 | Alain Giletti, France | 1978 | Charles Tickner, United States | 1971–72 | Beatrix Schuba, Austria |
| 1961 | No competition | 1979 | Vladimir Kovalev, U.S.S.R. | 1973 | Karen Magnusson, Canada |
| 1962 | Donald Jackson, Canada | 1980 | Jan Hoffman, East Germany | 1974 | Christine Errath, East Germany |
| 1963 | Don McPherson, Canada | 1981 | Scott Hamilton, United States | | |
| 1964 | Manfred Schnelldorfer, West Germany | 1982 | Scott Hamilton, United States | 1975 | Dianne de Leeuw, Netherlands |
| | | **Women** | | 1976 | Dorothy Hamill, United States |
| 1965 | Alain Calmat, France | | | 1977 | Linda Fratianne, United States |
| 1966–68 | Emmerich Danzer, Austria | 1956–60 | Carol Heiss, United States | 1978 | Anett Poetzsch, East Germany |
| 1969–70 | Tim Wood, United States | 1961 | No competition | 1979 | Linda Fratianne, United States |
| 1971–73 | Ondrej Nepela, Czechoslovakia | 1962–64 | Sjoukje Dijkstra, Netherlands | 1980 | Anett Poetzsch, East Germany |
| 1974 | Jan Hoffman, East Germany | 1965 | Petra Burka, Canada | 1981 | Denise Biellmann, Switzerland |
| 1975 | Sergei Yolkov, U.S.S.R. | 1966–68 | Peggy Fleming, United States | 1982 | Elaine Zayak, United States |
| 1976 | John Curry, Britain | 1969–70 | Gabriele Seyfert, East Germany | | |
| 1977 | Vladimir Kovelov, U.S.S.R. | | | | |

## U.S. CHAMPIONS

**Men**

| | | | | | |
|---|---|---|---|---|---|
| 1946–52 | Richard Button | 1972 | Ken Shelley | 1957–60 | Carol Heiss |
| 1953–56 | Hayes Jenkins | 1973–75 | Gordon McKellen | 1961 | Laurence Owen |
| 1957–60 | David Jenkins | 1976 | Terry Kubicka | 1962 | Barbara Roles Pursley |
| 1961 | Bradley Lord | 1977–80 | Charles Tickner | 1963 | Lorraine Hanlon |
| 1962 | Monty Hoyt | 1981 | Scott Hamilton | 1964–68 | Peggy Fleming |
| 1963 | Tommy Litz | 1982 | Scott Hamilton | 1969–73 | Janet Lynn |
| 1964 | Scott Allen | | | 1974–76 | Dorothy Hamill |
| 1965 | Gary Visconti | **Women** | | 1977–80 | Linda Fratianne |
| 1966 | Scott Allen | 1943–48 | Gretchen Merrill | 1981 | Elaine Zayak |
| 1967 | Gary Visconti | 1949–50 | Yvonne Sherman | 1982 | Rosalynn Sumners |
| 1968–70 | Tim Wood | 1951 | Sonya Klopfer | | |
| 1971 | John M. Petkevich | 1952–56 | Tenley Albright | | |

### UNITED STATES CHAMPIONS—1982
(Indianapolis, Ind., Jan. 27-30, 1982)

Men's singles—Scott Hamilton, Denver, Colo.
Women's singles—Rosalynn Sumners, Edmonds, Wash.
Pairs—Peter and Caitlin Carruthers, Wilmington, Del.
Dance—Judy Blumberg, Colorado Springs, and Michael Seibert, Indianapolis
Junior dance—Amanda Newman, Short Hills, N.J., and Jerry Santoferrara, Syracuse, N.Y.

### WORLD CHAMPIONS—1982
(Copenhagen, Denmark, March 9-13, 1982)

Men's singles—Scott Hamilton, Denver, Colo.
Women's singles—Elaine Zayak, Paramus, N.J.
Pairs—Sabine Baess and Tassilo Thierbach, East Germany
Dance—Jayne Torvill and Christopher Dean, Britain

# SWIMMING

## WORLD RECORDS—MEN
(Through Oct. 4, 1982)
Approved by International Swimming Federation (F.I.N.A.)
(F.I.N.A. discontinued acceptance of records in yards in 1968)

| Distance | Record | Holder | Country | Where Made | Date |
|---|---|---|---|---|---|
| **Freestyle** | | | | | |
| 100 Meters | 0:49.36 | Rowdy Gaines | U.S. | Austin, Tex. | April 3, 1981 |
| 200 Meters | 1:48.93 | Rowdy Gaines | U.S. | Mission Viejo, Calif. | July 20, 1982 |
| 400 Meters | 3:49.57 | Vladimir Salnikov | U.S.S.R. | Moscow | March 12, 1982 |
| 800 Meters | 7:52.83 | Vladimir Salnikov | U.S.S.R. | Moscow | Feb. 15, 1982 |
| 1,500 Meters | 14:56.35 | Vladimir Salnikov | U.S.S.R. | Moscow | March 13, 1982 |
| **Backstroke** | | | | | |
| 100 Meters | 0:55.49 | John Naber | U.S. | Montreal | July 19, 1976 |
| 200 Meters | 1:59.19 | John Naber | U.S. | Montreal | July 24, 1976 |
| **Breaststroke** | | | | | |
| 100 Meters | 1:02.53 | Steve Lundquist | U.S. | Indianapolis, Ind. | Aug. 17, 1982 |
| 200 Meters | 2:14.77 | Victor Davis | Canada | Guayaquil, Ecuador | Aug. 5, 1982 |
| **Butterfly** | | | | | |
| 100 Meters | 0:53.81 | William Paulus | U.S. | Austin, Tex. | April 3, 1981 |
| 200 Meters | 1:58.01 | Craig Beardsley | U.S. | Kiev, U.S.S.R. | Aug. 22, 1981 |
| **Individual Medley** | | | | | |
| 200 Meters | 2:02.25 | Alex Baumann | Canada | Brisbane, Australia | Oct. 3, 1982 |
| 400 Meters | 4:19.78 | Ricardo Prado | Brazil | Guayaquil, Ecuador | Aug. 1, 1982 |
| **Freestyle Relays** | | | | | |
| 400 Meters | 3:19.26 | National Team | U.S. | Guayaquil, Ecuador' | Aug. 7, 1982 |
| (Chris Cavanaugh, Robin Leamy, David McCagg, Rowdy Gaines) | | | | | |
| 800 Meters | 7:20.82 | National Team | U.S. | West Berlin | Aug. 24, 1978 |
| (Bruce Furniss, Bill Forrester, Bobby Hackett, Rowdy Gaines) | | | | | |
| **Medley Relay** | | | | | |
| 400 Meters | 3:40.84 | National Team | U.S. | Guayaquil, Ecuador | Aug. 7, 1982 |
| (Rick Carey, Steve Lundquist, Matt Gribble, Rowdy Gaines) | | | | | |

## WORLD RECORDS—WOMEN

| Distance | Record | Holder | Country | Where made | Date |
|---|---|---|---|---|---|
| **Freestyle** | | | | | |
| 100 Meters | 0:54.79 | Barbara Krause | East Germany | Moscow | July 21, 1980 |
| 200 Meters | 1:58.23 | Cynthia Woodhead | U.S. | Tokyo | Sept. 3, 1979 |
| 400 Meters | 4:06.28 | Tracey Wickham | Australia | West Berlin | Aug. 24, 1978 |
| 800 Meters | 8:24.62 | Tracey Wickham | Australia | Edmonton, Canada | Aug. 5, 1978 |
| 1,500 Meters | 16:04.49 | Kim Linehan | U.S. | Ft. Lauderdale, Fla. | Aug. 19, 1979 |
| **Backstroke** | | | | | |
| 100 Meters | 1:00.86 | Rica Reinisch | East Germany | Moscow | July 23, 1980 |
| 200 Meters | 2:09.91 | Cornelia Sirch | East Germany | Guayaquil, Ecuador | Aug. 7, 1982 |
| **Breaststroke** | | | | | |
| 100 Meters | 1:08.60 | Ute Geweniger | East Germany | Split, Yugoslavia | Sept. 8, 1981 |
| 200 Meters | 2:28.36 | Lina Kachushite | U.S.S.R. | Potsdam | April 6, 1979 |
| **Butterfly** | | | | | |
| 100 Meters | 0:57.93 | Mary T. Meagher | U.S. | Brown Deer, Wis. | Aug. 16, 1981 |
| 200 Meters | 2:05.96 | Mary T. Meagher | U.S. | Brown Deer, Wis. | Aug. 13, 1981 |
| **Individual Medley** | | | | | |
| 200 Meters | 2:11.73 | Ute Geweniger | East Germany | East Berlin | July 4, 1981 |
| 400 Meters | 4:36.10 | Petra Schneider | East Germany | Guayaquil, Ecuador | Aug. 1, 1982 |

**Freestyle Relay**

| | | | | | |
|---|---|---|---|---|---|
| 400 Meters | 3:42.71 | National Team | East Germany | Moscow | July 27, 1980 |
| 800 Meters | 8:07.44 | Mission Viejo A | U.S. | Milwaukee | Aug. 14, 1981 |

**Medley Relay**

| | | | | | |
|---|---|---|---|---|---|
| 400 Meters | 4:05.88 | National Team | East Germany | Guayaquil, Ecuador | Aug. 7, 1982 |

(Kristin Otto, Ute Geweniger, Ines Geissler, Birgit Meineke)

## U.S. SHORT–COURSE SWIMMING RECORDS

(Listed by Amateur Athletic Union)

## MEN
### Freestyle

| | |
|---|---|
| 50 yards—Robin Leamy, 1981 | 0:19.36 |
| 100 yards—Rowdy Gaines, 1981 | 0:42.38 |
| 100 yards—Rowdy Gaines, 1980 | 0:43.16 |
| 100 yards—Andy Coan, 1979 | 0:43.25 |
| 100 yards—Jonty Skinner, 1978 | 0:43.29[1] |
| 100 yards—Joe Bottom, 1977 | 0:43.49 |
| 200 yards—Rowdy Gaines, 1981 | 1:33.80 |
| 200 yards—Rowdy Gaines, 1980 | 1:34.57 |
| 200 yards—Andy Coan, 1979 | 1:35.62 |
| 200 yards—Jim Montgomery, 1977 | 1:35.67 |
| 500 yards—Brian Goodell, 1978 | 4:16.40 |
| 500 yards—Brian Goodell, 1979 | 4:16.43 |
| 1,000 yards—Jeff Kostoff, 1982 | 8:49.97 |
| 1,650 yards—Brian Goodell, 1979 | 14:47.27 |
| 1,650 yards—Rafael Escalas, 1981 | 14:53.90[1] |
| 1,650 yards—Brian Goodell, 1979 | 14:54.13 |
| 1,650 yards—Brian Goodell, 1978 | 14:54.54 |

### Backstroke

| | |
|---|---|
| 100 yards—Dave Bottom, 1982 | 0:48.94 |
| 100 yards—Clay Britt, 1981 | 0:49.08 |
| 200 yards—Wladar Sandor, 1982 | 1:45.22[1] |
| 200 yards—Rick Carey, 1982 | 1:45.80 |

### Breaststroke

| | |
|---|---|
| 100 yards—Steve Lundquist, 1981 | 0:52.93 |
| 100 yards—Steve Lundquist, 1980 | 0:53.59 |
| 100 yards—Steve Lundquist, 1979 | 0:54.08 |
| 100 yards—Graham Smith, 1977 | 0:54.91[1] |
| 100 yards—Scott Spann, 1977 | 0:55.19 |
| 200 yards—Steve Lundquist, 1981 | 1:55.01 |
| 200 yards—Bill Barrett, 1980 | 1:58.43 |
| 200 yards—Steve Lundquist, 1979 | 1:59.18 |
| 200 yards—Graham Smith, 1977 | 2:00.05[1] |
| 200 yards—Nick Nevid, 1978 | 2:00.53 |

### Butterfly

| | |
|---|---|
| 100 yards—Scott Spann, 1981 | 0:47.22 |
| 100 yards—Par Arvidsson, 1980 | 0:47.34[1] |
| 100 yards—Par Arvidsson, 1979 | 0:47.76[1] |
| 100 yards—Joe Bottom, 1977 | 0:47.77 |
| 200 yards—Craig Beardsley, 1982 | 1:43.81 |
| 200 yards—Craig Beardsley, 1982 | 1:44.10 |
| 200 yards—Craig Beardsley, 1981 | 1:44.15 |
| 200 yards—Par Arvidsson, 1980 | 1:44.43[1] |

### Individual Medley

| | |
|---|---|
| 200 yards—Bill Barrett, 1982 | 1:45.00 |
| 200 yards—Bill Barrett, 1981 | 1:45.01 |
| 400 yards—Ricardo Prado, 1982 | 3:47.97[1] |
| 400 yards—Jesse Vassallo, 1981 | 3:48.16 |

### Relays

| | |
|---|---|
| 400–yard freestyle—U.C.L.A., 1982 | 2:53.15 |
| 400–yard freestyle—Mission Viejo, 1981 | 2:53.86 |
| 400–yard freestyle—Tennessee, 1979 | 2:54.54 |
| 400–yard freestyle—Gatorade S.C., 1978 | 2:55.27 |
| 800–yard freestyle—Florida Aquatic Club, 1979 | 6:25.42 |
| 800–yard freestyle—Auburn, 1981 | 6:26.49 |
| 800–yard freestyle—Florida A.C., 1978 | 6:29.81 |
| 400–yard medley—Texas, 1981 | 3:12.93 |
| 400–yard medley—California-Berkeley, 1979 | 3:15.22[1] |
| 400–yard medley—Indiana, 1977 | 3:17.14[1] |
| 400–yard medley—Auburn, 1977 | 3:17.62 |

## WOMEN
### Freestyle

| | |
|---|---|
| 50 yards—Jill Sterkel, 1981 | 0:22.41 |
| 100 yards—Jill Sterkel, 1982 | 0:48.61 |
| 100 yards—Jill Sterkel, 1980 | 0:48.76 |
| 100 yards—Cynthia Woodhead, 1979 | 0:49.39 |
| 100 yards—Jill Sterkel, 1979 | 0:49.55 |
| 100 yards—Tracy Caulkins, 1978 | 0:49.58 |
| 200 yards—Cynthia Woodhead, 1979 | 1:44.10 |
| 200 yards—Marybeth Linzmeier, 1982 | 1:45.82 |
| 500 yards—Tracy Caulkins, 1979 | 4:36.25 |
| 500 yards—Cynthia Woodhead, 1978 | 4:39.94 |
| 1,650 yards—Kim Linehan, 1979 | 15:49.10 |
| 1,650 yards—Cynthia Woodhead, 1978 | 15:55.15 |

### Backstroke

| | |
|---|---|
| 100 yards—Sue Walsh, 1982 | 0:54.81 |
| 100 yards—Linda Jezek, 1978 | 0:54.94 |
| 200 yards—Linda Jezek, 1978 | 1:57.79 |

### Breaststroke

| | |
|---|---|
| 100 yards—Tracy Caulkins, 1979 | 1:01.82 |
| 100 yards—Tracy Caulkins, 1979 | 1:02.06 |
| 100 yards—Tracy Caulkins, 1978 | 1:02.20 |
| 200 yards—Tracy Caulkins, 1980 | 2:11.46 |
| 200 yards—Tracy Caulkins, 1978 | 2:14.07 |

### Butterfly

| | |
|---|---|
| 100 yards—Jill Sterkel, 1981 | 0:53.10 |
| 100 yards—Mary T. Meagher, 1980 | 0:53.18 |
| 100 yards—Jill Sterkel, 1979 | 0:53.76 |
| 100 yards—Diane Johannigman, 1978 | 0:54.11 |
| 200 yards—Mary T. Meagher, 1980 | 1:53.21 |
| 200 yards—Nancy Hogshead, 1978 | 1:55.74 |

### Individual Medley

| | |
|---|---|
| 200 yards—Tracy Caulkins, 1979 | 1:57.86 |
| 200 yards—Tracy Caulkins, 1978 | 1:59.33 |
| 400 yards—Tracy Caulkins, 1979 | 4:08.09 |
| 400 yards—Tracy Caulkins, 1978 | 4:11.38 |

### Relays

| | |
|---|---|
| 200–yard freestyle—Stanford, 1981 | 1:31.12 |
| 400–yard freestyle—Stanford, 1981 | 3:19.70 |
| 400–yard freestyle—Nashville A.C., 1979 | 3:20.51 |
| 400–yard freestyle—Nashville A.C., 1978 | 3:20.69 |
| 800–yard freestyle—Mission Viejo S.C., 1979 | 7:15.14 |
| 800–yard freestyle—U.S. Team, 1976 | 7:15.64 |
| 200–yard medley—Florida, 1982 | 1:42.10 |
| 400–yard medley—Florida, 1982 | 3:40.99 |

1. Open American record by non-U.S. competitors.

## U.S. SHORT-COURSE CHAMPIONSHIPS—1982

(Gainesville, Fla., April 7–10, 1982)

**INDOORS**
**Men's Events**

50–yd freestyle—Siong Ang, Houston  0:19.86
100–yd freestyle—Rowdy Gaines, Winter Haven, Fla.0:43.64
200–yd freestyle—Rowdy Gaines  1:35.17
500–yd freestyle—Jeff Kostoff, Upland, Calif.  4:19.39
1,000–yd freestyle—Jeff Kostoff  8:49.97[1][2]
1,650–yd freestyle—Jeff Kostoff  14:52.39
100–yd backstroke—Dave Bottom, Danville, Calif.  0:48.94[1][2]
200–yd backstroke—Sandor Wladar, Hungary  1:45.22[2]
100–yd butterfly—David Cowell, Belpre, Ohio  0:47.89
200–yd butterfly—Craig Beardsley, Harrington Park, N.J.  1:43.81[1]
100–yd breaststroke—Steve Lundquist, Jonesboro, Ga.  0:53.84
200–yd breaststroke—John Moffett, Newport Beach, Calif.  1:59.44
200–yd individual medley—Roger Von Jouanne, Southern Illinois  1:48.41
400–yd individual medley—Ricardo Prado, Mission Viejo, Calif.  3:47.97[2]
400–yd freestyle relay—Mission Viejo (Calif.) A Team  2:55.01
800–yd freestyle relay—Florida Aquatic Swim Team A (Bill Sawchuk, John Hillencamp, Steve Wood, Geoff Gaberino)  6:27.94
400–yd medley relay—Mission Viejo Nadadores A Team (Jay Yarid, Bill Barrett, Bob Placak, Robin Leamy)  3:16.22

1. American record. 2. United States Open record.

**Women's Events**

50–yd freestyle—Dana Torres, Tandem Swim Club, Calif.  0:22.44
100–yd freestyle—Jill Sterkel, Austin, Tex.  0:48.94
200–yd freestyle—Cynthia Woodhead, Mission Viejo, Calif.  1:45.46
500–yd freestyle—Tiffany Cohen, Mission Viejo, Calif.  4:39.97
1,000–yd freestyle—Tiffany Cohen  9:34.61
1,650–yd freestyle—Tiffany Cohen  15:58.52
100–yd backstroke—Debbie Risen, Overland Park, Kan.  0:55.49
200–yd backstroke—Tracy Caulkins, Nashville, Tenn.1:57.77
100–yd breaststroke—Tracy Caulkins  1:02.41
200–yd breaststroke—Kim Rhodenbaugh, Cincinnati2:14.17
100–yd butterfly—Jill Sterkel  0:53.20
200–yd butterfly—Mary T. Meagher, Louisville, Ky.1:53.37
200–yd individual medley—Tracy Caulkins  1:58.94
400–yd freestyle relay—Mission Viejo (Calif.) A Team  3:20.68
800–yd freestyle relay—Mission Viejo Nadadores A Team (Tiffany Cohen, Marybeth Linzmeier, Julie Williams, Cynthia Woodhead)  7:10.55[1][2]
400–yd medley relay—Nashville A Team (Amy Caulkins, Tracy Caulkins, Patty King, Libby Pruden)  3:44.01

1. American record. 2. United States Open record.

## U.S. LONG-COURSE CHAMPIONSHIPS

(Indianapolis, Ind., Aug. 18–21, 1982)

**Men's Events**

50–m freestyle—Ping Siong Ang, Singapore and Univ. of Houston  0:22.69
100–m freestyle—Rowdy Gaines, Winter Haven, Fla. 0:50.27
200–m freestyle—Rowdy Gaines  1:49.64
400–m freestyle—Bruce Hayes, Mission Viejo, Calif. 3:54.80
800–m freestyle—Tony Corbisiero, Bayside, N.Y.  7:58.50[1]
1,500–m freestyle—Jeff Kostoff, Upland, Calif.  15:17.77
100–m breaststroke—Steve Lundquist, Jonesboro, Ga.  1:02.53[2]
200–m breaststroke—John Moffet, Costa Mesa, Calif.2:17.88
100–m backstroke—Mark Rhodenbaugh, Cincinnati  0:56.90
200–m backstroke—Steve Barnicoat, Mission Viejo, Calif.  2:02.91
100–m butterfly—David Cowell, Belpre, Ohio  0:54.61
200–m butterfly—Craif Beardsley, Gainesville, Fla.  1:59.01
200–m ind. medley—Bill Barrett, Mission Viejo, Calif.2:04.03
400–m ind. medley—Ricardo Prado, Mission Viejo, Calif.  4:22.54
400–m medley relay—Mission Viejo Nadadores (Jay Yarid, Bill Barrett, John Critchfield, Robin Leamy)  3:46.96
800–m freestyle relay—Mission Viejo Nadadores (Bruce Hayes, Bill Barrett, John Hillencamp, Rich Saeger)  7:29.14
400–m freestyle relay—Mission Viejo Nadadores (Rich Saeger, Bill Barrett, Stuart MacDonald, Robin Leamy)  3:21.89[1]

**Women's Events**

50–m freestyle—Dara Torres, Beverly Hills, Calif.  0:26.13
100–m freestyle—Paige Zemina, Fort Lauderdale, Fla.0:57.45
200–m freestyle—Sarah Linke, Walnut Creek, Calif.  2:01.25
400–m freestyle—Tiffany Cohen, Mission Viejo, Calif.4:11.61
800–m freestyle—Marybeth Linzmeier, Mission Viejo, Calif.  8:35.48
1,500–m freestyle—Karin LaBerge, Doylestown, Pa.16:18.94
100–m breaststroke—Kim Rhodenbaugh, Cincinnati  1:10.79
200–m breaststroke—Beverly Acker, Richmond, Ky.  2:35.45
100–m backstroke—Sue Walsh, Hamburg, N.Y.  1:02.48[1]
200–m backstroke—Tracy Caulkins, Nashville, Tenn. 2:15.53
100–m butterfly—Mary T. Meagher, Louisville, Ky.  0:59.75
200–m butterfly—Mary T. Meagher  2:07.14
200–m ind. medley—Tracy Caulkins  2:15.66
400–m ind. medley—Tracy Caulkins  4:44.26
400–m medley relay—Cincinnati Marlins (Kim Nicholson, Kim Rhodenbaugh, Betsy Mitchell, Beth Washut)  4:15.19
800–m freestyle relay—Mission Viejo Nadadores (Marybeth Linzmeier, Cynthia Woodhead, Tiffany Cohen, Vera Barker)  8:17.00
400–m freestyle relay—Mission Viejo Nadadores (Susan Habernigg, Cynthia Woodhead, Julie Williams, Marybeth Linzmeier)  3:49.36
Combined team—Mission Viejo Nadadores  1,255 pts

1. American record. 2. World record.

## U.S. INDOOR DIVING CHAMPIONSHIPS—1982

(Brown Deer, Wis., April 13–17, 1982)

**INDOOR**

| Men's Events | Pts |
|---|---|
| 1 meter—Ron Merriott, Kimball | 603.57 |
| 3 meter—Ron Merriott | 610.44 |
| Platform—Dan Watson, Danvers Y | 531.99 |
| High point winner—Ron Merriott | |
| Team—Mission Viejo Nadadores | 103 |

| Women's Events | |
|---|---|
| 1 meter—Megan Neyer, Mission Viejo Nadadores | 427.38 |
| 3 meter—Megan Neyer | 512.40 |
| Platform—Wendy Wyland, Mission Viejo | 367.59 |
| High point winner—Megan Neyer | |
| Team—Mission Viejo Nadadores | 155 |

## OUTDOOR

(Pittsburgh, Pa., Aug. 17–21, 1982)

| Men's Events | Pts |
|---|---|
| 1 meter—Greg Louganis, Mission Viejo, Calif. | 626.13 |
| 3 meter—Greg Louganis | 703.14 |
| Platform—Bruce Kimball, Ann Arbor, Mich. | 603.63 |
| Team—Mission Viejo, Calif. | |

**Women's Events**

| | |
|---|---|
| 1 meter—Megan Neyer, Mission Viejo, Calif. | 468.27 |
| 3 meter—Kelly McCormick, Columbus, Ohio | 513.57 |
| Platform—Wendy Wyland, Mission Viejo, Calif. | 427.14 |
| Team—Mission Viejo, Calif. | |

## NATIONAL COLLEGIATE ATHLETIC ASSOCIATION

(Brown Deer, Wis., March 25–27, 1982)

| | |
|---|---|
| 50–yd freestyle—Robin Leamy, U.C.L.A. | 0:19.85 |
| 100–yd freestyle—Robin Leamy | 0:43.59 |
| 200–yd freestyle—Pelle Holmertz, California | 1:36.46 |
| 500–yd freestyle—Andy Astbury, Arizona State | 4:18.15 |
| 1,650–yd freestyle—Arne Borgstrom, Alabama | 15:02.24 |
| 100–yd backstroke—Clay Britt, Texas | 0:49.09 |
| 200–yd backstroke—Rick Carey, Texas | 1:46.01 |
| 100–yd breaststroke—Steve Lundquist, Southern Methodist | 0:53.09 |
| 200–yd breaststroke—Steve Lundquist | 1:56.84 |
| 100–yd butterfly—Matt Gribble, Miami | 0:47.35 |
| 200–yd butterfly—Craig Beardsley, Florida | 1:44.10[1] |
| 200–yd individual medley—Bill Barrett, U.C.L.A. | 1:45.00[1] |
| 400–yd individual medley—Jeff Float, Southern California | 3:49.00 |
| 400–yd freestyle relay—U.C.L.A. (Bill Barrett, Chris Silva, Stuart MacDonald, Robin Leamy) | 2:53.15[1] |
| 800–yd freestyle relay—California (Paolo Revelli, P.A. Magnuson, Todd Trowbridge, Pelle Holmertz) | 6:28.94 |
| 400–yd medley relay—Texas (Jim Britt, Nick Nevid, Bill Paulus, Eric Finical) | 3:14.24 |
| 1–m dive—Robert Bollinger, Indiana | 554.95 pts |
| 3–m dive—Ron Merriott, Michigan | 600.30 pts |
| Team—U.C.L.A. | 219 pts |

1. American record.

## ASSOCIATION FOR INTERCOLLEGIATE ATHLETICS FOR WOMEN—1982

(Austin, Tex., March 17–20, 1982)

| | |
|---|---|
| 50–yd freestyle—Jill Sterkel, Texas | 0:22.59 |
| 100–yd freestyle—Jill Sterkel | 0:48.61[1] |
| 200–yd freestyle—Jill Sterkel | 1:46.47[1] |

| | |
|---|---|
| 500–yd freestyle—Kim Linehan, Texas | 4:44.12 |
| 1,650–yd freestyle—Kim Linehan | 16:18.50 |
| 50–yd backstroke—Marci Ballard, Ohio State | 0:26.97 |
| 100–yd backstroke—Elaine Palmer, Brown | 0:57.61 |
| 200–yd backstroke—Elaine Palmer | 2:02.60 |
| 50–yd breaststroke—Amanda Martin, Southern Illinois | 0:29.36 |
| 100–yd breaststroke—Jeanne Childs, Hawaii | 1:02.08[2] |
| 200–yd breaststroke—Jeanne Childs | 2:11.90[2] |
| 50–yd butterfly—Jill Sterkel | 0:24.03[1] |
| 100–yd butterfly—Jill Sterkel | 0:53.49 |
| 200–yd butterfly—Kim Linehan | 2:00.21 |
| 100–yd ind. medley—Carol Borgmann, Texas | 0:57.40 |
| 200–yd ind. medley—Carol Borgmann | 2:03.55 |
| 400–yd ind. medley—Sue Cahill, Michigan | 4:20.86 |
| 200–yd medley relay—Florida State University | 1:42.86 |
| 400–yd medley relay—Texas | 3:45.37 |
| 200–yd freestyle relay—Florida State University | 1:33.50 |
| 400–yd freestyle relay—Texas | 3:21.46 |
| 800–yd freestyle relay—Princeton | n.a. |
| 1–meter dive—Lona Foss, Indiana | 449.55 pts[2] |
| 3–meter dive—Kelly McCormick, Ohio State | 550.20 pts[2] |
| Team—Texas | 755 pts |

1. American record. 2. A.I.A.W. record. n.a. = not available.

## NATIONAL ASSOCIATION OF INTERCOLLEGIATE ATHLETICS—1982

(Burnaby, British Columbia, March 4–6, 1982)

| | |
|---|---|
| 50–m freestyle—Steve Koga, Willamette (Ore.) University | 0:23.42 |
| 100–m freestyle—Steve Koga | 0:50.98[1] |
| 200–m freestyle—Dan Sullivan, Drury | 1:52.78[1] |
| 400–m freestyle—Dan Sullivan | 4:00.55[1] |
| 1,500–m freestyle—Russell Dale, Simon Fraser University | 16:05.51 |
| 100–m backstroke—Sean Allison, Drury | 0:58.00[1] |
| 200–m backstroke—Bryce Fleming, Simon Fraser | 2:08.30[1] |
| 100–m breaststroke—Ray Markle, Drury | 1:06.06 |
| 200–m breaststroke—Ray Markle | 2:23.53[1] |
| 100–m butterfly—Thomas Ullrich, Denver | 0:56.59[1] |
| 200–m butterfly—Roger Bird, Drury | 2:09.14 |
| 200–m ind. medley—Paul Stanford, Denver | 2:09.12[1] |
| 400–m ind. medley—Paul Stanford | 4:33.76 |
| 400–m medley relay—Drury College | 3:53.47[1] |
| 400–m freestyle relay—Denver | 3:28.18[1] |
| 800–m freestyle relay—Drury | 7:39.81 |
| 1–meter dive—Mike Lewis, Drury | 460.53 pts |
| 3–meter dive—Mike Lewis | 455.50 pts |
| Team—Drury College | 456 pts |

1. N.A.I.A. record.

# PADDLE TENNIS

*Source:* Murray Geller, Executive-Secretary, U.S. Paddle Tennis Association

## NATIONAL OPEN CHAMPIONSHIPS—1982

(Santa Monica, Calif., July 31–Aug. 1, 1982)

Men's singles—Mark Rifenbark, Los Angeles
Men's doubles—Jeff Fleitman, Brooklyn, N.Y., and Sol Hauptman, Santa Monica, Calif.
Women's singles—Carolyn Dadian, Venice, Calif.

## WOMEN'S EAST COAST CHAMPIONSHIPS—1982

Singles—Mary Ellen Stewart, St. Augustine, Fla.

# PLATFORM TENNIS

## UNITED STATES CHAMPIONS—1982
### American Platform Tennis Association

Open singles* (Apple Platform Tennis Club, New York City)—Doug Russell, New York City, defeated Gregg Brents, White Plains, N.Y., in final

Men's doubles—Stephen Baird, Harrison, N.Y., and Rich Maier, Allendale, N.J.

Women's doubles (Montclair Golf Club, West Orange, N.Y.)—Evonne Hackenberg, Kalamazoo, Mich., and Hilary Hilton Marold, Glen Ellyn, Ill.

Mixed doubles (Sleepy Hollow Country Club, Scarborough, N.Y.)—Doug Russell and Hilary Marold.

* Open is for men and women.

# GYMNASTICS

## WORLD CHAMPIONSHIPS—1981*
(Moscow, Soviet Union, Nov. 22–29, 1981)

### Men's Events

| | Pts |
|---|---|
| All–around—Yuri Kovolev, Soviet Union | 118.375 |
| Floor exercises—Yuri Kovolev | 19.775 |
| Pommel horse—Tie between Xiaopong Li, China, and Michael Nikolai, Soviet Union | 19.9 |
| Still rings—Aleksandr Dityatin, Soviet Union | 19.825 |
| Parallel bars—Tie between Aleksandr Dityatin, Soviet Union, and Koji Gushiken, Japan | 19.825 |
| Vault—Ralph Peter Heman, East Germany | 19.9 |
| Horizontal bars—Aleksandr Tkachev, Soviet Union | 19.9 |
| Team—Soviet Union | 586.95 |

### Women's Events

| | Pts |
|---|---|
| All–around—Olga Bicherova, Soviet Union | 78.5 |
| Floor exercises—Natalie Menko, Soviet Union | 19.85 |
| Balance beam—Maxi Gnauck, East Germany | 19.525 |
| Uneven parallel bars—Maxi Gnauck | 19.9 |
| Vault—Maxi Gnauck | 19.675 |
| Team—Soviet Union | 389.3 |

*World championships are held every two years, on odd-numbered years. The next competition will be held in the Fall of 1983 in Budapest, Hungary.

## NATIONAL COLLEGIATE ATHLETIC ASSOCIATION

### Men's Division I
(Lincoln, Neb., April 2–4, 1982)

All–around—Peter Vidmar, U.C.L.A.
Floor exercise—Steve Elliott, Nebraska
Pommel horse—Peter Vidmar and Steve Jennings, New Mexico (tie)
Still rings—Jim Hartung, Nebraska
Vault—Steve Elliott and Randy Wickstrom, California-Berkeley (tie)
Horizontal bars—Peter Vidmar
Team—Nebraska, 286.45 pts

### Women's Division I
(Salt Lake City, Utah, March 25–27, 1982)

| | Pts |
|---|---|
| All–around—Sue Stednitz, Utah | 37.20 |
| Balance beam—Sue Stednitz | 18.7 |
| Floor exercise—Mary Ayotte-Law, Oregon State | 18.85 |
| Vault—Elaine Alfano, Utah | 18.9 |
| Uneven parallel bars—Lisa Shirk, Pittsburgh | 19.0 |
| Team—Utah | 148.6 |

# QUARTER HORSE RACING—1982

Kansas Futurity (Ruidoso Downs, N.M., purse: $760,000)—Chicks Etta Wind (Rudy Bustamante, jockey)
Rainbow Futurity (Ruidoso Downs, N.M., purse: $617,514)—Yankee Wind
Skoal Dash for Cash Futurity (Los Alamitos, Calif., purse: $750,000)—Sail on Bunny (Gary Sumpter, jockey)
Kindergarten (Los Alamitos, Calif., purse: $715,000)—Sail on Bunny
Champion of Champions (Los Alamitos, Calif., purse: $700,000)—Denim N Diamonds (Jerry Nicodemus, jockey)

## ASSOCIATION FOR INTERCOLLEGIATE ATHLETICS FOR WOMEN

### DIVISION I
(Memphis, Tenn., April 2–3, 1982)

| | Pts |
|---|---|
| All–around—Ann Woods, Florida | 37.05 |
| Balance beam—Lynn McDonnell, Florida | 18.65 |
| Floor exercise—Ann Woods | 18.65 |
| Uneven parallel bars—Ann Woods | 18.85 |
| Vault—Kathy Niebel, Georgia | 18.65 |
| Team—Florida | 143.90 |

### DIVISION II
(Denver, Colo., March 26–27, 1982)

| | Pts |
|---|---|
| All–around—Karen Beer, Denver | 36.80 |
| Balance beam—Karen Beer | 18.70 |
| Floor exercise—Karen Beer | 18.10 |
| Uneven parallel bars—Karen Beer | 18.75 |
| Vault—Margot Todd, Centenary College | 18.40 |
| Team—University of Denver | 141.30 |

### DIVISION III
(Keene, N.H., March 19–20, 1982)

| | Pts |
|---|---|
| All–around—Tari Gould, Gustavus Adolphus | 16.75 |
| Balance beam—Patty Ritter, Pittsburgh–Johnstown | 17.30 |
| Floor exercise—Lisa Harlan, Texas Woman's University | 17.45 |
| Uneven parallel bars—Tari Gould | 16.75 |
| Vault—Gretchen Gunderson, Gustavus Adolphus | 17.75 |
| Team—Gustavus Adolphus, St. Peter, Minn. | 133.55 |

## WORLD CUP*
(Toronto, Oct. 24–26, 1980)

### Men's Events
All around—Bogdan Makuz, Soviet Union
Floor exercise—Roland Brueckner, East Germany
Horizontal bar—Tie among Makuz, Koji Gushiken, Japan, and Toshiomi Nishikii, Japan
Still rings—Tie between Makuz and Yubin Huang, China
Pommel horse—Roland Brueckner, East Germany
Parallel bars—Yuejiu Li, China
Vault—Roland Brueckner, East Germany

### Women's Events
All around—Stella Zakharova, U.S.S.R.
Floor exercise—Maxi Gnauck, East Germany
Balance beam—Elena Naymoushina, U.S.S.R.
Vault—Stella Zakharova, U.S.S.R.
Uneven parallel bars—Maxi Gnauck, East Germany

*The World Cup was not contested in 1981. The 1982 Cup competition was scheduled for Oct. 22–24 in Zagreb, Yugoslavia.

# EQUESTRIAN EVENTS—1982

World Cup jumping (Goteborg, Sweden)—Melanie Smith, United States, riding Calypso. Runnerup: Paul Schockemohle, West Germany; third: tie between Hugo Simon, Austria, and John Whitaker, Britain
World Horse Trial (Luhmuehlen, West Germany)—Lucinda Green, Britain. Team: Britain
World dressage—Team: West Germany

# BOXING

Whether it be called pugilism, prize fighting or boxing, there is no tracing "the Sweet Science" to any definite source. Tales of rivals exchanging blows for fun, fame or money go back to earliest recorded history and classical legend. There was a mixture of boxing and wrestling called the "pancratium" in the ancient Olympic Games and in such contests the rivals belabored one another with hands fortified with heavy leather wrappings that were sometimes studded with metal. More than one Olympic competitor lost his life at this brutal exercise.

There was little law or order in pugilism until Jack Broughton, one of the early champions of England, drew up a set of rules for the game in 1743. Broughton, called "the father of English boxing," also is credited with having invented boxing gloves. However, these gloves—or "mufflers" as they were called—were used only in teaching "the manly art of self-defense" or in training bouts. All professional championship fights were contested with "bare knuckles" until 1892, when John L. Sullivan lost the heavyweight championship of the world to James J. Corbett in New Orleans in a bout in which both contestants wore regulation gloves.

The Broughton rules were superseded by the London Prize Ring Rules of 1838. The 8th Marquis of Queensberry, with the help of John G. Chambers, put forward the "Queensberry Rules" in 1866, a code that called for gloved contests. Amateurs took quickly to the Queensberry Rules, the professionals slowly.

## HISTORY OF WORLD HEAVYWEIGHT CHAMPIONSHIP FIGHTS

(Bouts in which a new champion was crowned)

*Source: Nat Fleischer's Ring Boxing Encyclopedia and Record Book*, published and copyrighted by The Ring Book Shop, Inc., 120 West 31st St., New York, N.Y. 10001.

| Date | Where held | Winner, weight, age | Loser, weight, age | Rounds | Referee |
|---|---|---|---|---|---|
| Sept. 7, 1892 | New Orleans, La. | James J. Corbett, 178 (26) | John L. Sullivan, 212 (33) | 21 | Prof. John Duffy |
| March 17, 1897 | Carson City, Nev. | Bob Fitzsimmons, 167 (34) | James J. Corbett, 183 (30) | KO 14 | George Siler |
| June 9, 1899 | Coney Island, N.Y. | James J. Jeffries, 206 (24)[1] | Bob Fitzsimmons, 167 (37) | KO 11 | George Siler |
| Feb. 23, 1906 | Los Angeles | Tommy Burns, 180 (24)[2] | Marvin Hart, 188 (29) | 20 | James J. Jeffries |
| Dec. 26, 1908 | Sydney, N.S.W. | Jack Johnson, 196 (30) | Tommy Burns, 176 (27) | KO 14 | Hugh McIntosh |
| April 5, 1915 | Havana, Cuba | Jess Willard, 230 (33) | Jack Johnson, 205½ (37) | KO 26 | Jack Welch |
| July 4, 1919 | Toledo, Ohio | Jack Dempsey, 187 (24) | Jess Willard, 245 (37) | KO 3 | Ollie Pecord |
| Sept. 23, 1926 | Philadelphia | Gene Tunney, 189 (28)[3] | Jack Dempsey, 190 (31) | 10 | Pop Reilly |
| June 12, 1930 | New York | Max Schmeling, 188 (24) | Jack Sharkey, 197 (27) | WF 4 | Jim Crowley |
| June 21, 1932 | Long Island City | Jack Sharkey, 205 (29) | Max Schmeling, 188 (26) | 15 | Gunboat Smith |
| June 29, 1933 | Long Island City | Primo Carnera, 260½ (26) | Jack Sharkey, 201 (30) | KO 6 | Arthur Donovan |
| June 14, 1934 | Long Island City | Max Baer, 209½ (25) | Primo Carnera, 263¼ (27) | KO 11 | Arthur Donovan |
| June 13, 1935 | Long Island City | Jim Braddock, 193¾ (29) | Max Baer, 209½ (26) | 15 | Jack McAvoy |
| June 22, 1937 | Chicago | Joe Louis, 197¼ (23) | Jim Braddock, 197 (31) | KO 8 | Tommy Thomas |
| June 22, 1949 | Chicago | Ezzard Charles, 181¾ (27)[4] | Joe Walcott, 195½ (35) | 15 | Davey Miller |
| Sept. 27, 1950 | New York | Ezzard Charles, 184½ (29)[5] | Joe Louis, 218 (36) | 15 | Mark Conn |
| July 18, 1951 | Pittsburgh | Joe Walcott, 194 (37) | Ezzard Charles, 182 (30) | KO 7 | Buck McTiernan |
| Sept. 23, 1952 | Philadelphia | Rocky Marciano, 184 (29)[6] | Joe Walcott, 196 (38) | KO 13 | Charley Daggert |
| Nov. 30, 1956 | Chicago | Floyd Patterson, 182¼ (21) | Archie Moore, 187¾ (42) | KO 5 | Frank Sikora |
| June 26, 1959 | New York | Ingemar Johansson, 196 (26) | Floyd Patterson, 182 (24) | KO 3 | Ruby Goldstein |
| June 20, 1960 | New York | Floyd Patterson, 190 (25) | Ingemar Johansson, 194¾ (27) | KO 5 | Arthur Mercante |
| Sept. 25, 1962 | Chicago | Sonny Liston, 214 (28) | Floyd Patterson, 189 (27) | KO 1 | Frank Sikora |
| Feb. 25, 1964 | Miami Beach, Fla. | Cassius Clay, 210 (22)[7] | Sonny Liston, 218 (30) | KO 7 | Barney Felix |
| March 4, 1968 | New York | Joe Frazier, 204½ (24)[8] | Buster Mathis, 243½ (23) | KO 11 | Arthur Mercante |
| April 27, 1968 | Oakland, Calif. | Jimmy Ellis, 197 (28)[9] | Jerry Quarry, 195 (22) | 15 | Elmer Costa |
| Feb. 16, 1970 | New York | Joe Frazier, 205 (26)[10] | Jimmy Ellis, 201 (29) | KO 5 | Tony Perez |
| Jan. 22, 1973 | Kingston, Jamaica | George Foreman, 217½ (24) | Joe Frazier, 214 (29) | KO 2 | Arthur Mercante |
| Oct. 30, 1974 | Kinshasa, Zaire | Muhammad Ali, 216½ (32) | George Foreman, 220 (26) | KO 8 | Zack Clayton |
| Feb. 15, 1978 | Las Vegas, Nev. | Leon Spinks, 197 (25) | Muhammad Ali, 224½ (36) | 15 | Howard Buck |
| June 9, 1978 | Las Vegas, Nev. | Larry Holmes, 212 (28)[11] | Ken Norton, 220 (32) | 15 | Mills Lans |
| Sept. 15, 1978 | New Orleans | Muhammad Ali, 221 (36)[12] | Leon Spinks, 201 (25) | 15 | Lucien Joubert |
| Oct. 20, 1979 | Pretoria, S. Africa | John Tate, 240 (24)[13] | Gerrie Coetzee, 222 (24) | 15 | Carlos Berrocal |
| March 31, 1980 | Knoxville, Tenn. | Mike Weaver, 207½ (27) | John Tate, 232 (25) | KO 15 | Ernesto Magana Ansorena |

1. Jeffries retired as champion in March 1905. He named Marvin Hart and Jack Root as leading contenders and agreed to referee their fight in Reno, Nev., on July 3, 1905, with the stipulation that he would term the winner the champion. Hart, 190 (28), knocked out Root, 171 (29), in the 12th round. 2. Burns claimed the title after defeating Hart. 3. Tunney retired as champion after defeating Tom Heeney on July 26, 1928. 4. After Louis announced his retirement as champion on March 1, 1949, Charles won recognition from the National Boxing Association as champion by defeating Walcott. 5. Charles gained undisputed recognition as champion by defeating Louis, who came out of retirement. 6. Retired as champion April 27, 1956. 7. The World Boxing Association later withdrew its recognition of Clay as champion and declared the winner of a bout between Ernie Terrell and Eddie Machen would gain its version of the title. Terrell, 199 (25), won a 15-round decision from Machen, 192 (32), in Chicago on March 5, 1965. Clay, 212¼ (25) and Terrell, 212½ (27) met in Houston on Feb. 6, 1967, Clay winning a 15-round decision. 8. Winner recognized by New York, Massachusetts, Maine, Illinois, Texas and Pennsylvania to fill vacated title when Clay was stripped of championship for failing to accept U. S. Induction. 9. Bout was final of eight-man tournament to fill Clay's place and is recognized by World Boxing Association. 10. Bout settled controversy over title. 11. Holmes won World Boxing Council title after W.B.C. had withdrawn recognition of Spinks, March 18, 1978, and awarded its title to Norton. W.B.C. said Spinks had reneged on agreement to fight Norton 12. Ali regained World Boxing Association championship. 13. Tate won W.B.A. title after Ali retired and left it vacant.

# CHAMPIONSHIP BOUTS—1982
### (Through Aug. 20, 1982)

## Junior Flyweight
### (108 pound limit)

Amado Ursua of Mexico knocked out Hilario Zapata of Panama in the second round to win the World Boxing Council title on Feb. 6 at Panama City. Zapata was making the 9th defense of the title he won by beating Shigeo Nakajima of Japan in March of 1980. In April, Ursua lost the title on a split decision to Tadashi Tomori of Japan in a 15–rounder in Tokyo and then in July Zapata got the title back by defeating Tomori, also on a split decision, at Kanazawa, Japan.

Katsuo Tokashiki of Japan, who won the W.B.A. version of the title in December 1981, retained it in his 1st defense with an 8th–round knockout of countryman Masaharu Inami in Tokyo.

## Flyweight
### (112 pound limit)

There were several new champions crowned during the year and the succession was complicated. Santos Laciar of Mexico lost his W.B.A. title to Luis Ibarra of Panama in 1981. Ibarra then lost it to Juan Herrera of Mexico in December 1981. Then Laciar reclaimed it with a 13th–round knockout of Herrera in May. Shoji Uguma of Japan, who won the W.B.C. title in 1980, lost it to Antonio Avelar of Mexico in 1981. Avelar lost it in turn to Prudencio Cardona of Colombia, who was dethroned in August by Freddie Castillo of Mexico.

## Junior Bantamweight
### (115 pound limit)

Kim Chul Ho of South Korea, who won the crown in January 1981 with a knockout of Rafael Orono of Venezuela, made two successful defenses in the first half of the year. He scored an 8th–round knockout of Koki Ishii of Japan on Feb. 10 at Taegu, South Korea. On July 4, at Taejon, South Korea, the 21–year–old Kim battled to a 15–round draw with Raul Valdez of Mexico to retain the W.B.C. title. The 28–year–old Mexican was warned several times against holding and butting.

Jiro Wantanabe of Japan took the W.B.A. title from Rafael Pedroza of Panama with a unanimous 15–round decision at Tokyo in April, then made a successful defense in July with a 9th–round knockout of Gustavo Ballas in Osaka, Japan.

## Bantamweight
### (118 pound limit)

Jeff Chandler of Philadelphia remained unbeaten and retained his W.B.A. title with a 6th–round knockout of Johnny Carter, also from Philadelphia, on March 27. The two fighters had been high school classmates in Philadelphia. The 25–year–old Chandler knocked Carter down with a left hook midway in the 6th, then pummeled him before referee Frank Cappuccino stopped the fight at 2:28 of the 6th. Chandler had lost only once—as an amateur to Carter in December 1975. He raised his pro record to 28–0–2, with 15 knockouts. It was the 5th defense of the title he won in 1980 by knocking out Julian Solis in the 14th round at Miami.

Lupe Pintor, who has held the W.B.C. crown since 1979, retained it again in July. The popular Mexican champion stopped Seung Hoon Lee of Korea with an 11th–round knockout in Los Angeles.

## Junior Featherweight
### (122 pound limit)

Sergio Palma of Argentina successfully defended his W.B.A. crown for the fifth time, scoring a unanimous decision over Jorge Lujan of Panama at Cordoba, Argentina, on Jan. 16. Each weighed 122 pounds. Palma, who was on the offensive for most of the 15–round bout, posted his 47th victory against 4 losses and 3 draws. Lujan is a former W.B.A. bantamweight champion.

In his next defense, on June 12 at Miami Beach, Palma lost his title on a 15–round unanimous decision to Leo Cruz of the Dominican Republic. Cruz connected with a straight right hand to close Palma's left eye in the 4th round and pounded the eye the rest of the bout. Cruz lifted his record to 45 victories, 5 losses and 1 draw, with 17 knockouts.

Wilfredo Gomez, the W.B.C. champion from Puerto Rico, made two title defenses through July. He knocked out Juan (Kid) Meza at 2:28 of the 6th round at Atlantic City on March 27. On June 11, at Las Vegas, Nev., as part of the undercard to the Holmes-Cooney heavyweight title fight, he scored a 10th–round knockout over Juan Antonio Lopez of Mexico. Gomez has 36 career victories, all by knockouts, has lost only once and fought one draw. All of his 15 title defenses have ended in knockout victories—a stunning record for any weight division. Against Meza, a 26–year–old who lives in Hawthorne, Calif., Gomez was warned several times for hitting low.

## Featherweight
### (128 pound limit)

Eusebio Pedroza surpassed Abe Attell's record of 13 successful defenses of the title when he won a unanimous decision from Juan LaPorte of New York and retained his W.B.A. crown. The 28–year–old champion was penalized a point in the 8th round for low blows and a point in the 14th for using his elbows. But his 3–inch reach advantage was too much for his opponent and he was able to set up LaPorte for solid rights with a persistent left jab. Pedroza, whose record is 33–3, is unbeaten since July 1976. The 5'–8" Panamanian champion received $65,000 and $150,000 from Latin American TV rights. LaPorte received $40,000 for the bout at Atlantic City on Jan. 24.

Salvador Sanchez, the W.B.C. champion, settled for a unanimous decision after throwing all he had at Jorge (Rocky) Garcia in their title bout at Dallas, May 8. The Mexican champion tried desperately to score a knockout, but Garcia weathered his best flurries. It was Sanchez's 8th title defense and the 1st title fight in Dallas in 14 years. Sanchez raised his record to 42–1–1. Sanchez, regarded by boxing experts as one of the finest ever to battle in the division, knocked out Azumah Nelson in the 15th round at Madison Square Garden in New York in July and it proved to be his last bout. Shortly after the fight, Sanchez was killed in an auto accident in Mexico.

## Junior Lightweight
### (130 pound limit)

Rolando Navarette of the Philippines retained the W.B.C. title by knocking out Choi Chung Il of South Korea in the 11th round at Manila on Jan. 16. The 24–year–old champion survived a 5th–round knockdown and came back to beat the 20–year–old challenger. Choi was taken to a hospital for observation. He suffered a broken nose and an injured right arm, and complained of pain in the groin.

Sammy Serrano of Puerto Rico lost his W.B.A. title at Santiago, Chile, on June 6 after a doctor ruled in the 11th round he could not continue because of a deep cut over his eye. But Serrano was reinstated as champion two weeks later by the W.B.A., which ruled that Serrano's cut was inflicted by an illegal head butt. Benedicto Villablanca of Chile was declared the winner, becoming the first Chilean to win a world title, when the bout was halted by the referee, Jesus Celis of Venezuela. Serrano had dominated the fight through 10 rounds and appeared on his way to winning the 15th defense of the title he won in 1976. The W.B.A. Championship Committee, on appeal from Serrano, voided the bout, however, and reinstated Serrano as titleholder.

Rafael Limon of Mexico, a former champion, regained the W.B.C. title in May by knocking out Navarette in the 12th round at Las Vegas.

## Lightweight
(135 pound limit)

Arturo Frias, from Montebello, Calif., making his first title defense, kept the W.B.A. lightweight crown at Los Angeles on Jan. 30. The ring doctor halted the fight with Ernesto Espana of Caracas, Venezuela in the 9th round because of cuts inflicted on the champion by butts from Espana.

Frias was cut over the left eye in the 2nd round and slashed under the same eye in the 9th. Frias was ahead on all cards at the time. Frias won the title on Dec. 5, 1981, by knocking out Claude Noel of Trinidad in the 8th round. Frias lifted his record to 24–1. He had lost previously only to Espana, whose record slipped to 34–4. The 25–year–old Frias earned $125,000; Espana, 27, received $40,000.

Alexis Arguello, the W.B.C. champion, kept his title with a 6th–round knockout of Bubba Busceme at Beaumont, Tex., Busceme's hometown, on Feb. 13. Arguello, with a 74–4 record, scored his 60th knockout. He stunned Busceme with a left hook, then following with a series of punches that led to the knockout at 2:35 of the round.

At Las Vegas, on May 22, Arguello survived a 1st–round knockdown and came back to knock out Andrew Ganigan, a Hawaiian, in the 5th round. The Nicaraguan champion earned $400,000, Ganigan $130,000. The victory was the 19th straight in a title fight for Arguello, one of six fighters to win titles in three weight divisions.

The W.B.A. title changed hands on May 8 at Las Vegas, when Ray (Boom Boom) Mancini, of Youngstown, Ohio, stopped Frias with six seconds left in the 1st round. Mancini took the title in his second attempt in seven months. He suffered his only defeat in 24 bouts in October 1981 when he was knocked out in the 14th by Arguello in a W.B.C. title match. Mancini put Frias down midway in the round, then pursued the attack with 25 to 30 punches to the head before the referee Richard Green halted the action. Mancini retained the title with a 6th–round knockout of Ernesto Espana in July at Warren, Ohio.

## Junior Welterweight
(140 pound limit)

Aaron Pryor, the W.B.A. champion, made two defenses and raised his unbeaten record to 31–0 through the Fourth of July. Pryor's first defense of the year came on March 21 at Atlantic City when he knocked out Miguel Montilla of the Dominican Republic at 42 seconds of the 12th round. Pryor had never been forced to go a full 10 rounds in winning 29 previous fights. The knockout was Pryor's 22nd in a row and 28th in 30 bouts. The 26–year–old Pryor scored another knockout on July 4 at Cincinnati, his hometown, stopping Akio Kameda of Japan at 1:44 of the 6th round. Kameda was knocked down twice in the 6th before the fight was halted. He was floored five times in the bout.

Leroy Haley, from Las Vegas, dethroned Saoul Mamby, from New York City, on an upset majority decision to take the W.B.C. title on June 26 at Highland Heights, Ohio. Haley, who had been the fourth–ranked contender, raised his record to 45–2–2. The 29–year–old champion outscored Mamby on the cards of two judges, 145–142 and 148–144. The third judge scored for Mamby 144–143. The defense was the sixth for Mamby, 35, who won the title on Feb. 23, 1980. His record is 33–13–5.

## Welterweight
(147 pound limit)

Sugar Ray Leonard, in his first defense since he became undisputed champion by defeating Thomas Hearns in September 1981, lost the 1st round on the cards of the three judges, then swarmed back to knock out Bruce Finch at 1:50 of the 3rd round on Feb. 15 at Reno, Nev. Leonard floored Finch twice in the 2nd round. In the 3rd, a left hook buckled the challenger's knees and two left-right combinations sent him to the canvas for the last time. Leonard received $1 million for the fight. In June, Leonard underwent surgery for a detached retina and the injury left the status of his boxing future in doubt.

## Junior Middleweight
(154 pound limit)

Wilfred Benitez, the 23–year–old Puerto Rican champion, kept the W.B.C. title with a unanimous decision over Roberto Duran of Panama at Las Vegas on Jan. 30. Benitez kept the 30–year–old Duran off balance with straight right–hand leads and scored with an effective jab and combinations. The loss was Duran's third in 77 pro fights. Benitez's record was raised to 43–1–1. His only loss was to Sugar Ray Leonard. He received more than $1 million for the bout. Duran, who received $750,000, won only four rounds on the cards of the three judges. Benitez weighed 152¼, Duran 152½.

Davey Moore of New York captured the W.B.A. crown on Feb. 2 at Tokyo by knocking out Tadashi Mihara of Japan in the 6th round. It was the ninth victory and sixth straight knockout for the unbeaten, 22–year–old Moore, who knocked Mihara down three times in the 6th. Under rules agreed upon before the fight, three knockdowns in one round would constitute a knockout. The defense was the first for Mihara, who won the crown in November 1981 after the division title was vacated by Sugar Ray Leonard.

Moore continued winning on April 26 at Johannesburg, South Africa, where he knocked out Charlie Weir, a South African who went down five times and was counted out at 25 seconds of the 5th round. A crowd of 45,000 saw the fight. Moore weighed 152 and Weir 151¾. Moore won again in July, stopping Ayub Kalule in the 10th round at Atlantic City.

## Middleweight
(160 pound limit)

Marvelous Marvin Hagler, the undisputed champion, stopped Bill (Caveman) Lee at 67 seconds of the 1st round on March 7 at Atlantic City. It was the first one–round knockout in a world title fight in more than three and a half years, covering more than 275 bouts. Hagler scored the 45th knockout of his career that shows 54 victories, 2 defeats, and 2 draws. The previous 1st–round knockout in a title match was on June 3, 1978, when Alexis Arguello stopped Diego Alcala in a W.B.C. junior lightweight fight. It was the first 1st–round knockout in the middleweight division since Aug. 25, 1950, when Sugar Ray Robinson stopped Jose Basora in 52 seconds. The 29–year–old Hagler weighed 158, and Lee, 26, scaled 159½. Lee's record is 20–3.

## Light Heavyweight
(175 pound limit)

Michael Spinks registered knockouts in title bouts in February, April, and June in retaining the W.B.A. crown. At Atlantic City on Feb. 13, he battered Mustapha Wassaja, a Ugandan, with four successive left hooks for a 6th–round knockout. He floored Murray Sutherland, from Bay City, Mich., three times in the 8th round and was declared the winner by an automatic knockout in the same Atlantic City ring on April 11. On June 12, again at the Playboy Hotel and Casino ballroom, he posted his 21st straight victory when the referee stopped the bout with Jerry Celestine at 1:58 of the 8th round.

Dwight Braxton, making his first defense since winning the W.B.C. title in December 1981 from Matthew Saad Muhammad, dominated Jerry Martin from the start. He floored Martin twice in the 2nd round and stopped him with a relentless assault in the 6th, when he opened a cut over Martin's right eye. Braxton, from Camden, N.J., weighed 175 pounds. His record is 17–1–1. Martin, from Antigua, West Indies, weighed 173½. His record is 22–4. In a rematch with Matthew Saad Muhammad at Philadelphia, Braxton was clearly superior as he scored a 6th–round knockout.

## Junior Heavyweight
(190 pound limit)

In the new weight division, Ossie Ocasio of Puerto Rico used left hooks and jabs to defeat Robbie Williams of South Africa and take the W.B.A. title on a 15–round split decision. It was the W.B.A.'s first championship bout since the weight division was created. Ocasio weighed 188½, Williams 186¼. A cut under William's left eye hampered him from the 8th round on in the bout at Johannesburg, South Africa, on Feb. 13.

S.T. Gordon of Los Angeles dethroned Carlos DeLeon of Puerto Rico with a knockout at 2:51 of the 2nd round at Highland Heights, Ohio, on June 27 to win the W.B.C. crown. DeLeon, who had won his title in 1981, had made a successful defense against Marvin Camel in February at Atlantic City, scoring an 8th–round knockout.

### Heavyweight

Larry Holmes, the undefeated W.B.C. champion, fought 12 dangerous rounds with Gerry Cooney on June 11 before he knocked out the previously unbeaten 25–year–old challenger at 2:52 of the 13th round at Las Vegas. It was the 40th victory, 30 by knockout, for Holmes and the 11th knockout victory in his 12 defenses of the title. The 32–year–old champion bloodied Cooney's left eye and nose from a two–fisted barrage in the 13th, putting on one of his finest performances. Cooney was penalized 2 points in the 9th and 1 point in the 11th for low blows. The fight was the richest in boxing history, grossing more than $40 million, including pay TV and other ancillary rights. Each fighter earned more than $8 million. Postponed once because of an injury to Cooney's shoulder, the fight was one of the most highly publicized in boxing history. Cooney made a game effort to stay with the champion and, surprisingly, through 12 rounds he trailed Holmes by only 2 points on the scorecards of two judges. Holmes weighed 212½ pounds, Cooney 225½. It was Cooney's only loss in 26 fights.

## OTHER WORLD BOXING TITLEHOLDERS

(Through Aug. 20, 1982)

### Light Heavyweight

| | | | | |
|---|---|---|---|---|
| 1903 | Jack Root, George Gardner | 1950–52 | Joey Maxim | (WBC), Marvin Johnson |
| 1903–05 | Bob Fitzsimmons | 1952–61 | Archie Moore[3] | (WBC) |
| 1905–12 | Philadelphia Jack O'Brien[1] | 1961–63 | Harold Johnson | 1979 Mike Rossman (WBA), Victor |
| 1912–16 | Jack Dillon | 1963–65 | Willie Pastrano | Galindez (WBA), Marvin |
| 1916–20 | Battling Levinsky | 1965–66 | José Torres | Johnson (WBC), Matthew |
| 1920–22 | Georges Carpentier | 1966–67 | Dick Tiger | (Franklin) Saad |
| 1923 | Battling Siki | 1968 | Dick Tiger, Bob Foster | Muhammad (WBC) |
| 1923–25 | Mike McTigue | 1969–70 | Bob Foster | 1980 Matthew Saad Muhammad |
| 1925–26 | Paul Berlenbach | 1971 | Vicente Rondon (WBA), Bob | (WBC), Marvin Johnson |
| 1926–27 | Jack Delaney[2] | | Foster (WBC) | (WBA), Eddie (Gregory) |
| 1927 | Mike McTigue | 1972–73 | Bob Foster (WBA, WBC) | Mustafa Muhammad |
| 1927–29 | Tommy Loughran | 1974 | John Conteh (WBA), Bob | (WBA) |
| 1930 | Jimmy Slattery | | Foster (WBC)[1 4] | 1981 Matthew Saad Muhammad |
| 1930–34 | Maxie Rosenbloom | 1975–76 | Victor Galindez (WBA), John | (WBC), Eddie Mustafa |
| 1934–35 | Bob Olin | | Conteh (WBC) | Muhammad (WBA), |
| 1935–39 | John Henry Lewis | 1977 | Victor Galindez (WBA), John | Michael Spinks (WBA), |
| 1939 | Melio Bettina | | Conteh (WBC)[4], Miguel | Dwight Braxton (WBC) |
| 1939–41 | Billy Conn[2] | | Cuello (WBC) | 1982 Dwight Braxton (WBC), |
| 1941 | Anton Christoforidis (NBA) | 1978 | Victor Galindez (WBA), Mike | Michael Spinks (WBA) |
| 1941–48 | Gus Lesnevich | | Rossman (WBA), Miguel | |
| 1948–50 | Freddie Mills | | Cuello (WBC), Mate Parlov | |

1. Retired. 2. Abandoned title. 3. NBA withdrew recognition in 1961, New York Commission in 1962; recognized thereafter only by California and Europe. 4. WBC withdrew recognition.

### Middleweight

| | | | | |
|---|---|---|---|---|
| 1867–72 | Tom Chandler | | Ken Overlin, Billy Soose, | 1967 Nino Benvenuti, Emile Griffith |
| 1872–81 | George Rooke | | Tony Zale[4] | 1968 Emile Griffith, Nino Benvenuti |
| 1881–82 | Mike Donovan[1] | 1941–47 | Tony Zale | 1969 Nino Benvenuti |
| 1884–91 | Jack (Nonpareil) Dempsey | 1947–48 | Rocky Graziano | 1970 Nino Benvenuti, Carlos Mon- |
| 1891–97 | Bob Fitzsimmons[2] | 1948 | Tony Zale | zon |
| 1908 | Stanley Ketchel, Billy Papke | 1948–49 | Marcel Cerdan | 1971–73 Carlos Monzon |
| 1908–10 | Stanley Ketchel[3] | 1949–51 | Jake LaMotta | 1974–75 Carlos Monzon (WBA), |
| 1913 | Frank Klaus | 1952 | Ray Robinson, Randy Turpin | Rodrigo Valdez (WBC) |
| 1913–14 | George Chip | 1951–52 | Ray Robinson[1] | 1976 Carlos Monzon (WBA, WBC), |
| 1914–17 | Al McCoy | 1953–55 | Carl Olson | Rodrigo Valdez (WBC) |
| 1917–20 | Mike O'Dowd | 1955–57 | Ray Robinson[5] | 1977 Carlos Monzon (WBA, |
| 1920–23 | Johnny Wilson | 1957 | Gene Fullmer, Ray Robinson | WBC)[1], Rodrigo Valdez |
| 1923–26 | Harry Greb | 1957–58 | Carmen Basilio | (WBA, WBC) |
| 1926 | Tiger Flowers | 1958–60 | Ray Robinson[6] | 1978 Rodrigo Valdez, Hugo Corro |
| 1926–31 | Mickey Walker[2] | 1960–61 | Paul Pender[7] | 1979 Hugo Corro, Vito Antuofermo |
| 1931–41 | Gorilla Jones, Ben Jeby, | 1959–62 | Gene Fullmer (NBA) | 1980 Vito Antuofermo, Alan |
| | Marcel Thil, Lou Brouillard, | 1961–62 | Terry Downes[1] | Minter, Marvin Hagler |
| | Vince Dundee, Teddy | 1962 | Paul Pender[1] | 1981 Marvin Hagler |
| | Yarosz, Babe Risko, | 1962–63 | Dick Tiger | 1982 Marvelous Marvin Hagler |
| | Freddy Steele, Al Hostak, | 1963–65 | Joey Giardello | |
| | Solly Kreiger, Fred | 1965–66 | Dick Tiger | |
| | Apostoli, Ceferino Garcia, | 1966 | Emile Griffith | |

1. Retired. 2. Abandoned title. 3. Died. 4. National Boxing Association and New York Commission disagreed on champions. Those listed were accepted by one or the other until Zale gained world-wide recognition. 5. Ended retirement in 1954. 6. NBA withdrew recognition. 7. Recognized by New York, Massachusetts, and Europe.

## Welterweight

| | | | | | |
|---|---|---|---|---|---|
| 1892–94 | Mysterious Billy Smith | 1933 | Young Corbett 3rd | 1969 | Curtis Cokes, José Napoles |
| 1894–96 | Tommy Ryan | 1933–34 | Jimmy McLarnin, Barney Ross | 1970 | José Napoles, Billy Backus |
| 1896 | Kid McCoy[2] | 1934–35 | Jimmy McLarnin | 1971 | Billy Backus, José Napoles |
| 1896– | | 1935–38 | Barney Ross | 1972–74 | José Napoles |
| 1900 | Mysterious Billy Smith | 1938–40 | Henry Armstrong | 1975 | José Napoles (WBA, WBC)[3], |
| 1900 | Rube Ferns | 1940–41 | Fritzie Zivic | | Angel Espada (WBA), John |
| 1900–01 | Matty Matthews | 1941–46 | Freddie Cochrane | | Stracey (WBC) |
| 1901 | Ruby Ferns | 1946 | Marty Servo[1] | 1976 | Angel Espada (WBA), José |
| 1901–04 | Joe Walcott | 1946–51 | Ray Robinson[2] | | Cuevas (WBA), John |
| 1904 | Dixie Kid[2] | 1951 | Johnny Bratton (NBA) | | Stracey (WBC), Carlos |
| 1904–06 | Joe Walcott | 1951–54 | Kid Gavilan | | Palomino (WBC) |
| 1906–07 | Honey Mellody | 1954–55 | Johnny Saxton | 1977–78 | José Cuevas (WBA), Carlos |
| 1907 | Mike (Twin) Sullivan[2] | 1955 | Tony DeMarco | | Palomino (WBC) |
| 1915–19 | Ted Lewis | 1955–56 | Carmen Basilio | 1979 | José Cuevas (WBA), Carlos |
| 1919–22 | Jack Britton | 1956 | Johnny Saxton | | Palomino (WBC), Wilfredo |
| 1922–26 | Mickey Walker | 1956–57 | Carmen Basilio[2] | | Benitez (WBC) |
| 1926–27 | Pete Latzo | 1958 | Virgil Akins | 1980 | Jose Cuevas (WBA), Sugar |
| 1927–29 | Joe Dundee | 1959–60 | Don Jordan | | Ray Leonard (WBC), |
| 1929–30 | Jackie Fields | 1960–61 | Benny (Kid) Paret | | Roberto Duran (WBC), |
| 1930 | Young Jack Thompson | 1961 | Emile Griffith | | Thomas Hearns (WBA) |
| 1930–31 | Tommy Freeman | 1961–62 | Benny (Kid) Paret | 1981 | Ray Leonard (WBC), Thomas |
| 1931 | Young Jack Thompson | 1962–63 | Emile Griffith, Luis Rodriguez | | Hearns (WBA), Ray |
| 1931–32 | Lou Brouillard | 1963–66 | Emile Griffith[2] | | Leonard (WBC,WBA) |
| 1932–33 | Jackie Fields | 1966–69 | Curtis Cokes | 1982 | Ray Leonard |

1. Retired. 2. Abandoned title. 3. WBA withdrew recognition.

## Lightweight

| | | | | | |
|---|---|---|---|---|---|
| 1869–99 | Kid Lavigne | 1947–51 | Ike Williams | 1974 | Roberto Duran (WBA), |
| 1899– | | 1951–52 | James Carter | | Rodolfo Gonzalez (WBC), |
| 1902 | Frank Erne | 1952 | Lauro Salas | | Guts Ishimatsu (WBC) |
| 1902–08 | Joe Gans | 1952–54 | James Carter | 1975 | Roberto Duran (WBA), Guts |
| 1908–10 | Battling Nelson | 1954 | Paddy DeMarco | | Ishimatsu (WBC) |
| 1910–12 | Ad Wolgast | 1954–55 | James Carter | 1976 | Roberto Duran (WBA), Guts |
| 1912–14 | Willie Ritchie | 1955–56 | Wallace Smith | | Ishimatsu (WBC), Esteban |
| 1914–17 | Freddy Welsh | 1956–62 | Joe Brown | | De Jesus (WBC) |
| 1917–25 | Benny Leonard[1] | 1962–65 | Carlos Ortiz | 1977 | Roberto Duran (WBA), Este- |
| 1925 | Jimmy Goodrich | 1965 | Ismael Laguna | | ban De Jesus (WBC) |
| 1925–26 | Rocky Kansas | 1965–68 | Carlos Ortiz | 1978 | Roberto Duran (WBA, WBC) |
| 1926–30 | Sammy Mandell | 1968 | Teo Cruz | 1979 | Roberto Duran[2]; Jim Watt |
| 1930 | Al Singer | 1969 | Teo Cruz, Mando Ramos | | (WBC), Ernesto Espana |
| 1930–33 | Tony Canzoneri | 1970 | Mando Ramos, Ismael | | (WBA) |
| 1933–35 | Barney Ross[2] | | Laguna, Ken Buchanan | 1980 | Ernesto Espana (WBA), |
| 1935–36 | Tony Canzoneri | 1971 | Ken Buchanan (WBA), Mando | | Hilmer Kenty (WBA), Jim |
| 1936–38 | Lou Ambers | | Ramos (WBC), Pedro Car- | | Watt (WBC) |
| 1938–39 | Henry Armstrong | | rasco (WBC) | 1981 | Hilmer Kenty (WBA), Sean |
| 1939–40 | Lou Ambers | 1972 | Ken Buchanan (WBA), | | O'Grady (WBA), James |
| 1940–41 | Lew Jenkins | | Roberto Duran (WBA), | | Watt (WBC), Alexis |
| 1941–42 | Sammy Angott[1] | | Pedro Carrasco (WBC), | | Arguello (WBC), Arturo |
| 1943–47 | Beau Jack (N.Y.), Bob | | Mando Ramos (WBC), | | Frias (WBA) |
| | Montgomery (N.Y.), | | Chango Carmona (WBC), | 1982 | Arturo Frias (WBA), Ray |
| | Sammy Angott (NBA), | | Rodolfo Gonzalez (WBC) | | Mancini (WBA), Alexis |
| | Juan Zurita (NBA), Ike | 1973 | Roberto Duran (WBA), | | Arguello (WBC) |
| | Williams (NBA) | | Rodolfo Gonzalez (WBC) | | |

1. Retired. 2. Abandoned title.

## Featherweight

| | | | | | |
|---|---|---|---|---|---|
| 1889 | Dal Hawkins[1] | | | 1964–67 | Vicente Saldivar[2] |
| 1890 | Billy Murphy | 1932 | Tommy Paul (NBA), Kid | 1968 | Howard Winstone, José |
| 1892– | | | Chocolate (N.Y.) | | Legra,[3] Paul Rojas (WBA), |
| 1900 | George Dixon | 1933–36 | Freddie Miller | | Sho Saijo (WBA) |
| 1900–01 | Terry McGovern | 1936–37 | Petey Sarron | 1969 | Sho Saijo (WBA), Johnny |
| 1901 | Young Corbett[1] | 1937–38 | Henry Armstrong[1] | | Famechon[3] |
| 1901–12 | Abe Attell | 1938–40 | Joey Archibald | 1970 | Sho Saijo (WBA), Johnny |
| 1912–23 | Johnny Kilbane | 1940–41 | Harry Jefra, Joey Archibald | | Famechon,[3] Vicente |
| 1923 | Eugene Criqui | 1941–42 | Chalky Wright | | Salvidar,[3] Kuniaki Shibata[3] |
| 1923–25 | Johnny Dundee[1] | 1942–48 | Willie Pep | 1971 | Sho Saijo (WBA), Antonio |
| 1925–27 | Louis (Kid) Kaplan[1] | 1948–49 | Sandy Saddler[2] | | Gomez (WBA), Kuniaki |
| 1927–28 | Benny Bass | 1949–50 | Willie Pep | | Shibata (WBC) |
| 1928 | Tony Canzoneri | 1950–57 | Sandy Saddler | 1972 | Antonio Gomez (WBA), |
| 1928–29 | Andre Routis | 1957–59 | Kid Bassey | | Ernesto Marcel (WBA), |
| 1929–32 | Battling Battalino[1] | 1959–63 | Davey Moore | | Kuniaki Shibata (WBC), |
| | | 1963–64 | Sugar Ramos | | |

| | | | |
|---|---|---|---|
| | Clemente Sanchez (WBC),[2] José Legra (WBC) | | Bobby Chacon (WBC), Ruben Olivares (WBC), David Kotey (WBC) | 1979 | Lopez (WBC) Eusebio Pedrosa (WBA), Danny Lopez (WBC) |
| 1973 | Ernesto Marcel (WBA), José Legra (WBC), Eder Jofre (WBC) | 1976 | Alexis Arguello (WBA),[2] David Kotey (WBC), Danny Lopez (WBC) | 1980 | Eusebio Pedroza (WBA), Danny Lopez (WBC), Salvador Sanchez (WBC) |
| 1974 | Ernesto Marcel (WBA),[2] Ruben Olivares (WBA), Alexis Arguello (WBA), Eder Jofre (WBC), Bobby Chacon (WBC) | 1977 | Rafael Ortega (WBA), Danny Lopez (WBC) | 1981 | Eusebio Pedroza (WBA), Salvador Sanchez (WBC) |
| 1975 | Alexis Arguello (WBA), | 1978 | Rafael Ortega (WBA), Cecilio Lastra (WBA), Eusebio Pedrosa (WBA), Danny | 1982 | Eusebio Pedroza (WBA), Salvador Sanchez (WBC)[4] |

1. Abandoned title. 2. Retired. 3. Recognized in Europe, Mexico, and Orient. 4. Killed in auto accident.

## Bantamweight

| | | | | | |
|---|---|---|---|---|---|
| 1890–92 | George Dixon[1] | 1940–42 | Lou Salica | | Rodolfo Martinez (WBC), |
| 1894–99 | Jimmy Barry[2] | 1942–46 | Manuel Ortiz | | Rafael Herrera (WBC) |
| 1899– | | 1947 | Manuel Ortiz, Harold Dade | 1974 | Arnold Taylor (WBA), Soo |
| 1900 | Terry McGovern[1] | 1948–50 | Manuel Ortiz | | Hwan Hong (WBA), Rafael |
| 1901 | Harry Harris[1] | 1950–52 | Vic Toweel | | Herrera (WBC), Rodolfo |
| 1902–03 | Harry Forbes | 1952–54 | Jimmy Carruthers[2] | | Martinez (WBC) |
| 1903–04 | Frankie Neil | 1954–55 | Robert Cohen | 1975 | Soo Hwan Hong (WBA), |
| 1904 | Joe Bowker[1] | 1956 | Robert Cohen, Mario | | Alfonso Zamora (WBA), |
| 1905–07 | Jimmy Walsh[1] | | D'Agata, Raul Macias | | Rodolfo Martinez (WBC) |
| 1910–14 | Johnny Coulon | | (NBA) | 1976 | Alfonso Zamora (WBA), |
| 1914–17 | Kid Williams | 1957 | Mario D'Agata, Alphonse | | Rodolfo Martinez (WBC), |
| 1917–20 | Pete Herman | | Halimi | | Carlos Zarate (WBC) |
| 1920 | Joe Lynch | 1958–59 | Alphonse Halimi | 1977 | Alfonso Zamora (WBA), |
| 1920–21 | Joe Lynch, Pete Herman, Johnny Buff | 1959–60 | Jose Becerra[2] | | Jorge Lujan (WBA), Carlos Zarate (WBC) |
| | | 1960–61 | Alphonse Halimi[4] | | |
| 1922 | Johnny Buff, Joe Lynch | 1961–62 | Johnny Caldwell[4] | 1978 | Jorge Lujan (WBA), Carlos |
| 1923 | Joe Lynch | 1961–65 | Eder Jofre | | Zarate (WBC) |
| 1924 | Joe Lynch, Abe Goldstein | 1965–68 | Masahika (Fighting) Harada | 1979 | Jorge Lujan (WBA), Carlos |
| 1924 | Abe Goldstein, Eddie (Cannonball) Martin | 1968 | Masahika (Fighting) Harada, Lionel Rose | | Zarate (WBC), Lupe Pintor (WBC) |
| 1925 | Eddie (Cannonball) Martin, Charlie (Phil) Rosenberg[3] | 1969 | Lionel Rose, Ruben Olivares | 1980 | Jorge Lujan (WBA), Lupe Pintor (WBC), Julian Solis |
| | | 1970 | Ruben Olivares, Chucho Castillo | | (WBA) Jeff Chandler (WBA) |
| 1927–28 | Bud Taylor (NBA)[1] | | | | |
| 1929–34 | Al Brown | 1971 | Chucho Castillo, Ruben Olivares | 1981 | Lupe Pintor (WBC), Jeff Chandler (WBA) |
| 1935 | Al Brown, Baltazar Sangchili | | | | |
| 1936 | Baltazar Sangchili, Tony Marino, Sixto Escobar | 1972 | Ruben Olivares, Rafael Herrera, Enrique Pinder | 1982 | Lupe Pintor (WBC), Jeff Chandler (WBA) |
| 1937 | Sixto Escobar, Harry Jeffra | 1973 | Enrique Pinder (WBA), Romeo Anaya (WBA), Arnold Taylor (WBA) | | |
| 1938 | Harry Jeffra, Sixto Escobar | | | | |
| 1939–40 | Sixto Escobar[2] | | | | |

1. Abandoned title. 2. Retired. 3. Deprived of title for failing to make weight. 4. Recognized in Europe.

## Flyweight

| | | | | | |
|---|---|---|---|---|---|
| 1916–23 | Jimmy Wilde | 1966 | Walter McGown, Chartchai Chionoi | | Betulio Gonzalez (WBC), Shoji Oguma (WBC) |
| 1923–25 | Pancho Villa[1] | | | | |
| 1925 | Frankie Genaro | 1966–68 | Charchai Chionoi | 1975 | Susumu Hanagata (WBA), |
| 1925–27 | Fidel La Barba[2] | 1969 | Bernabe Villacampa, Efran Torres (WBA) | | Erbito Salavarria (WBA), Shoji Oguma (WBC), |
| 1927–31 | Corporal Izzy Schwartz, Frankie Genaro, Emile (Spider) Pladner, Midget Wolgast, Young Perez[3] | 1970 | Bernabe Villacampa, Chartchai Chionoi, Erbito Salavarria, Berkrerk Chartvanchai (WBA), Masao Ohba (WBA) | 1976 | Miguel Canto (WBC) Erbito Salavarria (WBA), Alfonso Lopez (WBA), Guty Espadas (WBA), Miguel Canto (WBC) |
| 1932–35 | Jackie Brown | | | | |
| 1935–38 | Bennie Lynch[4] | 1971 | Masao Ohba (WBA), Erbito Salavarria (WBC) | 1977 | Guty Espadas (WBA), Miguel Canto (WBC) |
| 1939 | Peter Kane[4] | | | | |
| 1943–47 | Jackie Paterson[1] | 1972 | Masao Ohba (WBA), Erbito Salavarria (WBC), Betulio Gonzalez (WBC), Venice Borkorsor (WBC) | 1978 | Guty Espadas (WBA), Betulio Gonzalez (WBA), Miguel Canto (WBC) |
| 1947–50 | Rinty Monaghan[2] | | | | |
| 1950 | Terry Allen | | | | |
| 1950–52 | Dado Marino | | | | |
| 1952–54 | Yoshio Shirai | 1973 | Masao Ohba (WBA), Chartchai Chionoi (WBA), Venice Borkorsor (WBC), Betulio Gonzalez (WBC) | 1979 | Betulio Gonzalez (WBA), Miguel Canto (WBC), Park Chan-Hee (WBC) |
| 1954–60 | Pascual Perez | | | | |
| 1960–62 | Pone Kingpetch | | | | |
| 1962–63 | Masahika (Fighting) Harada | | | | |
| 1963–64 | Hiroyuki Ebihara | 1974 | Chartchai Chionoi (WBA), Susumu Hanagata (WBA), | 1980 | Luis Ibarra (WBA), Kim Tae Shik (WBA), Park Chan-Hee (WBC), Shoji Oguma (WBC) Peter |
| 1964–65 | Pone Kingpetch | | | | |
| 1965–66 | Salvatore Burrini | | | | |

| | | | |
|---|---|---|---|
| 1981 | Mathebula (WBA) Shoji Oguma (WBC), Peter Mathebula (WBA), Santos Laciar (WBA), Luis Ibarra (WBA), Juan Herrera (WBA), Antonio Avelar (WBC) | 1982 | Juan Herrera (WBA), Prudencio Cardona (WBC), Santos Laciar (WBA), Antonio Avelar (WBC), Freddie Castillo (WBC) |

1. Died. 2. Retired. 3. Claimants to NBA and New York Commission titles. 4. Abandoned title.

## FIGHTER OF THE YEAR
Selected by *The Ring* Magazine.

| | | | | | |
|---|---|---|---|---|---|
| 1928 | Gene Tunney | 1941 | Joe Louis | 1955 | Rocky Marciano |
| 1929 | Tommy Loughran | 1942 | Ray Robinson | 1956 | Floyd Patterson |
| 1930 | Max Schmeling | 1943 | Fred Apostoli | 1957 | Carmen Basilio |
| 1931 | Tommy Loughran | 1944 | Beau Jack | 1958 | Ingemar Johansson |
| 1932 | Jack Sharkey | 1945 | Willie Pep | 1959 | Ingemar Johansson |
| 1933 | No award | 1946 | Tony Zale | 1960 | Floyd Patterson |
| 1934 | Barney Ross and Tony Canzoneri | 1947 | Gus Lesnevich | 1961 | Joe Brown |
| 1935 | Barney Ross | 1948 | Ike Williams | 1962 | Dick Tiger |
| 1936 | Joe Louis | 1949 | Ezzard Charles | 1963 | Cassius Clay |
| 1937 | Henry Armstrong | 1950 | Ezzard Charles | 1964 | Emile Griffith |
| 1938 | Joe Louis | 1951 | Ray Robinson | 1965 | Dick Tiger |
| 1939 | Joe Louis | 1952 | Rocky Marciano | 1966 | No award |
| 1940 | Billy Conn | 1953 | Bobo Olson | 1967 | Joe Frazier |
| | | 1954 | Rocky Marciano | 1968 | Nino Benvenuti |

| | |
|---|---|
| 1969 | Jose Napoles |
| 1970–71 | Joe Frazier |
| 1972 | Carlos Monzon and Muhammad Ali |
| 1973 | George Foreman |
| 1974–75 | Muhammad Ali |
| 1976 | George Foreman |
| 1977 | Carlos Zarate |
| 1978 | Muhammand Ali |
| 1979 | Sugar Ray Leonard |
| 1980 | Thomas Hearns |
| 1981 | Sugar Ray Leonard |

# BOXING—AMATEUR

## U.S. AMATEUR CHAMPIONSHIPS—1982

### U.S. Amateur Boxing Federation
(Charlotte, N.C., April 12–17, 1982)

106 lb—Mario Lesperance, Vallejo, Calif.
112 lb—Steve McCrory, Detroit, Mich.
119 lb—Floyd Favors, Capitol Heights, Md.
125 lb—Orlando Johnson, Chicago
132 lb—Pernell Whitaker, Norfolk, Va.
139 lb—Henry Hughes, Cleveland, Ohio
147 lb—Mark Breland, Brooklyn, N.Y.
156 lb—Dennis Milton, Bronx, N.Y.
165 lb—Michael Grogan, Atlanta
178 lb—Bennie Heard, Augusta, Ga.
201 lb—Elmer Martin, United States Navy
Over 201 lb—Tyrell Biggs, Philadelphia

### WORLD CHAMPIONSHIPS—1982
(Munich, West Germany, May 15, 1982)

106 lb—Ismail Mustafov, Bulgaria
112 lb—Yuri Alexandrov, Soviet Union
119 lb—Floyd Favors, United States
125 lb—Adolfo Hortz, Cuba
132 lb—Angel Herrera, Cuba
139 lb—Carlos Garcia, Cuba
147 lb—Mark Breland, United States
156 lb—Aleksandr Koshkin, Soviet Union
165 lb—Bernardo Comas, Cuba
178 lb—Pablo Romero, Cuba
Heavyweight—Aleksandr Yagubkin, Soviet Union
Super heavyweight—Tyrone Biggs, United States

### NATIONAL GOLDEN GLOVES CHAMPIONS—1982
(Kansas City, Mo., April 4, 1982)

106 lb—Jose Rosario, Jersey City, N.J.
112 lb—Jesse Benavides, Corpus Christi, Tex.
119 lb—Meldrick Taylor, Philadelphia
125 lb—Shelton LeBlanc, Lafayette, La.
139 lb—Timmy Rabon, Lafayette, La.
147 lb—Roman George, Lafayette, La.
156 lb—Sanderline Williams, Cleveland, Ohio
165 lb—Arthel Lawhorn, Detroit, Mich.
178 lb—Keith Vining, Detroit, Mich.
Heavyweight—Earl Lewis, Cleveland, Ohio
Superheavyweight—Warren Thompson, Baltimore, Md.
Team—Lafayette, La.
Outstanding boxer—Jesse Benavides

# LUGE

## UNITED STATES CHAMPIONSHIPS
(Lake Placid, N.Y., Feb. 16–17, 1982)

Men—Frank Masley, Newark, Del.
Women—Erica Terwillegar, Lake Placid, N.Y.
Men's doubles—Terry Morgan, Saranac Lake, N.Y., and Bo Jamieson, Hudson, Ohio
Women's junior—Erica Terwillegar
Women's youth division—Cammy Myler, Willsboro, N.Y.
Men's junior—Christian Bochniowicz, Old Forge, Pa.
Men's junior doubles—Christian Bochniowicz and Duncan Kennedy, Lake Placid, N.Y.

## WORLD JUNIOR CHAMPIONS
(Lake Placid, N.Y., Jan. 23–24, 1982)

Men—Hans–Joachim Shurack, East Germany
Women—Elena Buslaeva, Soviet Union
Men's doubles—Jorg Hoffmann and Jocher Pietzsch, East Germany

## WORLD CHAMPIONS*
(Hammarstrand, Sweden, Feb. 1–3, 1981)

Men—Sergei Damilin, Soviet Union
Women—Melitta Sollman, East Germany
*The world championship was not contested in 1982.

# HORSE RACING

Ancient drawings on stone and bone prove that horse racing is at least 3000 years old, but Thoroughbred Racing is a modern development. Practically every thoroughbred in training today traces its registered ancestry back to one or more of three sires that arrived in England about 1728 from the Near East and became known, from the names of their owners, as the Byerly Turk, the Darley Arabian, and the Godolphin Arabian. The Jockey Club (English) was founded at Newmarket in 1750 or 1751 and became the custodian of the Stud Book as well as the court of last resort in deciding turf affairs.

Horse racing took place in this country before the Revolution, but the great lift to the breeding industry came with the importation in 1798, by Col. John Hoomes of Virginia, of Diomed, winner of the Epsom Derby of 1780. Diomed's lineal descendants included such famous stars of the American turf as American Eclipse and Lexington. From 1800 to the time of the Civil War there were race courses and breeding establishments plentifully scattered through Virginia, North Carolina, South Carolina, Tennessee, Kentucky, and Louisiana.

The oldest stake event in North America is the Queen's Plate, a Canadian fixture that was first run in the Province of Quebec in 1836. The oldest stake event in the United States is The Travers, which was first run at Saratoga in 1864. The gambling that goes with horse racing and trickery by jockeys, trainers, owners, and track officials caused attacks on the sport by reformers and a demand among horse racing enthusiasts for an honest and effective control of some kind, but nothing of lasting value to racing came of this until the formation in 1894 of The Jockey Club.

## "TRIPLE CROWN" WINNERS IN THE UNITED STATES[1]

### (Kentucky Derby, Preakness and Belmont Stakes)

| Year | Horse | Owner | Year | Horse | Owner |
|------|-------|-------|------|-------|-------|
| 1919 | Sir Barton | J. K. L. Ross | 1946 | Assault | Robert J. Kleberg |
| 1930 | Gallant Fox | William Woodward | 1948 | Citation | Warren Wright |
| 1935 | Omaha | William Woodward | 1973 | Secretariat | Meadow Stable |
| 1937 | War Admiral | Samuel D. Riddle | 1977 | Seattle Slew | Karen Taylor |
| 1941 | Whirlaway | Warren Wright | 1978 | Affirmed | Louis Wolfson |
| 1943 | Count Fleet | Mrs. John Hertz | | | |

1. Statistics relative to thoroughbred racing in this publication are reproduced from the *American Racing Manual*, by special permission of the copyright owners. TRIANGLE PUBLICATIONS, INC. Reproduction prohibited.

## KENTUCKY DERBY

Churchill Downs; 3-year-olds; 1 1/4 miles.

| Year | Winner | Jockey | Wt. | Win val. | Year | Winner | Jockey | Wt. | Win val. |
|------|--------|--------|-----|----------|------|--------|--------|-----|----------|
| 1875 | Aristides | O. Lewis | 100 | $2,850 | 1909 | Wintergreen | V. Powers | 117 | $ 4,850 |
| 1876 | Vagrant | R. Swim | 97 | 2,950 | 1910 | Donau | F. Herbert | 117 | 4,850 |
| 1877 | Baden Baden | W. Walker | 100 | 3,300 | 1911 | Meridian | G. Archibald | 117 | 4,850 |
| 1878 | Day Star | J. Carter | 100 | 4,050 | 1912 | Worth | C. H. Shilling | 117 | 4,850 |
| 1879 | Lord Murphy | C. Schauer | 100 | 3,550 | 1913 | Donerail | R. Goose | 117 | 5,475 |
| 1880 | Fonso | G. Lewis | 105 | 3,800 | 1914 | Old Rosebud | J. McCabe | 114 | 9,125 |
| 1881 | Hindoo | J. McLaughlin | 105 | 4,410 | 1915 | Regret | J. Notter | 112 | 11,450 |
| 1882 | Apollo | B. Hurd | 102 | 4,560 | 1916 | George Smith | J. Loftus | 117 | 9,750 |
| 1883 | Leonatus | W. Donohue | 105 | 3,760 | 1917 | Omar Khayyam | C. Borel | 117 | 16,600 |
| 1884 | Buchanan | I. Murphy | 110 | 3,990 | 1918 | Exterminator | W. Knapp | 114 | 14,700 |
| 1885 | Joe Cotton | E. Henderson | 110 | 4,630 | 1919 | Sir Barton | J. Loftus | 112 1/2 | 20,825 |
| 1886 | Ben Ali | P. Duffy | 118 | 4,890 | 1920 | Paul Jones | T. Rice | 126 | 30,375 |
| 1887 | Montrose | I. Lewis | 118 | 4,200 | 1921 | Behave Yourself | C. Thompson | 126 | 38,450 |
| 1888 | Macbeth II | G. Covington | 115 | 4,740 | 1922 | Morvich | A. Johnson | 126 | 46,775 |
| 1889 | Spokane | T. Kiley | 118 | 4,970 | 1923 | Zev | E. Sande | 126 | 53,600 |
| 1890 | Riley | I. Murphy | 118 | 5,460 | 1924 | Black Gold | J. D. Mooney | 126 | 52,775 |
| 1891 | Kingman | I. Murphy | 122 | 4,680 | 1925 | Flying Ebony | E. Sande | 126 | 52,950 |
| 1892 | Azra | A. Clayton | 122 | 4,230 | 1926 | Bubbling Over | A. Johnson | 126 | 50,075 |
| 1893 | Lookout | E. Kunze | 122 | 4,090 | 1927 | Whiskery | L. McAtee | 126 | 51,000 |
| 1894 | Chant | F. Goodale | 122 | 4,020 | 1928 | Reigh Count | C. Lang | 126 | 55,375 |
| 1895 | Halma | J. Perkins | 122 | 2,970 | 1929 | Clyde Van Dusen | L. McAtee | 126 | 53,950 |
| 1896 | Ben Brush | W. Simms | 117 | 4,850 | 1930 | Gallant Fox | E. Sande | 126 | 50,725 |
| 1897 | Typhoon II | F. Garner | 117 | 4,850 | 1931 | Twenty Grand | C. Kurtsinger | 126 | 48,725 |
| 1898 | Plaudit | W. Simms | 117 | 4,850 | 1932 | Burgoo King | E. James | 126 | 52,350 |
| 1899 | Manuel | F. Taral | 117 | 4,850 | 1933 | Brokers Tip | D. Meade | 126 | 48,925 |
| 1900 | Lieut. Gibson | J. Boland | 117 | 4,850 | 1934 | Cavalcade | M. Garner | 126 | 28,175 |
| 1901 | His Eminence | J. Winkfield | 117 | 4,850 | 1935 | Omaha | W. Saunders | 126 | 39,525 |
| 1902 | Alan-a-Dale | J. Winkfield | 117 | 4,850 | 1936 | Bold Venture | I. Hanford | 126 | 37,725 |
| 1903 | Judge Himes | H. Booker | 117 | 4,850 | 1937 | War Admiral | C. Kurtsinger | 126 | 52,050 |
| 1904 | Elwood | F. Prior | 117 | 4,850 | 1938 | Lawrin | E. Arcaro | 126 | 47,050 |
| 1905 | Agile | J. Martin | 122 | 4,850 | 1939 | Johnstown | J. Stout | 126 | 46,350 |
| 1906 | Sir Huon | R. Troxler | 117 | 4,850 | 1940 | Gallahadion | C. Bierman | 126 | 60,150 |
| 1907 | Pink Star | A. Minder | 117 | 4,850 | 1941 | Whirlaway | E. Arcaro | 126 | 61,275 |
| 1908 | Stone Street | A. Pickens | 117 | 4,850 | 1942 | Shut Out | W. D. Wright | 126 | 64,225 |

| Year | Winner | Jockey | Wt. | Win val. | Year | Winner | Jockey | Wt. | Win val. |
|------|--------|--------|-----|----------|------|--------|--------|-----|----------|
| 1943 | Count Fleet | J. Longden | 126 | $ 60,725 | 1963 | Chateaugay | B. Baeza | 126 | $108,900 |
| 1944 | Pensive | C. McCreary | 126 | 64,675 | 1964 | Northern Dancer | W. Hartack | 126 | 114,300 |
| 1945 | Hoop Jr. | E. Arcaro | 126 | 64,850 | 1965 | Lucky Debonair | W. Shoemaker | 126 | 112,000 |
| 1946 | Assault | W. Mehrtens | 126 | 96,400 | 1966 | Kauai King | D. Brumfield | 126 | 120,500 |
| 1947 | Jet Pilot | E. Guerin | 126 | 92,160 | 1967 | Proud Clarion | R. Ussery | 126 | 119,700 |
| 1948 | Citation | E. Arcaro | 126 | 83,400 | 1968 | Forward Pass[1] | I. Valenzuela | 126 | 122,600 |
| 1949 | Ponder | S. Brooks | 126 | 91,600 | 1969 | Majestic Prince | W. Hartack | 126 | 113,200 |
| 1950 | Middleground | W. Boland | 126 | 92,650 | 1970 | Dust Commander | M. Manganello | 126 | 127,800 |
| 1951 | Count Turf | C. McCreary | 126 | 98,050 | 1971 | Canonero II | G. Avila | 126 | 145,500 |
| 1952 | Hill Gail | E. Arcaro | 126 | 96,300 | 1972 | Riva Ridge | R. Turcotte | 126 | 140,300 |
| 1953 | Dark Star | H. Moreno | 126 | 90,050 | 1973 | Secretariat | R. Turcotte | 126 | 155,050 |
| 1954 | Determine | R. York | 126 | 102,050 | 1974 | Cannonade | A. Cordero, Jr. | 126 | 274,000 |
| 1955 | Swaps | W. Shoemaker | 126 | 108,400 | 1975 | Foolish Pleasure | J. Vasquez | 126 | 209,600 |
| 1956 | Needles | D. Erb | 126 | 123,450 | 1976 | Bold Forbes | A. Cordero, Jr. | 126 | 165,200 |
| 1957 | Iron Liege | W. Hartack | 126 | 107,950 | 1977 | Seattle Slew | J. Cruguet | 126 | 214,700 |
| 1958 | Tim Tam | I. Valenzuela | 126 | 116,400 | 1978 | Affirmed | S. Cauthen | 126 | 186,900 |
| 1959 | Tomy Lee | W. Shoemaker | 126 | 119,650 | 1979 | Spectacular Bid | R. Franklin | 126 | 228,650 |
| 1960 | Venetian Way | W. Hartack | 126 | 114,850 | 1980 | Genuine Risk | J. Vasquez | 126 | 250,550 |
| 1961 | Carry Back | J. Sellers | 126 | 120,500 | 1981 | Pleasant Colony | J. Velasquez | 126 | 317,200 |
| 1962 | Decidedly | W. Hartack | 126 | 119,650 | 1982 | Gato del Sol | E. Delahoussaye | 126 | 417,600 |

1. Dancer's Image finished first but was disqualified after traces of drug were found in system.

## PREAKNESS STAKES

Pimlico; 3-year-olds; 1³/₁₆ miles; first race 1873.

| Year | Winner | Jockey | Wt. | Win val. | Year | Winner | Jockey | Wt. | Win val. |
|------|--------|--------|-----|----------|------|--------|--------|-----|----------|
| 1919 | Sir Barton | J. Loftus | 126 | $ 24,500 | 1956 | Fabius | W. Hartack | 126 | $ 84,250 |
| 1930 | Gallant Fox | E. Sande | 126 | 51,925 | 1957 | Bold Ruler | E. Arcaro | 126 | 65,250 |
| 1931 | Mate | G. Ellis | 126 | 48,225 | 1958 | Tim Tam | I. Valenzuela | 126 | 97,900 |
| 1932 | Burgoo King | E. James | 126 | 50,375 | 1959 | Royal Orbit | W. Harmatz | 126 | 136,200 |
| 1933 | Head Play | C. Kurtsinger | 126 | 26,850 | 1960 | Bally Ache | R. Ussery | 126 | 121,000 |
| 1934 | High Quest | R. Jones | 126 | 25,175 | 1961 | Carry Back | J. Sellers | 126 | 126,200 |
| 1935 | Omaha | W. Saunders | 126 | 25,325 | 1962 | Greek Money | J. Rotz | 126 | 135,800 |
| 1936 | Bold Venture | G. Woolf | 126 | 27,325 | 1963 | Candy Spots | W. Shoemaker | 126 | 127,500 |
| 1937 | War Admiral | C. Kurtsinger | 126 | 45,600 | 1964 | Northern Dancer | W. Hartack | 126 | 124,200 |
| 1938 | Dauber | M. Peters | 126 | 51,875 | 1965 | Tom Rolfe | R. Turcotte | 126 | 128,100 |
| 1939 | Challedon | G. Seabo | 126 | 53,710 | 1966 | Kauai King | D. Brumfield | 126 | 129,000 |
| 1940 | Bimelech | F.A. Smith | 126 | 53,230 | 1967 | Damascus | W. Shoemaker | 126 | 141,500 |
| 1941 | Whirlaway | E. Arcaro | 126 | 49,365 | 1968 | Forward Pass | I. Valenzuela | 126 | 142,700 |
| 1942 | Alsab | B. James | 126 | 58,175 | 1969 | Majestic Prince | W. Hartack | 126 | 129,500 |
| 1943 | Count Fleet | J. Longden | 126 | 43,190 | 1970 | Personality | E. Belmonte | 126 | 151,300 |
| 1944 | Pensive | C. McCreary | 126 | 60,075 | 1971 | Canonero II | G. Avila | 126 | 137,400 |
| 1945 | Polynesian | W.D. Wright | 126 | 66,170 | 1972 | Bee Bee Bee | E. Nelson | 126 | 135,300 |
| 1946 | Assault | W. Mehrtens | 126 | 96,620 | 1973 | Secretariat | R. Turcotte | 126 | 129,900 |
| 1947 | Faultless | D. Dodson | 126 | 98,005 | 1974 | Little Current | M. Rivera | 126 | 156,000 |
| 1948 | Citation | E. Arcaro | 126 | 91,870 | 1975 | Master Derby | D. McHargue | 126 | 158,100 |
| 1949 | Capot | T. Atkinson | 126 | 79,985 | 1976 | Elocutionist | J. Lively | 126 | 129,700 |
| 1950 | Hill Prince | E. Arcaro | 126 | 56,115 | 1977 | Seattle Slew | J. Cruguet | 126 | 138,600 |
| 1951 | Bold | E. Arcaro | 126 | 83,110 | 1978 | Affirmed | S. Cauthen | 126 | 136,200 |
| 1952 | Blue Man | C. McCreary | 126 | 86,135 | 1979 | Spectacular Bid | R. Franklin | 126 | 165,300 |
| 1953 | Native Dancer | E. Guerin | 126 | 65,200 | 1980 | Codex | A. Cordero | 126 | 180,600 |
| 1954 | Hasty Road | J. Adams | 126 | 91,600 | 1981 | Pleasant Colony | J. Velasquez | 126 | 270,800 |
| 1955 | Nashua | E. Arcaro | 126 | 67,550 | 1982 | Aloma's Ruler | J. Kaenel | 126 | 209,900 |

## BELMONT STAKES

Belmont Park; 3-year-olds; 1¹/₂ miles.

Run at Jerome Park 1867 to 1890; at Morris Park 1890–94; at Belmont Park 1905–62; at Aqueduct 1963–67. Distance 1⁵/₈ miles prior to 1874; reduced to 1¹/₂ miles, 1874; reduced to 1¹/₄ miles, 1890; reduced to 1¹/₈ miles, 1893; increased to 1¹/₄ miles, 1895; increased to 1³/₈ miles, 1896; reduced to 1¹/₄ miles in 1904; increased to 1¹/₂ miles, 1926.

| Year | Winner | Jockey | Wt. | Win val. | Year | Winner | Jockey | Wt. | Win val. |
|------|--------|--------|-----|----------|------|--------|--------|-----|----------|
| 1919 | Sir Barton | J. Loftus | 126 | $ 11,950 | 1940 | Bimelech | F.A. Smith | 126 | $ 35,030 |
| 1930 | Gallant Fox | E. Sande | 126 | 66,040 | 1941 | Whirlaway | E. Arcaro | 126 | 39,770 |
| 1931 | Twenty Grand | C. Kurtsinger | 126 | 58,770 | 1942 | Shut Out | E. Arcaro | 126 | 44,520 |
| 1932 | Faireno | T. Malley | 126 | 55,120 | 1943 | Count Fleet | J. Longden | 126 | 35,340 |
| 1933 | Hurryoff | M. Garner | 126 | 49,490 | 1944 | Bounding Home | G.L. Smith | 126 | 55,000 |
| 1934 | Peace Chance | W.D. Wright | 126 | 43,410 | 1945 | Pavot | E. Arcaro | 126 | 56,675 |
| 1935 | Omaha | W. Saunders | 126 | 35,480 | 1946 | Assault | W. Mehrtens | 126 | 75,400 |
| 1936 | Granville | J. Stout | 126 | 29,800 | 1947 | Phalanx | R. Donoso | 126 | 78,900 |
| 1937 | War Admiral | C. Kurtsinger | 126 | 38,020 | 1948 | Citation | E. Arcaro | 126 | 77,700 |
| 1938 | Pasteurized | J. Stout | 126 | 34,530 | 1949 | Capot | T. Atkinson | 126 | 60,900 |
| 1939 | Johnstown | J. Stout | 126 | 37,020 | 1950 | Middleground | W. Boland | 126 | 61,350 |

| Year | Winner | Jockey | Wt. | Win val. | Year | Winner | Jockey | Wt. | Win val. |
|---|---|---|---|---|---|---|---|---|---|
| 1951 | Counterpoint | D. Gorman | 126 | 82,000 | 1967 | Damascus | W. Shoemaker | 126 | 104,950 |
| 1952 | One Count | E. Arcaro | 126 | 82,400 | 1968 | Stage Door Johnny | H. Gustines | 126 | 117,700 |
| 1953 | Native Dancer | E. Guerin | 126 | 82,500 | 1969 | Arts and Letters | B. Baeza | 126 | 104,050 |
| 1954 | High Gun | E. Guerin | 126 | 89,000 | 1970 | High Echelon | J. Rotz | 126 | 115,000 |
| 1955 | Nashua | E. Arcaro | 126 | 83,700 | 1971 | Pass Catcher | R. Blum | 126 | 97,710 |
| 1956 | Needles | D. Erb | 126 | 83,600 | 1972 | Riva Ridge | R. Turcotte | 126 | 93,540 |
| 1957 | Gallant Man | W. Shoemaker | 126 | 77,300 | 1973 | Secretariat | R. Turcotte | 126 | 90,120 |
| 1958 | Cavan | P. Anderson | 126 | 73,440 | 1974 | Little Current | M. Rivera | 126 | 101,970 |
| 1959 | Sword Dancer | W. Shoemaker | 126 | 93,525 | 1975 | Avatar | W. Shoemaker | 126 | 116,160 |
| 1960 | Celtic Ash | W. Hartack | 126 | 96,785 | 1976 | Bold Forbes | A. Cordero, Jr. | 126 | 117,000 |
| 1961 | Sherluck | B. Baeza | 126 | 104,900 | 1977 | Seattle Slew | J. Cruguet | 126 | 109,080 |
| 1962 | Jaipur | W. Shoemaker | 126 | 109,550 | 1978 | Affirmed | S. Cauthen | 126 | 110,580 |
| 1963 | Chateauguay | B. Baeza | 126 | 101,700 | 1979 | Coastal | R. Hernandez | 126 | 161,400 |
| 1964 | Quadrangle | M. Ycaza | 126 | 110,850 | 1980 | Temperence Hill | E. Maple | 126 | 176,220 |
| 1965 | Hail to All | J. Sellers | 126 | 104,150 | 1981 | Summing | G. Martens | 126 | 170,580 |
| 1966 | Amberoid | W. Boland | 126 | 117,700 | 1982 | Conquistador Cielo | L. Pincay, Jr. | 126 | 159,720 |

## TRIPLE CROWN RACES—1982

(For 3–year–olds, carrying 126 pounds; jockeys in parentheses)

**Kentucky Derby** (Churchill Downs, Lousiville, Ky., May 1; gross purse: $522,600; 1¼ miles)—1. Gato del Sol (Eddie Delahoussaye), owned by Arthur Hancock III and Leone J. Peters; mutuel returns: $44.40, 19.00, 9.40. 2. Laser Light (Maple) $17.00, 9.20. 3. Reinvested (MacBeth) $4.40. 4. Water Bank (Castaneda). 5. Muttering (Pincay). 6. Rockwall (Valdivieso). 7. Air Forbes Won (Cordero). 8. Star Gallant (Shoemaker). 9. Majesty Prince (Hernandez). 10. Cupecoy's Joy [1] (Santiago). 11. El Baba (Brumfield). 12. Wavering Monarch (Romero). 13. Cassalaria (McHargue). 14. Royal Roberto (Rivera). 15. Music Leader (Day). 16. Bold Style (Fell). 17. Wolfie's Rascal (Velasquez). 18. New Discovery (Bailey). 19. Real Dare (Guidry). Time: 2:02 2/5. Winner's purse: $417,600. Margin of victory: 2½ lengths. Attendance: 141,009.

1. Filly, carried 121 pounds.

**Preakness Stakes** (Pimlico, Baltimore, Md., May 15; gross purse: $279,900; 1³/₁₆ miles)—1. Aloma's Ruler (Jack Kaenel), owned by Nathan Scherr; mutuel returns: $15.80, 4.60, 3.60. 2. Linkage (Shoemaker) $2.60, 2.60. 3. Cut Away (Bailey) $6.00. 4. Bold Style (Moyers). 5. Laser Light (Maple). 6. Reinvested (MacBeth). 7. Water Bank (Castaneda) Time: 1:55 ²/₅. Winner's purse: $209,900. Margin of victory: half–length. Attendance: 80,724.

**Belmont Stakes** (Elmont, N.Y., June 5; gross purse: $266,200; 1½ miles)—1. Conquistador Cielo (Laffit Pincay Jr.), owned by Henryk de Kwiatkowski; mutuel returns: $10.20, 7.40, 6.80. 2. Gato del Sol (Delahoussaye) $8.00, 6.40. 3. Illuminate (Velasquez) $6.40. 4. Linkage (Shoemaker). 5. High Ascent (Lovato). 6. Lejoil (Samyn). 7. Estoril (Fell). 8. Royal Roberto (Cordero). 9. Aloma's Ruler (Kaenel). 10. Anemal (Martens). 11. Cut Away (Bailey). Time: 2:28 ⅕. Winner's purse: $159,720. Margin of victory: 14½ lengths. Attendance: 45,128.

# POWERBOAT RACING

## BENIHANA GRAND PRIX

(Point Pleasant, N.J., July 14, 1982)

Open Class I—Benihana, Rocky Aoki, Englewood, N.J., 30–foot Active; 2 hours, 35 minutes, 33 seconds
Sports Class II—El Boss, Willie Diaz, Miami, Fla., 30–foot Shadow, 1:22:48
Modified Class III—Seahawk, Sal Magluta, Miami, Fla., 31–foot Seahawk, 1:36:56
Pro Stock IV—Fox, Gene Whipp, Sarasota, Fla., 30–foot Velocity, 1:44:05
Class V—K & K Outboard, Kenny Kalibat, Island Park, N.Y., 23–foot Ghost, 2:05:21
Bacardi Trophy (Miami, Fla.)—Jerry Jacoby, Westbury, N.Y.

## ECLIPSE AWARDS—1981

The Eclipse Awards in thoroughbred racing are given on the basis of voting by three groups: the Daily Racing Form, the National Turf Writers Association, and the racing secretaries at tracks that are members of the Thoroughbred Racing Association.

| | |
|---|---|
| Horse of the year and best older male horse | John Henry |
| 2–year–old colt | Deputy Minister |
| 2–year–old filly | Before Dawn |
| 3–year–old colt | Pleasant Colony |
| 3–year–old filly | Wayward Lass |
| Older filly or mare | Relaxing |
| Male turf horse | John Henry |
| Female turf horse | De La Rose |
| Sprinter | Guilty Conscience |
| Steeplechase | Zaccio |

# FENCING

## UNITED STATES CHAMPIONS—1982
### U.S. Fencing Association

Men's foil—Michael Marx, Salle Auriol, Portland, Ore.
Men's epee—Lee Shelley, Salle Orsi, Rutherford, N.J.
Men's saber—Peter Westwood, New York Fencers Club, New York City
Women's foil—Jana Angelakis, Tanner City Fencing Club, Peabody, Mass.
Women's epee—Vincent Bradford, Pentathlon Center, San Antonio, Tex.
Men's foil team—New York Fencers Club
Men's saber team—New York Athletic Club
Men's epee team—United States Modern Pentathlon, Fort Sam Houston, Tex.
Women's foil team—Tanner City Fencing Club, Peabody, Mass.

## WORLD CHAMPIONSHIPS—1982

Men's foil—Aleksandr Romankov, Soviet Union
Men's epee—Jeno Pap, Hungary
Men's saber—Viktor Krovopouskov, Soviet Union
Women's foil—Naila Giliazova, Soviet Union
Men's foil team—Soviet Union
Men's epee team—France
Men's saber team—Hungary
Women's foil team—Italy

## NORTH AMERICAN CUP—1982

Men's foil—Greg Massialas, United States
Men's epee—Lee Shelley, United States
Men's saber—Peter Westwood, United States
Women's foil—Jana Angelakis, United States

# TRACK AND FIELD

Running, jumping, hurdling and throwing weights—track and field sports, in other words—are as natural to young people as eating, drinking and breathing. Unorganized competition in this form of sport goes back beyond the Cave Man era. Organized competition begins with the first recorded Olympic Games in Greece, 776 B.C., when Coroebus of Elis won the only event on the program, a race of approximately 200 yards. The Olympic Games, with an ever-widening program of events, continued until "the glory that was Greece" had faded and "the grandeur that was Rome" was tarnished, and finally were abolished by decree of Emperor Theodosius I of Rome in A.D. 394. The Tailteann Games of Ireland are supposed to have antedated the first Olympic Games by some centuries, but we have no records of the specific events and winners thereof.

Professional contests of speed and strength were popular at all times and in many lands, but the widespread competition of amateur athletes in track and field sports is a comparatively modern development. The first organized amateur athletic meet of record was sponsored by the Royal Military Academy at Woolwich, England, in 1849. Oxford and Cambridge track and field rivalry began in 1864, and the English amateur championships were established in 1866. In the United States such organizations as the New York Athletic Club and the Olympic Club of San Francisco conducted track and field meets in the 1870s, and a few colleges joined to sponsor a meet in 1874. The success of the college meet led to the formation of the Intercollegiate Association of Amateur Athletes of America and the holding of an annual set of championship games beginning in 1876. The Amateur Athletic Union, organized in 1888, has been the ruling body in American amateur athletics since that time. In 1980, The Athletics Congress of the U.S.A. took over the governing of track and field from the A.A.U.

## WORLD RECORDS—MEN

(Through Sept. 19, 1982)
Recognized by the International Athletic Federation
The I.A.A.F. decided late in 1976 not to recognize records in yards except for the one-mile run.
The I.A.A.F. also requires automatic timing for all records for races of 400 meters or less.

| Event | Record | Holder | Home Country | Where Made | Date |
|---|---|---|---|---|---|
| **Running** | | | | | |
| 100 m | 0:09.95 | Jim Hines | U.S. | Mexico City | Oct. 14, 1968 |
| 200 m | 0:19.72 | Pietro Mennea | Italy | Mexico City | Sept. 17, 1979 |
| 400 m | 0:43.86 | Lee Evans | U.S. | Mexico City | Oct. 18, 1968 |
| 800 m | 1:41.8 | Sebastian Coe | England | Florence, Italy | June 10, 1981 |
| 1,000 m | 2:12.40 | Sebastian Coe | England | Oslo, Norway | July 11, 1981 |
| 1,500 m | 3:31.36 | Steve Ovett | England | Koblenz, W. Ger. | Aug. 27, 1980 |
| 1 mile | 3:47.33 | Sebastian Coe | England | Brussels | Aug. 28, 1981 |
| 2,000 m | 4:51.4 | John Walker | New Zealand | Oslo | June 30, 1976 |
| 3,000 m | 7:32.1 | Henry Rono | Kenya | Oslo | June 27, 1978 |
| 3,000 m steeplechase | 8:05.4 | Henry Rono | Kenya | Seattle, Wash. | May 13, 1978 |
| 5,000 m | 13:00.42 | David Moorcroft | England | Oslo | July 7, 1982 |
| 10,000 m | 27:22.4 | Henry Rono | Kenya | Vienna, Austria | June 11, 1978 |
| 25,000 m | 1:13:55.8 | Toshihiko Seko | Japan | Christchurch, N.Z. | March 22, 1981 |
| 30,000 m | 1:29:18.8 | Toshihiko Seko | Japan | Christchurch, N.Z. | March 22, 1981 |
| 20,000 m | 57:24.2 | Jos Hermans | Netherlands | Papandal, Neth. | May 1, 1976 |
| 1 hour | 13 mi. 24 yd | Jos Hermans | Netherlands | Papandal, Neth. | May 1, 1976 |
| **Walking** | | | | | |
| 20,000 m | 1:20.06.8 | Daniel Bautista | Mexico | Montreal | Oct. 17, 1979 |
| 2 hours | 17 mi. 1,092 yd | Ralph Kowalsky | East Germany | East Berlin | March 28, 1982 |
| 30,000 m | 2:06.54 | Ralph Kowalksy | East Germany | East Berlin | March 28, 1982 |
| 50,000 m | 3:41:39 | Raul Gonzales | Mexico | Bergen, Norway | May 25, 1979 |
| **Hurdles** | | | | | |
| 110 m | 0:12.93 | Renaldo Nehemiah | U.S. | Zurich, Switzerland | Aug. 19, 1981 |
| 400 m | 0:47.13 | Edwin Moses | U.S. | Milan, Italy | July 3, 1980 |
| **Relay Races** | | | | | |
| 400 m (4x100) | 0:38.03 | National Team | U.S. | Dusseldorf, W. Ger. | Sept. 3, 1977 |
| 800 m (4x200) | 1:20.26 | So. California | U.S. | Tempe, Ariz. | May 27, 1978 |
| | | (Joel Andrews, James Sanford, Billy Mullins, Clancy Edwards) | | | |
| 1,600 m (4x400) | 2:56.16 | National Team | U.S. | Mexico City | Oct. 20, 1968 |
| | | (Vince Matthews, Ron Freeman, Larry James, Lee Evans) | | | |
| 3,200 m (4x800) | 7:03.89 | National Team | Britain | London | Aug. 30, 1982 |
| | | (Peter Elliott, Garry Cook, Steve Cram, Sebastian Coe) | | | |
| **Field Events** | | | | | |
| High jump | 7 ft 8¾ in. | Gerd Wessig | East Germany | Moscow | Aug. 1, 1980 |

| | | | | | |
|---|---|---|---|---|---|
| Long jump | 29 ft 2½ in. | Bob Beamon | U.S. | Mexico City | Oct. 18, 1976 |
| Triple jump | 58 ft 8¼ in. | Joao Oliveira | Brazil | Mexico City | Oct. 15, 1975 |
| Pole vault | 19 ft ¾ in. | Vladimir Polyakov | U.S.S.R. | Tbilisi, U.S.S.R. | June 26, 1981 |
| Shotput | 72 ft 8 in. | Udo Beyer | East Germany | Goteborg, Sweden | July 6, 1978 |
| Discus throw | 233 ft 5 in. | Wolfgang Schmidt | East Germany | East Berlin | Aug. 9, 1978 |
| Javelin throw | 317 ft 4 in. | Ferenc Paragi | Hungary | Tata, Hungary | April 23, 1980 |
| Hammer Throw | 275 ft 6 in. | Sergei Litvinov | U.S.S.R. | Moscow | June 3, 1982 |
| Decathlon | 8,743 pts | Daley Thompson | England | Athens | Sept. 7–8, 1982 |

## WORLD RECORDS—WOMEN

| Event | Record | Holder | Home Country | Where Made | Date |
|---|---|---|---|---|---|
| **Running** | | | | | |
| 100 m | 0:10.88 | Marlies Goehr | East Germany | Dresden, E. Ger. | July 1, 1977 |
| 200 m | 0:21.71 | Marita Koch | East Germany | Karl Marx Stadt | June 10, 1979 |
| 400 m | 0:48.15 | Marita Koch | East Germany | Athens | Sept. 8, 1982 |
| 800 m | 1:53.42 | Nadezhda Olizaryenko | U.S.S.R. | Moscow | June 27, 1980 |
| 1,500 m | 3:52.47 | Tatyana Kazankina | U.S.S.R. | Zurich, Switz. | Aug. 13, 1980 |
| 1 mile | 4:17.44 | Maricica Puica | Rumania | Rieti, Italy, | Sept. 16, 1982 |
| 3,000 m | 8:26.78 | Svetlana Ulmasova, | U.S.S.R. | Kiev, U.S.S.R. | July 25, 1982 |
| 5,000 m | 15:08.26 | Mary Decker | United States | Eugene, Ore. | June 5, 1982 |
| 10,000 m | 31:35.3 | Mary Decker | United States | Eugene, Ore. | July 17, 1982 |
| **Hurdles** | | | | | |
| 100 m | 0:12.36 | Grazyna Rabsztyn | Poland | Warsaw | June 13, 1980 |
| 400 m | 0:54.28 | Karin Rossley | East Germany | Jena, E. Ger. | May 17, 1980 |
| **Relay Races** | | | | | |
| 400 m (4x100) | 0:41.60 | National Team | East Germany | Moscow | Aug. 1, 1980 |
| | | (Romy Mueller, Barbel Woeckel, Ingrid Auerwald, Marlies Goehr) | | | |
| 800 m (4x200) | 1:28.15 | National Team | East Germany | Jena, E. Ger. | July 9, 1980 |
| | | (Marlies Goehr, Romy Mueller, Barbel Woeckel, Marita Koch) | | | |
| 1,600 m (4x400) | 3:19.05 | National Team | East Germany | Athens | Sept. 11, 1982 |
| | | (Kirsten Siemon, Sabine Busch, Dagmar Ruebsam, Marita Koch) | | | |
| 3,200 m (4x800) | 7:52.3 | National Team | U.S.S.R. | Podolsk, U.S.S.R. | Aug. 16, 1976 |
| | | (Tatyana Providokhina, Vera Gerasimova, Svetlana Styrkina, Tatyana Kazankina) | | | |
| **Field Events** | | | | | |
| High jump | 6 ft 7½ in. | Ulrike Meyfarth | West Germany | Athens | Sept. 8, 1982 |
| Long jump | 23 ft 7½ in. | Vali Ionescu | Romania | Bucharest | Aug. 8, 1982 |
| Shotput | 73 ft 4¼ in. | Ilona Slupianek | East Germany | Celje, Yugoslavia | May 2, 1980 |
| Discus throw | 235 ft 7 in. | Maria Vergova | Bulgaria | Sofia, Bulgaria | July 13, 1980 |
| Javelin throw | 237 ft 6 in. | Tiina Lillak | Finland | Helsinki | July 29, 1982 |
| Heptathlon | 6,717 pts | Ramona Neubert | East Germany | Kiev, U.S.S.R. | June 27, 1981 |

## AMERICAN RECORDS—MEN
### Officially approved by The Athletics Congress

| Event | Record | Holder | Where Made | Date |
|---|---|---|---|---|
| **Running** | | | | |
| 100 m | 0:09.95 | Jim Hines | Mexico City | Oct. 14, 1968 |
| 200 m | 0:19.83 | Tommie Smith | Mexico City | Oct. 16, 1968 |
| 400 m | 0:43.86 | Lee Evans | Mexico City | Oct. 16, 1968 |
| 800 m | 1:43.9 | Richard Wohlhuter | Stockholm | July 18, 1974 |
| 1,000 m | 2:13.9 | Richard Wohlhuter | Oslo | July 30, 1974 |
| 1,500 m | 3:31.96 | Steve Scott | Koblenz, W. Ger. | Aug. 26, 1981 |
| 1 mile | 3:47.69 | Steve Scott | Oslo, Norway | July 7, 1982 |
| 2,000 m | 4:54.71 | Steve Scott | Ingelheim, W. Germany | Aug. 31, 1982 |
| 3,000 m | 7:36.68 | Steve Scott | Ingelheim, W. Germany | Sept. 1, 1981 |
| 5,000 m | 13:11.93 | Alberto Salazar | Oslo | July 7, 1982 |
| 10,000 m | 27:25.61 | Alberto Salazar | Oslo | June 26, 1982 |
| 20,000 m | 58:15.0 | Bill Rodgers | Boston | Aug. 9, 1977 |
| 25,000 m | 1:14:12 | Bill Rodgers | Saratoga, Calif. | Feb. 21, 1979 |
| 30,000 m | 1:31:50 | Bill Rodgers | Saratoga, Calif. | Feb. 21, 1979 |
| 1 hour | 12 mi. 997 yds | Bill Rodgers | Saratoga, Calif. | Feb. 21, 1979 |
| 3,000 m steeplechase | 8:15.68 | Henry Marsh | Eugene, Ore. | June 28, 1980 |

## Hurdles

| | | | | |
|---|---|---|---|---|
| 110 m | 0:12.93 | Renaldo Nehemiah | Zurich, Switzerland | Aug. 19, 1981 |
| 400 m | 0:47.13 | Edwin Moses | Milan, Italy | July 3, 1980 |

## Relay Races

| | | | | |
|---|---|---|---|---|
| 400 m (4x100) | 0:38.03 | U.S. Team | Dusseldorf, W. Ger. | Sept. 3, 1977 |
| | | (Bill Collins, Steve Riddick, Cliff Wiley, Steve Williams) | | |
| 800 m (4x200) | 1:20.26 | Southern California | Tempe, Ariz. | May 27, 1978 |
| | | (Joe Andrews, James Sanford, Billy Mullins, Clancy Edwards) | | |
| 1,600 m (4x400) | 2:56.16 | U.S. Team | Mexico City | Oct. 20, 1968 |
| | | (Vince Matthews, Ron Freeman, Larry James, Lee Evans) | | |
| 3,200 m (4x800) | 7:10.4 | U. of Chicago T.C. | Durham, N.C. | May 12, 1973 |
| | | (Tom Bach, Ken Sparks, Lowell Paul, Rick Wohlhuter) | | |

## Field Events

| | | | | |
|---|---|---|---|---|
| High jump | 7 ft 7¼ in. | Dwight Stones | Philadelphia | Aug. 14, 1982 |
| Long jump | 29 ft 2½ in. | Bob Beamon | Mexico City | Oct. 18, 1968 |
| Triple jump | 57 ft 7½ in. | Willie Banks | Sacramento, Calif. | June 21, 1981 |
| Pole vault | 18 ft 10¼ in. | Dave Volz | Nice, France | Aug. 14, 1982 |
| Shotput | 72 ft 3 in. | David Laut | Koblentz, W. Germany | Aug. 25, 1982 |
| | | Brian Oldfield | Modesto, Calif. | May 16, 1981 |
| Discus throw | 237 ft 4 in. | Ben Plucknett | Stockholm | July 7, 1981 |
| Javelin throw | 314 ft 3 in. | Bob Roggy | Stuttgart, W. Germany | Aug. 29, 1982 |
| Hammer throw | 243 ft 11 in. | Dave McKenzie | Durham, N.C. | June 27, 1982 |

## AMERICAN RECORDS—WOMEN

| Event | Record | Holder | Where Made | Date |
|---|---|---|---|---|
| **Running** | | | | |
| 100 m | 0:10.90 | Evelyn Ashford | Colorado Springs | July 22, 1981 |
| 200 m | 0:21.83 | Evelyn Ashford | Montreal | Aug. 24, 1979 |
| 400 m | 0:50.62 | Rosalyn Bryant | Montreal | July 28, 1976 |
| 800 m | 1:57.9 | Madeline Jackson | College Park, Md. | Aug. 7, 1976 |
| 1,500 m | 3:59.43 | Mary Decker | Zurich, Switzerland | Aug. 13, 1980 |
| 1 mile | 4:18.08 | Mary Decker | Paris | July 9, 1982 |
| 3,000 m | 8:29.71 | Mary Decker | Oslo, Norway | July 7, 1982 |
| 5,000 m | 15:08.26 | Mary Decker | Eugene, Ore. | June 5, 1982 |
| 10,000 m | 31:35.3 | Mary Decker | Eugene, Ore. | July 17, 1982 |
| **Hurdles** | | | | |
| 100 m | 0:12.79 | Stephanie Hightower | Karl–Marx–Stadt, E. Germany | July 10, 1982 |
| 400 m | 0:56.16 | Esther Mahr | Sittard, Netherlands | Aug. 15, 1980 |
| **Relay Races** | | | | |
| 400 m (4x100) | 0:42.29 | United States Team | Karl–Marx–Stadt, E. Germany | July 9, 1982 |
| | | (Alice Brown, Florence Griffith, Randy Givens, Diane Williams) | | |
| 800 m (4x200) | 1:32.6 | U.S. National Team | Bourges, France | June 23, 1979 |
| | | (Wanda Hooker, Karen Hawkins, Chandra Cheeseborough, Brenda Morehead) | | |
| 1,600 m (4x400) | 3:22.81 | U.S. Team | Montreal | July 31, 1976 |
| | | (Debra Sapenter, Sheila Ingram, Pam Jiles, Rosalyn Bryant) | | |
| **Field Events** | | | | |
| High jump | 6 ft 6 in. | Coleen Sommer | Durham, N.C. | June 26, 1982 |
| Long jump | 22 ft 11½ in. | Jodi Anderson | Eugene, Ore. | June 28, 1980 |
| Shotput | 62 ft 7¾ in. | Maren Seidler | Walnut, Calif. | June 16, 1979 |
| Discus throw | 207 ft 5 in. | Lorna Griffin | Long Beach, Calif. | May 24, 1980 |
| Javelin throw | 227 ft 5 in. | Kathy Schmidt | Furth, W. Ger. | Sept. 11, 1977 |
| Heptathlon | 6,458 pts | Jane Frederick | Goleta, Calif. | July 17–18, 1982 |

## HISTORY OF THE RECORD FOR THE MILE RUN

| Time | Athlete | Country | Year | Location |
|---|---|---|---|---|
| 4:36.5 | Richard Webster | England | 1865 | England |
| 4:29.0 | William Chinnery | England | 1868 | England |
| 4:28.8 | Walter Gibbs | England | 1868 | England |
| 4:26.0 | Walter Slade | England | 1874 | England |
| 4:24.5 | Walter Slade | England | 1875 | London |

| Time | Athlete | Country | Year | Location |
|---|---|---|---|---|
| 4:23.2 | Walter George | England | 1880 | London |
| 4:21.4 | Walter George | England | 1882 | London |
| 4:18.4 | Walter George | England | 1884 | Birmingham, England |
| 4:18.2 | Fred Bacon | Scotland | 1894 | Edinburgh, Scotland |
| 4:17.0 | Fred Bacon | Scotland | 1895 | London |
| 4:15.6 | Thomas Conneff | United States | 1895 | Travers Island, N.Y. |
| 4:15.4 | John Paul Jones | United States | 1911 | Cambridge, Mass. |
| 4:14.4 | John Paul Jones | United States | 1913 | Cambridge, Mass. |
| 4:12.6 | Norman Taber | United States | 1915 | Cambridge, Mass. |
| 4:10.4 | Paavo Nurmi | Finland | 1923 | Stockholm |
| 4:09.2 | Jules Ladoumegue | France | 1931 | Paris |
| 4:07.6 | Jack Lovelock | New Zealand | 1933 | Princeton, N.J. |
| 4:06.8 | Glenn Cunningham | United States | 1934 | Princeton, N.J. |
| 4:06.4 | Sydney Wooderson | England | 1937 | London |
| 4:06.2 | Gundar Hägg | Sweden | 1942 | Göteborg, Sweden |
| 4:06.2 | Arne Andersson | Sweden | 1942 | Stockholm |
| 4:04.6 | Gunder Hägg | Sweden | 1942 | Stockholm |
| 4:02.6 | Arne Andersson | Sweden | 1943 | Göteborg, Sweden |
| 4:01.6 | Arne Andersson | Sweden | 1944 | Malmö, Sweden |
| 4:01.4 | Gunder Hägg | Sweden | 1945 | Malmö, Sweden |
| 3:59.4 | Roger Bannister | England | 1954 | Oxford, England |
| 3:58.0 | John Landy | Australia | 1954 | Turku, Finland |
| 3:57.2 | Derek Ibbotson | England | 1957 | London |
| 3:54.5 | Herb Elliott | Australia | 1958 | Dublin |
| 3:54.4 | Peter Snell | New Zealand | 1962 | Wanganui, N.Z. |
| 3:54.1 | Peter Snell | New Zealand | 1964 | Auckland, N.Z. |
| 3:53.6 | Michel Jazy | France | 1965 | Rennes, France |
| 3:51.3 | Jim Ryun | United States | 1966 | Berkeley, Calif. |
| 3:51.1 | Jim Ryun | United States | 1967 | Bakersfield, Calif. |
| 3:51.0 | Filbert Bayi | Tanzania | 1975 | Kingston, Jamaica |
| 3:49.4 | John Walker | New Zealand | 1975 | Göteborg, Sweden |
| 3:49.0 | Sebastian Coe | England | 1979 | Oslo |
| 3:48.8 | Steve Ovett | England | 1980 | Oslo |
| 3:48.53 | Sebastian Coe | England | 1981 | Zurich, Switzerland |
| 3:48.40 | Steve Ovett | England | 1981 | Koblenz, W. Ger. |
| 3:47.33 | Sebastian Coe | England | 1981 | Brussels |

## WORLD'S FASTEST INDOOR MILES

| Time | Athlete | Country | Date | Location |
|---|---|---|---|---|
| 3:50.6 | Eamonn Coghlan | Ireland | Feb. 20, 1981 | San Diego |
| 3:51.8 | Steve Scott[1] | United States | Feb. 20, 1981 | San Diego |
| 3:52.6 | Eamonn Coghlan | Ireland | Feb. 16, 1979 | San Diego |
| 3:52.8 | John Walker[2] | New Zealand | Feb. 20, 1981 | San Diego |
| 3:52.8 | John Walker | New Zealand | Feb. 19, 1982 | San Diego |
| 3:52.9 | Eamonn Coghlan | Ireland | Feb. 15, 1980 | Los Angeles |
| 3:53.0 | Steve Scott[1] | United States | Feb. 15, 1980 | Los Angeles |
| 3:53.0 | Eamonn Coghlan | Ireland | Feb. 6, 1981 | New York |
| 3:53.6 | Ray Flynn[3] | Ireland | Feb. 20, 1981 | San Diego |
| 3:53.6 | Tom Byers[1] | United States | Feb. 19, 1982 | San Diego |
| 3:53.7 | Steve Scott | United States | Jan. 30, 1981 | Los Angeles |
| 3:53.8 | Ray Flynn | Ireland | Feb. 6, 1981 | New York |
| 3:54.1 | Steve Scott[1] | United States | Feb. 16, 1979 | San Diego |
| 3:54.1 | Ray Flynn[2] | Ireland | Feb. 19, 1982 | San Diego |
| 3:54.3 | Eamonn Coghlan[1] | Ireland | Jan. 30, 1981 | Los Angeles |
| 3:54.4 | Ray Flynn[2] | Ireland | Jan. 30, 1981 | Los Angeles |
| 3:54.5 | Filbert Bayi[2] | Tanzania | Feb. 15, 1980 | Los Angeles |
| 3:54.7 | Steve Lacy[2] | United States | Feb. 16, 1979 | San Diego |
| 3:54.7 | Thomas Wessinghage[2] | West Germany | Feb. 6, 1981 | New York |
| 3:54.9 | Ray Flynn | Ireland | Feb. 13, 1981 | Inglewood, Calif. |
| 3:55.0 | Tony Waldrop | United States | Feb. 17, 1974 | San Diego |
| 3:55.0 | Dick Buerkle | United States | Jan. 13, 1978 | College Park, Md. |
| 3:55.0 | Eamonn Coghlan | Ireland | Feb. 9, 1979 | New York |
| 3:55.0 | Steve Scott[3] | United States | Feb. 6, 1981 | New York |
| 3:55.0 | Steve Scott[3] | United States | Feb. 19, 1982 | San Diego |
| 3:55.2 | John Walker[1] | New Zealand | Feb. 13, 1981 | Inglewood, Calif. |
| 3:55.3 | Steve Scott | United States | Feb. 21, 1981 | Daly City, Calif. |
| 3:55.37 | Steve Scott | United States | Feb. 12, 1982 | New York |
| 3:55.4 | Niall O'Shaughnessy | Ireland | Jan. 28, 1977 | Columbia, Mo. |
| 3:55.41 | Tom Byers[1] | United States | Feb. 12, 1982 | New York |
| 3:55.5 | Filbert Bayi | Tanzania | Feb. 22, 1980 | San Diego |

| | | | | |
|---|---|---|---|---|
| 3:55.5 | Sydney Maree[1] | South Africa | Feb. 21, 1981 | Daly City, Calif. |
| 3:55.55 | Eamonn Coghlan | Ireland | Jan. 31, 1981 | Dallas |
| 3:55.62 | John Walker[2] | New Zealand | Feb. 12, 1982 | New York |
| 3:55.6 | Steve Lacy[3] | United States | Feb. 15, 1980 | Los Angeles |
| 3:55.63 | Eamonn Coghlan | Ireland | Feb. 13, 1981 | Toronto |
| 3:55.7 | Wilson Waigwa | Kenya | Feb. 18, 1977 | San Diego |
| 3:55.7 | Eamonn Coghlan[1] | Ireland | Feb. 22, 1980 | San Diego |
| 3:55.8 | Marty Liquori | United States | Feb. 7, 1975 | Philadelphia |
| 3:55.8 | John Walker[2] | New Zealand | Feb. 22, 1980 | San Diego |
| 3:55.87 | Wilson Waigwa | Kenya | Jan. 31, 1981 | Dallas |
| 3:56.0 | Eamonn Coghlan | Ireland | Feb. 17, 1978 | San Diego |
| 3:56.0 | Tom Byers[2] | United States | Feb. 13, 1981 | Inglewood, Calif. |
| 3:56.1 | Filbert Bayi | Tanzania | Feb. 27, 1976 | New York |
| 3:56.1 | Eamonn Coghlan | Ireland | Jan. 20, 1979 | Los Angeles |

1. Finished second. 2. Finished third. 3. Finished fourth.

## WORLD'S FASTEST OUTDOOR MILES

| Time | Athlete | Country | Date | Location |
|---|---|---|---|---|
| 3:47.33 | Sebastian Coe | England | Aug. 28, 1981 | Brussels |
| 3:47.69 | Steve Scott | United States | July 7, 1982 | Oslo |
| 3:48.40 | Steve Ovett | England | Aug. 26, 1981 | Koblenz, W. Ger. |
| 3:48.53 | Sebastian Coe | England | Aug. 19, 1981 | Zurich |
| 3:48.53 | Steve Scott | United States | June 26, 1982 | Oslo |
| 3:48.8 | Steve Ovett | England | July 1, 1980 | Oslo |
| 3:48.83 | Sydney Maree | United States | Sept. 9, 1981 | Rieti, Italy |
| 3:48.85 | Sydney Maree[1] | United States | June 26, 1982 | Oslo |
| 3:48.95 | Sebastian Coe | England | July 17, 1979 | Oslo |
| 3:49.08 | John Walker[1] | New Zealand | July 7, 1982 | Oslo |
| 3:49.25 | Steve Ovett | England | July 11, 1981 | Oslo |
| 3:49.34 | David Moorcroft[2] | England | June 26, 1982 | Oslo |
| 3:49.4 | John Walker | New Zealand | Aug. 12, 1975 | Goteborg, Sweden |
| 3:49.44 | Sydney Maree | United States | July 13, 1982 | Cork, Eire |
| 3:49.45 | Mike Boit[1] | Kenya | Aug. 28, 1981 | Brussels |
| 3:49.50 | John Walker[3] | New Zealand | June 26, 1982 | Oslo |
| 3:49.57 | Steve Ovett | England | Aug. 31, 1979 | London |
| 3:49.66 | Steve Ovett | England | July 14, 1981 | Lausanne, Switz. |
| 3:49.67 | Jose–Luis Gonzalez[1] | Spain | July 11, 1981 | Oslo |
| 3:49.68 | Steve Scott[2] | United States | July 11, 1981 | Oslo |
| 3:49.72 | Steve Scott | United States | Aug. 25, 1982 | Koblenz, W. Ger. |
| 3:49.74 | Mike Boit[1] | Kenya | Aug. 19, 1981 | Zurich |
| 3:49.75 | Sydney Maree[1] | United States | Aug. 25, 1982 | Koblenz, W. Ger. |
| 3:49.77 | Ray Flynn[2] | Eire | July 7, 1982 | Oslo |
| 3:49.92 | Steve Cram[1] | England | July 13, 1982 | Cork, Eire |
| 3:49.93 | Sydney Maree | United States | Sept. 16, 1981 | Aichach, W. Ger. |
| 3:49.95 | Steve Cram[2] | England | Aug. 19, 1981 | Zurich |
| 3:50.03 | John Walker[2] | New Zealand | July 13, 1982 | Cork, Eire |
| 3:50.12 | John Walker[3] | New Zealand | Aug. 19, 1981 | Zurich |
| 3:50.19 | Thomas Wessinghage[2] | West Germany | Aug. 25, 1982 | Koblenz, W. Ger. |
| 3:50.23 | Steve Ovett[1] | England | Sept. 9, 1981 | Rieti, Italy |
| 3:50.26 | John Walker[3] | New Zealand | July 11, 1981 | Oslo |
| 3:50.34 | Todd Harbour[4] | United States | July 11, 1981 | Oslo |
| 3:50.38 | Steve Cram[5] | England | July 11, 1981 | Oslo |
| 3:50.38 | Pierre Deleze[3] | Switzerland | Aug. 25, 1982 | Koblenz, W. Ger. |
| 3:50.51 | Mike Boit[1] | Kenya | Sept. 16, 1981 | Aichach, W. Ger. |
| 3:50.54 | Ray Flynn[4] | Eire | June 26, 1982 | Oslo |
| 3:50.55 | Ray Flynn[4] | Eire | Aug. 25, 1982 | Koblenz, W. Ger. |
| 3:50.56 | Thomas Wessinghage[1] | West Germany | Aug. 31, 1979 | London |
| 3:50.58 | John Walker | New Zealand | Mar. 19, 1981 | Auckland, N.Z. |
| 3:50.65 | Graham Williamson[3] | England | July 13, 1982 | Cork. Eire |
| 3:50.84 | Tom Byers[5] | United States | Aug. 25, 1982 | Koblenz, W. Ger. |
| 3:50.87 | Jose–Luis Gonzalez[1] | Spain | July 14, 1981 | Lausanne, Switz. |
| 3:50.91 | Thomas Wessinghage[6] | West Germany | July 11, 1981 | Oslo |
| 3:50.95 | Thomas Wessinghage[4] | West Germany | Aug. 19, 1981 | Zurich |
| 3:51.0 | Filbert Bayi | Tanzania | May 17, 1975 | Kingston, Jamaica |
| 3:51.1 | Jim Ryun | United States | June 23, 1967 | Bakersfield, Calif. |

1. Finished second. 2. Finished third. 3. Finished fourth. 4. Finished fifth. 5. Finished sixth. 6. Finished seventh. NOTE: Professional marks not included.

# HISTORY OF THE POLE VAULT

(Some of early dates are the winning heights of A.A.U. champion for that year, used to show progression from one foot level to the next. Figures from A.A.U. records and *Track & Field News*.)

**Bamboo Poles**

| | | |
|---|---|---|
| 1877 | G. McNichol | 9 ft 7 in. |
| 1879 | W. J. Van Houten | 10 ft 4¾ in. |
| 1883 | Hugh Baxter | 11 ft 0½ in. |
| 1904 | Norman Dole | 12 ft 1³/₁₀ in. |
| 1912 | Robert Gardner | 13 ft 1 in. |
| 1927 | Sabin Carr | 14 ft 0 in. |
| 1940 | Cornelius Warmerdam | 15 ft 1 in. |
| 1942 | Cornelius Warmerdam | 15 ft 7¾ in. |

**Metal Poles**

| | | |
|---|---|---|
| 1957 | Bob Gutowski | 15 ft 8¼ in. |
| 1960 | Don Bragg | 15 ft 9¼ in. |

**Fiberglas Poles**

| | | |
|---|---|---|
| 1961 | George Davis | 15 ft 10¼ in. |
| 1962 | John Uelses | 16 ft 0¾ in. |
| 1962 | Dave Tork | 16 ft 2 in. |
| 1962 | Pentti Nikula | 16 ft 2½ in. |
| 1963 | John Pennel | 16 ft 4 in. |
| 1963 | Brian Sternberg | 16 ft 5 in. |
| 1963 | John Pennel | 16 ft 6¾ in. |
| 1963 | Brian Sternberg | 16 ft 8 in. |

| | | |
|---|---|---|
| 1963 | John Pennel | 16 ft 10 in. |
| 1963 | John Pennel | 17 ft 0¾ in. |
| 1964 | Fred Hansen | 17 ft 4 in. |
| 1966 | Bob Seagren | 17 ft 5½ in. |
| 1966 | John Pennel | 17 ft 6¼ in. |
| 1967 | Bob Seagren | 17 ft 0 in. |
| 1967 | Paul Wilson | 17 ft 7¾ in. |
| 1968 | Bob Seagren | 17 ft 9 in. |
| 1969 | John Pennel | 17 ft 10¼ in. |
| 1970 | Wolfgang Norwig | 17 ft 10½ in. |
| 1970 | Chris Papanicolaou | 18 ft 0¼ in. |
| 1972 | Kjell Isaksson | 18 ft 1 in. |
| 1972 | Kjell Isaksson | 18 ft 2 in. |
| 1972 | Kjell Isaksson, Bob Seagren | 18 ft 4¼ in. |
| 1972 | Bob Seagren | 18 ft 5¾ in. |
| 1975 | Dave Roberts | 18 ft 6½ in. |
| 1976 | Earl Bell | 18 ft 7¼ in. |
| 1976 | Dave Roberts | 18 ft 8¼ in. |
| 1980 | Thierry Vigneron | 18 ft 10¼ in. |
| 1980 | Philippe Houvion | 18 ft 11 in. |
| 1980 | Wladyslaw Kozakiewicz | 18 ft 11½ in. |
| 1981 | Thierry Vigneron | 19 ft ¼ in. |
| 1981 | Vladimir Polyakov | 19 ft ¾ in. |

# UNITED STATES MARATHON CHAMPIONS

(26 miles, 385 Yards)

**Boston Marathon**

| | | |
|---|---|---|
| 1970 | Ron Hill, England | 2:10:30 |
| 1971 | Alvaro Meija, Colombia | 2:18:45 |
| 1972 | Olavi Suomalainen, Finland | 2:15:39 |
| 1973 | Jon Anderson, Eugene, Ore. | 2:16:03 |
| 1974 | Neil Cusack, Ireland | 2:13:39 |
| 1975 | William H. Rodgers, Boston | 2:09:55 |
| 1976 | Jack Fultz, Arlington, Va. | 2:20:19 |
| 1977 | Jerome Drayton, Toronto | 2:14:46 |
| 1978 | William H. Rodgers, Melrose, Mass. | 2:10:13 |
| 1979 | William H. Rodgers, Melrose, Mass. | 2:09.27 |
| 1980 | William H. Rodgers, Melrose, Mass. | 2:12:11 |
| 1981 | Toshihiko Seko, Japan | 2:09:26 |
| 1982 | Alberto Salazar, Eugene, Ore. | 2:08:51 |

**Amateur Athletic Union**

| | | |
|---|---|---|
| 1970 | Bob Fitts, Wisconsin | 2:24:11 |
| 1971 | Ken Moore, Portland, Ore. | 2:16:49 |
| 1972 | Edmund Norris, Brockton, Mass. | 2:24:42.8 |
| 1973 | Doug Schmenk | 2:15:48 |
| 1974 | Ron Wayne, Eugene, Ore. | 2:18:52 |
| 1975 | Gary Tuttle, Beverly Hills Strider | 2:17:27 |
| 1976 | Gary Tuttle, Los Angeles | 2:15:15 |
| 1977 | Not Held | |
| 1978 | Carl Hatfield, West Va. T.C. | 2:17.20 |
| 1979 | Tom Antczak, Rockford, Ill. | 2:15.28 |

**The Athletics Congress**

| | | |
|---|---|---|
| 1980 | Paul Richardson, Ames, Iowa | 2:13:54* |

*Time not recognized because course was too short.

# CROSS COUNTRY RACE CHAMPIONS

**The Athletics Congress**

(A.A.U. before 1980)

(10,000 Meters)

| | |
|---|---|
| 1971 | Frank Shorter, Gainesville, Fla.; Florida T.C. |
| 1972 | Frank Shorter, Gainesville, Fla.; Florida T.C. |
| 1973 | Frank Shorter, Gainesville, Fla.; Florida T.C. |
| 1974 | John Ngeno, Kenya; Colorado T.C. |
| 1975 | Greg Fredericks, Philadelphia; Colorado T.C. |
| 1976 | Rick Rojas, San Diego; Jamul Toads |
| 1977 | Nick Rose, England; Colorado T.C. |
| 1978 | Greg Meyer, Boston; Mason Dixon A.C. |
| 1979 | Alberto Salazar, Boston; Greater Boston T.C. |
| 1980 | Jon Sinclair, Boulder, Colo. Victory A.C. |
| 1981 | Adrian Royle, Reno, Nev.; Athletics West |

**N.C.A.A. (University)**

(10,000 meters)

| | |
|---|---|
| 1973 | Steve Prefontaine, Oregon; Oregon |
| 1974 | Nick Rose, Western Kentucky; Oregon |

| | |
|---|---|
| 1975 | Craig Virgin, Illinois; Texas-El Paso |
| 1976 | Henry Rono, Wash. State; Texas-El Paso |
| 1977 | Henry Rono, Wash. State; Oregon |
| 1978 | Alberto Salazar, Oregon; Texas-El Paso |
| 1979 | Henry Rono, Washington State; Texas-El Paso |
| 1980 | Suleiman Nyambui, Texas-El Paso, Texas-El Paso |
| 1981 | Matthews Motshwaraten, Texas-El Paso; Texas-El Paso |

**N.C.A.A. (College)**

(10,000 meters)

| | |
|---|---|
| 1975 | Div. II: Ralph Serna, Calif.-Irvine; Calif.-Irvine |
| | Div. III: Vin Fleming, Lowell; N. Central Illinois |
| 1976 | Div. II: Ralph Serna, Calif.-Irvine; Calif.-Irvine |
| | Div. III: Dale Cramer, Carleton; N. Central Illinois |

1977 Div. II: Michael Boltman, N.D. State; E. Illinois
Div. III: Dale Kramer, Carleton; Occidental
1978 Div. II: Jim Schankel, Cal Poly, San Luis Opisbo;
Cal Poly, San Luis Opisbo
Div. III: Dan Henderson, Wheaton; N. Cent. Illinois
1979 Div. II: Jim Schankel, Cal Poly, San Luis Opisbo
Div. III: Steve Hunt, Boston State; North Central, Ill.
1980 Div. II: Gary Henry, Pembroke State; Humboldt State
Div. III: Jeff Millman, North Central; Carleton
1981 Div. II: Mark Conover, Humboldt State; Millersville
State
Div. III: Mark Whalley, Principia; North Central

**N.A.I.A.**
(5 Miles)
1973 Tony Brien, Marymount; Eastern New Mexico
1974 Mike Boit, Eastern New Mexico; Eastern New Mexico
1975 Mike Boit, Eastern New Mexico; Edinboro State

1976 John Kebiro, Eastern New Mexico; Edinboro State
1977 Garry Henry, Pembroke State; Adams State
1978 Kelly Jensen, So. Oregon; Pembroke State
1979 Sam Montoya, Adams State; Adams State
1980 Pat Porter, Adams State; Adams State
1981 Pat Porter, Adams State; Adams State

## CROSS-COUNTRY WORLD CHAMPIONSHIPS—1982
(Rome, Italy, March 21, 1982)

| | |
|---|---|
| Men—Mohammad Kedir, Ethiopia | 33:40.5 |
| Women—Maricica Puica, Romania | 14:38.9 |
| Junior men—Zurabachew Gelaw, Ethiopia | 22:45.3 |
| Men's team—Ethiopia | 98 pts |
| Women's team—Soviet Union | 44 pts |
| Junior men's team—Ethiopia | 12 pts |

## WORLD AND AMERICAN BEST PERFORMANCES IN INDOOR TRACK

The International Amateur Athletic Union does not recognize indoor records. The following best performances, often called world records, are from lists provided by The Athletics Congress of the United States and *Track and Field News*, published in Los Altos, Calif., Bert Nelson, editor and publisher.

### MEN
#### Running

| | |
|---|---|
| 50 yards—Stanley Floyd, Los Angeles, 1982 | 0:05.22 |
| 60 yards—Stanley Floyd, Dallas, 1981 | 0:06.04 |
| 70 yards—Herb McFarland, Louisville, Ky. | 0:06.7 |
| 100 yards—Don Quarrie, Pocatello, Idaho, 1971 | 0:09.3 |
| Carl Lawson, Pocatello, Idaho, 1971 | 0:09.3 |
| Cliff Branch, Pocatello, Idaho, 1972 | 0:09.3 |
| 300 yards—Terron Wright, Bloomington, Ind., 1981 | 0:29.26 |
| 440 yards—Tommie Smith, Louisville, Ky., 1967 | 0:46.2 |
| Deon Hogan (Am.), Lincoln, Neb., 1981 | 0:47.20 |
| 500 yards—Lee Evans, College Park, Md., 1971 | 0:54.4 |
| Pro—Larry James, Salt Lake City, Utah, 1973 | 0:53.9 |
| 600 yards—Martin McGrady, New York, 1970 | 1:07.6 |
| 880 yards—Ralph Doubell, Albuquerque N.M., 1969 | 1:47.9 |
| Mark Belger (Am.), College Park, Md., 1978 | 1:48.1 |
| Tom Von Ruden (Am.), College Park, Md., 1971 | 1:48.5 |
| 1,000 yards—Don Paige, Inglewood, Calif., 1982 | 2:04.7 |
| Mile—Eamonn Coghlan, San Diego, 1981 | 3:50.6 |
| Steve Scott (Am.), San Diego, 1981 | 3:51.8 |
| 2 miles—Emiel Puttemans, Berlin, 1973 | 8:13.2 |
| Doug Padilla (Am.) San Diego, 1982 | 8:16.8 |
| 3 miles—Emiel Puttemans, Pentin, Belgium, 1976 | 12:54.6 |
| Alberto Salazar (Am.), New York, 1981 | 12:56.6 |

#### Running—Metric Distances

| | |
|---|---|
| 50 meters—Manfred Koket, East Germany, 1971 | 0:05.4 |
| Bill Gaines (Am.), Highland Park, N.J., 1968 | 0:05.4 |
| James Sanford (Am.), San Diego, 1981 | 0:05.61 |
| 60 meters—Houston McTear, New York, 1978 | 0:06.11 |
| 70 meters—Helmut Kornig, Germany, 1932 | 0:07.5 |
| Ira Murchison (Am.), United States | 0:07.5 |
| Pro—John Carlos, Pocatello, Idaho, 1974 | 0:07.3 |
| 100 meters—Eugen Ray, East Berlin, 1976 | 0:10.16 |
| Pro—Warren Edmonson, Pocatello, Idaho, 1973 | 0:10.2 |
| 200 meters—Erwin Skamrahl, Dortmund, West Germany, 1982 | 0:20.99 |
| Mel Lattany (Am.), Milan, Italy, 1982 | 0:21.25 |
| 300 meters—Pietro Mennea, Italy, 1978 | 0:32.83 |
| Cliff Wiley (Am.), Saskatchewan, 1981 | 0:33.33 |
| 400 meters—Hartmut Weber, West Germany, 1981 | 0:45.96 |
| Bill Green (Am.), Sherbrooke, Quebec, 1981 | 0:46.08 |
| 500 meters—Herman Frazier, Long Beach, Calif., 1979 | 1:01.2 |

| | |
|---|---|
| Pro—Lee Evans, Pocatello, Idaho, 1973 | 1:02 |
| 600 meters—Coloman Trabado, Madrid, 1982 | 1:17.2 |
| Fred Sowerby (Am.), Newark, Del. 1982 | 1:17.60 |
| Pro—Lee Evans, Pocatello, Idaho, 1977 | 1:16.7 |
| 800 meters—Sabastian Coe, England, 1981 | 1:46.0 |
| Ted Nelson (Am.), Berlin, 1965 | 1:47.4 |
| 1,000 meters—Paul-Heinz Wellmann, West Germany, 1976 | 2:19.1 |
| Tom Byers (Am.), Louisville, Ky., 1982 | 2:19.5 |
| Pro—Chris Fisher, Daly City, Calif., 1973 | 2:19.7 |
| 1,500 meters—Eamonn Coghlan, San Diego, 1981 | 3:35.6 |
| Steve Smith (Am.), San Diego, 1981 | 3:36.0 |
| 2,000 meters—Steve Scott, Louisville, Ky., 1981 | 4:58.6 |
| 3,000 meters—Emiel Puttemans, Berlin, 1973 | 7:39.2 |
| Steve Scott (Am.), Long Beach, Calif., 1980 | 7:45.2 |
| 5,000 meters—Suleiman Nyambui, New York, 1981 | 13:20.4 |
| Doug Padilla (Am.), New York, 1982 | 13:20.55 |

#### Hurdles

| | |
|---|---|
| 50 yards—Renaldo Nehemiah, Toronto, 1982 | 0:05.92 |
| 60 yards—Renaldo Nehemiah, Dallas, 1982 | 0:06.82 |
| 50 meters—Renaldo Nehemiah, Edmonton, 1979 | 0:06.36 |
| 60 meters—Andre Prokofyev, Vilnius, 1979 | 0:07.54 |
| Renaldo Nehemiah, (Am.), Montreal, 1979 | 0:07.62 |

#### Walking

| | |
|---|---|
| 1,500 meters—Jim Heiring, East Rutherford, N.J., 1982 | 5:27.1 |
| Mile—Jim Heiring, Richfield, Ohio, 1982 | 5:47.39 |
| 3,000 meters—Yevgeny Yavsyukov, Montreal, 1979 | 11.31.1 |
| 2 miles—Jim Heiring, Kansas City, Mo., 1982 | 12:20.6 |
| 3 miles—Antoli Soloman, Toronto, 1978 | 19:40.0 |

#### Relays

| | |
|---|---|
| 1,600 meters—West Germany, Dortmund, West Germany, 1981 | 3:34.38 |
| 880 yards—Idaho State, Pocatello, Idaho, 1979 | 1:26.9 |
| Mile—Pacific Coast Club, Pocatello, Idaho, 1971 | 3:09.4 |
| 2 miles—Univ. of Chicago, T.C., Louisville, Ky., 1974 | 7:20.8 |
| 4 miles—Villanova, Hanover, N.H., 1976 | 16:19 |
| Sprint medley—Philadelphia T.C., New York, 1980 | 2:01.1 |
| Distance medley—Villanova, Louisville, Ky., 1980 | 9:38.4 |

## Field Events

| | |
|---|---|
| High jump—Dietmar Mogenburg, West Germany, 1980 | 7 ft 8¾ in. |
| Jeff Woodard (Am.), New York, 1981 | 7 ft 7¾ in. |
| Long jump—Carl Lewis, East Rutherford, N.J., 1982 | 28 ft 1 in. |
| Triple jump—Willie Banks, San Diego, 1982 | 57 ft 1½ in. |
| Pole Vault—Billy Olson, Kansas City, Mo., 1982 | 18 ft 10 in. |
| Pro—Steve Smith, New York, 1975 | 18 ft 5 in. |
| Shotput—George Woods, Inglewood, Calif., 1974 | 72 ft 2¾ in. |
| Brian Oldfield (pro), El Paso, Tex., 1975 | 72 ft 6½ in. |
| 35-pound weight throw—Yuri Syedikh, Montreal, 1979 | 76 ft 11¾ in. |
| Ed Kania (Am.), Princeton, N.J., 1981 | 73 ft 4 in. |
| Penthathlon—Daley Thompson, Canyon, Tex., 1982 | 4.314 pts |

## WOMEN
### Running

| | |
|---|---|
| 50 yards—Andrea Lynch, Toronto, 1978 | 0:05.80 |
| Deandra Carney (Am.), Toronto, 1978 | 0:05.68 |
| Evelyn Ashford (Am.), Toronto, 1981 | 0:05.83 |
| 60 yards—Evelyn Ashford, New York, 1982 | 0:06.54 |
| 100 yards—Marita Koch, East Berling, 1979 | 0:10.40 |
| Wilma Rudolph (Am.), Tennessee State, 1960 | 0:10.70 |
| 220 yards—Chandra Cheeseborough, New York, 1982 | 0:23.25 |
| 300 yards—Merlene Ottey, Cedar Falls, Neb., 1982 | 0:32.63 |
| Randy Givens (Am.), Cedar Falls, Neb., 1982 | 0:34.07 |
| 440 yards—Rosalyn Bryant, New York, 1977 | 0:53.20 |
| 500 yards—Rosalyn Bryant, San Diego, 1977 | 1:03.30 |
| Janine MacGregor, Inglewood, Calif., 1982 | 1:03.30 |
| 600 yards—Delisa Walton, Cedar Falls, Neb., 1982 | 1:17.38 |
| 880 yards—Mary Decker, San Diego, 1980 | 1:59.70 |
| 1,000 yards—Mary Decker, Inglewood, Calif., 1978 | 2:23.80 |
| Mile—Mary Decker Tabb, San Diego, 1982 | 4:20.5 |
| 2 miles—Joan Hansen, New York, 1982 | 9:37.03 |

### Running—Metric Distances

| | |
|---|---|
| 50 meters—Jeanette Bolden, Edmonton, Alberta, 1981 | 0:06.13 |
| 60 meters—Marlies Gohr, East Germany, 1980 | 0:07.10 |
| Brenda Moorehead (Am.), Louisville, Ky., 1980 | 0:07.28 |
| 100 meters—Marlies Gohr, East Berlin, 1979 | 0:11.30 |
| Mamie Rallins (Am.), San Diego, 1975 | 0:12.40 |
| 200 meters—Gesine Walther, Budapest, 1982 | 0:22.64 |
| 300 meters—Merlene Ottey, Lincoln, Neb., 1981 | 0:33.12 |
| Janet Dodson (Am.), Morgantown, W. Va., 1982 | 0:37.54 |
| 400 meters—Jarmila Kratochvilova, Milan, Italy, 1982 | 0:49.59 |
| Sharon Dabney (Am.), Italy, 1978 | 0:53.27 |
| 500 meters—Lorna Forde, Hanover, N.H., 1978 | 1:10.50 |
| 600 meters—Anita Weiss, East Berlin, 1980 | 1:26.20 |
| Chris Muller (Am.), Columbia, Mo., 1980 | 1:28.80 |
| 800 meters—Olga Vakrusheva, Moscow, 1980 | 1:58.40 |
| Mary Decker (Am.), San Diego, 1980 | 1:58.90 |
| 1,000 meters—Bridgette Kraus, West Germany 1978 | 2:34.80 |
| Francie Larrieu (Am.), Los Angeles, 1975 | 2:40.20 |
| 1,500 meters—Mary Decker, New York, 1980 | 4:00.80 |
| 2,000 meters—Francie Larrieu, Edmonton, Alberta, 1981 | 5:55.2 |
| 3,000 meters—Mary Decker Tabb, Inglewood, Calif., 1982 | 8:47.3 |

### Hurdles

| | |
|---|---|
| 50 yards—Johanna Klier, Toronto, 1978 | 0:06.20 |
| Deby LaPlante (Am.), Toronto, 1978 | 0:06.37 |
| 60 yards—Candy Young, New York, 1982 | 0:07.37 |
| Stephanie Hightower, New York, 1982 | 0:07.37 |
| 60 yards—Stephanie Hightower, New York, 1980 | 0:07.47 |
| 70 yards—Mamie Rallins, Chicago, 1970 | 0:08.80 |
| Deby LaPlante, Louisville, Ky., 1976 | 0:08.80 |
| 50 meters—Annelie Ehrhardt, Berlin, 1973 | 0:06.74 |
| Sofia Bielczyzk, Grenoble, France, 1981 | 0:06.74 |
| Candy Young (Am.), Edmonton, Alberta, 1979 | 0:06.95 |
| 60 meters—Sofia Bielczyzk, Poland, 1980 | 0:07.77 |
| Stephanie Hightower, (Am.), Milan, Italy, 1982 | 0:08.04 |
| 100 meters—Annelie Ehrhardt, East Germany, 1976 | 0:13.12 |
| Patty van Wolvelaere (Am.), New York, 1974 | 0:13.20 |

### Walking

| | |
|---|---|
| Mile—Susan Brodock, New York, 1978 | 7:01.70 |
| 1,500 meters—Susan Brodock, Toronto, 1976 | 6:42.90 |

### Relays

| | |
|---|---|
| 640 yards—Tennessee State, New York, 1981 | 1:08.99 |
| 880 yards—Tennessee State, Louisville, Ky., 1980 | 1:37.80 |
| 880 yard medley relay—Tennessee State, New York, 1981 | 1:42.17 |
| Mile—Los Angeles Mercurettes, New York, 1981 | 3:40.46 |
| 2 miles—Soviet Union, 1972 | 8:41.60 |
| Distance medley—Virginia, Princeton, N.J., 1982 | 11:19.39 |

### Field Events

| | |
|---|---|
| Long jump—Svyetlana Vanyushina, Vilnius, U.S.S.R., 1982 | 22 ft 5 in. |
| Veronica Bell (Am.), New York, 1982 | 21 ft 11¾ in. |
| High jump—Coleen Rienstra, Ottawa, 1982 | 6 ft 6¾ in. |
| Shotput—Helena Fibingerova, Czechoslovakia, 1977 | 73 ft 9¾ in. |
| Maren Seidler (Am.), West Germany, 1978 | 61 ft 2¼ in. |

## THE ATHLETICS CONGRESS NATIONAL CHAMPIONSHIPS

### INDOOR

(Madison Square Garden, New York, Feb. 26, 1982)

### Men's Events

| | |
|---|---|
| 60 yd—Ron Brown, Arizona State | 0:06.14 |
| 600 yd—Fred Sowerby, D.C. International | 1:09.50 |
| 1,000 yd—Don Paige, Athletic Attic | 2:05.81[1] |
| 440 yd—Walter McCoy, Athletic Attic | 0:48.24 |
| Mile—Jim Spivey, Indiana University | 3:57.04 |
| 3 Miles—Paul Cummings, Pacific Coast Club | 13:00.52 |
| 60-yd hurdles—Tony Campbell, Maccabi Track Club | 0:07.13 |
| 2-mile walk—Jim Heiring, Athletic Attic | 12:24.82[1] |
| Sprint medley relay—Athletic Attic (Ron Nelson, Floyd Brown, Vescoe Bradley, Terron Wright) | 2:03.98 |
| 2-mile relay—University of Richmond (Ed Koech, Phil Norgate, Barnabas Kipkorior, Julian Spooner) | 7:28.14[1] |
| Mile relay—Morgan State (Gary Goodman, Mitch Lovett, Carlton McNorton, Ed Yearwood) | 3:13.46 |
| Long jump—Carl Lewis, (Houston) unattached | 28 ft ¾ in.[1] |
| Triple jump—Keith Connor, Southern Methodist | 55 ft 11 in.[1] |
| High jump—Dwight Stones, Pacific Coast Club | 7 ft 4½ in. |
| Pole vault—Billy Olson, Pacific Coast Club | 18 ft 6½ in. |
| Shotput—Jeff Baum, University of Chicago | 65 ft 10½ in. |
| 35-lb weight throw—Ed Kania, Pacific Coast Club | 70 ft ½ in. |
| Team—Athletic Attic | 38 pts |
| Outstanding athlete—Carl Lewis | |

### Women's Events

| | |
|---|---|
| 60 yd—Evelyn Ashford, Medalist Track Club | 0:06.54[1] |
| 220 yd—Chandra Cheeseborough, Tennessee State (Miss Cheeseborough set world best in heat of 0:23.25) | 0:23.46 |
| 440 yd—Maxine Underwood, Boston International A.C. | 0:54.55[2] |
| 880 yd—Leann Warren, University of Oregon | 2:04.61 |
| Mile—Cathie Twomey, Athletics West | 4:32.92[1] |
| 2 miles—Joan Hansen, Athletics West | 9:37.03[3] |
| 60-yd hurdles—Stephanie Hightower, Los Angeles Naturites | 0:07.38[1] |
| Mile walk—Susan Brodock, Southern California Road Runners | 7:14 |
| 640-yd relay—Tennessee State (Chandra Cheeseborough, Wanda Fort, Sheryl Pernell, Ernestine Davis) | 1:09.36 |
| 880-yd medley relay—Tennessee State (Judith Pollion, Wanda Fort, Sheryl Pernell, Chandra Cheeseborough) | 1:44.26 |
| Mile relay—Atoms Track Club (Stephanie Vega, Dorionne McClure, Lorna Forde, Diane Dixon) | 3:40.54 |
| High jump—Coleen Rienstra, Wilt's Athletic Club | 6 ft 3¼ in.[1] |
| Long jump—Veronica Bell, Southern California | 21 ft 11¾ in.[1][4] |
| Shotput—Marita Walton, University of Maryland | 55 ft 11¾ in. |

1. Meet record. 2. National high school record. 3. World best. 4. American record.

## THE ATHLETICS CONGRESS NATIONAL CHAMPIONSHIPS—1982

(Knoxville, Tenn., June 18–20, 1982)

### OUTDOOR
### Men's Events

| | |
|---|---|
| 100 m—Carl Lewis, Santa Monica Track Club | 0:10.11 |
| 200 m—Calvin Smith, Athletic Attic | 0:20.47 |
| 400 m—Cliff Wiley, unattached | 0:45.05 |
| 800 m—James Robinson, Inner City Athletic Club | 1:46.12 |
| 1,500 m—Steve Scott, Sub 4 Track Club | 3:34.92[1] |
| 3,000-m steeplechase—Henry Marsh, Athletics West | 8:22.94 |
| 5,000 m—Matt Centrowitz, New York Athletic Club | 13:31.96 |
| 10,000 m—Craig Virgin, Front Runner Track Club | 28:33.02 |
| 20,000-m walk—Jim Heiring, Athletic Attic | 1:30:21.8 |
| 110-m hurdles—Willie Gault, Athletic Attic | 0:13.54 |
| 400-m hurdles—David Patrick, Athletics West | 0:48.57 |
| High jump—Milt Ottey, Philadelphia Pioneers | 7 ft 5¾ in. |
| Pole vault—Tie between Dan Ripley, Pacific Coast Club, and Billy Olson, Pacific Coast Club | 18 ft 9¼ in.[2] |
| Long jump—Carl Lewis, Santa Monica Track Club | 27 ft 10 in. |
| Triple jump—Robert Cannon, Athletic Attic | 55 ft ¾ in. |
| Shot-put—Kevin Akins, Ohio State | 69 ft 9½ in. |
| Discus—Louis Delis, Cuba | 225 ft 5 in. |
| Hammer—David McKenzie, unattached | 235 ft 2 in. |
| Javelin—Bob Roggy, Athletics West | 289 ft 9 in.[1] |

1. Meet record. 2. American record.

### Women's Events

| | |
|---|---|
| 100 m—Evelyn Ashford, Medalist Track Club | 0:10.96[1] |
| 200 m—Merlene Ottey, Los Angeles Naturite–Jamaica | 0:22.17[1] |
| 400 m—Denean Howard, Los Angeles Naturite | 0:50.87[1] |
| 800 m—Delisa Walton, Los Angeles Naturite | 2:00.91 |
| 1,500 m—Miss Decker Tabb, Athletics West | 4:03.37[1] |
| 3,000 m—Francie Larrieu-Smith, New Balance Track Club | 8:58.66 |
| 10,000 m—Kim Schurpfeil, Stanford Track Club | 33:35.88 |
| 100—m hurdles—Stephanie Hightower, Los Angeles Naturite | 0:12.86[2] |
| 400-m hurdles—Tammy Etienne, Metroplex Striders | 0:56.55 |
| 5,000-m walk—Susan Liers-Westerfield, Island Track Club | 24:56.6 |
| 400-m relay—Wilt's Athletic Club (Brenda Morehead, Jeannette Bolden, Alice Brown, Florence Griffith) | 0:43.45 |
| 800-m relay—Wilt's Athletic Club (Brenda Morehead, Jeanette Bolden, Alice Brown, Arlise Emerson) | 1:36.79 |
| 1,600-m relay—Los Angeles Naturite (Sharon Dabney, Denean Howard, Sherry Howard, Rosalyn Bryant) | 3:28.68 |
| 3,200-m relay—Stanford Track Club (Evonne Hannus, Regina Jacobs, June Griffith, Tami Essington) | 8:22.26[1] |
| High jump—Debbie Brill, Pacific Coast Club | 6 ft 4 in. |
| Long jump—Carol Lewis, Willingboro, N.J. | 22 ft 4½ in. |
| Shot-put—Maria Sarria, Cuba | 61 ft 8¼ in. |
| Discus—Ria Stalman, Los Angeles Naturite | 203 ft 10 in. |
| Javelin—Lynda Huges, Oregon | 202 ft 3 in. |

1. Meet record. 2. Ties American record.

## N.C.A.A. CHAMPIONSHIPS—1982

### INDOOR

(Pontiac, Mich., March 12–13, 1982)

| | |
|---|---|
| 60 yd—Rod Richardson, Texas A. and M. | 0:06.07[1] |
| 440 yd—Anthony Ketcham, Houston | 0:47.47 |
| 600 yd—Eugene Sanders, Mississippi Valley | 1:08.51[1] |
| 880 yd—David Patrick, Tennessee | 1:49.94 |
| 1,000 yd—John Stephens, Arkansas | 2:07.37 |
| Mile—Suleiman Nyambui, Texas–El Paso | 4:00.65 |
| 2 miles—Suleiman Nyambui | 8:38.91 |
| 3 miles—Gabriel Kamau, Texas–El Paso | 13:07.81[1] |
| 60-yd hurdles—Tony Campbell, Southern California | 0:07.14 |
| Mile relay—Oklahoma (Freddie Wilson, Donald Bly, Coty Duling, Dannie Cater) | 3:11.07[1] |
| 2-mile relay—Richmond (Edwin Koech, Julian Spooner, Phil Norgate, Sosthenes Bitok) | 7:24.48 |
| Distance medley relay—Georgetown (John Padati, Patrick McCabe, Kevin King, John Gregorek) | 9:45.97 |
| Long jump—Gilbert Smith, Texas–Arlington | 26 ft 1 in. |
| High jump—Leo Williams, Navy | 7 ft 5¾ in.[1] |
| Pole vault—Doug Lytle, Kansas State | 17 ft 9¾ in. |
| Triple jump—Keith Connor, Southern Methodist | 55 ft 3 in. |
| 35-lb weight throw—Tore Johnsen, Texas–El Paso | 70 ft 3¼ in. |
| Shotput—Mike Lehmann, Illinois | 67 ft 7¾ in. |
| Team—Texas–El Paso | 67 pts |

1. Meet record.

### OUTDOOR

(Provo, Utah, May 31–June 5, 1982)

### Men's Events

| | |
|---|---|
| 100 m—Stanley Floyd, Houston | 0:10.03[1] |
| 200 m—James Butler, Oklahoma State | 0:20.07 |
| 400 m—Kasheef Hassan, Oregon State | 0:45.47 |
| 800 m—David Mack, Oregon | 1:48.00 |
| 1,500 m—Jim Spivey, Indiana | 3:45.42 |

| | |
|---|---|
| 3,000 steeplechase—Richard Tuwei, Washington State | 8:42.73 |
| 5,000 m—Suleiman Nyambui, Texas-El Paso | 13:54.09 |
| 10,000 m—Suleiman Nyambui | 29:03.54 |
| 110-m hurdles—Milan Stewart, Southern California | 0:13.53 |
| 400-m hurdles—David Patrick, Tennessee | 0:48.44[1] |
| 400-m relay—Houston (Charles Young, Mark McNeil, Anthony Ketchum, Stanley Floyd) | 0:38.53[2] |
| 1,600-m relay—Mississippi State (Michael Hadley, George Washington, Michael Moore, Daryl Jones) | 3:03.49 |
| Discus—Dean Crouser, Oregon | 207 ft 4 in. |
| Javelin—Brian Crouser, Oregon | 274 ft 7 in. |
| Shot-Put—Dean Crouser, Oregon | 68 ft 4¼ in. |
| Hammer—Richard Olsen, Southern Methodist | 240 ft 6 in. |
| Pole vault—Dave Kenworthy, Southern California | 18 ft 2½ in. |
| High jump—Milt Ottey, Texas-El Paso | 7 ft 7¼ in.[3] |
| Triple jump—Keith Connor, Southern Methodist | 57 ft 7¾ in.[2] |
| Long jump—Vance Johnson, Arizona | 26 ft 11¼ in. |
| Decathlon—Trond Skramstad, Mount St. Mary's | 7,770 pts |
| Team—Texas-El Paso | 105 pts |

1. Meet record. 2. Collegiate record. 3. Tied collegiate record.

**Women's Events**[1]

| | |
|---|---|
| 100 m—Merlene Ottey, Nebraska | 0:10.97 |
| 200 m—Florence Griffith, U.C.L.A. | 0:23.20 |
| 400 m—Marita Payne, Florida State | 0:52.01 |
| 800 m—Delisa Walton, Tennessee | 2:05.22 |
| 1,500 m—Leann Warren, Oregon | 4:17.90 |
| 3,000 m—Ceci Hopp, Stanford | 9:28.92 |
| 5,000 m—Kathy Bryant, Tennessee | 16:10.41 |
| 10,000 m—Kim Schnurpfeil, Stanford | n.a. |
| 100-m hurdles—Benita Fitzgerald, Tennessee | 0:13.13 |
| 400-m hurdles—Tonja Brown, Florida State | 0:56.46 |
| High jump—Disa Gisladdottir, Alabama | 6 ft 1¼ in. |
| Long jump—Jennifer Innis, California State-Los Angeles | 21 ft 9½ in. |
| Shot-Put—Meg Ritchie, Arizona | 55 ft 5¼ in. |
| Discus—Meg Ritchie | 202 ft |
| Javelin—Karin Smith, California Poly-San Luis Obispo | 206 ft 8 in. |
| 400-m relay—Nebraska (Kristen Engle, Alicia McQueen, Rhonda Blanford, Merlene Ottey) | 0:43.72 |
| 1,600-m relay—Tennessee (Cathy Rattray, Sharieffa Barksdale, Joetta Clark, Delisa Walton) | 3:28.55[2] |
| Heptathlon—Jackie Joyner, U.C.L.A. | 6,099 pts |
| Team—U.C.L.A. | 153 pts |

1. First time women's N.C.A.A. competition was held. 2. Collegiate record. n.a. = not available.

---

## NATIONAL ATHLETIC CONGRESS RELAY CHAMPIONSHIPS

(New Brunswick, N. J., July 4, 1982)

| | |
|---|---|
| 400 meters—New York Pioneer Club (Michael McKnight, Brian Denman, Brady Crain, Elliott Quow) | 0:40.6 |
| 800 meters—New York Pioneer Club (Brady Crain, Brian Denman, Derrick Peynado, Elliott Quow) | 1:26.1 |
| 1,600 meters—BOHAA Club of New York (Dennis Duckworth, Nigel Gabriel, Gordon Hinds, Richard Louis) | 3:09.7 |
| 3,200 meters—Fort Lee Athletic Attic (Jim McKeon, John Borgese, Ray Oglesby, Tavo Rivera) | 7:36.3 |
| Sprint medley—Alliance Track Club of Long Island (Kevin Price, Alfred Daley, Hubert Blue, Larry Brooks) | 3:22.6[1] |
| 6,000 meters—New York Athletic Club (John Malone, John Hunter, Vince Draddy, Jim DiRienzo) | 15:34.6[1] |
| Distance medley—New York Athletic Club (Brian McNellis, Tim Hanlon, John Hunter, Ross Donoghue) | 9:45.0[1] |
| 440-meter shuttle hurdles—Shore Athletic Club (Joe Myatt, Bob Beaman, John Charniga, Leon Devero) | 0:57.3 |
| Team—Fort Lee Athletic Attic | 42 pts |

1. Meet record.

---

## ASSOCIATION FOR INTERCOLLEGIATE ATHLETICS FOR WOMEN

(Cedar Falls, Iowa, March 12–13, 1982)

### Indoor

| | |
|---|---|
| 60 yd—Merlene Ottey, Nebraska | 0:06.61 |
| 300 yd—Merlene Ottey, Nebraska | 0:32.63[1][2] |
| 440 yd—Lori McCauley, Rutgers | 0:55.12 |
| 600 yd—Delisa Walton, Tennessee | 1:17.38[1][2][3] |
| 880 yd—Doriane McClive, Cornell | 2:05.34 |
| 1,000 yd—Goetta Clark, Tennessee | 2:26.70 |
| Mile—Darleen Beckford, Harvard | 4:38.30 |
| 2 miles—Bernadette Badigan, Kentucky | 9:58.22 |
| 3 miles—Kellie Cathy, Oklahoma | 15:18.47[4] |
| 60-yd hurdles—Benita Fitzgerald, Tennessee | 0:07.54 |
| 880-yd relay—Nebraska (Ottey, Gorham, Blanford, James) | 1:37.70[5] |
| Mile relay—Texas (Sherfield, Walker, Bean, Coleman) | 3:44.66[5] |
| 2-mile relay—Florida State (Coomber, Borovicha, Wood, Brown) | 8:47.26[4] |
| Distance medley relay—Virginia (Nicholoson, Hatchett, Welch, Haworth) | 11:21.92[4] |
| Long jump—Donna Thomas, North Texas State | 20 ft 8½ in. |
| High jump—Gale Charmaine, Arizona | 6 ft 1¾ in. |
| Shot-put—Rosemary Blauch, Tennessee | 54 ft 11¾ in. |
| Pentathlon—Julie White, Boston University | 4,268 pts |
| Team—Nebraska | 84 pts |

1. World best. 2. U.S. collegiate best. 3. American best. 4. New event, record. 5. Meet record.

### Outdoor

(College Station, Tex., May 27–29, 1982)

| | |
|---|---|
| 100 m—Colleen Hanna, Iowa State | 0:11.73 |
| 200 m—Merry Johnson, West Texas State | 0:23.57 |
| 400 m—Merry Johnson | 0:52.43 |
| 800 m—Louise Romo, California—Berkeley | 2:04.39[1] |
| 1,500 m—Rose Thomson, Wisconsin—Madison | 4:18.78 |
| 3,000 m—Andrea Marek, Purdue | 9:16.18 |
| 5,000 m—Midde Hamrin, Lamar University | 16:03.75[1] |
| 10,000 m—Midde Hamrin | 33:37.68 |
| 100-m hurdles—Lori Dinello, Florida | 0:13.48 |
| 400-m hurdles—Edna Brown, Temple | 0:57.17[1] |
| 400-m relay—Texas—Austin (H. Denny, S. Bean, D. Sherfield, S. Shurr) | 0:46.04 |
| 800-m relay—Texas—Austin (D. Hollie, S. Shurr, D. Sherfield, R. Coleman) | 1:39.92 |
| 1,600-m relay—Texas—Austin (D. Sherfield, F. Walker, S. Bean, R. Coleman) | 3:37.66 |
| 3,200-m relay—Texas—Austin (S. Neugebauer, R. Coleman, F. Walker, T. Arnold) | 8:39.67[1] |
| Long jump—Pat Johnson, Wisconsin—Madison | 21 ft 4¾ in.[1] |
| Javelin—Lorri Kokkola, Texas—Austin | 170 ft 10 in. |
| Shotput—Sandy Burke, Northeastern | 52 ft 2¾ in. |
| Discus—Penny Neer, Michigan | 183 ft |
| High jump—Carolyn Ford, Lamar University | 6 ft ½ in.[1] |
| Hepthathlon—Kathy Raugust, California—Berkeley | 5,514 pts |
| Team—Texas—Austin | 82 pts |

1. A.I.A.W. record.

# TENNIS

Lawn tennis is a comparatively modern modification of the ancient game of court tennis. Major Walter Clopton Wingfield thought that something like court tennis might be played outdoors on lawns, and in December, 1873, at Nantclwyd, Wales, he introduced his new game under the name of *Sphairistike* at a lawn party. The game was a success and spread rapidly, but the name was a total failure and almost immediately disappeared when all the players and spectators began to refer to the new game as "lawn tennis." In the early part of 1874, a young lady named Mary Ewing Outerbridge returned from Bermuda to New York, bringing with her the implements and necessary equipment of the new game, which she had obtained from a British Army supply store in Bermuda. Miss Outerbridge and friends played the first game of lawn tennis in the United States on the grounds of the Staten Island Cricket and Baseball Club in the spring of 1874.

For a few years, the new game went along in haphazard fashion until about 1880, when standard measurements for the court and standard equipment within definite limits became the rule. In 1881, the U.S. Lawn Tennis Association (whose name was changed in 1975 to U.S. Tennis Association) was formed and conducted the first national championship at Newport, R.I. The international matches for the Davis Cup began with a series between the British and United States players on the courts of the Longwood Cricket Club, Chestnut Hill, Mass., in 1900, with the home players winning.

Professional tennis, which got its start in 1926 when the French star Suzanne Lenglen was paid $50,000 for a tour, received full recognition in 1968. Staid old Wimbledon, the London home of what are considered the world championships, let the pros compete. This decision ended a long controversy over open tennis and changed the format of the competition. The United States championships were also opened to the pros and the site of the event, long held at Forest Hills, N.Y., was shifted to the National Tennis Center in Flushing Meadows, N.Y., in 1978. Pro tours for men and women became worldwide in play that continued throughout the year.

## DAVIS CUP CHAMPIONSHIPS

No matches in 1901, 1910, 1915–18, and 1940–45.

| | | | | | |
|---|---|---|---|---|---|
| 1900 | United States 3, British Isles 0 | 1930 | France 4, United States 1 | 1960 | Australia 4, Italy 1 |
| 1902 | United States 3, British Isles 2 | 1931 | France 3, Great Britain 1 | 1961 | Australia 5, Italy 0 |
| 1903 | British Isles 4, United States 1 | 1932 | France 3, United States 2 | 1962 | Australia 5, Mexico 0 |
| 1904 | British Isles 5, Belgium 0 | 1933 | Great Britain 3, France 2 | 1963 | United States 3, Australia 2 |
| 1905 | British Isles 5, United States 0 | 1934 | Great Britain 4, United States 1 | 1964 | Australia 3, United States 2 |
| 1906 | British Isles 5, United States 0 | 1935 | Great Britain 5, United States 0 | 1965 | Australia 4, Spain 1 |
| 1907 | Australasia 3, British Isles 2 | 1936 | Great Britain 3, Australia 2 | 1966 | Australia 4, India 1 |
| 1908 | Australasia 3, United States 2 | 1937 | United States 4, Great Britain 1 | 1967 | Australia 4, Spain 1 |
| 1909 | Australasia 5, United States 0 | 1938 | United States 3, Australia 2 | 1968 | United States 4, Australia 1 |
| 1911 | Australasia 5, United States 0 | 1939 | Australia 3, United States 2 | 1969 | United States 5, Romania 0 |
| 1912 | British Isles 3, Australasia 2 | 1946 | United States 5, Australia 0 | 1970 | United States 5, West Germany 0 |
| 1913 | United States 3, British Isles 2 | 1947 | United States 4, Australia 1 | 1971 | United States 3, Romania 2 |
| 1914 | Australasia 3, United States 2 | 1948 | United States 5, Australia 0 | 1972 | United States 3, Romania 2 |
| 1919 | Australasia 4, British Isles 1 | 1949 | United States 4, Australia 1 | 1973 | Australia 5, United States 0 |
| 1920 | United States 5, Australasia 0 | 1950 | Australia 4, United States 1 | 1974 | South Africa (Default by India) |
| 1921 | United States 5, Japan 0 | 1951 | Australia 3, United States 2 | 1975 | Sweden 3, Czechoslovakia 2 |
| 1922 | United States 4, Australasia 1 | 1952 | Australia 4, United States 1 | 1976 | Italy 4, Chile 1 |
| 1923 | United States 4, Australasia 1 | 1953 | Australia 3, United States 2 | 1977 | Australia 3, Italy 1 |
| 1924 | United States 5, Australasia 0 | 1954 | United States 3, Australia 2 | 1978 | United States 4, Britain 1 |
| 1925 | United States 5, France 0 | 1955 | Australia 5, United States 0 | 1979 | United States 5, Italy 0 |
| 1926 | United States 4, France 1 | 1956 | Australia 5, United States 0 | 1980 | Czechoslovakia 3, Italy 2 |
| 1927 | France 3, United States 2 | 1957 | Australia 3, United States 2 | 1981 | United States 3, Argentina 1 |
| 1928 | France 4, United States 1 | 1958 | United States 3, Australia 2 | | |
| 1929 | France 3, United States 2 | 1959 | Australia 3, United States 2 | | |

## FEDERATION CUP CHAMPIONSHIPS

World team competition for women conducted by International Lawn Tennis Federation

| | | | | | |
|---|---|---|---|---|---|
| 1963 | United States 2, Australia 1 | 1970 | Australia 3, West Germany 0 | 1977 | United States 2, Australia 1 |
| 1964 | Australia 2, United States 1 | 1971 | Australia 3, Britain 0 | 1978 | United States 2, Australia 1 |
| 1965 | Australia 2, United States 1 | 1972 | South Africa 2, Britain 1 | 1979 | United States 3, Australia 0 |
| 1966 | United States 3, West Germany 0 | 1973 | Australia 3, South Africa 0 | 1980 | United States 3, Australia 0 |
| 1967 | United States 2, Britain 0 | 1974 | Australia 2, United States 1 | 1981 | United States 3, Britain 0 |
| 1968 | Australia 3, Netherlands 0 | 1975 | Czechoslovakia 3, Australia 0 | 1982 | United States 3, West Germany 0 |
| 1969 | United States 2, Australia 1 | 1976 | United States 2, Australia 1 | | |

## FOUR PLAYERS WIN GRAND SLAM OF TENNIS

Only four players, two men and two women, have won the Grand Slam of Tennis by winning the Australian, French, Wimbledon, and United States singles championships. Rod Laver of Australia did it twice, in 1962 and again in 1969 when the tourneys were opens. Don Budge, an American, was the first to complete the slam in 1938. Maureen Connolly of California in 1953 was the first woman to take the four titles. Margaret Smith Court of Australia won them all in 1970.

# U.S. CHAMPIONS
## Singles—Men

**NATIONAL**

| | | | | | | | |
|---|---|---|---|---|---|---|---|
| 1881–87 | Richard D. Sears | 1915 | William Johnston | 1944–45 | Frank Parker | 1968 | Arthur Ashe[3] |
| 1888–89 | Henry Slocum, Jr. | 1916 | R. N. William II | 1946–47 | Jack Kramer | 1969 | Stan Smith[3] |
| 1890–92 | Oliver S. Campbell | 1917–18 | R. Lindley Murray[2] | 1948–49 | Richard Gonzales | | |
| | | 1919 | William Johnston | 1950 | Arthur Larsen | **OPEN** | |
| | | 1920–25 | Bill Tilden | 1951–52 | Frank Sedgman | 1968 | Arthur Ashe |
| 1893–94 | Robert D. Wrenn | 1926–27 | Jean Rene Lacoste | 1953 | Tony Trabert | 1969 | Rod Laver |
| 1895 | Fred H. Hovey | 1928 | Henri Cochet | 1954 | Vic Seixas | 1970 | Ken Rosewall |
| 1896–97 | Robert D. Wrenn | 1929 | Bill Tilden | 1955 | Tony Trabert | 1971 | Stan Smith |
| 1898– | | 1930 | John H. Doeg | 1956 | Ken Rosewall | 1972 | Ilie Nastase |
| 1900 | Malcolm Whitman | 1931–32 | Ellsworth Vines | 1957 | Mal Anderson | 1973 | John Newcombe |
| 1901–02 | William A. Larned | 1933–34 | Fred J. Perry | 1958 | Ashley Cooper | 1974 | Jimmy Connors |
| 1903 | Hugh L. Doherty | 1935 | Wilmer L. Allison | 1959–60 | Neale Fraser | 1975 | Manuel Orantes |
| 1904 | Holcombe Ward | 1936 | Fred J. Perry | 1961 | Roy Emerson | 1976 | Jimmy Connors |
| 1905 | Beals C. Wright | 1937–38 | Don Budge | 1962 | Rod Laver | 1977 | Guillermo Vilas |
| 1906 | William J. Clothier | 1939 | Robert L. Riggs | 1963 | Rafael Osuna | 1978 | Jimmy Connors |
| 1907–11 | William A. Larned | 1940 | Donald McNeill | 1964 | Roy Emerson | 1979 | John McEnroe |
| 1912–13 | Maurice McLoughlin[1] | 1941 | Robert L. Riggs | 1965 | Manuel Santana | 1980–81 | John McEnroe |
| | | 1942 | Fred Schroeder | 1966 | Fred Stolle | 1982 | Jimmy Connors |
| 1914 | R. N. Williams II | 1943 | Joseph Hunt | 1967 | John Newcombe | | |

## Singles—Women

**NATIONAL**

| | | | | | | | |
|---|---|---|---|---|---|---|---|
| 1887 | Ellen F. Hansel | 1904 | May Sutton | 1931 | Helen Wills Moody | 1962 | Margaret Smith |
| 1888–89 | Bertha Townsend | 1905 | Elisabeth H. Moore | 1932–35 | Helen Jacobs | 1963–64 | Maria Bueno |
| 1890 | Ellen C. Roosevelt | | | 1936 | Alice Marble | 1965 | Margaret Smith |
| 1891–92 | Mabel E. Cahill | 1906 | Helen Homans | 1937 | Anita Lizana | 1966 | Maria Bueno |
| 1893 | Aline M. Terry | 1907 | Evelyn Sears | 1938–40 | Alice Marble | 1967 | Billie Jean King |
| 1894 | Helen R. Helwig | 1908 | Maud Bargar-Wallach | 1941 | Sarah Palfrey Cooke | 1968–69 | Margaret Smith Court[3] |
| 1895 | Juliette P. Atkinson | 1909–11 | Hazel V. Hotchkiss | 1942–44 | Pauline Betz | | |
| 1896 | Elisabeth H. Moore | 1912–14 | Mary K. Browne | 1945 | Sarah Cooke | **OPEN** | |
| | | 1915–18 | Molla Bjurstedt | 1946 | Pauline Betz | 1968 | Virginia Wade |
| 1897–98 | Juliette P. Atkinson | 1919 | Hazel Hotchkiss Wightman | 1947 | Louise Brough | 1969–70 | Margaret Court |
| 1899 | Marion Jones | | | 1948–50 | Margaret Osborne duPont | 1971–72 | Billie Jean King |
| 1900 | Myrtle McAteer | 1920–22 | Molla Bjurstedt Mallory | 1951–53 | Maureen Connolly | 1973 | Margaret Court |
| 1901 | Elisabeth H. Moore | | | 1954–55 | Doris Hart | 1974 | Billie Jean King |
| | | 1923–25 | Helen N. Wills | 1956 | Shirley Fry | 1975–78 | Chris Evert |
| 1902 | Marion Jones | 1926 | Molla B. Mallory | 1957–58 | Althea Gibson | 1979 | Tracy Austin |
| 1903 | Elisabeth H. Moore | 1927–29 | Helen N. Wills | 1959 | Maria Bueno | 1980 | Chris Evert Lloyd |
| | | 1930 | Betty Nuthall | 1960–61 | Darlene Hard | 1981 | Tracy Austin |
| | | | | | | 1982 | Chris Evert Lloyd |

## Doubles—Men

**NATIONAL**

| | | | | | | |
|---|---|---|---|---|---|---|
| 1920 | Bill Johnston–C. J. Griffin | 1942 | Gardnar Mulloy–Bill Talbert | 1957 | Ashley Cooper–Neale Fraser |
| 1921–22 | Bill Tilden–Vincent Richards | 1943 | Jack Kramer–Frank Parker | 1958 | Ham Richardson–Alex Olmedo |
| 1923 | Bill Tilden–B. I. C. Norton | 1944 | Don McNeill–Bob Falkenburg | 1959–60 | Neale Fraser–Roy Emerson |
| 1924 | H. O. Kinsey–R. G. Kinsey | 1945 | Gardnar Mulloy–Bill Talbert | 1961 | Chuck McKinley–Dennis Ralston |
| 1925–26 | Vincent Richards–R. N. Williams II | 1946 | Gardnar Mulloy–Bill Talbert | | |
| | | 1947 | Jack Kramer–Fred Schroeder | 1962 | Rafael Osuna–Antonio Palafox |
| 1927 | Bill Tilden–Frank Hunter | 1948 | Gardnar Mulloy–Bill Talbert | 1963–64 | Chuck McKinley–Dennis Ralston |
| 1928 | G. M. Lott, Jr.–V. Hennessy | 1949 | John Bromwich–William Sidwell | | |
| 1929–30 | G. M. Lott, Jr.–J. H. Doeg | | | 1965–66 | Fred Stolle–Roy Emerson |
| 1931 | W. L. Allison–John Van Ryn | 1950 | John Bromwich–Frank Sedgman | 1967 | John Newcombe–Tony Roche |
| 1932 | E. H. Vines, Jr.–Keith Gledh | | | 1968 | Stan Smith–Bob Lutz[3] |
| 1933–34 | G. M. Lott, Jr.–L. R. Stoefen | 1951 | Frank Sedgman–Ken McGregor | 1969 | Richard Crealy–Allan Stone[3] |
| 1935 | W. L. Allison–John Van Ryn | 1952 | Vic Seixas–Mervyn Rose | | |
| 1936 | Don Budge–Gene Mako | 1953 | Mervyn Rose–Rex Hartwig | **OPEN** | |
| 1937 | G. von Cramm–H. Henkel | 1954 | Vic Seixas–Tony Trabert | 1968 | Stan Smith–Bob Lutz |
| 1938 | Don Budge–Gene Mako | 1955 | Kosei Kamo–Atsushi Miyagi | 1969 | Fred Stolle–Ken Rosewall |
| 1939 | A. K. Quist–J. E. Bromwich | 1956 | Lewis Hoad–Ken Rosewall | 1970 | Nikki Pilic–Fred Barthes |
| 1940–41 | Jack Kramer–F. R. Schroeder | | | | |

1. Challenge round abandoned in 1912. 2. Patriotic Tournament in 1917. 3. With the inaugural of the Open Tournament in 1968, the United States Lawn Tennis Association held a national championship at Longwood, Chestnut Hill, Mass. which barred contract professionals in 1968 and 1969.

| 1971 | John Newcombe–Roger Taylor | 1975 | Jimmy Connors–Ilie Nastase | 1979 | John McEnroe–Peter Fleming |
|---|---|---|---|---|---|
| 1972 | Cliff Drysdale–Roger Taylor | 1976 | Marty Riessen–Tom Okker | 1980 | Stan Smith–Bob Lutz |
| 1973 | John Newcombe–Owen Davidson | 1977 | Frew McMillan–Bob Hewitt | 1981 | John McEnroe–Peter Fleming |
| 1974 | Bob Lutz–Stan Smith | 1978 | Bob Lutz–Stan Smith | 1982 | Kevin Curren–Steve Denton |

## Doubles—Women

### NATIONAL

| 1924 | G. W. Wightman–Helen Wills |
|---|---|
| 1925 | Mary K. Browne–Helen Wills |
| 1926 | Elizabeth Ryan–Eleanor Goss |
| 1927 | L. A. Godfree–Ermyntrude Harvey |
| 1928 | Hazel Hotchkiss Wightman–Helen Wills |
| 1929 | Phoebe Watson–L. R. C. Michell |
| 1930 | Betty Nuthall–Sarah Palfrey |
| 1931 | Betty Nuthall–E. B. Wittingstall |
| 1932 | Helen Jacobs–Sarah Palfrey |
| 1933 | Betty Nuthall–Freda James |
| 1934 | Helen Jacobs–Sarah Palfrey |
| 1935 | Helen Jacobs–Sarah Palfrey Fabyan |
| 1936 | Marjorie G. Van Ryn–Carolin Babcock |
| 1937–40 | Sarah Palfrey Fabyan–Alice Marble |
| 1941 | Sarah Palfrey Cooke–Margaret Osborne |
| 1942–47 | A. Louise Brough–Margaret Osborne |
| 1948–50 | A. Louise Brough–Margaret O. duPont |
| 1951–54 | Doris Hart–Shirley Fry |
| 1955–57 | A. Louise Brough–Margaret O. duPont |
| 1958–59 | Darlene Hard–Jeanne Arth |
| 1960 | Darlene Hard–Maria Bueno |
| 1961 | Darlene Hard–Lesley Turner |
| 1962 | Darlene Hard–Maria Bueno |
| 1963 | Margaret Smith–Robyn Ebbern |
| 1964 | Karen Hantze Susman–Billie Jean Moffitt |
| 1965 | Nancy Richey–Carole Caldwell Graebner |
| 1966 | Nancy Richey–Maria Bueno |
| 1967 | Billie Jean King–Rosemary Casals |
| 1968 | Margaret Court–Maria Bueno[3] |
| 1969 | Margaret Court–Virginia Wade[3] |

### OPEN

| 1968 | Maria Bueno–Margaret Court |
|---|---|
| 1969 | Darlene Hard–Francoise Durr |
| 1970 | Margaret Court–Judy Dalton |
| 1971 | Rosemary Casals–Judy Dalton |
| 1972 | Francoise Durr–Betty Stove |
| 1973 | Margaret Court–Virginia Wade |
| 1974 | Billie Jean King–Rosemary Casals |
| 1975 | Margaret Court–Virginia Wade |
| 1976 | Linky Boshoff–Ilana Kloss |
| 1977 | Martina Navratilova–Betty Stove |
| 1978 | Billie Jean King–Martina Navratilova |
| 1979 | Betty Stove–Wendy Turnbull |
| 1980 | Billie Jean King–Martina Navratilova |
| 1981 | Kathy Jordan–Anne Smith |
| 1982 | Rosemary Casals–Wendy Turnbull |

1. Challenge round abandoned in 1912. 2. Patriotic Tournament in 1917. 3. With the inaugural of the Open Tournament in 1968, the United States Lawn Tennis Association held a national championship at Longwood, Chestnut Hill, Mass. which barred contract professionals in 1968 and 1969.

## U.S. INDOOR CHAMPIONS

### Singles—Men

| 1964 | Charles McKinley | 1972 | Stan Smith |
|---|---|---|---|
| 1965 | Erik Lundquist | 1973–75 | Jimmy Connors |
| 1966 | Charles Pasarell | 1976 | Ilie Nastase |
| 1967 | Charles Pasarell | 1977 | Bjorn Borg |
| 1968 | Cliff Richey | 1978–79 | Jimmy Connors |
| 1969 | Stan Smith | 1980 | John McEnroe |
| 1970 | Ilie Nastase | 1981 | Gene Mayer |
| 1971 | Clark Graebner | 1982 | Johan Kriek |

### Singles—Women

| 1964 | Mary Ann Eisel | 1972 | Not held |
|---|---|---|---|
| 1965 | Nancy Richey | 1973 | Evonne Goolagong |
| 1966 | Billie Jean King | 1974 | Billie Jean King |
| 1967 | Billie Jean King | 1975 | Martina Navratilova |
| 1968 | Billie Jean King | 1976 | Virginia Wade |
| 1969 | Mary Ann Eisel | 1977–82 | Not held |
| 1970 | Mary Ann Curtis | | |
| 1971 | Billie Jean King | | |

### Doubles—Men

| 1967 | Arthur Ashe–Charles Pasarell |
|---|---|
| 1968 | Thomas Koch–Tom Okker |
| 1969 | Stan Smith–Bob Lutz |
| 1970 | Arthur Ashe–Stan Smith |
| 1971 | Manuel Orantes–Juan Gisbert |
| 1972 | Manuel Orantes–Andres Gimeno |
| 1973 | Juan Gisbert–Jurgen Fassbender |
| 1974 | Jimmy Connors–Frew McMillan |
| 1975 | Jimmy Connors–Ilie Nastase |
| 1976–77 | Sherwood Stewart–Fred McNair |
| 1978 | Brian Gottfried–Raul Ramirez |
| 1979 | Wojtek Fibak–Tom Okker |
| 1980 | John McEnroe–Brian Gottfried |
| 1981 | Gene Mayer–Sandy Mayer |
| 1982 | Kevin Curren–Steve Denton |

### Doubles—Women

| 1967 | Carol Aucamp–Mary Ann Eisel |
|---|---|
| 1968 | Rosemary Casals–Billie Jean King |
| 1969 | Mary Ann Eisel–Valerie Ziegenfuss |
| 1970 | Peaches Bartkowicz–Nancy Richey |
| 1971 | Billie Jean King–Rosemary Casals |
| 1972 | Not held |
| 1973 | Olga Morozova–Marina Kroshina |
| 1974 | Not held |
| 1975 | Billie Jean King–Rosemary Casals |
| 1976 | Rosemary Casals–Francoise Durr |
| 1977–82 | Not held |

## BRITISH (WIMBLEDON) CHAMPIONS
(Amateur from inception in 1877 through 1967)

### Singles—Men

| | | | | | |
|---|---|---|---|---|---|
| 1908–09 | Arthur Gore | 1929 | Jean Cochet | 1950 | Budge Patty | 1964–65 | Roy Emerson |
| 1910–13 | A. F. Wilding | 1930 | Bill Tilden | 1951 | Richard Savitt | 1966 | Manuel Santana |
| 1914 | N. E. Brookes | 1931 | S. B. Wood | 1952 | Frank Sedgman | 1967 | John Newcombe |
| 1919 | G. L. Patterson | 1932 | Ellsworth Vines | 1953 | Vic Siexas | 1968–69 | Rod Laver |
| 1920–21 | Bill Tilden | 1933 | J. H. Crawford | 1954 | Jaroslav Drobny | 1970–71 | John Newcombe |
| 1922 | G. L. Patterson | 1934–36 | Fred Perry | 1955 | Tony Trabert | 1972 | Stan Smith |
| 1923 | William Johnston | 1937–38 | Don Budge | 1956–57 | Lewis Hoad | 1973 | Jan Kodes |
| 1924 | Jean Borotra | 1939 | Robert L. Riggs | 1958 | Ashley Cooper | 1974 | Jimmy Connors |
| 1925 | Rene Lacoste | 1946 | Yvon Petra | 1959 | Alex Olmedo | 1975 | Arthur Ashe |
| 1926 | Jean Borotra | 1947 | Jack Kramer | 1960 | Neale Fraser | 1976–80 | Bjorn Borg |
| 1927 | Henri Cochet | 1948 | R. Falkenburg | 1961–62 | Rod Laver | 1981 | John McEnroe |
| 1928 | Rene Lacoste | 1949 | Fred Schroeder | 1963 | Chuck McKinley | 1982 | Jimmy Connors |

### Singles—Women

| | | | | | |
|---|---|---|---|---|---|
| 1919–23 | Lenglen | 1937 | D. E. Round | 1959–60 | Maria Bueno | 1972–73 | Billie Jean King |
| 1924 | Kathleen McKane | 1938 | Helen Wills Moody | 1961 | Angela Mortimer | 1974 | Chris Evert |
| 1925 | Lenglen | 1939 | Alice Marble | 1962 | Karen Susman | 1975 | Billie Jean King |
| 1926 | Godfree | 1946 | Pauline M. Betz | 1963 | Margaret Smith | 1976 | Chris Evert |
| 1927–29 | Helen Wills | 1947 | Margaret Osborne | 1964 | Maria Bueno | 1977 | Virginia Wade |
| 1930 | Helen Wills Moody | 1948–50 | A. Louise Brough | 1965 | Margaret Smith | 1978–79 | Martina |
| 1931 | Frl. C. Aussen | 1951 | Doris Hart | 1966–67 | Billie Jean King | | Navratilova |
| 1932–33 | Helen Wills Moody | 1952–54 | Maureen Connolly | 1968 | Billie Jean King | 1980 | Evonne Goolagong |
| 1934 | D. E. Round | 1955 | A. Louise Brough | 1969 | Ann Jones | | Cawley |
| 1935 | Helen Wills Moody | 1956 | Shirley Fry | 1970 | Margaret Court | 1981 | Chris Evert Lloyd |
| 1936 | Helen Jacobs | 1957–58 | Althea Gibson | 1971 | Evonne Goolagong | 1982 | Martina Navratilova |

### Doubles—Men

| | | | | | |
|---|---|---|---|---|---|
| 1953 | K. Rosewall–L. Hoad | 1964 | Fred Stolle–Bob Hewitt | 1976 | Brian Gottfried–Raul Ramirez |
| 1954 | R. Hartwig–M. Rose | 1965 | John Newcombe–Tony Roche | 1977 | Ross Case–Geoff Masters |
| 1955 | R. Hartwig–L. Hoad | | | 1978 | Frew McMillan–Bob Hewitt |
| 1956 | L. Hoad–K. Rosewall | 1966 | John Newcombe–Ken Fletcher | 1979 | Peter Fleming–John McEnroe |
| 1957 | Gardnar Mulloy–Budge Patty | 1967 | Bob Hewitt–Frew McMillan | 1980 | Peter McNamara–Paul |
| 1958 | Sven Davidson–Ulf Schmidt | 1968–70 | John Newcombe–Tony Roche | | McNamee |
| 1959 | Roy Emerson–Neale Fraser | 1971 | Rod Laver–Roy Emerson | 1981 | John McEnroe–Peter Fleming |
| 1960 | Dennis Ralston–Rafael Osuna | 1972 | Bob Hewitt–Frew McMillan | 1982 | Paul McNamee–Peter |
| 1961 | Roy Emerson–Neale Fraser | 1973 | Jimmy Connors–Ilie Nastase | | McNamara |
| 1962 | Fred Stolle–Bob Hewitt | 1974 | John Newcombe–Tony Roche | | |
| 1963 | Rafael Osuna–Antonio Palafox | 1975 | Vitas Gerulaitis–Sandy Mayer | | |

### Doubles—Women

| | | | | | |
|---|---|---|---|---|---|
| 1956 | Althea Gibson–Angela Buxton | 1965 | Billie Jean Moffitt–Maria Bueno | 1975 | Ann Kiyomura–Kazuko Sawamatsu |
| 1957 | Althea Gibson–Darlene Hard | 1966 | Nancy Richey–Maria Bueno | 1976 | Chris Evert–Martina Navratilova |
| 1958 | Althea Gibson–Maria Bueno | 1967–68 | Billie Jean King–Rosemary Casals | 1977 | Helen Cawley–JoAnne Russell |
| 1959 | Darlene Hard–Jeanne Arth | 1969 | Margaret Court–Judy Tegart | 1978 | Wendy Turnbull–Kerry Reid |
| 1960 | Darlene Hard–Maria Bueno | 1970–71 | Billie Jean King–Rosemary Casals | 1979 | Billie Jean King–Martina Navratilova |
| 1961 | Karen Hantze–Billie Jean Moffitt | 1972 | Billie Jean King–Betty Stove | 1980 | Kathy Jordan–Anne Smith |
| 1962 | Karen Hantze Susman–Billie Jean Moffitt | 1973 | Billie Jean King–Rosemary Casals | 1981 | Martina Navratilova–Pam Shriver |
| 1963 | Darlene Hard–Maria Bueno | 1974 | Evonne Goolagong–Peggy Michel | 1982 | Pam Shriver–Martina Navratilova |
| 1964 | Margaret Smith–Les Turnerley | | | | |

## UNITED STATES CHAMPIONSHIPS—1982

### Open

(Flushing Meadows, N.Y., Aug. 31–Sept. 12, 1982)

Men's singles—Final: Jimmy Connors, Miami Beach, Fla., defeated Ivan Lendl, Czechoslovakia, 6–3, 6–2, 4–6, 6–4. Semifinals: Connors defeated Guillermo Vilas, Argentina, 6–1, 3–6, 6–2, 6–3; Lendl defeated John McEnroe, Douglaston, N.Y., 6–4, 6–4, 7–6.

Women's singles—Final: Chris Evert Lloyd, Amelia Island, Fla., defeated Hana Mandlikova, Czechoslovakia, 6–3, 6–1. Semifinals: Mrs. Lloyd defeated Andrea Jaeger, Lincolnshire, Ill., 6–1, 6–2; Miss Mandlikova defeated Pam Shriver, Lutherville, Md., 6–4, 2–6, 6–2.

Men's doubles—Final: Kevin Curren, South Africa, and Steve Denton, Driscoll, Tex., defeated Victor Amaya, Louisville, Ky., and Hank Pfister, Los Gatos, Calif., 6–2, 6–7, 5–7, 6–2, 6–4.

Women's doubles—Final: Rosemary Casals, Sausalito, Calif., and Wendy Turnbull, Australia, defeated Barbara Potter, Woodbury, Conn., and Sharon Walsh, Novato, Calif., 6–4, 6–4.

Mixed doubles—Final: Anne Smith, Dallas, Tex., and Kevin Curren defeated Barbara Potter and Ferdi Taygan, Framingham, Mass., 6–7, 7–6, 7–6.

Junior boys singles—Final: Pat Cash, Australia, defeated Guy Forget, France, 6–3, 6–3.

Junior girls singles—Final: Beth Herr, Dayton, Ohio, defeated Gretchen Rush, Pittsburgh, 6–3, 6–1.

### National Clay Court

(Indianapolis, Aug. 2–8, 1982)

Men's singles final—Jose Higueras, Spain, defeated Jimmy Arias, Grand Island, N.Y., 7–5, 5–7, 6–3.

Women's singles final—Virginia Ruzici, Romania, defeated Helena Sukova, Czechoslovakia, 6–2, 6–0.

Men's doubles final—Sherwood Stewart, Houston, Tex., and Ferdy Taygan, Framingham, Mass., defeated Robbie Venter, South Africa, and Baline Willenborg, Miami Shores, Fla., 6–4, 7–5.

Women's doubles final—Ivanna Madruga–Osses, Argentina, and Katherine Tanvier, France, defeated Joanne Russell, Naples, Fla., and Virginia Ruzici, Romania, 7–5, 7–6.

### World Championship Tennis

(Dallas, April 29–May 2, 1982)

Final—Ivan Lendl, Czechoslovakia, defeated John McEnroe, Douglaston, N.Y., 6–2, 3–6, 6–3.

### U.S. National Indoor

(Memphis, Tenn., Feb. 8–14, 1982)

Singles final—Johan Kriek, Naples, Fla., defeated John McEnroe, Douglaston, N.Y., 6–3, 3–6, 6–4. Doubles final—Kevin Curren, South Africa and Steve Denton, Driscoll., Tex., defeated McEnroe and Peter Fleming, Seabrook Island, S.C., 7–6, 4–6, 6–2.

### U.S. Pro Indoor

(Philadelphia, Jan. 25–31, 1982)

Final—John McEnroe, Douglaston, N.Y., defeated Jimmy Connors, Miami Beach, Fla., 6–3, 6–3, 6–1.

### U.S. Pro

(Brookline, Mass., July 12–19, 1982)

Singles final—Guillermo Vilas, Argentina, defeated Mel Purcell, Murray, Ky., 6–4, 6–0. Doubles final—Steve Meister and Craig Wittus, United States, defeated Freddie Sauer and Schalk van der Merwe, South Africa, 6–2, 6–3.

## OTHER 1982 CHAMPIONSHIPS

### Wimbledon Open

Men's singles—Jimmy Connors, Belleville, Ill., defeated John McEnroe, Douglaston, N.Y., 3–6, 6–3, 6–7, 7–6, 6–4.

Women's singles—Martina Navratilova, Fort Lauderdale, Fla., defeated Chris Evert Lloyd, Fort Lauderdale, Fla., 6–1, 3–6, 6–2.

Men's doubles—Paul McNamee and Peter McNamara, Australia, defeated John McEnroe and Peter Fleming, United States, 6–3, 6–2.

Women's doubles—Pam Shriver and Martina Navratilova, United States, defeated Kathy Jordan and Anne Smith, United States, 6–4, 6–1.

Mixed doubles—Kevin Curren, South Africa, and Anne Smith, United States, defeated John Lloyd, Britain, and Wendy Turnbull, Australia, 2–6, 6–3, 7–5.

### French Open

Men's singles—Mats Wilander, Sweden, defeated Guillermo Vilas, Argentina, 1–6, 7–6, 6–0, 6–4.

Women's singles—Martina Navratilova, Dallas, defeated Andrea Jaeger, Lincolnshire, Ill., 7–6, 6–1.

Men's doubles—Sherwood Stewart and Ferdi Taygan, United States, defeated Hans Gildemeister and Belus Prajoux, Chile, 7–5, 6–3, 1–1, retired (Gildemeister injured his back and could not continue).

Women's doubles—Martina Navratilova and Anne Smith, United States, defeated Rosemary Casals, United States, and Wendy Turnbull, Australia, 6–3, 6–4.

### Australian Open

(Men's events at Melbourne, Australia, Dec. 26, 1981-Jan. 2, 1982)

(Women's events at Melbourne, Australia, Nov. 30-Dec. 5, 1981)

Men's singles—Johan Kriek, South Africa, defeated Steve Denton, Driscoll, Tex., 6–2, 7–6, 6–7, 6–4.

Women's singles—Martina Navratilova, Dallas, defeated Chris Evert Lloyd, Fort Lauderdale, Fla., 6–7, 6–4, 7–5.

Men's doubles—Mark Edmondson and Kim Warwick, Australia, defeated Hank Pfister and John Sadri, United States, 6–3, 7–6.

Women's doubles—Kathy Jordan and Anne Smith, United States, defeated Martina Navratilova and Pam Shriver, United States, 6–2, 7–5.

## DAVIS CUP RESULTS—1981
## Final Round (Championship Competition)

United States 3, Argentina 1 (At Cincinnati, Ohio)
John McEnroe (U.S.) defeated Guillermo Vilas (A), 6–3, 6–2, 6–2; Jose–Luis Clerc (A) defeated Roscoe Tanner (U.S.), 7–5, 6–3, 8–6; Peter Fleming and McEnroe (U.S.) defeated Clerc–Vilas, 6–3, 4–6, 6–4, 4–6, 11–9; McEnroe defeated Clerc, 7–5, 5–7, 3–6, 6–3, 6–3. Tanner vs. Vilas suspended at 11 games to 10 in the first set, Tanner.

### Semifinal Round

United States 5, Australia 0 (At Portland, Ore.)
Argentina 5, Britain 0 (At Buenos Aires)

### Quarterfinal Round

Argentina 3, Romania 2 (At Timisoara)
Britain 4, New Zealand 1 (At Christchurch)
Australia 3, Sweden 1 (At Baastad)
United States 4, Czechoslovakia 1 (At Flushing Meadows)

### First Round

Argentina 3, Federal Republic of Germany 2 (At Munich)
Romania 3, Brazil 2 (At Timisoara)
Britain 3, Italy 2 (At Brighton)
New Zealand 5, Korea 0 (At Seoul)
Sweden 5, Japan 0 (At Yokohama)
Australia 3, France 2 (At Lyons)
Czechoslovakia 3, Switzerland 2 (At Zurich)
United States 3, Mexico 2 (At Carlsbad, Calif.)

## MEN'S FINAL TENNIS EARNINGS—1981

| Player | Amount |
| --- | --- |
| John McEnroe | $991,000 |
| Ivan Lendl | 846,037 |
| Jimmy Connors | 405,872 |
| Guillermo Vilas | 402,261 |
| Jose–Luis Clerc | 327,375 |
| Vitas Gerulaitis | 288,475 |
| Heinz Gunthardt | 278,642 |
| Peter McNamara | 273,066 |
| Eliot Teltscher | 267,630 |
| Roscoe Tanner | 245,380 |

## WOMEN'S FINAL TENNIS EARNINGS—1981

| Player | Amount |
| --- | --- |
| Martina Navratilova | $865,437 |
| Chris Evert Lloyd | 572,162 |
| Tracy Austin | 453,409 |
| Andrea Jaeger | 392,115 |
| Pam Shriver | 366,530 |
| Hana Mandlikova | 339,602 |
| Wendy Turnbull | 225,161 |
| Anne Smith | 192,311 |
| Sylvia Hanika | 190,898 |
| Virginia Ruzici | 179,115 |

# ROWING

Rowing goes back so far in history that there is no possibility of tracing it to any particular aboriginal source. The oldest rowing race still on the calendar is the "Doggett's Coat and Badge" contest among professional watermen of the Thames (England) that began in 1715. The first Oxford-Cambridge race was held at Henley in 1829. Competitive rowing in the United States began with matches between boats rowed by professional oarsmen of the New York water front. They were oarsmen who rowed the small boats that plied as ferries from Manhattan Island to Brooklyn and return, or who rowed salesmen down the harbor to meet ships arriving from Europe. Since the first salesman to meet an incoming ship had some advantage over his rivals, there was keen competition in the bidding for fast boats and the best oarsmen. This gave rise to match races.

Amateur boat clubs sprang up in the United States between 1820 and 1830 and seven students of Yale joined together to purchase a four-oared lap-streak gig in 1843. The first Harvard-Yale race was held Aug. 3, 1852, on Lake Winnepesaukee, N.H. The first time an American college crew went abroad was in 1869 when Harvard challenged Oxford and was defeated on the Thames. There were early college rowing races on Lake Quinsigamond, near Worcester, Mass., and on Saratoga Lake, N.Y., but the Intercollegiate Rowing Association in 1895 settled on the Hudson, at Poughkeepsie, as the setting for the annual "Poughkeepsie Regatta." In 1950 the I.R.A. shifted its classic to Marietta, Ohio, and in 1952 it was moved to Syracuse, N.Y. The National Association of Amateur Oarsmen, organized in 1872, has conducted annual championship regattas since that time.

## INTERCOLLEGIATE ROWING ASSOCIATION REGATTA
### (Varsity Eight-Oared Shells)

Rowed at 4 miles, Poughkeepsie, N.Y., 1895–97, 1899–1916, 1925–32, 1934–41. Rowed at 3 miles, Saratoga, N.Y., 1898; Poughkeepsie, 1921–24, 1947–49; Syracuse, N.Y., 1952–1963, 1965–67. Rowed at 2,000 meters, Syracuse, N.Y., 1964 and from 1968 on. Rowed at 2 miles, Ithaca, N.Y., 1920; Marietta, Ohio, 1950–51. Suspended 1917–19, 1933, 1942–46.

| Year | Time | First | Second | Year | Time | First | Second |
|------|------|-------|--------|------|------|-------|--------|
| 1895 | 21:25 | Columbia | Cornell | 1939 | 18:12 3/5 | California | Washington |
| 1896 | 19:59 | Cornell | Harvard | 1940 | 22:42 | Washington | Cornell |
| 1897 | 20:47 4/5 | Cornell | Columbia | 1941 | 18:53 3/10 | Washington | California |
| 1898 | 15:51 1/2 | Pennsylvania | Cornell | 1947 | 13:59 1/5 | Navy | Cornell |
| 1899 | 20:04 | Pennsylvania | Wisconsin | 1948 | 14:06 2/5 | Washington | California |
| 1900 | 19:44 3/5 | Pennsylvania | Wisconsin | 1949 | 14:42 3/5 | California | Washington |
| 1901 | 18:53 1/5 | Cornell | Columbia | 1950 | 8:07.5 | Washington | California |
| 1902 | 19:03 3/5 | Cornell | Wisconsin | 1951 | 7:50.5 | Wisconsin | Washington |
| 1903 | 18:57 | Cornell | Georgetown | 1952 | 15:08.1 | Navy | Princeton |
| 1904 | 20:22 3/5 | Syracuse | Cornell | 1953 | 15:29.6 | Navy | Cornell |
| 1905 | 20:29 | Cornell | Syracuse | 1954 | 16:04.4 | Navy[1] | Cornell |
| 1906 | 19:36 4/5 | Cornell | Pennsylvania | 1955 | 15:49.9 | Cornell | Pennsylvania |
| 1907 | 20:02 2/5 | Cornell | Columbia | 1956 | 16:22.4 | Cornell | Navy |
| 1908 | 19:24 1/5 | Syracuse | Columbia | 1957 | 15:26.6 | Cornell | Pennsylvania |
| 1909 | 19:02 | Cornell | Columbia | 1958 | 17:12.1 | Cornell | Navy |
| 1910 | 20:42 1/5 | Cornell | Pennsylvania | 1959 | 18:01.7 | Wisconsin | Syracuse |
| 1911 | 20:10 4/5 | Cornell | Columbia | 1960 | 15:57 | California | Navy |
| 1912 | 19:31 2/5 | Cornell | Wisconsin | 1961 | 16:49.2 | California | Cornell |
| 1913 | 19:28 3/5 | Syracuse | Cornell | 1962 | 17:02.9 | Cornell | Washington |
| 1914 | 19:37 4/5 | Columbia | Pennsylvania | 1963 | 17:24 | Cornell | Navy |
| 1915 | 19:36 3/5 | Cornell | Stanford | 1964 | 6:31.1 | California | Washington |
| 1916 | 20:15 2/5 | Syracuse | Cornell | 1965 | 16:51.3 | Navy | Cornell |
| 1920 | 11:02 3/5 | Syracuse | Cornell | 1966 | 16:03.4 | Wisconsin | Navy |
| 1921 | 14:07 | Navy | California | 1967 | 16:13.9 | Pennsylvania | Wisconsin |
| 1922 | 13:33 3/5 | Navy | Washington | 1968 | 6:15.6 | Pennsylvania | Washington |
| 1923 | 14:03 1/5 | Washington | Navy | 1969 | 6:30.4 | Pennsylvania | Dartmouth |
| 1924 | 15:02 | Washington | Wisconsin | 1970 | 6:39.3 | Washington | Wisconsin |
| 1925 | 19:24 4/5 | Navy | Washington | 1971 | 6:06 | Cornell | Washington |
| 1926 | 19:28 3/5 | Washington | Navy | 1972 | 6:22.6 | Pennsylvania | Brown |
| 1927 | 20:57 | Columbia | Washington | 1973 | 6:21 | Wisconsin | Brown |
| 1928 | 18:35 4/5 | California | Columbia | 1974 | 6:33 | Wisconsin | Mass. Inst. of Technology |
| 1929 | 22:58 | Columbia | Washington | | | | |
| 1930 | 21:42 | Cornell | Syracuse | 1975 | 6:08.2 | Wisconsin | M.I.T. |
| 1931 | 18:54 1/5 | Navy | Cornell | 1976 | 6:31 | California | Princeton |
| 1932 | 19:55 | California | Cornell | 1977 | 6:32.4 | Cornell | Pennsylvania |
| 1934 | 19:44 | California | Washington | 1978 | 6:39.5 | Syracuse | Brown |
| 1935 | 18:52 | California | Cornell | 1979 | 6:26.4 | Brown | Wisconsin |
| 1936 | 19:09 3/5 | Washington | California | 1980 | 6:46 | Navy | Northeastern |
| 1937 | 18:33 3/5 | Washington | Navy | 1981 | 5:57.3 | Cornell | Navy |
| 1938 | 18:19 | Navy | California | 1982 | 5:57.5 | Cornell | Princeton |

1. Disqualified.

## COLLEGIATE—1982

**Intercollegiate Rowing Association**

(Lake Onondaga, Syracuse, N.Y., June 3–5, 1982)
(All races at 2,000 meters.)

Eights—1. Cornell, 5 minutes 57.5 seconds. 2. Princeton, 5:59.6; 3. Syracuse, 6:01.2; 4. Navy, 6:01.7; 5. Brown, 6:02.3; 6. Boston University, 6:03.6.

| | |
|---|---|
| Junior varsity eights—Navy | 6:01.4 |
| Freshman eights—California | 6:08.3 |
| Pairs with coxswain—Northeastern | 8:02.3 |
| Pairs without coxswain—Wisconsin | 7:26.5 |
| Fours with coxswain—Wisconsin | 6:54.1 |
| Fours without coxswain—Pennsylvania | 6:46.2 |
| Freshman fours—Navy | 7:03 |

## U.S. MEN'S CHAMPIONSHIPS
## U.S. Rowing Association

(Stony Creek Metropark, Mich., July 16–18, 1982)

| | |
|---|---|
| Lightweight ¼-mile dash—Bill Belden, Fairmount Rowing Club | 1:16.47 |
| Intermediate doubles—Fairmount Rowing Association | 6:54.40 |
| Intermediate lightweight doubles—Woodstock, Canada | 6:52.80 |
| Intermediate fours with coxswain—Vesper Boat Club B team, Philadelphia | 6:46.00 |
| Elite Lightweight fours without coxswain—Lightweight Camp | 6:23.80 |
| Elite fours with coxswain—Vesper B.C., Philadelphia | 6:36.4 |
| Intermediate pairs without coxswain—Detroit Boat Club C team | 7:14.16 |
| Elite Lightweight singles—Paul Fuchs, Detroit Boat Club | 7:05.9 |
| Intermediate lightweight singles—D. Chandler, Durham R.A. | 7:31.00 |
| Intermediate singles—M. Totta, New York Athletic Club | 7:21.19 |
| Elite pairs without coxswain—Detroit Boat Club | 6:47.9 |
| Elite Lightweight Eight—Lightweight Camp | 5:52.41 |
| Lightweight quads—Malta Rowing Association | 6:14.80 |
| Elite singles—P. McGowan, Ridley Graduates, Canada | 7:18.02 |
| Intermediate eights—New York Athletic Club | 6:07.8 |
| Intermediate Lightweight eights—West Side Rowing Club | 6:09.77 |
| Quarter-mile singles—Jim Dietz, New York Athletic Club | 1:12.9 |
| Senior doubles—Vesper Boat Club, Philadelphia | 6:50.75 |
| Senior lightweight doubles—Malta Rowing Association | 6:46.2 |
| Senior fours with coxswain—New York Athletic Club | 6:37.36 |
| Elite fours without coxswain—Vesper Boat Club, Philadelphia | 6:32.80 |
| Senior lightweight fours without coxswain—New York Athletic Club | 6:36.3 |
| Senior quads—Vesper Boat Club, Philadelphia | 6:16.77 |
| Senior pairs without coxswain—Jablonic-Erickson | 7:00.4 |
| Elite doubles—Ridley Graduates, Canada | 6:29.2 |
| Elite pairs with coxswain—Detroit Boat Club | 7:17.5 |
| Elite lightweight doubles—St. Catherines, Canada | 6:41.1 |
| Senior singles—Sean Colgan, University of Pennsylvania | 7:17.8 |
| Senior lightweight singles—E. Lentz, Malta R.A. | 7:20.7 |
| Elite lightweight fours with coxswain—Vesper Boat Club, Phila. | 6:54.99 |
| Elite lightweight pairs without coxswain—Ecorse Boat Club, Detroit | 7:17.3 |
| Senior lightweight eight—New York Athletic Club | 6:11.8 |
| Senior eights—Vesper Boat Club, Philadelphia | 6:04.5 |
| Elite quads—Ridley/Burnaby, Canada | 6:06.1 |
| Elite eights—Lightweight Camp | 5:50.68 |

## U.S. WOMEN'S CHAMPIONSHIPS

(Lake Waramaug, Conn., June 17–21, 1982)

| | |
|---|---|
| Senior fours—College Boat Club | 3:45.1 |
| Lightweight quads—Durham Boat Club | 3:59.0 |
| Elite singles—Judy Geer, Dartmouth Rowing Club | 3:59.1 |
| Intermediate singles—Eileen O'Rourke, New York Rowing Association | 4:10.2 |
| High School eight—Lakeside High School | 3:34.7 |
| Flyweight fours—West Side Rowing Association | 4:20.8 |
| Lightweight pairs—Potomac River Development Center | 4:29.9 |
| Elite Quads—Boston/Dartmouth/California–Irvine | 3:45.6 |
| Senior doubles—Bachelors Barge Club | 4:02.0 |
| Lightweight singles—Billie Brown, Harbor City Boat Club | 4:29.5 |
| Elite pairs—Lake Washington A team | 3:58.5 |
| Junior quads—Durham Boat Club B team | 3:50.9 |
| Lightweight eights—Lightweight Development Camp | 3:30.4 |
| Junior doubles—Durham Boat Club C team | 3:44.5 |
| Elite fours—College Boat Club | 3:24.0 |
| Lightweight singles dash—Beth Stickney, Dartmouth Rowing Club | 1:55.5 |
| High school fours—Durham Boat Club | 3:34.3 |
| Elite doubles—Dartmouth Rowing Club | 3:28.2 |
| Lightweight fours—Pioneer Valley Rowing Association | 3:39.2 |
| Senior eights—Lightweight Dev. Camp/Boston Univ. | 3:14.2 |
| Elite singles dash—Ann Marden, 1980 Rowing Club | 1:43.8 |
| Lightweight doubles—Pioneer Valley Rowing Association | 3:50.2 |
| Elite eights—College Boat Club | 3:06.2 |
| Junior points trophy—Durham Boat Club | 251 pts |
| Lightweight points trophy—Pioneer Valley Rowing Association | 59½ pts |
| All events trophy—Pioneer Valley Rowing Association | 87 pts |

## WORLD CHAMPIONSHIPS—1982

| | |
|---|---|
| Fours with coxswain—East Germany | 6:19.04 |
| Doubles sculls—Norway | 6:23.66 |
| Pairs without coxswain—Norway | 6:41.98 |
| Singles sculls—East Germany | 7:00.67 |
| Pairs with coxswain—Italy | 6:59.63 |
| Fours without coxswain—Switzerland | 6:10.41 |
| Fours without coxswain (small)—United States | 6:15.19 |
| Quads—East Germany | 5:55.50 |
| Eights—New Zealand | 5:36.39 |

**Lightweights**

| | |
|---|---|
| Men's singles—Austria | 7:12.57 |
| Men's fours without coxswain—Italy | 6:17.79 |
| Men's doubles—Italy | 6:34.85 |
| Men's eights—Italy | 5:49.45 |
| Men's eights (small)—United States | 5:56.92 |
| Women's fours with coxswain—Soviet Union | 3:17.16 |
| Women's doubles—Soviet Union | 3:19.47 |
| Women's pairs without coxswain—East Germany | n.a. |
| Women's pairs without coxswain (small)—United States | n.a. |
| Women's singles—Soviet Union | 3:42.83 |
| Women's doubles—Soviet Union | 3:07.58 |
| Women's eights—Soviet Union | 2:57.97 |

n.a.=not available.

# SLED DOG RACING

## INTERNATIONAL CHAMPIONSHIPS—1982

Unlimited–dog class—Peter Norberg, Tuktoyartur, N.W.T. (14.7 miles, 46 minutes, 38.02 seconds, 16 dogs)

Five–dog class—Dan Larkin, Buena Vista, Calif. (6.5 miles, 20:41.35)

Junior Iditarod—Tom Osmar, Clam Gulch, Alaska (130 miles, 12 hours, 31 minutes, 41.10 seconds)

# HARNESS RACING

Oliver Wendell Holmes, the famous Autocrat of the Breakfast Table, wrote that the running horse was a gambling toy but the trotting horse was useful and, furthermore, "horse-racing is not a republican institution; horse-trotting is." Oliver Wendell Holmes was a born-and-bred New Englander, and New England was the nursery of the harness racing sport in America. Pacers and trotters were matters of local pride and prejudice in Colonial New England, and, shortly after the Revolution, the Messenger and Justin Morgan strains produced many winners in harness racing "matches" along the turnpikes of New York, Connecticut, Rhode Island, Massachusetts, Vermont, and New Hampshire.

There was English thoroughbred blood in Messenger and Justin Morgan, and, many years later, it was blended in Rysdyk's Hambletonian, foaled in 1849. Hambletonian was not particularly fast under harness but his descendants have had almost a monopoly of prizes, titles, and records in the harness racing game. Hambletonian was purchased as a foal with its dam for a total of $124 by William Rysdyk of Goshen, N.Y., and made a modest fortune for the purchaser.

Trotters and pacers often were raced under saddle in the old days, and, in fact, the custom still survives in some places in Europe. Dexter, the great trotter that lowered the mile record from 2:19¾ to 2:17¼ in 1867, was said to handle just as well under saddle as when pulling a sulky. But as sulkies were lightened in weight and improved in design, trotting under saddle became less common and finally faded out in this country.

## WORLD RECORDS
Established in a Race or Against Time at One Mile
*Source:* Research Specialist, United States Trotting Association

### Trotting on Mile Track

| | Record | Holder | Driver | Where Made | Year |
|---|---|---|---|---|---|
| All Age | 1:54⅘¹ | Lindy's Crown | Howard Beissinger | DuQuoin, Ill. | 1980 |
| | 1:54⅘* | Nevele Pride | Stanley Dancer | Indianapolis | 1969 |
| 2-year-old | 1:56⅗* | Star Investment, f | William Herman | Lexington, Ky. | 1979 |
| 3-year-old | 1:55¹ | Speedy Somolli | Howard Beissinger | DuQuoin, Ill. | 1978 |
| | | Florida Pro | George Sholty | DuQuoin, Ill. | 1978 |
| 4-year-old | 1:54⅘¹ | Lindy's Crown | Howard Beissinger | DuQuoin, Ill. | 1980 |
| | 1:54⅘* | Nevele Pride | Stanley Dancer | Indianapolis | 1969 |

### Trotting on Five-Eighths Mile Track

| | | | | | |
|---|---|---|---|---|---|
| All Age | 1:57⅕¹ | Lindy's Crown | Howard Beissinger | Wilmington, Del. | 1980 |
| 2-year-old | 2:00⅕¹ | Smokin Yankee | Stanley Dancer | Laurel, Md. | 1980 |
| 3-year-old | 1:58¹ | Keystone Sister | Delvin Miller | Meadow Lands, Pa. | 1981 |
| 4-year-old | 1:57⅕¹ | Lindy's Crown | Howard Beissinger | Wilmington, Del. | 1980 |

### Trotting on Half-Mile Track

| | | | | | |
|---|---|---|---|---|---|
| All Age | 1:56⅘¹ | Nevele Pride | Stanley Dancer | Saratoga Springs, N.Y. | 1969 |
| 2-year-old | 2:00¹ | Incredible Nevele | Glen Garnsey | Delaware, Ohio | 1981 |
| 3-year-old | 1:58¹ | Incredible Nevele | Glen Garnsey | Saratoga Springs, N.Y. | 1982 |
| 4-year-old | 1:56⅘¹ | Nevele Pride | Stanley Dancer | Saratoga Springs, N.Y. | 1969 |

### Pacing on Mile Track

| | Record | Holder | Driver | Where Made | Year |
|---|---|---|---|---|---|
| All Age | 1:51⅗¹ | Trenton | Tommy Haughton | Springfield, Ill. | 1982 |
| | 1:49⅕* | Niatross | Clint Galbraith | Lexington, Ky. | 1980 |
| 2-year-old | 1:53⅘¹ | Merger | John Campbell | Lexington, Ky. | 1981 |
| 3-year-old | 1:51⅗¹ | Trenton | Tommy Haughton | Springfield, Ill. | 1982 |
| | 1:49⅕* | Niatross | Clint Galbraith | Lexington, Ky. | 1980 |
| 4-year-old | 1:52* | Steady Star | Joe O'Brien | Lexington, Ky. | 1971 |

### Pacing on Five-Eighths Mile Track

| | | | | | |
|---|---|---|---|---|---|
| All Age | 1:53⅖¹ | Storm Damage | Joe O'Brien | Meadow Lands, Pa. | 1980 |
| 2-year-old | 1:56⅕¹ | French Chef | Stanley Dancer | Columbus, Ky. | 1980 |
| 3-year-old | 1:53⅖¹ | Storm Damage | Joe O'Brien | Meadow Lands, Pa. | 1980 |
| 4-year-old | 1:54⅖¹ | Direct Scooter | Warren Cameron | Windsor, Ontario | 1980 |

### Pacing on Half-Mile Track

| | | | | | |
|---|---|---|---|---|---|
| All Age | 1:54⅗¹ | Temujin | Clarence Martin | Delaware, Ohio | 1982 |
| 2-year-old | 1:56⅕¹ | Temujin | Clarence Martin | Louisville, Ky. | 1981 |
| 3-year-old | 1:54⅗¹ | Temujin | Clarence Martin | Delaware, Ohio | 1982 |
| 4-year-old | 1:55⅖¹ | Bandelier | Joe O'Brien | Delaware, Ohio | 1981 |

1. Record set in race. *Record set in time trial. f=filly.

## HARNESS RACING RECORDS FOR THE MILE

**Trotters**

| Time | Trotter, age, driver | Year |
|---|---|---|
| 2:00 | Lou Dillon, 5, Millard Sanders | 1903 |
| 1:58½ | Lou Dillon, 5, Millard Sanders | 1903 |
| 1:58 | Uhlan, 8, Charles Tanner | 1912 |
| 1:58 | Peter Manning, 5, T. W. Murphy | 1921 |
| 1:57¾ | Peter Manning, 5, T. W. Murphy | 1921 |
| 1:57 | Peter Manning, 6, T. W. Murphy | 1922 |
| 1:56¾ | Peter Manning, 6, T. W. Murphy | 1922 |
| 1:56¾ | Greyhound, 5, Sep Palin | 1937 |
| 1:56 | Greyhound, 5, Sep Palin | 1937 |
| 1:55¼ | Greyhound, 6, Sep Palin | 1938 |
| 1:54⅘ | Nevele Pride, 4, Stanley Dancer | 1969 |

**Pacers**

| Time | Pacer, age, driver | Year |
|---|---|---|
| 2:00½ | John R. Gentry, 7, W.J. Andrews | 1896 |
| 1:59¼ | Star Pointer, 8, D. McClary | 1897 |
| 1:59 | Dan Patch, 7, M. E. McHenry | 1903 |
| 1:56¼ | Dan Patch, 7, M. E. McHenry | 1903 |
| 1:56 | Dan Patch, 8, H. C. Hersey | 1904 |
| 1:55 | Billy Direct, 4, Vic Fleming | 1938 |
| 1:55 | Adios Harry, 4, Luther Lyons | 1955 |
| 1:54⅗ | Adios Butler, 4, Paige West | 1960 |
| 1:54 | Bret Hanover, 4, Frank Ervin | 1966 |
| 1:53⅗ | Bret Hanover, 4, Frank Ervin | 1966 |
| 1:52 | Steady Star, 4, Joe O'Brien | 1971 |
| 1:49⅕ | Niatross, 3, Clint Galbraith | 1980 |

## HARNESS HORSE OF THE YEAR

Chosen in poll conducted by United States Trotting Association in conjunction with the U.S. Harness Writers Assn.

| | | | | | |
|---|---|---|---|---|---|
| 1959 | Bye Bye Byrd, Pacer | 1967 | Nevele Pride, Trotter | 1975 | Savoir, Trotter |
| 1960 | Adios Butler, Pacer | 1968 | Nevele Pride, Trotter | 1976 | Keystone Ore, Pacer |
| 1961 | Adios Butler, Pacer | 1969 | Nevele Pride, Trotter | 1977 | Green Speed, Trotter |
| 1962 | Su Mac Lad, Trotter | 1970 | Fresh Yankee, Trotter | 1978 | Abercrombie, Pacer |
| 1963 | Speedy Scot, Trotter | 1971 | Albatross, Pacer | 1979 | Niatross, Pacer |
| 1964 | Bret Hanover, Pacer | 1972 | Albatross, Pacer | 1980 | Niatross, Pacer |
| 1965 | Bret Hanover, Pacer | 1973 | Sir Dalrae, Pacer | 1981 | Fan Hanover, Pacer |
| 1966 | Bret Hanover, Pacer | 1974 | Delmonica Hanover, Trotter | | |

## HISTORY OF TRADITIONAL HARNESS RACING STAKES

### The Hambletonian

Three-year-old trotters. One mile. Guy McKinney won first race at Syracuse in 1926; held at Goshen, N.Y., 1930–1942, 1944–1956; at Yonkers, N.Y., 1943; at Du Quoin, Ill., 1957–1980. In 1981 and 1982 the race was held at the Meadowlands in East Rutherford, N.J.

| Year | Winner | Driver | Best time | Total purse |
|---|---|---|---|---|
| 1967 | Speedy Streak | Del Cameron | 2:00 | 122,650 |
| 1968 | Nevele Pride | Stanley Dancer | 1:59⅖ | 116,190 |
| 1969 | Lindy's Pride | Howard Beissinger | 1:57⅗ | 124,910 |
| 1970 | Timothy T. | John Simpson, Jr. | 1:58⅖[1] | 143,630 |
| 1971 | Speedy Crown | Howard Beissinger | 1:57⅖ | 129,770 |
| 1972 | Super Bowl | Stanley Dancer | 1:56⅖ | 119,090 |
| 1973 | Flirth | Ralph Baldwin | 1:57⅕ | 144,710 |
| 1974 | Christopher T | Billy Haughton | 1:58⅗ | 160,150 |
| 1975 | Bonefish | Stanley Dancer | 1:59[2] | 232,192 |
| 1976 | Steve Lobell | Billy Haughton | 1:56⅖ | 263,524 |
| 1977 | Green Speed | Billy Haughton | 1:55⅗ | 284,131 |
| 1978 | Speedy Somolli | Howard Beissinger | 1:55[3] | 241,280 |
| 1979 | Legend Hanover | George Sholty | 1:56⅕ | 300,000 |
| 1980 | Burgomeister | Billy Haughton | 1:56⅗ | 293,570 |
| 1981 | Shiaway St. Pat | Ray Remmen | 2:01⅕[4] | 838,000 |
| 1982 | Speed Bowl | Tommy Haughton | 1:56⅘ | 875,750 |

1. By Formal Notice. 2. By Yankee Bambino. 3. By Speedy Somolli and Florida Pro. 4. By Super Juan.

### Little Brown Jug

Three-year-old pacers. One Mile. Raced at Delaware County Fair Grounds, Delaware, Ohio.

| | | | | |
|---|---|---|---|---|
| 1967 | Best of All | Jim Hackett | 1:59[1] | 84,778 |
| 1968 | Rum Customer | Billy Haughton | 1:59⅗ | 104,226 |
| 1969 | Laverne Hanover | Billy Haughton | 2:00⅖ | 109,731 |
| 1970 | Most Happy Fella | Stanley Dancer | 1:57⅕ | 100,110 |
| 1971 | Nansemond | Herve Filion | 1:57⅖ | 102,994 |
| 1972 | Strike Out | Keith Waples | 1:56⅗ | 104,916 |
| 1973 | Melvin's Woe | Joe O'Brien | 1:57⅗ | 120,000 |
| 1974 | Ambro Omaha | Billy Haughton | 1:57 | 132,630 |
| 1975 | Seatrain | Ben Webster | 1:57[2] | 147,813 |
| 1976 | Keystone Ore | Stanley Dancer | 1:56⅘[3] | 153,799 |
| 1977 | Governor Skipper | John Chapman | 1:56⅕ | 150,000 |
| 1978 | Happy Escort | William Popfinger | 1:55⅖[4] | 186,760 |
| 1979 | Hot Hitter | Herve Filion | 1:55⅗ | 226,455 |
| 1980 | Niatross | Clint Galbraith | 1:54⅘ | 207,361 |
| 1981 | Fan Hanover | Glen Garnsey | 1:56[5] | 243,799 |
| 1982 | Merger | John Campbell | 1:56⅗ | 328,900 |

1. By Nardin's Byrd. 2. By Armbro Ranger. 3. By Falcon Almahurst. 4. By Falcon Almahurst. 5. By Seahawk Hanover.

# GOLF

It may be that golf originated in Holland—historians believe it did—but certainly Scotland fostered the game and is famous for it. In fact, in 1457 the Scottish Parliament, disturbed because football and golf had lured young Scots from the more soldierly exercise of archery, passed an ordinance that "futeball and golf be utterly cryit doun and nocht usit." James I and Charles I of the royal line of Stuarts were golf enthusiasts, whereby the game came to be known as "the royal and ancient game of golf."

The golf balls used in the early games were leather-covered and stuffed with feathers. Clubs of all kinds were fashioned by hand to suit individual players. The great step in spreading the game came with the change from the feather ball to the gutta-percha ball about 1850. In 1860, formal competition began with the establishment of an annual tournament for the British Open championship. There are records of "golf clubs" in the United

States as far back as colonial days but no proof of actual play before John Reid and some friends laid out six holes on the Reid lawn in Yonkers, N.Y., in 1888 and played there with golf balls and clubs brought over from Scotland by Robert Lockhart. This group then formed the St. Andrews Golf Club of Yonkers, and golf was established in this country.

However, it remained a rather sedate and almost aristocratic pastime until a 20-year-old ex-caddy, Francis Ouimet of Boston, defeated two great British professionals, Harry Vardon and Ted Ray, in the United States Open championship at Brookline, Mass., in 1913. This feat put the game and Francis Ouimet on the front pages of the newspapers and stirred a wave of enthusiasm for the sport. The greatest feat so far in golf history is that of Robert Tyre Jones, Jr., of Atlanta, who won the British Open, the British Amateur, the U.S. Open, and the U.S. Amateur titles in one year, 1930.

## U.S. OPEN CHAMPIONS

| Year | Winner | Score | Where played | Year | Winner | Score | Where played |
|---|---|---|---|---|---|---|---|
| 1895 | Horace Rawlins | 173 | Newport | 1938 | Ralph Guldahl | 284 | Cherry Hills |
| 1896 | James Foulis | 152 | Shinnecock Hills | 1939 | Byron Nelson[1] | 284 | Philadelphia |
| 1897 | Joe Lloyd | 162 | Chicago | 1940 | Lawson Little[1] | 287 | Canterbury |
| 1898[3] | Fred Herd | 328 | Myopia | 1941 | Craig Wood | 284 | Colonial |
| 1899 | Willie Smith | 315 | Baltimore | 1942–45 | No tournaments[5] | | |
| 1900 | Harry Vardon | 313 | Chicago | 1946 | Lloyd Mangrum[1] | 284 | Canterbury |
| 1901 | Willie Anderson[1] | 331 | Myopia | 1947 | Lew Worsham[1] | 282 | St. Louis |
| 1902 | Laurie Auchterlonie | 307 | Garden City | 1948 | Ben Hogan | 276 | Riviera |
| 1903 | Willie Anderson[1] | 307 | Baltusrol | 1949 | Cary Middlecoff | 286 | Medinah |
| 1904 | Willie Anderson | 303 | Glen View | 1950 | Ben Hogan[1] | 287 | Merion |
| 1905 | Willie Anderson | 314 | Myopia | 1951 | Ben Hogan | 287 | Oakland Hills |
| 1906 | Alex Smith | 295 | Onwentsia | 1952 | Julius Boros | 281 | Northwood |
| 1907 | Alex Ross | 302 | Philadelphia | 1953 | Ben Hogan | 283 | Oakmont |
| 1908 | Fred McLeod[1] | 322 | Myopia | 1954 | Ed Furgol | 284 | Baltusrol |
| 1909 | George Sargent | 290 | Englewood | 1955 | Jack Fleck[1] | 287 | Olympic |
| 1910 | Alex Smith[1] | 298 | Philadelphia | 1956 | Cary Middlecoff | 281 | Oak Hill |
| 1911 | John McDermott[1] | 307 | Chicago | 1957 | Dick Mayer[1] | 298 | Inverness |
| 1912 | John McDermott | 294 | Buffalo | 1958 | Tommy Bolt | 283 | Southern Hills |
| 1913 | Francis Ouimet[1][2] | 304 | Brookline | 1959 | Bill Casper, Jr. | 282 | Winged Foot |
| 1914 | Walter Hagen | 290 | Midlothian | 1960 | Arnold Palmer | 280 | Cherry Hills |
| 1915 | Jerome D. Travers[2] | 297 | Baltusrol | 1961 | Gene Littler | 281 | Oakland Hills |
| 1916 | Charles Evans, Jr.[2] | 286 | Minikahda | 1962 | Jack Nicklaus[1] | 283 | Oakmont |
| 1917–18 | No tournaments[4] | | | 1963 | Julius Boros[1] | 293 | Country Club |
| 1919 | Walter Hagen[2] | 301 | Brae Burn | 1964 | Ken Venturi | 278 | Congressional |
| 1920 | Edward Ray | 295 | Inverness | 1965 | Gary Player[1] | 282 | Bellerive |
| 1921 | Jim Barnes | 289 | Columbia | 1966 | Bill Casper[1] | 278 | Olympic |
| 1922 | Gene Sarazen | 288 | Skokie | 1967 | Jack Nicklaus | 275 | Baltusrol |
| 1923 | R. T. Jones, Jr.[1][2] | 296 | Inwood | 1968 | Lee Trevino | 275 | Oak Hill |
| 1924 | Cyril Walker | 297 | Oakland Hills | 1969 | Orville Moody | 281 | Champions G. C. |
| 1925 | Willie Macfarlane[1] | 291 | Worcester | 1970 | Tony Jacklin | 281 | Hazeltine |
| 1926 | R. T. Jones, Jr.[2] | 293 | Scioto | 1971 | Lee Trevino[1] | 280 | Merion |
| 1927 | Tommy Armour[1] | 301 | Oakmont | 1972 | Jack Nicklaus | 290 | Pebble Beach |
| 1928 | Johnny Farrell[1] | 294 | Olympia Fields | 1973 | Johnny Miller | 279 | Oakmont |
| 1929 | R. T. Jones, Jr.[1][2] | 294 | Winged Foot | 1974 | Hale Irwin | 287 | Winged Foot |
| 1930 | R. T. Jones, Jr.[2] | 287 | Interlachen | 1975 | Lou Graham[1] | 287 | Medinah |
| 1931 | Billy Burke[1] | 292 | Inverness | 1976 | Jerry Pate | 277 | Atlanta A.C. |
| 1932 | Gene Sarazen | 286 | Fresh Meadow | 1977 | Hubert Green | 278 | Southern Hills |
| 1933 | John Goodman[2] | 287 | North Shore | 1978 | Andy North | 285 | Cherry Hills |
| 1934 | Olin Dutra | 293 | Merion | 1979 | Hale Irwin | 284 | Inverness |
| 1935 | Sam Parks, Jr. | 299 | Oakmont | 1980 | Jack Nicklaus | 272 | Baltusrol |
| 1936 | Tony Manero | 282 | Baltusrol | 1981 | David Graham | 273 | Merion |
| 1937 | Ralph Guldahl | 281 | Oakland Hills | 1982 | Tom Watson | 282 | Pebble Beach |

1. Winner in playoff. 2. Amateur. 3. In 1898, competition was extended to 72 holes. 4. In 1917, Jock Hutchison, with a 292, won an Open Patriotic Tournament for the benefit of the American Red Cross at Whitemarsh Valley Country Club. 5. In 1942, Ben Hogan, with a 271 won a Hale American National Open Tournament for the benefit of the Navy Relief Society and USO at Ridgemoor Country Club.

## U.S. AMATEUR CHAMPIONS

| | | | | | | | |
|---|---|---|---|---|---|---|---|
| 1895 | Charles B. Macdonald | 1920 | Charles Evans, Jr. | 1946 | Ted Bishop | 1966 | Gary Cowan[1] |
| 1896–97 | H. J. Whigham | 1921 | Jesse P. Guilford | 1947 | Robert Riegel | 1967 | Bob Dickson |
| 1898 | Findlay S. Douglas | 1922 | Jess W. Sweetser | 1948 | Willie Turnesa | 1968 | Bruce Fleisher |
| 1899 | H. M. Harriman | 1923 | Max R. Marston | 1949 | Charles Coe | 1969 | Steven Melnyk |
| 1900–01 | Walter J. Travis | 1924–25 | R. T. Jones Jr. | 1950 | Sam Urzetta | 1970 | Lanny Wadkins |
| 1902 | Louis N. James | 1926 | George Von Elm | 1951 | Billy Maxwell | 1971 | Gary Cowan |
| 1903 | Walter J. Travis | 1927–28 | R. T. Jones Jr. | 1952 | Jack Westland | 1972 | Vinny Giles 3d |
| 1904–05 | H. Chandler Egan | 1929 | H. R. Johnston | 1953 | Gene Littler | 1973[3] | Craig Stadler |
| 1906 | Eben M. Byers | 1930 | R. T. Jones, Jr. | 1954 | Arnold Palmer | 1974 | Jerry Pate |
| 1907–08 | Jerome D. Travers | 1931 | Francis Ouimet | 1955–56 | Harvie Ward | 1975 | Fred Ridley |
| 1909 | Robert A. Gardner | 1932 | Ross Somerville | 1957 | Hillman Robbins | 1976 | Bill Sander |
| 1910 | W. C. Fownes, Jr. | 1933 | G. T. Dunlap, Jr. | 1958 | Charles Coe | 1977 | John Fought |
| 1911 | Harold H. Hilton | 1934–35 | Lawson Little | 1959 | Jack Nicklaus | 1978 | John Cook |
| 1912–13 | Jerome D. Travers | 1936 | John W. Fischer | 1960 | Deane Beman | 1979 | Mark O'Meara |
| 1914 | Francis Ouimet | 1937 | John Goodman | 1961 | Jack Nicklaus | 1980 | Hal Sutton |
| 1915 | Robert A. Gardner | 1938 | Willie Turnesa | 1962 | Labron Harris, Jr. | 1981 | Nathaniel Crosby |
| 1916 | Charles Evans, Jr. | 1939 | Marvin H. Ward | 1963 | Deane Beman | 1982 | Jay Sigel |
| 1919 | S. D. Herron | 1940 | R. D. Chapman | 1964 | Bill Campbell | | |
| | | 1941 | Marvin H. Ward | 1965[2] | Robert Murphy, Jr. | | |

1. Winner in playoff. 2. Tourney switched to medal play through 1972. 3. Return to match play.

## U.S. P.G.A. CHAMPIONS

| | | | | | | | |
|---|---|---|---|---|---|---|---|
| 1916 | Jim Barnes | 1939 | Henry Picard | 1955 | Doug Ford | 1970 | Dave Stockton |
| 1919 | Jim Barnes | 1940 | Byron Nelson | 1956 | Jack Burke, Jr. | 1971 | Jack Nicklaus |
| 1920 | Jock Hutchison | 1941 | Victor Ghezzi | 1957 | Lionel Hebert | 1972 | Gary Player |
| 1921 | Walter Hagen | 1942 | Sam Snead | 1958[2] | Dow Finsterwald | 1973 | Jack Nicklaus |
| 1922–23 | Gene Sarazen | 1944 | Bob Hamilton | 1959 | Bob Rosburg | 1974 | Lee Trevino |
| 1924–27 | Walter Hagen | 1945 | Byron Nelson | 1960 | Jay Hebert | 1975 | Jack Nicklaus |
| 1928–29 | Leo Diegel | 1946 | Ben Hogan | 1961 | Jerry Barber[1] | 1976 | Dave Stockton |
| 1930 | Tommy Armour | 1947 | Jim Ferrier | 1962 | Gary Player | 1977 | Lanny Wadkins[1] |
| 1931 | Tom Creavy | 1948 | Ben Hogan | 1963 | Jack Nicklaus | 1978 | John Mahaffey |
| 1932 | Olin Dutra | 1949 | Sam Snead | 1964 | Bobby Nichols | 1979 | David Graham[1] |
| 1933 | Gene Sarazen | 1950 | Chandler Harper | 1965 | Dave Marr | 1980 | Jack Nicklaus |
| 1934 | Paul Runyan | 1951 | Sam Snead | 1966 | Al Geiberger | 1981 | Larry Nelson |
| 1935 | Johnny Revolta | 1952 | Jim Turnesa | 1967 | Don January[1] | 1982 | Ray Floyd |
| 1936–37 | Denny Shute | 1953 | Walter Burkemo | 1968 | Julius Boros | | |
| 1938 | Paul Runyan | 1954 | Chick Harbert | 1969 | Ray Floyd | | |

1. Winner in playoff. 2. Switched to medal play.

## THE MASTERS TOURNAMENT WINNERS
Augusta National Golf Club, Augusta, Ga.

| Year | Winner | Score | Year | Winner | Score | Year | Winner | Score |
|---|---|---|---|---|---|---|---|---|
| 1934 | Horton Smith | 284 | 1952 | Sam Snead | 286 | 1968 | Bob Goalby | 277 |
| 1935 | Gene Sarazen[1] | 282 | 1953 | Ben Hogan | 274 | 1969 | George Archer | 281 |
| 1936 | Horton Smith | 285 | 1954 | Sam Snead[1] | 289 | 1970 | Billy Casper[1] | 279 |
| 1937 | Byron Nelson | 283 | 1955 | Cary Middlecoff | 279 | 1971 | Charles Coody | 279 |
| 1938 | Henry Picard | 285 | 1956 | Jack Burke | 289 | 1972 | Jack Nicklaus | 286 |
| 1939 | Ralph Guldahl | 279 | 1957 | Doug Ford | 283 | 1973 | Tommy Aaron | 283 |
| 1940 | Jimmy Demaret | 280 | 1958 | Arnold Palmer | 284 | 1974 | Gary Player | 278 |
| 1941 | Craig Wood | 280 | 1959 | Art Wall, Jr. | 284 | 1975 | Jack Nicklaus | 276 |
| 1942 | Byron Nelson[1] | 280 | 1960 | Arnold Palmer | 282 | 1976 | Ray Floyd | 271 |
| 1943–45 | No Tournaments | | 1961 | Gary Player | 280 | 1977 | Tom Watson | 276 |
| 1946 | Herman Keiser | 282 | 1962 | Arnold Palmer[1] | 280 | 1978 | Gary Player | 277 |
| 1947 | Jimmy Demaret | 281 | 1963 | Jack Nicklaus | 286 | 1979 | Fuzzy Zoeller[1] | 280 |
| 1948 | Claude Harmon | 279 | 1964 | Arnold Palmer | 276 | 1980 | Severiano Ballesteros | 275 |
| 1949 | Sam Snead | 282 | 1965 | Jack Nicklaus | 271 | 1981 | Tom Watson | 280 |
| 1950 | Jimmy Demaret | 283 | 1966 | Jack Nicklaus[1] | 288 | 1982 | Craig Stadler[1] | 284 |
| 1951 | Ben Hogan | 280 | 1967 | Gay Brewer, Jr. | 280 | | | |

1. Winner in playoff.

## U.S. WOMEN'S AMATEUR CHAMPIONS

| | | | | | | | |
|---|---|---|---|---|---|---|---|
| 1916 | Alexa Stirling | 1925 | Glenna Collett | 1935 | Glenna Collett Vare | 1939–40 | Betty Jameson |
| 1919–20 | Alexa Stirling | 1926 | Helen Stetson | | | 1941 | Mrs. Frank Newell |
| 1921 | Marion Hollins | 1927 | Mrs. M. B. Horn | 1936 | Pamela Barton | 1946 | Mildred Zaharias |
| 1922 | Glenna Collett | 1928–30 | Glenna Collett | 1937 | Mrs. J. A. Page, Jr. | 1947 | Louise Suggs |
| 1923 | Edith Cummings | 1931 | Helen Hicks | | | 1948 | Grace Lenczyk |
| 1924 | Dorothy Campbell Hurd | 1932–34 | Virginia Van Wie | 1938 | Patty Berg | 1949 | Mrs. D. G. Porter |

| Year | Winner | Year | Winner | Year | Winner | Year | Winner |
|---|---|---|---|---|---|---|---|
| 1950 | Beverly Hanson | 1959 | Barbara McIntire | 1967 | Lou Dill | 1976 | Donna Horton |
| 1951 | Dorothy Kirby | 1960 | JoAnne Gunderson | 1968 | JoAnne G. Carner | 1977 | Beth Daniel |
| 1952 | Jacqueline Pung | 1961 | Anne Quast Decker | 1969 | Catherine Lacoste | 1978 | Cathy Sherk |
| 1953 | Mary Lena Faulk | | | 1970 | Martha Wilkinson | 1979 | Carolyn Hill |
| 1954 | Barbara Romack | 1962 | JoAnne Gunderson | 1971 | Laura Baugh | 1980 | Juli Inkster |
| 1955 | Patricia Lesser | 1963 | Anne Quast Welts | 1972 | Mary Ann Budke | 1981 | Juli Inkster |
| 1956 | Marlene Stewart | 1964 | Barbara McIntire | 1973 | Carol Semple | 1982 | Juli Inkster |
| 1957 | JoAnne Gunderson | 1965 | Jean Ashley | 1974 | Cynthia Hill | | |
| 1958 | Anne Quast | 1966 | JoAnne Gunderson | 1975 | Beth Daniel | | |

## U.S. WOMEN'S OPEN CHAMPIONS

| Year | Winner | Score | Year | Winner | Score | Year | Winner | Score |
|---|---|---|---|---|---|---|---|---|
| 1946 | Patty Berg (match play) | — | 1959 | Mickey Wright | 287 | 1973 | Susie Berning | 299 |
| 1947 | Betty Jameson | 295 | 1960 | Betsy Rawls | 291 | 1973 | Susie Berning | 290 |
| 1948 | Mildred D. Zaharias | 300 | 1961 | Mickey Wright | 293 | 1974 | Sandra Haynie | 295 |
| 1949 | Louise Suggs | 291 | 1962 | Murle Lindstrom | 301 | 1975 | Sandra Palmer | 295 |
| 1950 | Mildred D. Zaharias | 291 | 1963 | Mary Mills | 289 | 1976 | JoAnne Carner | 292 |
| 1951 | Betsy Rawls | 293 | 1964 | Mickey Wright[1] | 290 | 1977 | Hollis Stacy | 292 |
| 1952 | Louise Suggs | 284 | 1965 | Carol Mann | 290 | 1978 | Hollis Stacy | 289 |
| 1953 | Betsy Rawls[1] | 302 | 1966 | Sandra Spuzich | 297 | 1979 | Jerilyn Britz | 284 |
| 1954 | Mildred D. Zaharias | 291 | 1967 | Catherine LaCoste | 294 | 1980 | Amy Alcott | 280 |
| 1955 | Fay Crocker | 299 | 1968 | Susie Berning | 289 | 1981 | Pat Bradley | 279 |
| 1956 | Katherine Cornelius[1] | 302 | 1969 | Donna Caponi | 294 | 1982 | Janet Alex | 283 |
| 1957 | Betsy Rawls | 299 | 1970 | Donna Caponi | 287 | | | |
| 1958 | Mickey Wright | 290 | 1971 | JoAnne Carner | 288 | | | |

1. Winner in playoff. 2. Amateur.

## BRITISH OPEN CHAMPIONS

(First tournament, held in 1860, was won by Willie Park, Sr.)

| Year | Winner | Score | Year | Winner | Score | Year | Winner | Score |
|---|---|---|---|---|---|---|---|---|
| 1920 | George Duncan | 303 | 1939 | R. Burton | 290 | 1964 | Tony Lema | 279 |
| 1921 | Jock Hutchison[1] | 296 | 1946 | Sam Snead | 290 | 1965 | Peter Thomson | 285 |
| 1922 | Walter Hagen | 300 | 1947 | Fred Daly | 294 | 1966 | Jack Nicklaus | 282 |
| 1923 | A. G. Havers | 295 | 1948 | Henry Cotton | 283 | 1967 | Roberto de Vicenzo | 278 |
| 1924 | Walter Hagen | 301 | 1949 | Bobby Locke[1] | 283 | 1968 | Gary Player | 289 |
| 1925 | Jim Barnes | 300 | 1950 | Bobby Locke | 279 | 1969 | Tony Jacklin | 280 |
| 1926 | R. T. Jones, Jr. | 291 | 1951 | Max Faulkner | 285 | 1970 | Jack Nicklaus[1] | 283 |
| 1927 | R. T. Jones, Jr. | 285 | 1952 | Bobby Locke | 287 | 1971 | Lee Trevino | 278 |
| 1928 | Walter Hagen | 292 | 1953 | Ben Hogan | 282 | 1972 | Lee Trevino | 278 |
| 1929 | Walter Hagen | 292 | 1954 | Peter Thomson | 283 | 1973 | Tom Weiskopf | 276 |
| 1930 | R. T. Jones, Jr. | 291 | 1955 | Peter Thomson | 281 | 1974 | Gary Player | 282 |
| 1931 | Tommy Armour | 296 | 1956 | Peter Thomson | 286 | 1975 | Tom Watson[1] | 279 |
| 1932 | Gene Sarazen | 283 | 1957 | Bobby Locke | 279 | 1976 | Johnny Miller | 279 |
| 1933 | Denny Shute[1] | 292 | 1958 | Peter Thomson[1] | 278 | 1977 | Tom Watson | 268 |
| 1934 | Henry Cotton | 283 | 1959 | Gary Player | 284 | 1978 | Jack Nicklaus | 281 |
| 1935 | A. Perry | 283 | 1960 | Kel Nagle | 278 | 1979 | Severiano Ballesteros | 283 |
| 1936 | A. H. Padgham | 287 | 1961 | Arnold Palmer | 284 | 1980 | Tom Watson | 271 |
| 1937 | Henry Cotton | 290 | 1962 | Arnold Palmer | 276 | 1981 | Bill Rogers | 276 |
| 1938 | R. A. Whitcombe | 295 | 1963 | Bob Charles[1] | 277 | 1982 | Tom Watson | 284 |

1. Winner in playoff.

## MEN'S U.S. OPEN—1982

[Pebble Beach (Calif.) Golf Links, June 17–20, 1982]

| | | | | | |
|---|---|---|---|---|---|
| Tom Watson | 72 | 72 | 68 | 70—282 | $60,000 |
| Jack Nicklaus | 74 | 70 | 71 | 69—284 | 34,506 |
| Bobby Clampett | 71 | 73 | 72 | 70—286 | 14,967 |
| Dan Pohl | 72 | 74 | 70 | 70—286 | 14,967 |
| Bill Rogers | 70 | 73 | 69 | 74—286 | 14,967 |
| Gary Koch | 78 | 73 | 69 | 67—287 | 8,011 |
| Jay Haas | 75 | 74 | 70 | 68—287 | 8,011 |
| Lanny Wadkins | 73 | 76 | 67 | 71—287 | 8,011 |
| David Graham | 73 | 72 | 69 | 73—287 | 8,011 |
| Calvin Peete | 71 | 72 | 72 | 73—288 | 6,332 |
| Bruce Devlin | 70 | 69 | 75 | 74—288 | 6,332 |

Leaders—18 holes, Bruce Devlin and Bill Rogers, 70; 36 holes, Bruce Devlin, 139; 54 holes, Tom Watson and Bill Rogers, 212.

## MASTERS TOURNAMENT—1982

(Augusta, Ga., April 8–11, 1982)

| | | | | | |
|---|---|---|---|---|---|
| Craig Stadler* | 75 | 69 | 67 | 73—284 | $64,000 |
| Dan Pohl | 75 | 75 | 67 | 67—284 | 39,000 |
| Severiano Ballesteros | 73 | 73 | 68 | 71—285 | 21,000 |
| Jerry Pate | 74 | 73 | 67 | 71—285 | 21,000 |
| Tom Watson | 77 | 69 | 70 | 71—287 | 13,500 |
| Tom Kite | 76 | 69 | 73 | 69—287 | 13,500 |
| Ray Floyd | 74 | 72 | 69 | 74—289 | 11,067 |
| Curtis Strange | 74 | 70 | 73 | 72—289 | 11,067 |
| Larry Nelson | 79 | 71 | 70 | 69—289 | 11,067 |
| Fuzzy Zoeller | 72 | 76 | 70 | 72—290 | 8,550 |
| Mark Hayes | 74 | 73 | 73 | 70—290 | 8,550 |
| Andy Bean | 75 | 72 | 73 | 70—290 | 8,550 |
| Tom Weiskopf | 75 | 72 | 68 | 75—290 | 8,550 |
| Bob Gilder | 79 | 71 | 66 | 75—291 | 6,700 |

*Won playoff on first extra hole.

## P.G.A. CHAMPIONSHIP—1982
(Southern Hills Country Club, Tulsa, Okla., Aug. 5–8, 1982)

| | | | | | |
|---|---|---|---|---|---|
| Ray Floyd | 63 | 69 | 68 | 72—272 | $65,000 |
| Lanny Wadkins | 71 | 68 | 69 | 67—275 | 45,000 |
| Fred Couples | 67 | 71 | 72 | 66—276 | 25,000 |
| Calvin Peete | 69 | 70 | 68 | 69—276 | 25,000 |
| Jerry Haas | 71 | 66 | 68 | 72—277 | 16,000 |
| Jim Simons | 68 | 67 | 73 | 69—277 | 16,000 |
| Bob Gilder | 66 | 68 | 72 | 72—278 | 11,000 |
| Tom Kite | 73 | 70 | 70 | 67—280 | 7,919 |
| Lonnie Hinkle | 70 | 68 | 71 | 71—280 | 7,919 |
| Tom Watson | 72 | 69 | 71 | 68—280 | 7,919 |
| Jerry Pate | 72 | 69 | 70 | 69—280 | 7,919 |

## BRITISH OPEN—1982
(Troon, Scotland, July 15–18, 1982)

| | | | | | |
|---|---|---|---|---|---|
| Tom Watson | 69 | 71 | 74 | 70—284 | $57,600 |
| Nick Price | 69 | 69 | 74 | 73—285 | 34,750 |
| Peter Oosterhuis | 74 | 67 | 74 | 70—285 | 34,750 |
| Nick Faldo | 73 | 73 | 71 | 69—286 | 19,800 |
| Des Smyth | 70 | 69 | 74 | 73—286 | 19,800 |
| Masahiro Kuramoto | 71 | 73 | 71 | 71—286 | 19,800 |
| Tom Purtzer | 76 | 66 | 75 | 69—286 | 19,800 |
| Sandy Lyle | 74 | 66 | 73 | 74—287 | 15,550 |
| Fuzzy Zoeller | 73 | 71 | 73 | 70—287 | 15,550 |
| Bobby Clampett | 67 | 66 | 78 | 77—288 | 13,230 |
| Jack Nicklaus | 77 | 70 | 72 | 69—288 | 13,230 |

## U.S. WOMEN'S OPEN—1982
(Sacramento, Calif., July 22–25, 1982)

| | | | | | |
|---|---|---|---|---|---|
| Janet Alex | 70 | 73 | 72 | 68—283 | $27,315 |
| JoAnne Carner | 69 | 70 | 75 | 75—289 | 10,659 |
| Beth Daniel | 71 | 71 | 71 | 76—289 | 10,659 |
| Donna White | 70 | 74 | 73 | 72—289 | 10,659 |
| Sandra Haynie | 70 | 74 | 74 | 71—289 | 10,659 |
| Susie McAllister | 77 | 70 | 75 | 71—293 | 5,673 |
| Carole Jo Callison | 76 | 69 | 72 | 77—294 | 4,540 |
| Nancy Lopez | 78 | 73 | 74 | 69—294 | 4,540 |
| Vicki Tabor | 70 | 76 | 75 | 73—294 | 4,540 |
| Beverly Cooper | 73 | 72 | 76 | 74—295 | 3,637 |
| Stephanie Farwig | 75 | 76 | 72 | 72—295 | 3,637 |
| Muffin Spencer–Devlin | 76 | 71 | 76 | 72—295 | 3,637 |

## L.P.G.A. CHAMPIONSHIP—1982
(Jack Nicklaus Sports Center, Kings Island, Ohio, June 10–13, 1982)

| | | | | | |
|---|---|---|---|---|---|
| Jan Stephenson | 69 | 69 | 70 | 71—279 | $30,000 |
| JoAnne Carner | 71 | 70 | 71 | 69—281 | 19,600 |
| Janet Alex | 72 | 72 | 72 | 67—283 | 12,000 |
| Pam Gietzen | 72 | 69 | 71 | 71—283 | 12,000 |
| Amy Alcott | 74 | 68 | 72 | 70—284 | 7,500 |
| Kathy Young | 72 | 74 | 70 | 68—284 | 7,500 |
| Beth Daniel | 69 | 70 | 71 | 75—285 | 5,866 |
| Hollis Stacy | 73 | 70 | 69 | 73—285 | 5,866 |
| Sandra Haynie | 73 | 69 | 73 | 70—285 | 5,866 |
| Sally Little | 71 | 73 | 71 | 71—286 | 4,800 |
| Sandra Palmer | 70 | 70 | 74 | 72—286 | 4,800 |

## 1982 COLLEGIATE GOLF CHAMPIONS
## NATIONAL COLLEGIATE ATHLETIC ASSOCIATION

Division I—Men: Individual: Billy Ray Brown, Houston, 280; Team: Houston; 1,141. Women: Individual: Kathy Baker, Tulsa, 295; Team: Tulsa, 1,191.
Division II—Individual: Vic Wilk, California State–Northridge, 288; Team: Florida Southern, 1,181.
Division III—Individual: Cliff Smith, California State–Stanislaus, 295; Team: Ramapo, 1,200.

## FINAL 1981 LEADING L.P.G.A. EARNINGS

| Player | Amount | Player | Amount |
|---|---|---|---|
| Beth Daniel | $206,977 | Nancy Lopez | $165,679 |
| JoAnne Carner | 206,648 | Amy Alcott | 149,089 |
| Pat Bradley | 197,050 | Sally Little | 142,251 |
| Donna Caponi | 193,916 | Hollis Stacy | 138,908 |
| Jan Stephenson | 180,528 | Kathy Whitworth | 134,937 |

## FINAL 1981 LEADING P.G.A. EARNINGS

| Player | Amount | Player | Amount |
|---|---|---|---|
| Tom Kite | $375,699 | Jerry Pate | $280,627 |
| Ray Floyd | 359,360 | Hale Irwin | 276,499 |
| Tom Watson | 347,660 | Craig Stadler | 218,829 |
| Bruce Lietzke | 343,446 | Curtis Strange | 201,513 |
| Bill Rogers | 315,411 | Larry Nelson | 193,342 |

## 1982 LEADING L.P.G.A. EARNINGS
(Through Aug. 22, 1982)

| Player | Amount | Player | Amount |
|---|---|---|---|
| JoAnne Carner | $248,109 | Jerry Pate | $234,141 |
| Sally Little | 214,510 | Bob Gilder | 230,998 |
| Sandra Haynie | 212,820 | Calvin Peete | 223,111 |
| Beth Daniel | 201,298 | Jack Nicklaus | 217,645 |
| Patty Sheehan | 169,817 | Bruce Lietzke | 210,928 |

## 1982 LEADING P.G.A. EARNINGS
(Through Aug. 22, 1982)

| Player | Amount | Player | Amount |
|---|---|---|---|
| Ray Floyd | $331,809 | Hollis Stacy | $145,340 |
| Craig Stadler | 328,101 | Amy Alcott | 143,145 |
| Tom Kite | 308,076 | Nancy Lopez | 126,397 |
| Tom Watson | 296,715 | Jan Stephenson | 121,893 |
| Lanny Wadkins | 290,138 | Kathy Whitworth | 111,839 |

## U.S.G.A. SENIORS CHAMPIONSHIP—1982
(Portland, Ore., July 8–11, 1982)
(For professionals and amateurs 50 and older)

| | | | | | |
|---|---|---|---|---|---|
| Miller Barber | 72 | 74 | 71 | 65—282 | $28,648 |
| Gene Littler | 73 | 69 | 76 | 68—286 | 12,519 |
| Dan Sikes | 75 | 69 | 72 | 70—286 | 12,519 |
| Bob Goalby | 72 | 71 | 74 | 72—289 | 6,532 |
| Gay Brewer | 73 | 70 | 75 | 73—291 | 4,813 |
| Arnold Palmer | 73 | 71 | 73 | 74—291 | 4,813 |
| Ken Towns | 71 | 74 | 72 | 75—292 | 3,942 |
| Charles Sifford | 76 | 71 | 77 | 69—293 | 3,572 |
| Jack Fleck | 73 | 72 | 75 | 74—294 | 3,282 |
| Bob Gajda | 75 | 74 | 72 | 74—295 | 2,890 |
| H. Johnson | 74 | 73 | 72 | 76—295 | 2,890 |

## MEN'S U.S. AMATEUR
(Brookline, Mass., Aug. 31–Sept. 5, 1982)

Final (36 holes)—Jay Sigel, Philadelphia, defeated David Tolley, Roanoke, Va., 8 and 7, in final
Semifinals—Sigel defeated Richard Fehr, Seattle, Wash., 1 up, and Tolley defeated Jim Hallet, South Yarmouth, Mass., 1 up

## WOMEN'S U.S. AMATEUR
(Colorado Springs, Colo., Aug. 17–22, 1982)

Final (36 holes)—Juli Inkster, Los Altos, Calif., defeated Cathy Hanlon, Palos Verdes Estates, Calif., 4 and 3
Semifinals—Miss Inkster defeated Lisa Kluver, Alexandria, Minn., 3 and 2; Miss Hanlon defeated Lindy Goggin, Australia, 6 and 4

## OTHER 1982 PGA TOUR WINNERS

(Through Aug. 22, 1982)

| | |
|---|---|
| Tucson Open—Craig Stadler (266) | $54,000 |
| Bob Hope Classic—Ed Fiori* (335) | 50,000 |
| Phoenix Open—Lanny Wadkins (263) | 54,000 |
| San Diego Open—Johnny Miller (270) | 54,000 |
| Crosby Pro-Am—Jim Simons (274) | 54,000 |
| Hawaii Open—Wayne Levi (277) | 58,500 |
| Los Angeles Open—Tom Watson* (271) | 54,000 |
| Doral Open—Andy Bean (278) | 54,000 |
| Bay Hill Classic—Tom Kite* (278) | 54,000 |
| Inverrary Classic—Hale Irwin (269) | 72,000 |
| Tournament Players Championship—Jerry Pate (280) | 90,000 |
| Heritage Classic—Tom Watson* (280) | 54,000 |
| Greensboro Open—Danny Edwards (285) | 54,000 |
| Tournament of Champions—Lanny Wadkins (280) | 63,000 |
| Tallahassee Open—Bob Shearer (272) | 18,000 |
| USF&G Classic—Scott Hoch (206) | 54,000 |
| Nelson Classic—Bob Gilder (266) | 63,000 |
| Houston Open—Ed Sneed* (275) | 63,000 |
| Colonial Invitational—Jack Nicklaus (273) | 63,000 |
| Atlanta Classic—Keith Fergus* (273) | 54,000 |
| Memorial Tournament—Ray Floyd (281) | 63,000 |
| Kemper Open—Craig Stadler (275) | 72,000 |
| Memphis Open—Ray Floyd (271) | 72,000 |
| Westchester Classic—Bob Gilder (261) | 72,000 |
| Western Open—Tom Weiskopf (276) | 63,000 |
| Milwaukee Open—Calvin Peete (274) | 45,000 |
| Quad Cities Open—Payne Stewart (268) | 36,000 |
| Anheuser-Busch Classic—Calvin Peete (203) | 63,000 |
| Canadian Open—Bruce Lietzke (277) | 76,500 |
| Hartford Open—Tim Norris (259) | 54,000 |

*Won playoff.

## OTHER 1982 L.P.G.A. TOUR WINNERS

(Through Aug. 22, 1982)

| | |
|---|---|
| Whirlpool—Hollis Stacy* (282) | $18,750 |
| Elizabeth Arden Classic—JoAnne Carner (283) | 18,750 |
| S&H Classic—Hollis Stacy (204) | 18,750 |
| Bent Tree Classic—Beth Daniel (276) | 22,500 |
| Arizona Copper—Ayako Okamoto* (281) | 18,750 |
| Sun City Classic—Beth Daniel* (278) | 15,000 |
| Olympia Gold—Sally Little (288) | 22,500 |
| J&B Scotch—Nancy Lopez (279) | 30,000 |
| Kemper—Amy Alcott (286) | 26,250 |
| Dinah Shore Classic—Sally Little (278) | 45,000 |
| CPC International—Kathy Whitworth (281) | 22,500 |
| Orlando Classic—Patty Sheehan (209) | 22,500 |
| Birmingham Classic—Beth Daniel (203) | 15,000 |
| UVB Classic—Sally Little* (208) | 18,750 |
| Lady Michelob—Kathy Whitworth (207) | 22,500 |
| Chrysler Classic—Cathy Morse (216) | 18,750 |
| Borning Classic—Sandra Spuzich* (280) | 18,750 |
| McDonald's Kids—JoAnne Carner (276) | 37,500 |
| Lady Keystone—Jan Stephenson (211) | 30,000 |
| Rochester—Sandra Haynie (276) | 30,000 |
| Jackson Classic—Sandra Haynie (280) | 30,000 |
| West Virginia—Hollis Stacy* (209) | 18,750 |
| Mayflower—Sally Little (275) | 30,000 |
| Columbia Savings—Beth Daniel (276) | 30,000 |
| Boston Five—Sandra Palmer (281) | 26,250 |
| WUI Classic—Beth Daniel (276) | 18,750 |

*Won playoff.

# SOCCER

## WORLD CUP

| | | | | | | | |
|---|---|---|---|---|---|---|---|
| 1930 | Uruguay | 1946 | No competition | 1962 | Brazil | 1978 | Argentina |
| 1934 | Italy | 1950 | Uruguay | 1966 | England | 1982 | Italy |
| 1938 | Italy | 1954 | West Germany | 1970 | Brazil | | |
| 1942 | No competition | 1958 | Brazil | 1974 | West Germany | | |

### WORLD CUP—1982 SEMIFINALS

(Madrid, Spain, July 8, 1982)

Italy 2, Poland 0
West Germany 5, France 4 (penalty kicks)

### FINAL

(Madrid, Spain, July 11, 1982)

Italy 3, West Germany 1

### THIRD PLACE

(Madrid, Spain, July 10, 1982)

Poland 3, France 2

The following are the results of matches played by the four teams which reached the semifinals:

**Italy (Group C)**

Italy 0, Poland 0
Italy 1, Peru 1
Italy 1, Cameroon 1
Italy 2, Argentina 1
Italy 3, Brazil 2

**Poland (Group A)**

Poland 0, Italy 0
Poland 0, Cameroon 0
Poland 5, Peru 1

Poland 3, Belgium 0
Poland 0, Soviet Union 0

**West Germany (Group B)**

West Germany 1, Algeria 2
West Germany 4, Chile 1
West Germany 1, Austria 0
West Germany 0, England 0
West Germany 2, Spain 1

**France (Group D)**

France 1, England 3
France 4, Kuwait 1
France 1, Czechoslovakia 1
France 1, Austria 0
France 4, Northern Ireland 1

### MAJOR INDOOR SOCCER LEAGUE FINAL STANDING—1982

**EASTERN DIVISION**

| | W | L | Pct | GB |
|---|---|---|---|---|
| New York | 36 | 8 | .818 | — |
| Pittsburgh | 31 | 13 | .705 | 5 |
| Baltimore | 27 | 17 | .614 | 9 |
| Buffalo | 24 | 20 | .545 | 12 |
| New Jersey | 17 | 27 | .386 | 19 |

| Cleveland | 15 | 29 | .341 | 21 |
| Philadelphia | 11 | 33 | .250 | 25 |

## WESTERN DIVISION

| St. Louis | 28 | 16 | .636 | — |
| Wichita | 27 | 17 | .614 | 1 |
| Memphis | 20 | 24 | .455 | 8 |
| Denver | 19 | 25 | .432 | 9 |
| Phoenix | 17 | 27 | .386 | 11 |
| Kansas City | 14 | 30 | .318 | 14 |

## CHAMPIONSHIP PLAYOFFS
### Quarterfinal Round

New York defeated Buffalo, 2 games to 1
Baltimore defeated Pittsburgh, 2 games to 1
St. Louis defeated Denver, 2 games to 0
Wichita defeated Memphis, 2 games to 1

### Semifinal Round

New York defeated Baltimore, 2 games to 0
St. Louis defeated Wichita, 2 games to 1

### Final

New York defeated St. Louis, 3 games to 2

## LEADING N.A.S.L. SCORERS—1982

| | GP | G | A | Pts |
|---|---|---|---|---|
| Giorgio Chinaglia, Cosmos | 32 | 20 | 15 | 55 |
| Karl–Heinz Granitza, Chicago | 32 | 20 | 9 | 49 |
| Peter Ward, Seattle | 32 | 18 | 18 | 49 |
| Ricardo Alonzo, Jacksonville | 30 | 21 | 4 | 46 |
| Laurie Abrahams, Tulsa | 31 | 17 | 10 | 44 |
| Neill Roberts, Toronto | 28 | 17 | 8 | 42 |
| Ace Ntsoelengoe, Toronto | 32 | 14 | 12 | 40 |
| Mark Peterson, Seattle | 31 | 17 | 5 | 39 |
| David Byrne, Toronto | 32 | 8 | 23 | 39 |
| Godfrey Ingram, San Jose | 31 | 17 | 3 | 37 |
| Alan Willey, Montreal | 27 | 15 | 7 | 37 |
| Branko Segota, Fort Lauderdale | 29 | 12 | 13 | 37 |

## OUTDOOR SOCCER
## NORTH AMERICAN SOCCER LEAGUE
### Final Standing—1982

| | W | L | GF | GA | BP[1] | Pts |
|---|---|---|---|---|---|---|
| **EASTERN DIVISION** | | | | | | |
| Cosmos | 23 | 9 | 73 | 52 | 67 | 203 |
| Montreal Manic | 19 | 13 | 60 | 43 | 49 | 159 |
| Toronto Blizzard | 17 | 15 | 64 | 47 | 49 | 151 |
| Chicago Sting | 13 | 19 | 56 | 67 | 53 | 129 |
| **SOUTHERN DIVISION** | | | | | | |
| Fort Lauderdale Strikers | 18 | 14 | 64 | 74 | 57 | 163 |
| Tulsa Roughnecks | 16 | 16 | 69 | 57 | 59 | 151 |
| Tampa Bay Rowdies | 12 | 20 | 47 | 77 | 42 | 112 |
| Jacksonville Tea Men | 11 | 21 | 41 | 71 | 39 | 105 |
| **WESTERN DIVISION** | | | | | | |
| Seattle Sounders | 18 | 14 | 72 | 48 | 60 | 166 |
| San Diego Sockers | 19 | 13 | 71 | 54 | 54 | 162 |
| Vancouver Whitecaps | 20 | 12 | 58 | 48 | 46 | 160 |
| Portland Timbers | 14 | 18 | 49 | 44 | 42 | 122 |
| San Jose Earthquake | 13 | 19 | 47 | 62 | 38 | 114 |
| Edmonton Drillers | 11 | 21 | 38 | 65 | 33 | 93 |

1. A bonus point is awarded for each goal scored to a maximum of three a game, excluding overtimes and shootouts; teams receive 6 points for each victory in regulation time or overtime, but only 4 points for winning a game decided by a shootout.

## CHAMPIONSHIP PLAYOFF—1982

(San Diego, Calif. Sept. 18, 1982)
Cosmos 1, Seattle 0
  (Scoring: Chinaglia 0)

### Semifinals

Cosmos defeated San Diego, 2 games to 0
Seattle defeated Ft. Lauderdale, 2 games to 1

## N.A.S.L. INDOOR SOCCER—1982
## FINAL STANDING

### ATLANTIC CONFERENCE
### Central Division

| | W | L | Pct | GB |
|---|---|---|---|---|
| Chicago | 12 | 6 | .667 | — |
| Tampa Bay | 11 | 7 | .611 | 1 |
| Tulsa | 10 | 8 | .556 | 2 |

### Eastern Division

| Montreal | 9 | 9 | .500 | — |
|---|---|---|---|---|
| Toronto | 8 | 10 | .444 | 1 |
| Jacksonville | 7 | 11 | .389 | 2 |
| Cosmos | 6 | 12 | .333 | 3 |

### PACIFIC CONFERENCE
### Western Division

| San Diego | 10 | 8 | .556 | — |
|---|---|---|---|---|
| Portland | 7 | 11 | .389 | 3 |
| San Jose | 5 | 13 | .278 | 5 |

### Northwest Division

| Edmonton | 13 | 5 | .722 | — |
|---|---|---|---|---|
| Vancouver | 10 | 8 | .556 | 3 |
| Seattle | 9 | 9 | .500 | 4 |

## CHAMPIONSHIP PLAYOFFS
### Quarterfinal Round

Tulsa defeated Chicago, 2 games to 1
Tampa Bay defeated Montreal, 2 games to 1
Edmonton defeated Seattle, 2 games to 0
San Diego defeated Vancouver, 2 games to 0

### Semifinal Round

Tampa Bay defeated Tulsa, 2 games to 1
San Diego defeated Edmonton, 2 games to 0

### Final

San Diego 9, Tampa Bay 7
San Diego 10, Tampa Bay 5 (San Diego won series 2 games to 0)

# COURT TENNIS

## UNITED STATES CHAMPIONS—1982

Men's open—Wayne Davies, New York City
Men's amateur—Gene Scott, New York City
Men's seniors—Bill Vogt, Philadelphia
Men's amateur doubles—O.M. Phipps and Gene Scott, New York City
Men's open doubles—Wayne Davies and O.M. Phipps

# SURFING—1982

World men's amateur—Tom Curren, Santa Barbara, Calif.
World women's amateur—Jerry Gill, Australia

# YACHTING

## AMERICA'S CUP RECORD

First race in 1851 around Isle of Wight, Cowes, England. First defense and all others through 1920 held 30 miles off New York Bay. Races since 1930 held 30 miles off Newport, R.I. Conducted as one race only in 1851 and 1870; best four-of-seven basis, 1871; best two-of-three, 1876–1887; best three-of-five, 1893–1901; best four-of-seven, since 1930. Figures in parentheses indicate number of races won.

| Year | Winner and owner | Loser and owner |
|---|---|---|
| 1851 | AMERICA (1), John C. Stevens, U.S. | AURORA, T. Le Marchant, England[1] |
| 1870 | MAGIC (1), Franklin Osgood, U.S. | CAMBRIA, James Ashbury, England[2] |
| 1871 | COLUMBIA (2), Franklin Osgood, U.S.[3] | LIVONIA (1), James Ashbury, England |
|  | SAPPHO (2), William P. Douglas, U.S. | |
| 1876 | MADELEINE (2), John S. Dickerson, U.S. | COUNTESS OF DUFFERIN, Chas. Gifford, Canada |
| 1881 | MISCHIEF (2), J. R. Busk, U.S. | ATALANTA, Alexander Cuthbert, Canada |
| 1885 | PURITAN (2), J. M. Forbes-Gen. Charles Paine, U.S. | GENESTA, Sir Richard Sutton, England |
| 1886 | MAYFLOWER (2), Gen. Charles Paine, U.S. | GALATEA, Lt. William Henn, England |
| 1887 | VOLUNTEER (2), Gen. Charles Paine, U.S. | THISTLE, James Bell et al, Scotland |
| 1893 | VIGILANT (3), C. Oliver Iselin et al., U.S. | VALKYRIE II, Lord Dunraven, England |
| 1895 | DEFENDER (3), C. O. Iselin-W. K. Vanderbilt-E. D. Morgan, U.S. | VALKYRIE III, Lord Dunraven-Lord Lonsdale-Lord Wolverton, England |
| 1899 | COLUMBIA (3), J. P. Morgan-C. O. Iselin, U.S. | SHAMROCK I, Sir Thomas Lipton, Ireland |
| 1901 | COLUMBIA (3), Edwin D. Morgan, U.S. | SHAMROCK II, Sir Thomas Lipton, Ireland |
| 1903 | RELIANCE (3), Cornelius Vanderbilt et al., U.S. | SHAMROCK III, Sir Thomas Lipton, Ireland |
| 1920 | RESOLUTE (3), Henry Walters et al., U.S. | SHAMROCK IV (2), Sir Thomas Lipton, Ireland |
| 1930 | ENTERPRISE (4), Harold S. Vanderbilt et al., U.S. | SHAMROCK V, Sir Thomas Lipton, Ireland |
| 1934 | RAINBOW (4), Harold S. Vanderbilt, U.S. | ENDEAVOUR (2), T. O. M. Sopwith, England |
| 1937 | RANGER (4), Harold S. Vanderbilt, U.S. | ENDEAVOUR II, T. O. M. Sopwith, England |
| 1958 | COLUMBIA (4), Henry Sears et al., U.S. | SCEPTRE, Hugh Goodson et al., England |
| 1962 | WEATHERLY (4), Henry D. Mercer et al., U.S. | GRETEL (1), Sir Frank Packer et al., Australia |
| 1964 | CONSTELLATION (4), New York Y.C. Syndicate, U.S. | SOVEREIGN (0), J. Anthony Bowden, England |
| 1967 | INTREPID (4), New York Y.C. Syndicate, U.S. | DAME PATTIE (0), Sydney (Aust.) Syndicate |
| 1970 | INTREPID (4), New York Y.C. Syndicate, U.S. | GRETEL II (1), Sydney (Aust.) Syndicate |
| 1974 | COURAGEOUS (4), New York, N.Y. Syndicate, U.S. | SOUTHERN CROSS (0), Sydney (Aust.) Syndicate |
| 1977 | COURAGEOUS (4), New York, N.Y. Syndicate, U.S. | AUSTRALIA (0), Sun City (Aust.) Syndicate |
| 1980 | FREEDOM (4), New York, N.Y. Syndicate, U.S. | AUSTRALIA (1), Alan Bond et al, Australia |

1. Fourteen British yachts started against America; Aurora finished second. 2. Cambria sailed against 23 U.S. yachts and finished tenth. 3. Columbia was disabled in the third race, after winning the first two; Sappho substituted and won the fourth and fifth.

## YACHTING—1982

Newport–to–Bermuda Race (635 miles, held every 2 years)— Corrected time winner: Brigadoon, Class B, 57-foot sloop, skippered by Robert Morton, handicapped under Measurement Handicap System, 2 days 20 hours 42 seconds. First to finish: Nirvana, Class A, 81-foot Maxi, skippered by M.H. Green, handicapped under International Offshore Rule, elapsed time: 2:14:29:16

Chicago–to–Mackinac Island (Lake Michigan, 333 miles)— Corrected time winner: Leading Edge, 40-foot sloop, skippered by Eugene Mondry, 41 hours 38 minutes 27 seconds. First to finish: Heritage, 63-foot sloop, skippered by Don Wildman, elapsed time: 48:45:18

Onion Patch National Team Series (Hamilton, Bermuda)— Canada (Ontario), 711 points

# KARATE

## AMATEUR ATHLETIC UNION NATIONAL CHAMPIONSHIPS

(Palatine, Ill., July 25, 1982)

Open heavyweight class—Bob Allen, New Orleans, La.
80–kilogram class—Terrance Tokey Hill, Chillicothe, Ohio
75–kilogram class—John DiPasquale, Chicago
70–kilogram class—Michael Sledge, New York City
60–kilogram–and–under class—George Gino, Cleveland, Ohio

# SHUFFLEBOARD

## U.S.-INTERNATIONAL PRO WORLD CHAMPIONSHIP

(Lakeland, Fla., Jan. 28–30, 1982)

Men—Jason Baade and Len deBoer, Lakeland, Fla.
Women—Therese Charbonneau, St. Petersburg, Fla., and Thea Harris, Fort Myers, Fla.

# DUCKPIN BOWLING

## NATIONAL CHAMPIONSHIPS—1982

(Providence, R.I.)

### National Duckpin Bowling Congress

| | |
|---|---|
| Men's singles—Bart Matteson, East Taunton, Mass. | 568 |
| Women's singles—Pat Smith, Warwick, R.I. | 523 |
| Men's doubles—Thomas Bohara Sr. and Len Gdula, Norwich, Conn. | 1,037 |
| Women's doubles—Carol Deshong, Riverside, R.I., and Anne Mello, Rehoboth, R.I. | 913 |
| Championship Team—Legion Major No. 3, Cranston, R.I. | 2,200 |
| Class A Teams—Walko Five, Fall River, Mass. | 2,164 |
| Class B Teams—Rhode Island Paper Box, Cranston, R.I. | 2,065 |
| Class C Teams—Samor Funeral Home, Bridgeport, Conn. | 1,897 |
| Class D Teams—Moss Trucking, Charlotte, N.C. | 1,763 |

# AUTO RACING

## INDIANAPOLIS 500

| Year | Winner | Car | Time | mph | Second place |
|------|--------|-----|------|-----|--------------|
| 1911 | Ray Harroun | Marmon | 6:42:08 | 74.59 | Ralph Mulford |
| 1912 | Joe Dawson | National | 6:21:06 | 78.72 | Teddy Tetzloff |
| 1913 | Jules Goux | Peugeot | 6:35:05 | 75.93 | Spencer Wishart |
| 1914 | René Thomas | Delage | 6:03:45 | 82.47 | Arthur Duray |
| 1915 | Ralph DePalma | Mercedes | 5:33:55.51 | 89.84 | Dario Resta |
| 1916[1] | Dario Resta | Peugeot | 3:34:17 | 84.00 | Wilbur D'Alene |
| 1919 | Howard Wilcox | Peugeot | 5:40:42.87 | 88.05 | Eddie Hearne |
| 1920 | Gaston Chevrolet | Monroe | 5:38:32 | 88.62 | René Thomas |
| 1921 | Tommy Milton | Frontenac | 5:34:44.65 | 89.62 | Roscoe Sarles |
| 1922 | Jimmy Murphy | Murphy Special | 5:17:30.79 | 94.48 | Harry Hartz |
| 1923 | Tommy Milton | H. C. S. Special | 5:29:50.17 | 90.95 | Harry Hartz |
| 1924 | L. L. Corum–Joe Boyer | Dusenberg Special | 5:05:23.51 | 98.23 | Earl Cooper |
| 1925 | Peter DePaolo | Dusenberg Special | 4:56:39.45 | 101.13 | Dave Lewis |
| 1926[2] | Frank Lockhart | Miller Special | 4:10:14.95 | 95.904 | Harry Hartz |
| 1927 | George Souders | Dusenberg Special | 5:07:33.08 | 97.54 | Earl DeVore |
| 1928 | Louis Meyer | Miller Special | 5:01:33.75 | 99.48 | Lou Moore |
| 1929 | Ray Keech | Simplex Special | 5:07:25.42 | 97.58 | Louis Meyer |
| 1930 | Billy Arnold | Miller–Hartz Special | 4:58:39.72 | 100.448 | Shorty Cantlon |
| 1931 | Louis Schneider | Bowes Special | 5:10:27.93 | 96.629 | Fred Frame |
| 1932 | Fred Frame | Miller–Hartz Special | 4:48:03.79 | 104.144 | Howard Wilcox |
| 1933 | Louis Meyer | Tydol Special | 4:48:00.75 | 104.162 | Wilbur Shaw |
| 1934 | Bill Cummings | Boyle Products Special | 4:46:05.20 | 104.863 | Mauri Rose |
| 1935 | Kelly Petillo | Gilmore Special | 4:42:22.71 | 106.240 | Wilbur Shaw |
| 1936 | Louis Meyer | Ring Free Special | 4:35:03.39 | 109.069 | Ted Horn |
| 1937 | Wilbur Shaw | Shaw–Gilmore Special | 4:24:07.80 | 113.580 | Ralph Hepburn |
| 1938 | Floyd Roberts | Burd Piston Ring Special | 4:15:58.40 | 117.200 | Wilbur Shaw |
| 1939 | Wilbur Shaw | Boyle Special | 4:20:47.39 | 115.035 | Jimmy Snyder |
| 1940 | Wilbur Shaw | Boyle Special | 4:22:31.17 | 114.277 | Rex Mays |
| 1941 | Floyd Davis–Mauri Rose | Noc–Out Hose Clamp Special | 4:20:36.24 | 115.117 | Rex Mays |
| 1946 | George Robson | Thorne Engineering Special | 4:21:26.71 | 114.820 | Jimmy Jackson |
| 1947 | Mauri Rose | Blue Crown Special | 4:17:52.17 | 116.338 | Bill Holland |
| 1948 | Mauri Rose | Blue Crown Special | 4:10:23.33 | 119.814 | Bill Holland |
| 1949 | Bill Holland | Blue Crown Special | 4:07:15.97 | 121.327 | Johnny Parsons |
| 1950[3] | Johnnie Parsons | Wynn's Friction Proof Special | 2:46:55.97 | 124.002 | Bill Holland |
| 1951 | Lee Wallard | Belanger Special | 3:57:38.05 | 126.244 | Mike Nazaruk |
| 1952 | Troy Ruttman | Agajanian Special | 3:52:41.88 | 128.922 | Jim Rathmann |
| 1953 | Bill Vukovich | Fuel Injection Special | 3:53:01.69 | 128.740 | Art Cross |
| 1954 | Bill Vukovich | Fuel Injection Special | 3:49:17.27 | 130.840 | Jim Bryan |
| 1955 | Bob Sweikert | John Zink Special | 3:53:59.13 | 128.209 | Tony Bettenhausen |
| 1956 | Pat Flaherty | John Zink Special | 3:53:28.84 | 128.490 | Sam Hanks |
| 1957 | Sam Hanks | Belond Exhaust Special | 3:41:14.25 | 135.601 | Jim Rathmann |
| 1958 | Jimmy Bryan | Belond A–P Special | 3:44:13.80 | 133.791 | George Amick |
| 1959 | Rodger Ward | Leader Card 500 Roadster | 3:40:49.20 | 135.857 | Jim Rathmann |
| 1960 | Jim Rathmann | Ken–Paul Special | 3:36:11.36 | 138.767 | Rodger Ward |
| 1961 | A. J. Foyt | Bowes Special | 3:35:37.49 | 139.130 | Eddie Sachs |
| 1962 | Rodger Ward | Leader Card Special | 3:33:50.33 | 140.293 | Len Sutton |
| 1963 | Parnelli Jones | Agajanian Special | 3:29:35.40 | 143.137 | Jim Clark |
| 1964 | A. J. Foyt | Offenhauser Special | 3:23:35.83 | 147.350 | Rodger Ward |
| 1965 | Jim Clark | Lotus–Ford | 3:19:05.34 | 150.686 | Parnelli Jones |
| 1966 | Graham Hill | Lola–Ford | 3:27:52.53 | 144.317 | Jim Clark |
| 1967[4] | A. J. Foyt | Coyote–Ford | 3:18:24.22 | 151.207 | Al Unser |
| 1968 | Bobby Unser | Eagle–Offenhauser | 3:16:13.76 | 152.882 | Dan Gurney |
| 1969 | Mario Andretti | STP Hawk–Ford | 3:11:14.71 | 156.867 | Dan Gurney |
| 1970 | Al Unser | P. J. Colt–Ford | 3:12:37.04 | 155.749 | Mark Donohue |
| 1971 | Al Unser | P. J. Colt–Ford | 3:10:11.56 | 157.735 | Peter Revson |
| 1972 | Mark Donohue | McLaren–Offenhauser | 3:04:05.54 | 162.962 | Al Unser |
| 1973[5] | Gordon Johncock | Eagle–Offenhauser | 2:05:26.59 | 159.036 | Bill Vukovich |
| 1974 | Johnny Rutherford | McLaren–Offenhauser | 3:09:10.06 | 158.589 | Bobby Unser |
| 1975[6] | Bobby Unser | Eagle–Offenhauser | 2:54:55.08 | 149.213 | Johnny Rutherford |
| 1976[7] | Johnny Rutherford | McLaren–Offenhauser | 1:42:52.48 | 148.725 | A. J. Foyt |
| 1977 | A. J. Foyt | Coyote–Foyt | 3:05:57.16 | 161.331 | Tom Sneva |
| 1978 | Al Unser | Lola–Cosworth | 3:05:54.99 | 161.363 | Tom Sneva |
| 1979 | Rick Mears | Penske–Cosworth | 3:08:27.97 | 158.899 | A. J. Foyt |
| 1980 | Johnny Rutherford | Chaparral–Cosworth | 3:29:59.56 | 142.862 | Tom Sneva |
| 1981[8] | Bobby Unser | Eagle–Offenhauser | 3:35:41.78 | 139.029 | Mario Andretti |

| 1982 | Gordon Johncock | Wildcat—Cosworth | 3:05:09.14 | 162.029 | Rick Mears |

1. 300 miles. 2. Race ended at 400 miles because of rain. 3. Race ended at 345 miles because of rain. 4. Race, postponed after 18 laps because of rain on May 30, was finished on May 31. 5. Race postponed May 28 and 29 was cut to 332.5 miles because of rain, May 30. 6. Race ended at 435 miles because of rain. 7. Race ended at 255 miles because of rain. 8. Andretti was awarded the victory the day after the race after Bobby Unser, whose car finished first, was penalized one lap and dropped from first place to second for passing other cars illegally under a yellow caution flag. Unser appealed the decision to the U.S. Auto Club and was upheld. A panel ruled the penalty was too severe and instead fined Unser $40,000, but restored the victory to him.

## U.S. AUTO CLUB
## NATIONAL CHAMPIONS

| | | | | | | | |
|---|---|---|---|---|---|---|---|
| 1910 | Ray Harroun | 1926 | Harry Hartz | 1950 | Henry Banks | 1968 | Bobby Unser |
| 1911 | Ralph Mulford | 1927 | Peter DePaolo | 1951 | Tony Bettenhausen | 1969 | Mario Andretti |
| 1912 | Ralph DePalma | 1928–29 | Louis Meyer | | | 1970 | Al Unser |
| 1913 | Earl Cooper | 1930 | Billy Arnold | 1952 | Chuck Stevenson | 1971–72 | Joe Leonard |
| 1914 | Ralph DePalma | 1931 | Louis Schneider | 1953 | Sam Hanks | 1973 | Roger McCluskey |
| 1915 | Earl Cooper | 1932 | Bob Carey | 1954 | Jimmy Bryan | 1974 | Bobby Unser |
| 1916 | Dario Resta | 1933 | Louis Meyer | 1955 | Bob Sweikert | 1975 | A. J. Foyt |
| 1917 | Earl Cooper | 1934 | Bill Cummings | 1956–57 | Jimmy Bryan | 1976 | Gordon Johncock |
| 1918 | Ralph Mulford | 1935 | Kelly Petillo | 1958 | Tony Bettenhausen | 1977–78 | Tom Sneva |
| 1919 | Howard Wilcox | 1936 | Mauri Rose | | | 1979 | A. J. Foyt |
| 1920 | Gaston Chevrolet | 1937 | Wilbur Shaw | 1959 | Rodger Ward | 1980 | Johnny Rutherford |
| 1921 | Tommy Milton | 1938 | Floyd Roberts | 1960–61 | A. J. Foyt | 1981–82 | George Snider |
| 1922 | James Murphy | 1939 | Wilbur Shaw | 1962 | Rodger Ward | | |
| 1923 | Eddie Hearne | 1940–41 | Rex Mays | 1963–64 | A. J. Foyt | | |
| 1924 | James Murphy | 1946–48 | Ted Horn | 1965–66 | Mario Andretti | | |
| 1925 | Peter DePaolo | 1949 | Johnnie Parsons | 1967 | A. J. Foyt | | |

## NATIONAL ASSOCIATION FOR STOCK CAR AUTO RACING
## (NASCAR) GRAND NATIONAL CHAMPIONS

| | | | | | | | |
|---|---|---|---|---|---|---|---|
| 1949 | Red Byron | 1956–57 | Buck Baker | 1966 | David Pearson | 1976–78 | Cale Yarborough |
| 1950 | Bill Rexford | 1958–59 | Lee Petty | 1967 | Richard Petty | 1979 | Richard Petty |
| 1951 | Herb Thomas | 1960 | Rex White | 1968–69 | David Pearson | 1980 | Dale Earnhardt |
| 1952 | Tim Flock | 1961 | Ned Jarrett | 1970 | Bobby Isaac | 1981 | Darrell Waltrip |
| 1953 | Herb Thomas | 1962–63 | Joe Weatherly | 1971–72 | Richard Petty | | |
| 1954 | Lee Petty | 1964 | Richard Petty | 1973 | Benny Parsons | | |
| 1955 | Tim Flock | 1965 | Ned Jarrett | 1974–75 | Richard Petty | | |

## WORLD GRAND PRIX DRIVER CHAMPIONS

| | | | |
|---|---|---|---|
| 1950 | Giuseppe Farina, Italy, Alfa Romeo | 1967 | Denis Hulme, New Zealand, Brabham-Repco |
| 1951 | Juan Fangio, Argentina, Alfa Romeo | 1968 | Graham Hill, England, Lotus-Ford |
| 1952 | Alberto Ascari, Italy, Ferrari | 1969 | Jackie Stewart, Scotland, Matra-Ford |
| 1953 | Alberto Ascari, Italy, Ferrari | 1970 | Jochen Rindt, Austria, Lotus-Ford |
| 1955 | Juan Fangio, Argentina, Maserati, Mercedes-Benz | 1971 | Jackie Stewart, Scotland, Tyrrell-Ford |
| 1955 | Juan Fangio, Argentina, Mercedes-Benz | 1972 | Emerson Fittipaldi, Brazil, Lotus-Ford |
| 1956 | Juan Fangio, Argentina, Lancia-Ferrari | 1973 | Jackie Stewart, Scotland, Tyrrell-Ford |
| 1957 | Juan Fangio, Argentina, Masserati | 1974 | Emerson Fittipaldi, Brazil, McLaren-Ford |
| 1958 | Mike Hawthorn, England, Ferrari | 1975 | Niki Lauda, Austria, Ferrari |
| 1959 | Jack Brabham, Australia, Cooper | 1976 | James Hunt, Britain, McLaren-Ford |
| 1960 | Jack Brabham, Australia, Cooper | 1977 | Niki Lauda, Austria, Ferrari |
| 1961 | Phil Hill, United States, Ferrari | 1978 | Mario Andretti, Nazareth, Pa., Lotus |
| 1962 | Graham Hill, England, BRM | 1979 | Jody Scheckter, South Africa |
| 1963 | Jim Clark, Scotland, Lotus-Ford | 1980 | Alan Jones, Australia |
| 1964 | John Surtees, England, Ferrari | 1981 | Nelson Piquet, Brazil |
| 1965 | Jim Clark, Scotland, Lotus-Ford | 1982 | Kiki Rosberg, Finland |
| 1966 | Jack Brabham, Australia, Brabham-Repco | | |

## GRAND PRIX RACING EVENTS—1982
### (Through Aug. 29, 1982)

**Formula One Competition**

South Africa (Kyalami, South Africa, Jan. 23)—Alain Prost, France; driving a Renault-turbo; 1 hour 32 minutes 8.4 seconds; 128.59 miles per hour

Brazil (Rio de Janiero, March 21)—Nelson Piquet, Brazil; Brabham; 1:43:54.760; 114.086 mph

Long Beach (Long Beach, Calif., April 4)—Niki Lauda, Austria; McLaren; 81.4 mph

San Marino (Imola, Italy, April 25)—Didier Pironi, France; Ferrari; 1:36:38.887; 116.9 mph

Belgium (Zolder, Belgium, May 9)—John Watson, Britain; McLaren-Cosworth; 1:35:41.995; 116.19 mph

Monaco (Monte Carlo, Monaco, May 23)—Riccardo Patrese, Italy; Brabham-Ford; 1:54:11.259; 82.21 mph

Detroit (Detroit, Mich., June 6)—John Watson, Britain; McLaren-Cosworth; 1:58:4.043; 78.2 mph

Canada (Montreal, June 13)—Nelson Piquet, Brazil; Brabham BT-50; 104.22 mph

Dutch (Zandvoort, The Netherlands, July 3)—Didier Pironi, France; Ferrari; 1:38:03.25; 116.386 mph

Britain (Brands Hatch, England, July 18)—Niki Lauda, Austria; McLaren; 1:35:33.812; 124.7 mph

France (LeCastellet, France, July 25)—Rene Arnoux, France; Renault; 1:33:33.217; 125.0 mph

Germany (Hockenheim, West Germany, Aug. 8)—Patrick Tambay, France; Ferrari; 1:27:25.17; 130.42 mph
Austria (Zeltweg, Austria, Aug. 15)—Elio de Angelis, Italy; Lotus; 1:25:02.212; 138.1 mph
Switzerland (Dijon, France, Aug. 29)—Keke Rosberg, Finland; Williams; 1:33:50.32; 122.286 mph

## U.S. AUTO CLUB

### 1982 Triple Crown Races

Indianapolis 500 (Indianapolis Motor Speedway, May 30, 500 miles)—1. Gordon Johncock, Coldwater, Mich.; STP Wildcat —Cosworth; 200 laps; 3:05:9.14; 162.029 mph; first—place prize; $290,609. 2. Rick Mears, Bakersfield, Calif.; Penske-Ford; 200 laps. 3. Pancho Carter, Brownsburg, Ind.; March-Cosworth; 199 laps. 4. Tom Sneva, Spokane, Wash.; Texaco Star March; 197 laps. 5. Al Unser, Albuquerque, N.M., Longworth–Cosworth, 197 laps.
Pocono 500 (Pocono International Raceway, Long Pond, Pa., Aug. 15, 500 miles)—Rick Mears, Bakersfield, Calif., Penske PC–10 Ford; 3:25:39; 145.879 mph; 200 laps; $66,435. 2. Kevin Cogan, Redondo Beach, Calif.; Penske PC–10 Ford; 200 laps. 3. Bobby Rahal, Columbus, Ohio; 82C Cosworth; 197 laps. 4. Geoff Brabham, San Clemente, Calif.; March-Cosworth, 197 laps. 5. Tony Bettenhausen, Speedway, Ind.; March–Cosworth.

## FINAL 1981 WINSTON CUP GRAND NATIONAL POINT LEADERS

| | |
|---|---|
| Darrell Waltrip | 4,880 |
| Bobby Allison | 4,827 |
| Harry Gant | 4,210 |
| Terry Labonte | 4,052 |
| Jody Ridley | 4,002 |
| Ricky Rudd | 3,988 |
| Dale Earnhardt | 3,975 |
| Richard Petty | 3,880 |
| Dave Marcis | 3,507 |
| Benny Parsons | 3,449 |

## FINAL 1981 NASCAR LEADING MONEY-WINNERS

| | |
|---|---|
| Darrell Waltrip | $693,342 |
| Bobby Allison | 644,311 |
| Richard Petty | 389,214 |
| Ricky Rudd | 381,968 |
| Dale Earnhardt | 347,113 |
| Terry Labonte | 334,987 |
| Benny Parsons | 287,949 |
| Harry Gant | 280,047 |
| Jody Ridley | 257,318 |
| Neil Bonnett | 181,670 |

## OTHER 1982 CHAMPIONSHIP AUTO RACES
### Championship Auto Racing Team (CART) Events

Kraco Phoenix 150 (Phoenix, Ariz., March 28, 150 miles)—Rick Mears, Bakersfield, Calif.; Penske P-C 10 Ford; 1 hour 15 minutes 48.231 seconds; 118.727 mph; $19,415
Stroh's 200 (Atlanta, Ga., March 1, 200 miles)—Rick Mears; Penske P–C 10 Ford; 1:13:10; 164,750 mph; $22,974
Gould Rex Mays 150 (Milwaukee, Wis., June 13, 150 miles)— Gordon Johncock, Coldwater, Mich.; ST Wildcat; 1:10:52.79; 126.978 mph; $19,979

Budweiser 500 kilometers (Cleveland, Ohio, July 4)—Bobby Rahal, Columbus, Ohio; Red Roof March; 3:03:44; 101.234 mph; $42,341
Norton 500 (Norton, Mich., July 18, 500 miles)—Gordon Johncock; ST Wildcat; 3:14:54; 153.925 mph; $89,303
Tony Bettenhausen 200 (Milwaukee, Wis., Aug. 1, 200 miles) —Tom Sneva, Paradise Valley, Ariz.; Texaco Star March; 1:49:57.54; 109.132 mph; $23,079
Domino's Pizza Pocono 500 (Pocono, Pa., Aug. 15, 500 miles) —Rick Mears, Penske P–C 10 Ford; 3:25:39; 145.879 mph; $66,435
Aircal 500 kilometers (Riverside, Calif., Aug. 29)—Rick Mears; Penske P–C 10 Ford; 2:42:14; 115.955 mph; $33,391

## NATIONAL ASSOCIATION FOR STOCK CAR RACING (NASCAR)—1982
(Through races of Aug. 22, 1982)

Daytona 500 (Daytona Beach, Fla., Feb. 14, 500 miles)— Bobby Allison, Hueytown, Ala., Buick, 3 hours 14 minutes 49 seconds; average speed: 153.991 mph; total purse: $927,625; winner's purse: $120,630
Richmond 500 (Richmond, Va., Feb. 21, 216.8 miles)—Dave Marcis, Averys Creek, N.C.; Chevrolet; 1:51:30; 72.914 mph; $187,655; $19,145
Valleydale 500 (Bristol, Tenn., March 14, 266.5 miles)—Darrell Waltrip, Franklin, Tenn.; Buick; 2:49:52; 94.025 mph; $179,-175; $26,520
Coca-Cola 500 (Atlanta, Ga., March 21, 500 miles)—Darrell Waltrip; Buick; 3:29:58; 124.824 mph; $300,775; $49,615
Hodgdon Carolina 500 (Rockingham, N.C., March 28, 500 miles)—Cale Yarborough, Timmonsville, S.C.; Buick; 4:35:27; 108.992 mph; $232,665; $17,360
CRC Chemicals Rebel 500 (Darlington, S.C., April 4, 500 miles) —Dale Earnhardt, Kannapolis, N.C.; Ford; 4:03:27; 123.554 mph; $267,025; $31,450
Northwestern Bank 400 (North Wilkesboro, N.C., April 18, 250 miles)—Darrell Waltrip; Buick; 2:33:37; 97.646 mph; $181,-390; $32,300
Virginia National Bank 500 (Martinsville, Va., April 25, 262.5 miles)—Harry Gant, Taylorsville, N.C.; Buick; 3:30:01; 75.073 mph; $203,750; $26,795
Winston 500 (Talladega, Ala., May 2, 500 miles)—Darrell Waltrip; Buick; 3:11:19; 156.697 mph; $398,575; $44,250
Cracker Barrel 420 (Nashville, Tenn., May 8, 250.3 miles)— Darrell Waltrip; Buick; 2:59:52; 83.502 mph; $159,225; $24,-025
Mason-Dixon 500 (Dover, Del., May 16, 500 miles)—Bobby Allison; Chevrolet; 4:09:43; 120.136 mph; $224,300; $25,350
World 600 (Harrisburg, N.C., May 30, 600 miles)—Neil Bonnett, Hueytown, Ala.; Ford; 4:36:48; 130.058 mph; $430,325; $50,650
Van Scoy Diamond Mine 500 (Pocono, Pa., June 6, 500 miles) —Bobby Allison; Buick; 4:24:08; 113.579 mph; $250,525; $25,500
Budweiser 400 (Riverside, Calif., June 13, 400 kilometers)— Tim Richmond, Ashland, Ohio; Buick; 2:23:51; 103.816 mph; $217,400; $21,530
Gabriel 400 (Brooklyn, Mich., June 20, 400 miles)—Cale Yarborough; Buick; 3:23:13; 118.101 mph; $295,325; $24,700
Firecracker 400 (Daytona Beach, Fla., July 4, 400 miles)— Bobby Allison; Buick; 2:27:09; 163.099 mph; $318,675; $42,-100
Busch Nashville 420 (Nashville, Tenn., July 10, 250 miles)— Darrell Waltrip; Buick; 2:53:35; 86.524 mph; $158,575; $22,-025
Mountain Dew 500 (Mt. Pocono, Pa., July 25, 500 miles)— Bobby Allison; Buick; 4:19:45; 115.496 mph; $261,075; $24,-200
Talladega 500 (Talladega, Ala., Aug. 1, 500 miles)—Darrell Waltrip; Buick; 2:58:26; 168.157 mph; $351,725; $58,770
Champion Spark Plug 400 (Brooklyn, Mich., Aug. 22, 400 miles) —Bobby Allison; Buick; 2:45:53; 136.454 mph; $267,905; $26,900

## LITTLE LEAGUE WORLD SERIES

| | | | | | |
|---|---|---|---|---|---|
| 1947 | Williamsport, Pa. | 1959 | Hamtramck, Mich. | 1971 | Taiwan (Nationalist China) |
| 1948 | Lock Haven, Pa. | 1960 | Levittown, Pa. | 1972 | Taiwan (Nationalist China) |
| 1949 | Hammonton, N.J. | 1961 | El Cajon, Calif. | 1973 | Taiwan (Nationalist China) |
| 1950 | Houston, Tex. | 1962 | San Jose, Calif. | 1974 | Taiwan (Nationalist China) |
| 1951 | Stamford, Conn. | 1963 | Granada Hills, Calif. | 1975 | Lakewood Township, N.J. |
| 1952 | Norwalk, Conn. | 1964 | Staten Island, N.Y. | 1976 | Tokyo, Japan |
| 1953 | Birmingham, Ala. | 1965 | Windsor Locks, Conn. | 1977 | Tapei, Taiwan |
| 1954 | Schenectady, N.Y. | 1966 | Houston, Tex. | 1978–79 | Pintung, Taiwan |
| 1955 | Morrisville, Pa. | 1967 | West Tokyo, Japan | 1980 | Hua Lian, Taiwan |
| 1956 | Roswell, N.M. | 1968 | Wakayama, Japan | 1981 | Taiwan |
| 1957 | Monterrey, Mexico | 1969 | Taiwan (Nationalist China) | 1982 | Kirkland, Wash. |
| 1958 | Monterrey, Mexico | 1970 | Wayne, N.J. | | |

# SOFTBALL

*Source:* Amateur Softball Association.

## Amateur Champions

| | | | | | |
|---|---|---|---|---|---|
| 1959 | Aurora (Ill.) Sealmasters | 1969 | Raybestos Cardinals, Stratford, Conn. | 1977 | Billard Barbell, Reading, Pa. |
| 1960 | Clearwater (Fla.) Bombers | | | 1978 | Reading, Pa. |
| 1961 | Aurora (Ill.) Sealmasters | 1971 | Welty Way, Cedar Rapids, Iowa | 1979 | Midland, Mich. |
| 1962–63 | Clearwater (Fla.) Bombers | 1972 | Raybestos Cardinals, Stratford, Conn. | 1980 | Peterbilt Western, Seattle |
| 1964 | Burch Gage & Tool, Detroit | | | 1981 | Archer Daniels Midland, Decatur, Ill. |
| 1965 | Aurora (Ill.) Sealmasters | 1973 | Clearwater (Fla.) Bombers | | |
| 1966 | Clearwater (Fla.) Bombers | 1974 | Santa Rosa (Calif.) | 1982 | Peterbilt Western, Seattle |
| 1967 | Aurora (Ill.) Sealmasters | 1975 | Rising Sun Hotel, Reading, Pa. | | |
| 1968 | Clearwater (Fla.) Bombers | 1976 | Raybestos Cardinals, Stratford, Conn. | | |

### YOUTH TOURNAMENTS—1982

Boys 16–18 fast pitch—Prescott Merchants, Prescott, Ariz.

Boys 18 and under slow pitch—Turner's, Franklin, Ohio

Boys 13–15 fast pitch—Ludd's Team and Trophy House, Peoria, Ill.

Boys 13–15 slow pitch—The Swampfrogs, Pembrook Pines, Fla.

Boys 12 and under fast pitch—Baton Rouge, La.

Boys 12 and under slow pitch—East Denison, Cleveland, Ohio

Girls 16–18 fast pitch—Santa Monica Raiders, Santa Monica, Calif.

Girls 16–18 slow pitch—PDS Sunshiners, Jacksonville, Fla.

Girls 13–15 fast pitch—Tri-Valley Shilos, Sylmer, Calif.

Girls 13–15 slow pitch—The Mets, Satellite Beach, Fla.

Girls 12 and under fast pitch—Gordon's, Buena Park, Calif.

Girls 12 and under slow pitch—River City Rebels, Jacksonville, Fla.

### WORLD CHAMPION—1982*

Women's fast pitch—New Zealand

*Men's world championship not contested in 1982.

### AMATEUR SOFTBALL ASSOCIATION CHAMPIONS—1982

Men's major fast pitch—Peterbilt Western, Seattle

Women's major fast pitch—Raybestos Brakettes, Stamford, Conn.

Women's Class A fast pitch—San Diego Astros, San Diego, Calif.

Men's Class A fast pitch—Tee House, Stockton, Calif.

Men's major slow pitch—Triangle, Minneapolis, Minn.

Women's major slow pitch—Stompers, Richmond, Va.

Men's major industrial slow pitch—Sikorsky Aircraft, Shelton, Conn.

Women's industrial slow pitch—Provident Vets, Chattanooga, Tenn.

Men's Class A slow pitch—Lawson Auto Parts, Altamonte Springs, Fla.

Women's Class A slow pitch—Circle K Roadrunners, Phoenix, Ariz.

Men's Class A industrial slow pitch—General Dynamics, Detroit, Mich.

Men's modified slow pitch—Sylvestro's, Staten Island, N.Y.

Men's church slow pitch—Grace Methodist Black, Oklahoma City, Okla.

Women's church slow pitch—First Baptist Church, Tallahassee, Fla.

# VOLLEYBALL

## U.S. VOLLEYBALL ASSOCIATION CHAMPIONSHIPS

(Hilo, Hawaii, May 11–15, 1982)

**National Champions**

Men—Chuck's Steak House National, Los Angeles; runnerup: Olympic Club, San Francisco.

Women—Monarch, Honolulu; runnerup: Gym Master, Logan, Utah.

Senior men—Outrigger Canoe Club, Honolulu; runnerup: Legends Restaurant, Long Beach, Calif.

Senior women—South Bay Spoilers, Hermosa Beach, Calif.; runnerup: Alumnae, San Francisco.

Golden masters—Outrigger Canoe Club, Honolulu; runnerup, Virginia Beach, Va.

### N.C.A.A. CHAMPIONSHIPS

(Muncie, Ind., May 7–8, 1982)

**Men**

Final—U.C.L.A. defeated Penn State.

Third place—Southern California defeated Ohio State.

**Women**

Division I—Southern California

Division II—Sacramento State

Division III—University of California–San Diego

### A.I.A.W. CHAMPIONSHIPS

Division I—Texas–Austin

Division II—Hawaii–Hilo

Division III—LaVerne

# BASEBALL

The popular tradition that baseball was invented by Abner Doubleday at Cooperstown, N.Y., in 1839 has been enshrined in the Hall of Fame and National Museum of Baseball erected in that town, but research has proved that a game called "Base Ball" was played in this country and England before 1839. The first team baseball as we know it was played at the Elysian Fields, Hoboken, N.J., on June 19, 1846, between the Knickerbockers and the New York Nine. The next fifty years saw a gradual growth of baseball and an improvement of equipment and playing skill.

Historians have it that the first pitcher to throw a curve was William A. (Candy) Cummings in 1867. The Cincinnati Red Stockings were the first all-professional team, and in 1869 they played 64 games without a loss. The standard ball of the same size and weight, still the rule, was adopted in 1872. The first catcher's mask was worn in 1875. The National League was organized in 1876. The first chest protector was worn in 1885. The three-strike rule was put on the books in 1887, and the four-ball

ticket to first base was instituted in 1889. The pitching distance was lengthened to 60 feet 6 inches in 1893, and the rules have been modified only slightly since that time.

The American League, under the vigorous leadership of B. B. Johnson, became a major league in 1901. Judge Kenesaw Mountain Landis, by action of the two major leagues, became Commissioner of Baseball in 1921, and upon his death (1944), Albert B. Chandler, former United States Senator from Kentucky, was elected to that office (1945). Chandler failed to obtain a new contract and was succeeded by Ford C. Frick (1951), the National League president. Frick retired after the 1965 season, and William D. Eckert, a retired Air Force lieutenant general, was named to succeed him. Eckert resigned under pressure in December, 1968. Bowie Kuhn, a New York attorney, became interim commissioner for one year in February. His appointment was made permanent with two seven-year contracts until August 1983.

## BASEBALL PLAYERS' STRIKE HALTED 1981 SEASON FOR 7 WEEKS

A seven-week strike by major league players began on June 12 and disrupted the 1981 baseball season, canceled 713 games, caused heavy financial losses in all 26 big-league cities, and created confusion and ill-feelings among fans, players, and officials.

The major issue stemmed from a disagreement between the players and the club owners over compensation for the signing of free agents. The two sides finally worked out an agreement and the strike ended on Aug. 1. An arrangement under which teams losing a ranking free agent would receive a professional player as compensation as well as a selection in the amateur free-agent draft was the key to the accord. It also resolved a service credit issue for the players for the time lost during the strike. Service credit is used to determine eligibility for free agency and salary arbitration.

The players were allowed a week to get into con-dition and the season resumed on Aug. 10. The All-Star Game at Cleveland, postponed from its original date of July 14 because of the strike, was played on Aug. 9. Rescheduling the championship season became a problem. Normally the regular-season winners in the two divisions—Eastern and Western—in the National and American leagues meet in a best-of-five-game playoff series for their respective league pennants.

Because the 162-game regular season was shortened, officials decided to split the season into two halves. The four leaders in the two leagues when the strike began were declared champions of the first half. The four leaders in the second half were also declared champions. Those teams played off in a preliminary, or miniseries, playoff round. The survivors played off for their respective league pennants and the right to move on to the World Series, which started on Oct. 20, much later than usual.

### AMERICAN LEAGUE*
### (Final Standing—1981)

#### EASTERN DIVISION
#### FIRST-HALF SEASON

| Team | W | L | Pct | GB |
|---|---|---|---|---|
| New York Yankees* | 34 | 22 | .607 | — |
| Baltimore Orioles | 31 | 23 | .574 | 2 |
| Milwaukee Brewers | 31 | 25 | .554 | 3 |
| Detroit Tigers | 31 | 26 | .544 | 3½ |
| Boston Red Sox | 30 | 26 | .536 | 4 |
| Cleveland Indians | 26 | 24 | .520 | 5 |
| Toronto Blue Jays | 16 | 42 | .276 | 19 |

#### WESTERN DIVISION

| | W | L | Pct | GB |
|---|---|---|---|---|
| Oakland A's* | 37 | 23 | .617 | — |
| Texas Rangers | 33 | 22 | .600 | 1½ |
| Chicago White Sox | 31 | 22 | .585 | 2½ |
| California Angels | 31 | 29 | .517 | 6 |
| Kansas City Royals | 20 | 30 | .400 | 12 |
| Seattle Mariners | 21 | 36 | .368 | 14½ |
| Minnesota Twins | 17 | 39 | .304 | 28 |

### SECOND-HALF SEASON
#### EASTERN DIVISION

| | W | L | Pct | GB |
|---|---|---|---|---|
| Milwaukee Brewers* | 31 | 22 | .585 | — |
| Boston Red Sox | 29 | 23 | .558 | 1½ |
| Detroit Tigers | 29 | 23 | .558 | 1½ |
| Baltimore Orioles | 28 | 23 | .549 | 2 |
| Cleveland Indians | 26 | 27 | .491 | 5 |
| New York Yankees | 25 | 26 | .490 | 5 |
| Toronto Blue Jays | 21 | 27 | .438 | 7½ |

#### WESTERN DIVISION

| | W | L | Pct | GB |
|---|---|---|---|---|
| Kansas City Royals* | 30 | 23 | .566 | — |
| Oakland A's | 27 | 22 | .551 | 1 |
| Texas Rangers | 24 | 26 | .480 | 4½ |
| Minnesota Twins | 24 | 29 | .453 | 6 |
| Seattle Mariners | 23 | 29 | .442 | 6½ |
| Chicago White Sox | 23 | 30 | .434 | 7 |
| California Angels | 20 | 30 | .400 | 8½ |

*Qualified for postseason playoffs.

## AMERICAN LEAGUE PLAYOFFS
### EASTERN DIVISION—Preliminary Round
**1st game, Milwaukee, Oct. 7**

| | | | | | |
|---|---|---|---|---|---|
| New York | 000 | 400 | 001—5 | 13 | 1 |
| Milwaukee | 011 | 010 | 000—3 | 8 | 3 |

Guidry, Davis (5), Gossage (8); Haas, Bernard (4), McClure (5), Slaton (6), Fingers (8). Winner: Davis; Loser: Haas. Home run: New York: Gamble. Attendance: 35,064.

**2nd game, Milwaukee, Oct. 8**

| | | | | | |
|---|---|---|---|---|---|
| New York | 000 | 100 | 002—3 | 7 | 0 |
| Milwaukee | 000 | 000 | 000—0 | 7 | 0 |

Righetti, Davis (7), Gossage (7); Caldwell, Slaton (9). Winner: Righetti; Loser: Caldwell. Home runs: New York: Piniella, Jackson. Attendance: 26,395.

**3rd game, New York, Oct. 9**

| | | | | | |
|---|---|---|---|---|---|
| Milwaukee | 000 | 000 | 320—5 | 9 | 0 |
| New York | 000 | 100 | 200—3 | 8 | 2 |

Lerch, Fingers (7); John, May (8). Winner: Fingers; Loser: John. Home runs: Milwaukee: Simmons, Molitor. Attendance: 54,171.

**4th game, New York, Oct. 10**

| | | | | | |
|---|---|---|---|---|---|
| Milwaukee | 000 | 200 | 000—2 | 4 | 2 |
| New York | 000 | 001 | 000—1 | 5 | 0 |

Vuckovich, Easterly (6), Slaton (7), McClure (8), Fingers (9); Reuschel, R. Davis (7). Winner: Vuckovich; Loser: Reuschel. Attendance: 52,077.

**5th game, New York, Oct. 11**

| | | | | | |
|---|---|---|---|---|---|
| Milwaukee | 011 | 000 | 100—3 | 8 | 0 |
| New York | 000 | 400 | 12x—7 | 13 | 0 |

Haas, Caldwell (4), Bernard (4), McClure (6), Slaton (7), Easterly (8), Vuckovich (8); Guidry, Righetti (5), Gossage (8). Winner: Righetti; Loser: Haas. Home runs: Milwaukee: Thomas; New York: Jackson, Gamble, Cerone. Attendance: 47,505.

### WESTERN DIVISION—Preliminary Round
**1st game, Kansas City, Oct. 6**

| | | | | | |
|---|---|---|---|---|---|
| Oakland | 000 | 300 | 010—4 | 8 | 2 |
| Kansas City | 000 | 000 | 000—0 | 4 | 1 |

Norris; Leonard, Martin (9). Winner: Norris; Loser: Leonard. Home runs: Oakland: Gross, Murphy. Attendance: 40,592.

**2nd game, Kansas City, Oct. 7**

| | | | | | |
|---|---|---|---|---|---|
| Oakland | 100 | 000 | 010—2 | 10 | 1 |
| Kansas City | 000 | 010 | 000—1 | 6 | 0 |

McCatty; Jones, Quisenberry (9). Winner: McCatty; Loser: Jones. Attendance: 40,274.

**3rd game, Oakland, Oct. 9**

| | | | | | |
|---|---|---|---|---|---|
| Kansas City | 000 | 100 | 000—1 | 10 | 0 |
| Oakland | 101 | 200 | 00X—4 | 7 | 0 |

Gura, Martin (4); Langford, Underwood (8), Beard (8). Winner: Langford; Loser: Gura. Home run: Oakland: McKay. Attendance: 40,002.

### CHAMPIONSHIP ROUND
**1st game, New York, Oct. 13**

| | | | | | |
|---|---|---|---|---|---|
| Oakland | 000 | 010 | 000—1 | 6 | 1 |
| New York | 300 | 000 | 00X—3 | 7 | 1 |

Norris, Underwood (8); John, Davis (7), Gossage (8). Winner: John; Loser: Norris. Attendance: 55,740.

**2nd game, New York, Oct. 14**

| | | | | | |
|---|---|---|---|---|---|
| Oakland | 001 | 200 | 000—3 | 11 | 1 |
| New York | 100 | 701 | 40x—13 | 19 | 0 |

McCatty, Beard (4), Jones (5), Kingman (7), Owchinko (7); May, Frazier (4). Winner: Frazier; Loser: McCatty. Home runs: New York: Piniella, Nettles. Attendance: 48,497.

**3rd game, Oakland, Oct. 15**

| | | | | | |
|---|---|---|---|---|---|
| New York | 000 | 001 | 003—4 | 10 | 2 |
| Oakland | 000 | 000 | 000—0 | 5 | 0 |

Righetti, Davis (7), Gossage (9); Keough, Underwood (9). Winner: Righetti; Loser: Keough. Home run: New York: Randolph. Attendance: 47,302.

## NATIONAL LEAGUE*
### (Final Standing—1981)

### EASTERN DIVISION
#### FIRST-HALF SEASON

| Team | W | L | Pct | GB |
|---|---|---|---|---|
| Philadelphia Phillies* | 34 | 21 | .618 | — |
| St. Louis Cardinals | 30 | 20 | .600 | 1½ |
| Montreal Expos | 30 | 25 | .545 | 4 |
| Pittsburgh Pirates | 25 | 23 | .521 | 5½ |
| New York Mets | 17 | 34 | .333 | 15 |
| Chicago Cubs | 15 | 37 | .288 | 17½ |

#### WESTERN DIVISION

| | W | L | Pct | GB |
|---|---|---|---|---|
| Los Angeles Dodgers* | 36 | 21 | .632 | — |
| Cincinnati Reds | 35 | 21 | .625 | ½ |
| Houston Astros | 28 | 29 | .491 | 8 |
| Atlanta Braves | 25 | 29 | .463 | 9½ |
| San Francisco Giants | 27 | 32 | .458 | 10 |
| San Diego Padres | 23 | 33 | .411 | 12½ |

#### SECOND-HALF SEASON
### EASTERN DIVISION

| | W | L | Pct | GB |
|---|---|---|---|---|
| Montreal Expos* | 30 | 23 | .566 | — |
| St. Louis Cardinals | 29 | 23 | .558 | ½ |
| Philadelphia Phillies | 25 | 27 | .481 | 4½ |
| New York Mets | 24 | 28 | .462 | 5½ |
| Chicago Cubs | 23 | 28 | .451 | 6 |
| Pittsburgh Pirates | 21 | 33 | .389 | 9½ |

#### WESTERN DIVISION

| | W | L | Pct | GB |
|---|---|---|---|---|
| Houston Astros* | 33 | 20 | .623 | — |
| Cincinnati Reds | 31 | 21 | .596 | 1½ |
| San Francisco Giants | 29 | 23 | .558 | 3½ |
| Los Angeles Dodgers | 27 | 26 | .509 | 6 |
| Atlanta Braves | 25 | 27 | .481 | 7½ |
| San Diego Padres | 18 | 36 | .333 | 15½ |

*Qualified for postseason playoffs.

## NATIONAL LEAGUE PLAYOFFS
### EASTERN DIVISION—Preliminary Round
**1st game, Montreal, Oct. 7**

| | | | | | |
|---|---|---|---|---|---|
| Philadelphia | 010 | 000 | 000—1 | 10 | 1 |
| Montreal | 110 | 100 | 00X—3 | 8 | 0 |

Carlton, R. Reed (7); Rogers, Reardon (9). Winner: Rogers; Loser: Carlton. Home run: Philadelphia: Moreland. Attendance: 34,327.

**2nd game, Montreal, Oct. 8**

| | | | | | |
|---|---|---|---|---|---|
| Philadelphia | 000 | 000 | 010—1 | 6 | 2 |
| Montreal | 012 | 000 | 00X—3 | 7 | 0 |

Ruthven, Brusstar (5), Lyle (7), McGraw (8); Gullickson, Reardon (8). Winner: Gullickson; Loser: Ruthven. Home run:

Montreal: Carter. Attendance: 45,896.

### 3rd game, Philadelphia, Oct. 9

| | | | | | |
|---|---|---|---|---|---|
| Montreal | 010 | 000 | 010—2 | 8 | 4 |
| Philadelphia | 020 | 002 | 20X—6 | 13 | 0 |

Burris, Lee (6), Sosa (7); Christenson, Lyle (7), R. Reed (8). Winner: Christenson; Loser: Burris. Attendance: 36,835.

### 4th game, Philadelphia, Oct. 10 (10 innings)

| | | | | | | |
|---|---|---|---|---|---|---|
| Montreal | 000 | 112 | 100 | 0—5 | 10 | 1 |
| Philadelphia | 202 | 001 | 000 | 1—6 | 9 | 0 |

Sanderson, Bahnsen (3), Sosa (5), Fryman (6), Reardon (7); Noles, Brusstar (5), Lyle (6), R. Reed (7), McGraw (8). Winner: McGraw; Loser: Reardon. Home runs: Montreal: Carter. Philadelphia: Schmidt, Matthews, G. Vukovich. Attendance: 38,818.

### 5th game, Philadelphia, Oct. 11

| | | | | | |
|---|---|---|---|---|---|
| Montreal | 000 | 021 | 000—3 | 8 | 1 |
| Philadelphia | 000 | 000 | 000—0 | 6 | 0 |

Rogers; Carlton, R. Reed (9). Winner: Rogers; Loser: Carlton. Attendance: 47,384.

### WESTERN DIVISION—Preliminary Round
### 1st game, Houston, Oct. 6

| | | | | | |
|---|---|---|---|---|---|
| Los Angeles | 000 | 000 | 1000—1 | 2 | 0 |
| Houston | 000 | 001 | 002—3 | 8 | 0 |

Valenzuela, Stewart (9); Ryan. Winner: Ryan; Loser: Stewart. Home runs: Los Angeles: Garvey; Houston: Ashby. Attendance: 44,836

### 2nd game, Houston, Oct. 7 (11 innings)

| | | | | | | |
|---|---|---|---|---|---|---|
| Los Angeles | 000 | 000 | 000 | 00—0 | 9 | 1 |
| Houston | 000 | 000 | 000 | 01—1 | 9 | 0 |

Reuss, S. Howe (10), Stewart (11), Forster (11), Niedenfuer (11); Niekro, D. Smith (10), Sambito (11). Winner: Sambito; Loser: Stewart. Attendance: 42,398

### 3rd game, Los Angeles, Oct. 9

| | | | | | |
|---|---|---|---|---|---|
| Houston | 001 | 000 | 000—1 | 3 | 2 |
| Los Angeles | 300 | 000 | 03X—6 | 10 | 0 |

Knepper, LaCorte (6), Sambito (8), B. Smith (8); Hooton, S. Howe (8), Welch (8). Winner: Hooton; Loser: Knepper. Home runs: Houston: A. Howe; Los Angeles: Garvey. Attendance: 46,820.

### 4th game, Los Angeles, Oct. 10

| | | | | | |
|---|---|---|---|---|---|
| Houston | 000 | 000 | 001—1 | 4 | 0 |
| Los Angeles | 000 | 010 | 10X—2 | 4 | 0 |

Ruhle; Valenzuela. Winner: Valenzuela; Loser: Ruhle. Home run: Los Angeles: Guerrero. Attendance: 55,983.

### 5th game, Los Angeles, Oct. 11

| | | | | | |
|---|---|---|---|---|---|
| Houston | 000 | 000 | 000—0 | 5 | 3 |
| Los Angeles | 000 | 003 | 10X—4 | 7 | 2 |

Ryan, D. Smith (7), LaCorte (7); Reuss. Winner: Reuss; Loser: Ryan. Attendance: 55,979.

### CHAMPIONSHIP ROUND
### 1st game, Los Angeles, Oct. 13

| | | | | | |
|---|---|---|---|---|---|
| Montreal | 000 | 000 | 001—1 | 9 | 0 |
| Los Angeles | 020 | 000 | 03X—5 | 8 | 0 |

Gullickson, Reardon (8); Hooton, Welch (8), Howe (9). Winner: Hooton; Loser: Gullickson. Home runs: Los Angeles: Guerrero, Scioscia. Attendance: 51,273.

### 2nd game, Los Angeles, Oct. 14

| | | | | | |
|---|---|---|---|---|---|
| Montreal | 020 | 001 | 000—3 | 10 | 1 |
| Los Angeles | 000 | 000 | 000—0 | 5 | 1 |

Burris; Valenzuela, Niedenfuer (7), Forster (7), Pena (7), Castillo (9). Winner: Burris; Loser: Valenzuela. Attendance: 53,463.

### 3rd game, Montreal, Oct. 16

| | | | | | |
|---|---|---|---|---|---|
| Los Angeles | 000 | 100 | 000—1 | 7 | 0 |
| Montreal | 000 | 004 | 00X—4 | 7 | 1 |

Ruess, Pena (8); Rogers. Winner: Rogers; Loser: Reuss. Home run: Montreal: White. Attendance: 54,372.

### 4th game, Montreal, Oct. 17

| | | | | | |
|---|---|---|---|---|---|
| Los Angeles | 001 | 000 | 024—7 | 12 | 1 |
| Montreal | 000 | 100 | 000—1 | 5 | 1 |

Hooton, Welch (8), Howe (9); Gullickson, Fryman (8), Sosa (9), Lee (9). Winner: Hooton; Loser: Gullickson. Home run: Los Angeles: Garvey. Attendance: 54,499.

### 5th game, Montreal, Oct. 19

| | | | | | |
|---|---|---|---|---|---|
| Los Angeles | 000 | 010 | 001—2 | 6 | 0 |
| Montreal | 100 | 000 | 000—1 | 3 | 1 |

Valenzuela, Welch (9); Burris, Rogers (9). Winner: Valenzuela; Loser: Rogers. Home runs: Los Angeles: Monday. Attendance: 36,491.

## AMERICAN LEAGUE LEADERS—1981

| | |
|---|---|
| Batting—Carney Lansford, Boston | .336 |
| Runs—Rickey Henderson, Oakland | 89 |
| Hits—Rickey Henderson, Oakland | 135 |
| Runs batted in—Eddie Murray, Baltimore | 78 |
| Doubles—Cecil Cooper, Milwaukee | 35 |
| Triples—John Castino, Minnesota | 9 |
| Home runs—Eddie Murray, Baltimore | 22 |
| Dwight Evans, Boston | 22 |
| Bobby Grich, California | 22 |
| Tony Armas, Oakland | 22 |
| Stolen Bases—Rickey Henderson, Oakland | 56 |
| Pitching | |
| Victories—Jack Morris, Detroit | 14 |
| Dennis Martinez, Baltimore | 14 |
| Bill Vuckovich, Milwaukee | 14 |
| Steve McCatty, Oakland | 14 |
| Earned-run average—Steve McCatty, Oakland | 2.32 |
| Strikeouts—Len Barker, Cleveland | 127 |
| Shutouts—Steve McCatty, Oakland | 4 |
| Ken Forsch, California | 4 |
| Richard Dotson, Chicago | 4 |
| Doc Medich, Texas | 4 |

## NATIONAL LEAGUE LEADERS—1981

| | |
|---|---|
| Batting—Bill Madlock, Pittsburgh | .341 |
| Runs—Mike Schmidt, Philadelphia | 78 |
| Hits—Pete Rose, Philadelphia | 140 |
| Runs batted in—Mike Schmidt, Philadelphia | 91 |
| Doubles—Bill Buckner, Chicago | 35 |
| Triples—Craig Reynolds, Houston | 12 |
| Gene Richards, San Diego | 12 |
| Home runs—Mike Schmidt, Philadelphia | 31 |
| Stolen bases—Tim Raines, Montreal | 71 |
| Pitching— | |
| Victories—Tom Seaver, Cincinnati | 14 |
| Earned-run average—Nolan Ryan, Houston | 1.69 |
| Strikeouts—Fernando Valenzuela, Los Angeles | 180 |
| Shutouts—Fernando Valenzuela, Los Angeles | 8 |

## AMERICAN LEAGUE AVERAGES—1981
(Unofficial)

### Batting—Club

| | AB | R | H | HR | RBI | PCT |
|---|---|---|---|---|---|---|
| Boston | 3,820 | 519 | 1,052 | 90 | 493 | .275 |
| Chicago | 3,615 | 476 | 982 | 76 | 435 | .272 |
| Texas | 3,582 | 452 | 968 | 49 | 418 | .270 |
| Kansas City | 3,562 | 397 | 952 | 61 | 381 | .267 |
| Cleveland | 3,507 | 431 | 922 | 38 | 397 | .263 |
| Milwaukee | 3,743 | 493 | 961 | 97 | 477 | .257 |
| Detroit | 3,599 | 427 | 922 | 65 | 403 | .256 |
| California | 3,688 | 476 | 944 | 97 | 439 | .256 |
| New York | 3,528 | 421 | 889 | 100 | 403 | .252 |
| Seattle | 3,780 | 436 | 950 | 89 | 405 | .251 |
| Baltimore | 3,516 | 429 | 883 | 88 | 408 | .251 |
| Oakland | 3,678 | 458 | 910 | 104 | 429 | .247 |
| Minnesota | 3,776 | 378 | 884 | 48 | 358 | .234 |
| Toronto | 3,521 | 329 | 797 | 61 | 315 | .226 |

### Batting Leaders

| Player/team | AB | R | H | HR | RBI | PCT |
|---|---|---|---|---|---|---|
| Lansford, Boston | 399 | 61 | 134 | 4 | 52 | .336 |
| Gibson, Detroit | 290 | 41 | 95 | 9 | 40 | .329 |
| Paciorek, Seattle | 405 | 50 | 132 | 14 | 66 | .326 |
| C. Cooper, Milwaukee | 416 | 70 | 133 | 12 | 60 | .320 |
| R. Henderson, Oakland | 423 | 89 | 135 | 6 | 35 | .319 |
| Hargrove, Cleveland | 322 | 44 | 102 | 2 | 49 | .317 |
| G. Brett, Kansas City | 347 | 42 | 109 | 6 | 43 | .314 |
| Zisk, Seattle | 357 | 42 | 111 | 16 | 55 | .311 |
| Oliver, Texas | 421 | 53 | 130 | 4 | 55 | .309 |
| Remy, Boston | 358 | 55 | 110 | 0 | 31 | .307 |
| Murphy, New York | 320 | 44 | 98 | 6 | 32 | .306 |
| Carew, California | 364 | 57 | 111 | 2 | 21 | .305 |
| Murray, Baltimore | 378 | 57 | 115 | 22 | 78 | .304 |
| Grich, California | 352 | 56 | 107 | 22 | 61 | .304 |
| Wilson, Kansas City | 439 | 54 | 133 | 1 | 32 | .303 |
| Lemon, Chicago | 328 | 51 | 99 | 9 | 50 | .302 |
| Almon, Chicago | 349 | 46 | 105 | 4 | 40 | .301 |
| Evans, Boston | 412 | 84 | 122 | 22 | 71 | .296 |
| B. Bell, Texas | 360 | 44 | 106 | 10 | 64 | .294 |
| Winfield, New York | 388 | 52 | 114 | 13 | 68 | .294 |
| Burleson, California | 431 | 53 | 126 | 5 | 33 | .292 |
| Miller, Boston | 316 | 38 | 92 | 2 | 33 | .291 |
| Harrah, Cleveland | 361 | 64 | 105 | 5 | 44 | .291 |
| Baines, Chicago | 280 | 43 | 80 | 10 | 41 | .286 |
| Rivers, Texas | 399 | 62 | 114 | 3 | 26 | .286 |
| Stapleton, Boston | 355 | 45 | 101 | 10 | 42 | .285 |

### Leading Pitchers
(110 or more innings)

| Player/team | IP | H | BB | SO | W | L | ERA |
|---|---|---|---|---|---|---|---|
| McCatty, Oakland | 186 | 140 | 61 | 91 | 14 | 7 | 2.32 |
| Stewart, Baltimore | 112 | 89 | 57 | 57 | 4 | 8 | 2.33 |
| Lamp, Chicago | 127 | 103 | 43 | 71 | 7 | 6 | 2.41 |
| John, New York | 140 | 135 | 39 | 50 | 9 | 8 | 2.64 |
| Burns, Chicago | 157 | 139 | 49 | 108 | 10 | 6 | 2.64 |
| Gura, Kansas City | 172 | 139 | 35 | 61 | 11 | 8 | 2.72 |
| Guidry, New York | 127 | 101 | 26 | 104 | 11 | 5 | 2.76 |
| Blyleven, Cleveland | 159 | 145 | 40 | 107 | 11 | 7 | 2.89 |
| Forsch, California | 153 | 143 | 27 | 55 | 11 | 7 | 2.94 |
| Leonard, Kansas City | 202 | 202 | 41 | 107 | 13 | 11 | 2.99 |
| Langford, Oakland | 195 | 190 | 58 | 84 | 12 | 10 | 3.00 |
| Petry, Detroit | 141 | 115 | 57 | 79 | 10 | 9 | 3.00 |

## NATIONAL LEAGUE AVERAGES—1981
(Unofficial)

### Batting—Club

| | AB | R | H | HR | RBI | PCT |
|---|---|---|---|---|---|---|
| Philadelphia | 3,665 | 491 | 1,002 | 69 | 453 | .273 |
| Cincinnati | 3,637 | 464 | 972 | 64 | 429 | .267 |
| St. Louis | 3,538 | 464 | 936 | 50 | 431 | .265 |
| Los Angeles | 3,751 | 450 | 984 | 82 | 427 | .262 |
| Pittsburgh | 3,576 | 407 | 920 | 55 | 384 | .257 |
| Houston | 3,693 | 394 | 948 | 45 | 369 | .257 |
| San Diego | 3,758 | 382 | 963 | 32 | 350 | .256 |
| San Francisco | 3,765 | 427 | 941 | 63 | 399 | .256 |
| New York | 3,493 | 348 | 868 | 57 | 323 | .249 |
| Montreal | 3,591 | 443 | 883 | 81 | 407 | .246 |
| Atlanta | 3,642 | 395 | 886 | 64 | 366 | .243 |
| Chicago | 3,546 | 370 | 838 | 57 | 348 | .236 |

### Batting Leaders

| Player/team | AB | R | H | HR | RBI | PCT |
|---|---|---|---|---|---|---|
| Madlock, Pittsburgh | 279 | 35 | 95 | 6 | 45 | .341 |
| Rose, Philadelphia | 431 | 73 | 140 | 0 | 33 | .325 |
| Baker, Los Angeles | 400 | 48 | 128 | 9 | 49 | .320 |
| Schmidt, Philadelphia | 354 | 78 | 112 | 31 | 91 | .316 |
| Buckner, Chicago | 421 | 45 | 131 | 10 | 75 | .311 |
| Griffey, Cincinnati | 396 | 64 | 123 | 2 | 34 | .310 |
| May, San Francisco | 316 | 20 | 98 | 2 | 33 | .310 |
| Brooks, New York | 358 | 34 | 110 | 4 | 38 | .307 |
| Concepcion, Cincinnati | 421 | 57 | 129 | 5 | 67 | .306 |
| Hernandez, St. Louis | 376 | 65 | 115 | 8 | 48 | .306 |
| Cromartie, Montreal | 358 | 41 | 109 | 6 | 42 | .304 |
| Raines, Montreal | 313 | 61 | 95 | 5 | 37 | .304 |
| Salazar, San Diego | 400 | 37 | 121 | 3 | 38 | .303 |
| Dawson, Montreal | 394 | 71 | 119 | 24 | 64 | .302 |
| T. Kennedy, San Diego | 382 | 32 | 115 | 2 | 41 | .301 |
| Matthews, Philadelphia | 359 | 62 | 108 | 8 | 67 | .301 |
| Guerrero, Los Angeles | 347 | 46 | 104 | 12 | 48 | .300 |
| A. Howe, Houston | 361 | 43 | 107 | 3 | 36 | .296 |
| Foster, Cincinnati | 414 | 64 | 122 | 22 | 90 | .295 |
| Henderson, Chicago | 287 | 32 | 84 | 5 | 35 | .293 |
| Oberkfell, St. Louis | 376 | 43 | 110 | 2 | 45 | .293 |
| Washington, Atlanta | 320 | 37 | 93 | 5 | 37 | .291 |
| Bonilla, San Diego | 369 | 30 | 107 | 1 | 25 | .290 |
| Durham, Chicago | 328 | 42 | 95 | 10 | 35 | .290 |
| Cey, Los Angeles | 312 | 42 | 90 | 13 | 50 | .288 |
| Herndon, San Francisco | 364 | 48 | 105 | 5 | 41 | .288 |
| Templeton, St. Louis | 333 | 47 | 96 | 1 | 33 | .288 |
| Richards, San Diego | 393 | 47 | 113 | 3 | 42 | .288 |

### Leading Pitchers
(110 or More Innings)

| Player/team | IP | H | BB | SO | W | L | ERA |
|---|---|---|---|---|---|---|---|
| Ryan, Houston | 149 | 99 | 68 | 140 | 11 | 5 | 1.69 |
| Knepper, Houston | 157 | 128 | 38 | 75 | 9 | 5 | 2.18 |
| Hooton, Los Angeles | 142 | 124 | 33 | 74 | 11 | 6 | 2.28 |
| Reuss, Los Angeles | 153 | 138 | 27 | 51 | 10 | 4 | 2.29 |
| Carlton, Philadelphia | 190 | 152 | 62 | 179 | 13 | 4 | 2.42 |
| Blue, San Francisco | 125 | 97 | 54 | 63 | 8 | 6 | 2.45 |
| Valenzuela, Los Angeles | 192 | 140 | 61 | 180 | 13 | 7 | 2.48 |
| Seaver, Cincinnati | 166 | 120 | 66 | 87 | 14 | 2 | 2.55 |
| Sutton, Houston | 159 | 132 | 29 | 104 | 11 | 9 | 2.60 |

# FIELD HOCKEY—1982

World Cup men—Pakistan
International Cup women—Netherlands

# BIATHLON

## WORLD CHAMPIONSHIPS—1982

Men's 10 kilometers—Erik Kvalfoss, Norway
Men's 20 kilometers—Frank Ullrich, East Germany
World Cup—Frank Ullrich

### WORLD SERIES—1981
Los Angeles Dodgers (NL) defeated New York Yankees (AL), 4 games to 2

#### 1st Game—New York, Oct. 20

**LOS ANGELES (NL)**

| | AB | R | H | BI |
|---|---|---|---|---|
| Lopes, 2b | 3 | 1 | 0 | 0 |
| Russell, ss | 3 | 0 | 0 | 0 |
| Johnstone, ph | 1 | 0 | 1 | 1 |
| Stewart, p | 0 | 0 | 0 | 0 |
| Baker, lf | 2 | 0 | 1 | 1 |
| Garvey, 1b | 4 | 0 | 1 | 0 |
| Cey, 3b | 4 | 0 | 1 | 0 |
| Guerrero, cf | 3 | 0 | 0 | 0 |
| Monday, rf | 4 | 0 | 0 | 0 |
| Yeager, c | 3 | 1 | 1 | 1 |
| Landreaux, ph | 1 | 0 | 0 | 0 |
| Reuss, p | 1 | 0 | 0 | 0 |
| Castillo, p | 0 | 0 | 0 | 0 |
| Goltz, p | 0 | 0 | 0 | 0 |
| Sax, ph | 1 | 0 | 0 | 0 |
| Niedenfuer, p | 0 | 0 | 0 | 0 |
| Thomas, ss | 0 | 1 | 0 | 0 |
| **Total** | **30** | **3** | **5** | **3** |

**NEW YORK (AL)**

| | AB | R | H | BI |
|---|---|---|---|---|
| Randolph, 2b | 3 | 0 | 0 | 0 |
| Mumphrey, cf | 3 | 2 | 2 | 0 |
| Winfield, lf | 3 | 0 | 0 | 1 |
| Piniella, rf | 4 | 1 | 2 | 1 |
| Watson, 1b | 3 | 1 | 2 | 3 |
| Nettles, 3b | 3 | 0 | 0 | 0 |
| Cerone, c | 3 | 0 | 0 | 0 |
| Milbourne, ss | 4 | 1 | 0 | 0 |
| Guidry, p | 2 | 0 | 0 | 0 |
| Davis, p | 0 | 0 | 0 | 0 |
| Gossage, p | 0 | 0 | 0 | 0 |
| **Total** | **28** | **5** | **6** | **5** |

| | | | | | | |
|---|---|---|---|---|---|---|
| Los Angeles | 000 | 000 | 000—0 |
| New York | 000 | 010 | 02X—3 |

E—Milbourne, Lopes, Stewart. DR—Los Angeles. LOB—Los Angeles 6, New York 9. 2B—Milbourne. S—John, Murcer. SF—Randolph.

| | IP | H | R | ER | BB | SO |
|---|---|---|---|---|---|---|
| **Los Angeles** | | | | | | |
| Hooton (L) | 6 | 3 | 1 | 0 | 4 | 1 |
| Forster | 1 | 0 | 0 | 0 | 1 | 0 |
| Howe | 1/3 | 2 | 2 | 2 | 0 | 0 |
| Stewart | 2/3 | 1 | 0 | 0 | 1 | 1 |
| **New York** | | | | | | |
| John (W) | 7 | 3 | 0 | 0 | 0 | 4 |
| Gossage (S) | 2 | 1 | 0 | 0 | 1 | 3 |

Hooton pitched to 2 batters in the seventh. Time of game—2:29. Attendance—56,505

#### 3rd Game—Los Angeles, Oct. 23

**NEW YORK (AL)**

| | AB | R | H | BI |
|---|---|---|---|---|
| Randolph, 2b | 2 | 0 | 0 | 0 |
| Mumphrey, cf | 5 | 0 | 0 | 0 |
| Winfield, lf | 3 | 0 | 0 | 0 |
| Piniella, rf | 5 | 1 | 1 | 0 |
| Watson, 1b | 4 | 1 | 2 | 1 |
| Cerone, c | 4 | 2 | 2 | 1 |
| Rodriguez, 3b | 4 | 0 | 2 | 0 |
| Milbourne, ss | 2 | 0 | 2 | 1 |
| Righetti, p | 1 | 0 | 0 | 0 |
| Frazier, p | 1 | 0 | 0 | 0 |
| May, p | 0 | 0 | 0 | 0 |
| Murcer, ph | 1 | 0 | 0 | 0 |
| Davis, p | 0 | 0 | 0 | 0 |
| **Total** | **32** | **4** | **9** | **3** |

**LOS ANGELES (NL)**

| | AB | R | H | BI |
|---|---|---|---|---|
| Lopes, 2b | 4 | 1 | 2 | 0 |
| Russell, ss | 5 | 1 | 2 | 0 |
| Baker, lf | 4 | 0 | 0 | 0 |
| Garvey, 1b | 4 | 1 | 2 | 0 |
| Cey, 3b | 2 | 2 | 2 | 3 |
| Guerrero, cf | 3 | 0 | 1 | 1 |
| Monday, rf | 2 | 0 | 1 | 0 |
| Thomas, rf | 1 | 0 | 0 | 0 |
| Yeager, c | 1 | 0 | 0 | 0 |
| Scioscia, c | 3 | 0 | 1 | 0 |
| Valenzuela, p | 3 | 0 | 0 | 0 |
| **Total** | **32** | **5** | **11** | **4** |

| | | | | |
|---|---|---|---|---|
| New York | 022 | 000 | 000—4 |
| Los Angeles | 300 | 020 | 00X—5 |

E—Lopes. DP—New York 2, Los Angeles 3. LOB—New York 9, Los Angeles 9. 2B—Lopes, Cerone, Watson, Guerrero. HR—Cey, Watson, Cerone. S—Righetti, Lopes.

| | IP | H | R | ER | BB | SO |
|---|---|---|---|---|---|---|
| **New York** | | | | | | |
| Righetti | 2 | 5 | 3 | 3 | 2 | 1 |
| Frazier (L) | 2 | 3 | 2 | 2 | 2 | 1 |
| May | 3 | 2 | 0 | 0 | 0 | 2 |
| Davis | 1 | 1 | 0 | 0 | 0 | 1 |
| **Los Angeles** | | | | | | |
| Valenzuela (W) | 9 | 9 | 4 | 4 | 7 | 6 |

HBP—by Righetti (Guerrero). Time of game—3:04. Attendance—56,236.

#### 2nd Game—New York, Oct. 21

**LOS ANGELES (NL)**

| | AB | R | H | BI |
|---|---|---|---|---|
| Lopes, 2b | 3 | 0 | 0 | 0 |
| Monday, ph | 1 | 0 | 0 | 0 |
| Howe, p | 0 | 0 | 0 | 0 |
| Stewart, p | 0 | 0 | 0 | 0 |
| Russell, ss | 4 | 0 | 1 | 0 |
| Baker, lf | 4 | 0 | 0 | 0 |
| Garvey, 1b | 3 | 0 | 2 | 0 |
| Cey, 3b | 4 | 0 | 0 | 0 |
| Guerrero, rf | 4 | 0 | 0 | 0 |
| Landreaux, cf | 3 | 0 | 0 | 0 |
| Yeager, c | 2 | 0 | 0 | 0 |
| Johnstone, ph | 1 | 0 | 0 | 0 |
| Scioscia, c | 0 | 0 | 0 | 0 |
| Hooton, p | 2 | 0 | 0 | 0 |
| Forster, p | 0 | 0 | 0 | 0 |
| Smith, ph | 1 | 0 | 1 | 0 |
| Sax, 2b | 0 | 0 | 0 | 0 |
| **Total** | **32** | **0** | **4** | **0** |

**NEW YORK (AL)**

| | AB | R | H | BI |
|---|---|---|---|---|
| Mumphrey, cf | 3 | 0 | 0 | 0 |
| Milbourne, ss | 4 | 0 | 1 | 1 |
| Winfield, lf | 4 | 0 | 0 | 0 |
| Gamble, rf | 2 | 0 | 0 | 0 |
| Piniella, ph | 1 | 0 | 1 | 0 |
| Brown, rf | 0 | 1 | 0 | 0 |
| Nettles, 3b | 4 | 1 | 2 | 0 |
| Watson, 1b | 4 | 0 | 2 | 1 |
| Cerone, c | 2 | 0 | 0 | 0 |
| Randolph, 2b | 2 | 1 | 0 | 1 |
| John, p | 1 | 0 | 0 | 0 |
| Murcer, ph | 0 | 0 | 0 | 0 |
| Gossage, p | 1 | 0 | 0 | 0 |
| **Total** | **27** | **3** | **6** | **3** |

| | | | | |
|---|---|---|---|---|
| Los Angeles | 000 | 010 | 020—3 |
| New York | 301 | 100 | 00X—5 |

DP—Los Angeles. LOB—Los Angeles 5, New York 6. 2B—Piniella. HR—Watson, Yeager. SB—Mumphrey, Piniella. S—Guidry. SF—Baker.

| | IP | H | R | ER | BB | SO |
|---|---|---|---|---|---|---|
| **Los Angeles** | | | | | | |
| Reuss (L) | 2 2/3 | 5 | 4 | 4 | 0 | 2 |
| Castillo | 1 | 0 | 1 | 1 | 5 | 0 |
| Goltz | 1/3 | 0 | 0 | 0 | 0 | 0 |
| Niedenfuer | 3 | 1 | 0 | 0 | 0 | 0 |
| Stewart | 1 | 0 | 0 | 0 | 1 | 0 |
| **New York** | | | | | | |
| Guidry (W) | 7 | 4 | 1 | 1 | 2 | 6 |
| Davis | 0 | 0 | 2 | 2 | 2 | 0 |
| Gossage (S) | 2 | 1 | 0 | 0 | 0 | 2 |

PB—Cerone. Time of game—2:32. Attendance—56,470.

## COLLEGE BASEBALL

### 1982 CHAMPIONS

N.C.A.A. Division I—Miami (Fla.) defeated Wichita State, 9–3, in title game

N.A.I.A.—Grand Canyon (Ariz.) College defeated Lewis & Clark (Idaho) State, 10–6, in title game

## 4th Game—Los Angeles, Oct. 24

**NEW YORK (AL)**     **LOS ANGELES (NL)**

| | AB | R | H | BI | | AB | R | H | BI |
|---|---|---|---|---|---|---|---|---|---|
| Randolph, 2b | 5 | 3 | 2 | 1 | Lopes, 2b | 5 | 2 | 2 | 2 |
| Milbourne, ss | 4 | 1 | 1 | 1 | Russell, ss | 5 | 0 | 1 | 1 |
| Winfield, lf, cf | 4 | 0 | 0 | 0 | Garvey, 1b | 5 | 1 | 3 | 0 |
| Jackson, rf | 3 | 2 | 3 | 1 | Cey, 3b | 5 | 0 | 2 | 2 |
| Gamble, lf | 4 | 1 | 2 | 1 | Baker, lf | 5 | 1 | 1 | 0 |
| Brown, cf | 0 | 0 | 0 | 0 | Monday, rf | 3 | 1 | 1 | 0 |
| Piniella, lf | 1 | 0 | 0 | 0 | Thomas, cf | 1 | 0 | 0 | 0 |
| Watson, 1b | 3 | 0 | 1 | 2 | Guerrero, rf | 3 | 0 | 2 | 0 |
| Cerone, c | 5 | 0 | 2 | 1 | Scioscia, c | 1 | 1 | 0 | 0 |
| Robertson, ph | 0 | 0 | 0 | 0 | Yeager, c | 0 | 0 | 0 | 1 |
| Rodriguez, 3b | 4 | 0 | 2 | 0 | Welch, p | 0 | 0 | 0 | 0 |
| Foote, ph | 1 | 0 | 0 | 0 | Goltz, p | 0 | 0 | 0 | 0 |
| Reuschel, p | 2 | 0 | 0 | 0 | Landreaux, ph | 1 | 1 | 1 | 0 |
| May, p | 1 | 0 | 0 | 0 | Forster, p | 0 | 0 | 0 | 0 |
| Davis, p | 0 | 0 | 0 | 0 | Smith, ph | 1 | 0 | 0 | 0 |
| Frazier, p | 1 | 0 | 0 | 0 | Niedenfuer, p | 0 | 0 | 0 | 0 |
| John, p | 0 | 0 | 0 | 0 | Johnstone, ph | 1 | 1 | 1 | 2 |
| Murcer, ph | 1 | 0 | 0 | 0 | Howe, p | 0 | 0 | 0 | 0 |
| **Total** | **39** | **7** | **13** | **7** | **Total** | **36** | **8** | **14** | **8** |

| | | | | | | | |
|---|---|---|---|---|---|---|---|
| New York | 2 1 1 | 0 0 2 | 0 1 0—7 |
| Los Angeles | 0 0 2 | 0 1 3 | 2 0 X—8 |

E—Russell, Jackson, Howe. LOB—New York 12, Los Angeles 10. 2B—Milbourne, Landreaux, Garvey, Monday. 3B—Randolph. HR—Randolph, Johnstone, Jackson. SB—Winfield, Lopes 2. S—Milbourne, Scioscia, Howe. SF—Watson, Yeager.

| | IP | H | R | ER | BB | SO |
|---|---|---|---|---|---|---|
| **New York** | | | | | | |
| Reuschel | 3 | 6 | 2 | 2 | 1 | 2 |
| May | 1⅓ | 2 | 1 | 1 | 0 | 1 |
| Davis | 1 | 2 | 3 | 2 | 1 | 2 |
| Frazier (L) | ⅔ | 2 | 2 | 2 | 1 | 0 |
| John | 2 | 2 | 0 | 0 | 0 | 2 |
| **Los Angeles** | | | | | | |
| Welch | 0 | 3 | 2 | 2 | 1 | 0 |
| Goltz | 3 | 4 | 2 | 2 | 1 | 2 |
| Forster | 1 | 1 | 0 | 0 | 2 | 0 |
| Niedenfuer | 2 | 2 | 2 | 0 | 1 | 0 |
| Howe (W) | 3 | 3 | 1 | 1 | 0 | 1 |

Time of game—3:32. Attendance—56,242.

## 5th Game—Los Angeles, Oct. 25

**NEW YORK (AL)**     **LOS ANGELES (NL)**

| | AB | R | H | BI | | AB | R | H | BI |
|---|---|---|---|---|---|---|---|---|---|
| Randolph, 2b | 3 | 0 | 0 | 0 | Lopes, 2b | 3 | 0 | 0 | 0 |
| Milbourne, ss | 4 | 0 | 1 | 0 | Russell, ss | 4 | 0 | 0 | 0 |
| Winfield, cf | 4 | 0 | 1 | 0 | Garvey, 1b | 4 | 0 | 1 | 0 |
| Jackson, rf | 4 | 1 | 1 | 0 | Cey, 3b | 2 | 0 | 0 | 0 |
| Gossage, p | 0 | 0 | 0 | 0 | Landreaux, cf | 0 | 0 | 0 | 0 |
| Watson, 1b | 3 | 0 | 0 | 0 | Baker, lf | 4 | 0 | 0 | 0 |
| Piniella, lf | 4 | 0 | 2 | 1 | Guerrero, rf | 3 | 1 | 1 | 1 |
| Brown, pr | 0 | 0 | 0 | 0 | Yeager, c | 3 | 1 | 2 | 1 |
| Cerone, c | 4 | 0 | 0 | 0 | Thomas, cf | 3 | 0 | 0 | 0 |
| Rodriguez, 3b | 3 | 0 | 0 | 0 | Reuss, p | 2 | 0 | 0 | 0 |
| Guidry, p | 3 | 0 | 0 | 0 | **Total** | **28** | **2** | **4** | **2** |
| Mumphrey, cf | 0 | 0 | 0 | 0 | | | | | |
| **Total** | **32** | **1** | **5** | **1** | | | | | |

## RUGBY—1982

Five Nations—Ireland
United States champion—Old Blues, Berkeley, Calif.
United States college—California

---

| | | | |
|---|---|---|---|
| New York | 0 1 0 | 0 0 0 | 0 0 0—1 |
| Los Angeles | 0 0 0 | 0 0 0 | 2 0 X—2 |

E—Lopes 3. DP—Los Angeles 2. LOB—New York 7, Los Angeles 6. 2B—Jackson, Yeager. HR—Guerrero, Yeager. SB—Lopes, Landreaux.

| | IP | H | R | ER | BB | SO |
|---|---|---|---|---|---|---|
| **New York** | | | | | | |
| Guidry (L) | 7 | 4 | 2 | 2 | 2 | 9 |
| Gossage | 1 | 0 | 0 | 0 | 1 | 0 |
| **Los Angeles** | | | | | | |
| Reuss (W) | 9 | 5 | 1 | 1 | 3 | 6 |

HBP—by Gossage (Cey). Time of game—2:19. Attendance—56,115.

## 6th Game—New York, Oct. 28

**LOS ANGELES (NL)**     **NEW YORK (AL)**

| | AB | R | H | BI | | AB | R | H | BI |
|---|---|---|---|---|---|---|---|---|---|
| Lopes, 2b | 4 | 2 | 1 | 0 | Randolph, 2b | 3 | 1 | 2 | 1 |
| Russell, ss | 4 | 0 | 2 | 1 | Mumphrey, cf | 5 | 0 | 1 | 0 |
| Garvey, 1b | 4 | 1 | 1 | 0 | Winfield, lf | 4 | 0 | 0 | 0 |
| Cey, 3b | 3 | 1 | 2 | 1 | Jackson, rf | 5 | 0 | 0 | 0 |
| Thomas, 3b | 2 | 1 | 0 | 1 | Watson, 1b | 5 | 0 | 0 | 0 |
| Baker, lf | 5 | 2 | 2 | 0 | Nettles, 3b | 3 | 0 | 2 | 0 |
| Guerrero, cf | 5 | 1 | 3 | 5 | Rodriguez, 3b | 1 | 1 | 1 | 0 |
| Monday, rf | 3 | 0 | 1 | 0 | Cerone, c | 3 | 0 | 0 | 0 |
| Landreaux, cf | 1 | 0 | 0 | 0 | Milbourne, ss | 2 | 0 | 0 | 0 |
| Yeager, c | 5 | 0 | 1 | 1 | John, p | 1 | 0 | 0 | 0 |
| Hooton, p | 2 | 1 | 0 | 0 | Murcer, ph | 1 | 0 | 0 | 0 |
| Howe, p | 2 | 0 | 0 | 0 | Frazier, p | 0 | 0 | 0 | 0 |
| **Total** | **40** | **9** | **13** | **9** | Davis, p | 0 | 0 | 0 | 0 |
| | | | | | Reuschel, p | 0 | 0 | 0 | 0 |
| | | | | | Gamble, ph | 0 | 0 | 0 | 0 |
| | | | | | Piniella, ph | 1 | 0 | 1 | 1 |
| | | | | | May, p | 0 | 0 | 0 | 0 |
| | | | | | Brown, ph | 1 | 0 | 0 | 0 |
| | | | | | LaRoche, p | 0 | 0 | 0 | 0 |
| | | | | | **Total** | **35** | **2** | **7** | **2** |

| | | | |
|---|---|---|---|
| Los Angeles | 0 0 0 | 1 3 4 | 0 1 0—9 |
| New York | 0 0 1 | 0 0 1 | 0 0 0—2 |

E—Milbourne, Nettles, Lopes. LOB—Los Angeles 10, New York 12. 2B—Nettles, Randolph. 3B—Guerrero. HR—Randolph, Guerrero. SB—Lopes, Russell, Randolph. S—Russell.

| | IP | H | R | ER | BB | SO |
|---|---|---|---|---|---|---|
| **Los Angeles** | | | | | | |
| Hooton (W) | 5⅓ | 5 | 2 | 2 | 5 | 2 |
| Howe (S) | 3⅔ | 2 | 0 | 0 | 1 | 3 |
| **New York** | | | | | | |
| John | 4 | 6 | 1 | 1 | 0 | 2 |
| Frazier (L) | 1 | 4 | 3 | 3 | 0 | 1 |
| Davis | ⅓ | 1 | 3 | 2 | 2 | 1 |
| Reuschel | ⅔ | 1 | 1 | 0 | 2 | 0 |
| May | 2 | 1 | 1 | 1 | 1 | 2 |
| LaRoche | 1 | 0 | 0 | 0 | 0 | 2 |

Time of game—3:09. Attendance—56,513.

## SQUASH TENNIS

### UNITED STATES OPEN CHAMPION—1982

Men's open singles—Gary Squires, New Haven, Conn., defeated Stuart MacFarlane, New York City, 15–12, 15–6, 15–9, in final. Semifinals: MacFarlane defeated David Stafford, Bronxville, N.Y., and Squires defeated Bill Rubin, White Plains, N.Y.

## MAJOR LEAGUE ALL-STAR GAME

| Year | Date | Winning league and manager | Runs | Losing league and manager | Runs | Winning pitcher | Losing pitcher | Site | Paid attendance |
|---|---|---|---|---|---|---|---|---|---|
| 1933 | July 6 | A.L. (Mack) | 4 | N.L. (McGraw) | 2 | Gomez | Hallahan | Chicago A.L. | 47,595 |
| 1934 | July 10 | A.L. (Cronin) | 9 | N.L. (Terry) | 7 | Harder | Mungo | New York N.L. | 48,363 |
| 1935 | July 8 | A.L. (Cochrane) | 4 | N.L. (Frisch) | 1 | Gomez | Walker | Cleveland A.L. | 69,831 |
| 1936 | July 7 | N.L. (Grimm) | 4 | A.L. (McCarthy) | 3 | J. Dean | Grove | Boston N.L. | 25,556 |
| 1937 | July 7 | A.L. (McCarthy) | 8 | N.L. (Terry) | 3 | Gomez | J. Dean | Washington A.L. | 31,391 |
| 1938 | July 6 | N.L. (Terry) | 4 | A.L. (McCarthy) | 1 | Vander Meer | Gomez | Cincinnati N.L. | 27,067 |
| 1939 | July 11 | A.L. (McCarthy) | 3 | N.L. (Hartnett) | 1 | Bridges | Lee | New York A.L. | 62,892 |
| 1940 | July 9 | N.L. (McKechnie) | 4 | A.L. (Cronin) | 0 | Derringer | Ruffing | St. Louis N.L. | 32,373 |
| 1941 | July 8 | A.L. (Baker) | 7 | N.L. (McKechnie) | 5 | E. Smith | Passeau | Detroit A.L. | 54,674 |
| 1942 | July 6 | A.L. (McCarthy) | 3 | N.L. (Durocher) | 1 | Chandler | Cooper | New York A.L. | 34,178 |
| 1943 | July 13[1] | A.L. (McCarthy) | 5 | N.L. (Southworth) | 3 | Leonard | Cooper | Philadelphia A.L. | 31,938 |
| 1944 | July 11[1] | N.L. (Southworth) | 7 | A.L. (McCarthy) | 1 | Raffensberger | Hughson | Pittsburgh N.L. | 29,589 |
| 1946 | July 9 | A.L. (O'Neill) | 12 | N.L. (Grimm) | 0 | Feller | Passeau | Boston A.L. | 34,906 |
| 1947 | July 8 | A.L. (Cronin) | 2 | N.L. (Dyer) | 1 | Shea | Sain | Chicago N.L. | 41,123 |
| 1948 | July 13 | A.L. (Harris) | 5 | N.L. (Durocher) | 2 | Raschi | Schmitz | St. Louis A.L. | 34,009 |
| 1949 | July 12 | A.L. (Boudreau) | 11 | N.L. (Southworth) | 7 | Trucks | Newcombe | Brooklyn N.L. | 32,577 |
| 1950 | July 11 | N.L. (Shotton) | 4 | A.L. (Stengel) | 3[3] | Blackwell | Gray | Chicago A.L. | 46,127 |
| 1951 | July 10 | N.L. (Sawyer) | 8 | A.L. (Stengel) | 3 | Maglie | Lopat | Detroit A.L. | 52,075 |
| 1952 | July 8 | N.L. (Durocher) | 3 | A.L. (Stengel) | 2[4] | Rush | Lemon | Philadelphia N.L. | 32,785 |
| 1953 | July 14 | N.L. (Dressen) | 5 | A.L. (Stengel) | 1 | Spahn | Reynolds | Cincinnati N.L. | 30,846 |
| 1954 | July 13 | A.L. (Stengel) | 11 | N.L. (Alston) | 9 | Stone | Conley | Cleveland A.L. | 68,751 |
| 1955 | July 12 | N.L. (Durocher) | 6 | A.L. (Lopez) | 5[5] | Conley | Sullivan | Milwaukee N.L. | 45,643 |
| 1956 | July 10 | N.L. (Alston) | 7 | A.L. (Stengel) | 3 | Friend | Pierce | Washington A.L. | 28,843 |
| 1957 | July 9 | A.L. (Stengel) | 6 | N.L. (Alston) | 5 | Bunning | Simmons | St. Louis N.L. | 30,693 |
| 1958 | July 8 | A.L. (Stengel) | 4 | N.L. (Haney) | 3 | Wynn | Friend | Baltimore A.L. | 48,829 |
| 1959[2] | July 7 | N.L. (Haney) | 5 | A.L. (Stengel) | 4 | Antonelli | Ford | Pittsburgh N.L. | 35,277 |
| | Aug. 3 | A.L. (Stengel) | 5 | N.L. (Haney) | 3 | Walker | Drysdale | Los Angeles N.L. | 55,105 |
| 1960[2] | July 11 | N.L. (Alston) | 5 | A.L. (Lopez) | 3 | Friend | Monbouquette | Kansas City A.L. | 30,619 |
| | July 13 | N.L. (Alston) | 6 | A.L. (Lopez) | 0 | Law | Ford | New York A.L. | 38,362 |
| 1961[2] | July 11 | N.L. (Murtaugh) | 5 | A.L. (Richards) | 4[6] | Miller | Wilhelm | San Francisco N.L. | 44,115 |
| | July 31 | N.L. (Murtaugh) | 1 | A.L. (Richards) | 1[7] | — | — | Boston A.L. | 31,851 |
| 1962[2] | July 10 | N.L. (Hutchinson) | 3 | A.L. (Houk) | 1 | Marichal | Pascual | Washington A.L. | 45,480 |
| | July 30 | A.L. (Houk) | 9 | N.L. (Hutchinson) | 4 | Herbert | Mahaffey | Chicago N.L. | 38,359 |
| 1963 | July 9 | N.L. (Dark) | 5 | A.L. (Houk) | 3 | Jackson | Bunning | Cleveland A.L. | 44,160 |
| 1964 | July 7 | N.L. (Alston) | 7 | A.L. (Lopez) | 4 | Marichal | Radatz | New York N.L. | 50,850 |
| 1965 | July 13 | N.L. (March) | 6 | A.L. (Lopez) | 5 | Koufax | McDowell | Minnesota A.L. | 46,706 |
| 1966 | July 12 | N.L. (Alston) | 2 | A.L. (Mele) | 1[6] | Perry | Richert | St. Louis N.L. | 49,926 |
| 1967 | July 11 | N.L. (Alston) | 2 | A.L. (Bauer) | 1[8] | Drysdale | Hunter | Anaheim N.L. | 46,309 |
| 1968 | July 9 | N.L. (Schoendienst) | 1 | A.L. (Williams) | 0 | Drysdale | Tiant | Houston N.L. | 48,321 |
| 1969 | July 23 | N.L. (Schoendienst) | 9 | A.L. (M. Smith) | 3 | Carlton | Stottlemyre | Washington A.L. | 45,259 |
| 1970 | July 14 | N.L. (Hodges) | 5 | A.L. (Weaver) | 4[5] | Osteen | Wright | Cincinnati N.L. | 51,838 |
| 1971 | July 13 | A.L. (Weaver) | 6 | N.L. (Anderson) | 4 | Blue | Ellis | Detroit A.L. | 53,559 |
| 1972 | July 25 | N.L. (Murtaugh) | 4 | A.L. (Weaver) | 3[6] | McGraw | McNally | Atlanta N.L. | 53,107 |
| 1973 | July 24[1] | N.L. (Anderson) | 7 | A.L. (Williams) | 1 | Wise | Blyleven | Kansas City A.L. | 40,849 |
| 1974 | July 23[1] | N.L. (Berra) | 7 | A.L. (Williams) | 2 | Brett | Tiant | Pittsburgh N.L. | 50,706 |
| 1975 | July 15[1] | N.L. (Alston) | 6 | A.L. (Dark) | 3 | Matlack | Hunter | Milwaukee A.L. | 51,540 |
| 1976 | July 13 | N.L. (Anderson) | 7 | A.L. (D. Johnson) | 1 | R. Jones | Fidrych | Philadelphia N.L. | 63,974 |
| 1977 | July 19[1] | N.L. (Anderson) | 7 | A.L. (Martin) | 5 | Sutton | Palmer | New York A.L. | 56,683 |
| 1978 | July 11[1] | N.L. (Lasorda) | 7 | A.L. (Martin) | 3 | Sutter | Gossage | San Diego N.L. | 51,549 |
| 1979 | July 17[1] | N.L. (Lasorda) | 7 | A.L. (Lemon) | 6 | Sutter | Kern | Seattle A.L. | 58,905 |
| 1980 | July 8[1] | N.L. (Tanner) | 4 | A.L. (Weaver) | 2 | Reuss | John | Los Angeles N.L. | 56,088 |
| 1981 | Aug. 9[1] | N.L. (Green) | 5 | A.L. (Frey) | 4 | Blue | Fingers | Cleveland*A.L. | 72,086 |
| 1982 | July 13[1] | N.L. (Lasorda) | 4 | A.L. (Martin) | 1 | Rogers | Eckersley | Montreal N.L. | 59,057 |

1. Night game. 2. Two games. 3. Fourteen innings. 4. Five innings, rain. 5. Twelve innings. 6. Ten innings. 7. Called because of rain after nine innings. 8. Fifteen innings. NOTE: No game in 1945. *Game was originally scheduled for July 14, but was put off because of players' strike.

## PAWTUCKET WINS LONGEST GAME IN 33RD INNING

The Pawtucket Red Sox and the Rochester Red Wings of the International League played one of the most bizarre games and the longest in baseball history during 1981. Pawtucket won it, 3–2, after 33 innings, 67 days after it had begun. The teams made 39 hits in the marathon that lasted 8 hours 25 minutes of actual playing time. The Class AAA game started on April 18 at McCoy Stadium in Pawtucket, R.I., and was tied at 2–2 when it was called at 4:07 in the morning by order of the league president. On Rochester's next visit to Pawtucket, June 23, the teams resumed the game and took only 18 minutes to decide the outcome. Miami and St. Petersburg of the Florida State League had played 29 innings on June 14, 1966, the previous longest game. Miami won, 4–3. In the major leagues the longest game was played on May 2, 1920, between the Brooklyn Dodgers and Boston Braves. It went 26 innings and was called with the teams tied at 1–1.

## NATIONAL BASEBALL HALL OF FAME
Cooperstown, N.Y.

### Fielders

| Member | Active years | Member | Active years | Member | Active years |
|---|---|---|---|---|---|
| Aaron, Henry (Hank) | 1954–1976 | Duffy, Hugh | 1888–1906 | Maranville, Walter (Rabbit) | 1912–1935 |
| Anson, Adrian (Cap) | 1876–1897 | Evers, John | 1902–1919 | Mathews, Edwin | 1952–1968 |
| Appling, Lucius (Luke) | 1930–1950 | Ewing, William | 1880–1897 | Mays, Willie | 1951–1973 |
| Averill, H. Earl | 1929–1941 | Flick, Elmer | 1898–1910 | McCarthy, Thomas | 1884–1896 |
| Baker, J. Frank (Home Run) | 1908–1922 | Foxx, James | 1925–1945 | McGraw, John J. | 1891–1906 |
| Bancroft, David | 1915–1930 | Frisch, Frank | 1919–1937 | Medwick, Joseph (Ducky) | 1932–1948 |
| Banks, Ernest | 1953–1971 | Gehrig, H. Louis (Lou) | 1923–1939 | Mize, John (The Big Cat) | 1936–1953 |
| Beckley, Jacob | 1888–1907 | Gehringer, Charles | 1924–1942 | Musial, Stanley | 1941–1963 |
| Bell, James (Cool Papa)[1] | 1920–1947 | Gibson, Josh[1] | 1929–1946 | O'Rourke, James | 1876–1894 |
| Berra, Lawrence (Yogi) | 1946–1965 | Goslin, Leon (Goose) | 1921–1938 | Ott, Melvin | 1926–1947 |
| Bottomley, James | 1922–1937 | Greenberg, Henry (Hank) | 1933–1947 | Rice, Edgar (Sam) | 1915–1934 |
| Boudreau, Louis | 1938–1952 | Hafey, Charles (Chick) | 1924–1937 | Robinson, Frank | 1956–1976 |
| Bresnahan, Roger | 1897–1915 | Hamilton, William | 1888–1901 | Robinson, Jack | 1947–1956 |
| Brouthers, Dennis | 1879–1896 | Hartnett, Charles (Gabby) | 1922–1941 | Robinson, Wilbert | 1886–1902 |
| Burkett, Jesse | 1890–1905 | Heilmann, Harry | 1914–1932 | Roush, Edd | 1913–1931 |
| Campanella, Roy | 1948–1957 | Herman, William | 1931–1947 | Ruth, George (Babe) | 1914–1935 |
| Carey, Max | 1910–1929 | Hooper, Harry | 1909–1925 | Schalk, Raymond | 1912–1929 |
| Chance, Frank | 1898–1914 | Hornsby, Rogers | 1915–1937 | Sewell, Joseph | 1920–1933 |
| Charleston, Oscar[1] | 1915–1954 | Irvin, Monford (Monte)[1] | 1939–1956 | Simmons, Al | 1924–1944 |
| Clarke, Fred | 1894–1915 | Jackson, Travis | 1922–1936 | Sisler, George | 1915–1930 |
| Clemente, Roberto | 1955–1972 | Jennings, Hugh | 1891–1918 | Snider, Edwin D. (Duke) | 1947–1964 |
| Cobb, Tyrus | 1905–1928 | Johnson, William (Judy)[1] | 1921–1937 | Speaker, Tristram | 1907–1928 |
| Cochrane, Gordon (Mickey) | 1925–1937 | Kaline, Albert W. | 1953–1974 | Terry, William | 1923–1936 |
| Collins, Edward | 1906–1930 | Keeler, William (Wee Willie) | 1892–1910 | Thompson, Samuel | 1885–1906 |
| Collins, James | 1895–1908 | Kelley, Joseph | 1891–1908 | Tinker, Joseph | 1902–1916 |
| Comiskey, Charles | 1882–1894 | Kelly, George | 1915–1932 | Traynor, Harold (Pie) | 1920–1937 |
| Combs, Earle | 1924–1935 | Kelly, Michael (King) | 1878–1893 | Wagner, John (Honus) | 1897–1917 |
| Connor, Roger | 1880–1897 | Kiner, Ralph | 1946–1955 | Wallace, Roderick (Bobby) | 1894–1918 |
| Crawford, Samuel | 1899–1917 | Klein, Charles H. (Chuck) | 1928–1944 | Waner, Lloyd | 1927–1945 |
| Cronin, Joseph | 1926–1945 | Lajoie, Napoleon | 1896–1916 | Waner, Paul | 1926–1945 |
| Cuyler, Hazen (Kiki) | 1921–1938 | Leonard, Walter (Buck)[1] | 1933–1955 | Ward, John (Monte) | 1878–1894 |
| Delahanty, Edward | 1888–1903 | Lindstrom, Frederick | 1924–1936 | Wheat, Zachariah | 1909–1927 |
| Dickey, William | 1928–1946 | Lloyd, John Henry[1] | 1905–1931 | Williams, Theodore | 1939–1960 |
| Dihigo, Martin[1] | 1923–1945 | Mantle, Mickey | 1951–1968 | Wilson, Lewis R. (Hack) | 1923–1934 |
| DiMaggio, Joseph | 1936–1951 | Manush, Henry (Heinie) | 1923–1939 | Youngs, Ross (Pep) | 1917–1926 |

### Pitchers

| Member | Active years | Member | Active years | Member | Active years |
|---|---|---|---|---|---|
| Alexander, Grover | 1911–1930 | Grove, Robert (Lefty) | 1925–1941 | Pennock, Herbert | 1912–1934 |
| Bender, Charles (Chief) | 1903–1925 | Haines, Jesse | 1918–1937 | Plank, Edward | 1901–1917 |
| Brown, Mordecai (3-Finger) | 1903–1916 | Hoyt, Waite | 1918–1938 | Radbourn, Charles (Hoss) | 1880–1891 |
| Chesbro, John | 1899–1909 | Hubbell, Carl | 1928–1943 | Rixey, Eppa | 1912–1933 |
| Clarkson, John | 1882–1894 | Johnson, Walter | 1907–1927 | Roberts, Robert (Robin) | 1948–1966 |
| Coveleski, Stanley | 1912–1928 | Joss, Adrian | 1902–1910 | Ruffing, Charles (Red) | 1924–1947 |
| Dean, Jerome (Dizzy) | 1930–1947 | Keefe, Timothy | 1880–1893 | Rusie, Amos | 1889–1901 |
| Faber, Urban (Red) | 1914–1933 | Koufax, Sanford (Sandy) | 1955–1966 | Spahn, Warren | 1942–1965 |
| Feller, Robert | 1936–1956 | Lemon, Robert | 1946–1958 | Vance, Arthur (Dazzy) | 1915–1935 |
| Ford, Edward (Whitey) | 1950–1967 | Lyons, Theodore | 1923–1946 | Waddell, George | 1897–1910 |
| Foster, Andrew (Rube) | 1897–1926 | Marquard, Richard (Rube) | 1908–1925 | Walsh, Edward | 1904–1917 |
| Galvin, James (Pud) | 1876–1892 | Mathewson, Christopher | 1900–1916 | Welch, Michael (Mickey) | 1880–1892 |
| Gibson, Bob | 1959–1975 | McGinnity, Joseph | 1899–1908 | Wynn, Early | 1939–1963 |
| Gomez, Vernon (Lefty) | 1930–1943 | Nichols, Charles (Kid) | 1890–1906 | Young, Denton (Cy) | 1890–1911 |
| Griffith, Clark | 1891–1914 | Paige, LeRoy (Satchel)[1] | 1926–1965 | | |
| Grimes, Burleigh | 1916–1934 | | | | |

### Officials and Others

| | | | |
|---|---|---|---|
| Barrow, Edward[2,3] | Evans, William G.[5,3] | Klem, William[5] | Spalding, Albert G.[6] |
| Bulkeley, Morgan G.[3] | Frick, Ford C.[7,3] | Landis, Kenesaw M.[7] | Stengel, Charles D.[8] |
| Cartwright, Alexander[3] | Giles, Warren C.[3] | Lopez, Alfonso R.[8] | Weiss, George M.[3] |
| Chadwick, Henry[4] | Harridge, William[3] | Mack, Connie[2,3] | Wright, George[6] |
| Chandler, A.B.[7] | Harris, Stanley R.[8] | MacPhail, Leland S.[3] | Wright, Harry[6,2] |
| Conlan, John[5] | Hubbard, R. Calvin[5] | McCarthy, Joseph V.[2] | Yawkey, Thomas[3] |
| Connolly, Thomas[5] | Higgins, Miller J.[2] | McKechnie, William B.[2] | |
| Cummings, William A.[6] | Johnson, B. Bancroft[3] | Rickey, W. Branch[2,3] | |

1. Negro league player selected by special committee. 2. Manager. 3. Executive. 4. Writer-statistician. 5. Umpire. 6. Early player. 7. Commissioner. 8. Player-manager

# OTHER LIFETIME BATTING, PITCHING, AND BASE–RUNNING RECORDS

Sources: *Baseball Record Book*, published and copyrighted by The Sporting News, St. Louis, Mo. 63166, and *The Book of Baseball Records*, published and copyrighted by Seymour Siwoff, New York, N.Y. 10036

## Hits (3,000 or More)

| | |
|---|---|
| Ty Cobb | 4,191 |
| Pete Rose | 3,869 |
| Henry Aaron | 3,771 |
| Stan Musial | 3,630 |
| Tris Speaker | 3,515 |
| Honus Wagner | 3,430 |
| Carl Yastrzemski | 3,318 |
| Eddie Collins | 3,311 |
| Willie Mays | 3,283 |
| Nap Lajoie | 3,251 |
| Paul Waner | 3,152 |
| Cap Anson | 3,081 |
| Lou Brock | 3,023 |
| Al Kaline | 3,007 |
| Roberto Clemente | 3,000 |

## Earned-Run Average[1]

| | |
|---|---|
| Walter Johnson | 2.37 |
| Grover Alexander | 2.56 |
| Tom Seaver* | 2.60 |
| Whitey Ford | 2.74 |
| Jim Palmer* | 2.78 |
| Stanley Coveleski | 2.88 |
| Juan Marichal | 2.89 |
| Wilbur Cooper | 2.89 |
| Bob Gibson | 2.91 |
| Carl Mays | 2.92 |
| Don Drysdale | 2.95 |
| Bert Blyleven* | 2.95 |
| Carl Hubbell | 2.98 |
| Gaylord Perry* | 2.99 |
| Steve Carlton* | 3.00 |

## Runs Scored

| | |
|---|---|
| Ty Cobb | 2,245 |
| Henry Aaron | 2,174 |
| Babe Ruth | 2,174 |
| Willie Mays | 2,062 |
| Pete Rose* | 1,995 |
| Stan Musial | 1,949 |
| Lou Gehrig | 1,888 |
| Tris Speaker | 1,881 |
| Mel Ott | 1,859 |

| | |
|---|---|
| Frank Robinson | 1,829 |
| Eddie Collins | 1,816 |
| Ted Williams | 1,798 |
| Carl Yastrzemski* | 1,778 |
| Charlie Gehringer | 1,774 |
| Jimmie Foxx | 1,751 |
| Honus Wagner | 1,740 |
| Willie Keeler | 1,720 |
| Cap Anson | 1,712 |
| Jesse Burkett | 1,708 |
| Billy Hamilton | 1,690 |
| Mickey Mantle | 1,677 |
| John McPhee | 1,674 |
| George Van Haltren | 1,650 |

## Strikeouts, Pitching

| | |
|---|---|
| Walter Johnson | 3,508 |
| Nolan Ryan* | 3,494 |
| Gaylord Perry* | 3,452 |
| Steve Carlton* | 3,434 |
| Tom Seaver* | 3,163 |
| Bob Gibson | 3,117 |
| Ferguson Jenkins* | 3,096 |
| Jim Bunning | 2,855 |
| Mickey Lolich | 2,832 |
| Cy Young | 2,819 |
| Don Sutton* | 2,792 |
| Phil Niekro* | 2,784 |
| Warren Spahn | 2,583 |
| Bob Feller | 2,581 |
| Tim Keefe | 2,538 |
| Christy Mathewson | 2,505 |

## Home Runs (350 or More)

| | |
|---|---|
| Henry Aaron | 755 |
| Babe Ruth | 714 |
| Willie Mays | 660 |
| Frank Robinson | 586 |
| Harmon Killebrew | 573 |
| Mickey Mantle | 536 |
| Jimmie Foxx | 534 |
| Ted Williams | 521 |
| Willie McCovey | 521 |
| Eddie Mathews | 512 |

| | |
|---|---|
| Ernie Banks | 512 |
| Mel Ott | 511 |
| Lou Gehrig | 493 |
| Stan Musial | 475 |
| Willie Stargell* | 475 |
| Reggie Jackson* | 464 |
| Carl Yastrzemski* | 442 |
| Billy Williams | 426 |
| Duke Snider | 407 |
| Al Kaline | 399 |
| Frank Howard | 382 |
| Orlando Cepeda | 379 |
| Norm Cash | 377 |
| Johnny Bench* | 377 |
| Rocky Colavito | 374 |
| Gil Hodges | 370 |
| Ralph Kiner | 369 |
| Tony Perez* | 363 |
| Joe DiMaggio | 361 |
| Lee May* | 360 |
| Johnny Mize | 359 |
| Yogi Berra | 358 |
| Dick Allen | 351 |

## Shutouts

| | |
|---|---|
| Walter Johnson | 110 |
| Grover Alexander | 90 |
| Christy Mathewson | 83 |
| Cy Young | 77 |
| Ed Plank | 64 |
| Warren Spahn | 63 |
| Ed Walsh | 58 |
| James Galvin | 57 |
| Bob Gibson | 56 |
| Don Sutton* | 56 |
| Tom Seaver* | 54 |
| Jim Palmer* | 53 |
| Gaylord Perry* | 52 |
| Steve Carlton* | 52 |
| Juan Marichal | 52 |

## Strikeouts, Batting[1]

| | |
|---|---|
| Willie Stargell* | 1,912 |
| Reggie Jackson* | 1,810 |

| | |
|---|---|
| Bobby Bonds | 1,757 |
| Lou Brock | 1,730 |
| Mickey Mantle | 1,710 |
| Harmon Killebrew | 1,699 |
| Tony Perez* | 1,694 |
| Dick Allen | 1,556 |
| Lee May* | 1,552 |
| Willie McCovey | 1,550 |
| Frank Robinson | 1,532 |
| Willie Mays | 1,526 |
| Eddie Mathews | 1,487 |
| Frank Howard | 1,460 |
| Jim Wynn | 1,427 |

## Bases on Balls[1]

| | |
|---|---|
| Babe Ruth | 2,056 |
| Ted Williams | 2,019 |
| Mickey Mantle | 1,734 |
| Carl Yastrzemski* | 1,732 |
| Mel Ott | 1,708 |
| Joe Morgan* | 1,625 |
| Eddie Yost | 1,614 |
| Stan Musial | 1,599 |
| Harmon Killebrew | 1,559 |
| Lou Gehrig | 1,508 |
| Willie Mays | 1,464 |
| Jimmie Foxx | 1,452 |
| Eddie Mathews | 1,444 |
| Frank Robinson | 1,420 |
| Henry Aaron | 1,402 |

## Stolen Bases

| | |
|---|---|
| Lou Brock | 938 |
| Billy Hamilton | 937 |
| Ty Cobb | 892 |
| Walter Latham | 791 |
| Harry Stovey | 744 |
| Eddie Collins | 743 |
| Max Carey | 738 |
| Honus Wagner | 720 |
| Tom Brown | 697 |
| Joe Morgan* | 663 |
| Bert Campaneris | 643 |

*Active player through 1982. 1. Through 1981 season.

## RECORD OF WORLD SERIES GAMES

Source: *The Book of Baseball Records*, published by Seymour Siwoff, New York City.

**Figures in parentheses for winning pitchers (WP) and losing pitchers (LP) indicate the game number in the series**

**1903**—Boston A.L. 5 (Jimmy Collins); Pittsburgh N.L. 3 (Fred Clarke). WP—Bos.: Dinneen (2, 6, 8), Young (5, 7); Pitts.: Phillippe (1, 3, 4). LP—Bos.: Young (1), Hughes (3), Dinneen (4); Pitts.: Leever (2, 6), Kennedy (5), Phillippe (7, 8).

**1904**—No series.

**1905**—New York N.L. 4 (John J. McGraw); Philadelphia A.L. 1 (Connie Mack). WP—N.Y.: Mathewson (1, 3, 5); McGinnity (4); Phila.: Bender (2). LP—N.Y.: McGinnity (2); Phila.: Plank (1, 4), Coakley (3), Bender (5).

**1906**—Chicago A.L. 4 (Fielder Jones); Chicago N.L. 2 (Frank Chance). WP—Chi.: A.L.: Altrock (1), Walsh (3, 5), White (6); Chi.: N.L.: Reulbach (2), Brown (4). LP—Chi. A.L.: White (2), Altrock (4); Chi.: N.L.: Brown (1, 6), Pfeister (3, 5).

**1907**—Chicago N.L. 4 (Frank Chance); Detroit A.L. 0 (Hugh Jennings). First game tied 3–3, 12 innings. WP—Pfeister (2), Reulbach (3), Overall (4), Brown (5). LP—Mullin (2, 5), Siever (3), Donovan (4).

**1908**—Chicago N.L. 4 (Frank Chance); Detroit A.L. 1 (Hugh

Jennings). WP—Chi.: Brown (1, 4), Overall (2, 5); Det.: Mullin (3). LP—Chi.: Pfeister (3); Det.: Summers (1, 4), Donovan (2, 5).

**1909**—Pittsburgh N.L. 4 (Fred Clarke); Detroit A.L. 3 (Hugh Jennings). WP—Pitts.: Adams (1, 5, 7), Maddox (3); Det.: Donovan (2), Mullin (4, 6). LP—Pitts.: Camnitz (2), Leifield (4), Willis (6); Det.: Mullin (1), Summers (3, 5), Donovan (7).

**1910**—Philadelphia A.L. 4 (Connie Mack); Chicago N.L. 1 (Frank Chance). WP—Phila.: Bender (1), Coombs (2, 3, 5); Chi.: Brown (4). LP—Phila.: Bender (4); Chi.: Overall (1), Brown (2, 5), McIntyre (3).

**1911**—Philadelphia A.L. 4 (Connie Mack); New York N.L. 2 (John J. McGraw). WP—Phila.: Plank (2), Coombs (3), Bender (4, 6); N.Y.: Mathewson (1), Crandall (5). LP—Phila.: Bender (1), Plank (5); N.Y.: Marquard (2), Mathewson (3, 4), Ames (6).

**1912**—Boston A.L. 4 (J. Garland Stahl); New York N.L. 3 (John J. McGraw). Second game tied, 6–6, 11 innings. WP—Bos.:

Wood (1, 4, 8), Bedient (5); N.Y.: Marquard (3, 6), Tesreau (7). LP—Bos.: O'Brien (3, 6), Wood (7); N.Y.: Tesreau (1, 4), Mathewson (5, 8).

**1913**—Philadelphia A.L. 4 (Connie Mack); New York N.L. 1 (John J. McGraw). WP—Phila.: Bender (1, 4), Bush (3), Plank (5); N.Y.: Mathewson (2); LP—Phila.: Plank (2); N.Y.: Marquard (1), Tesreau (3), Demaree (4), Mathewson (5).

**1914**—Boston N.L. 4 (George Stallings); Philadelphia A.L. 0 (Connie Mack). WP—Rudolph (1, 4), James (2, 3). LP—Bender (1), Plank (2), Bush (3), Shawkey (4).

**1915**—Boston A.L. 4 (Bill Carrigan); Philadelphia N.L. 1 (Pat Moran). WP—Bos.: Foster (2, 5), Leonard (3), Shore (4); Phila.: Alexander (1). LP—Bos.: Shore (1); Phila.: Mayer (2), Alexander (3), Chalmers (4), Rixey (5).

**1916**—Boston A.L. 4 (Bill Carrigan); Brooklyn N.L. 1 (Wilbert Robinson). WP—Bos.: Shore (1, 5), Ruth (2), Leonard (4); Bklyn.: Coombs (3). LP—Bos.: Mays (3); Bklyn.: Marquard (1, 4), Smith (5), Pfeffer (5).

**1917**—Chicago A.L. 4 (Clarence Rowland); New York N.L. 2 (John J. McGraw). WP—Chi.: Cicotte (1), Faber (2, 5, 6); N.Y.: Benton (3), Schupp (4). LP—Chi.: Cicotte (4), Faber (4); N.Y.: Sallee (1, 5), Anderson (2), Benton (6).

**1918**—Boston A.L. 4 (Ed Barrow); Chicago N.L. 2 (Fred Mitchell). WP—Bos.: Ruth (1, 4), Mays (3, 6); Chi.: Tyler (2), Vaughn (5). LP—Bos.: Bush (2), Jones (5); Chi.: Vaughn (1, 3), Douglas (4), Tyler (6).

**1919**—Cincinnati N.L. 5 (Pat Moran); Chicago A.L. 3 (William Gleason). WP—Cin.: Ruether (1), Sallee (2), Ring (4), Eller (5, 8); Chi.: Kerr (3, 6), Cicotte (7). LP—Cin.: Fisher (3), Ring (4), Sallee (7); Chi.: Cicotte (1, 4), Williams (2, 5, 8).

**1920**—Cleveland A.L. 5 (Tris Speaker); Brooklyn N.L. 2 (Wilbert Robinson). WP—Cleve.: Coveleski (1, 4, 7), Bagby (5), Mails (6); Bklyn.: Grimes (2), Smith (3). LP—Cleve.: Bagby (2), Caldwell (4). Bklyn.: Marquard (1), Cadore (4), Grimes (5, 7), Smith (6).

**1921**—New York N.L. 5 (John J. McGraw); New York A.L. 3 (Miller Huggins). WP—N.Y. N.L.: Barnes (3, 6), Douglas (4, 7), Nehf (8); N.Y. A.L.: Mays (1), Hoyt (2, 5). LP—N.Y. N.L.: Nehf (2, 5), Douglas (3). N.Y. A.L.: Quinn (3), Mays (4, 7), Shawkey (6), Hoyt (8).

**1922**—New York N.L. 4 (John J. McGraw); New York A.L. 0 (Miller Huggins). Second game tied 3–3, 10 innings. WP—Ryan (1), Scott (3), McQuillan (4), Nehf (5); LP—Bush (1, 5), Hoyt (3), Mays (4).

**1923**—New York A.L. 4 (Miller Huggins); New York N.L. 2 (John J. McGraw). WP—N.Y. A.L.: Pennock (2, 6), Shawkey (4), Bush (5); N.Y. N.L.: Ryan (1), Nehf (3). LP—N.Y. A.L.: Bush (1), Jones (3); N.Y. N.L.: McQuillan (2), Scott (4), Bentley (5), Nehf (6).

**1924**—Washington A.L. 4 (Bucky Harris); New York N.L. 3 (John J. McGraw). WP—Wash.: Zachary (2, 6), Mogridge (4), Johnson (7); N.Y.: Nehf (1), McQuillan (3), Bentley (5). LP—Wash.: Johnson (1, 5), Marberry (3); N.Y.: Bentley (2, 7), Barnes (4), Nehf (6).

**1925**—Pittsburgh N.L. 4 (Bill McKechnie); Washington A.L. 3 (Bucky Harris). WP—Pitts.: Aldridge (2, 5), Kremer (6, 7); Wash.: Johnson (1, 4), Ferguson (3). LP—Pitts.: Meadows (1), Kremer (3), Yde (4); Wash.: Coveleski (2, 5), Ferguson (6), Johnson (7).

**1926**—St. Louis N.L. 4 (Rogers Hornsby); New York A.L. 3 (Miller Huggins). WP—St. L.: Alexander (2, 6), Haines (3, 7); N.Y.: Pennock (1, 5), Hoyt (4). LP—St. L.: Sherdel (1, 5), Reinhart (4); N.Y.: Shocker (2), Ruether (3), Shawkey (6), Hoyt (7).

**1927**—New York A.L. 4 (Miller Huggins); Pittsburgh N.L. 0 (Donie Bush). WP—Hoyt (1), Pipgras (2), Pennock (3), Moore (4). LP—Kremer (1), Aldridge (2), Meadows (3), Miljus (4).

**1928**—New York A.L. 4 (Miller Huggins); St. Louis N.L. 0 (Bill McKechnie). WP—Hoyt (1, 4), Pipgras (2), Zachary (3). LP—Sherdel (1, 4), Alexander (2), Haines (3).

**1929**—Philadelphia A.L. 4 (Connie Mack); Chicago N.L. 1 (Joe McCarthy). WP—Phila.: Ehmke (1), Earnshaw (2), Rommel (4), Walberg (5); Chi.: Bush (3). LP—Phila.: Earnshaw

Chi.: Root (1), Malone (2, 5), Blake (4).

**1930**—Philadelphia A.L. 4 (Connie Mack); St. Louis N.L. 2 (Gabby Street). WP—Phila.: Grove (1, 5), Earnshaw (2, 6); St. L.: Hallahan (3), Haines (4). LP—Phila.: Walberg (3), Grove (4); St. L.: Grimes (1, 5), Rhem (2), Hallahan (6).

**1931**—St. Louis N.L. 4 (Gabby Street); Philadelphia A.L. 3 (Connie Mack). WP—St. L.: Hallahan (2, 6), Grimes (3, 7); Phila.: Grove (1, 6), Earnshaw (4). LP—St. L.: Derringer (1, 6), Johnson (4); Phila.: Earnshaw (2, 7), Grove (3), Hoyt (5).

**1932**—New York A.L. 4 (Joe McCarthy); Chicago N.L. 0 (Charles Grimm). WP—Ruffing (1), Gomez (2), Pipgras (3), Moore (4). LP—Bush (1), Warneke (2), Root (3), May (4).

**1933**—New York N.L. 4 (Bill Terry); Washington A.L. 1 (Joe Cronin). WP—N.Y.: Hubbell (1, 4), Schumacher (2), Luque (5); Wash.: Whitehill (3). LP—N.Y.: Fitzsimmons (3); Wash.: Stewart (1), Crowder (2), Weaver (4), Russell (5).

**1934**—St. Louis N.L. 4 (Frank Frisch); Detroit A.L. 3 (Mickey Cochrane). WP—St. L.: J. Dean (1, 7), P. Dean (3, 6); Det.: Rowe (2), Auker (4), Bridges (5). LP—St. L.: W. Walker (2, 4), J. Dean (3); Det.: Crowder (1), Bridges (3), Rowe (6), Auker (7).

**1935**—Detroit A.L. 4 (Mickey Cochrane); Chicago N.L. 2 (Charles Grimm). WP—Det.: Bridges (2, 6), Rowe (3), Crowder (4); Chi.: Warneke (1, 5); LP—Det.: Rowe (1, 5); Chi.: Root (2), French (3, 6), Carleton (4).

**1936**—New York A.L. 4 (Joe McCarthy); New York N.L. 2 (Bill Terry). WP—N.Y. A.L.: Gomez (2, 6), Hadley (3), Pearson (4); N.Y. N.L.: Hubbell (1), Schumacher (5); LP—N.Y. A.L.: Ruffing (1), Malone (6); N.Y. N.L.: Schumacher (2), Fitzsimmons (3, 6), Hubbell (4).

**1937**—New York A.L. 4 (Joe McCarthy); New York N.L. 1 (Bill Terry). WP—N.Y. A.L.: Gomez (1, 5), Ruffing (2), Pearson (3); N.Y. N.L.: Hubbell (4). LP—N.Y. A.L.: Hadley (4); N.Y. N.L.: Hubbell (1), Melton (2, 5), Schumacher (3).

**1938**—New York A.L. 4 (Joe McCarthy); Chicago N.L. 0 (Gabby Hartnett). WP—Ruffing (1, 4), Gomez (2), Pearson (3). LP—Lee (1, 4), Dean (2), Bryant (3).

**1939**—New York A.L. 4 (Joe McCarthy); Cincinnati N.L. 0 (Bill McKechnie). WP—Ruffing (1), Pearson (2), Hadley (3), Murphy (4). LP—Derringer (1), Walters (2, 4), Thompson (3).

**1940**—Cincinnati N.L. 4 (Bill McKechnie); Detroit A.L. 3 (Del Baker). WP—Cin.: Walters (2, 6), Derringer (4, 7); Det.: Newsom (1, 5), Bridges (3). LP—Cin.: Derringer (1), Turner (3), Thompson (5); Det.: Rowe (2, 6), Trout (4), Newsom (7).

**1941**—New York A.L. 4 (Joe McCarthy); Brooklyn N.L. 1 (Leo Durocher). WP—N.Y.: Ruffing (1), Russo (3), Murphy (4), Bonham (5); Bklyn: Wyatt (2). LP—N.Y.: Chandler (2); Bklyn: Davis (1), Casey (3, 4), Wyatt (5).

**1942**—St. Louis N.L. 4 (Billy Southworth); New York A.L. 1 (Joe McCarthy). WP—St. L.: Beazley (2, 5), White (3), Lanier (4); N.Y.: Ruffing (1). LP—St. L.: Cooper (1); N.Y.: Bonham (2), Chandler (3), Donald (4), Ruffing (5).

**1943**—New York A.L. 4 (Joe McCarthy); St. Louis N.L. 1 (Billy Southworth). WP—N.Y.: Chandler (1, 5), Borowy (3), Russo (4); St. L.: Cooper (2). LP—N.Y.: Bonham (2); St. L.: Lanier (1), Brazle (3), Brecheen (4), Cooper (5).

**1944**—St. Louis N.L. 4 (Billy Southworth); St. Louis A.L. 2 (Luke Sewell). WP—St. L. N.L.: Donnelly (2), Brecheen (4), Cooper (5), Lanier (6); St. L. A.L.: Galehouse (1), Kramer (3). LP—St. L. N.L.: Cooper (1), Wilks (3); St. L. A.L.: Muncrief (2), Jakucki (4), Galehouse (5), Potter (6).

**1945**—Detroit A.L. 4 (Steve O'Neill); Chicago N.L. 3 (Charles Grimm). WP—Det.: Trucks (2), Trout (4), Newhouser (5, 7); Chi.: Borowy (1, 6), Passeau (3). LP—Det.: Newhouser (1), Overmire (3), Trout (6); Chi.: Wyse (2), Prim (4), Borowy (5, 7).

**1946**—St. Louis N.L. 4 (Eddie Dyer); Boston A.L. 3 (Joe Cronin). WP—St. L.: Brecheen (2, 6, 7), Munger (4); Bos.: Johnson (1), Ferriss (3), Dobson (5). LP—St. L.: Pollet (1), Dickson (3), Brazle (5); Bos.: Harris (2, 6), Hughson (4), Klinger (7).

**1947**—New York A.L. 4 (Bucky Harris); Brooklyn N.L. 3 (Burt Shotton). WP—N.Y.: Shea (1, 5), Reynolds (2), Page (7);

Bklyn.: Casey (3, 4), Branca (6). LP—N.Y.: Newsom (3), Bevens (4), Page (6); Bklyn.: Branca (1), Lombardi (2), Barney (5), Gregg (7).

**1948**—Cleveland A.L. 4 (Lou Boudreau); Boston N.L. 2 (Billy Southworth). WP—Cleve.: Lemon (2, 6), Bearden (3), Gromek (4); Bos.: Sain (1), Spahn (5). LP—Cleve.: Feller (1, 5); Bos.: Spahn (2), Bickford (3), Sain (4), Voiselle (6).

**1949**—New York A.L. 4 (Casey Stengel); Brooklyn N.L. 1 (Burt Shotton). WP—N.Y.: Reynolds (1), Page (3), Lopat (4), Raschi (5); Bklyn.: Roe (2). LP—N.Y.: Raschi (2); Bklyn.: Newcombe (1, 4), Branca (3), Barney (5).

**1950**—New York A.L. 4 (Casey Stengel); Philadelphia N.L. 0 (Eddie Sawyer). WP—Raschi (1), Reynolds (2), Ferrick (3), Ford (4). LP—Konstanty (1), Roberts (2), Meyer (3), Miller (4).

**1951**—New York A.L. 4 (Casey Stengel); New York N.L. 2 (Leo Durocher). WP—N.Y. A.L.: Lopat (2, 5), Reynolds (4), Raschi (6); N.Y. N.L.: Koslo (1), Hearn (3). LP—N.Y. A.L.: Reynolds (1), Raschi (3); N.Y. N.L.: Jansen (2, 5), Maglie (4), Koslo (6).

**1952**—New York A.L. 4 (Casey Stengel); Brooklyn N.L. 3 (Chuck Dressen). WP—N.Y.: Raschi (2, 6), Reynolds (4, 7); Bklyn.: Black (1), Roe (3), Erskine (5). LP—N.Y.: Reynolds (1), Lopat (3), Sain (5); Bklyn.: Erskine (3), Black (4, 7), Loes (6).

**1953**—New York A.L. 4 (Casey Stengel); Brooklyn N.L. 2 (Chuck Dressen). WP—N.Y.: Sain (1), Lopat (2), McDonald (5), Reynolds (6); Bklyn.: Erskine (3), Loes (4). LP—N.Y.: Raschi (3), Ford (4); Bklyn.: Labine (1, 6), Roe (2), Podres (5).

**1954**—New York N.L. 4 (Leo Durocher); Cleveland A.L. 0 (Al Lopez). WP—Grissom (1), Antonelli (2), Gomez (3), Liddle (4). LP—Lemon (1, 4), Wynn (2), Garcia (3).

**1955**—Brooklyn N.L. 4 (Walter Alston); New York A.L. 3 (Casey Stengel). WP—Bklyn.: Podres (3, 7), Labine (4), Craig (5); N.Y.: Ford (1, 6), Byrne (2). LP—Bklyn.: Newcombe (1), Loes (2), Spooner (6); N.Y.: Turley (3), Larsen (4), Grim (5), Byrne (7).

**1956**—New York A.L. 4 (Casey Stengel); Brooklyn N.L. 3 (Walter Alston). WP—N.Y.: Ford (3), Sturdivant (4), Larsen (5), Kucks (7); Bklyn.: Maglie (1), Bessent (2), Labine (6). LP—N.Y.: Ford (1), Morgan (2), Turley (4); Bklyn.: Craig (3), Erskine (4), Maglie (5), Newcombe (7).

**1957**—Milwaukee N.L. 4 (Fred Haney); New York A.L. 3 (Casey Stengel). WP—Mil.: Burdette (2, 5, 7), Spahn (4); N.Y.: Ford (1), Larsen (4), Turley (6). LP—Mil.: Spahn (1), Buhl (3), Johnson (6); N.Y.: Shantz (2), Grim (4), Ford (5), Larsen (7).

**1958**—New York A.L. 4 (Casey Stengel); Milwaukee N.L. 3 (Fred Haney). WP—N.Y.: Larsen (3), Turley (5, 7), Duren (6); Mil.: Spahn (1, 4), Burdette (2). LP—N.Y.: Duren (1), Turley (2), Ford (4); Mil.: Rush (3), Burdette (5, 7), Spahn (6).

**1959**—Los Angeles N.L. 4 (Walter Alston); Chicago A.L. 2 (Al Lopez). WP—L.A.: Podres (2), Drysdale (3), Sherry (4, 6); Chi.: Wynn (1), Shaw (5). LP—L.A.: Craig (1), Koufax (5); Chi.: Shaw (2), Donovan (3), Staley (4), Wynn (6).

**1960**—Pittsburgh N.L. 4 (Danny Murtaugh); New York A.L. 3 (Casey Stengel). WP—Pitts.: Law (1, 4), Haddix (5, 7); N.Y.: Turley (2), Ford (3, 6). LP—Pitts.: Friend (2, 6), Mizell (3); N.Y.: Ditmar (1, 5), Terry (4, 7).

**1961**—New York A.L. 4 (Ralph Houk); Cincinnati N.L. 1 (Fred Hutchinson). WP—N.Y.: Ford (1, 4), Arroyo (3), Daley (5); Cin.: Jay (2). LP—N.Y.: Terry (2); Cin.: O'Toole (1, 4), Purkey (3), Jay (5).

**1962**—New York A.L. 4 (Ralph Houk); San Francisco N.L. 3 (Al Dark). WP—N.Y.: Ford (1), Stafford (3), Terry (5, 7); S.F.: Sanford (2), Larsen (4), Pierce (6). LP—N.Y.: Terry (2), Coates (4), Ford (6); S.F.: O'Dell (1), Pierce (3), Sanford (5, 7).

**1963**—Los Angeles N.L. 4 (Walter Alston); New York A.L. 0 (Ralph Houk). WP—Koufax (1, 4), Podres (2), Drysdale (3). LP—Ford (1, 4), Downing (2), Bouton (3).

**1964**—St. Louis N.L. 4 (Johnny Keane); New York A.L. 3 (Yogi Berra). WP—St. L.: Sadecki (1), Craig (4), Gibson (5, 7);

N.Y.: Stottlemyre (2), Bouton (3, 6). LP—St. L.: Gibson (2), Schultz (3), Simmons (6); N.Y.: Ford (1), Downing (4), Mikkelsen (5), Stottlemyre (7).

**1965**—Los Angeles N.L. 4 (Walter Alston); Minnesota A.L. 3 (Sam Mele). WP—L.A.: Osteen (3), Drysdale (4), Koufax (5, 7); Minn.: Grant (1, 6), Kaat (2). LP—L.A.: Drysdale (1), Koufax (2), Osteen (6); Minn.: Pascual (3), Grant (4), Kaat (5, 7).

**1966**—Baltimore A.L. 4 (Hank Bauer); Los Angeles N.L. 0 (Walter Alston). WP—Drabowsky (1), Palmer (2), Bunker (3), McNally (4). LP—Drysdale (1, 4), Koufax (2), Osteen (3).

**1967**—St. Louis N.L. 4 (Red Schoendienst); Boston A.L. 3 (Dick Williams). WP—St. L.: Gibson (1, 4, 7), Briles (3); Bos.: Lonborg (2, 5), Wyatt (6). LP—St. L.: Hughes (2), Carlton (5), Lamabe (6); Bos.: Santiago (1, 4), Bell (3), Lonborg (7).

**1968**—Detroit A.L. 4 (Mayo Smith); St. Louis N.L. 3 (Red Schoendienst). WP—Det.: Lolich (2, 5, 7), McLain (6); St. L.: Gibson (1, 4), Washburn (3). LP—Det.: McLain (1, 4), Wilson (3); St. L.: Briles (2), Hoerner (5), Washburn (6), Gibson (7).

**1969**—New York N.L. 4 (Gil Hodges); Baltimore A.L. 1 (Earl Weaver). WP—N.Y.: Koosman (2, 5), Gentry (3), Seaver (4); Balt.: Cuellar (1). LP—N.Y.: Seaver (1); Balt.: McNally (2), Palmer (3), Hall (4), Watt (5).

**1970**—Baltimore A.L. 4 (Earl Weaver); Cincinnati N.L. 1 (Sparky Anderson) 1. WP—Balt.: Palmer (1), Phoebus (2), McNally (3), Cuellar (5); Cin.: Carroll (4). LP—Cin.: Nolan (1), Wilcox (2), Cloninger (3), Merritt (5); Balt.: Watt (4).

**1971**—Pittsburgh N.L. 4 (Danny Murtaugh); Baltimore A.L. 3 (Earl Weaver). WP—Pitts.: Blass (3, 7), Kison (4), Briles (5); Balt.: McNally (1, 6), Palmer (2). LP—Pitts.: Ellis (1), R. Johnson (2), Miller (6); Balt.: Cuellar (3, 7), Watt (4) McNally (5).

**1972**—Oakland A.L. 4 (Dick Williams); Cincinnati N.L. (Sparky Anderson) 3. WP—Oakland: Holtzman (1), Hunter (2, 7), Fingers (4); Cincinnati: Billingham (3), Grimsley (5, 6). LP—Oakland: Odom (3), Fingers (5), Blue (6); Cincinnati: Nolan (1), Grimsley (2), Carroll (4), Borbon (7).

**1973**—Oakland A.L. 4 (Dick Williams); New York N.L. 3 (Yogi Berra). WP—Oakland: Holtzman (1, 7), Lindblad (3), Hunter (6). New York: McGraw (2), Matlack (4), Koosman (5). LP—Oakland: Fingers (2), Holtzman (4), Blue (5). New York: Matlack (1, 7) Parker (3), Seaver (6).

**1974**—Oakland A.L. 4 (Al Dark); Los Angeles N.L. 1 (Walter Alston). WP—Oakland: Fingers (1), Hunter (3), Holtzman (4), Odom (5). Los Angeles: Sutton (1). LP—Oakland: Blue (2), Los Angeles: Messersmith (1, 4), Downing (3), Marshall (5).

**1975**—Cincinnati N.L. 4 (Sparky Anderson); Boston A.L. 3 (Darrell Johnson). WP—Cincinnati: Eastwick (2-3), Gullett (5), Carroll (7); Boston: Tiant (1-4), Wise (6). LP—Cincinnati: Gullett (1), Norman (4), Darcy (6); Boston: Drago (2), Willoughby (3), Cleveland (5), Burton (7).

**1976**—Cincinnati N.L. 4 (Sparky Anderson); New York A.L. 0 (Billy Martin). WP—Gullett (1), Billingham (2), Zachry (3), Nolan (4). LP—Alexander (1), Hunter (2), Ellis (3), Figueroa (4).

**1977**—New York A.L. 4 (Billy Martin); Los Angeles N.L. 2 (Tom Lasorda). WP—New York: Lyle (1), Torrez (3,6), Guidry (4); Los Angeles: Hooton (2), Sutton (5). LP—New York: Hunter (2), Gullett (5); Los Angeles: Rhoden (1), John (3), Rau (4), Hooton (6).

**1978**—New York A.L. 4 (Bob Lemon), Los Angeles N.L. 2 (Tom Lasorda). WP—New York: Guidry (3), Gossage (4); Beattie (5), Hunter (6); Los Angeles: John (1), Hooton (2). LP—New York: Figuero (1), Hunter (2); Los Angeles: Sutton (3-6), Welch (4), Hooton (5).

**1979**—Pittsburgh N.L. 4 (Chuck Tanner), Baltimore A.L. 3 (Earl Weaver); WP—Pittsburgh: D. Robinson (2), Blyleven (5), Candelaria (6), Jackson (7); Baltimore: Flanagan (1), McGregor (3), Stoddard (4). LP—Pittsburgh: Kison (1), Candelaria (3), Tekulve (4); Baltimore: Stanhouse (2), Flana-

gan (5), Palmer (6), McGregor (7).
**1980**—Philadelphia N.L. 4 (Dallas Green), Kansas City A.L. 2 (Jim Frey); WP—Philadelphia: Walk (1), Carlton (2), McGraw (5), Carlton (6); Kansas City: Quisenberry (3), Leonard (4). LP—Philadelphia: McGraw (3), Christenson (4); Kansas City: Leonard (1), Quisenberry (2), Quisenberry (5), Gale (6).
**1981**—Los Angeles N.L. 4 (Tom Lasorda), New York A.L. 2 (Bob Lemon); WP—Los Angeles: Valenzuela (3), Howe (4),

Reuss (5), Hooton (6); New York: Guidry (1), John (2). LP—Los Angeles: Reuss (1), Hooton (2); New York: Frazier (3), Frazier (4), Guidry (5), Frazier (6).
**1982**—St. Louis N.L. 4 (Whitey Herzog), Milwaukee A.L. (Harvey Kuenn); WP—St. Louis: Sutter (2), Andujar (3), Stuper (6), Andujar (7). Milwaukee: Caldwell (1), Slaton (4), Caldwell (5). LP—St. Louis: Forsch (1), Bair (4), Forsch (5). Milwaukee: McClure (2), Vuckovich (3), Sutton (6), McClure (7).

## WORLD SERIES CLUB STANDING (THROUGH 1982)

| | Series | Won | Lost | Pct. | | Series | Won | Lost | Pct. |
|---|---|---|---|---|---|---|---|---|---|
| Oakland (A) | 3 | 3 | 0 | 1.000 | Detroit (A) | 8 | 3 | 5 | .375 |
| Pittsburgh (N) | 7 | 5 | 2 | .714 | New York (N-Giants) | 14 | 5 | 9 | .357 |
| St. Louis (N) | 13 | 9 | 4 | .692 | Washington (A) | 3 | 1 | 2 | .333 |
| New York (A) | 33 | 22 | 11 | .667 | Philadelphia (N) | 3 | 1 | 2 | .333 |
| Cleveland (A) | 3 | 2 | 1 | .667 | Chicago (N) | 10 | 2 | 8 | .200 |
| Boston (A) | 8 | 5 | 3 | .625 | Brooklyn (N) | 9 | 1 | 8 | .111 |
| Philadelphia (A) | 8 | 5 | 3 | .625 | St. Louis (A) | 1 | 0 | 1 | .000 |
| Los Angeles (N) | 8 | 4 | 4 | .500 | San Francisco (N) | 1 | 0 | 1 | .000 |
| New York (N-Mets) | 2 | 1 | 1 | .500 | Minnesota (A) | 1 | 0 | 1 | .000 |
| Milwaukee (A) | 2 | 1 | 1 | .500 | Kansas City (A) | 1 | 0 | 1 | .000 |
| Boston (N) | 2 | 1 | 1 | .500 | Milwaukee (A) | 1 | 0 | 1 | .000 |
| Chicago (A) | 4 | 2 | 2 | .500 | | | | | |
| Cincinnati (N) | 8 | 4 | 4 | .500 | **Recapitulation** | | | | |
| Baltimore (A) | 5 | 2 | 3 | .400 | | | | | |

| | Won |
|---|---|
| American League | 45 |
| National League | 34 |

## SINGLE GAME AND SINGLE SERIES RECORDS

Most hits game—5, Paul Molitor, Milwaukee A.L., first game vs. St. Louis, N.L., 1982.
Most 4-hit games, series—2, Robin Yount, Milwaukee A.L., first and fifth games vs. St. Louis N.L., 1982.
Most hits inning—2, held by many players.
Most hits series—13 (7 games) Bobby Richardson, New York A.L., 1964; Lou Brock, St. Louis N.L., 1968; 12 (6 games) Billy Martin, New York A.L., 1953; 12 (8 games) Buck Herzog, New York N.L., 1912; Joe Jackson, Chicago A.L., 1919; 10 (4 games) Babe Ruth, New York A.L., 1928; 9 (5 games) held by 7 players.
Most home runs, series—5 (6 games) Reggie Jackson, New York A.L., 1977; 4 (7 games) Babe Ruth, New York A.L., 1926; Duke Snider, Brooklyn N.L., 1952, 1955; Hank Bauer, New York A.L., 1958; Gene Tenace, Oakland A.L., 1972; 4 (4 games) Lou Gehrig, New York A.L., 1928; 3 (6 games) Babe Ruth, New York A.L., 1923; Ted Kluszewski, Chicago A.L., 1959; 3 (5 games) Donn Clendenon, New York Mets N.L., 1969.
Most home runs, game—3, Babe Ruth, New York A.L., 1926 and 1928; Reggie Jackson, New York A.L., 1977.
Most strikeouts, series—12 (6 games) Willie Wilson, Kansas City A.L., 1980; 11 (7 games) Ed Mathews, Milwaukee N.L., 1958; Wayne Garrett, New York N.L., 1973; 10 (8 games)

George Kelly, New York N.L., 1921; 9 (6 games) Jim Bottomley, St. Louis N.L., 1930; 8 (5 games) Rogers Hornsby, Chicago N.L., 1924; Duke Snider, Brooklyn N.L., 1949; 7 (4 games) Bob Muesel, New York A.L., 1927.
Most stolen bases, game—3, Honus Wagner, Pittsburgh N.L., 1909; Willie Davis, Los Angeles N.L., 1965; Lou Brock, St. Louis N.L., 1967 and 1968.
Most strikeouts by pitcher, game—17, Bob Gibson, St. Louis N.L. 1968.
Most strikeouts by pitcher in succession—6, Horace Eller, Cincinnati N.L., 1919; Moe Drabowsky, Baltimore A.L., 1966.
Most strikeouts by pitcher, series—35 (7 games) Bob Gibson, St. Louis N.L., 1968; 28 (8 games) Bill Dinneen, Boston A.L., 1903; 23 (4 games) Sandy Koufax, Los Angeles, 1963; 20 (6 games) Chief Bender, Philadelphia A.L., 1911; 18 (5 games) Christy Mathewson, New York N.L., 1905.
Most bases on balls, series—11 (7 games) Babe Ruth, New York A.L., 1926; Gene Tenace, Oakland A.L., 1973; 9 (6 games) Willie Randolph, New York A.L., 1981; 7 (5 games) James Sheckard, Chicago N.L., 1910; Mickey Cochrane, Philadelphia A.L., 1929; Joe Gordon, New York A.L., 1941; 7 (4 games) Hank Thompson, New York N.L., 1954.
Most consecutive scoreless innings, one series—27, Christy Mathewson, New York N.L., 1905.

## LIFETIME WORLD SERIES RECORDS

Most hits—71, Yogi Berra, New York A.L., 1947, 1949–53, 1955–58, 1960–63.
Most runs—42, Mickey Mantle, New York A.L., 1951–53, 1955–58, 1960–64.
Most runs batted in—40, Mickey Mantle, New York A.L., 1951–53, 1955–58, 1960–64.
Most home runs—18, Mickey Mantle, New York A.L., 1951–53, 1955–58, 1960–64.
Most bases on balls—43, Mickey Mantle, New York A.L., 1951–53, 1955–58, 1960–64.
Most strikeouts—54, Mickey Mantle, New York A.L., 1951–53, 1955–58, 1960–64.
Most stolen bases—14, Eddie Collins, Philadelphia A.L. 1910–11, 13–14; Chicago A.L., 1917, 1919. Lou Brock, St. Louis N.L., 1964, 67–68.

Most victories, pitcher—10, Whitey Ford, New York A.L., 1950, 1953, 1955–58, 1960–64.
Most times member of winning team—10, Yogi Berra, New York A.L., 1947, 1949–53, 1956, 1958, 1961–62.
Most victories, no defeats—6, Vernon Gomez, New York A.L., 1932, 1936(2), 1937(2), 1938.
Most shutouts—4, Christy Mathewson, New York N.L., 1905 (3), 1913.
Most innings pitched—146, Whitey Ford, New York A.L., 1950, 1953, 1955–58, 1960–1964.
Most consecutive scoreless innings—33⅔, Whitey Ford, New York A.L., 1960 (18), 1961 (14), 1962 (1⅔).
Most strikeouts by pitcher—94, Whitey Ford, New York A.L., 1950, 1953, 1955–58, 1960–64.

## AMERICAN LEAGUE HOME RUN CHAMPIONS

| Year | Player, team | No. | Year | Player, team | No. | Year | Player, team | No. |
|---|---|---|---|---|---|---|---|---|
| 1901 | Nap Lajoie, Phila. | 13 | 1930 | Babe Ruth, N.Y. | 49 | 1959 | Rocky Colavito, Cleve., and | |
| 1902 | Ralph Seybold, Phila. | 16 | 1931 | Lou Gehrig, N.Y., and | | | Harmon Killebrew, Wash. | 42 |
| 1903 | Buck Freeman, Bost. | 13 | | Babe Ruth, N.Y. | 46 | 1960 | Mickey Mantle, N.Y. | 40 |
| 1904 | Harry Davis, Phila. | 10 | 1932 | Jimmy Foxx, Phila. | 58 | 1961 | Roger Maris, N.Y. | 61 |
| 1905 | Harry Davis, Phila. | 8 | 1933 | Jimmy Foxx, Phila. | 48 | 1962 | Harmon Killebrew, Minn. | 48 |
| 1906 | Harry Davis, Phila. | 12 | 1934 | Lou Gehrig, N.Y. | 49 | 1963 | Harmon Killebrew, Minn. | 45 |
| 1907 | Harry Davis, Phila. | 8 | 1935 | Jimmy Foxx, Phila., and | | 1964 | Harmon Killebrew, Minn. | 49 |
| 1908 | Sam Crawford, Det. | 7 | | Hank Greenberg, Det. | 36 | 1965 | Tony Conigliaro, Bost. | 32 |
| 1909 | Ty Cobb, Det. | 9 | 1936 | Lou Gehrig, N.Y. | 49 | 1966 | Frank Robinson, Balt. | 49 |
| 1910 | J. Garland Stahl, Bost. | 10 | 1937 | Joe DiMaggio, N.Y. | 46 | 1967 | Carl Yastrzemski, Bost., and | |
| 1911 | Franklin Baker, Phila. | 9 | 1938 | Hank Greenberg, Det. | 58 | | Harmon Killebrew, Minn. | 44 |
| 1912 | Franklin Baker, Phila. | 10 | 1939 | Jimmy Foxx, Bost. | 35 | 1968 | Frank Howard, Wash. | 44 |
| 1913 | Franklin Baker, Phila. | 12 | 1940 | Hank Greenberg, Det. | 41 | 1969 | Harmon Killebrew, Minn. | 49 |
| 1914 | Franklin Baker, Phila., and | | 1941 | Ted Williams, Bost. | 37 | 1970 | Frank Howard, Wash. | 44 |
| | Sam Crawford, Det. | 8 | 1942 | Ted Williams, Bost. | 36 | 1971 | Bill Melton, Chicago | 33 |
| 1915 | Robert Roth, Chi.-Cleve. | 7 | 1943 | Rudy York, Det. | 34 | 1972 | Dick Allen, Chicago | 37 |
| 1916 | Wally Pipp, N.Y. | 12 | 1944 | Nick Etten, N.Y. | 22 | 1973 | Reggie Jackson, Oak. | 32 |
| 1917 | Wally Pipp, N.Y. | 9 | 1945 | Vern Stephens, St. L. | 24 | 1974 | Dick Allen, Chicago | 32 |
| 1918 | Babe Ruth, Bost., and | | 1946 | Hank Greenberg, Det. | 44 | 1975 | Reggie Jackson, Oak., and | |
| | Clarence Walker, Phila. | 11 | 1947 | Ted Williams, Bost. | 32 | | George Scott, Mil. | 36 |
| 1919 | Babe Ruth, Bost. | 29 | 1948 | Joe DiMaggio, N.Y. | 39 | 1976 | Graig Nettles, N.Y. | 32 |
| 1920 | Babe Ruth, N.Y. | 54 | 1949 | Ted Williams, Bost. | 43 | 1977 | Jim Rice, Boston | 39 |
| 1921 | Babe Ruth, N.Y. | 59 | 1950 | Al Rosen, Cleve. | 37 | 1978 | Jim Rice, Boston | 46 |
| 1922 | Ken Williams, St. L. | 39 | 1951 | Gus Zernial, Chi.-Phila. | 33 | 1979 | Gorman Thomas, Milwaukee | 45 |
| 1923 | Babe Ruth, N.Y. | 41 | 1952 | Larry Doby, Cleve. | 32 | 1980 | Reggie Jackson, N.Y., and | |
| 1924 | Babe Ruth, N.Y. | 46 | 1953 | Al Rosen, Cleve. | 43 | | Ben Oglivie, Mil. | 41 |
| 1925 | Bob Meusel, N.Y. | 33 | 1954 | Larry Doby, Cleve. | 32 | 1981* | Tony Armas, Oak., Dwight | |
| 1926 | Babe Ruth, N.Y. | 47 | 1955 | Mickey Mantle, N.Y. | 37 | | Evans, Bost., Bobby Grich, | |
| 1927 | Babe Ruth, N.Y. | 60 | 1956 | Mickey Mantle, N.Y. | 52 | | Calif., and Eddie Murray, | |
| 1928 | Babe Ruth, N.Y. | 54 | 1957 | Roy Sievers, Wash. | 42 | | Balt. (tie) | 22 |
| 1929 | Babe Ruth, N.Y. | 46 | 1958 | Mickey Mantle, N.Y. | 42 | 1982 | Gorman Thomas, Mil., and | |
| | | | | | | | Reggie Jackson, Calif. | 39 |

*Split season because of player strike.

## AMERICAN LEAGUE BATTING CHAMPIONS

| Year | Player, team | Avg | Year | Player, team | Avg | Year | Player, team | Avg |
|---|---|---|---|---|---|---|---|---|
| 1901 | Nap Lajoie, Phila. | .422 | 1929 | Lew Fonseca, Cleve. | .369 | 1957 | Ted Williams, Bost. | .388 |
| 1902 | Ed Delahanty, Wash. | .376 | 1930 | Al Simmons, Phila. | .381 | 1958 | Ted Williams, Bost. | .328 |
| 1903 | Nap Lajoie, Cleve. | .355 | 1931 | Al Simmons, Phila. | .390 | 1959 | Harvey Kuenn, Det. | .353 |
| 1904 | Nap Lajoie, Cleve. | .381 | 1932 | Dale Alexander, Det.-Bost. | .367 | 1960 | Pete Runnels, Bost. | .320 |
| 1905 | Elmer Flick, Cleve. | .306 | 1933 | Jimmy Foxx, Phila. | .356 | 1961 | Norman Cash, Det. | .361 |
| 1906 | George Stone, St. L. | .358 | 1934 | Lou Gehrig, N.Y. | .363 | 1962 | Pete Runnels, Bost. | .326 |
| 1907 | Ty Cobb, Det. | .350 | 1935 | Buddy Myer, Wash. | .349 | 1963 | Carl Yastrzemski, Bost. | .321 |
| 1908 | Ty Cobb, Det. | .324 | 1936 | Luke Appling, Chi. | .388 | 1964 | Tony Oliva, Minn. | .323 |
| 1909 | Ty Cobb, Det. | .377 | 1937 | Charley Gehringer, Det. | .371 | 1965 | Tony Oliva, Minn. | .321 |
| 1910 | Ty Cobb, Det. | .385 | 1938 | Jimmy Foxx, Bost. | .349 | 1966 | Frank Robinson, Balt. | .316 |
| 1911 | Ty Cobb, Det. | .420 | 1939 | Joe DiMaggio, N.Y. | .381 | 1967 | Carl Yastrzemski, Bost. | .326 |
| 1912 | Ty Cobb, Det. | .410 | 1940 | Joe DiMaggio, N.Y. | .352 | 1968 | Carl Yastrzemski, Bost. | .301 |
| 1913 | Ty Cobb, Det. | .390 | 1941 | Ted Williams, Bost. | .406 | 1969 | Rod Carew, Minn. | .332 |
| 1914 | Ty Cobb, Det. | .368 | 1942 | Ted Williams, Bost. | .356 | 1970 | Alex Johnson, Calif. | .329 |
| 1915 | Ty Cobb, Det. | .369 | 1943 | Luke Appling, Chi. | .328 | 1971 | Tony Oliva, Minn. | .337 |
| 1916 | Tris Speaker, Cleve. | .386 | 1944 | Lou Boudreau, Cleve. | .327 | 1972 | Rod Carew, Minn. | .318 |
| 1917 | Ty Cobb, Det. | .383 | 1945 | George Sternweiss, N.Y. | .309 | 1973 | Rod Carew, Minn. | .350 |
| 1918 | Ty Cobb, Det. | .382 | 1946 | Mickey Vernon, Wash. | .353 | 1974 | Rod Carew, Minn. | .364 |
| 1919 | Ty Cobb, Det. | .384 | 1947 | Ted Williams, Bost. | .343 | 1975 | Rod Carew, Minn. | .359 |
| 1920 | George Sisler, St. L. | .407 | 1948 | Ted Williams, Bost. | .369 | 1976 | George Brett, Kansas City | .333 |
| 1921 | Harry Heilmann, Det. | .394 | 1949 | George Kell, Det. | .343 | 1977 | Rod Carew, Minn. | .388 |
| 1922 | George Sisler, St. L. | .420 | 1950 | Billy Goodman, Bost. | .354 | 1978 | Rod Carew, Minn. | .333 |
| 1923 | Harry Heilmann, Det. | .403 | 1951 | Ferris Fain, Phila. | .344 | 1979 | Fred Lynn, Boston | .333 |
| 1924 | Babe Ruth, N.Y. | .378 | 1952 | Ferris Fain, Phila. | .327 | 1980 | George Brett, Kansas City | .390 |
| 1925 | Harry Heilmann, Det. | .393 | 1953 | Mickey Vernon, Wash. | .337 | 1981* | Carney Lansford, Bost. | .336 |
| 1926 | Heinie Manush, Det. | .378 | 1954 | Bobby Avila, Cleve. | .341 | 1982 | Willie Wilson, Kansas City | .332 |
| 1927 | Harry Heilmann, Det. | .398 | 1955 | Al Kaline, Det. | .340 | | | |
| 1928 | Goose Goslin, Wash. | .379 | 1956 | Mickey Mantle, N.Y. | .353 | | | |

*Split season because of player strike.

## NATIONAL LEAGUE HOME RUN CHAMPIONS

| Year | Player, team | No. | Year | Player, team | No. | Year | Player, team | No. |
|---|---|---|---|---|---|---|---|---|
| 1876 | George Hall, Phila. Athletics | 5 | 1911 | Frank Schulte, Chi. | 21 | 1946 | Ralph Kiner, Pitts. | 23 |
| 1877 | George Shaffer, Louisville | 3 | 1912 | Henry Zimmerman, Chi. | 14 | 1947 | Ralph Kiner, Pitts., and | |
| 1878 | Paul Hines, Providence | 4 | 1913 | Cliff Cravath, Phila. | 19 | | John Mize, N.Y. | 51 |
| 1879 | Charles Jones, Bost. | 9 | 1914 | Cliff Cravath, Phila. | 19 | 1948 | Ralph Kiner, Pitts., and | |
| 1880 | James O'Rourke, Bost., and | | 1915 | Cliff Cravath, Phila. | 24 | | John Mize, N.Y. | 40 |
| | Harry Stovey, Worcester | 6 | 1916 | Davis Robertson, N.Y., and | | 1949 | Ralph Kiner, Pitts. | 54 |
| 1881 | Dan Brouthers, Buffalo | 8 | | Fred Williams, Chi. | 12 | 1950 | Ralph Kiner, Pitts. | 47 |
| 1882 | George Wood, Det. | 7 | 1917 | Davis Robertson, N.Y., and | | 1951 | Ralph Kiner, Pitts. | 42 |
| 1883 | William Ewing, N.Y. | 10 | | Cliff Cravath, Phila. | 12 | 1952 | Ralph Kiner, Pitts., and | |
| 1884 | Ed Williamson, Chi. | 27 | 1918 | Cliff Cravath, Phila. | 8 | | Hank Sauer, Chi. | 37 |
| 1885 | Abner Dalrymple, Chi. | 11 | 1919 | Cliff Cravath, Phila. | 12 | 1953 | Ed Mathews, Mil. | 47 |
| 1886 | Arthur Richardson, Det. | 11 | 1920 | Cy Williams, Phila. | 15 | 1954 | Ted Kluszewski, Cin. | 49 |
| 1887 | Roger Connor, N.Y., and | | 1921 | George Kelly, N.Y. | 23 | 1955 | Willie Mays, N.Y. | 51 |
| | Wm. O'Brien, Wash. | 17 | 1922 | Rogers Hornsby, St. L. | 42 | 1956 | Duke Snider, Bklyn. | 43 |
| 1888 | Roger Connor, N.Y. | 14 | 1923 | Cy Williams, Phila. | 41 | 1957 | Henry Aaron, Mil. | 44 |
| 1889 | Sam Thompson, Phila. | 20 | 1924 | Jacques Fournier, Bklyn. | 27 | 1958 | Ernie Banks, Chi. | 47 |
| 1890 | Tom Burns, Bklyn., and | | 1925 | Rogers Hornsby, St. L. | 39 | 1959 | Ed Mathews, Mil. | 46 |
| | Mike Tiernan, N.Y. | 13 | 1926 | Hack Wilson, Chi. | 21 | 1960 | Ernie Banks, Chi. | 41 |
| 1891 | Harry Stovey, Bost., and | | 1927 | Hack Wilson, Chi., and | | 1961 | Orlando Cepeda, San Fran. | 46 |
| | Mike Tiernan, N.Y. | 16 | | Cy Williams, Phila. | 30 | 1962 | Willie Mays, San Fran. | 49 |
| 1892 | Jim Holliday, Cin. | 13 | 1928 | Hack Wilson, Chi., and | | 1963 | Henry Aaron, Mil., and | |
| 1893 | Ed Delahanty, Phila. | 19 | | Jim Bottomley, St. L. | 31 | | Willie McCovey, San Fran. | 44 |
| 1894 | Hugh Duffy, Bost., and | | 1929 | Chuck Klein, Phila. | 43 | 1964 | Willie Mays, San Fran. | 47 |
| | Robert Lowe, Bost. | 18 | 1930 | Hack Wilson, Chi. | 56 | 1965 | Willie Mays, San Fran. | 52 |
| 1895 | Bill Joyce, Wash. | 17 | 1931 | Chuck Klein, Phila. | 31 | 1966 | Henry Aaron, Atlanta | 44 |
| 1896 | Ed Delahanty, Phila., and | | 1932 | Chuck Klein, Phila., and | | 1967 | Henry Aaron, Atlanta | 39 |
| | Sam Thompson, Phila. | 13 | | Mel Ott, N.Y. | 38 | 1968 | Willie McCovey, San Fran. | 36 |
| 1897 | Nap Lajoie, Phila. | 10 | 1933 | Chuck Klein, Phila. | 28 | 1969 | Willie McCovey, San Fran. | 45 |
| 1898 | James Collins, Bost. | 14 | 1934 | Mel Ott, N.Y., and | | 1970 | Johnny Bench, Cin. | 45 |
| 1899 | John Freeman, Wash. | 25 | | Rip Collins, St. L. | 35 | 1971 | Willie Stargell, Pitts. | 48 |
| 1900 | Herman Long, Bost. | 12 | 1935 | Wally Berger, Bost. | 34 | 1972 | Johnny Bench, Cin. | 40 |
| 1901 | Sam Crawford, Cin. | 16 | 1936 | Mel Ott, N.Y. | 33 | 1973 | Willie Stargell, Pitts. | 44 |
| 1902 | Tom Leach, Pitts. | 6 | 1937 | Mel Ott, N.Y., and Joe | | 1974 | Mike Schmidt, Phila. | 36 |
| 1903 | James Sheckard, Bklyn. | 9 | | Medwick, St. L. | 31 | 1975 | Mike Schmidt, Phila. | 38 |
| 1904 | Harry Lumley, Bklyn. | 9 | 1938 | Mel Ott, N.Y. | 36 | 1976 | Mike Schmidt, Phila. | 38 |
| 1905 | Fred Odwell, Cin. | 9 | 1939 | John Mize, St. L. | 28 | 1977 | George Foster, Cin. | 52 |
| 1906 | Tim Jordan, Bklyn. | 12 | 1940 | John Mize, St. L. | 43 | 1978 | George Foster, Cin. | 40 |
| 1907 | David Brain, Bost. | 10 | 1941 | Dolph Camilli, Bklyn. | 34 | 1979 | Dave Kingman, Chicago | 48 |
| 1908 | Tim Jordan, Bklyn. | 12 | 1942 | Mel Ott, N.Y. | 30 | 1980 | Mike Schmidt, Phila. | 48 |
| 1909 | John Murray, N.Y. | 7 | 1943 | Bill Nicholson, Chi. | 29 | 1981* | Mike Schmidt, Phila. | 31 |
| 1910 | Fred Beck, Bost., and | | 1944 | Bill Nicholson, Chi. | 33 | 1982 | Dave Kingman, N.Y. | 37 |
| | Frank Schulte, Chi. | 10 | 1945 | Tommy Holmes, Bost. | 28 | | | |

*Split season because of player strike.

## NATIONAL LEAGUE BATTING CHAMPIONS

| Year | Player, Team | Avg | Year | Player, Team | Avg | Year | Player, Team | Avg |
|---|---|---|---|---|---|---|---|---|
| 1876 | Roscoe Barnes, Chicago | .404 | 1894 | Hugh Duffy, Boston | .438 | 1912 | Henry Zimmerman, Chicago | .372 |
| 1877 | Jim White, Boston | .385 | 1895 | Jesse Burkett, Cleveland | .423 | 1913 | Jake Daubert, Brooklyn | .350 |
| 1878 | Abner Dalrymple, Mil. | .356 | 1896 | Jesse Burkett, Cleveland | .410 | 1914 | Jake Daubert, Brooklyn | .329 |
| 1879 | Cap Anson, Chicago | .407 | 1897 | Willie Keeler, Baltimore | .432 | 1915 | Larry Doyle, New York | .320 |
| 1880 | George Gore, Chicago | .365 | 1898 | Willie Keeler, Baltimore | .379 | 1916 | Hal Chase, Cincinnati | .339 |
| 1881 | Cap Anson, Chicago | .399 | 1899 | Ed Delahanty, Phila. | .408 | 1917 | Edd Roush, Cincinnati | .341 |
| 1882 | Dan Brouthers, Buffalo | .367 | 1900 | Honus Wagner, Pittsburgh | .381 | 1918 | Zack Wheat, Brooklyn | .335 |
| 1883 | Dan Brouthers, Buffalo | .371 | 1901 | Jesse Burkett, St. Louis | .382 | 1919 | Edd Roush, Cincinnati | .321 |
| 1884 | James O'Rourke, Buffalo | .350 | 1902 | Clarence Beaumont, Pitts. | .357 | 1920 | Rogers Hornsby, St. Louis | .370 |
| 1885 | Roger Connor, N. Y. | .371 | 1903 | Honus Wagner, Pittsburgh | .355 | 1921 | Rogers Hornsby, St. Louis | .397 |
| 1886 | King Kelly, Chicago | .388 | 1904 | Honus Wagner, Pittsburgh | .349 | 1922 | Rogers Hornsby, St. Louis | .401 |
| 1887 | Cap Anson, Chicago | .421 | 1905 | Cy Seymour, Cincinnati | .377 | 1923 | Rogers Hornsby, St. Louis | .384 |
| 1888 | Cap Anson, Chicago | .343 | 1906 | Honus Wagner, Pittsburgh | .339 | 1924 | Rogers Hornsby, St. Louis | .424 |
| 1889 | Dan Brouthers, Boston | .373 | 1907 | Honus Wagner, Pittsburgh | .350 | 1925 | Rogers Hornsby, St. Louis | .403 |
| 1890 | John Glasscock, N. Y. | .336 | 1908 | Honus Wagner, Pittsburgh | .354 | 1926 | Gene Hargrave, Cincinnati | .353 |
| 1891 | William Hamilton, Phila. | .338 | 1909 | Honus Wagner, Pittsburgh | .339 | 1927 | Paul Waner, Pittsburgh | .380 |
| 1892 | Dan Brouthers, Bklyn., and | | 1910 | Sherwood Magee, | | 1928 | Rogers Hornsby, Boston | .387 |
| | Clarence Childs, Cleve. | .335 | | Philadelphia | .331 | 1929 | Lefty O'Doul, Phila. | .398 |
| 1893 | Hugh Duffy, Boston | .378 | 1911 | Honus Wagner, Pittsburgh | .334 | 1930 | Bill Terry, N. Y. | .401 |

| Year | Player, Team | Avg | Year | Player, Team | Avg | Year | Player, Team | Avg |
|------|-------------|-----|------|-------------|-----|------|-------------|-----|
| 1931 | Chick Hafey, St. Louis | .349 | 1949 | Jackie Robinson, Brooklyn | .342 | 1967 | Roberto Clemente, Pitts. | .357 |
| 1932 | Lefty O'Doul, Brooklyn | .368 | 1950 | Stan Musial, St. Louis | .346 | 1968 | Pete Rose, Cincinnati | .335 |
| 1933 | Chuck Klein, Phila. | .368 | 1951 | Stan Musial, St. Louis | .355 | 1969 | Pete Rose, Cincinnati | .348 |
| 1934 | Paul Waner, Pittsburgh | .362 | 1952 | Stan Musial, St. Louis | .336 | 1970 | Rico Carty, Atlanta | .366 |
| 1935 | Arky Vaughan, Pittsburgh | .385 | 1953 | Carl Furillo, Brooklyn | .344 | 1971 | Joe Torre, St. Louis | .363 |
| 1936 | Paul Waner, Pittsburgh | .373 | 1954 | Willie Mays, N. Y. | .345 | 1972 | Billy Williams, Chicago | .333 |
| 1937 | Joe Medwick, St. Louis | .374 | 1955 | Richie Ashburn, Phila. | .338 | 1973 | Pete Rose, Cincinnati | .338 |
| 1938 | Ernie Lombardi, Cin. | .342 | 1956 | Henry Aaron, Mil. | .328 | 1974 | Ralph Garr, Atlanta | .353 |
| 1939 | John Mize, St. Louis | .349 | 1957 | Stan Musial, St. Louis | .351 | 1975 | Bill Madlock, Chicago | .354 |
| 1940 | Debs Garms, Pittsburgh | .355 | 1958 | Richie Ashburn, Phila. | .350 | 1976 | Bill Madlock, Chicago | .339 |
| 1941 | Pete Reiser, Brooklyn | .343 | 1959 | Henry Aaron, Mil. | .355 | 1977 | Dave Parker, Pittsburgh | .338 |
| 1942 | Ernie Lombardi, Boston | .330 | 1960 | Dick Groat, Pittsburgh | .325 | 1978 | Dave Parker, Pittsburgh | .334 |
| 1943 | Stan Musial, St. Louis | .357 | 1961 | Roberto Clemente, Pitts. | .351 | 1979 | Keith Hernandez, St. Louis | .344 |
| 1944 | Dixie Walker, Brooklyn | .357 | 1962 | Tommy Davis, L. A. | .346 | 1980 | Bill Buckner, Chicago | .324 |
| 1945 | Phil Cavarretta, Chicago | .355 | 1963 | Tommy Davis, L. A. | .326 | 1981* | Bill Madlock, Pittsburgh | .341 |
| 1946 | Stan Musial, St. Louis | .365 | 1964 | Roberto Clemente, Pitts. | .339 | 1982 | Al Oliver, Montreal | .331 |
| 1947 | Harry Walker, St. L.-Phila. | .363 | 1965 | Roberto Clemente, Pitts. | .329 | | | |
| 1948 | Stan Musial, St. Louis | .376 | 1966 | Matty Alou, Pittsburgh | .342 | | | |

*Split season because of player strike.

## AMERICAN LEAGUE PENNANT WINNERS

| Year | Club | Manager | Won | Lost | Pct | Year | Club | Manager | Won | Lost | Pct |
|------|------|---------|-----|------|-----|------|------|---------|-----|------|-----|
| 1901 | Chicago | Clark C. Griffith | 83 | 53 | .610 | 1943[1] | New York | Joseph V. McCarthy | 98 | 56 | .636 |
| 1902 | Philadelphia | Connie Mack | 83 | 53 | .610 | 1944 | St. Louis | Luke Sewell | 89 | 65 | .578 |
| 1903[1] | Boston | Jimmy Collins | 91 | 47 | .659 | 1945[1] | Detroit | Steve O'Neill | 88 | 65 | .575 |
| 1904[2] | Boston | Jimmy Collins | 95 | 59 | .617 | 1946 | Boston | Joseph E. Cronin | 104 | 50 | .675 |
| 1905 | Philadelphia | Connie Mack | 92 | 56 | .622 | 1947[1] | New York | Stanley R. Harris | 97 | 57 | .630 |
| 1906[1] | Chicago | Fielder A. Jones | 93 | 58 | .616 | 1948[1] | Cleveland | Lou Boudreau | 97 | 58 | .626 |
| 1907 | Detroit | Hugh A. Jennings | 92 | 58 | .613 | 1949[1] | New York | Casey Stengel | 97 | 57 | .630 |
| 1908 | Detroit | Hugh A. Jennings | 90 | 63 | .588 | 1950[1] | New York | Casey Stengel | 98 | 56 | .636 |
| 1909 | Detroit | Hugh A. Jennings | 98 | 54 | .645 | 1951[1] | New York | Casey Stengel | 98 | 56 | .636 |
| 1910[1] | Philadelphia | Connie Mack | 102 | 48 | .680 | 1952[1] | New York | Casey Stengel | 95 | 59 | .617 |
| 1911[1] | Philadelphia | Connie Mack | 101 | 50 | .669 | 1953[1] | New York | Casey Stengel | 99 | 52 | .656 |
| 1912[1] | Boston | J. Garland Stahl | 105 | 47 | .691 | 1954 | Cleveland | Al Lopez | 111 | 43 | .721 |
| 1913[1] | Philadelphia | Connie Mack | 96 | 57 | .627 | 1955 | New York | Casey Stengel | 96 | 58 | .623 |
| 1914 | Philadelphia | Connie Mack | 99 | 53 | .651 | 1956[1] | New York | Casey Stengel | 97 | 57 | .630 |
| 1915[1] | Boston | William F. Carrigan | 101 | 50 | .669 | 1957 | New York | Casey Stengel | 98 | 56 | .636 |
| 1916[1] | Boston | William F. Carrigan | 91 | 63 | .591 | 1958[1] | New York | Casey Stengel | 92 | 62 | .597 |
| 1917[1] | Chicago | Clarence H. Rowland | 100 | 54 | .649 | 1959 | Chicago | Al Lopez | 94 | 60 | .610 |
| 1918[1] | Boston | Ed Barrow | 75 | 51 | .595 | 1960 | New York | Casey Stengel | 97 | 57 | .630 |
| 1919 | Chicago | William Gleason | 88 | 52 | .629 | 1961[1] | New York | Ralph Houk | 109 | 53 | .673 |
| 1920[1] | Cleveland | Tris Speaker | 98 | 56 | .636 | 1962[1] | New York | Ralph Houk | 96 | 66 | .593 |
| 1921 | New York | Miller J. Huggins | 98 | 55 | .641 | 1963 | New York | Ralph Houk | 104 | 57 | .646 |
| 1922 | New York | Miller J. Huggins | 94 | 60 | .610 | 1964 | New York | Yogi Berra | 99 | 63 | .611 |
| 1923[1] | New York | Miller J. Huggins | 98 | 54 | .645 | 1965 | Minnesota | Sam Mele | 102 | 60 | .630 |
| 1924[1] | Washington | Stanley R. Harris | 92 | 62 | .597 | 1966[1] | Baltimore | Hank Bauer | 97 | 63 | .606 |
| 1925 | Washington | Stanley R. Harris | 96 | 55 | .636 | 1967 | Boston | Dick Williams | 92 | 70 | .568 |
| 1926 | New York | Miller J. Huggins | 91 | 63 | .591 | 1968[1] | Detroit | Mayo Smith | 103 | 59 | .636 |
| 1927[1] | New York | Miller J. Huggins | 110 | 44 | .714 | 1969 | Baltimore[3] | Earl Weaver | 109 | 53 | .673 |
| 1928[1] | New York | Miller J. Huggins | 101 | 53 | .656 | 1970[1] | Baltimore[3] | Earl Weaver | 108 | 54 | .667 |
| 1929[1] | Philadelphia | Connie Mack | 104 | 46 | .693 | 1971 | Baltimore[4] | Earl Weaver | 101 | 57 | .639 |
| 1930[1] | Philadelphia | Connie Mack | 102 | 52 | .662 | 1972[1] | Oakland[5] | Dick Williams | 93 | 62 | .600 |
| 1931 | Philadelphia | Connie Mack | 107 | 45 | .704 | 1973[1] | Oakland[6] | Dick Williams | 94 | 68 | .580 |
| 1932 | New York | Joseph V. McCarthy | 107 | 47 | .695 | 1974[1] | Oakland[6] | Alvin Dark | 90 | 72 | .556 |
| 1933 | Washington | Joseph E. Cronin | 99 | 53 | .651 | 1975 | Boston[4] | Darrell Johnson | 95 | 65 | .594 |
| 1934 | Detroit | Gordon Cochrane | 101 | 53 | .656 | 1976 | New York[7] | Billy Martin | 97 | 62 | .610 |
| 1935[1] | Detroit | Gordon Cochrane | 93 | 58 | .616 | 1977[1] | New York[7] | Billy Martin | 100 | 62 | .617 |
| 1936[1] | New York | Joseph V. McCarthy | 102 | 51 | .667 | 1978[1] | New York[7] | Billy Martin | | | |
| 1937[1] | New York | Joseph V. McCarthy | 102 | 52 | .662 | | | and Bob Lemon | 100 | 63 | .613 |
| 1938[1] | New York | Joseph V. McCarthy | 99 | 53 | .651 | 1979 | Baltimore[8] | Earl Weaver | 102 | 57 | .642 |
| 1939[1] | New York | Joseph V. McCarthy | 106 | 45 | .702 | 1980 | Kansas City[9] | Jim Frey | 97 | 65 | .599 |
| 1940 | Detroit | Delmar D. Baker | 90 | 64 | .584 | 1981 | New York[10] | Gene Michael–Bob | | | |
| 1941[1] | New York | Joseph V. McCarthy | 101 | 53 | .656 | | | Lemon | 59 | 48 | .551* |
| 1942 | New York | Joseph V. McCarthy | 103 | 51 | .669 | 1982 | Milwaukee[11] | Harvey Kuenn | 95 | 67 | .586 |

*Split season because of player strike. 1. World Series winner. 2. No World Series. 3. Defeated Minnesota, Western Division winner, in playoff. 4. Defeated Oakland, Western Division Leader, in playoff. 5. Defeated Detroit, Eastern Division winner, in playoff. 6. Defeated Baltimore, Eastern Division winner, in playoff. 7. Defeated Kansas City, Western Division winner, in playoff. 8. Defeated California, Western Division winner, in playoff. 9. Defeated New York, Eastern Division winner, in playoff. 10. Defeated Oakland, Western Division winner, in playoff. 11. Defeated California, Western Division winner, in playoff.

## NATIONAL LEAGUE PENNANT WINNERS

| Year | Club | Manager | Won | Lost | Pct | Year | Club | Manager | Won | Lost | Pct |
|------|------|---------|-----|------|-----|------|------|---------|-----|------|-----|
| 1876 | Chicago | Albert G. Spalding | 52 | 14 | .788 | 1930 | St. Louis | Gabby Street | 92 | 62 | .597 |
| 1877 | Boston | Harry Wright | 31 | 17 | .646 | 1931 | St. Louis[1] | Gabby Street | 101 | 53 | .656 |
| 1878 | Boston | Harry Wright | 41 | 19 | .683 | 1932 | Chicago | Charles J. Grimm | 90 | 64 | .584 |
| 1879 | Providence | George Wright | 55 | 23 | .705 | 1933 | New York[1] | William H. Terry | 91 | 61 | .599 |
| 1880 | Chicago | Adrian C. Anson | 67 | 17 | .798 | 1934 | St. Louis[1] | Frank F. Frisch | 95 | 58 | .621 |
| 1881 | Chicago | Adrian C. Anson | 56 | 28 | .667 | 1935 | Chicago | Charles J. Grimm | 100 | 54 | .649 |
| 1882 | Chicago | Adrian C. Anson | 55 | 29 | .655 | 1936 | New York | William H. Terry | 92 | 62 | .597 |
| 1883 | Boston | John F. Morrill | 63 | 35 | .643 | 1937 | New York | William H. Terry | 95 | 57 | .625 |
| 1884 | Providence | Frank C. Bancroft | 84 | 28 | .750 | 1938 | Chicago | Gabby Hartnett | 89 | 63 | .586 |
| 1885 | Chicago | Adrian C. Anson | 87 | 25 | .777 | 1939 | Cincinnati | William B. McKechnie | 97 | 57 | .630 |
| 1886 | Chicago | Adrian C. Anson | 90 | 34 | .726 | 1940 | Cincinnati[1] | William B. McKechnie | 100 | 53 | .654 |
| 1887 | Detroit | W. H. Watkins | 79 | 45 | .637 | 1941 | Brooklyn | Leo E. Durocher | 100 | 54 | .649 |
| 1888 | New York | James J. Mutrie | 84 | 47 | .641 | 1942 | St. Louis[1] | William H. Southworth | 106 | 48 | .688 |
| 1889 | New York | James J. Mutrie | 83 | 43 | .659 | 1943 | St. Louis | William H. Southworth | 105 | 49 | .682 |
| 1890 | Brooklyn | William H. McGunnigle | 86 | 43 | .667 | 1944 | St. Louis[1] | William H. Southworth | 105 | 49 | .682 |
| 1891 | Boston | Frank G. Selee | 87 | 51 | .630 | 1945 | Chicago | Charles J. Grimm | 98 | 56 | .636 |
| 1892 | Boston | Frank G. Selee | 102 | 48 | .680 | 1946 | St. Louis[1] | Edwin H. Dyer | 98 | 58 | .628 |
| 1893 | Boston | Frank G. Selee | 86 | 44 | .662 | 1947 | Brooklyn | Burton E. Shotton | 94 | 60 | .610 |
| 1894 | Baltimore | Edward H. Hanlon | 89 | 39 | .695 | 1948 | Boston | William H. Southworth | 91 | 62 | .595 |
| 1895 | Baltimore | Edward H. Hanlon | 87 | 43 | .669 | 1949 | Brooklyn | Burton E. Shotton | 97 | 57 | .630 |
| 1896 | Baltimore | Edward H. Hanlon | 90 | 39 | .698 | 1950 | Philadelphia | Edwin H. Sawyer | 91 | 63 | .591 |
| 1897 | Boston | Frank G. Selee | 93 | 39 | .705 | 1951 | New York | Leo E. Durocher | 98 | 59 | .624 |
| 1898 | Boston | Frank G. Selee | 102 | 47 | .685 | 1952 | Brooklyn | Charles W. Dressen | 96 | 57 | .630 |
| 1899 | Brooklyn | Edward H. Hanlon | 88 | 42 | .677 | 1953 | Brooklyn | Charles W. Dressen | 105 | 49 | .682 |
| 1900 | Brooklyn | Edward H. Hanlon | 82 | 54 | .603 | 1954 | New York[1] | Leo E. Durocher | 97 | 57 | .630 |
| 1901 | Pittsburgh | Fred C. Clarke | 90 | 49 | .647 | 1955 | Brooklyn[1] | Walter Alston | 98 | 55 | .641 |
| 1902 | Pittsburgh | Fred C. Clarke | 103 | 36 | .741 | 1956 | Brooklyn | Walter Alston | 93 | 61 | .604 |
| 1903 | Pittsburgh | Fred C. Clarke | 91 | 49 | .650 | 1957 | Milwaukee[1] | Fred Haney | 95 | 59 | .617 |
| 1904 | New York[2] | John J. McGraw | 106 | 47 | .693 | 1958 | Milwaukee | Fred Haney | 92 | 62 | .597 |
| 1905 | New York[1] | John J. McGraw | 105 | 48 | .686 | 1959 | Los Angeles[1] | Walter Alston | 88 | 68 | .564 |
| 1906 | Chicago | Frank L. Chance | 116 | 36 | .763 | 1960 | Pittsburgh[1] | Danny Murtaugh | 95 | 59 | .617 |
| 1907 | Chicago[1] | Frank L. Chance | 107 | 45 | .704 | 1961 | Cincinnati | Fred Hutchinson | 93 | 61 | .604 |
| 1908 | Chicago[1] | Frank L. Chance | 99 | 55 | .643 | 1962 | San Francisco | Alvin Dark | 103 | 62 | .624 |
| 1909 | Pittsburgh[1] | Fred C. Clarke | 110 | 42 | .724 | 1963 | Los Angeles[1] | Walter Alston | 99 | 63 | .611 |
| 1910 | Chicago | Frank L. Chance | 104 | 50 | .675 | 1964 | St. Louis[1] | Johnny Keane | 93 | 69 | .574 |
| 1911 | New York | John J. McGraw | 99 | 54 | .647 | 1965 | Los Angeles[1] | Walter Alston | 97 | 65 | .599 |
| 1912 | New York | John J. McGraw | 103 | 48 | .682 | 1966 | Los Angeles | Walter Alston | 95 | 67 | .586 |
| 1913 | New York | John J. McGraw | 101 | 51 | .664 | 1967 | St. Louis[1] | Red Schoendienst | 101 | 60 | .627 |
| 1914 | Boston[1] | George T. Stallings | 94 | 59 | .614 | 1968 | St. Louis | Red Schoendienst | 97 | 65 | .599 |
| 1915 | Philadelphia | Patrick J. Moran | 90 | 62 | .592 | 1969 | New York[1][3] | Gil Hodges | 100 | 62 | .617 |
| 1916 | Brooklyn | Wilbert Robinson | 94 | 60 | .610 | 1970 | Cincinnati[4] | Sparky Anderson | 102 | 60 | .630 |
| 1917 | New York | John J. McGraw | 98 | 56 | .636 | 1971 | Pittsburgh[1][5] | Danny Murtaugh | 97 | 65 | .599 |
| 1918 | Chicago | Fred L. Mitchell | 84 | 45 | .651 | 1972 | Cincinnati[4] | Sparky Anderson | 95 | 59 | .617 |
| 1919 | Cincinnati[1] | Patrick J. Moran | 96 | 44 | .686 | 1973 | New York[6] | Yogi Berra | 82 | 79 | .509 |
| 1920 | Brooklyn | Wilbert Robinson | 93 | 61 | .604 | 1974 | Los Angeles[6] | Walter Alston | 102 | 60 | .630 |
| 1921 | New York[1] | John J. McGraw | 94 | 59 | .614 | 1975 | Cincinnati[1][4] | Sparky Anderson | 108 | 54 | .667 |
| 1922 | New York[1] | John J. McGraw | 93 | 61 | .604 | 1976 | Cincinnati[7][1] | Sparky Anderson | 102 | 60 | .630 |
| 1923 | New York | John J. McGraw | 95 | 58 | .621 | 1977 | Los Angeles[7] | Tom Lasorda | 98 | 64 | .605 |
| 1924 | New York | John J. McGraw | 93 | 60 | .608 | 1978 | Los Angeles[7] | Tom Lasorda | 95 | 67 | .586 |
| 1925 | Pittsburgh[1] | William B. McKechnie | 95 | 58 | .621 | 1979[1] | Pittsburgh[6] | Chuck Tanner | 98 | 64 | .605 |
| 1926 | St. Louis[1] | Rogers Hornsby | 89 | 65 | .578 | 1980[1] | Philadelphia[8] | Dallas Green | 91 | 71 | .562 |
| 1927 | Pittsburgh | Donie Bush | 94 | 60 | .610 | 1981 | Los Angeles[1][9] | Tom Lasorda | 63 | 47 | .573* |
| 1928 | St. Louis | William B. McKechnie | 95 | 59 | .617 | 1982[1] | St. Louis[10] | Whitey Herzog | 92 | 70 | .568 |
| 1929 | Chicago | Joseph V. McCarthy | 98 | 54 | .645 | | | | | | |

*Split season because of player strike. 1. World Series winner. 2. No World Series. 3. Defeated Atlanta, Western Division winner, in playoff. 4. Defeated Pittsburgh, Eastern Division winner, in playoff. 5. Defeated San Francisco, Western Division winner, in playoff. 6. Defeated Cincinnati, Western Division winner, in playoff. 7. Defeated Philadelphia, Eastern Division winner, in playoff. 8. Defeated Houston, Western Division winner, in playoff. 9. Defeated Montreal, Eastern Division winner, in playoff. 10. Defeated Atlanta, Western Division winner, in playoff.

## GAYLORD PERRY JOINS 300-VICTORY CLUB

Gaylord Perry, the 44-year-old right-hander for the Seattle Mariners, became only the 15th pitcher in baseball history to record 300 victories in 1982. Perry, who pitched for seven teams in both major leagues over 21 years, won his 300th on May 6. He is the only pitcher to win the Cy Young Award, for best pitcher of the year, in both major leagues. He finished the 1982 season with a 10–12 won-lost record and 307 career victories. He is also third in career strikeouts, with 3,452, behind Walter Johnson, the leader with 3,508, and Nolan Ryan of Houston, who is second with 3,494.

## MOST VALUABLE PLAYERS
(Baseball Writers Association selections)

### American League
| | |
|---|---|
| 1931 | Lefty Grove, Philadelphia |
| 1932–33 | Jimmy Foxx, Philadelphia |
| 1934 | Mickey Cochrane, Detroit |
| 1935 | Hank Greenberg, Detroit |
| 1936 | Lou Gehrig, New York |
| 1937 | Charlie Gehringer, Detroit |
| 1938 | Jimmy Foxx, Boston |
| 1939 | Joe DiMaggio, New York |
| 1940 | Hank Greenberg, Detroit |
| 1941 | Joe DiMaggio, New York |
| 1942 | Joe Gordon, New York |
| 1943 | Spurgeon Chandler, New York |
| 1944–45 | Hal Newhouser, Detroit |
| 1946 | Ted Williams, Boston |
| 1947 | Joe DiMaggio, New York |
| 1948 | Lou Boudreau, Cleveland |
| 1949 | Ted Williams, Boston |
| 1950 | Phil Rizzuto, New York |
| 1951 | Yogi Berra, New York |
| 1952 | Bobby Shantz, Philadelphia |
| 1953 | Al Rosen, Cleveland |
| 1954–55 | Yogi Berra, New York |
| 1956–57 | Mickey Mantle, New York |
| 1958 | Jackie Jensen, Boston |
| 1959 | Nellie Fox, Chicago |
| 1960–61 | Roger Maris, New York |
| 1962 | Mickey Mantle, New York |
| 1963 | Elston Howard, New York |
| 1964 | Brooks Robinson, Baltimore |
| 1965 | Zoilo Versalles, Minnesota |
| 1966 | Frank Robinson, Baltimore |
| 1967 | Carl Yastrzemski, Boston |
| 1968 | Dennis McLain, Detroit |
| 1969 | Harmon Killebrew, Minnesota |
| 1970 | John (Boog) Powell, Baltimore |
| 1971 | Vida Blue, Oakland |
| 1972 | Dick Allen, Chicago |
| 1973 | Reggie Jackson, Oakland |
| 1974 | Jeff Burroughs, Texas |
| 1975 | Fred Lynn, Boston |
| 1976 | Thurman Munson, New York |
| 1977 | Rod Carew, Minnesota |
| 1978 | Jim Rice, Boston |
| 1979 | Don Baylor, California |
| 1980 | George Brett, Kansas City |
| 1981 | Rollie Fingers, Milwaukee |

### National League
| | |
|---|---|
| 1931 | Frank Frisch, St. Louis |
| 1932 | Chuck Klein, Philadelphia |
| 1933 | Carl Hubbell, New York |
| 1934 | Dizzy Dean, St. Louis |
| 1935 | Gabby Hartnett, Chicago |
| 1936 | Carl Hubbell, New York |
| 1937 | Joe Medwick, St. Louis |
| 1938 | Ernie Lombardi, Cincinnati |
| 1939 | Bucky Walters, Cincinnati |
| 1940 | Frank McCormick, Cincinnati |
| 1941 | Dolph Camilli, Brooklyn |
| 1942 | Mort Cooper, St. Louis |
| 1943 | Stan Musial, St. Louis |
| 1944 | Marty Marion, St. Louis |
| 1945 | Phil Cavarretta, Chicago |
| 1946 | Stan Musial, St. Louis |
| 1947 | Bob Elliott, Boston |
| 1948 | Stan Musial, St. Louis |
| 1949 | Jackie Robinson, Brooklyn |
| 1950 | Jim Konstanty, Philadelphia |
| 1951 | Roy Campanella, Brooklyn |
| 1952 | Hank Sauer, Chicago |
| 1953 | Roy Campanella, Brooklyn |
| 1954 | Willie Mays, New York |
| 1955 | Roy Campanella, Brooklyn |
| 1956 | Don Newcombe, Brooklyn |
| 1957 | Henry Aaron, Milwaukee |
| 1958–59 | Ernie Banks, Chicago |
| 1960 | Dick Groat, Pittsburgh |
| 1961 | Frank Robinson, Cincinnati |
| 1962 | Maury Wills, Los Angeles |
| 1963 | Sandy Koufax, Los Angeles |
| 1964 | Ken Boyer, St. Louis |
| 1965 | Willie Mays, San Francisco |
| 1966 | Roberto Clemente, Pittsburgh |
| 1967 | Orlando Cepeda, St. Louis |
| 1968 | Bob Gibson, St. Louis |
| 1969 | Willie McCovey, San Francisco |
| 1970 | Johnny Bench, Cincinnati |
| 1971 | Joe Torre, St. Louis |
| 1972 | Johnny Bench, Cincinnati |
| 1973 | Pete Rose, Cincinnati |
| 1974 | Steve Garvey, Los Angeles |
| 1975–76 | Joe Morgan, Cincinnati |
| 1977 | George Foster, Cincinnati |
| 1978 | Dave Parker, Pittsburgh |
| 1979 | Willie Stargell, Pittsburgh |
| 1979 | Keith Hernandez, St. Louis |
| 1980 | Mike Schmidt, Philadelphia |
| 1981 | Mike Schmidt, Philadelphia |

## CY YOUNG AWARD

| | |
|---|---|
| 1956 | Don Newcombe, Brooklyn N.L. |
| 1957 | Warren Spahn, Milwaukee N.L. |
| 1958 | Bob Turley, New York A.L. |
| 1959 | Early Wynn, Chicago A.L. |
| 1960 | Vernon Law, Pittsburgh, N.L. |
| 1961 | Whitey Ford, New York A.L. |
| 1962 | Don Drysdale, Los Angeles N.L. |
| 1963 | Sandy Koufax, Los Angeles N.L. |
| 1964 | Dean Chance, Los Angeles A.L. |
| 1965 | Sandy Koufax, Los Angeles N.L. |
| 1966 | Sandy Koufax, Los Angeles N.L. |
| 1967 | Jim Lonborg, Boston A.L.; Mike McCormick, San Francisco N.L. |
| 1968 | Dennis McLain, Detroit A.L.; Bob Gibson, St. Louis N.L. |
| 1969 | Mike Cuellar, Baltimore, and Dennis McLain, Detroit, tied in A.L.; Tom Seaver, N.Y. N.L. |
| 1970 | Jim Perry, Minnesota A.L.; Bob Gibson, St. Louis N.L. |
| 1971 | Vida Blue, Oakland A.L.; Ferguson Jenkins, Chicago N.L. |
| 1972 | Gaylord Perry, Cleveland A.L.; Steve Carlton, Phila. N.L. |
| 1973 | Jim Palmer, Baltimore A.L.; Tom Seaver, New York N.L. |
| 1974 | Catfish Hunter, Oakland A.L.; Mike Marshall, Los Angeles N.L. |
| 1975 | Jim Palmer, Baltimore A.L.; Tom Seaver, New York N.L. |
| 1976 | Jim Palmer, Baltimore A.L.; Randy Jones, San Diego N.L. |
| 1977 | Sparky Lyle, N.Y., A.L.; Steve Carlton, Philadelphia N.L. |
| 1978 | Ron Guidry, N.Y., A.L.; Gaylord Perry, San Diego N.L. |
| 1979 | Mike Flanagan, Baltimore, A.L.; Bruce Sutter, Chicago, N.L. |
| 1980 | Steve Stone, Baltimore, A.L.; Steve Carlton, Philadelphia, N.L. |
| 1981 | Rollie Fingers, Milwaukee, A.L.; Fernando Valenzuela, Los Angeles, N.L. |

## ROOKIE OF THE YEAR
(Baseball Writers Association selections)

### American League
| | |
|---|---|
| 1949 | Roy Sievers, St. Louis |
| 1950 | Walt Dropo, Boston |
| 1951 | Gil McDougald, New York |
| 1952 | Harry Byrd, Philadelphia |
| 1953 | Harvey Kuenn, Detroit |
| 1954 | Bob Grim, New York |
| 1955 | Herb Score, Cleveland |
| 1956 | Luis Aparicio, Chicago |
| 1957 | Tony Kubek, New York |
| 1958 | Albie Pearson, Washington |
| 1959 | Bob Allison, Washington |
| 1960 | Ron Hansen, Baltimore |
| 1961 | Don Schwall, Boston |
| 1962 | Tom Tresh, New York |
| 1963 | Gary Peters, Chicago |
| 1964 | Tony Oliva, Minnesota |
| 1965 | Curt Blefary, Baltimore |
| 1966 | Tommy Agee, Chicago |
| 1967 | Rod Carew, Minnesota |
| 1968 | Stan Bahnsen, New York |
| 1969 | Lou Piniella, Kansas City |
| 1970 | Thurman Munson, New York |
| 1971 | Chris Chambliss, Cleveland |
| 1972 | Carlton Fisk, Boston |
| 1973 | Alonzo Bumbry, Baltimore |
| 1974 | Mike Hargrove, Texas |
| 1975 | Fred Lynn, Boston |
| 1976 | Mark Fidrych, Detroit |
| 1977 | Eddie Murray, Baltimore |
| 1978 | Lou Whitaker, Detroit |
| 1979 | Alfredo Griffin, Toronto |
| 1979 | John Castino, Minnesota |
| 1980 | Joe Charboneau, Cleveland |
| 1981 | Dave Righetti, New York |

### National League
| | |
|---|---|
| 1949 | Don Newcombe, Brooklyn |
| 1950 | Sam Jethroe, Boston |
| 1951 | Willie Mays, New York |
| 1952 | Joe Black, Brooklyn |
| 1953 | Jim Gilliam, Brooklyn |
| 1954 | Wally Moon, St. Louis |
| 1955 | Bill Virdon, St. Louis |
| 1956 | Frank Robinson, Cincinnati |

| | | | |
|---|---|---|---|
| 1957 | Jack Sanford, Philadelphia | 1966 | Tommy Helms, Cincinnati | 1975 | John Montefusco, San Francisco |
| 1958 | Orlando Cepeda, San Francisco | 1967 | Tom Seaver, New York | 1976 | Pat Zachry, Cincinnati |
| 1959 | Willie McCovey, San Francisco | 1968 | Johnny Bench, Cincinnati | 1977 | Andre Dawson, Montreal |
| 1960 | Frank Howard, Los Angeles | 1969 | Ted Sizemore, Los Angeles | 1978 | Bob Horner, Atlanta |
| 1961 | Billy Williams, Chicago | 1970 | Carl Morton, Montreal | 1979 | Rick Sutcliffe, Los Angeles |
| 1962 | Ken Hubbs, Chicago | 1971 | Earl Williams, Atlanta | 1980 | Steve Howe, Los Angeles |
| 1963 | Pete Rose, Cincinnati | 1972 | Jon Matlack, New York | 1981 | Fernando Valenzuela, Los Angeles |
| 1964 | Richie Allen, Philadelphia | 1973 | Gary Matthews, San Francisco | | |
| 1965 | Jim Lefebvre, Los Angeles | 1974 | Bake McBride, St. Louis | | |

## MAJOR LEAGUE LIFETIME RECORDS

*Source:* The Book of Baseball Records, published and copyrighted by Seymour Siwoff, New York, N.Y. 10036.

### Leading Batters, by Average
(Over 2,000 Hits)

| | Years | At Bats | Hits | Avg |
|---|---|---|---|---|
| Ty Cobb | 24 | 11,429 | 4,191 | .367 |
| Rogers Hornsby | 23 | 8,173 | 2,930 | .358 |
| Dan Brouthers | 19 | 6,725 | 2,349 | .349 |
| Ed Delahanty | 16 | 7,493 | 2,593 | .346 |
| Tris Speaker | 22 | 10,196 | 3,515 | .345 |
| Willie Keeler | 19 | 8,564 | 2,955 | .345 |
| Ted Williams | 19 | 7,706 | 2,654 | .345 |
| Billy Hamilton | 14 | 6,262 | 2,157 | .344 |
| Harry Heilmann | 17 | 7,787 | 2,660 | .342 |
| Babe Ruth | 22 | 8,399 | 2,873 | .342 |
| Jesse Burkett | 16 | 8,389 | 2,872 | .342 |
| Bill Terry | 14 | 6,428 | 2,193 | .341 |
| Lou Gehrig | 17 | 8,001 | 2,721 | .340 |
| George Sisler | 15 | 8,267 | 2,812 | .340 |
| Nap Lajoie | 21 | 9,589 | 3,251 | .339 |
| Cap Anson | 22 | 9,084 | 3,081 | .339 |
| Sam Thompson | 15 | 6,004 | 2,016 | .336 |
| Al Simmons | 20 | 8,761 | 2,927 | .334 |
| Eddie Collins | 25 | 9,949 | 3,311 | .333 |
| Paul Waner | 20 | 9,459 | 3,152 | .333 |
| Stan Musial | 22 | 10,972 | 3,630 | .331 |
| Rod Carew* | 16 | 8,071 | 2,672 | .331 |
| Heinie Manush | 17 | 7,653 | 2,524 | .330 |
| Hugh Duffy | 17 | 6,999 | 2,307 | .330 |
| Honus Wagner | 21 | 10,427 | 3,430 | .329 |
| Joe DiMaggio | 13 | 6,821 | 2,214 | .325 |
| Jimmie Foxx | 20 | 8,134 | 2,646 | .325 |

*Active player.

### Leading Pitchers
(Over 250 Victories)

| | Years | W | L | Pct |
|---|---|---|---|---|
| Cy Young | 22 | 511 | 315 | .619 |
| Walter Johnson | 21 | 416 | 279 | .599 |
| Grover Alexander | 20 | 373 | 208 | .642 |
| Christy Mathewson | 17 | 373 | 188 | .665 |
| James Galvin | 15 | 365 | 309 | .542 |
| Warren Spahn | 21 | 363 | 245 | .597 |
| Charles Nichols | 15 | 360 | 202 | .641 |
| Tim Keefe | 14 | 346 | 225 | .606 |
| John Clarkson | 12 | 328 | 175 | .652 |
| Eddie Plank | 17 | 325 | 190 | .631 |
| Mickey Welch | 13 | 316 | 214 | .596 |
| Hoss Radbourne | 11 | 308 | 191 | .617 |
| Gaylord Perry* | 21 | 307 | 251 | .550 |
| Lefty Grove | 20 | 300 | 141 | .680 |
| Early Wynn | 23 | 300 | 244 | .551 |
| Steve Carlton* | 18 | 285 | 184 | .608 |
| Robin Roberts | 19 | 286 | 245 | .539 |
| Tony Mullane | 14 | 282 | 221 | .561 |
| Jim Kaat* | 24 | 283 | 236 | .545 |
| Ferguson Jenkins* | 18 | 278 | 217 | .561 |
| Red Ruffing | 22 | 273 | 225 | .548 |
| Burleigh Grimes | 19 | 270 | 212 | .560 |
| Bob Feller | 18 | 266 | 162 | .621 |
| Eppa Rixey | 21 | 266 | 251 | .515 |
| Gus Weyhing | 14 | 265 | 236 | .529 |
| Jim McCormick | 10 | 264 | 217 | .549 |
| Tom Seaver* | 16 | 264 | 156 | .628 |
| Jim Palmer* | 17 | 263 | 145 | .645 |
| Ted Lyons | 21 | 260 | 230 | .531 |
| Phil Niekro* | 19 | 257 | 220 | .539 |
| Red Faber | 20 | 254 | 212 | .545 |
| Carl Hubbell | 16 | 253 | 154 | .622 |
| Bob Gibson | 17 | 251 | 174 | .591 |

*Active player.

## BASEBALL'S PERFECTLY PITCHED GAMES[1]
### (no opposing runner reached base)

| | |
|---|---|
| John Richmond—Worcester vs. Cleveland (NL) June 12, 1880 | 1–0 |
| John M. Ward—Providence vs. Buffalo (NL) June 17, 1880 | 5–0 |
| Cy Young—Boston vs. Philadelphia (AL) May 5, 1904 | 3–0 |
| Addie Joss—Cleveland vs. Chicago (AL) Oct. 2, 1908 | 1–0 |
| Ernest Shore[2]—Boston vs. Washington (AL) June 23, 1917 | 4–0 |
| Charles Robertson—Chicago vs. Detroit (AL) April 30, 1922 | 2–0 |
| Don Larsen[3]—New York (AL) vs. Brooklyn (NL) Oct. 8, 1956 | 2–0 |
| Jim Bunning—Philadelphia vs. New York (NL) June 21, 1964 | 6–0 |
| Sandy Koufax—Los Angeles vs. Chicago (NL) Sept. 9, 1965 | 1–0 |
| Jim Hunter—Oakland vs. Minnesota (AL) May 8, 1968 | 4–0 |
| Len Barker—Cleveland vs. Toronto (AL) May 15, 1981 | 3–0 |

1. Harvey Haddix, of Pittsburgh, pitched 12 perfect innings against Milwaukee (NL), May 26, 1959 but lost game in 13th on error and hit. 2. Shore, relief pitcher for Babe Ruth who walked first batter before being ejected by umpire, retired 26 batters who faced him and baserunner was out stealing. 3. World Series.

# MAJOR LEAGUE INDIVIDUAL ALL-TIME RECORDS

Highest Batting Average—.442, James O'Neill, St. Louis, A.A., 1887; .438, Hugh Duffy, Boston, N.L., 1894 (Since 1900—.424, Rogers Hornsby, St. Louis, N.L., 1924; .422, Nap Lajoie, Phil., A.L., 1901)

Most Times at Bat—12,364, Henry Aaron, Milwaukee N.L., 1954–65; Atlanta N.L., 1966–74; Milwaukee A.L., 1975–76.

Most Years Batted .300 or Better—23, Ty Cobb, Detroit A.L., 1906–26, Philadelphia A.L., 1927–28.

Most hits—4,191, Ty Cobb, Detroit A.L., 1905–26, Philadelphia A.L., 1927–28.

Most Hits, Season—257, George Sisler, St. Louis A.L., 1920.

Most Hits, Game (9 innings)—7, Wilbert Robinson, Baltimore N.L., 6 singles, 1 double, 1892. Rennie Stennett, Pittsburgh N.L., 4 singles, 2 doubles, 1 triple, 1975.

Most Hits, Game (extra innings)—9, John Burnett, Cleveland A.L., 18 innings, 7 singles, 2 doubles, 1932.

Most Hits in Succession—12, Mike Higgins, Boston A.L., in four games, 1938; Walt Dropo, Detroit A.L., in three games, 1952.

Most Consecutive Games Batted Safely—56, Joe DiMaggio, New York A.L., 1941.

Most Runs—2,244, Ty Cobb, Detroit A.L., 1905–26, Philadelphia A.L., 1927–28.

Most Runs, Season—196, William Hamilton, Philadelphia N.L., 1894. (Since 1900—177, Babe Ruth, New York A.L., 1921.)

Most Runs, Game—7, Guy Hecker, Louisville A.A., 1886. (Since 1900—6, by Mel Ott, New York N.L., 1934, 1944; Johnny Pesky, Boston A.L., 1946; Frank Torre, Milwaukee N.L., 1957.)

Most Runs Batted In—2,297, Henry Aaron, Milwaukee N.L., 1954–1965; Atlanta N.L., 1966–74; Milwaukee A.L., 1975–76.

Most Runs Batted in, Season—190, Hack Wilson, Chicago N.L., 1930.

Most Runs Batted In, Game—12, Jim Bottomley, St. Louis N.L., 1924.

Most Home Runs—755, Henry Aaron, Milwaukee N.L., 1954–1965; Atlanta N.L., 1966–74; Milwaukee A.L., 1975–76.

Most Home Runs, Season—61, Roger Maris, New York A.L., 1961 (162-game season); 60, Babe Ruth, New York A.L., 1927 (154-game season)

Most Home Runs with Bases Filled—23, Lou Gehrig, New York A.L., 1927–39.

Most 2-Base Hits—793, Tris Speaker, Boston A.L., 1907–15, Cleveland A.L., 1916–26, Washington A.L., 1927, Philadelphia A.L., 1928.

Most 2-Base Hits, Season—67, Earl Webb, Boston A.L., 1931.

Most 2-base Hits, Game—4, by many.

Most 3-Base Hits—312, Sam Crawford, Cincinnati N.L., 1899–1902, Detroit A.L., 1903–17.

Most 3-Base Hits, Season—36, Owen Wilson, Pittsburgh N.L., 1912.

Most 3-Base Hits, Game—4, George Strief, Philadelphia A.A., 1885; William Joyce, New York N.L., 1897. (Since 1900—3, by many.)

Most Games Played—3,298, Henry Aaron, Milwaukee N.L., 1954–1965; Atlanta, N.L., 1966–74; Milwaukee A.L., 1975–76.

Most Consecutive Games Played—2,130, Lou Gehrig, New York A.L., 1925–39.

Most Bases on Balls—2,056, Babe Ruth, Boston A.L., 1914–19; New York A.L., 1920–34, Boston N.L., 1935.

Most Bases on Balls, Season—170, Babe Ruth, New York A.L., 1923.

Most Bases on Balls, Game—6, Jimmy Foxx, Boston A.L., 1938.

Most Strikeouts, Season—189, Bobby Bonds, San Francisco N.L., 1970.

Most Strikeouts, Game (9 innings)—5, by many.

Most Strikeouts, Game (extra innings)—6, Carl Weilman, St. Louis A.L., 15 innings, 1913; Don Hoak, Chicago N.L., 17 innings, 1956; Fred Reichardt, California A.L., 17, innings, 1966; Billy Cowan, California A.L., 20, 1971; Cecil Cooper, Boston A.L., 15, 1974.

Most pinch-hits, lifetime—150, Manny Mota, S.F., 1962; Pitt., 1963–68; Montreal, 1969; L.A., 1969–80, N.L.

Most Pinch-hits, season—25, Jose Morales, Montreal N.L., 1976.

Most consecutive pinch-hits—9, Dave Philley, Phil., N.L., 1958 (8), 1959 (1).

Most pinch-hit home runs, lifetime—18, Gerald Lynch, Pitt.-Cin. N.L., 1957–66.

Most pinch-hit home runs, season—6, Johnny Frederick, Brooklyn, N.L., 1932.

Most stolen bases, lifetime (since 1900)—938, Lou Brock, Chicago N.L. 1961–64; St. Louis, N.L. 1964–79.

Most stolen bases, season—156, Harry Stovey, Phil., A.A., 1888. Since 1900: 130, Rickey Henderson, Oak., A.L., 1982; 118, Lou Brock, St. Lou., 1974.

Most stolen bases, game—7, George Gore, Chicago N.L. 1881; William Hamilton, Philadelphia N.L. 1894. (Since 1900—6, Eddie Collins, Philadelphia A.L., 1912.)

Most times stealing home, lifetime—35, Ty Cobb, Detroit-Phil. A.L., 1905–28.

# MAJOR LEAGUE ALL-TIME PITCHING RECORDS

Most Games Won—511, Cy Young, Cleveland N.L., 1890–98, St. Louis N.L., 1899–1900, Boston A.L., 1901–08, Cleveland A.L., 1909–11, Boston N.L., 1911.

Most Games Won, Season—60, Hoss Radbourne, Providence N.L., 1884. (Since 1900—41, Jack Chesbro, New York A.L., 1904.)

Most Consecutive Games Won—24, Carl Hubbell, New York N.L., 1936 (16) and 1937 (8).

Most Consecutive Games Won, Season—19, Tim Keefe, New York N.L., 1888; Rube Marquard, New York N.L., 1912.

Most Years Won 20 or More Games—16, Cy Young, Cleveland N.L., 1891–98, St. Louis N.L., 1899–1900, Boston A.L., 1901–04, 1907–08.

Most Shutouts—113, Walter Johnson, Wash. A.L., 1907–27.

Most Shutouts, Season—16, Grover Alexander, Philadelphia N.L., 1916.

Most Consecutive Shutouts—6, Don Drysdale, Los Angeles, N.L., 1968.

Most Consecutive Scoreless Innings—58, Don Drysdale, Los Angeles, N.L., 1968.

Most Strikeouts—3,508, Walter Johnson, Washington A.L. 1907–27.

Most Strikeouts, Season—505, Matthew Kilroy, Baltimore A.A., 1886. (Since 1900—383, Nolan Ryan, California, A.L., 1973.)

Most Strikeouts, Game—21, Tom Cheney, Washington A.L. 1962, 16 innings. Nine innings: 19, Charles McSweeney, Providence N.L., 1884; Hugh Dailey, Chicago U.A., 1884. (Since 1900—19, Steve Carlton, St. Louis N.L. vs. New York, Sept. 15, 1969; Tom Seaver, New York N.L. vs. San Diego, April 22, 1970; Nolan Ryan, California A.L. vs. Boston, Aug. 12, 1974.)

Most Consecutive Strikeouts—10, Tom Seaver, New York N.L. vs. San Diego, April 22, 1970.

Most Games, Season—106, Mike Marshall, Los Angeles, N.L., 1974.

Most Complete Games, Season—74, William White, Cincinnati N.L., 1879. (Since 1900—48, Jack Chesbro, New York A.L., 1904.)

## MAJOR LEAGUE ATTENDANCE RECORDS

Single game—78,672, San Francisco at Los Angeles (N.L.), April 18, 1958. (At Memorial Coliseum.)

Doubleheader—84,587, New York at Cleveland (A.L.), Sept. 12, 1954.

Night—78,382, Chicago at Cleveland (A.L.), Aug. 20, 1948.

Season, home—3,608,881, Los Angeles (N.L.), 1982.

Season, road—2,461,240, New York (A.L.), 1980.

Season, league—23,080,449, American League, 1982.

Season, both leagues—44,584,943, 1982.

World Series, single game—92,706, Chicago (A.L.) at Los Angeles (N.L.), Oct. 6, 1959.

World Series, all games (6)—420,784, Chicago (A.L.) and Los Angeles (N.L.), 1959.

## MOST HOME RUNS IN ONE SEASON
### (45 or More)

| HR | Player/Team | Year | HR | Player/Team | Year |
|---|---|---|---|---|---|
| 61 | Roger Maris, New York (AL) | 1961 | 48 | Jimmy Foxx, Philadelphia (AL) | 1933 |
| 60 | Babe Ruth, New York (AL) | 1927 | 48 | Harmon Killebrew, Minnesota (AL) | 1962 |
| 59 | Babe Ruth, New York (AL) | 1921 | 48 | Willie Stargell, Pittsburgh (NL) | 1971 |
| 58 | Jimmy Foxx, Philadelphia (AL) | 1932 | 48 | Dave Kingman, Chicago (NL) | 1979 |
| 58 | Hank Greenberg, Detroit (AL) | 1938 | 48 | Mike Schmidt, Philadelphia (NL) | 1980 |
| 56 | Hack Wilson, Chicago (NL) | 1930 | 47 | Babe Ruth, New York (AL) | 1926 |
| 54 | Babe Ruth, New York (AL) | 1920 | 47 | Ralph Kiner, Pittsburgh (NL) | 1950 |
| 54 | Babe Ruth, New York (AL) | 1928 | 47 | Ed Mathews, Milwaukee (NL) | 1953 |
| 54 | Ralph Kiner, Pittsburgh (NL) | 1949 | 47 | Ernie Banks, Chicago (NL) | 1958 |
| 54 | Mickey Mantle, New York (AL) | 1961 | 47 | Willie Mays, San Francisco (NL) | 1964 |
| 52 | Mickey Mantle, New York (AL) | 1956 | 47 | Henry Aaron, Atlanta (NL) | 1971 |
| 52 | Willie Mays, San Francisco (NL) | 1965 | 47 | Reggie Jackson, Oakland (AL) | 1969 |
| 52 | George Foster, Cincinnati (NL) | 1977 | 46 | Babe Ruth, New York (AL) | 1924 |
| 51 | Ralph Kiner, Pittsburgh (NL) | 1947 | 46 | Babe Ruth, New York (AL) | 1929 |
| 51 | John Mize, New York (NL) | 1947 | 46 | Babe Ruth, New York (AL) | 1931 |
| 51 | Willie Mays, New York (NL) | 1955 | 46 | Lou Gehrig, New York (AL) | 1931 |
| 50 | Jimmy Foxx, Boston (AL) | 1938 | 46 | Joe DiMaggio, New York (AL) | 1937 |
| 49 | Babe Ruth, New York (AL) | 1930 | 46 | Ed Mathews, Milwaukee (NL) | 1959 |
| 49 | Lou Gehrig, New York (AL) | 1934 | 46 | Orlando Cepeda, San Francisco (NL) | 1961 |
| 49 | Lou Gehrig, New York (AL) | 1936 | 46 | Jim Rice, Boston (AL) | 1978 |
| 49 | Ted Kluszewski, Cincinnati (NL) | 1954 | 45 | Harmon Killebrew, Minnesota (AL) | 1963 |
| 49 | Willie Mays, San Francisco (NL) | 1962 | 45 | Willie McCovey, San Francisco (NL) | 1969 |
| 49 | Harmon Killebrew, Minnesota (AL) | 1964 | 45 | Johnny Bench, Cincinnati (NL) | 1970 |
| 49 | Frank Robinson, Baltimore (AL) | 1966 | 45 | Gorman Thomas, Milwaukee (AL) | 1979 |
| 49 | Harmon Killebrew, Minnesota (AL) | 1969 | 45 | Henry Aaron, Milwaukee (NL) | 1962 |

# RODEO

## PROFESSIONAL RODEO COWBOY ASSOCIATION, ALL AROUND COWBOY

| | | | | | |
|---|---|---|---|---|---|
| 1953 | Bill Linderman | 1962 | Tom Nesmith | 1975 | Leo Camarillo and Tom Ferguson |
| 1954 | Buck Rutherford | 1963–65 | Dean Oliver | 1976–79 | Tom Ferguson |
| 1955 | Casey Tibbs | 1966–70 | Larry Mahan | 1980 | Paul Tierney |
| 1956–59 | Jim Shoulders | 1971–72 | Phil Lyne | 1981 | Jimmie Cooper |
| 1960 | Harry Tompkins | 1973 | Larry Mahan | | |
| 1961 | Benny Reynolds | 1974 | Tom Ferguson | | |

# CURLING

## WORLD CHAMPIONSHIPS—1982

Men (Garmisch-Partenkirchen, West Germany, March 29–April 4, 1982)—Canada, Al Hackner, skip (defeated Switzerland, 9–7, in final)

Women (Geneva, Switzerland, March 21–27, 1982)—Denmark, Helena Blach, skip (defeated Sweden, 8–7, in final)

## UNITED STATES CHAMPIONSHIPS—1982

Men (Brookline, Mass., Feb. 28–March 6, 1982)—Madison, Wis., Steve Brown, skip

Women (Bowling Green, Ohio)—Illinois, Ruth Schwenker, skip (defeated North Dakota, 11–3, in final)

Mixed (Madison, Wis., March 15–19, 1982)—Minnesota, Bemidji, Mark Haluptzak, skip (defeated Illinois, Willamette, 8–2, in final)

Junior—Seattle, Wash., Dale Risling, skip (defeated Minnesota in final)

# TUMBLING—1982

World men's champion—Steve Elliott, Amarillo, Tex.

Women's champion—Jill Hollenbeck, Rockford, Ill.

World men's trampoline champion—Carl Furrer, Britain

World women's trampoline champion—Ruth Keller, Switzerland

## MAJOR LEAGUE BALL PARK STATISTICS*

lf—Left–field foul line; cf—center field; rf—right–field foul line

| Club, nickname, and grounds | Distance, feet | | | Seating capacity | Record Attendance[4] | | |
|---|---|---|---|---|---|---|---|
| | lf | cf | rf | | Day game | Double-header[3] | Night game |
| **American League** | | | | | | | |
| Baltimore Orioles—Memorial Stadium | 309 | 405 | 309 | 53,208 | 51,798 | 46,796 | 51,649 |
| Boston Red Sox—Fenway Park | 315 | 390 | 302 | 33,536 | 36,350 | 41,766 | 36,228 |
| California Angels—Anaheim Stadium | 333 | 404 | 370 | 67,335 | 42,655 | 37,768 | 53,591 |
| Chicago White Sox—Comiskey Park | 352 | 402 | 375 | 44,492 | 51,560 | 55,555 | 53,940 |
| Cleveland Indians—Municipal Stadium | 320 | 400 | 320 | 74,208 | 74,420 | 84,587 | 78,382 |
| Detroit Tigers—Tiger Stadium | 340 | 440 | 325 | 52,687 | 57,888 | 58,369 | 56,586 |
| Kansas City Royals—Royals Stadium | 330 | 410 | 330 | 40,635 | 41,329 | 40,525 | 41,860 |
| Milwaukee Brewers—County Stadium | 362 | 402 | 362 | 53,192 | 55,120 | 49,054 | 52,968 |
| Minnesota Twins—Metropolitan Stadium[5] | 385 | 407 | 367 | 54,711 | 46,963 | 43,419 | 45,890 |
| New York Yankees—Yankee Stadium[1] | 387 | 417 | 353 | 57,545 | 73,205 | 81,841 | 74,747 |
| Oakland A's—Oakland Coliseum | 330 | 397 | 330 | 50,255 | 48,758 | 48,592 | 47,741 |
| Seattle Mariners—Kingdome | 316 | 410 | 316 | 59,438 | 47,353 | 25,344 | 57,762 |
| Texas Rangers—Arlington Stadium | 330 | 400 | 330 | 41,284 | 40,078 | 24,241 | 41,097 |
| Toronto Blue Jays—Exhibition Stadium | 330 | 400 | 330 | 43,737 | 44,649 | 41,308 | 39,347 |
| **National League** | | | | | | | |
| Atlanta Braves—Atlanta Stadium | 330 | 402 | 330 | 52,785 | 51,275 | 46,489 | 53,775 |
| Chicago Cubs—Wrigley Field | 355 | 400 | 353 | 37,272 | 46,572 | 46,965 | No lights |
| Cincinnati Reds—Riverfront Stadium | 330 | 404 | 330 | 52,392 | 53,390 | 52,147 | 52,315 |
| Houston Astros—Astrodome | 340 | 406 | 340 | 45,000 | 49,442 | 42,648 | 50,908 |
| Los Angeles Dodgers—Dodger Stadium[2] | 330 | 400 | 330 | 56,000 | 78,672 | 53,856 | 67,550 |
| Montreal Expos—Olympic Stadium | 325 | 404 | 325 | 58,838 | 57,592 | 59,282 | 57,121 |
| New York Mets—Shea Stadium | 338 | 410 | 338 | 55,300 | 56,738 | 57,175 | 56,658 |
| Philadelphia Phillies—Veterans Stadium | 330 | 408 | 330 | 65,454 | 60,120 | 40,720 | 63,283 |
| Pittsburgh Pirates—Three Rivers Stadium | 335 | 400 | 335 | 54,499 | 51,726 | 49,412 | 48,846 |
| St. Louis Cardinals—Busch Memorial Stadium | 330 | 414 | 330 | 50,222 | 50,548 | 49,743 | 50,340 |
| San Diego Padres—Jack Murphy Stadium | 330 | 420 | 330 | 51,362 | 42,142 | 43,373 | 50,569 |
| San Francisco Giants—Candlestick Park | 335 | 400 | 335 | 58,000 | 56,196 | 50,924 | 55,920 |

*At end of 1981 season. 1. Distance and capacity after rebuilding; attendance records prior to rebuilding. 2. Played also in Los Angeles Coliseum. 3. Two day games. 4. Through 1981 season. 5. Moved into Hubert H. Humphrey Metrodome for 1982 season; distance for 1982, attendance figures through 1981.

## MAJOR LEAGUE FRANCHISE SHIFTS AND ADDITIONS

1953—Boston Braves (N.L.) became Milwaukee Braves. Home attendance, last season in Boston (1952), 281,278; first season in Milwaukee (1953), 1,826,397.

1954—St. Louis Browns (A.L.) became Baltimore Orioles. Home attendance, last season in St. Louis (1953), 297,238; first season in Baltimore (1954), 1,060,910.

1955—Philadelphia Athletics (A.L.) became Kansas City Athletics. Home attendance, last season in Phila. (1954), 627,-100; first season in K.C. (1955), 1,393,054.

1958—New York Giants (N.L.) became San Francisco Giants. Home attendance, last season in New York (1957), 653,923; first season in San Francisco (1958), 1,272,625.

1958—Brooklyn Dodgers (N.L.) became Los Angeles Dodgers. Home attendance, last season in Brooklyn (1957), 1,028,258; first season in Los Angeles (1958), 1,845,556.

1961—Washington Senators (A.L.) became Minnesota Twins. Home attendance, last season in Washington (1960), 743,-404; first season in Minneapolis-St. Paul (1961), 1,256,722.

1961—Los Angeles Angels (later renamed the California Angels) enfranchised by the American League.

1961—Washington Senators enfranchised by the American League (a new team, replacing the former Washington club,

whose franchise was moved to Minneapolis-St. Paul).

1962—Houston Colt .45's (later renamed the Houston Astros) enfranchised by the National League.

1962—New York Mets enfranchised by the National League. Home attendance, first season (1962), 922,530.

1966—Milwaukee Braves (N.L.) became Atlanta Braves. Home attendance, last season in Milwaukee (1965), 555,584; first season in Atlanta (1966), 1,539,801.

1968—Kansas City Athletics (A.L.) became Oakland Athletics.

1969—Two major leagues each added two teams for totals of 12 and split into two divisions. American League additions: Kansas City Royals and Seattle Pilots; National League additions: Montreal Expos and San Diego Padres. The Division leaders met for the league championship and the two league winners met in the World Series.

1970—Seattle franchise was shifted to Milwaukee, with final court approval coming on March 31. Club was renamed Milwaukee Brewers.

1971—Washington franchise shifted at end of season to Dallas-Fort Worth Texas Rangers with field at Arlington, Tex.

1977—Seattle and Toronto began play in American League.

## MAJOR LEAGUE BASEBALL BREAKS ATTENDANCE RECORD IN 1982

Major league baseball attendance rose to 44,584,943 in 1982, breaking a record set in 1979 when the 26 teams drew 43,550,398 fans to the ball parks. The American League also broke a mark it set in 1979, drawing 23,080,440 in 1982 compared with the previous record of 22,371,979. The Los Angeles Dodgers broke their own home attendance record by drawing 3,608,881 fans, bettering the figure of 3,347,845 of 1978, which was the previous record for a major league team.

# MAJOR LEAGUE BASEBALL—1982

## AMERICAN LEAGUE
### (Final Standing—1982)

**EASTERN DIVISION**

| Team | W | L | Pct | GB |
|---|---|---|---|---|
| Milwaukee Brewers | 95 | 67 | .586 | — |
| Baltimore Orioles | 94 | 68 | .580 | 1 |
| Boston Red Sox | 89 | 73 | .549 | 6 |
| Detroit Tigers | 83 | 79 | .512 | 12 |
| New York Yankees | 79 | 83 | .488 | 16 |
| Cleveland Indians | 78 | 84 | .481 | 17 |
| Toronto Blue Jays | 78 | 84 | .481 | 17 |

**WESTERN DIVISION**

| Team | W | L | Pct | GB |
|---|---|---|---|---|
| California Angels | 93 | 69 | .574 | — |
| Kansas City Royals | 90 | 72 | .556 | 3 |
| Chicago White Sox | 87 | 75 | .537 | 6 |
| Seattle Mariners | 76 | 86 | .469 | 17 |
| Oakland A's | 68 | 94 | .420 | 25 |
| Texas Rangers | 64 | 98 | .395 | 29 |
| Minnesota Twins | 60 | 102 | .370 | 33 |

### AMERICAN LEAGUE PLAYOFFS—1982
**1st game, Anaheim, Calif., Oct. 5**

| | | | | | | | |
|---|---|---|---|---|---|---|---|
| Milwaukee | 021 | 000 | 000 | — | 3 | 7 | 2 |
| California | 104 | 210 | 00X | — | 8 | 10 | 0 |

Caldwell, Slaton (4), Ladd (7), Bernard (8); John. Winner: John. Loser: Caldwell. Home Runs: Milwaukee: Thomas. California: Lynn. Attendance: 64,406.

**2nd game, Anaheim, Calif., Oct. 6**

| | | | | | | | |
|---|---|---|---|---|---|---|---|
| Milwaukee | 000 | 020 | 000 | — | 2 | 5 | 0 |
| California | 021 | 100 | 00X | — | 4 | 6 | 0 |

Vuckovich; Kison. Winner: Kison. Loser: Vuckovich. Home Runs: Milwaukee: Molitor. California: Reggie Jackson. Attendance: 64,179.

**3rd game, Milwaukee, Oct. 8**

| | | | | | | | |
|---|---|---|---|---|---|---|---|
| California | 000 | 000 | 030 | — | 3 | 8 | 0 |
| Milwaukee | 000 | 300 | 20X | — | 5 | 6 | 0 |

Zahn, Witt (4), Hassler (7); Sutton, Ladd (8). Winner: Sutton. Loser: Zahn. Home Runs: California: Boone. Milwaukee: Molitor. Attendance: 50,135.

**4th game, Milwaukee, Oct. 9**

| | | | | | | | |
|---|---|---|---|---|---|---|---|
| California | 000 | 001 | 040 | — | 5 | 5 | 3 |
| Milwaukee | 030 | 301 | 02X | — | 9 | 9 | 2 |

John, Goltz (4), Sanchez (8); Haas, Slaton (8). Winner: Haas. Loser: John. Home Runs: California: Baylor. Milwaukee: Brouhard. Attendance: 51,003.

**5th game, Milwaukee, Oct. 10**

| | | | | | | | |
|---|---|---|---|---|---|---|---|
| California | 101 | 100 | 000 | — | 3 | 11 | 1 |
| Milwaukee | 100 | 100 | 20X | — | 4 | 6 | 4 |

Kison, Sanchez (6), Hassler (7); Vuckovich, McClure (7), Ladd (9). Winner: McClure. Loser: Sanchez. Home Runs: Milwaukee: Oglivie. Attendance: 54,968.

### AMERICAN LEAGUE LEADERS—1982

| | |
|---|---|
| Batting—Willie Wilson, Kansas City | .332 |
| Runs—Paul Molitor, Milwaukee | 136 |
| Hits—Robin Yount, Milwaukee | 210 |
| Runs batted in—Hal McRae, Kansas City | 133 |
| Doubles—Robin Yount, Milwaukee | 46 |
| Triples—Willie Wilson, Kansas City | 15 |
| Home runs—Gorman Thomas, Milwaukee, and Reggie Jackson, California | 39 |
| Stolen bases—Rickey Henderson, Oakland | 130 |

**Pitching**

| | |
|---|---|
| Victories—LaMarr Hoyt, Chicago | 19 |
| Earned run average—Rick Sutcliffe, Cleveland | 2.96 |
| Strikeouts—Floyd Bannister, Seattle | 209 |
| Shutouts—Dave Stieb, Toronto | 5 |

## NATIONAL LEAGUE
### (Final Standing—1982)

**EASTERN DIVISION**

| Team | W | L | Pct | GB |
|---|---|---|---|---|
| St. Louis Cardinals | 92 | 70 | .568 | — |
| Philadelphia Phillies | 89 | 73 | .549 | 3 |
| Montreal Expos | 86 | 76 | .531 | 6 |
| Pittsburgh Pirates | 84 | 78 | .519 | 8 |
| Chicago Cubs | 73 | 89 | .451 | 19 |
| New York Mets | 65 | 97 | .401 | 27 |

**WESTERN DIVISION**

| Team | W | L | Pct | GB |
|---|---|---|---|---|
| Atlanta Braves | 89 | 73 | .549 | — |
| Los Angeles Dodgers | 88 | 74 | .543 | 1 |
| San Francisco Giants | 87 | 75 | .537 | 2 |
| San Diego Padres | 81 | 81 | .500 | 8 |
| Houston Astros | 77 | 85 | .475 | 12 |
| Cincinnati Reds | 61 | 101 | .377 | 28 |

### NATIONAL LEAGUE PLAYOFFS—1982
**1st game, St. Louis, Oct. 6**

| | | | | | | | |
|---|---|---|---|---|---|---|---|
| Atlanta | 000 | 000 | 000 | — | 0 | 3 | 0 |
| St. Louis | 001 | 005 | 01X | — | 7 | 14 | 0 |

Perez, Bedrosian (6), Moore (6), Walk (9); Forsch. Winner: Forsch. Loser: Perez. Attendance: 53,008.

**2nd game, St. Louis, Oct. 9**

| | | | | | | | |
|---|---|---|---|---|---|---|---|
| Atlanta | 002 | 010 | 000 | — | 3 | 6 | |
| St. Louis | 100 | 001 | 011 | — | 4 | 9 | |

P. Niekro, Garber (7); Stuper, Bair (7), Sutter (8). Winner: Sutter. Loser: Garber. Attendance: 53,408.

**3rd game, Atlanta, Oct. 10**

| | | | | | | | |
|---|---|---|---|---|---|---|---|
| St. Louis | 040 | 010 | 001 | — | 6 | 12 | |
| Atlanta | 000 | 000 | 200 | — | 2 | 6 | |

Andujar, Sutter (7); Camp, Perez (2), Moore (5), Mahler (7), Bedrosian (8), Garber (9). Winner: Andujar. Loser: Camp. Home Runs: St. Louis: McGee. Attendance: 52,173.

### NATIONAL LEAGUE LEADERS—1982

| | |
|---|---|
| Batting—Al Oliver, Montreal | .33 |
| Runs—Lonnie Smith, St. Louis | 12 |
| Hits—Al Oliver, Montreal | 20 |
| Runs batted in—Al Oliver, Montreal | 1 |
| Doubles—Al Oliver, Montreal | |
| Triples—Dick Thon, Houston | |
| Home runs—Dave Kingman, New York | |
| Stolen bases—Tim Raines, Montreal | |

**Pitching**

| | |
|---|---|
| Victories—Steve Carlton, Philadelphia | |
| Earned run average—Steve Rogers, Montreal | 2. |
| Strikeouts—Steve Carlton, Philadelphia | 2 |
| Shutouts—Steve Carlton, Philadelphia | |

## AMERICAN LEAGUE AVERAGES—1982
(Unofficial)

### Batting—Club

| | AB | R | H | HR | RBI | PCT |
|---|---|---|---|---|---|---|
| Kansas City | 5,629 | 784 | 1,603 | 132 | 746 | .285 |
| Milwaukee | 5,733 | 891 | 1,599 | 216 | 843 | .279 |
| Boston | 5,596 | 753 | 1,536 | 136 | 705 | .274 |
| California | 5,532 | 814 | 1,518 | 186 | 760 | .274 |
| Chicago | 5,575 | 786 | 1,523 | 136 | 747 | .273 |
| Detroit | 5,590 | 729 | 1,489 | 177 | 684 | .266 |
| Baltimore | 5,557 | 774 | 1,478 | 179 | 735 | .266 |
| Cleveland | 5,559 | 683 | 1,458 | 109 | 639 | .262 |
| Toronto | 5,526 | 651 | 1,447 | 106 | 605 | .262 |
| Minnesota | 5,545 | 657 | 1,427 | 148 | 623 | .257 |
| New York | 5,526 | 709 | 1,417 | 161 | 666 | .256 |
| Seattle | 5,626 | 651 | 1,431 | 130 | 613 | .254 |
| Texas | 5,445 | 590 | 1,354 | 115 | 558 | .249 |
| Oakland | 5,448 | 691 | 1,287 | 149 | 659 | .236 |

### Batting Leaders

| Player/Team | AB | R | H | HR | RBI | PCT |
|---|---|---|---|---|---|---|
| Wilson, Kansas City | 585 | 87 | 194 | 3 | 46 | .332 |
| Yount, Milwaukee | 635 | 129 | 210 | 29 | 114 | .331 |
| Carew, California | 523 | 88 | 167 | 3 | 44 | .319 |
| Murray, Baltimore | 550 | 87 | 174 | 32 | 110 | .316 |
| Cooper, Milwaukee | 654 | 104 | 205 | 32 | 121 | .313 |
| Paciorek, Chicago | 382 | 49 | 119 | 11 | 55 | .312 |
| Garcia, Toronto | 597 | 89 | 185 | 5 | 42 | .310 |
| Rice, Boston | 573 | 86 | 177 | 24 | 97 | .309 |
| McRae, Kansas City | 613 | 91 | 189 | 27 | 133 | .308 |
| Harrah, Cleveland | 602 | 100 | 183 | 25 | 78 | .304 |
| Molitor, Milwaukee | 666 | 136 | 201 | 19 | 71 | .302 |
| DeCinces, California | 575 | 94 | 173 | 30 | 97 | .301 |
| Lansford, Boston | 482 | 65 | 145 | 11 | 63 | .301 |
| Hrbek, Minnesota | 532 | 82 | 160 | 23 | 92 | .301 |
| Brett, Kansas City | 552 | 101 | 166 | 21 | 82 | .301 |
| Mumphrey, New York | 477 | 76 | 143 | 9 | 68 | .300 |
| Lynn, California | 472 | 89 | 141 | 21 | 86 | .299 |
| White, Kansas City | 524 | 71 | 156 | 11 | 56 | .298 |
| Bochte, Seattle | 509 | 58 | 151 | 12 | 70 | .297 |
| Bell, Texas | 537 | 62 | 159 | 13 | 67 | .296 |
| Gantner, Milwaukee | 447 | 48 | 132 | 4 | 43 | .295 |
| Bonnell, Toronto | 437 | 59 | 128 | 6 | 49 | .293 |
| Evans, Boston | 609 | 122 | 178 | 32 | 98 | .292 |
| Zisk, Seattle | 503 | 61 | 147 | 21 | 61 | .292 |
| Luzinski, Chicago | 583 | 87 | 170 | 18 | 102 | .292 |
| Herndon, Detroit | 614 | 92 | 179 | 23 | 88 | .292 |

### Leading Pitchers
(15 or more decisions)

| Player/Team | IP | H | BB | SO | W | L | ERA |
|---|---|---|---|---|---|---|---|
| Spillner, Cleveland | 133 | 117 | 45 | 90 | 12 | 10 | 2.49 |
| Quisenberry, Kansas City | 136 | 126 | 12 | 46 | 9 | 7 | 2.57 |
| Sutcliffe, Cleveland | 216 | 174 | 98 | 142 | 14 | 8 | 2.96 |
| Stanley, Boston | 168 | 161 | 50 | 83 | 12 | 7 | 3.10 |
| Palmer, Baltimore | 227 | 195 | 63 | 103 | 15 | 5 | 3.13 |
| Kison, California | 142 | 120 | 44 | 86 | 10 | 5 | 3.17 |
| Petry, Detroit | 246 | 220 | 100 | 132 | 15 | 9 | 3.22 |
| Stieb, Toronto | 288 | 271 | 75 | 141 | 17 | 14 | 3.25 |
| Underwood, Oakland | 153 | 136 | 68 | 79 | 10 | 6 | 3.29 |
| Vuckovich, Milwaukee | 223 | 234 | 102 | 105 | 18 | 6 | 3.34 |
| Beattie, Seattle | 172 | 149 | 65 | 140 | 8 | 12 | 3.34 |
| Bannister, Seattle | 247 | 225 | 77 | 209 | 12 | 13 | 3.33 |
| Hoyt, Chicago | 239 | 248 | 48 | 124 | 19 | 15 | 3.53 |
| Wilcox, Detroit | 193 | 187 | 85 | 112 | 12 | 10 | 3.62 |
| Tudor, Boston | 195 | 215 | 59 | 146 | 13 | 10 | 3.63 |
| Castillo, Minnesota | 218 | 194 | 85 | 124 | 13 | 11 | 3.66 |
| Udjur, Detroit | 178 | 150 | 69 | 86 | 10 | 10 | 3.69 |
| John, California (N.Y.) | 221 | 239 | 39 | 68 | 14 | 12 | 3.69 |
| Clancy, Toronto | 266 | 251 | 77 | 139 | 16 | 14 | 3.71 |
| Zahn, California | 229 | 225 | 65 | 81 | 18 | 8 | 3.73 |
| Eckersley, Boston | 224 | 228 | 43 | 127 | 13 | 13 | 3.73 |
| Blue, Kansas City | 181 | 163 | 80 | 103 | 13 | 12 | 3.78 |
| Righetti, New York | 183 | 155 | 108 | 163 | 11 | 10 | 3.79 |
| Guidry, New York | 222 | 216 | 69 | 162 | 14 | 8 | 3.81 |
| Koosman, Chicago | 173 | 194 | 38 | 88 | 11 | 7 | 3.84 |

## NATIONAL LEAGUE AVERAGES—1982
(Unofficial)

### Batting—Club

| | AB | R | H | HR | RBI | PCT |
|---|---|---|---|---|---|---|
| Pittsburgh | 5,614 | 724 | 1,535 | 134 | 688 | .273 |
| St. Louis | 5,455 | 685 | 1,439 | 67 | 632 | .264 |
| Los Angeles | 5,642 | 691 | 1,487 | 138 | 661 | .264 |
| Montreal | 5,557 | 697 | 1,454 | 133 | 656 | .262 |
| Philadelphia | 5,454 | 664 | 1,417 | 112 | 624 | .260 |
| Chicago | 5,531 | 676 | 1,436 | 102 | 647 | .260 |
| San Diego | 5,575 | 675 | 1,435 | 81 | 611 | .257 |
| Atlanta | 5,507 | 739 | 1,411 | 146 | 687 | .256 |
| San Francisco | 5,499 | 673 | 1,393 | 133 | 631 | .253 |
| Cincinnati | 5,479 | 545 | 1,375 | 82 | 496 | .251 |
| New York | 5,510 | 609 | 1,361 | 97 | 568 | .247 |
| Houston | 5,440 | 569 | 1,342 | 74 | 533 | .247 |

### Batting Leaders

| Player/Team | AB | R | H | HR | RBI | PCT |
|---|---|---|---|---|---|---|
| Oliver, Montreal | 617 | 90 | 204 | 22 | 109 | .331 |
| Madlock, Pittsburgh | 566 | 92 | 181 | 19 | 95 | .319 |
| Durham, Chicago | 539 | 84 | 168 | 22 | 90 | .312 |
| L. Smith, St. Louis | 592 | 120 | 182 | 8 | 69 | .307 |
| Buckner, Chicago | 657 | 93 | 201 | 15 | 105 | .306 |
| Guerrero, Los Angeles | 575 | 87 | 175 | 32 | 100 | .304 |
| Dawson, Montreal | 608 | 107 | 183 | 23 | 83 | .301 |
| Baker, Los Angeles | 570 | 80 | 171 | 23 | 88 | .300 |
| Hernandez, St. Louis | 579 | 79 | 173 | 7 | 94 | .299 |
| McGee, St. Louis | 422 | 43 | 125 | 4 | 56 | .296 |
| Pena, Pittsburgh | 497 | 53 | 147 | 11 | 63 | .296 |
| Kennedy, San Diego | 562 | 75 | 166 | 21 | 97 | .295 |
| Knight, Houston | 609 | 72 | 179 | 6 | 70 | .294 |
| Carter, Montreal | 557 | 91 | 163 | 29 | 97 | .293 |
| Morgan, San Francisco | 463 | 68 | 134 | 14 | 61 | .289 |
| Lezcano, San Diego | 470 | 73 | 136 | 16 | 84 | .289 |
| Oberkfell, St. Louis | 470 | 55 | 136 | 2 | 34 | .289 |
| Cedeno, Cincinnati | 492 | 52 | 142 | 8 | 57 | .289 |
| Diaz, Philadelphia | 525 | 69 | 151 | 18 | 85 | .288 |
| Concepcion, Cincinnati | 572 | 48 | 164 | 5 | 53 | .287 |
| Richards, San Diego | 521 | 63 | 149 | 3 | 28 | .286 |
| Landreaux, Los Angeles | 461 | 71 | 131 | 7 | 50 | .284 |
| Maddox, Philadelphia | 412 | 39 | 117 | 8 | 61 | .284 |
| Thompson, Pittsburgh | 550 | 87 | 156 | 31 | 101 | .284 |
| Jones, San Diego | 424 | 69 | 120 | 12 | 61 | .283 |

### Leading Pitchers
(15 or more decisions)

| | IP | H | BB | SO | W | L | ERA |
|---|---|---|---|---|---|---|---|
| Rogers, Montreal | 277 | 245 | 65 | 179 | 19 | 8 | 2.40 |
| J. Niekro, Houston | 270 | 224 | 64 | 130 | 17 | 12 | 2.47 |
| Andujar, St. Louis | 265 | 237 | 50 | 137 | 15 | 10 | 2.47 |
| Show, San Diego | 150 | 117 | 48 | 88 | 10 | 6 | 2.64 |
| Soto, Cincinnati | 257 | 202 | 71 | 274 | 14 | 13 | 2.79 |
| Tekulve, Pittsburgh | 128 | 113 | 46 | 66 | 12 | 8 | 2.87 |
| Valenzuela, Los Angeles | 285 | 247 | 83 | 199 | 19 | 13 | 2.87 |
| Candelaria, Pittsburgh | 174 | 166 | 37 | 133 | 12 | 7 | 2.94 |
| Breining, San Francisco | 143 | 146 | 52 | 98 | 11 | 6 | 3.08 |
| Carlton, Philadelphia | 295 | 253 | 86 | 286 | 23 | 11 | 3.10 |
| Reuss, Los Angeles | 254 | 232 | 50 | 138 | 18 | 11 | 3.11 |
| Krukow, Philadelphia | 208 | 211 | 82 | 138 | 13 | 11 | 3.12 |
| Lollar, San Diego | 232 | 192 | 87 | 150 | 16 | 9 | 3.13 |
| Laskey, San Francisco | 189 | 186 | 43 | 88 | 13 | 12 | 3.14 |

| | | | | | | | |
|---|---|---|---|---|---|---|---|
| Jenkins, Chicago | 217 | 221 | 68 | 134 | 14 | 15 | 3.15 |
| Ryan, Houston | 250 | 196 | 109 | 245 | 16 | 12 | 3.16 |
| Lea, Montreal | 177 | 145 | 56 | 115 | 12 | 10 | 3.24 |
| Swan, New York | 166 | 165 | 37 | 67 | 11 | 7 | 3.35 |
| Stuper, St. Louis | 136 | 137 | 55 | 53 | 9 | 7 | 3.36 |
| Berenyi, Cincinnati | 222 | 208 | 96 | 157 | 9 | 18 | 3.36 |
| Welch, Los Angeles | 235 | 199 | 81 | 176 | 16 | 11 | 3.36 |
| Sanderson, Montreal | 224 | 213 | 58 | 158 | 12 | 12 | 3.46 |
| Christenson, Philadelphia | 223 | 212 | 53 | 145 | 9 | 10 | 3.47 |
| Forsch, St. Louis | 233 | 238 | 54 | 69 | 15 | 9 | 3.48 |
| Gullickson, Montreal | 236 | 231 | 61 | 155 | 12 | 14 | 3.57 |

# WORLD SERIES—1982

St. Louis Cardinals (NL) defeated Milwaukee Brewers (AL), 4 games to 3

## 1st Game—St. Louis, Oct. 12

| MILWAUKEE (A) | AB | R | H | BI | ST. LOUIS (N) | AB | R | H | BI |
|---|---|---|---|---|---|---|---|---|---|
| Molitor, 3b | 6 | 1 | 5 | 2 | Herr, 2b | 3 | 0 | 0 | 0 |
| Yount, ss | 6 | 1 | 4 | 2 | L. Smith, lf | 4 | 0 | 0 | 0 |
| Cooper, 1b | 4 | 1 | 0 | 0 | Hernandez, 1b | 4 | 0 | 0 | 0 |
| Simmons, c | 5 | 1 | 2 | 1 | Hendrick, rf | 4 | 0 | 0 | 0 |
| Oglivie, lf | 4 | 1 | 0 | 0 | Tenace, dh | 3 | 0 | 0 | 0 |
| Thomas, cf | 4 | 0 | 1 | 1 | Porter, c | 3 | 0 | 2 | 0 |
| Howell, dh | 2 | 0 | 0 | 0 | Green, cf | 3 | 0 | 0 | 0 |
| Money, dh | 2 | 1 | 1 | 1 | Oberkfell, 3b | 3 | 0 | 1 | 0 |
| Moore, rf | 5 | 2 | 2 | 0 | O. Smith, ss | 3 | 0 | 0 | 0 |
| Gantner, 2b | 4 | 2 | 2 | 2 | Total | 30 | 0 | 3 | 0 |
| Total | 42 | 10 | 17 | 9 | | | | | |

| | | | | | | | | |
|---|---|---|---|---|---|---|---|---|
| Milwaukee | 200 | 112 | 004 | — | 10 | | | |
| St. Louis | 000 | 000 | 000 | — | 0 | | | |

E—Hernandez. DP—St. Louis. LOB—Milwaukee 10, St. Louis 4. 2B—Porter, Moore, Yount. 3B—Gantner. HR—Simmons. S—Gantner.

| | IP | H | R | ER | BB | SO |
|---|---|---|---|---|---|---|
| Milwaukee | | | | | | |
| Caldwell (W) | 9 | 3 | 0 | 0 | 1 | 3 |
| St. Louis | | | | | | |
| Forsch (L) | 5⅔ | 10 | 6 | 4 | 1 | 1 |
| Kaat | 1⅓ | 1 | 0 | 0 | 1 | 1 |
| LaPoint | 1⅔ | 3 | 2 | 2 | 1 | 0 |
| Lahti | ⅓ | 3 | 2 | 2 | 0 | 1 |

HBP—by Forsch (Howell). Time of game—2:30. Attendance—53,723.

## 2nd Game—St. Louis, Oct. 13

| MILWAUKEE (A) | AB | R | H | BI | ST. LOUIS (N) | AB | R | H | BI |
|---|---|---|---|---|---|---|---|---|---|
| Molitor, 3b | 5 | 1 | 2 | 0 | Herr, 2b | 3 | 1 | 1 | 1 |
| Yount, ss | 4 | 1 | 1 | 1 | Oberkfell, 3b | 3 | 1 | 2 | 1 |
| Cooper, 1b | 5 | 0 | 3 | 1 | Tenace, ph | 1 | 0 | 0 | 0 |
| Simmons, c | 3 | 1 | 1 | 1 | Ramsey, 3b | 0 | 0 | 0 | 0 |
| Oglivie, lf | 4 | 0 | 1 | 0 | Hernandez, 1b | 3 | 0 | 0 | 0 |
| Thomas, cf | 3 | 0 | 0 | 0 | Hendrick, rf | 3 | 2 | 0 | 0 |
| Howell, dh | 4 | 1 | 0 | 0 | Porter, c | 4 | 0 | 2 | 2 |
| Moore, rf | 4 | 0 | 2 | 1 | L. Smith, lf | 3 | 0 | 0 | 0 |
| Gantner, 2b | 3 | 0 | 0 | 0 | Iorg, dh | 2 | 0 | 1 | 0 |
| Total | 35 | 4 | 10 | 4 | Green, ph | 1 | 0 | 0 | 0 |
| | | | | | Braun, ph | 0 | 0 | 0 | 1 |
| | | | | | McGee, cf | 4 | 1 | 0 | 0 |
| | | | | | O. Smith, ss | 4 | 0 | 2 | 0 |
| | | | | | Total | 31 | 5 | 8 | 5 |

| | | | | | | | | |
|---|---|---|---|---|---|---|---|---|
| Milwaukee | 012 | 010 | 000 | — | 4 | | | |
| St. Louis | 002 | 002 | 01X | — | 5 | | | |

E—Oglivie. DP—St. Louis. LOB—Milwaukee 8, St. Louis 7. 2B—Moore, Herr, Yount, Porter, Cooper. HR—Simmons. SB—Molitor, McGee, Oberkfell, O. Smith.

| | IP | H | R | ER | BB | SO |
|---|---|---|---|---|---|---|
| Milwaukee | | | | | | |
| Sutton | 6 | 5 | 4 | 4 | 1 | 3 |
| McClure (L) | 1⅓ | 2 | 1 | 1 | 2 | 2 |
| Ladd | ⅔ | 1 | 0 | 0 | 2 | 0 |
| St. Louis | | | | | | |
| Stuper | 4 | 6 | 4 | 4 | 3 | 3 |
| Kaat | ⅔ | 1 | 0 | 0 | 0 | 0 |
| Bair | 2 | 1 | 0 | 0 | 0 | 3 |
| Sutter (W) | 2⅓ | 2 | 0 | 0 | 1 | 1 |

WP—Stuper, 2. Time of game—2:54. Attendance—53,723.

## 3rd Game—Milwaukee, Oct. 15

| ST. LOUIS (N) | AB | R | H | BI | MILWAUKEE (A) | AB | R | H | BI |
|---|---|---|---|---|---|---|---|---|---|
| Herr, 2b | 5 | 0 | 0 | 0 | Molitor, 3b | 4 | 0 | 0 | 0 |
| Oberkfell, 3b | 4 | 0 | 0 | 0 | Yount, ss | 3 | 1 | 0 | 0 |
| Hernandez, 1b | 4 | 0 | 0 | 0 | Cooper, 1b | 4 | 1 | 1 | 2 |
| Hendrick, rf | 2 | 1 | 1 | 0 | Simmons, c | 4 | 0 | 1 | 0 |
| Porter, c | 4 | 0 | 0 | 0 | Oglivie, lf | 4 | 0 | 0 | 0 |
| L. Smith, lf | 4 | 2 | 2 | 0 | Thomas, cf | 4 | 0 | 1 | 0 |
| Green, lf | 0 | 0 | 0 | 0 | Howell, dh | 2 | 0 | 0 | 0 |
| Iorg, dh | 4 | 1 | 1 | 0 | Money, dh | 1 | 0 | 0 | 0 |
| McGee, cf | 3 | 2 | 2 | 4 | Moore, rf | 3 | 0 | 0 | 0 |
| O. Smith, ss | 3 | 0 | 0 | 1 | Gantner, 2b | 3 | 0 | 2 | 0 |
| Total | 33 | 6 | 6 | 5 | Total | 32 | 2 | 5 | 2 |

| | | | | | | | | |
|---|---|---|---|---|---|---|---|---|
| St. Louis | 000 | 030 | 201 | — | 6 | | | |
| Milwaukee | 000 | 000 | 020 | — | 2 | | | |

E—Cooper, Gantner, Simmons, Hernandez. DP—St. Louis. LOB—St. Louis 4, Milwaukee 6. 2B—Gantner, L. Smith, Iorg. 3B—L. Smith. HRs—McGee 2; Cooper.

| | IP | H | R | ER | BB | SO |
|---|---|---|---|---|---|---|
| St. Louis | | | | | | |
| Andujar (W) | 6⅓ | 3 | 0 | 0 | 1 | 3 |
| Kaat | ⅓ | 1 | 0 | 0 | 0 | 1 |
| Bair | 0 | 0 | 0 | 0 | 1 | 0 |
| Sutter | 2⅓ | 1 | 2 | 2 | 1 | 1 |
| Milwaukee | | | | | | |
| Vuckovich (L) | 8⅔ | 6 | 6 | 4 | 3 | 1 |
| McClure | ⅓ | 0 | 0 | 0 | 0 | 0 |

Time of game—2:53. Attendance—56,556.

## HENDERSON OF A'S SETS STOLEN-BASES RECORD

Rickey Henderson of the Oakland A's broke the major league record for stolen bases in one season on Aug. 27, 1982, at Milwaukee when he stole his 119th base in the third inning. The previous record of 118 was held by Lou Brock of St. Louis and was set in 1974. Henderson had broken the American League stolen-bases mark in 1980 when he surpassed Ty Cobb's record of 96, set in 1915. Henderson finished the 1980 season with 100 stolen bases. In 1982 he completed the season with 130. The major league record for career stolen bases is held by Brock with 938.

## 4th Game—Milwaukee, Oct. 16

### ST. LOUIS (N)

| | AB | R | H | BI |
|---|---|---|---|---|
| Herr, 2b | 4 | 0 | 0 | 2 |
| Oberkfell, 3b | 2 | 2 | 1 | 0 |
| Tenace, ph | 1 | 0 | 0 | 0 |
| Hernandez, 1b | 4 | 0 | 0 | 0 |
| Hendrick, rf | 4 | 0 | 1 | 1 |
| Porter, c | 3 | 0 | 1 | 0 |
| L. Smith, lf | 4 | 1 | 1 | 0 |
| Iorg, dh | 4 | 0 | 2 | 1 |
| Green, pr | 0 | 0 | 0 | 0 |
| McGee, cf | 4 | 1 | 1 | 0 |
| O. Smith, ss | 3 | 1 | 1 | 0 |
| Total | 33 | 5 | 8 | 4 |

### MILWAUKEE (A)

| | AB | R | H | BI |
|---|---|---|---|---|
| Molitor, 3b | 4 | 1 | 0 | 0 |
| Yount, ss | 4 | 1 | 2 | 2 |
| Cooper, 1b | 4 | 1 | 2 | 1 |
| Simmons, c | 2 | 0 | 0 | 0 |
| Thomas, cf | 4 | 0 | 1 | 2 |
| Oglivie, lf | 3 | 1 | 1 | 0 |
| Money, dh | 4 | 2 | 2 | 0 |
| Moore, rf | 4 | 0 | 1 | 0 |
| Gantner, 2b | 4 | 1 | 1 | 1 |
| Total | 33 | 7 | 10 | 6 |

```
St. Louis      130  001  000  —  5
Milwaukee      000  010  60X  —  7
```

E—Gantner, Yount, LaPoint. DP—St. Louis 2; Milwaukee 2. LOB—St. Louis 6, Milwaukee 6. 2B—Oberkfell, Money, L. Smith, Iorg, Gantner. 3B—Oglivie. SB—McGee, Oberkfell. SF—Herr.

| | IP | H | R | ER | BB | SO |
|---|---|---|---|---|---|---|
| **St. Louis** | | | | | | |
| LaPoint | 6⅔ | 7 | 4 | 1 | 1 | 3 |
| Bair (L) | 0 | 1 | 2 | 0 | 1 | 0 |
| Kaat | 0 | 1 | 1 | 0 | 1 | 0 |
| Lahti | 1⅓ | 1 | 0 | 0 | 1 | 0 |
| **Milwaukee** | | | | | | |
| Haas | 5⅓ | 7 | 5 | 4 | 2 | 3 |
| Slaton (W) | 2 | 1 | 0 | 0 | 2 | 1 |
| McClure | 1⅔ | 0 | 0 | 0 | 0 | 2 |

WP—Hass, Kaat. Time of game—3:04. Attendance—56,560.

## 5th Game—Milwaukee, Oct. 17

### ST. LOUIS (N)

| | AB | R | H | BI |
|---|---|---|---|---|
| L. Smith, dh | 5 | 0 | 2 | 0 |
| Green, lf | 5 | 2 | 2 | 0 |
| Hernandez, 1b | 4 | 1 | 3 | 2 |
| Hendrick, rf | 5 | 0 | 3 | 2 |
| Porter, c | 5 | 0 | 1 | 0 |
| Ramsey, pr | 0 | 0 | 0 | 0 |
| McGee, cf | 5 | 0 | 1 | 0 |
| Oberkfell, 3b | 4 | 0 | 3 | 0 |
| Tenace, ph | 1 | 0 | 0 | 0 |
| Herr, 2b | 4 | 0 | 0 | 0 |
| O. Smith, ss | 3 | 1 | 0 | 0 |
| Total | 41 | 4 | 15 | 4 |

### MILWAUKEE (A)

| | AB | R | H | BI |
|---|---|---|---|---|
| Molitor, 3b | 4 | 1 | 1 | 1 |
| Yount, ss | 4 | 2 | 4 | 1 |
| Cooper, 1b | 4 | 0 | 1 | 1 |
| Simmons, c | 3 | 0 | 0 | 1 |
| Oglivie, lf | 4 | 1 | 2 | 0 |
| Thomas, cf | 4 | 0 | 0 | 0 |
| Money, dh | 3 | 1 | 0 | 0 |
| Moore, rf | 4 | 1 | 2 | 1 |
| Gantner, 2b | 4 | 0 | 1 | 1 |
| Total | 34 | 6 | 11 | 6 |

```
St. Louis      001  000  102  —  4
Milwaukee      101  010  12X  —  6
```

E—Forsch, Gantner, Herr. DP—St. Louis 2; Milwaukee. LOB—St. Louis 12, Milwaukee 7. 2B—Hernandez 2, Yount, Moore, Green. 3B—Green. HR—Yount. SB—L. Smith.

| | IP | H | R | ER | BB | SO |
|---|---|---|---|---|---|---|
| **St. Louis** | | | | | | |
| Forsch (L) | 7 | 8 | 4 | 3 | 2 | 3 |
| Sutter | 1 | 3 | 2 | 1 | 2 | 2 |
| **Milwaukee** | | | | | | |
| Caldwell (W) | 8⅓ | 14 | 4 | 4 | 2 | 3 |
| McClure | ⅔ | 1 | 0 | 0 | 0 | 1 |

Time of game—3:02. Attendance—56,562.

## 6th Game—St. Louis, Oct. 19

### MILWAUKEE (A)

| | AB | R | H | BI |
|---|---|---|---|---|
| Molitor, 3b | 4 | 0 | 1 | 0 |
| Yount, ss | 4 | 0 | 0 | 0 |
| Cooper, 1b | 4 | 0 | 0 | 0 |
| Simmons, c | 2 | 0 | 0 | 0 |
| Yost, c | 0 | 0 | 0 | 0 |
| Oglivie, lf | 4 | 0 | 1 | 0 |
| Thomas, cf | 3 | 0 | 0 | 0 |
| Edwards, cf | 0 | 0 | 0 | 0 |
| Money, dh | 3 | 0 | 0 | 0 |
| Moore, rf | 3 | 0 | 1 | 0 |
| Gantner, 2b | 3 | 1 | 1 | 0 |
| Total | 30 | 1 | 4 | 0 |

### ST. LOUIS (N)

| | AB | R | H | BI |
|---|---|---|---|---|
| L. Smith, lf | 3 | 1 | 1 | 0 |
| Green, lf | 1 | 1 | 0 | 0 |
| Oberkfell, 3b | 5 | 1 | 0 | 0 |
| Hernandez, 1b | 5 | 2 | 2 | 4 |
| Hendrick, rf | 4 | 2 | 1 | 2 |
| Porter, c | 4 | 1 | 1 | 2 |
| Brummer, c | 0 | 0 | 0 | 0 |
| Iorg, dh | 4 | 3 | 3 | 0 |
| McGee, cf | 4 | 1 | 1 | 1 |
| Herr, 2b | 3 | 1 | 2 | 2 |
| O. Smith, ss | 4 | 0 | 0 | 0 |
| Total | 38 | 13 | 12 | 10 |

```
Milwaukee      000  000  001  —   1
St. Louis      020  326  00X  —  13
```

E—Yount 2, Gantner 2, Oberkfell. DP—St. Louis 2. LOB—Milwaukee 4, St. Louis 3. 2B—Iorg 2, Herr, Gantner. 3B—Iorg. HR—Porter, Hernandez. SB—L. Smith. S—Herr.

| | IP | H | R | ER | BB | SO |
|---|---|---|---|---|---|---|
| **Milwaukee** | | | | | | |
| Sutton (L) | 4⅓ | 7 | 7 | 5 | 0 | 2 |
| Slaton | ⅔ | 0 | 0 | 0 | 0 | 0 |
| Medich | 2 | 5 | 6 | 4 | 1 | 0 |
| Bernard | 1 | 0 | 0 | 0 | 0 | 1 |
| **St. Louis** | | | | | | |
| Stuper (W) | 9 | 4 | 1 | 1 | 2 | 2 |

WP—Medich 2, Stuper. Balk—Sutton. Time of game—2:21. Attendance—53,723.

## 7th Game—St. Louis, Oct. 20

### MILWAUKEE (A)

| | AB | R | H | BI |
|---|---|---|---|---|
| Molitor, 3b | 4 | 1 | 2 | 0 |
| Yount, ss | 4 | 0 | 1 | 0 |
| Cooper, 1b | 3 | 0 | 1 | 1 |
| Simmons, c | 4 | 0 | 0 | 0 |
| Oglivie, lf | 4 | 1 | 1 | 1 |
| Thomas, cf | 4 | 0 | 0 | 0 |
| Howell, dh | 3 | 0 | 0 | 0 |
| Moore, rf | 3 | 0 | 1 | 0 |
| Gantner, 2b | 3 | 1 | 1 | 0 |
| Total | 32 | 3 | 7 | 2 |

### ST. LOUIS (N)

| | AB | R | H | BI |
|---|---|---|---|---|
| L. Smith, lf | 5 | 2 | 3 | 1 |
| Oberkfell, 3b | 3 | 0 | 0 | 0 |
| Tenace, ph | 0 | 0 | 0 | 0 |
| Ramsey, 3b | 1 | 1 | 0 | 0 |
| Hernandez, 1b | 3 | 1 | 2 | 2 |
| Hendrick, rf | 5 | 0 | 2 | 1 |
| Porter, c | 5 | 0 | 1 | 1 |
| Iorg, dh | 3 | 0 | 2 | 0 |
| Green, ph | 0 | 0 | 0 | 0 |
| Brauen, dh | 2 | 0 | 1 | 1 |
| McGee, cf | 5 | 1 | 1 | 0 |
| Herr, 2b | 3 | 0 | 1 | 0 |
| O. Smith, ss | 4 | 1 | 2 | 0 |
| Total | 39 | 6 | 15 | 6 |

```
Milwaukee      000  012  000  —  3
St. Louis      000  103  02X  —  6
```

E—Andujar. LOB—Milwaukee 3, St. Louis 13. 2B—Gantner, L. Smith 2. HR—Oglivie. SF—Cooper.

| | IP | H | R | ER | BB | SO |
|---|---|---|---|---|---|---|
| **Milwaukee** | | | | | | |
| Vuckovich | 5⅓ | 10 | 3 | 3 | 2 | 3 |
| McClure (L) | ⅓ | 2 | 1 | 1 | 1 | 0 |
| Haas | 2 | 1 | 2 | 2 | 1 | 1 |
| Caldwell | ⅓ | 2 | 0 | 0 | 0 | 0 |
| **St. Louis** | | | | | | |
| Andujar (W) | 7 | 7 | 3 | 2 | 0 | 1 |
| Sutter | 2 | 0 | 0 | 0 | 0 | 2 |

Time of game—2:50. Attendance—53,723.

# HANDBALL

## U.S.H.A. NATIONAL FOUR-WALL CHAMPIONS

| Singles | | | | | |
|---|---|---|---|---|---|
| 1960 | Jimmy Jacobs | 1978 | Fred Lewis | 1969 | Lou Kramberg-Lou Russo |
| 1961 | John Sloan | 1979 | Naty Alvarado | 1970 | Karl and Ruby Obert |
| 1962–63 | Oscar Obert | 1980 | Naty Alvarado | 1971 | Ray Neveau-Simie Fein |
| 1964–65 | Jimmy Jacobs | 1981 | Fred Lewis | 1972 | Kent Fusselman-Al Drews |
| 1966–67 | Paul Haber | 1982 | Naty Alvarado | 1973–74 | Ray Neveau-Simie Fein |
| 1968 | Simon (Stuffy) Singer | | | 1975 | Marty Decatur-Steve Lott |
| 1969–71 | Paul Haber | **Doubles** | | 1976 | Gary Rohrer-Dan O'Connor |
| 1972 | Fred Lewis | 1960 | Jimmy Jacobs-Dick Weisman | 1977 | Skip McDowell-Matt Kelly |
| 1973 | Terry Muck | 1961 | John Sloan-Vic Hershkowitz | 1978 | Stuffy Singer-Marty Decatur |
| 1974 | Fred Lewis | 1962–63 | Jimmy Jacobs-Marty Decatur | 1979 | Stuffy Singer-Marty Decatur |
| 1975 | Jay Bilyeu | 1964 | John Sloan-Phil Elbert | 1980 | Skip McDowell-Harry Robert-son |
| 1976 | Vern Roberts, Jr. | 1965 | Jimmy Jacobs-Marty Decatur | | |
| 1977 | Naty Alvarado | 1966 | Pete Tyson-Bob Lindsay | 1981 | Tom Kopatich-Jack Roberts |
| | | 1967–68 | Jimmy Jacobs-Marty Decatur | 1982 | Naty Alvarado-Vern Roberts |

## U.S. HANDBALL ASSOCIATION FOUR-WALL CHAMPIONS
(Tucson, Ariz., June 5-12, 1982)

Men's open singles—Naty Alvarado, Hesperia, Calif. (defeated Fred Lewis, Tucson, Ariz., 21–5, 21–9, in final)

Men's open doubles—Naty Alvarado and Vern Roberts, Chicago (defeated Jack Roberts and Tom Kopatich, Chicago, 21–10, 21–8, in final)

Women's open singles—Rosemary Bellini, New York (defeated Rossanna Ettinger, Long Beach, Calif., 21–12, 21–12, in final)

Women's doubles—Allison Roberts, Ohio, and Glorian Motal, Houston (defeated Rosemary Bellini, New York, and Sue Oakleaf, Texas, 13–21, 21–18, 11–2, in final)

23 and under singles—Alfonse Monreal, Texas (defeated Todd Worrell, Texas, 21–17, 21–14, in final)

35 and over singles—Larry Bookman, Colorado (defeated Larry Aguilar, California, 21–17, 21–12, in final)

40 and over singles—Pat Kirby, Tucson, Ariz. (defeated Ed Bellochio, Texas, 21–13, 21–6, in final)

40 and over doubles—Pat Kirby and Fred Munsch, New York, (defeated Jeff Capell and Joe McDonald, California, 21–14, 21–12, in final)

# BADMINTON

## WORLD CHAMPIONS—1982*

Men's singles—Rudy Hartono, Indonesia
Women's singles—Wiharjo Verawaty, Indonesia
Men's doubles—Ade Chandra and Christian Hadinata, Indonesia
Women's doubles—Nora Perry and Jane Webster, England
Mixed doubles—Christian Hadinata and Imelda Wigoeno, Indonesia

*World championships were not contested in 1981 and 1982. The 1983 championships are scheduled for May in Copenhagen, Denmark.

## UNITED STATES CHAMPIONSHIPS
(Countryside, Ill., April 7-10, 1982)

### Open

Men's singles—Gary Higgins, Alhambra, Calif.
Women's singles—Cheryl Carton, San Diego, Calif.
Men's doubles—Don Paup, Washington, D.C., and Bruce Pontow, Chicago
Women's doubles—Pam Brady, Flint, Mich., and Judianne Kelly, Costa Mesa, Calif.
Mixed doubles—Pam Brady and Danny Brady, Flint, Mich.

### Seniors
(San Diego, Calif., Jan. 21-23, 1982)

Men's singles—Tom Carmichael, Ortonville, Mich.
Men's doubles—Tom Carmichael and Jim Poole, Westminster, Calif.
Women's doubles—Helen Tibbetts, Torrance, Calif., and Vicky Toutz, Las Alamitos, Calif.
Mixed doubles—Jim Poole and Vicky Toutz

### Masters

Men's singles—Jim Bell, Ypsilanti, Mich.
Men's doubles—Tom Carmody, Freeport, La., and Dick Witte, St. Louis

Women's singles—Carlene Starkey, San Diego, Calif.
Women's doubles—Ruth Hoffman and Carlene Starkey, San Diego, Calif.
Mixed doubles—Bill Berry and Carlene Starkey, San Diego, Calif.

### Grand Masters

Men's singles—Ed Phillips, Warwick, R.I.
Men's doubles—John Forsythe, Canada, and Tom Graham, Canada
Women's singles—Mary Ann Wolfe, Seattle, Wash.
Women's doubles—Dorothy Tinline, Canada, and Ruth Hoffman, San Diego
Mixed doubles—Ed Phillips and Ruth Hoffman

### Juniors

Men's singles—Rodney Barton, Palo Alto, Calif.
Women's singles—Fran Hughes, Miller Place, N.Y.
Men's doubles—Rodney Barton and Marty French, Elmhurst, Ill.
Mixed doubles—Rodney Barton and Barb Morrison, DeKalb, Ill.

## ALL-ENGLAND CHAMPIONSHIPS
(Wembley, England, March 20-23, 1982)

Men's singles—Morton Frost, Denmark
Women's singles—Zhang Ailing, China
Men's doubles—R. Sidek and J. Sidek, Malaysia
Women's doubles—Liu Ying and Wu Dixi, China
Mixed doubles—M. Dew and Gillian Gilks, England

# BILLIARDS—1982

Men's world pocket billiards champion—Steve Mizerak, Fords, N.J.
Women's world pocket billiards champion—Jean Balukas, Brooklyn, N.Y.